D1067305

Confederate Colonels

Shades of Blue and Gray Series

**EDITED BY HERMAN HATTAWAY,
JON L. WAKELYN, AND CLAYTON E. JEWETT**

The Shades of Blue and Gray Series offers Civil War studies for the modern reader—Civil War buff and scholar alike. Military history today addresses the relationship between society and warfare. Thus biographies and thematic studies that deal with civilians, soldiers, and political leaders are increasingly important to a larger public. This series includes books that will appeal to Civil War Roundtable groups, individuals, libraries, and academics with a special interest in this era of American history.

Confederate Colonels

A BIOGRAPHICAL REGISTER

BRUCE S. ALLARDICE

UNIVERSITY OF MISSOURI PRESS

COLUMBIA AND LONDON

Copyright © 2008 by
The Curators of the University of Missouri
University of Missouri Press, Columbia, Missouri 65201
Printed and bound in the United States of America
All rights reserved
5   4   3   2   1   12   11   10   09   08

Library of Congress Cataloging-in-Publication Data

Allardice, Bruce S.
    Confederate colonels : a biographical register / Bruce S. Allardice.
        p. cm.
    Summary: "Allardice provides detailed biographical information on 1,583
Confederate colonels, both staff and line officers and members of all armies.
In his introduction, he explains how one became a colonel—the mustering
process, election of officers, reorganizing of regiments—and discusses
problems of the nominating process, seniority, and 'rank inflation'"
—Provided by publisher.
    ISBN 978-0-8262-1809-4 (alk. paper)
    1. Confederate States of America. Army—Officers—Biography.   2. Soldiers
—Confederate States of America—Biography.   3. United States—History—
Civil War, 1861–1865—Biography.   4. Confederate States of America. Army
—Organization.   5. Confederate States of America. Army—Recruiting,
enlistment, etc.   I. Title.
    E467.A39 2008
    973.7'820922—dc22
    [B]

                                                        2008018253

♾™ This paper meets the requirements of the
American National Standard for Permanence of Paper
for Printed Library Materials, Z39.48, 1984.

Designer: Kristie Lee
Typesetter: The Composing Room of Michigan, Inc.
Printer and binder: Maple-Vail Book Manufacturing Co.
Typefaces: Minion, Copperplate, and Goudy Handtooled

To Leslie
My "Dearest Friend"

CONTENTS

ACKNOWLEDGMENTS

The research for this book was immeasurably aided by the contributions of literally thousands of historians, genealogists, librarians, archivists, and descendants of the colonels. I wish there were space to acknowledge everyone properly. Hopefully they already know how grateful I am, and they can take satisfaction in their contribution to Civil War historiography. Any merit this book has is theirs; any errors, omissions, or unsubstantiated opinions remain my responsibility.

Robert K. Krick and his son Robert E. L. Krick deserve special mention for their pioneering research on the officer corps of the Army of Northern Virginia. They proved that a book of this type could be written. They also proved that the book-reading public desired such a book. On a more personal level, the two Bobs have generously given their time answering my questions and sharing their information, and debating whether the San Francisco Giants will finally win a pennant.

Special mention should also be given to Keith Bohannon, an expert on Georgia's war; Nat Hughes, prolific author and southern gentleman; Bryan Howerton, the living encyclopedia of Arkansas Confederates; Chris Ferguson, the biographer of Richmond's Hollywood Cemetery; Bob Davis of Wallace State University, genealogist extraordinaire; Art Bergeron; Greg Biggs; Tim Burgess; Ken Byrd; Dave Callihan; Clifton Cardin; Wayne Cosby; John Cothern; Chris Fonvielle; James Gabel; Lars Gjertveit; Bertil Haggman; Mike Hardy; Larry Hewitt; Diane Jacob; the late Homer Jones; Dean Letzring; Hayes Lowe; John Luckey; John Masters: Scott Mauger; Jim McGhee; Gerry Mogren; Jim Mundie; Randall Osborne; Richard Peterson; Alan Pitts; Jerry Ponder; Anthony Rushing; Judy Riffel; Justin Sanders; William Scaife; Barron T. Smith; Gordon B. Smith; Jonathan K. T. Smith; Marion O. Smith; David Sullivan; Phil Tucker; Mac Wyckoff;

Geoff Walden; Zack Waters; Raymond Watkins; Jeffrey C. Weaver; James E. Williams; Scott K. Williams; Terry Winschel; and countless others.

Thanks also to the people at University of Missouri Press, particularly Beverly Jarrett, editor in chief, and Jane Lago, managing editor.

And, finally, a big thanks to my Civil War friends who, even if they thought I was foolish to attempt this eight-year-long project, were considerate enough to keep their thoughts to themselves.

Confederate
Colonels

INTRODUCTION

"[The men] will go anywhere and do anything if properly led. But that is the difficulty—proper commanders—where can they be obtained?"

—Robert E. Lee to John Bell Hood, May 21, 1863

To an extent not always appreciated, the Confederacy's oft-beleaguered army, *not* the new Confederate government, *was* the Confederacy. The one million men who joined that army provided the flesh-and-blood commitment that enabled the fledgling country to endure four years of hellish, bloody war. Those men emerged with their honor, if not their country, intact. Several lengthy, though still frustratingly unsatisfying, books have been written on the Confederacy's generals. However, no comprehensive study has emerged on the army's colonels, the field officers who had the greatest life-or-death power over the average soldier. This book hopes to plug that gap in Civil War scholarship.

The laws passed by the Confederate Congress on February 28 and March 6, 1861, provided the legal framework for the Provisional Army of the Confederate States (PACS), the volunteer Confederate army that fought the war. Among other items, these laws provided that the Confederate government could accept volunteers tendered by the states and organized into regiments, with field officers (majors, lieutenant colonels, and colonels) chosen according to relevant state law.[1] In some states (Louisiana, for instance) the governor appointed the

---

1. "An Act to raise provisional forces for the Confederate States of America . . . ," February 28, 1861, in U.S. War Department, *War of the Rebellion: A Compilation of the Official Records of the Union and Confederate Armies,* 128 parts in 70 vols. (Washington, DC, 1880–1901), series IV, vol. 1, p. 117 (hereafter cited as *OR* with series followed by volume and page numbers). "An act to provide for the public defense . . . ," March 6, 1861, *OR,* series IV, 1:126.

colonels of the early regiments. Upon the turnover of these regiments to Confederate authorities, the appointed colonels would (under Confederate law) be commissioned as such by the Confederate government. Most states, however, allowed the volunteers to elect their own officers, including field officers.[2] Those elected would be formally commissioned by the Confederate government, to rank from the date the unit was mustered into Confederate service. The president was also authorized to accept individual volunteer companies and form regiments from them, with the field officers to be appointed by the president.[3]

These volunteer regiments usually signed up for one year's service.[4] In early 1862 Congress passed another law extending those one-year enlistments to three years. The law provided that existing one-year regiments had to reorganize themselves under the new law.[5] Essentially, the law treated the reorganized regiments as new regiments (more accurately, regiments reorganized under a new law), voiding the initial officer elections and instituting a new round of officer elections. Most of these reorganization elections took place in April and May 1862. Reelected officers retained their seniority based on the original date of commission. Officers not reelected were allowed to resign their commissions, with the newly elected colonels taking rank from the date of election.

A number of new regiments were raised and organized after the passage of this law. These regiments were generally allowed to elect their initial field officers, though increasingly as the war went on, the Confederate government or-

2. Throughout American history, tradition and state law dictated that private soldiers had the right to elect their own officers. The antebellum state militia laws generally provided for such elections, in which the politicking could become intense. After observing (with proper European disdain) a Confederate unit conduct its officer election, English reporter William H. Russell wrote, "The system of electing officers by ballot has made the camp as thoroughly a political arena as the poll districts in New Orleans" ("American Topics in Europe," *New York Times,* July 2, 1861).

3. See "An Act to raise an additional military force . . . ," May 8, 1861, *OR,* series IV, 1:302; act of March 6, 1861, *OR,* series IV, 1:126; and the Confederate War Department Circular, November 1861, *OR,* series IV, 1:766.

4. One year was the normal length of service of volunteer regiments in America's previous wars. See John K. Mahon, *History of the Militia and the National Guard* (New York and London: Macmillan, 1983).

5. The law of April 16, 1862 (*OR,* series IV, 1:1095), is of historical interest because it instituted conscription, making it the first national draft law in American history. The law provided for conscripting the units and men that did not choose to reorganize themselves. The soldiers voted out many competent but unpopular officers in favor of candidates who promised laxer discipline, but they also took this opportunity to elect men who had proved themselves in battle.

ganized unattached companies into regiments and directly appointed regimental field officers.

Congress also commissioned officers as provisional colonels (for example, Benjamin Anderson) to give them proper rank to recruit a regiment behind Union lines. The officers thus commissioned were given a time period (three or six months) to recruit a regiment, with the commission to become final if and when the regiment was mustered into Confederate service.

After 1862, promotion to colonel, to replace colonels who had died or resigned, was designed to be by seniority within the regiment, with the lieutenant colonel or other ranking officer succeeding to the colonelcy. The War Department would issue a commission to the new colonel, generally to take rank from the date the vacancy occurred.

This system had its flaws, the most notable being that a second in command would automatically succeed to the colonelcy whether or not that second in command was competent. The Confederate army soon recognized the need for a system to weed out incompetent field officers and promote more deserving juniors in their stead.[6] The army thus created examination boards, composed of generals and colonels, to test the prospective colonel on his knowledge of tactics and regulations. The boards also took testimony and recommendations from fellow officers into consideration. If the board rejected the applicant, the board could examine, and recommend for promotion to colonel, a more junior officer. In practice, a second in command could also waive his rights to promotion and allow a junior officer to be promoted over him.

With the exigencies of war, not every division or brigade was able to convene boards to fill every regimental vacancy. Predictably, elite combat divisions such as Pat Cleburne's were very active in convening boards, whereas divisions with less painstaking commanders hardly ever did so.

The detailed process by which a soldier would be promoted to colonel began with an appointment or election to the colonelcy, the appointment being made by a superior officer or the War Department. The president would then nominate that officer to the Confederate Senate. The Senate would vote to confirm or, in rare cases, reject the nominee. If the nominee was confirmed, the War Department would then issue a formal commission to the new colonel, the commission (normally) to date from the date of the election or the date the vacan-

---

6. The Union Army recognized this need as well and instituted similar examination boards.

cy occurred. The date of commission was very important to the officer, since it determined his seniority vis-à-vis other colonels.

Years could pass before an elected colonel actually received his commission, particularly for regiments in the Trans-Mississippi Department (covering Arkansas, Missouri, Texas, the Indian Territory, and West Louisiana) that after 1863 were cut off from direct communication with the capitol in Richmond. For example, Julius Andrews was officially appointed colonel of the Thirty-second Texas Cavalry on January 4, 1865, to rank from May 8, 1862, the date he'd been elected colonel. In those three years, Andrews had been commanding the regiment as colonel, had been paid as such, and had been obeyed as such.

In many instances the legal process could not be fully followed, through no fault of the War Department or the officer. Some appointed officers died before they could be confirmed and commissioned. The Senate rejected the nominations of others, and still others were appointed so late in the war that there simply wasn't time to complete the paperwork process. Another large-scale exception to the rules of promotion came about because of nonlegal "in the field" promotions by army commanders. Gen. Braxton Bragg, for one, zealously attempting to weed out incompetent officers from his Army of Tennessee, appointed officers from outside a regiment to fill vacancies. The regiments normally resented the outsider, and the nonpromoted officer would appeal to the War Department to overturn Bragg's action. In every instance, the War Department eventually declared Bragg's appointments illegal, though in the meantime the Bragg appointee exercised command as a colonel. In the last two years of the war the Trans-Mississippi Department could not directly communicate with the War Department. The department commander, Gen. E. Kirby Smith, assumed many of the president's civil duties, including assigning officers to serve as colonels, subject to eventual presidential approval. Historians have generally accepted the Bragg and Smith promotions as giving the promotee a valid claim to the title *colonel,* and they will be so accepted in this book. Other "promotions," by such junior generals as Gideon Pillow, were not at the time and have not subsequently been so accepted. These "colonels" are not in the biographical portion of this book but instead are listed in Appendix 3.

Murphy's law ("Whatever can go wrong, will") held true in the 1860s. Even the relatively simple-sounding promotion process could cause major problems. One such problem occurred in the Eighth Mississippi Infantry. In the initial multicandidate election for colonel of the Eighth, Capt. Greene C. Chandler received a plurality of votes. The Confederate mustering officer certified the election as official and Chandler as the colonel. One of the losers in the election, Lt. John C. Wilkinson, appealed to the War Department, which overturned the result on the grounds that an absolute majority, not a plurality, of votes was needed. Wilkinson won the subsequent election.[7] In the Fifth Mississippi Infantry the colonelship jockeyed back and forth between John Weir (elected by the troops, but rejected by an examining board) and John R. Dickens (appointed by Braxton Bragg after Weir was rejected). Eventually the secretary of war found Bragg's appointment illegal and ordered a new election that Weir again won. The Second Mississippi Cavalry was formed in 1862 by adding three unattached companies to James Gordon's existing Mississippi Cavalry Battalion. On the formation of the new regiment, Gordon simply assumed the colonelcy. When Capt. John L. McCarty (whom Gordon called "the most utterly worthless officer in the Regt.") organized, and won, an election to the colonelcy, Gordon arrested McCarty and kept him under arrest for over a year. Eventually the War Department found for McCarty on the point of law that a new election was required, and Gordon, to end the dispute, resigned. The Eleventh Texas Cavalry suffered most of the war with two competing sets of field officers. In 1862 Colonel Burks promoted Capt. Joseph M. Bounds of Company G to lieutenant colonel, on the mistaken belief that Bounds was the senior captain of the regiment. When Burks was killed in action at Stones River, Bounds succeeded to the colonelcy. It was later determined that another captain, George R. Reeves, had actually been the senior captain and should have received the promotion to lieutenant colonel. Gen. John Wharton, the brigade commander, thereupon appointed Reeves as colonel. Add in a disputed election for major, with the examining board rejecting the winning candidate, and the effect on regimental performance and discipline can only be imagined.[8]

In some cases the legal or actual existence of a regiment was in dispute. In the spring of 1862, the governor of Georgia ordered certain companies to be added to Asahel Littlefield's infantry battalion, raising that battalion to a regiment to be numbered the Thirty-third Georgia Infantry. However, only seven company commanders, instead of the required ten, were present at the called-

---

7. See Walter Chandler, ed., *Journals and Speeches of Greene C. Chandler* (Memphis: privately printed, 1953); Lynda Crist et al., eds., *The Papers of Jefferson Davis*, 11 vols. (Baton Rouge: Louisiana State University Press, 1983–), 8:351; and the compiled service records (CSRs) of Chandler and Wilkinson.

8. See the CSRs of the named officers. Neither the War Department nor the army ever straightened out the mess in the Eleventh Texas Cavalry.

for election to colonel of the Thirty-third, which Littlefield won. Subsequently, the three absent companies joined other regiments, invalidating both the formation of the Thirty-third and the election of a colonel. In the case of William E. Hughes, paroled in May 1865 as colonel of the Sixteenth Confederate Cavalry, it appears the War Department had no record of such a unit or even knew of its existence. The unit, if it existed at all, was organized in the mountains of north Alabama in 1865 from unattached partisan ranger companies. No evidence of any formal organization of the regiment, or election of a colonel, exists.[9]

Questions about seniority plagued some colonels. Col. William H. Parsons of the Twelfth Texas Cavalry commanded a brigade for nearly three years but never received promotion to general, due to a dispute over seniority with another colonel. Parsons's Twelfth formed as a state unit prior to the formation of George W. Carter's Nineteenth Texas Cavalry. However, the Nineteenth mustered into Confederate service prior to the Twelfth. Colonel Carter, an influential preacher, claimed (with some legal justification) to be senior to Parsons in date of commission. His superiors wished to promote the more competent Parsons to general and permanent command of the brigade, but Carter, claiming seniority, blocked that promotion. In the end, neither was promoted to general.[10] In the Eleventh Mississippi Infantry, Capts. Francis M. Green and William B. Lowry both claimed to be the senior captain and entitled to promotion. President Davis nominated Green as colonel, but the Confederate Congress, accepting Lowry's claim, rejected Green's nomination. The dispute was only "solved" by Green's death in 1864.[11]

The Confederate government recognized the need for staff (that is, nonregimental) officers and passed a variety of laws on the subject. Several of these laws created staff positions with a colonel's rank. For example, the law of February

9. See William E. Hughes, *The Journal of a Grandfather* (St. Louis: Nixon-Jones, 1912), for more on this "unit," which is listed on his parole as the "10th" Confederate Cavalry, a regiment that already existed and to which Hughes had no ties. I have tried, without success, to confirm that such a regiment actually was organized but found only indirect evidence that a regiment of some sort existed.

10. See Bruce Allardice, *More Generals in Gray* (Baton Rouge: Louisiana State University Press, 1995), for more on Parsons.

11. The whole, very complicated, story, is contained in President Davis's message to Congress, May 4, 1864, in *Journal of the Congress of the Confederate States of America, 1861–1865,* 7 vols. (Washington, DC, 1904–1905), 4:16. The dispute was one of law, with both sides conceding the military merits of both Lowry and Green.

26, 1861, provided that the Confederacy's adjutant general, quartermaster general, commissary general, and surgeon general be colonels.[12] The law of June 9, 1864, made the superintendent of the Niter and Mining Bureau a colonel.[13] Other laws authorized President Davis to appoint four aides, each to hold the rank and receive the pay of a colonel of cavalry.[14] Judges of military courts became colonels, as did certain staff officers of corps, army commanders, and commanders of artillery.[15] In one special instance, a secret clause in the treaty with the Creek Indian tribe provided that a colonel's rank and pay "for life" be given to the chief, Motey Kinnard.[16]

The Confederacy's surgeon general was the only medical officer to hold the substantive rank of colonel. An 1864 law provided that the medical directors of each Confederate army be given the pay and allotments of a colonel. It does not appear any actual commissions at that rank were ever issued to the medical directors.[17]

---

12. "An act for the establishment and organization of a general staff for the Army of the Confederate States of America," February 26, 1861, *OR*, series IV, 1:114. For an extensive overview of staff positions and their functions, see Robert E. L. Krick, *Staff Officers in Gray: A Biographical Register of Staff Officers in the Army of Northern Virginia* (Chapel Hill: University of North Carolina Press, 2003); J. Boone Bartholomees, *Buff Facings and Gilt Buttons: Staff and Headquarters Operations in the Army of Northern Virginia, 1861–1865* (Columbia: University of South Carolina Press, 1998). Many of these War Department appointments were made as part of the Confederate "regular" army, not the volunteer army (the PACS). The act of March 6, 1861, establishing the "regular" army (*OR*, series IV, 1:126) provided one colonel for each infantry regiment, and one each for the engineers, the artillery, and the cavalry. The "regular" army, envisioned as the Confederacy's equivalent of the prewar U.S. Army, never evolved beyond the appointing of such officers and the raising of a couple of companies of troops. The best, almost the only, examination of this "regular" army is Richard P. Weinert, *The Confederate Regular Army* (Shippensburg, PA: White Mane, 1991).

13. Act of June 9, 1864, *OR*, series IV, 3:492.

14. Act of April 2, 1862, *OR*, series IV, 1:1041. An earlier law (act of August 2, 1861, *OR*, series IV, 1:581) had provided for two such aides. A colonel of cavalry received fifteen dollars more pay per month than a colonel of infantry.

15. The act of June 14, 1864 (*OR*, series IV, 3:497), authorized for each army commander two assistant adjutant generals (AAG), one chief quartermaster (QM), one chief of ordnance (CO), one chief commissary, and one aide-de-camp (ADC) with the rank of colonel, as well as other staff officers of lesser rank. Each lieutenant general commanding an army corps was authorized two AAGs with colonel's rank. See also General Orders no. 44, April 29, 1864, *OR*, series IV, 3:352.

16. See *OR*, series I, 34, pt. 2:958.

17. Act of June 14, 1864, *OR*, series IV, 3:497. These medical directors are listed in Appendix 3.

What Role Did a Colonel Play in the Army?

The basic unit of Civil War era armies, and the unit the common soldier (when asked) most commonly identified himself as belonging to, was the regiment. Briefly, regiments in either army were to consist of ten companies, each with sixty-four to one hundred privates plus company officers, plus a few staff officers for each regiment. Each regiment was to be commanded by a colonel (a term that derives from the Italian *colonnello,* or officer in charge of a column). That colonel would be assisted by two other "field officers," a lieutenant colonel and a major.

Army regulations enjoined the colonel of a regiment to instruct the men in drill and in artillery practice, "to encourage useful occupations, and manly exercises and diversions among their men, and to repress dissipation and immorality"—a tall order for any officer! The colonel had the power to appoint the regimental adjutant and the noncommissoned staff of the regiment, nominate for appointment the regimental quartermaster (supply officer), and, upon recommendation of the company commanders, appoint the sergeants and corporals of the companies.

Numerous colonels, lieutenant colonels, and majors commanded a brigade (normally two to five regiments, and a brigadier general's command), or even a division, at one time or another due to the absence of their superiors.

The influence of an outstanding colonel on his regiment could be recognized throughout the army. The famous diarist Sam Watkins lauded Hume R. Field, his regiment's colonel, as "known by every soldier in the army" for bravery, an officer who molded the First Tennessee into a regiment fit to occupy "tight places." He "so trained his regiment that all the armies in the world could not whip it."[18]

What Is a "Confederate Army" Colonel?

The "Confederate Army" is generally envisioned as those volunteers clad in gray and butternut who followed Bobby Lee and Joe Johnston. Legally, almost all these men belonged to the Provisional Army of the Confederate States, the

18. Sam R. Watkins, *"Co. Aytch": A Side Show of the Big Show* (1900; rpt. New York: Collier, 1962), 52.

volunteer army already mentioned. A handful belonged to the never-fleshed-out Confederate "regular" army. Beyond these two organizations were a host of state-organized units and armies that fought for the South. These units and armies had their own colonels and generals and were often given legal recognition under Confederate law. These state armies included the regular militia of the eleven Confederate states; state armies organized in 1861, often in the interval between a state's secession and its joining the Confederacy, whose regiments may or may not have been transferred to Confederate service; state forces organized during the war, such as the Georgia militia division that fought in the Atlanta Campaign; and "allied" forces of a nonseceding state, such as the Missouri State Guard.[19]

Obviously, some "state" units such as the Georgia militia division saw far more actual combat than did many "Confederate" units. Under Confederate law, these state units, when serving with the Confederate army, were paid by the Confederate government and put under Confederate army orders. Under certain circumstances, "state" army officers could even issue orders to junior PACS officers.[20] Nevertheless, the colonels of these "state" units were not, under Confederate law, Confederate colonels. The rule followed in this book is the rule followed by the Confederate government: if the colonels were appointed/commissioned by the Confederate government, they are "Confederate" colonels; if they were appointed/commissioned by a state or other authority, they aren't.[21] Colonels of these "state" regiments and armies are listed in Appendix 2.

The Confederate army embraced not only the usual components of infantry, cavalry, artillery, partisan rangers, and staff but also local defense organizations denoted by such names as *reserves* or *local defense troops*. The Confederate Congress passed a number of laws establishing such units, whose personnel consisted of men too old or too young for field service, men detailed under the law to work in war industries, and men exempted from the draft. The units were restricted to service in a particular state or locality.[22] The Confederate govern-

---

19. These "state army" colonels are listed in Appendix 2. For more on the various state armies, see Allardice, *More Generals in Gray,* 7–9.

20. See, for example, the act of March 6, 1861, *OR,* series IV, 1:126.

21. See the opinion of the Confederate attorney general, August 26, 1861, in Rembert Patrick, ed., *The Opinions of the Confederate Attorneys General, 1861–1865* (Buffalo: Dennis, 1950), 26–32.

22. For the laws on local defense units, see General Order no. 86, June 22, 1863, *OR,* series IV, 2:602, which includes the text of the law of August 21, 1861. See also *OR,* series IV, 2:798, which covers the election of field officers by local defense troops. By 1864, local defense units

ment commissioned colonels of (among others) the Virginia and Georgia Local Defense Troops, as well as the North Carolina "Junior" and "Senior" Reserves. Other units in Texas and South Carolina, also denoted "Reserves," remained under state control. Still other reserve units (the Mississippi Cavalry
Reserves, for example), were transferred to Confederate control and thus became "Confederate" at the time of transfer.

One problem in determining who is a colonel arises in the twilight period
between a "state" regiment's formation and its transfer to Confederate authority. Cols. John F. Smith and James M. Norris, to name two, were, respectively,
colonels of the Second Mississippi State Cavalry and the Texas Frontier Regiment prior to their transfer from state to Confederate control. These officers
were colonels, and colonels of a regiment that became "Confederate," but since
they were colonels prior to the time of transfer they were never "Confederate"
colonels. William Lowry, who succeeded Smith as colonel of the Second Mississippi State Cavalry, *was* a colonel at the time of transfer and thus is included
here as a Confederate colonel.

Proof of Rank

Anyone who's read the *Official Records* or postwar literature is struck by the
number of Confederate officers termed *colonel*. At times after the war, claimed
disillusioned observers, it seemed as if every Confederate veteran was called
"colonel" or "general." In the 1890s one waggish newspaper observed, "it has
been a standing joke . . . that the Confederate army was composed almost wholly of staff officers, and that the number of colonels . . . was materially greater
than the number of male adult citizens."[23]

There are five main sources for this "rank inflation": (1) inexact giving of titles, particularly in the *Official Records,* where many lieutenant colonels were

---

had become a large portion of the total Southern fighting force. The best overview of these
local defense units is in Steven H. Newton, *Lost for the Cause: The Confederate Army in 1864*
(Mason City, IA: Savas, 2000). There was a bewildering variety of such units. The Sixty-
seventh and Sixty-eighth North Carolina Infantries, for example, were raised specifically for
service within North Carolina but had colonels appointed by the Confederate government.
Three regiments of Alabama Reserves transformed themselves into PACS regiments, the Sixty-
second, Sixty-third, and Sixty-fifth Alabama Infantry. Still other regiments of "detailed" men
were formed.

23. "Dixie's Many Colonels," *Chicago Tribune,* September 5, 1897. For more humor on this
subject, see "The Colonels and the Generals," *Atlanta Constitution,* June 9, 1907.

termed *colonel*; (2) mixing up of "state" and "Confederate" rank; (3) the award-
ing of "rank" by the United Confederate Veterans organization; (4) the popular
impression that if an officer commanded a regiment, even temporarily, he
should be considered an "acting" or "brevet" colonel, even if his substantive rank
was less; and (5) postwar popular sentiment. As explained long after the war by
a veteran's son, "All the home Southern people have such love and respect and
veneration for their old heroes, and they feel now that so few of them are left to
tell the story, that they by virtue of their valor and true heroism *ought* to be generals, colonels and majors. If not for that reason, we all think that they are now
entitled to promotion by reason of succession to the titles."[24]

This book follows Confederate law and the surviving government records in
determining an officer's true rank. The best evidence of PACS appointment to
colonel is reflected in each individual officer's compiled service record (CSR).
The lists of appointments to colonel in the National Archives, notably the War
Department appointment ledgers in Record Group 109, chapters 93 and 127,
also are of value.

Inevitably, problems of proof crop up. Officers such as Lysander Adams of
the Thirty-third Tennessee Infantry have service records in which they are referred to as "colonel" and are indexed by the National Archives as such. In
Adams's case, the appointment to colonel, if made at all, was made by Gen.
Leonidas Polk, who had no legal authority to so appoint. A. G. Greenwood has
a CSR as colonel of the Twenty-sixth Arkansas Infantry. In this instance Greenwood, the officer who mustered the Twenty-sixth into Confederate service, was
mistakenly listed as its colonel on the mustering papers. James E. Saunders, a
colonel of Alabama militia, served on Bedford Forrest's staff and in the *Official
Records* is referred to by his militia rank. A. J. Coupland allegedly was given a
temporary rank of colonel and authorized by the secretary of war to raise a regiment, but when his regiment (the Eleventh Texas Infantry) formally organized,
the men elected Coupland lieutenant colonel instead. When the colonelcy of the
Thirty-fourth Texas Cavalry fell vacant, the brigade commander promoted Maj.
M. W. Deavenport to fill the vacancy, but Deavenport had already resigned his
commission. In 1863, Brig. Gen. Gideon Pillow authorized Capt. James F.
Franklin to raise a regiment within Union lines in West Tennessee. It appears
Pillow (without legal authority) gave Franklin a temporary rank as colonel, but
the new regiment never completed its organization.

---

24. Sid S. Johnson, *Texans Who Wore the Gray* (Tyler, TX: privately printed, 1907), 307.

Other problems of proof involve otherwise deserving officers whose records of promotion were lost or who were promoted too late in the war for their promotions to be recorded. For example, the CSR of John W. Brown of the Seventh Texas Infantry does not show any rank higher than that of captain. However, there is abundant unofficial evidence that he was promoted to colonel in early 1865. The same is true for George Hampton of the Fourth Texas Cavalry and Benjamin Watson of the Nineteenth Texas Cavalry. The policy followed in this book is to allow flexibility in instances involving end-of-war promotions and Trans-Mississippi Department promotions, the two major instances where War Department records are lacking.

Statistics on the Colonels

A total of 1,583 officers of the Confederate army ended their careers as colonels. An additional 324 Confederate colonels received promotion to higher rank—brigadier general and above—making a total of 1,907 officers who held colonel's rank at one time or another.[25]

Of the 1,583 PACS colonels, 1,461 were primarily line officers and 122 primarily staff officers.[26] Of the colonels promoted to general, 280 were primarily line officers, 44 primarily staff.

Since the Southern army contained approximately seven hundred regiments,[27] the average Confederate regiment thus had two full colonels. Some

25. The Confederate generals who had been promoted from colonel are listed in Appendix 1.

26. For these purposes, "staff" colonels include all nonregimental colonels, such as those serving in the offices of the War Department, on the staffs of generals, in military courts, and as commanders of nonregimented artillery.

27. The Confederate army consisted of 693 regiments in the spring of 1864. This number does not include battalions, detached companies, and artillery batteries. It counts consolidated regiments, such as the Sixth/Seventh Arkansas Infantry of Cleburne's Division, as the two separate regiments they once were. A handful of new regiments were formed after this, and several regiments had been dissolved prior to 1864. These changes would not materially affect the conclusions herein.

In the spring of 1864 these regiments, and their colonels, served in the following armies and departments: Army of Northern Virginia, 181; Army of Tennessee, 181; Department of Alabama, Mississippi, and East Louisiana, 102; Department of East Tennessee, 21; Department of North Carolina and Southern Virginia, 51; Department of Richmond, 8; Department of South Carolina, Georgia, and Florida, 31; Department of Western Virginia, 11; Trans-Mississippi Department, 107 (Newton, *Lost for the Cause*). William F. Fox, *Regimental Losses in the American Civil War* (Albany, NY: Albany Pub. Co., 1889), lists 764 Confederate regiments in all, including multiple designations of the same regiment.

regiments had many more. The Eleventh Texas Cavalry, for example, had six colonels, due in part to disputes over promotion. The First Virginia Cavalry, First South Carolina Rifles, and Fourth Texas Infantry had six, six, and five colonels, respectively, the regiments losing many field officers in the bloody battles of Lee's Army. Other regiments, often garrison troops seeing little or no action, ended the war under their original colonel. In this one-colonel category were such old fighting regiments as the Twelfth Texas Cavalry, garrison regiments such as the Third South Carolina Cavalry, regiments raised late in the war such as the Sixty-first Alabama Infantry, and short-lived regiments such as the Thirty-ninth Virginia Infantry.

The following chart illustrates the breakdown by state of the units in which the colonels served. If a colonel served as such in both staff and line, or in two or more regiments, he is counted in each instance:

State	Colonels
Alabama	136
Arkansas	115
Florida	21
Georgia	169
Indian Territory	111
Kentucky	39
Louisiana	83
Mississippi	129
Missouri	60
North Carolina	148
South Carolina	89
Tennessee	163
Texas	128
Virginia	186
Confederate regiments	21
Staff	136

Virginia's total is the highest, in part because Virginia raised more regiments than did any other Confederate state, in part because practically all Virginia regiments served in the Army of Northern Virginia, the army with the highest rate of officer casualties. The overall state numbers are roughly proportional to the number of regiments each state raised.

Promotion. The "Wizard of the Saddle," Nathan Bedford Forrest, enjoyed perhaps the most spectacular rise in rank in military history. Enlisting in 1861 as a private, in fewer than four years he became a lieutenant general. In the improvised Confederate Army, quick promotions could be gained by deserving, and lucky, men. About 7.5 percent of all Confederate colonels entered service as privates and climbed the eight grades of rank to their colonelcy. At the other end of the spectrum, 17 percent of the colonels earned promotion to general.

Age. It was a young man's army and a young man's officer corps. The average Confederate colonel was just over thirty-two years of age in 1861. Since the war lasted four years, the average age when the officer became a colonel would be one to two years greater than their age in 1861. These figures are in line with Ezra Warner's studies on Confederate generals, which show an average beginning-of-war age of thirty-six for a brigadier general, thirty-seven for a major general, forty-one for a lieutenant general, and forty-eight for a full general. These figures are also in line with those compiled by Robert K. Krick for the field officers of the Army of Northern Virginia.[28] Colonels were born in almost every year from 1790 to 1844, with the most (ninety-three) being born in 1830. Six were born in the 1700s, and twenty-two after 1840.

The oldest man to become a Confederate colonel was probably a man who never really served in the Confederate Army. Motey Kinnard, the Creek Indian chief, signed a treaty of alliance with the Confederacy that provided that he be commissioned a colonel of cavalry, to be paid as such for life. No exact record of Chief Kinnard's birth exists, but family tradition has him born about 1790, making him seventy-one years old at the start of the war and seventy-four when he received his colonel's commission in 1864. Lewis G. De Russy of Louisiana, an "old army" officer, was sixty-five when the war started and sixty-six when commissioned as a colonel. Other colonels born in the 1700s were John Drew, James McKoin, Gaspard Tochman, and Angus McDonald.

Numerous claimants have been advanced for the honor of being the youngest Confederate colonel. The youngest man to become full colonel was the precocious James R. Hagood of South Carolina, a Citadel graduate born on November 26, 1844, who was sixteen when the war started and ten days short of his nineteenth birthday when commissioned as a colonel. Eight colonels were

---

28. Ezra J. Warner, *Generals in Gray: Lives of the Confederate Commanders* (Baton Rouge: Louisiana State University Press, 1959); Robert K. Krick, *Lee's Colonels: A Biographical Register of the Field Officers of the Army of Northern Virginia* (Dayton: Morningside, 1992).

born after 1841: George H. Carmical, Charles C. Floweree, John Higginbotham, William G. Burt, John W. Hinsdale, William L. Duff, William B. Lowry, and John Ed Murray. Forty-two future colonels were twenty or younger when the war started, and seven colonels—Burgwyn (born in 1841), Carmical, Duff, Floweree, Hagood, Higginbotham, and Murray—had not yet reached the tender age of twenty-one when they were commissioned.

Casualties. The war took its toll on the Confederate officer corps. A total of 252 colonels (16 percent) were killed or mortally wounded in action, and a further eight died in POW camps. Gettysburg claimed the most lives (nineteen) of any one battle. Five were killed in 1861, seventy-three in 1862, sixty in 1863, ninety-nine in 1864, and fifteen in 1865. Eighty died during the war of natural or noncombat causes. Reflecting the bloody fighting in Virginia, colonels of the Army of Northern Virginia, an army with fewer than half the Confederate regiments, accounted for 58 percent of the casualties, with the Western armies accounting for 33 percent and the Trans-Mississippi Department 9 percent.

Confederate colonels died in almost every year from 1861 to 1932. The most peacetime deaths occurred in 1889 (thirty-eight), with twenty to thirty deaths occurring in almost every year from 1865 to 1910. Of the colonels who survived the war, half were dead by 1896. The average age at death of those surviving the war was sixty-eight.

The first colonel to die was the unfortunate Seaborn M. Phillips of the Tenth Mississippi Infantry, who succumbed to "camp fever" at Pensacola, Florida, on May 23, 1861, little more than a month after Fort Sumter and little more than a month after he had become a colonel. The first colonels to be killed in action were Francis Bartow and Charles Fisher, both killed at First Manassas.[29] The last colonel to be killed in action was Charles A. L. Lamar, killed in a skirmish at Columbus, Georgia, on April 16, 1865. The beginning of the Great Depression coincided with the death of the last surviving Confederate colonel. John A. Wilson of the Twenty-fourth Tennessee Infantry "passed over the river" on March 19, 1932, in Bowie, Texas. The obituaries in the local newspapers failed to note that, with Wilson's death, an era had ended. At the age of ninety-four years and five months, Wilson was the second longest lived colonel, Michael Bulger having died at ninety-four years and ten months. At the other extreme was the

---

29. Bartow appears to have been the first Confederate colonel killed in action, some hours prior to Fisher. Colonel Edmund B. Holloway of the Missouri State Guard was killed by friendly fire in a June 13, 1861, skirmish in Missouri, one month prior to First Manassas.

shortest lived colonel, the highly regarded young John Ed Murray of the Fifth/ Thirteenth Arkansas, killed in the battle of Atlanta at the age of twenty-one years, five months. Thirty-six colonels lived into the 1920s.

William R. Calhoun survived enemy shells only to be killed by a subordinate (Alfred Rhett, who succeeded to his colonelcy) in an 1862 duel. R. T. P. Allen drowned while swimming. Reeves died from the bite of a rabid dog. Oliver died after hitting his head on an outhouse. Train accidents accounted for Alley, Clarke, Hagood, and Pate. Nine, including Anderson, Barry, Boyleston, and Brown, committed suicide. Woodruff and Wright had buildings fall on them during a fire. A relative accidentally shot Abercrombie, mistaking him for a burglar. Lowry, a western sheriff, was mortally wounded in a shootout. Bounds and Wilson were murdered by their men during the war, and at least eleven other colonels were murdered after the war. Henry Clay King died in prison after murdering an opposing lawyer.

Other losses. Nineteen colonels were thrown out of the army by court-martial or similar action, while many others, facing charges, chose to resign their commissions rather than risk trial. One in twelve Confederate colonels (136 in all) faced a court-martial at some point, most winning acquittal. Hundreds resigned their commissions, citing causes such as wounds or ill health (the most usual), advanced age, quarrels with fellow officers, poverty, and wishing to go home to take care of their families. Others were dropped from the army when their regiments ceased to exist due to consolidation with other regiments.

The single greatest loss among Confederate colonels did not occur at Gettysburg or Shiloh but rather at the army's 1862 reorganization elections. A Confederate law passed early in 1862 provided that existing regiments enlisted for one year's service must reorganize as three-year regiments.[30] As part of that reorganization, new elections for the regiments' field officers took place, mostly in April and May 1862. The inane but popular notion that troops should elect their officers had a predictably inane but popular result, throwing out huge numbers of deserving but unpopular officers, along with officers best characterized as "duds." No less than seventy-five regiments—one out of every four eligible—threw out their incumbent colonels.[31] Since at the time many regiments

---

30. The "Conscript Act" of April 16, 1862, *OR*, series IV, 1:1095.

31. On March 1, 1862, the secretary of war listed 369 regiments in all, 274 one-year regiments and 95 three-year regiments. Only the one-year regiments needed to reorganize. See *OR*, series IV, 1:962. For an overview of the reorganization, see Kevin C. Ruffner, "Before the Seven Days: The Reorganization of the Confederate Army in the Spring of 1862," in William J.

were commanded by officers of a lesser grade (lieutenant colonels or majors), while other colonels, facing reelection defeat, chose not to run, the removal rate was in reality far greater than the ostensible 26 percent. As a rule, the new electees were younger than the men they replaced, and often of very junior rank—lieutenants or captains.

Many harshly criticized these reelections, both at the time and subsequently. General Lee recognized the practical absurdity of reorganizing an army at a time when it was in contact with the enemy. Lee biographer Douglas Southall Freeman characterized officer elections as "rewarding those who had curried favor by laxity and demoting those who had enforced discipline." Some officers objected to elections on principle. Col. R. M. Cary of the Thirtieth Virginia, a strict disciplinarian, declined to run for reelection, being unwilling "to hold position conferred by those subject to his control." Elected nonetheless, Cary refused to accept and left the army.[32]

Turnover. Between elections, battle casualties, and resignations, regiments rarely had the same leader from one battle to the next. As one illustration, the Confederate army at Shiloh consisted of seventy-six regiments, but by the time of the next battle for these regiments (Perryville, Corinth, Baton Rouge or Stones River, five to eight months later), fifty-seven had a different commander, four had been broken up, and only fifteen (21 percent) had the same commander.

Place of birth/death. The list below shows the states of birth and death (where known) of the colonels:

State	Birth	Death
Alabama	108	105
Arkansas	4	68
Delaware	1	—
District of Columbia	7	22
Florida	8	43
Georgia	215	130
Indian Territory/Oklahoma	1	17

Miller, ed., *The Peninsula Campaign of 1862: Yorktown to Seven Days,* 3 vols. (Campbell, CA: Savas Woodbury, 1995–96), 1:47–70. In the Army of Northern Virginia, almost one field officer per regiment was thrown out by reelection. See Krick, *Lee's Colonels,* 16.

32. Freeman, *Robert E. Lee: A Biography,* 4 vols. (New York: Scribner's, 1934–35), 2:14–15, 26. Krick, *Lee's Colonels,* 88.

State	Birth	Death
Kentucky	101	34
Louisiana	35	71
Maryland	24	13
Mississippi	52	73
Missouri	16	30
North Carolina	176	78
South Carolina	203	61
Tennessee	211	118
Texas	51	38
Virginia	303[33]	161
West Virginia	—	13
Free States	70	67
Abroad	43	14

252 killed in action

8 died of disease in northern POW camps

63 unproved/disputed places of death

As can be seen, the overwhelming majority of colonels were born in the older southern states. Most colonels from the "western" states had been born in the east and then moved west. This westward movement, one that would have made Horace Greeley ("Go west, young man") proud, continued after the war. About 5 percent of the colonels hailed from the "Free" states of the Union, including eighteen from New York alone. More colonels were born in the North than in five of the eleven seceding states, and more colonels died in the North than died in Kentucky, Missouri, or Florida. About 3 percent were born abroad. Ireland furnished eleven colonels, Scotland nine, Germany seven, France five, England two, and Poland two, with Belgium, Sweden, Denmark, Wales, Canada, Cuba, and the Ottoman Empire furnishing one apiece. Most colonels remained in the South after Appomattox. Only 6 percent died outside the South, in such exotic places as Colombia (Samuel H. Lockett), Canada (John T. Wood), Italy (Thomas J. Page), Russia (James L. Orr), Mexico (A. A. Russell, J. C. Monroe), Brazil (Peter Hardeman, Arch S. Dobbins), and China (Alexander C. Jones).[34]

33. Birth totals for Virginia include what is now West Virginia, which was part of Virginia prior to the war.

34. Only 2.2 percent of whites in the eleven seceding states were Northern-born (per the 1860 census); thus, the Northern-born colonels exceeded their proportion in the Southern

Education. Compared to the present day, few antebellum Americans sought or received a college education. It is therefore surprising to see that over half (848, or 53 percent) of the colonels attended college, with many attending more than one college. No less than 116 attended the U.S. Military Academy at West Point. The University of Virginia was the second most attended, with 108. Seventy-three attended VMI, 51 the University of North Carolina, 44 the University of South Carolina, 43 the University of Georgia, and 41 Cumberland College in Tennessee. Many went North for their schooling, with 29 attending Yale, 18 Harvard, and 12 apiece Princeton and the University of Pennsylvania. One each attended the École des Ponts et Chaussées in France and the universities of Havana, Warsaw, and Berlin.

Prewar military background. Civil War officers are often derided as inexperienced amateurs. Although based on inadequate documentation, or no documentation at all, that stereotype contains more than a grain of truth. Yet no less than 720 (45 percent) of the colonels had some prewar military background. If more information were available as to antebellum militia officers, this total would doubtless be greater. The list below breaks down their military backgrounds:

Attended military colleges such as VMI	159
Attended military high schools	31
Total attending private or state-sponsored military schools	190
West Point graduate	67
West Point, nongraduate	49
U.S. Army, non–West Point	49
Total U.S. Army	165
U.S. Navy, Annapolis attendee	7
U.S. Navy, non-Annapolis	12
U.S. Marines	3
Total U.S. Navy	22
State militia	229
Mexican War volunteers	186
Indian War volunteers	40

population. The percentage of foreign-born colonels was slightly less than the percentage of foreign-born Southerners.

Attended foreign military schools	3
Veterans of foreign armies	14
Filibusterers, soldiers of fortune	18
Other	14
Minus duplicates with service in more than one category above	157
Total	**720**

This 45 percent figure compares favorably with the 64 percent figure for Confederate generals with prewar military experience. The dropoff simply was not as large as many historians have hitherto believed. Looked at from still other perspectives, the dropoff narrows even further. For example, if one includes the 324 colonels who became generals, the percentage of colonels with prewar military background jumps from 45 to 48 percent. And those colonels without any prewar military background largely achieved their rank after the first year of the war, with their year of actual Civil War service supplanting any lack of prewar experience.

The popular image of amateur officers is, at least at the level of colonel, a myth. On September 30, 1861, the Confederate War Department tabulated the 233 regiments it had records of, listing their colonels. Of the 233 listed, 186 (80 percent) had demonstrable prewar military background.[35] Of the remaining 47 regiments, many had a lieutenant colonel or major with the experience their colonel lacked. A sample from two Confederate states breaks down these figures further. Of the first wave of thirty-four Georgia regiments raised in 1861 (First through Thirtieth Infantry, plus four others), only thirteen (38 percent) chose colonels with no military background of any sort. The twenty-one colonels (62 percent) with a prewar military background comprised seven West Pointers, one non–West Point regular army officer, six officers in the volunteer militia, four Mexican War veterans, and three veterans of other wars. Of the thirteen colonels with no prewar experience, nine were backstopped by a lieutenant colonel or major with such experience. Louisiana shows a similar pattern. Of the first twenty-one Louisiana regiments, seventeen (81 percent) had colonels with pre-

35. The tabulation of regiments, and colonels, recognized by the War Department as of September 30, 1861, is in *OR*, series IV, 1:626. In the first major battle of the war, First Manassas, all of the brigades and 83 percent (thirty-eight of forty-six) of the regiments were headed by officers with prewar military background.

war experience, and three of the remaining four had experienced lieutenant colonels. When we add to these 1861 figures the men who were later commissioned as colonels (with rare exceptions, officers who had already served in the Confederate army), over 90 percent of line colonels had military experience at the time of their commissioning.

To an extent not always appreciated, Confederate regiments *were* commanded by men with military experience. However, the prewar military background of the men, as regular army lieutenants commanding a company or as privates in the Mexican War, did not always prepare them for the responsibilities of running a regiment. The problems that arose in the early days of the war stemmed from that limited experience, plus the dearth of experienced company officers and NCOs.

Several surprising patterns emerge from the statistics above. First, private military schools furnished more colonels than did West Point. VMI alone furnished seventy-three colonels—greater than the number of West Point graduates who became colonels. Second, the number of West Point nongraduates was almost as great as the number of graduates. Prior studies of West Point in the Confederacy have focused almost exclusively on the graduates, but based on these numbers more attention should be paid to those who did *not* graduate. Third, both state militia and Mexican War veterans outnumbered regular army veterans. Fourth, twenty-two naval veterans forsook service at sea in order to join the army.

Judging solely by the numbers of officers, only about 10 percent had prewar U.S. Army experience of any kind, while three times as many had other military background. The influence of the 10 percent on instruction and training could not, in any case, have been large and was dwarfed by the much larger numbers who had other military experience or no experience at all. While West Point–trained professional officers *commanded* the army, the army's regiments were *trained* and *led* largely by nonprofessionals.

There were also regional differences in the type of prewar military background. Virginia, for example, sent a relatively small volunteer contingent (one regiment) to the Mexican War but had the South's largest pool of West Point–trained officers and military school graduates. In contrast, Texas and Louisiana sent large contingents to the Mexican War (six regiments apiece) but had no long-established military schools or many West Point graduates. The colonels of these states' Civil War regiments reflect this imbalance. In general, the colonels of regiments from western states were more likely to be Mexican War veterans, and the colonels of eastern states more likely to boast of a formal military education.

The two main Confederate armies, the Army of Tennessee and the Army of Northern Virginia, drew their regiments from their home areas (the west and the east, respectively), and their colonels reflect this regional difference in experience. Another factor impacted the experience of the colonels of these two armies. In 1861, the Confederate government rushed the first-raised regiments, the regiments most likely to contain experienced officers, to Virginia to protect the capitol, while later-raised regiments were sent west, to an area then shielded by neutral Kentucky. This perfectly rational decision resulted in the cream of the Confederate army fighting in the east throughout the war. In January 1862, for example, of the sixty-nine regiments in the Western Department, thirty-four had as their original colonel an officer with no prewar military background. The Tennessee and Arkansas regiments, in particular, lacked experienced colonels. In the same month the Army in Virginia showed ninety regiments, of whom only fourteen lacked that prewar background, with a much higher percentage of the colonels being West Pointers.[36]

Of the Confederate states, Virginia, with its old army tradition and its VMI graduates, had the largest pool of potential officer candidates. Of Virginia's sixty-five initial regiments, sixty-one had colonels with a prewar military background. Arkansas, with no state-sponsored military school and only three prewar West Point graduates, had perhaps the scantiest pool of experienced officer candidates. Not surprisingly, the Confederate armies performed best in Virginia and worst in Arkansas.

Occupations. The majority of Southerners in 1861 farmed. The majority of the South's political leaders in 1861 were either farmers or lawyers. Not surprisingly, the majority of Confederate colonels were either farmers, lawyers, or politicians.

Because many colonels had more than one occupation (for example, many lawyers also owned plantations, and retired military officers usually started a second career), no exact breakdown of prewar occupations is possible. It should

36. For these two armies see *OR*, series I, 7:852 (January 31, 1862) and 5:1029 (January 14, 1862). For an overview of the contrasts between the eastern and western armies, see Richard M. McMurry, *Two Great Rebel Armies: An Essay in Confederate Military History* (Chapel Hill: University of North Carolina Press, 1989), esp. chaps. 6–7. For antebellum private military schools, see Bruce S. Allardice, "West Points of the Confederacy: Southern Military Schools and the Confederate Army," *Civil War History* 43:4 (December 1997): 310–31.

be noted, however, that among the colonels were eighty-six prewar physicians, thirty-eight ministers of religion, and sixty-seven newspaper editors, occupations not normally associated with a military career. It is clear that the common soldiers elected community leaders, and persons with education, to lead them, and the local minister or doctor was often one of the few educated men in the community. Only six manufacturers became colonels, a clear reflection of the South's essentially rural, nonindustrial prewar economy. Among the more unusual prewar lines of work were candy maker (George A. Smith); marble cutter (James Barr); saddle maker (Peter A. S. McGlashan); carpenter (Moses W. Smith); livery stable owner (Jeffrey Forrest); accountant (Samuel E. Baker); shoe salesman (William T. Barry); steamboat pilot (William A. Johnson); and sawmill owner (George W. Lee). Thirty-six members of the Confederate House and Senate served as colonels, as did three prewar and seven postwar U.S. senators, thirty-one prewar and thirty-five postwar U.S. congressmen, twenty-one prewar and postwar governors, and one future justice of the U.S. Supreme Court. Hundreds more colonels served in a state legislature or as a judge. One hundred and six colonels had been delegates to their state's secession convention.

Names. The names of Confederate army colonels overwhelmingly conformed to the norms of nineteenth-century Anglo-Saxon names. The era's standard first names predominated, with William and John the most common, followed by James, Robert, and Thomas. Fully 656 (41.4 percent) of the colonels shared these five first names. The next five most common first names were Charles, George, Joseph, Henry, and Samuel. There were no Ashleys, no Brets, no Rhetts, the kind of names one famous movie in particular loved to bestow on antebellum Southerners, but there were Gustaves, Adolphuses, an Ambrosio Jose, a Ludwig, two Pierres, and a Xavier. Smith and Jones led in last names with twenty-six apiece, followed by Brown (fourteen), Moore (thirteen), Williams (twelve), White (eleven), Harrison (ten), and Johnson (ten).

Burials. Hollywood Cemetery in Richmond has been called the "graveyard of the Confederacy." It is certainly the graveyard of colonels. No fewer than fifty-one colonels were buried there, including several colonels temporarily buried there after their deaths in battle. The next highest total is in Elmwood Cemetery, Memphis, with twenty-three. By state, the leading cemeteries are Oakwood in Montgomery, Alabama (twenty); Mt. Holly in Little Rock, Arkansas (six); Evergreen in Jacksonville, Florida (six); Rose Hill in Macon, Georgia (sixteen); Lexington in Lexington, Kentucky (twelve); Metairie in New Orleans, Louisiana (twelve); Greenwood in Jackson, Mississippi (ten); Bellefontaine in St. Louis, Missouri (eight); Oakdale in Wilmington, North Carolina (thirteen); Magnolia in Charleston, South Carolina (nine); Elmwood in Memphis, Tennessee (twenty-three); State Cemetery in Austin, Texas (eleven); and Hollywood in Richmond, Virginia (fifty-one). Outside the south, Woodlawn Cemetery in New York City has the most burials, with five.

USING THE REGISTER

It has been said that writing is the art of conveying the smallest number of facts using the greatest number of words. This biographical register reverses that admonition. Given the large number of officers to be covered (more than fifteen hundred) and the ever present dictates of book size and reader patience, it would be impractical to make the entries in fully composed prose. Instead, this roster is written using sentence fragments and numerous abbreviations, obeying the biblical injunction to "Let thy speech be short, comprehending much in few words." It is hoped that the reader will easily comprehend the information presented. Below are some notes to aid in that comprehension.

Standard information. The biographies contained in this book were written to contain, at a minimum, each officer's (1) date of birth; (2) place of birth; (3) college attended; (4) prewar residence and occupation; (5) prewar military experience; (6) spouse(s); (7) service record (ranks, units, dates of promotion); (8) instances of being wounded or captured; (9) postwar residence and occupation; (10) public/political posts held; (11) date of death; (12) place of death; and (13) place of burial. In addition, the biographies list (14) any published writings on the officer or manuscript collection of his papers and, whenever possible, include (15) a short quote from a contemporary illustrating the officer's character.

Geographic names. If an officer's entire life was spent in one state, the counties and cities listed in his biography will all be in that state. For example, in the beginning of his entry, Joseph Abney is noted as having been born in South Carolina, and all cities referred to subsequently in his entry are in South Carolina. If the officer moved to another state, once that "new" state is named, subsequent references are to places in that "new" state. Generally, battles that the officer participated in are named without designating the state where the battle occurred, the exception being battles so obscure that the average reader would have no idea where they were fought.

Regiments. Every scholar who has dealt with the Confederate Army becomes frustrated at some point with how the Confederacy labeled its regiments. The regiments often bore two or more numerical designations and were also designated by the name of the colonel, with the confusion becoming worse the farther west a regiment was raised. The state of Arkansas, in particular, seemed bent on bedeviling future historians. For example, the unit usually known as the Thirty-ninth Arkansas Infantry had at least nine monikers: Thirty-ninth Arkansas, Sixth Arkansas, Twentieth Arkansas, Twenty-first Arkansas, Sixth Trans-Mississippi Rifles, Cocke's Regiment, Hawthorne's Regiment, Johnson's Regiment, and Polk's Regiment. To add to the confusion, the Thirtieth Arkansas was briefly (and erroneously) called the Thirty-ninth, and the "real" Sixth, Twentieth, and Twenty-first Arkansas existed at the same time as the Thirty-ninth!

States organized regiments and gave these regiments names and/or numbers prior to their being mustered into the PACS, which accounts for part of the problem. Other regiments, organized late in the war in the Trans-Mississippi—for example, McGehee's (Forty-fourth) Arkansas (Mounted) Infantry—never were able to get their muster rolls to the War Department in Richmond so as to be officially recognized and numbered.

Confederate authorities sometimes changed the official designation of a unit. Coltart's Twenty-sixth Alabama was redesignated the Fiftieth Alabama. Company D of the Tenth Tennessee became Company I. The Twenty-sixth Georgia evolved into the Seventh Georgia Battalion and finally into the Sixty-first Georgia. The Sixth North Carolina Cavalry had its additional "state" designation of Sixty-fifth North Carolina Volunteers. Where relevant, these different official designations are noted in the register.

This work generally uses the regimental designations given in the National Archives microfilmed compiled service records—not because these designations are the best, but because they are most familiar to researchers. Exceptions to this approach will be specifically noted. Regimental designations are to infantry units unless they are specifically noted as being to a cavalry, artillery, or some other type of unit. Thus, "6th AR" refers to the Sixth Arkansas Infantry, while the Sixth Arkansas Cavalry is denoted "6th AR Cav."

Date of commission. In practice, the process of promotion to colonel involved five different relevant dates: those of election/appointment; nomination; confirmation; acceptance by the new colonel; and commission. Unless otherwise noted, the latter date, considered to be the date the colonel "ranked from," is the one given here. In the majority of cases, the date of commission is close to the date the promotion actually took place. Similarly, the date of resignation given is the date the resignation was accepted by the War Department, not the date the officer first submitted his letter of resignation. The officer's compiled service record supplies most of the dates given here, with other dates derived from independent sources.

In numerous instances, officers are shown as belonging to units that did not, technically, exist until a later time. This occurred primarily when a person joined an independent company that had not yet become part of a regimental organization or a unit that had not yet been accepted into Confederate service. For example, James Aiken's "Randolph Mountaineers" became Company D of the Thirteenth Alabama upon that regiment's organization, and Aiken's compiled service record reflects his service as being in that Company D. Thomas G. Bacon was elected colonel of the future Seventh South Carolina (at the time a state army unit) in March 1861. Bacon's compiled service record, and this roster, will reflect his commissioning as colonel on April 15, 1861, the date the regiment was accepted into Confederate service.

Place of burial. In many instances, officers killed in action were buried on the battlefield. In a number of biographies of the colonels killed in action, no place of burial is given. It can be assumed that the officer was buried on the battlefield, but the biographies do not note this unless proof of such burial has been found.

ABBREVIATIONS

The abbreviations listed below are not the only ones used in this book, but they are the ones an average reader may not be familiar with.

AAAG	acting assistant adjutant general
AADC	acting aide-de-camp
AAG	assistant adjutant general
AAIG	assistant adjutant and inspector general
ACS	assistant commissary of subsistence
ADC	aide-de-camp
Adj.	adjutant
AIG	adjutant inspector general
ANV	Army of Northern Virginia
Appmx.	paroled at Appomattox in April 1865
AQM	assistant quartermaster
Art.	Artillery
asst.	assistant
attd.	attended
Bn.	Battalion
Cav.	Cavalry
Co.	county or company, as appropriate
corp.	corporal
cos.	counties
CS	Confederate States
CSN	Confederate States Navy
CSR	Compiled Service Record
dist.	district

Div.	Division
exch.	exchanged
GDAH	Georgia Department of Archives and History
GMI	Georgia Military Institute
grad.	graduate
IG	inspector general
Inf.	Infantry
KIA	killed in action
KMI	Kentucky Military Institute
KSG	Kentucky State Guard
LDT	Local Defense Troops
MR	Mounted Rifles
MSG	Missouri State Guard
Mtd.	mounted
MWIA	mortally wounded in action
NYU	New York University
OO	ordnance officer
OR	*Official Records of the Civil War*
PACS	Provisional Army of the Confederate States
PAVA	Provisional Army of Virginia
PR	Partisan Rangers
Pvt.	private
QM	quartermaster
Regt.	Regiment
SCMA	South Carolina Military Academy, aka The Citadel
temp.	temporary
TMD	Trans-Mississippi Department
TSLA	Tennessee State Library and Archives
UAL	University of Alabama
UCV	United Confederate Veterans, a postwar veterans organization
UGA	University of Georgia, known in its early days as Franklin College
ULA	University of Louisiana
UMO	University of Missouri
UMS	University of Mississippi
UNC	University of North Carolina

unmd.	unmarried
UPA	University of Pennsylvania
USC	University of South Carolina, known then as South Carolina College
USMA	United States Military Academy (West Point)
USN	United States Navy
UTN	University of Tennessee (then East Tennessee University)
UTX	University of Texas
UVA	University of Virginia
VADC	volunteer aide-de-camp
VAHS	Virginia Historical Society
VMI	Virginia Military Institute
WIA	wounded in action
WMI	Western Military Institute, after 1854 a branch of the University of Nashville

William P. Adair, 2d Cherokee Mounted Rifles (Annie Abel, *The American Indian as Slaveholder and Secessionist* [Cleveland: A. H. Clark Co., 1919])

Benjamin E. Caudill, 13th Kentucky Cavalry (Kay Caudill Riecke)

David G. Cowand, 32d North Carolina (North Carolina Museum of History)

William L. Davidson, 7th North Carolina (Malcolm Marion)

James J. Diamond, 11th Texas Cavalry (Glynda Herndon)

Hume R. Feild, 1st Tennessee (Emily and Ronnie Townes collection)

Stuart W. Fisk, 25th Louisiana. (Kenneth Trist Urquhart)

Jeffrey E. Forrest, Forrest's Tennessee Cavalry (Mike Miner)

William Gilham, 21st Virginia (Virginia Military Institute Archives)

John Griffith, 11th/17th Arkansas (Bill Weldon)

Hiram L. Grinstead, 33d Arkansas (Mrs. M. A. Elliott, comp., *The Garden of Memory: Stories of the Civil War as Told by Veterans and Daughters of the Confederacy* [Camden, AR, 1911])

Matthew R. Hall, 48th Georgia (Margaret Monthan)

John M. Hughes, 25th
Tennessee (Emma Jean Carter)

William L. Jeffers, 8th Missouri
Cavalry (Jim McGhee)

Mathias Martin, 23d Tennessee
(Tennessee Division, Sons of
Confederate Veterans)

William S. McLemore, 4th
Tennessee Cavalry (John
Rucker)

Hugh R. Miller, 42d Mississippi
(Bob F. Thompson)

John S. Mosby, Mosby's
Virginia Rangers (NARA
530499)

George S. Patton, 22d Virginia (Virginia Military Institute Archives)

George C. Porter, 6th Tennessee (Tennessee Division, Sons of Confederate Veterans)

David Shanks, 12th Missouri Cavalry ("Confederate Veteran")

Thomas P. Shaw, 19th South Carolina. (Jeannette Broome)

Cyrus A. Sugg, 50th Tennessee (Barbara Dudley Brown)

James J. Turner, 30th Tennessee (Tennessee Division, Sons of Confederate Veterans)

The Register

Abercrombie, Robert Haden. Born Sept. 11, 1837, Cross Keys, Macon Co., AL. Grad. Cumberland U. Law School in 1859. Prewar lawyer in Tuskegee, AL. Md. Frances Gary. Capt. Co. H, 45th AL, March 14, 1862. Major, March 25, 1862. Lt. col., Oct. 28, 1863. WIA Franklin. Col., 1st AL Consolidated (consolidation of the 16th, 33d, and 45th AL), April 9, 1865. Postwar lawyer in Tuskegee and Gadsden. "A gentleman of the highest personal and professional standing." Accidentally shot and killed in Gadsden, June 8, 1891, by his son-in-law, who mistook Abercrombie for a chicken thief. Buried Tuskegee City Cemetery.

Abernathy, Alfred Harris. Born Feb. 26, 1822, Giles Co., TN. Grad. U. of Nashville, 1839. Teacher at Giles College. Circuit court clerk. Md. Elizabeth Todd Butler. Capt. Co. C, 53d TN, 1861. Col., Sept. 9, 1861. POW Fort Donelson. Exch. Sept. 1862. Resigned Sept. 26, 1862. Teacher at, and president of, Giles College postwar. Died May 7, 1889. Buried Maplewood Cemetery, Pulaski. Lt. Col. Lockhart said Col. Abernathy "makes no pretensions to military skill, but is certainly a gentleman and a scholar."

Abert, George William. Born April 28, 1829, Lowndes Co., MS. Attd. WMI and KMI. Md. Pattie V. Barry; Virginia Prentice. Sgt. Co. K, 14th MS, May 25, 1861. Capt. Co. E, 4th MS Cav. Bn. (later part of the 8th Confederate Cav.), Nov. 14, 1861. Discharged June 27, 1862, due to illness. Lt. col., 14th MS, Sept. 26, 1862. Col., Oct. 18, 1862. Resigned March 29, 1863, due to "phythesis" (tuberculosis). Detached to become post commander at Meridian, MS, Oct. 3, 1863. Cotton buyer in Columbus postwar. Died Dec. 16, 1912. Buried Friendship Cemetery, Columbus. According to friends, Abert was "patriotic almost to a fault" but physically unable to stand field duty.

Abney, Joseph Griffith Raleford. Born Dec. 2, 1819, Edgefield Dist., SC. Edgefield lawyer and newspaper editor prewar. State legislator. Officer in Mexican War. Md. Susan M. Miller. Capt. Co. A, 22d SC, Dec. 1861. Col., Jan. 29, 1862. Dropped at May 1862 reorganization. Major, 1st SC Bn. Sharpshooters, June 21, 1862. Major, 27th SC, Oct. 2, 1863. WIA Drewry's Bluff. Retired March 6, 1865. Returned to Edgefield after the war. Promoted ex-Confederate emigration to Brazil and may have lived there himself for a time. Died of his wounds, Feb. 2, 1870, Edgefield. Buried Willowbrook Baptist Cemetery, Edgefield. Gen. Hagood found Abney brave but indolent.

Adair, Thomas Nepoleon. Born April 11, 1834, near Winona, MS. Attd. medical college in Philadelphia and the U. of Nashville Med. School. Physician in Choctaw and Carroll Cos. prewar. Md. Elizabeth Frances Ross, his brother's widow. Sgt. Co. E, 4th MS, 1861. Major, Aug. 24, 1861. Escaped capture at Fort Donelson by rowing a dugout across the Cumberland River. Lt. col., Oct. 1, 1862. Twice WIA in Siege of Vicksburg. POW Vicksburg. Col., July 16, 1863. WIA Franklin in head. POW Fort Blakely, while commanding Sears's Brigade. Paroled Grenada, May 19, 1865. Physician and farmer in Montgomery Co. postwar. Moved to near Doddsville, MS, in 1895. Died Sept. 27, 1918, at his son's home in Doddsville. Buried Hays Creek Cemetery, Winona. In all, six Adair (also spelled "Adaire") brothers, and seven nephews, served in the Confederate army.

Adair, William Penn. Born April 15, 1830, near New Echota, GA, a mixed-blood Cherokee. Removed to the Indian Territory (OK) with the Cherokee tribe in 1837. Lawyer and tribal senator in the Flint Dist. prewar. Md. Sarah Adair; Susannah McIntosh Drew. 1st lt. and AQM, 1st Cherokee MR, 1861–62. POW July 3, 1862, Locust Grove, OK, and later exchanged. Col., 2d Cherokee MR, Feb. 3, 1863. Postwar lawyer and senator. Elected asst. chief of the Cherokees in 1879. Often represented Cherokee interests in Washington. Died Oct. 23, 1880, Washington, DC. Buried Tahlequah City Cemetery. One history calls Adair "magnetic, logical and frankly agreeable, the ablest and most brilliant of all Cherokees."

Adams, Charles W. Born Aug. 16, 1817, Boston, MA. Grew up in IN. Moved to Helena, AR, in 1835. Prewar lawyer, judge, cotton planter. Md. Lucy Everett. Delegate to AR Secession Convention, where he made lengthy speeches lauding secession. Major and QM, AR State Troops, 1861. Col., 23d AR, April 25, 1862. Transferred back to AR in the summer of 1862 and raised a new infantry regiment. Col., Adams's Regt. (aka 3d Regt., northwest division), mustered in Sept. 12, 1862. The raw regiment bolted at Prairie Grove, its first battle, and was soon (Dec. 16, 1862) dissolved. The regiment's lt. col., who panicked, was blamed for the debacle, but the disgrace touched Adams also. AAG and chief of staff to Gen. Hindman, fall of 1863. Commanded the Northern Sub-District of AR in 1864 with the rank of "acting brigadier general." Lawyer in Helena and Memphis postwar. Died Sept. 9, 1878, Memphis, of yellow fever. Buried Elmwood Cemetery, Memphis. Grandfather of Helen Keller. John N. Edwards bitterly criticized Adams's conduct as commander in northern AR, suggesting Adams favored cotton trading over fighting.

Adams, Fleming Wall. Born Nov. 19, 1828, Hanover Co., VA. Reared in Campbell Co. Attd. UVA. Studied law and moved to Handsboro, Harrison Co., MS. Unmd. Capt. Co. E (the "Adams Rifles"), 20th MS, May 20, 1861. "Gallant and courteous." Col., 38th MS, May 12, 1862. Injured on the field at Iuka. Resigned Sept. 24, 1862, due to his injuries and requested an appointment in the QM Dept. Lawyer in Brenham, TX, postwar. Died there March 13, 1871. Buried Masonic (aka Yellow Fever) Cemetery, Brenham.

Adams, Samuel. Born March 5, 1829, Abbeville Dist., SC. Grad. USC in 1850. Moved to Butler Co., AL in 1851. Teacher and lawyer in Conecuh Co. and Greenville. State representative 1857–61. Md. Dora, sister of Col. Hilary Herbert. 2d lt. Co. G, 9th AL, July 19, 1861. 1st lt., Sept. 6, 1861. Col., 33d AL upon its April 23, 1862, organization. WIA Perryville while leading a brigade. A "true patriot and Christian hero—a perfect specimen of a soldier and gentleman." KIA July 21, 1864, by a sharpshooter, in the fighting at Bald Hill near Atlanta. Buried Pioneer Cemetery, Greenville.

Aiken, David Wyatt. Born March 17, 1828, Winnsboro, SC. Grad. USC. Teacher and planter in the Abbeville Dist. prewar. Md. Martha Dubose Gaillard. Adj., 7th SC, March 9, 1861. Col., May 14, 1862. WIA Antietam (lung) so severely he was thought dead. Commanded post of Macon, GA, Aug. 1863–July 1864. Resigned July 14, 1864, due to his wounds. Printer and newspaper owner in Charleston postwar. Trustee of Davidson College. State representative 1865–66. US congressman 1877–87. Died April 6, 1887, Cokesbury. Buried Magnolia Cemetery, Greenwood, SC. Brother of Col. Hugh K. Aiken. War papers at USC. The brigade historian called Aiken "bold, fearless, and incorruptible."

Aiken, Hugh Kerr. Born July 5, 1822, Winnsboro, SC. Attd. USC. Planter in Winnsboro prewar. Moved to Charleston in 1856. Militia general. Md. Mary Gayle, daughter of Gov. John Gayle of AL. Lt. col., 16th SC Cav. Bn., July 21, 1862. Col., 6th SC Cav. (formed from the 16th Bn.), Nov. 1, 1862. Shot through the body at Trevilian Station. Led Butler's Brigade in the Carolinas Campaign. KIA Feb. 27, 1865, in a skirmish near Darlington, SC. Buried Sion Presbyterian Church, Winnsboro.

Aiken, James. Born Aug. 8, 1830, Fairfield Dist., SC. Grad. SCMA 1851 and taught school in SC. Moved to AL by 1854. Prewar teacher, state representative and lawyer in Randolph Co. Md. Mrs. Louisa McClelland. Capt. Co. D (the "Randolph Mountaineers"), 13th AL, July 19, 1861. Major, June 11, 1862. Lt. col., Jan. 4, 1863. Col., May 24, 1864. "A true soldier." WIA Seven Pines, Chancellorsville, and Bristoe Station. POW at High Bridge, April 1865. Postwar lawyer and judge in Gadsden. Died June 22, 1908, Gadsden. Buried Forrest Cemetery, Gadsden.

Alexander, Almerine M. Born c. 1821, KY. Moved to TX in the 1840s. North TX merchant, with stores in Dallas, Bonham, Sherman. Lived in all three towns at various times. Md. Sophia King; Josephine B. King. Col., 34th TX Cav., April

17, 1862. Resigned May 7, 1863, due to chronic illness. He moved to San Antonio and purchased vast quantities of cotton to ship to Mexico under contract with the state cotton board. The war ended before Alexander could reap the profits of this transaction. Died July 23, 1865, New Orleans. Buried Girod St. Cemetery, New Orleans. His nephew called him a businessman "of superior executive ability" but "addicted to intemperance." According to Sidney Jackman, Alexander admitted he "had no courage, and was utterly unfit for an officer."

Allen, James Walkinshaw. Born July 2, 1829, Woodstock, VA. Reared in Shenandoah Co. Grad. VMI. Teacher, farmer in Bedford Co. prewar. Md. Julia Pendleton. Col., 2d VA, April 28, 1861. WIA 1st Manassas. KIA Gaines's Mill, while leading the Stonewall Brigade. Buried Hollywood Cemetery; reburied Longwood Cemetery, Bedford Co. Gen. Winder praised Allen as "a true soldier and a gentleman." Brother of Col. R. C. Allen, 28th VA.

Allen, Lawrence Martin. Born Oct. 15, 1832, Buncombe Co., NC. Farmer in Marshall, Madison Co., NC, prewar. Court clerk. Md. Mary M. Peek. Pvt. Co. B, 16th NC, April 29, 1861. Capt. Co. H, 2d NC Bn., July 5, 1861. POW Roanoke Island. Paroled 2 weeks later. After exchange, raised Co. A, 5th NC Cav. Bn., 1862. Major, 64th NC, May 1, 1862. Col., July 20, 1862. Court-martialed Jan. 1863 for lying about the whereabouts of his adj. and reprimanded. Submitted resignation Aug. 1, 1863, citing "lameness" in his left leg, but the resignation was rejected at the request of the governor so that Allen could be court-martialed for his part in executing captured Unionist guerrillas (the "Shelton Laurel Massacre"). Found guilty and suspended from duty for 6 months. Resigned June 3, 1864. Left Madison Co. soon after the war, after indictment for murder for the "Shelton Laurel Massacre," and moved to Decatur, AR. Farmer and teacher there. Died Dec. 11, 1908, Decatur. Buried Decatur Cemetery. A captain in the 64th stated, "Colonel Allen was not an attractive man . . . but was chosen leader because he was known to be brave and fearless."

Allen, Robert Clotworthy. Born June 22, 1834, Shenandoah Co., VA. Grad. VMI. Lawyer in Salem prewar, partnering with future Col. William Watts. Major, 28th VA, July 1, 1861. Col., April 2, 1862. POW Williamsburg but soon escaped. WIA Gaines's Mill. KIA Gettysburg, near the stone wall during Pickett's Charge. Buried on the battlefield. Remains probably transferred to Hollywood Cemetery, Richmond. One soldier accused Allen of being "an unwarrantable military tyrant." Gen. Eppa Hunton criticized Allen for disobeying orders at 2d Manassas and regretted not having court-martialed him.

Allen, Robert Thomas Prichett. Born Sept. 26, 1813, Baltimore, MD. Grad. USMA 1834. Officer in US Army, 1834–36. Civil engineer, 1836–38. Professor of mathematics and engineering at Allegheny College and Transylvania U.

Methodist minister. Founder and Superintendent of KMI. Post Office agent in CA. Publisher, San Francisco *Pacific News*. President of Bastrop Military Institute in Bastrop, TX. Md. Julia Dickinson. Instructor at Camp Clark, 1861. Appointed col., 4th TX, in Sept. 1861, but the soldiers of the 4th, hearing of his reputation as a martinet, literally drove him out of camp. Col., 17th TX, June 7, 1862. WIA Milliken's Bend. Commanded Camp Ford, TX, prison camp, Dec. 1863–May 1864. Resigned July 27, 1864, due to ill health. Resumed superintendency of KMI after the war. Inventor of, among other things, a typewriter. Orange grower in FL. Drowned while swimming in the Kissimmee River near Orlando, FL, July 9, 1888. Buried Greenwood Cemetery, Orlando. His cadets called him "Rarin' Tearin' Pitchin'" Allen. His niece called him "a brilliant, but erratic character" of "misdirected talents." The middle name given above is from a letter of Allen's: it is usually but mistakenly given as "Pritchard."

Alley, Alexander Kelley. Born Jan. 26, 1831, Jasper, Marion Co., TN. Circuit court clerk in Marion Co. in 1860. Md. Mariah Craighead; Bettie Graham; Millie Bonner. Capt. Co. I, 36th TN, Jan. 4, 1862. Elected col. at May 1862 reorganization but never commissioned because the regiment had heavy desertions and not all companies participated in the election. Regiment was soon disbanded. Capt. Co. L, 35th TN (the old Co. I, 36th TN), Oct. 25, 1862. Paroled Greensboro, NC, in 1865. Operated a hotel in Tucker Springs, Bradley Co., postwar. Railroad agent. Died July 13, 1911, after being struck by a train. Buried Craighead (Hoge) Cemetery, near Jasper.

Allison, Robert Donaldson. Born Sept. 25, 1810, Orange Co., NC. Reared in TN. Farmer in Gordonsville, Smith Co. State representative 1849–51. Lt. col. in Mexican War. Md. Martha Tucker; Mrs. Louise G. Dowells. Capt. Co. F, 24th TN, July 19, 1861. Col., Aug. 6, 1861. Relieved from duty May 1862, by Gen. Cleburne, for failing to advance during a skirmish; Cleburne charged Allison "showed none of the qualities of an officer." Resigned July 2, 1862, due to failing health. Organized a squadron of cavalry in May 1863, which served in the Atlanta and Carolinas Campaigns. WIA six times during war. Farmer in McKinney, Collin Co., TX, postwar. Died Dec. 15, 1900, McKinney. Buried Pecan Grove Cemetery, McKinney.

Allston, Benjamin. Born Feb. 26, 1833, Charleston, SC. Grad. USMA 1853. Lt., US Army, 1853–57. Rice planter and Episcopal minister in Georgetown and Union, SC. Md. Ellen S. Robinson; Louise G. North. On staff of gov. of SC, early 1861. 1st lt., CS Regular Army, March 16, 1861. Major, PACS, June 20, 1861. Assigned to duty with 19th MS. Temporarily assigned to duty with 5th VA Cav., Jan. 13, 1862. Col., PACS, May 1862. Led cavalry brigade in east TN, summer of 1862. Captured Aug. 27, 1862, near Cumberland Gap. By Dec. 1862 IG on staff of Gen. Kirby Smith. Later IG of TMD. Paroled Shreveport, LA, June 7, 1865. Postwar minister in Georgetown. Died Jan. 15, 1900, Winnsboro, SC. Buried St. John's Episcopal Church, Winnsboro.

Amerine, John Porter Warner. Born April 27, 1823, McMinn Co., TN. Prewar Troy, AL, physician. Md. Lucy Meadows; Susan Meadows. Capt. Co. K, 37th AL, March 21, 1862. Major, May 13, 1862. Resigned July 28, 1862 to join staff of Gen. Little. Col., 57th AL (which he raised), April 13, 1863. Court-martialed and dismissed Dec. 18, 1863. Butler Co. physician postwar. Died May 11, 1876, Greenville, AL. Buried Magnolia Cemetery, Greenville.

Anderson, Benjamin M. Born c. 1836, KY, of a prominent Louisville family. Filibusterer with William Walker. Capt. in Walker's army. Wounded in Nicaragua before returning to the US. Clerk for a pork packing firm in Louisville in 1861. Unmd. Capt., "Davis Guards," April 26, 1861, a KY company (later Co. I, Taylor's 1st KY) that, since KY had not seceded, joined the 1st LA as Co. H. Capt. Co. I, 1st KY, May 2, 1861. Major, July 12, 1861. Transferred to 3d KY, July 20, 1861. Lt. col., 3d KY, Oct. 18, 1861. WIA Shiloh. Resigned June 1, 1862, due to his wounds. Commissioned col., to raise a regiment of PR behind Union lines in KY, and nominated to the Confederate Senate April 6, 1863. Nomination rejected, Feb. 17, 1864. Discouraged, he returned to Louisville and took an oath of loyalty. Involved in the planning phase of the "Northwest Conspiracy." Arrested in Dec. 1864, Anderson maintained his innocence, claiming that he had dropped out of the conspiracy. Brought to trial in Cincinnati. In the midst of the trial, Anderson seized a gun from a guard and shot himself. He died two days later, on Feb. 21, 1865. Buried in the family plot in Cave Hill Cemetery, Louisville. A newspaper report on the trial called Anderson "a young man of gentlemanly appearance and possessed of much ability." Anderson's suicide has been blamed on depression brought on by both sides calling him a traitor.

Anderson, Charles DeWitt. Born July 7, 1828, SC. Family moved in 1846 to TX, where his parents soon died. Attd. USMA 1846–48. Lt., US Army, 1856–61. Md. Lucy Hazard. 1st lt., CS Regular Army Engineers, March 16, 1861. Commanded detachment at Fort Morgan. Major, 20th AL, Dec. 9, 1861. Detached Feb. 15, 1862 to become AAG on staff of Gen. Gladden. Elected col., 21st AL, May 8, 1862. Commanded Fort Gaines in Mobile Bay. Surrendered Fort Gaines in 1864 after a brief siege. Anderson believed the old fort was about to be blown up and the garrison was close to mutiny. The surrender was bitterly criticized by his superior officers, but both the garrison and the Union besiegers agreed he had no other choice. Postwar civil engineer in Kansas and Galveston and Austin, TX. Keeper of Galveston lighthouse (which he built) during the 1900 hurricane. Died Nov. 21, 1901, Galveston. Buried Old Cahill Cemetery, Galveston, in an unmarked grave.

Anderson, Edward Clifford. Born Nov. 8, 1815, Savannah, GA. Lt., USN, 1834–50. Chatham Co. planter. Mayor of Savannah 1855–56, 1865–69, 1873–76. Md. Sarah Williamson. In GA state ordnance department, early 1861. Major of artillery, May 18, 1861. Government agent in England, purchasing army supplies, May–Nov. 1861. Inspector of Savannah batteries under Gen. Robert E. Lee, Dec. 1861. Lt. col., PACS, April 30, 1862. Col., July 9, 1862. Commanded batteries guarding Savannah. Offered post of asst. sec. of war in 1862 but declined. Commanded post of Charleston Jan.–Feb. 1865, after Savannah was evacuated. Postwar bank director and railroad president. Died Jan. 6, 1883, Savannah. Buried Laurel Grove Cemetery. Gen. McLaws found Anderson "a most valuable officer and an upright, honorable gentleman." Uncle of Gen. R. H. Anderson and Col. E. C. Anderson Jr. His war diary has been published.

Anderson, Edward Clifford, Jr. Born Jan. 7, 1838, Savannah, GA. Attd. UVA. Living with his father, a bank president, in Savannah in 1860. Md. Jane Randolph, granddaughter of Pres. Thomas Jefferson. 2d lt. "Georgia Hussars," Sept. 9, 1861. ADC to Gen. Hugh Mercer, Nov. 1861–April 1862. Capt. Co. B ("Randolph Rangers"), 24th GA Cav. Bn., July 21, 1862. Major, 7th GA Cav., Jan. 12, 1863. WIA Trevilian Station. Col., Dec. 1864. Banker in Savannah postwar. Died Sept. 27, 1876, Savannah, of yellow fever. Buried Laurel Grove Cemetery.

Anderson, John Hansford. Born Aug. 6, 1831, near Lebanon, TN. Attd. Irving College. Merchant in Nashville prewar. Md. Virginia A. Burnett. Capt. Co. C, 10th TN, May 17, 1861. Escaped capture at Fort Donelson by walking through the Union lines with Bushrod Johnson. Aide to Gen. Johnson at Shiloh and WIA there. Lt. col., 8th TN, July 21, 1862. Col., Jan. 1, 1863. WIA Chickamauga and Franklin. "[A]n able and gallant officer." Paroled Greensboro, May 1, 1865. Nashville merchant postwar. State representative 1875–77. Died Sept. 11, 1902, Nashville. Buried Mt. Olivet Cemetery.

Anderson, John Huske. Born April 26, 1839, Mobile, AL. Reared in Fayetteville, NC. Clerk there in 1860. Md. Mary Dobbin in 1861. Pvt. Co. H, 1st (Bethel) NC, April 17, 1861. Mustered out Nov. 12, 1861. 1st lt. Co. D, 48th NC, June 28, 1862. WIA and disabled in VA. Major, 2d Bn. NC Junior Reserves, May 31, 1864. Lt. col., July 16, 1864. Col., 2d NC Junior Reserves (formed from the 2d Bn.), Dec. 7, 1864. Paroled May 1, 1865, Greensboro. Lived in Fayetteville; Wilmington; and Brooklyn, NY, postwar. Managed a carting business. Died Nov. 17, 1891, Brooklyn, NY. Buried Greenwood Cemetery, Brooklyn. Gen. Holmes found Anderson an "excellent officer."

Anderson, Samuel Smith. Born Sept. 20, 1819, Cumberland Co., VA. Grad. USMA 1841. Officer in US Army 1841–61, earning two brevet promotions for service in Mexican War. Md. Harriet Tisdale. Adj. gen., VA state forces, early 1861. Appointed lt. col., PAVA, May 9, 1861. Major of artillery, CS Regular Army,

May 24, 1861. Staff officer in Dept. of Norfolk. Lt. col., Oct. 2, 1861. AAG TMD, 1862–65. Col., PACS, June 13, 1864 (promoted by Gen. Kirby Smith). Paroled Shreveport June 7, 1865, as lt. col. Postwar building contractor in New York City and Louisville, KY. Died Feb. 20, 1901, KY. Buried Cave Hill Cemetery, Louisville. A fellow staff officer called Anderson a "most accomplished and competent officer."

Anderson, Thomas Scott. Born c. 1827, TN. Brother of Gen. Patton Anderson. Known generally as "Scott" Anderson. Moved to TX in 1852. Lawyer in Austin, Dallas, and Columbus. Sec. of state of TX, 1857–59. Sgt. in Mexican War. Md. Mary McNeill Harper, sister of Col. Henry McNeill. Delegate to TX Secession Convention. Capt., TX militia. Lt. col., 6th TX Cav., Sept. 3, 1861. POW Arkansas Post. Exch. April 29, 1863. Lt. col., 3d TX State Troops, early 1864. Col., Anderson's TX Cav., April 27, 1864. In the spring of 1865 he was appointed IG of the Dist. of Texas and left his regiment. Paroled June 21, 1865, Houston. Lived in Eagle Lake, Colorado Co., postwar. Died Sept. 25, 1868, Eagle Lake. Probably buried Lakeview Cemetery, Eagle Lake, in an unmarked grave. An obituary called him "a man of brilliant intellectual achievements . . . as tender-hearted as a woman."

Andrews, Clinton Milton. Born Dec. 3, 1830, Rowan Co., NC. Reared in Greensboro. Attd. UNC. Grad. Lafayette College in PA. Bank cashier in Summerville. Ran a military school in Statesville. Md. Ellen M. Butz, "a Northern lady." Capt. Co. B, 2d NC Cav., June 21, 1861. Major, Sept. 6, 1862. Lt. col., Feb. 12, 1864. Col., Feb. 18, 1864. MWIA June 23, 1864, in a skirmish at Black & White, VA. Died of the effects of a leg amputation. Buried Fourth Creek Presbyterian Church, Statesville.

Andrews, Julius A. Born 1838, Columbus, GA. Reared in Columbus. Lived in Kaufman Co., then Marion Co., TX, prewar. Md. Tommie Theresa Freeman in 1867. Pvt. Co. D (the "Shreveport Greys"), 1st LA Bn. (Rightor's), April 20, 1861. Sgt. major, June 1, 1861. Discharged, Aug. 26, 1861. 1st lt., 1st TX Cav. Bn., Nov. 4, 1861. Adj., Nov. 4, 1861. Col., 32d TX Cav. (formed from the 1st Bn.), May 8, 1862. The 32d was dismounted and fought as infantry in the Army of TN. WIA (thigh) Chickamauga. Led Ector's Brigade in 1865 Mobile Campaign. Paroled May 9, 1865, Meridian, MS. Postwar merchant and traveling salesman. Cotton buyer. Lived in Enterprise, MS, and Fort Worth, TX. Indian agent in Idaho, where he was imprisoned for embezzlement. Moved to Mountain View, Kiowa Co., OK. Died Dec. 28, 1928, OK. Buried Mountain View Cemetery. In 1864 the officers of Ector's Brigade recommended him for promotion as "a thorough tactician . . . [who] frequently has commanded the brigade."

Armant, Leopold Ludger. Born June 10, 1835, Vacherie, LA. Attd. Georgetown U. and UVA. Grad. ULA in 1858. Attorney in St. James Parish prewar. State legislator. 1st lt. Co. A, 18th LA, Oct. 5, 1861. Capt., April 1862. Major, May 10, 1862. Col., July 19, 1862. 18th consolidated with Yellow Jacket Bn. in 1863 to form 18th Consolidated. KIA Mansfield, carrying his regiment's flag while leading a charge. Buried Mansfield City Cemetery after the battle; reburied St. James Cemetery, Convent, LA. Major Silas Grisamore found Armant "an accomplished officer and . . . an agreeable, social gentleman."

Armistead, Charles Gaines. Born c. 1826, NC. Lawyer in Yalobusha Co., MS, prewar. State representative and senator. Lt. col. of militia and ADC to the governor. Md. Frances E. Leigh. 4th Sgt. Co. H, 15th MS, May 29, 1861. Capt. and QM, 15th MS, June 17, 1861. WIA Mill Springs. In early 1863 a paymaster in the Dept. of MS and East LA. Later that year he wrote Pres. Davis offering to organize unattached companies into a new regiment. Col., 12th MS (aka 16th Confederate) Cav., Dec. 29, 1863. Shot in shoulder and side during the June 24, 1864, attack on Lafayette, GA. Often commanded a brigade and recommended for promotion to brigadier. Paroled May 14, 1865, Gainesville. Lawyer in Memphis, TN, postwar. Died June 28, 1869, Jackson, MS, at the state asylum, of his war wounds and the resulting insanity. Buried Jackson. One wartime inspector found Armistead "an intelligent gentleman whose gallantry is attested."

Armistead, Franck Stanley. Born April 1835, Upperville, VA. Brother of Gen. Lewis Armistead. His unusual first name derives from his grandmother. Reared in Fauquier Co. Grad. USMA 1856. Lt., US Army, 1856–61. Unmd. 1st lt., CS Regular Army, March 16, 1861. Capt. and AAG, Armistead's Brigade, April 28, 1862. WIA Seven Pines. Appointed lt. col., 21st GA, Aug. 14, 1862, but never joined the regiment. AAG to Gen. T. H. Holmes in the Dist. of AR, 1863–64. Col., 1st NC Junior Reserves, July 16, 1864. Commanded Junior Reserve Brigade in 1865. Gen. Holmes maneuvered to have his longtime staffer promoted to gen., but no action was taken by the War Dept. Paroled May 2, 1865. Hotel clerk in Wheeling, WVA, postwar. "Torpedo agent" (for oil company?) in WVA in 1880. Went insane in 1886. Died at Lakeland Hospital (the state lunatic asylum) in Louisville, KY, April 18, 1889. Buried Cave Hill Cemetery, Louisville, with a gravestone that gives a wrong year of death. Many sources jumble together his life and that of another Armistead, his cousin, a VMI attendee.

Armstrong, Joseph. Born July 9, 1836, Putnam Co., GA. Attd. Emory & Henry College and Cumberland U. Law School. Attorney in Macon prewar. ADC to his father, a general in the GA militia. Unmd. Capt. Co. I, 18th GA, June 22, 1861. WIA Gaines's Mill. Col., Jan. 6, 1864. Paroled April 15, 1865, Petersburg. Lawyer in Dooley Co. and Albany postwar. Died July 28, 1901, Gainesville. Buried Rose Hill Cemetery, Macon.

Arnett, William Wiley. Born Oct. 23, 1839, Marion Co., VA. Grad. Allegheny College in PA. Marion Co. lawyer prewar. Md. Sallie Stephenson in 1867. Pvt.

Co. A, 31st VA, April 1861. Appointed by the gov. of VA lt. col. VA state volunteers, May 22, 1861, and put in charge of a battalion later formed into the 25th VA. He resigned this commission Sept. 6, 1861, and went back to being a pvt. in the 31st. Capt., May 1, 1862. Resigned Sept. 23, 1862. Col., 20th VA Cav., Aug. 14, 1863. Lawyer in Berryville; St. Louis, MO; and Wheeling, WVA, postwar. State representative 1869–71. Lost race for Congress in 1896. Died Feb. 15, 1902, at his home in Wheeling. Buried Greenwood Cemetery, Wheeling.

Ashby, Henry Marshall. Born 1836, Fauquier Co., VA. Attd. William & Mary College. "Trader" in Chattanooga, TN, in 1860. Capt. Co. C, 4th TN Cav. Bn., July 6, 1861. Col., 2d TN Cav., May 24, 1862. Shot in the foot while on a raid into KY. Led a brigade in Wheeler's Corps in 1864. Commanded Humes's Div. at war's end. Paroled May 3, 1865, in NC. Moved to New York City after the war, then settled in Knoxville, TN. Killed July 10, 1868, Knoxville, during an argument with an ex-Union army officer. Buried Old Gray Cemetery, Knoxville. Fellow soldiers called Ashby "a born soldier" "who always put himself to the front." Cousin of Gen. Turner Ashby.

Ashcraft, Thomas Calvin. Born March 25, 1831, Perry Co., TN. Lawyer in Okolona, MS, in 1860. Md. Laura Noe. Capt. Co. E, 41st MS, Feb. 27, 1862. Resigned Aug. 29, 1864. WIA Perryville. Detached in 1863 to conscript bureau. Authorized Dec. 24, 1863, to raise a regiment for MS state service. Lt. col., 3d MS Cav. Bn., State Troops. Lt. col., Ashcraft's MS Cav. (aka 11th MS Cav.; formed from his State Troops battalion), May 4, 1864, when unit was mustered into Confederate service. Col., June 16, 1864. Unit consolidated with Ham's and Lowry's Regts., March 20, 1865. Died late 1865, Verona, MS.

Ashford, Frederick Augustus. Born April 19, 1830, Lawrence Co., AL. Prewar Lawrence Co. farmer. Unmd. Capt. Co. B, 16th AL, Aug. 6, 1861. Major, June 11, 1863. Lt. col., Oct. 7, 1863. Col., March 26, 1864. Called "an officer of very fine person and polished manners." KIA Franklin, Nov. 30, 1864. Buried Courtland, AL, probably in Ashford Cemetery.

Ashford, John. Born Sept. 6, 1837, Sampson Co., NC. Farmer in Sampson Co. prewar. Md. Eliza F. Hine. Capt., "Sampson Plowboys," Co. D, 38th NC, Oct. 22, 1861. Major, Aug. 21, 1862. Lt. col., Jan. 14, 1863. Col., June 18, 1864. WIA 2d Manassas (leg), Gettysburg, and Petersburg (March 30, 1865). Appmx. Farmer in Clinton postwar. Mortally wounded Jan. 3, 1889, in a boiler explosion at his Clinton soap factory. Died there Jan. 6, 1889. Buried Clinton Cemetery. Repeatedly cited for "gallantry" and "coolness" by his brigade commanders.

Atkinson, Edmund Nathan. Born Nov. 14, 1834, Marietta, GA. Grad. GMI. Camden Co. farmer prewar. Md. Elizabeth Lang in 1868. 1st lt. and adj., 26th GA, Oct. 22, 1861. Col., May 9, 1862. WIA (arm) and POW Fredericksburg while leading a brigade. Court-martialed Dec. 1863 for being drunk on duty but acquitted. POW Fisher's Hill. Released July 25, 1865. Camden Co. farmer postwar. Died June 17, 1884, Waycross, GA. Buried Lott Cemetery, Waycross.

August, Thomas Pearson. Born Oct. 1821, Fredericksburg, VA. Reared in Richmond. Richmond lawyer prewar. State representative 1850–51. State senator 1857–61. Militia captain. Officer in Mexican War. Unmd. Brig. gen., 2d Brigade, 4th Div., VA Militia in 1861. Col., 15th VA, May 17, 1861. WIA Malvern Hill (hip), disabling him for field duty. Assigned to Bureau of Conscription in 1862. Commander of a conscript camp in NC. The locals complained that a Virginian had been assigned to a NC command. Retired, disability, Dec. 31, 1864. Lawyer and city councilman postwar. Died July 31, 1869, Richmond. Buried Hollywood Cemetery. "[A] wag and punster by nature," "confessedly, the greatest wit of his day." However, a major in the 15th accused him of drunkenness.

Autry, James Lockhart. Born Jan. 28, 1830, near Jackson, TN. His father died at the Alamo, and the family moved to Holly Springs, MS. Educated at St. Thomas's Hall. Lawyer in Holly Springs. State representative 1854–59. State House speaker 1858–59. Md. Jennie Valiant. Lt. Co. B, 9th MS, Feb. 16, 1861. Lt. col., April 12, 1861. Relieved of command, Sept. 9, 1861. Lt. col., 27th MS, Nov. 1, 1861. Said to have been elected col., 9th MS, at that regiment's reorganization but declined the honor. His service record is silent on the asserted election. Commandant of the post of Vicksburg, summer of 1862, where, in response to a demand that he surrender the city, replied in the famous words "Mississippians don't know, and refuse to learn how, to surrender to an enemy." KIA Stones River, Dec. 31, 1862, while leading the 27th in the absence of its colonel (Thomas M. Jones). Buried Hillcrest Cemetery, Holly Springs. His wartime letters are at the TX State Archives.

Avery, Clark Moulton. Born Oct. 3, 1829, Burke Co., NC. Grad. UNC. Farmer near Morgantown, Burke Co. Elected to NC State Council in 1856. Delegate to NC Secession Convention. Md. Elizabeth T. Walton. Capt. Co. G, 1st (Bethel) NC, April 25, 1861. Lt. col., 33d NC, Sept. 20, 1861. Col., Jan. 17, 1862. POW New Bern, exch. Sept. 1862. WIA Chancellorsville, Gettysburg. WIA Wilderness. Left arm, right leg amputated. Died of his wounds June 18, 1864. Buried 1st Presbyterian Church, Morgantown. Brother of Col. I. E. Avery. "[A] brave and faithful officer, a true friend, and the knightliest of men."

Avery, Isaac Erwin. Born Dec. 20, 1828, "Swan Ponds" plantation, Burke Co., NC. Brother of Col. C. M. Avery. Attd. UNC. Farmer in Yancey and Burke Cos. Part owner of the Western NC Railroad. Unmd. Capt. Co. E, 6th NC, May 16, 1861. WIA 1st Manassas and Malvern Hill. Lt. col., June 1, 1862. Col., June 11, 1862. MWIA Gettysburg in the July 2 attack on Cemetery Hill, while leading

Hoke's Brigade. Died the next day. Buried Riverview Cemetery, Williamsport, MD; reburied Rose Hill Cemetery, Hagerstown. His last words, scrawled as he lay dying, were, "Tell my father I fell with my face to the enemy."

Avery, Isaac Wheeler. Born May 2, 1837, St. Augustine, FL. Grad. Oglethorpe U. Savannah lawyer prewar. Md. Sally H. Morris; Emma Bivings. Pvt., "Oglethorpe Light Infantry," 1861. Capt. Co. I, 23d GA Cav. Bn., Jan. 10, 1862. POW June 1, 1862, near Booneville, MS. Paroled 10 days later. Lt. col., Sept. 22, 1862. Col., 4th GA Cav. (later redesignated 12th), Jan. 30, 1863. WIA New Hope Church, which wound put him on crutches the remainder of his life. Put in command of Macon, GA, Home Guard, Dec. 1864. Often said to have been promoted to brig. the last month of the war. Lawyer in Dalton postwar. To Atlanta in 1869. Editor, Atlanta *Constitution.* Influential journalist and political leader. Wrote a standard history of Georgia. Died Sept. 8, 1897, Atlanta, buried Oakland Cemetery. Avery often led a brigade and won universal praise from his superiors; Gen. Wharton stated that "there was no better officer in his command."

Aylett, William Roane. Born May 14, 1833, King William Co., VA. Descendant of founding father Patrick Henry. Attd. UVA. King William Co. lawyer prewar. Md. Alice Brockenbrough. Capt. Co. D, 53d VA, May 13, 1861. Major, Aug. 29, 1862. Lt. col., Feb. 2, 1863. Col., March 5, 1863. WIA Gettysburg (in Pickett's Charge), Drewry's Bluff (in shoulder). POW Sayler's Creek. Released July 25, 1865. After Gettysburg he often led the Armistead-Barton Brigade as senior colonel but was always passed over for promotion to its permanent command in favor of officers from outside the brigade. Lawyer in King William Co. postwar. Commonwealth attorney. State legislator. Died Aug. 8, 1900, King William Co. Buried St. David's Episcopal Church, Aylett. Papers at VAHS.

Baber, Milton Dyer. Born Feb. 3, 1836, Ramsey, McLean Co., KY. Grad. U. of Louisville Law School, 1858. Prewar lawyer in Lawrence Co., AR. Delegate to AR Secession Convention. Md. Louisiana Watkins; Mrs. Margaret Raney Sloan. 1st lt., 7th AR, June 16, 1861. Capt., March 5, 1862. Returned to AR in May 1862. Capt. Co. D, 38th AR, July 12, 1862. Major, Aug. 2, 1862. Lt. col., April 1, 1863. Col., 45th AR Mounted Infantry, upon its organization in the summer of 1864. Led 45th in Price's Raid. POW Oct. 22, 1864, near Independence, MO. To Camp Douglas POW Camp, where he acted as the agent to distribute clothing to the prisoners. Paroled June 20, 1865. Postwar lawyer in Pocahontas and Walnut Ridge, Lawrence Co. 3d Circuit prosecuting attorney, 1866–68. Died July 5, 1894, at his Walnut Ridge home. Buried Smithville Cemetery.

Bacon, Thomas Glascock. Born June 24, 1812, Edgefield, SC. Educated at Pendleton Classical Institute. Clerk of court in Edgefield in 1860. Seminole and Mexican Wars veteran. Md. Angeline M. Gallman. Col., 7th SC, elected March

1861, commissioned into the PACS April 15, 1861. Accidentally shot himself in the thigh, March 1861. Dropped at May 4, 1862, reelection, declining to run due to failing health. Col., 5th SC State Reserves, 1862–63. Elected to State Senate in 1863. Businessman and farmer in Hamburg postwar. Died Sept. 25, 1876, Edgefield Co. Buried Willowbrook Baptist Cemetery, Edgefield.

Bagby, Arthur Pendleton. Born May 17, 1833, Claybourne, AL, son of a governor of AL. Grad. USMA 1852. Lt., US Army, 1852–53. Studied law. Lawyer in Mobile and (from 1858) Gonzales, TX. Md. Frances Taylor. Major, 7th TX Cav., Oct. 12, 1861. Court-martialed in 1862 for drunkenness during Sibley's New Mexico Campaign but exonerated despite overwhelming evidence of guilt. Lt. col., April 4, 1862. Col., Nov. 15, 1862. WIA (arm) at Berwick Bay. Led the Sibley-Green Brigade, 1863–64. Assigned to duty as brig. gen. March 17, 1864. Led a division of LA Cav., 1864–65. Assigned to duty as major gen., May 10, 1865. Postwar lawyer in Victoria and Halletsville. Editor, Victoria *Advocate.* Died Feb. 21, 1921, Halletsville. Buried Halletsville City Cemetery. A competent officer, often praised by his superiors.

Bailey, David Jackson. Born March 11, 1812, Lexington, GA. Privately tutored. Lawyer in Jackson, Butts Co., GA. Moved to Griffin in 1859. Longtime state representative and senator. US congressman 1851–55. Officer in Creek War. Delegate to GA Secession Convention. Md. Susan Grantland. Col., 30th GA, Oct. 7, 1861. Present through Nov. 1862. Griffin lawyer and planter postwar. State legislator. Died June 14, 1897, Griffin. Buried Oak Hill Cemetery, Griffin. A private in the 30th thought Bailey courageous but "does everything wrong."

Bailey, James Edmund. Born Aug. 15, 1822, Montgomery Co., TN. Attd. U. of Nashville. Clarksville lawyer prewar. State representative 1853–55. Elected to proposed TN Secession Convention as a Unionist. Delegate to 1861 Washington Peace Conference. On TN State Military Board in 1861. Md. Elizabeth Lusk. Capt. Co. A, 49th TN, Nov. 29, 1861. Col., Dec. 24, 1861. POW Fort Donelson. Resigned May 23, 1863, due to old age and chronic diarrhea. Appointed col. and judge, military court of Hardee's Corps, July 14, 1864. Paroled May 1, 1865, Greensboro. Clarksville lawyer and judge postwar. US senator 1877–81. Died Dec. 29, 1895, Clarksville. Buried Greenwood Cemetery. In 1863 Sen. Henry recommended Bailey for brigadier as "a man of decided ability and great energy; a true and gallant soldier."

Baird, Spruce McCoy. Born Oct. 8, 1814, Glasgow, KY. Lived prewar in Glasgow; Woodville, San Augustine and Nacogdoches, TX; and NM. Schoolteacher in KY. Lawyer in TX and NM. Rancher near Albuquerque, NM. Judge. Attorney general of NM. Md. Emmacetta C. Bowdry. Forced to leave NM in 1861, due to his pro-Southern leanings. Indicted for treason in 1862. Ranch confiscated. Helped recruit the 4th Cav., Arizona Brigade. Col., 4th AZ Cav., March 9, 1863. Paroled July 27, 1865, Austin. Lived in Golden, CO, postwar. Lawyer in CO and NM. Died June 5, 1872, Cimarron, NM, while attending court. Buried in an unmarked grave in Golden Cemetery. Gen. Magruder considered Baird "an officer and gentleman of much merit."

Baker, John Algernon. Born Sept. 19, 1830, Brunswick Co., NC. Attd. USC and Harvard Law School. Wilmington, NC, lawyer prewar. Md. six times, including Minnie Haywood, sister of Col. E. G. Haywood; Letitia Hargin; Susan Lawrence. 1st lt. Co. E, 1st NC Art., May 16, 1861. Capt. and VADC to Gen. French, 1862. Col., 3d NC Cav., Sept. 3, 1862. POW near Petersburg, VA, June 21, 1864. One of the "Immortal 600." Unlike his more resolute fellow prisoners, Baker took the oath of allegiance in March 1865, earning their contempt. Lived in Wilmington (lawyer there); the West Indies; and Charleston postwar. Roanoke, VA, lawyer in 1895. Died March 15, 1903, at St. Mary's Infirmary in Galveston. Buried Calvary Cemetery, Galveston. One diarist called Baker "notoriously unfit . . . confessedly ignorant & incompetent & inefficient" as colonel, so much so his officers asked him to resign. Other sources peg Baker as a drunk. On the plus side, one subordinate found him "the finest-looking man I ever saw," which may have had some connection to his being married six times.

Baker, John Harris. Born Aug. 7, 1824, Warren Co., GA. Pike Co. farmer prewar. Mexican War veteran. Md. Louisa Trice. Capt. Co. A, 13th GA, July 8, 1861. Major, Feb. 1, 1862. Lt. col., Sept. 17, 1862. POW Gettysburg, exch. May 4, 1864. Col., Dec. 14, 1863. WIA eight times during war. Led Evans's Brigade at Fort Stedman, where he was WIA "while in brave discharge of his duty." Sent to a Richmond hospital, thus missing the surrender at Appomattox. Paroled April 21, 1865. Pike Co. farmer postwar. State legislator. Died April 7, 1905, Pike Co. Buried Eastview Cemetery, Zebulon.

Baker, Samuel E. Born Nov. 5, 1828, MS. Bookkeeper in Natchez prewar. Md. Adeline Hester Foules. Capt. Co. D, 16th MS, April 25, 1861. Major, April 28, 1862. Col., Dec. 20, 1862. KIA Spotsylvania, May 12, 1864, in the fighting at the "Mule Shoe." One private called Baker "gallant and much beloved." Buried Natchez City Cemetery.

Baldwin, John Brown. Born Jan. 11, 1820, near Staunton, VA. Attd. UVA. Attorney in Staunton prewar. State representative 1848–61. Militia colonel. Delegate to VA Secession Convention. Md. Susan M. Peyton; Ann M. Lewis Peyton. Appointed col. and IG of VA State Troops (PAVA), April 23, 1861. Col., 52d VA, Aug. 19, 1861. Dropped at May 1862 reorganization. Confederate congressman 1862–65. Col. of a regiment of reserves. Attorney in Staunton postwar.

State representative 1865–67. Speaker of the VA House. Died Sept. 30, 1873, Staunton. Buried Thornrose Cemetery, Staunton. "As a man of intellect, he was almost unrivaled." Brother of Lt. Col. Briscoe Baldwin, ANV ordnance chief.

Ball, Charles Pollard. Born Aug. 16, 1837, Montgomery, AL. Attd. USMA, resigning Dec. 19, 1860 to go with his state. Md. Anna, daughter of Col. J. J. Seibels. Lt. of engineers in AL army at Pensacola, Feb. 1861. 2d lt., CS Regular Army, March 16, 1861. Served at Fort Morgan and with an artillery battery. Appointed major chief of artillery to Gen. Cleburne Oct. 22, 1862, but not confirmed. Reappointed major, Feb. 14, 1863 to be OO to Gen. Forney. POW Vicksburg and paroled. Col., 8th AL Cav., April 26, 1864. Paroled May 14, 1865, Gainesville. Railroad engineer and executive in AL postwar. Died Oct. 13, 1904, Montgomery of "paralysis." Buried Oakwood Cemetery, Montgomery. A fellow cadet called him "one of those rare young men who carry with them the fascinating mystery of promise . . . where nature has written leadership." Ball's sister married Gen. W. W. Allen.

Ball, Edward. Born 1825, SC. Planter in Barbour Co., AL, and later Randolph Co., GA. Clerk of the Randolph Co. Court at the time of his enlistment. Md. Harriet C. Howard. Capt. Co. H, 51st GA, March 1, 1862. Lt. col., March 22, 1862. Col., May 2, 1863. WIA Chancellorsville (heel). MWIA Cedar Creek. Died Nov. 13, 1864, Staunton, VA. Buried Staunton; reburied Rosedale Cemetery, Cuthbert, GA.

Ball, Lewis. Born Nov. 6, 1820, Laurens Co., SC. Baptist minister in Pontotoc Co., MS, prewar. Md. Mary Ann Hitt; Annie Suddoth; Adelia Suddoth. Capt. Co. B, 41st MS, Jan. 14, 1862. Major, March 1, 1864. WIA Kolb's Farm by a shell fragment that broke his collarbone, unfitting him for further field duty. Col., Aug. 31, 1864. Minister and farmer in Sunflower and Tippah Cos. postwar. Later moved to Clinton, Hinds Co. Died Nov. 30, 1896, on his farm near Clinton. Buried Clinton City Cemetery.

Ball, William Bernard. Born c. 1816, Chesterfield Co., VA. Grad. Jefferson Medical College. Physician in Chesterfield Co. prewar. Militia officer. Md. Laurie A. McCrae. Capt. Co. B, 4th VA Cav., April 1861. Lt. col., 15th VA Cav., April 1862. Col., Sept. 11, 1862. Furloughed Dec. 24, 1862, suffering from chronic liver disease. Detached (for health reasons) to the navy. Acting master, CSN, Sept. 30, 1863. Resigned from the navy, Dec. 31, 1863. Resigned as col., Feb. 28, 1864. Surgeon in Chesterfield Co. postwar. State commissioner of fish culture. Died Jan. 10, 1872, at the Exchange Hotel in Richmond. Buried first in Hollwood Cemetery, later in an unmarked grave at Maury Cemetery, Richmond. An obituary notes Ball's "coolness and courage" in battle.

Ballenger, Marcus Rowland. Born Jan. 10, 1827, SC. Physician in Floyd Co., GA, prewar. Md. Aphiah Moore. Capt. Co. C, 23d GA, Aug. 31, 1861. Major, Sept. 17, 1862. Lt. col., Aug. 20, 1864. Col., Jan. 5, 1865. Paroled Greensboro. Postwar physician in Floyd Springs. State legislator. Died Nov. 12, 1886, Floyd Springs, GA. Buried Floyd Springs Methodist Church Cemetery.

Ballentine, John Goff. Born May 20, 1825, Pulaski, TN. Grad. U. of Nashville and Harvard. Lawyer in Pulaski, Sardis, MS, and Memphis prewar. Md. Mary E. Laird. Pvt. Co. C ("Shelby County Dragoons"), 7th TN Cav., 1861. Capt., June 6, 1861. Col., Ballentine's MS Cav. (aka 2d MS PR—formed from unattached companies then on duty in northern MS), July 1, 1862. Served in MS and GA. WIA May 17, 1864, during the Atlanta Campaign. Paroled May 13, 1865, Memphis. Lawyer in Pulaski postwar. US congressman 1883–87. Died Nov. 23, 1915, Pulaski. Buried Maplewood Cemetery, Pulaski. One of his troopers found Ballentine "one of God's noblemen, kind to his men in war and always thoughtful of their comforts in battle or in camp."

Bane, John Pierson. Born Oct. 1835, Baneville, Giles Co., VA. Prewar farmer in Giles Co. Cattle rancher in Seguin, TX. Md. Julianna Grayson. Capt. Co. D, 4th TX, July 4, 1861. Major, Dec. 29, 1862. Lt. col., July 21, 1863. Col., April 29, 1864. WIA Gaines's Mill and Chickamauga. Assigned to recruiting duty in TX in 1864. Paroled Aug. 1865, San Antonio. Cattle rancher in Seguin to about 1880. Then moved to Montgomery Co., VA. Died May 14, 1887, at the Richmond Soldiers' Home. Buried Hollywood Cemetery.

Bankhead, Smith Pyne. Born Aug. 8, 1823, Fort Moultrie, SC, son of an army officer. Brother of Union Gen. Henry Bankhead. Attd. Georgetown U. and UVA. Capt. VA volunteers in Mexican War. To Memphis, TN, c. 1850. Editor and lawyer there. Md. Ada Garth. Capt., TN state artillery corps, early 1861. Capt., Bankhead's TN battery, 1861. Major, April 1, 1862. Chief of artillery of Polk's Corps at Shiloh. Col., Nov. 12, 1862. Chief of artillery of Dist. of TX. Appointed acting brig. gen. May 30, 1863, by Gen. Magruder (his cousin), to command the Northern Sub-District of TX. Recommissioned col. of art., Jan. 14, 1865, to rank from June 15, 1864. Postwar Memphis lawyer. Shot by an unknown assailant March 30, 1867, Memphis, dying the next day. Buried Elmwood Cemetery. Late in the war Gen. Magruder pushed Bankhead's promotion to general, but when the War Dept. reviewed Bankhead's file, it discovered that the papers on his 1862 promotion to colonel were lost, necessitating his recommissioning as colonel! The war ended before Bankhead's further promotion to general could be processed.

Barbour, William Morgan. Born Jan. 24, 1834, Rowan Co., NC. Grad. St. James College in MD. Wilkesboro lawyer. Md. Ada Alexander. Capt. Co. F, 37th

NC, Sept. 24, 1861. Lt. col., Nov. 20, 1861. Col., July 1, 1862. WIA Fredericks-burg (neck), Chancellorsville (arm). POW Spotsylvania. Exch. Aug. 3, 1864. WIA 2d Deep Bottom, Aug. 16, 1864 (leg). MWIA Jones Farm, Sept. 30, 1864. Died Oct. 3, 1864, in a Petersburg hospital. Buried Petersburg; reburied St. Paul's Episcopal Churchyard, Wilkesboro. His stone at St. Paul's gives his last name as "Barber," which appears to be the way he spelled it until midway through the war.

Barclay, William Paxton. Born c. 1828, TN. Lawyer in Union Co., GA, pre-war. He may be the William P. Barclay who lived in El Dorado Co., CA, in 1860, owned a mine and served in the state legislature. Lt. col., 23d GA, Aug. 31, 1861. Col., June 17, 1862. KIA Antietam. Brother of Lt. Col. Elihu Barclay, Phillips's Legion.

Barkuloo, William. Born Sept. 16, 1826, Brooklyn, NY. Clerk in Columbia, SC, in 1850. Moved to Fernandina, FL, and then to Brunswick, GA. Mexican War veteran with the Palmetto (SC) Regt. WIA Churubusco. In US Army. Sgt. of vol. militia (the "Brunswick Riflemen") in 1860. Member, Brunswick city council. Md. Eliza De Bruhl; Mary Margaret Anderson. Major, 8th GA Militia Bn., Jan. 1861. Col., 2d GA State Troops, Oct. 14, 1861. Col., 57th GA, Feb. 24, 1862. POW Vicksburg and exch. Often led Mercer's Brigade in the Atlanta Campaign. Left regiment in late 1864 and returned home. City Recorder of Brunswick postwar. Died Feb. 6, 1873, Brunswick. Buried Oak Grove Cemetery, Brunswick.

Barnes, Dixon. Born Oct. 9, 1816, Lancaster Dist., SC. Grad. USC. Wealthy planter in the Lancaster Dist. prewar. State representative 1844–48. State sena-tor 1848–52, 1854–56, 1860–62. Seminole War veteran. Md. Charlotte R. Brown; Mrs. Mary Masey Cunningham. Major, 2d SC Volunteers (State Troops), Jan. 1861. Capt. Co. I, 12th SC, Aug. 28, 1861. Lt. col., Sept. 1, 1861. Col., April 2, 1862. MWIA Antietam. Died Sept. 27, 1862, Charlestown, VA (now WVA). Buried Old Camp Creek Church, Lancaster. The brigade historian claimed Barnes, a "quiet gentleman with a long white beard," had "gallantry and cool-ness unsurpassed . . . the head and heart of his splendid regiment."

Barnett, Timothy ("Timbochee"). Born 1808, probably in AL. Creek tribal leader. Owned trading post in Wewoka Dist., Creek Nation, near the present We-tumpka, OK. Slave owner. Said to be the wealthiest man in the Creek Nation. Md. Mary ("Hoketa") Benson. Major, 2d Creek Cav., 1863. Col., probably late in the war, to succeed Chilly McIntosh. Barnett's service record, in common with other members of Indian units, is spotty. Treasurer of the Creek Nation post-war. Killed July 14, 1873, near his Wetumpka home. Barnett had killed a Semi-nole who'd been seeing his common-law wife, and a posse that was taking him to trial murdered him. Buried the original Wetumpka Cemetery, southeast of town. A fellow Indian officer said Barnett had "rather a domineering nature which sometimes led him into trouble."

Barr, James, Jr. Born Oct. 22, 1829, Brooklyn, NY. Moved to Jackson, MS, c. 1845. Marble cutter and monument maker prewar. Md. Frances Donnell. 3d lt. Co. A, 10th MS, Jan. 29, 1861. Capt., June 4, 1861. Major, April 23, 1862. Lt. col., Dec. 31, 1862. Col., March 10, 1863. WIA Stones River and absent sick much of 1863. WIA June 22, 1864, at Kolb's Farm, eventually losing his arm. Died July 25, 1864, in Macon, GA, of his wounds and after his ambulance crashed into a tree. Buried Macon, GA; reburied Greenwood Cemetery, Jackson, in Oct. 1868. Gen. Manigault found Barr "a cool, active, and brave officer."

Barrow, Robert James. Born Oct. 5, 1817, Edgecombe Co., NC. Reared in West Feliciana Parish, LA. Attd. UVA. Wealthy planter in West Feliciana Parish prewar. Md. Mary E. Crabb. Col., 4th LA, May 25, 1861. Resigned March 21, 1862, due to disability. Captured by Union forces Sept. 1864, in Point Coupee Parish, while going home to get a change of clothes. Imprisoned at Fort Lafayette. Exch. March 1865. Postwar planter in Wilkinson Co., MS. Impoverished by the war. Moved to New Orleans. Died Dec. 16, 1887, New Orleans. Buried West Feliciana Parish. A lieutenant of the 4th called Barrow "a nice old gentleman" but too elderly to command the regiment.

Barry, William T. Born c. 1829, Hartsville, TN. Mexican War veteran. "Drummer" (salesman) for a merchant house in Boonville, MO. Traveling salesman for a St. Louis boot store from 1856. Md. Mary J. Bozarth. In 1861 raised a company for the MSG in Henry Co. Capt. Co. H, 11th MO Cav. Bn., June 25, 1862. Major, 10th MO Cav. (formed in Dec. 1863 from the 11th Bn.), late in the war. Col., probably Feb. 27, 1865. Paroled as col. June 8, 1865. Traveling salesman for a St. Louis boot store postwar. Moved to Bentonville, AR, in 1880 and went into the livery business. Ran a hotel in Fayetteville, AR. Committed suicide in Pierce City, MO, Jan. 26, 1884, allegedly over financial reverses. Buried Evergreen Cemetery, Fayetteville. An obituary called him "beloved by his soldiers and highly esteemed by all who knew him."

Barry, William Taylor Sullivan. Born Dec. 10, 1821, Columbus, MS. Grad. Yale 1841. Lawyer in Columbus prewar. Owned large plantations in several counties in MS and many slaves. Speaker of the MS State House. US congressman 1853–55. Active secessionist. President of the MS Secession Convention. Md. Sally Fearn. Confederate congressman 1861–62, advocating such extreme measures as reopening the slave trade. Resigned to join the army. Capt. AAG on staff of Gen. Charles Clark, Sept. 9, 1861. Col., 35th MS, Jan. 27, 1862. POW Vicksburg and paroled. WIA Allatoona Pass (shoulder). Often led Sears's Brigade as senior colonel. POW Fort Blakely, exch. May 1, 1865. Paroled May 9,

1865, Meridian. Resumed his law practice postwar. Died Jan. 29, 1868, Columbus, of his wounds and of despair over the war's outcome. Buried Friendship Cemetery, Columbus. Gen. Maury called Barry a "capital fellow . . . one of the most popular and eloquent men of Mississippi. Gentle, genial, and humorous." Reuben Davis thought Barry "all orator [with] neither taste nor patience for the dry and ponderous details."

Barteau, Clark Russell. Born April 7, 1835, near Cleveland, OH. Attd. Wesleyan U. in OH. He visited the South in 1858 to view slavery firsthand and, liking what he saw, settled there. Teacher in Hartsville, TN. Principal of the Hartsville Male Academy. Newspaper editor. Ultrasecessionist, despite his Northern birth. Md. Mary Cosby; Zura Eckford. Pvt. Co. D, 7th TN Cav. Bn., Oct. 17, 1861. Lt. col., 2d TN Cav. (formed by merging the 1st and 7th Bns.), June 12, 1862. Col., June 8, 1863. Col., 22d TN Cav., May 10, 1864. Often led a brigade in Forrest's Cav. WIA Tupelo and at Murfreesboro Dec. 6, 1864, the latter wound (a leg fracture) disabling him from further service. Paroled May 15, 1865, Meridian. Lawyer in Aberdeen, MS, postwar. Moved practice to Memphis in 1870. Died Feb. 10, 1900, Memphis. Buried Elmwood Cemetery. A fellow soldier remembered Barteau as "a very cool man, but impetuous in action."

Bartow, Francis Stebbins. Born Sept. 6, 1816, Savannah, GA. Grad. UGA with first honors. Attd. Yale. Savannah lawyer and planter. Longtime state legislator and Whig Party stalwart. Officer in vol. militia. Secessionist leader. Delegate to GA Secession Convention. Md. Louisa Berrien, daughter of US senator John M. Berrien. Bartow's militia company helped seize Fort Pulaski in Jan. 1861. Elected to Provisional Confederate Congress in 1861. Chairman of its Military Affairs Committee. Resigned to join the army. Capt. Co. B, 8th GA, May 21, 1861. Col., June 1, 1861. KIA 1st Manassas, where he was leading a brigade as "acting general." Buried Laurel Grove Cemetery, Savannah. An orator of "great personal magnetism" but also a heavy drinker. A soldier in the 8th said of Bartow that "we all loved him like a father." In 1861 Cass Co., GA, was renamed Bartow Co. in his honor.

Bass, Frederick Samuel. Born Oct. 27, 1831, Brunswick Co., VA. Grad. VMI 1851. Taught in Petersburg, VA, and Warrenton, NC. In 1857 accepted a position as professor at Marshall College in Marshall, TX, a school with a cadet program. Md. Mary Ezell. Capt. Co. E, 1st TX (the "Marshall Guards") May 28, 1861. Major, Sept. 17, 1861. Lt. col., Jan. 5, 1864. Col., July 15, 1864. WIA Seven Days, Gettysburg, Chickamauga, Knoxville, Darbytown Road (Oct. 7, 1864). Led ANV's "Texas Brigade" at Appomattox. Said to have been appointed brig. gen. in 1865. Postwar president of Marshall U. and Jefferson (TX) College. Moved to Texarkana late in life. Admitted to the Austin, TX, Soldiers' Home in

1894, suffering from blindness. Died July 9, 1897, at the home. Buried State Cemetery, Austin. Gov. Culberson of TX said of Bass, "the golden age of the South produced few gentler and nobler men."

Bass, Thomas Coke. Born c. 1831, MS. Prewar lawyer in Aberdeen, MS. Moved to Sherman, TX, just before the war. Active secessionist. Md. Ada D. Hocker. In May 1861, he occupied the recently abandoned Fort Washita, Indian Territory, with a detachment. Col., 20th TX Cav., April 12, 1862. Fought at Prairie Grove and in the Indian Territory. Resigned March 1, 1864, due to lung disease. Postwar lawyer and editor in Sherman. Land agent. Died Sept. 22, 1878, Memphis, TN, of yellow fever. Probably buried Elmwood Cemetery, Memphis, in a mass grave for victims of that year's yellow fever epidemic. An army inspector termed Bass "an officer of no competency."

Bates, Joseph. Born Jan. 19, 1805, Mobile. AL businessman, state legislator. Gen. of AL militia. To Galveston, TX, in 1845. Mayor of Galveston. US marshal for Eastern TX. Rancher/farmer in Brazoria Co. Md. Mrs. Mary Love Morris. Appointed col. by Gen. Hebert Sept. 26, 1861, and authorized to raise a regiment. He raised 14 companies, but some were detached and the remaining companies could only constitute a battalion. Lt. col., Bates's TX Inf. Bn. June 14, 1862. Col., 13th TX (formed by adding new companies to Bates's Bn.), March 8, 1863. Commanded defense lines near Galveston. Served in LA in the summer of 1863. Postwar rancher/farmer in Brazoria Co. Died Feb. 18, 1888, Galveston. Buried Galveston Episcopal Cemetery. Gen. Magruder thought Bates "faithful and patriotic." A prisoner remembered his "long white hair" and "imposing appearance."

Battle, Joel Allen. Born Sept. 19, 1811, Davidson Co., TN. Davidson Co. farmer prewar. State representative 1851–52. Militia general. Seminole War veteran. Md. Sarah Searcy; Adeline Mosely. Capt. Co. C, 20th TN, May 17, 1861. Col., June 17, 1861. WIA and POW Shiloh. To Johnson's Island Prison. Not reelected at May 14, 1862, reorganization. Exch. Sept. 1862. Appointed TN state treasurer and served as such 1862–65. Hotel owner in Nashville postwar. Superintendent of the state prison. Died Aug. 23, 1872, Nashville. Buried the Battle family graveyard, Davidson Co. "Noble, generous, and brave to a fault" (in the words of a soldier of the 20th), Battle lost two sons in the war.

Baucum, George Franklin. Born Feb. 1, 1837, St. Charles, MO. Reared in Marshall Co., MS, and Memphis. Grocer in Searcy Co., AR, prewar. Md. Glovenin Critz; Katherine McRae, sister of Gen. Dandridge McRae. 1st lt. Co. A, Desha's AR Inf. Bn., Nov. 30, 1861. After Shiloh, battalion merged into 8th AR. Capt. Co. K, 8th AR, May 7, 1862. Major, May 8, 1862. WIA (foot) at Chickamauga. Lt. col., Dec. 20, 1862. Col., Nov. 16, 1863. Shot in the face at the Battle of Atlanta and invalided out of the army. On recruiting duty thereafter. Paroled May 18, 1865, Grenada. Grocer in Searcy postwar. Moved to Little Rock in 1885. Merchant, banker, plantation owner. Died July 29, 1905, Little Rock. Buried Oakland Cemetery, Little Rock. The town of Baucum, near Little Rock, is named for him.

Baxter, Eli Harris, Jr. Born Jan. 29, 1837, Hancock Co., GA. Attd. USMA 1853–54. Attd. UVA. Moved to Cherokee Co., TX, c. 1855. To Marshall, TX, in 1858. Lawyer. State legislator. Delegate to TX Secession Convention. Unmd. 1st lt. Co. E ("Marshall Guards"), 1st TX, 1861. Resigned March 18, 1862, to return to TX and recruit a company. Capt. Co. F, 28th TX Cav., May 10, 1862. Elected lt. col., May 17, 1862. In March 1864 the soldiers of the 28th, dissatisfied at being dismounted, mutinied. Baxter arrested the commanders of the five companies primarily involved. The officers, who had not known of the mutiny in advance, felt that Baxter was making them the scapegoats. Although quickly released, this arrest created a rift between Baxter and his company commanders. Col., April 8, 1864. WIA Mansfield (wrist). Houston lawyer postwar. Died Dec. 13, 1868, Bellville, TX. Buried Glenwood Cemetery, Houston. Capt. Peery of the 28th thought Harris was "one of the worst demagogues I have ever seen and is not a fair man I think."

Baylor, George Wythe. Born Aug. 24, 1832, Fort Gibson, Indian Territory. An uncle founded Baylor U. Col. John R. Baylor was his brother. Grew up in Fayette Co., TX. Attd. Rutersville College. Worked for US Army commissary dept. in San Antonio. Moved to California in 1854; to Weatherford TX, in 1859. Hunter. Listed in the 1860 census as "Indian fighter." Md. Sally Sydnor. 1st lt. Co. H (J. R. Baylor's) 2d TX MR, May 23, 1861. Regimental adj. Joined Gen. A. S. Johnston's staff at Shiloh and claimed to have cradled Johnston's head as he died. Lt. col., 2d TX Cav., AZ Brigade, 1862. Col., Feb. 1, 1863. Killed Maj. Gen. John Wharton, his corps commander, in a Houston hotel room in 1865, the killing the climax of a yearlong quarrel between the two over Baylor's handling of his regiment. He was tried for murder after the war but was acquitted. Paroled June 1, 1865, Galveston. Lived in Dallas and El Paso, TX, and Mexico postwar. Insurance agent. Noted Texas Ranger. State legislator. Farmer. Died March 27, 1916, San Antonio. Buried Confederate Cemetery, San Antonio. A subordinate called him "a hardy frontiersman who cared nothing for discipline . . . one of the best shots with firearms I ever saw." Baylor's reminiscences of frontier life have been published.

Baylor, John Robert. Born July 20, 1822, Paris, KY. Attd. Woodward College in Cincinnati. Weatherford, TX, rancher. Indian agent. State legislator. Newspaper editor. Like his brother George, a noted frontiersman and Indian fighter.

Md. Emily Harris. Elected lt. col., 2d TX MR, by TX Secession Convention, March 19, 1861. Appointed col., Dec. 15, 1861, by Gen. Sibley. With the 2d he seized the southern portion of what is now New Mexico. Confederate gov. of the New Mexico Territory, 1861–62. In 1862 he was commissioned col., to rank from May 29, to raise and command five battalions (the "Arizona Brigade") of PR. In Nov. 1862, with the recruiting well under way, the sec. of war revoked Baylor's commission and removed him from office. Baylor had recommended exterminating hostile Indians by poisoning their food supplies, an action too extreme for Pres. Davis but one Baylor thought much cheaper than bribery. Confederate congressman from TX, 1863–65. Recommissioned col., March 23, 1865, to raise a regiment of draft-exempt men for frontier service. Postwar lawyer, rancher in San Antonio and later Uvalde Co. Died Feb. 6, 1894, Montell, Uvalde Co. Buried Church of the Ascension Cemetery, Montell. A huge man with a hair-trigger temper, "anyone he liked was the best fellow in the world, and anyone he disliked was the damnest rascal living."

Baylor, William Smith Hanger. Born April 7, 1831, Augusta Co., VA. Grad. UVA and Washington College. Attorney in Staunton. Commonwealth attorney. Officer in vol. militia. Md. Mary H. Johnson. Capt. Co. L, 5th VA, April 1861. Elected col. at the original organization of the 5th VA, but this election (done prior to mustering in to Confederate service) was voided. Major, May 28, 1861. Lt. col., acting AAIG to Stonewall Jackson, Jan.–April 1862. Col., 5th VA, April 21, 1862. Led the Stonewall Brigade at 2d Manassas. KIA Aug. 30, 1862, 2d Manassas, while leading a counterattack. Buried Hebron Presbyterian Church, Augusta Co. Very brave and popular with his men and a favorite of Stonewall Jackson.

Beall, Lloyd James. Born Oct. 19, 1808, Fort Adams, RI. Son of an army officer. Grad. USMA 1830 (appointed from MD). US Army officer 1830–61, rising to the rank of major. Md. Frances A. Hayne, daughter of US senator Arthur Hayne of SC. Col., May 23, 1861. Commandant of the CS Marine Corps, 1861–65, with headquarters in Richmond. Postwar merchant in Richmond. City alderman, lost race for mayor. Died Nov. 10, 1887, Richmond, buried Hollywood Cemetery. Gen. Joseph Johnston thought Beall "eminently qualified for the grade of brigadier general."

Beard, James Hamilton. Born July 28, 1833, Lowndes Co., AL. Grew up in AL. Moved to LA in the 1850s, residing in Shreveport and then Kingston. Shreveport merchant prewar. Steamboat capt. Md. Catherine Tomkies. Capt., "Shreveport Grays," Jan. 1861 (mustered into Confederate service April 20, 1861). Company sent to Richmond, VA, and became Co. D, 1st LA Bn. Major, 1st LA Bn., Aug. 15, 1861. Unit disbanded May 1, 1862. Major, 11th LA Bn., May

14, 1862. Lt. col., Aug. 3, 1863. Col., Consolidated Crescent Regt. (the 11th Bn. was merged with the Crescent Regt. to form this new unit), Nov. 3, 1863. KIA Mansfield. Buried Evergreen Cemetery, Kingston. Beard's soldiers published a testimonial to his "amiability as a gentleman and an officer" and his devotion to his men.

Beattie, Taylor. Born July 4, 1837, Lafourche Parish, LA. Attd. UVA. Lawyer in Thibodeaux, LA. Md. Fannie O. Pugh. 1st lt. Co. A, 1st LA Regulars, April 1861. Capt., Sept. 30, 1861. Resigned Dec. 16, 1862. Acting judge advocate, c. Jan. 1863. Appointed col., May 1, 1863, to rank from Dec. 16, 1862, to be judge of the military court of Hardee's Corps. Postwar planter and lawyer in Thibodeaux. Unsuccessful candidate for Congress and for governor (as a Republican). Died Nov. 19, 1920, Thibodeaux. Buried on the Madewood Plantation Cemetery, near Napoleonville. Papers at Duke and UNC.

Beck, Benjamin. Born c. 1827, Henderson Co., NC. Merchant in Baldwin Co., GA, prewar. Noncom in 3d US Art. during Mexican War. Md. Mrs. Angeline Stubbs. Capt. Co. F, 9th GA, June 12, 1861. Col., Aug. 1, 1861. WIA 2d Manassas. Resigned March 16, 1864, due to a disability. While at home, he helped repel Stoneman's Raid on Macon. POW during the raid but released. Farmer, teacher, and lay preacher in Jones Co. postwar. Murdered there Nov. 16, 1884, by his stepsons, who had feuded with him over his wife's inheritance.

Beck, Franklin King. Born May 21, 1814, Duplin Co., NC. Attd. UAL and Georgetown U. Grad. Yale Law School, 1837. Prewar lawyer and planter in Camden, AL. State representative 1851–53, 1855–57. Delegate to AL Secession Convention. Md. Martha Tait. Col., 23d AL at Nov. 5, 1861, organization. POW at Vicksburg. Missed Atlanta Campaign due to a leg fracture. Returned to regiment after the fall of Atlanta. KIA at Resaca, GA, Oct. 12, 1864, by a cannon shot that hit a nearby tree, which fell and crushed his leg. Buried Resaca Confederate Cemetery. Memorial stone in Camden Cemetery. A "scholarly figure."

Beckham, Robert Franklin. Born May 6, 1837, Culpeper, VA. Grad. USMA 1859. Lt., US Army 1859–61. Unmd. Lt., CS Regular Army, March 16, 1861. Served with Groves's (later Pelham's) VA Battery. ADC on Gen. G. W. Smith's staff, 1861–62. Elected capt., Jeff Davis Art., March 31, 1862, but did not accept. Major of ordnance to Gen. G. W. Smith, Aug. 16, 1862. At Gen. Jeb Stuart's request, commanded Stuart's horse artillery after John Pelham's death. Promoted to col., Feb. 16, 1864, to take command of the artillery of Hood's Corps, Army of Tennessee. Chief of artillery, Army of Tennessee, July–Sept. 1864. MWIA by a shell fragment near Columbia, TN, Nov. 29, 1864, in skirmishing prior to Spring Hill. Died Dec. 5, 1864, in a house near Ashwood, TN. Buried St. John's Churchyard, Ashwood. Called "daring and efficient" in *OR*.

Bell, Hiram Parks. Born Jan. 19, 1827, Jackson Co., GA. Attorney in Cumming, GA, prewar. State representative and senator. Delegate to GA Secession Convention. GA commissioner to TN in 1861. Md. Virginia Lester (sister of Col. R. P. Lester); Anna Jordan. Pvt. Co. E, 43d GA, March 10, 1862. Capt. Co. I, March 1862. Lt. col., March 20, 1862. WIA (leg) Chickasaw Bayou. Col., May 17, 1863. Often ill. Elected to Confederate Congress in 1864. Cumming lawyer postwar. State representative and senator. US congressman 1873–75, 1877–79. Died Aug. 17, 1907, at his son's home in Atlanta. Buried Cumming Cemetery. Bell published his reminiscences in 1907, in which he wryly observed that he "perhaps had suffered more, and done less, than any soldier in the Confederate army."

Bell, James Madison. Born Oct. 15, 1826, near New Echota, GA. Prominent member of the Cherokee Tribe. Brother-in-law of Gen. Stand Watie. Farmer and stockman in the Indian Territory prewar. Md. Caroline Lynch. Capt. Co. D, 1st Cherokee MR, July 12, 1861. Lt. col., 2d Cherokee MR, Feb. 3, 1863. Col., June 6, 1863. Col., 1st Cherokee MR, June 1864. Farmer in the Canadian Dist. postwar. In Cherokee senate. Died March 22, 1915, at his home near Bernice, Craig Co., OK. Buried Bell-Watie Cemetery, Delaware Co.; reburied Polson Cemetery. Bell's Cherokee name was Colo-gotte-yon ("Dull Hoe").

Bell, Samuel Slade. Born June 1834, Currituck Co., NC. Lived prewar in NC, AL, MS, and Ashley Co., AR. Plantation owner. Md. M. J. Kirkpatrick; Mary E. Woodruff. Capt. Co. A, 37th (aka 29th) AR, March 15, 1862. Major, June 14, 1862. WIA Prairie Grove. Col., Dec. 21, 1862. WIA and POW Helena. Escaped from the train carrying him to Johnson's Island by jumping and returned to his regiment. Moved to Little Rock in 1866. Planter, merchant. Died Sept. 23, 1877, on his plantation near Hamburg, Ashley Co. Buried on his plantation. An obituary said of Bell, "No man in the army was better loved by his men."

Benavides, Santos. Born Jose Maria de los Santos Benavides, Nov. 1, 1823, Laredo, TX (then part of Mexico), descended from the founder of Laredo. Wealthy Laredo merchant prewar, known as the "merchant prince" of the Rio Grande. Attorney. Mayor of Laredo. Noted Texas Ranger. Md. Augustina Villareal. Capt., TX state cav., May 1861. Unit mustered in as Co. H, 33d TX Cav., Jan. 16, 1862, for 12 months. Major, 33d, May 2, 1863. Authorized in Nov. 1863 to raise a regiment in West TX to defend the Rio Grande Valley. Col., Benavides's TX Cav., 1864–65. Defended Laredo from Union attacks and won the thanks of the state legislature. "[A]n able, skillful commander" who "did not know the meaning of fear." Recommended for promotion to general. Paroled Laredo Aug. 18, 1865. Postwar Laredo merchant. State legislator. Died Nov. 9, 1891, Laredo. Buried Catholic Cemetery, Laredo. Benavides was undoubtedly the war's most distinguished Tejano Confederate.

Benbow, Henry Laurens. Born Oct. 25, 1829, Sumter Dist., SC. Attd. Cokesbury College. Planter in Clarendon Co. in 1860. Unmd. Lt. Co. D, Hampton Legion, June 19, 1861. Capt. Co. I, 23d SC, Nov. 15, 1861. Col., April 16, 1862. WIA 2d Manassas and Petersburg. WIA Five Forks in both hips and POW. Released June 15, 1865. Planter in Summerton postwar. Longtime state legislator. Died Dec. 21, 1907, at his Summerton home. Buried Manning Cemetery, Manning, SC. An old newspaper article claimed "no leader was ever loved more by his men." While in prison with his Five Forks wounds he met and shook hands with Pres. Lincoln.

Bennett, James Dearing. Born Nov. 9, 1816, Campbell Co., VA. Family moved to Smith Co., TN, in 1832. Schoolteacher, merchant, and farmer in Hartsville, Sumner Co., prewar. Seminole War veteran. Md. Martha Hutchinson. Lt. col., 7th TN Cav. Bn., Oct. 19, 1861. Resigned June 12, 1862, when his battalion was consolidated with the 1st TN Cav. Bn. to form the 2d TN Cav. and returned home to raise a regiment. Col., 9th TN Cav., Sept. 1, 1862. WIA near Goodlettsville, TN, Sept. 1862. Died Dec. 23, 1862 (per service record and gravestone: one source gives Jan. 23, 1863), of pneumonia, near Elizabethtown, KY. Buried Hartsville Cemetery. Gen. Duke found Bennett "high minded, brave, and generous" but a poor disciplinarian.

Bennett, Risdon Tyler. Born June 8, 1840, Wadesboro, NC. Attd. UNC and Davidson College. Grad. Cumberland U. in 1859. Lawyer in Anson Co., NC, prewar. Md. Kate Shepherd. Corporal Co. C, 14th NC, April 22, 1861. Sgt., June 1, 1861. Capt., Sept. 28, 1861. Lt. col., April 27, 1862. Col., July 5, 1862. WIA Antietam, Gettysburg (groin), Spotsylvania (mouth), and Cold Harbor (shoulder). POW Opequon Creek, exch. Feb. 27, 1865. Wadesboro attorney and farmer postwar. Judge. State representative 1872–74. US congressman 1883–87. Died July 21, 1913, Wadesboro. Buried Magnolia Heights Cemetery, west of Wadesboro. A voracious reader, noted orator, and colorful writer.

Berkeley, Norborne. Born March 31, 1828, VA. Grad. VMI. Loudoun Co. farmer prewar. Md. Lavinia Hart Berkeley. Major, 8th VA, April 1861. Lt. col., April 27, 1862. WIA (foot) and POW Gettysburg. Exch. March 18, 1864. Col., Aug. 9, 1863. Often absent due to chronic rheumatism. Resigned March 2, 1865. Paroled April 24, 1865, Richmond. Loudoun Co. farmer postwar. In charge of the farm program at VA A&M College, 1875–79. Died Jan. 12, 1911, Prince William Co. Buried St. Paul's Episcopal Church, Haymarket. The "gallant" Berkeley was one of four brothers who served in the 8th.

Best, Emory Fiske. Born March 28, 1840, Bladensburg, MD. Moved to Cassville, GA, in 1858. Grad. Cumberland U. Law School in 1860. Opened a law practice in Rome just prior to the war. Md. Mrs. Mary Hill. Lt. Co. C, 23d GA,

Aug. 31, 1861. Major, Aug. 31, 1861. Lt. col., Aug. 16, 1862. WIA Antietam. Col., Nov. 25, 1862. The 23d was largely captured at Chancellorsville while acting as a flank guard for Jackson's attack. Best was court-martialed for abandoning his men to avoid capture and dismissed from the service Dec. 23, 1863. Attorney in GA postwar. Attorney for the Dept. of the Interior in Washington, DC. Clerk in various government offices. Died April 23, 1912, DC. Buried Rose Hill Cemetery, Macon. Gen. Colquitt thought Best a "good drill officer" but "without judgment." A fine essay on Best's court-martial is in Gary Gallagher's 1996 book on Chancellorsville.

Bibb, Joseph Benajah. Born April 17, 1832, "Spring Hill," Elmore Co., AL. Prewar Montgomery lawyer and militia officer. Md. Martha Bibb, a cousin. Capt. of "minute men" at Fort Morgan, early 1861. Lt. col., 23d AL, Nov. 5, 1861. Col., Oct. 12, 1864. WIA Nashville. One veteran said, "his influence over the men was marvelous." Died Sept. 14, 1869, in Montgomery, of tuberculosis brought on by his war wound. Buried Oakwood Cemetery, Montgomery.

Biffle, Jacob Barnett. Born May 31, 1830, Maury Co., TN. Wayne Co. farmer prewar. Mexican War veteran. Md. Sarah Lusby. Capt. Co. B, 2d (Biffle's) TN Cav. Bn., c. July 1, 1861. Lt. col., 1862. Col., 6th TN Cav. (aka 1st, Wheeler's; formed from the 2d Bn.), May 1862. Dropped at June 12, 1862, reorganization and returned home to recruit a new regiment. Col., 19th (aka 9th) TN Cav., Oct. 3, 1862. Often led a brigade under Wheeler and Forrest. Cattle rancher in TX postwar. Shot and mortally wounded by one of his herders, Dec. 15, 1876. Died Jan. 2, 1877, near Gainesville. Buried Reed Cemetery, Myra, Cooke Co., TX. A biography of Biffle was published in 1991.

Bird, Edward. Born Sept. 30, 1825, Effingham Co., GA. Operated a timber and turpentine business in Effingham Co. prewar. Md. Eliza Ann Wilson. Capt. Co. A (the "Effingham Hussars"), 2d GA Cav. Bn., Sept. 7, 1861. Lt. col., May 17, 1862. Often detached to procure timber for the defenses of Savannah. Col., 5th GA Cav. (formed in 1863 from the 2d Bn.), July 26, 1864. Paroled May 3, 1865, Hillsboro, NC. Returned to Effingham Co. and his turpentine business after the war. Planter there. State representative 1880–81. Died April 15, 1893. Buried Guyton City Cemetery, Effingham Co.

Bird, William Capers. Born Jan. 7, 1835, Jefferson Co., FL. Attd. USC, Emory U. and UVA. Prewar lawyer and planter in Monticello, FL. Md. Carrie H. Brooks, daughter of Cong. Preston Brooks, 1865. 1st lt. Co. I, 1st FL, April 2, 1861. Capt., April 6, 1862. WIA Shiloh, while leading 1st FL Bn., and captured while recuperating. Exchanged. WIA and POW Perryville. Exchanged in mid-1863. Col., Dec. 16, 1862, but this appointment was canceled by the War Dept. on the mistaken belief that Bird had been killed. Reappointed col., Nov. 21, 1863. Judge advocate on Beauregard's staff. Postwar planter, lawyer in Monticello. US marshal, state senator, state treasurer. Died May 7, 1892, Monticello, buried Roseland Cemetery. A fellow prisoner said, "[A] more fearless, courteous, modest gentleman I have never met." Brother of Major Pickens Bird, 9th FL.

Bishop, William Harrison. Born Dec. 1834, Moorefield, Hardy Co., VA. Attd. Yale, though there's no record of him formally matriculating. Lawyer in Marion Co., MS, prewar. State representative 1859–61. Unmd. 1st lt. Co. F, 7th MS, Aug. 10, 1861. Col., May 8, 1862 (election). WIA Stones River. Regiment consolidated with 9th MS in 1863. MWIA Franklin, Nov. 30, 1864, dying that night. Buried McGavock Confederate Cemetery, Franklin. Gen. Patton Anderson thought Bishop "competent, able & efficient."

Bishop, William Preston. Born Aug. 19, 1841, Hancock Co., TN. Attd. Mossy Creek College. Practiced law in Lecompton, KS, and Hancock Co. prewar. Md. Mary McKamy; Emma Simpson; Emma Haggerd. 1st lt. Co. D, 29th TN, Aug. 13, 1861. Capt., 1862. WIA Stones River and Atlanta. Lt. col., probably Oct. 1864. Col., probably Dec. 1864. Led Vaughn's Brigade at Bentonville. Moved to TX in 1869. Teacher, trader, and farmer in Tarrant, Denton, and Collin Cos. State representative. To Frankford, Collin Co., in 1886. Died Jan. 7, 1901, Denton. Buried Frankford Cemetery.

Black, John Logan. Born July 12, 1830, York Dist., SC. Attd. USMA. Planter in Fairfield Dist. prewar. Md. Mary Peay Black; Eugenia T. Johnson. 1st lt. Co. E, 1st SC Regulars, March 6, 1861. Capt., May 1861. Lt. col., 1st SC Cav., Oct. 31, 1861. Col., June 25, 1862. WIA Upperville and 2d Brandy Station (hand). Regiment detached to duty in SC, 1864. Blacksburg planter postwar. Vice president, Magnetic Iron & Steel Ore Co. Died March 25, 1902, Blacksburg. Buried Aimwell Presbyterian Church near Woodward, SC. His family remembered him as "a very large man, bold and aggressive." Black's war memoirs have been published.

Black, William Thomas. Born Oct. 19, 1833, GA. Attd. GMI. Ellaville, Schley Co., attorney prewar. 2d lt. Co. K ("Schley Guards"), 5th GA, May 11, 1861. 1st lt. and adj., Oct. 7, 1861. Col., May 8, 1862. KIA Stones River, Dec. 31, 1862, shot in the head "while gallantly leading his brave regiment." A newspaper tribute praised his "pure morals and unimpeachable integrity." Buried Ellaville City Cemetery.

Blacknall, Charles Christopher. Born Dec. 4, 1830, Granville Co., NC. Brother of Major T. H. Blacknall, 37th AR. Farmer near Kittrell, Granville Co. Franklinton merchant in 1860. Md. Virginia Spencer. Capt. Co. G, 23d NC, June 11, 1861. Major, May 31, 1862. WIA Seven Pines. POW Chancellorsville, May 3,

1863. Paroled May 18, 1863. WIA (mouth and neck) and POW Gettysburg. Exch. March 1864. Lt. col., July 17, 1863. Col., Sept. 1, 1863. WIA Opequon Creek, losing a foot. Died of his wounds Nov. 6, 1864, near Winchester, VA. Buried Mt. Hebron Cemetery, Winchester. "[B]eloved . . . an ideal Confederate officer."

Blakey, David Taliaferro. Born Aug. 12, 1833, Montgomery, AL. Grad. UGA, 1851. Taught school in Tuskegee. Plantation owner in Bullock Co. Officer in vol. militia. Md. Mary S. Mabson. Enlisted June 27, 1861 in 3d AL. Promoted to sgt. of ordnance, at Mt. Vernon Arsenal, Sept. 12, 1861. Capt. Co. E, 1st AL Cav., c. Nov. 27, 1861. Major, Aug. 1862. Lt. col., Oct. 1862. Col., March 1863. WIA Dandridge. Paroled Charlotte May 3, 1865. Lawyer in Montgomery postwar. Died June 27, 1902, Montgomery. Buried Oakwood Cemetery.

Blandford, Mark Harden. Born July 13, 1826, Warren Co., GA. Attd. Mercer U. Lawyer in Buena Vista, GA. Sgt. in Mexican War. Md. Sarah C. Daniel. Capt. Co. K, 12th GA, June 15, 1861. Lt. col., Jan. 24, 1863. Resigned June 9, 1863, to enter the Confederate Congress. Commissioned col. of cav. and judge of a military court, July 24, 1863. Resigned Oct. 31, 1863. Columbus, GA, lawyer postwar. Justice, GA Supreme Court, 1872–80. Died Jan. 31, 1902, Columbus, buried Linwood Cemetery. "Rugged, rough, blunt and bright," according to a fellow congressman.

Blanding, James Douglass. Born June 26, 1821, Columbia, SC. Lawyer in Sumter prewar. Mayor. Mexican War veteran. Md. Leonora A. McFadden. Lt. col., 9th SC, April 8, 1861. Col., July 12, 1861. Regiment disbanded in 1862 at the expiration of its one-year enlistment. Blanding later tried to raise a battalion of PR. Sumter lawyer postwar. Trustee of Davidson College. Died Oct. 24, 1906, Heriot, SC. Buried Sumter Cemetery.

Bledsoe, Albert Taylor. Born Nov. 9, 1809, Frankfort, KY. Grad. USMA 1830. Lt., US Army, 1830–32. Episcopal minister. Lawyer in Springfield, IL, where he competed with Abraham Lincoln. Taught at UVA, UMS, Kenyon College and Miami U. of Ohio. Md. Harriet Coxe. Announced as col., 36th VA (PAVA), June 1, 1861, but regiment never raised. Transferred to War Dept. with that rank June 23, 1861. Asst. sec. of war, 1861–65. Bledsoe does not have a compiled service record. In 1864 he was sent to London to rally support for the Confederacy. Postwar author, living in Baltimore. Founded and edited the *Southern Review.* Wrote a book vindicating Jefferson Davis, his classmate at USMA. Died Dec. 8, 1877, Alexandria, VA. Buried UVA Cemetery, Charlottesville. One congressman called the erudite Bledsoe "not qualified for the office. He loses his papers."

Blythe, Andrew King. Born Jan. 27, 1818, TN. Lawyer in Lowndes and Yalobusha Cos., MS, prewar. State representative 1850–51. US consul to Havana

1856–58. Capt. in Mexican War. Md. Elizabeth A. Butler. Capt. Co. E, Blythe's (1st) MS Inf. Bn., April 27, 1861. Lt. col., Blythe's MS Inf. Bn., July 3, 1861. Col., Blythe's MS Regt. (formed from his battalion—renamed 44th MS in 1863), fall 1861. KIA the first day of Shiloh, while leading his regiment in an attack. A "perfectly courageous man . . . soft-hearted as a girl." Buried Friendship Cemetery, Columbus, MS.

Board, Francis Howard. Born Feb. 10, 1832, Moneta, Bedford Co., VA. Grad. Baltimore Medical College. Merchant in Bedford Co. prewar. Md. Buena Vista Arnold. Capt. Co. I, 58th VA, July 24, 1861. Lt. col., May 1, 1862. Behaved "most gallantly" at McDowell. WIA Gaines's Mill. Col., Oct. 30, 1862. KIA July 20, 1864, near Winchester, VA. Buried Stonewall Cemetery, Winchester.

Bonham, DeWitt Clinton. Born Jan. 5, 1819, Lancaster Co., PA. Cousin of Gen. M. L. Bonham of SC. Reared in PA. Attd. USMA 1835–38. Attorney in LA and MS. Planter in Issaquena Co., MS. Md. Mary Dameron. Col., 22d MS, Oct. 10, 1861. Died Dec. 24, 1861, Camp Beauregard, KY, of typhoid. Buried Cedar Hill Cemetery, Vicksburg. "[A] stern and inflexible disciplinarian."

Bonner, Thomas Reuben. Born Sept. 11, 1838, Holmes Co., MS. Family moved to Rusk, TX, in 1850. Prewar farmer, printer, ferry operator. Md. Cynthia A. Madden; Mary Davenport. Capt. Co. C, 18th TX, April 1, 1862. Major, Aug. 10, 1863. Lt. col., April 9, 1864. Col., April 30, 1864. Led 18th in the Red River Campaign. Postwar lawyer in Rusk. Banker in Tyler. Speaker of the TX State House. Died Aug. 30, 1891, Tyler. Buried Oakwood Cemetery, Tyler. "[A] man of fine ability."

Booker, Richard Anderson. Born Nov. 15, 1817, VA. Hotel keeper in Prince Edward Co. prewar. In VA legislature, 1861. Md. Virginia O. Brown; Harriet Crowder; Bettie E. Manning. Capt. Co. F, 18th VA, April 23, 1861. WIA 2d Manassas. Resigned May 5, 1863. Capt. Co. D, 3d VA Reserves, April 20, 1864. Col., Sept. 30, 1864. Paroled April 1865, Farmville. Newspaper publisher and tobacco merchant in Prince Edward Co. postwar. Died April 30, 1904, Farmville. Buried Farmville.

Bookter, Edwin Faust. Born Nov. 11, 1837, Richland Dist., SC. Attd. USC. Richland Dist. planter prewar. State representative 1860–61. Unmd. Capt. Co. D, 12th SC, Aug. 20, 1861. Major, Feb. 27, 1863. Lt. col., Nov. 17, 1863. Col., May 6, 1864. WIA Gaines's Mill, 2d Manassas, Wilderness. KIA Jones Farm, Sept. 30, 1864. Buried Mt. Pleasant Methodist Church, near Columbia. His gravestone inscription reads, "When the dead bolts deadliest fell, they reached no nobler breast than thine young, gallant Bookter."

Boone, Squire. Born April 13, 1830, Daviess Co., KY. Studied law in Grayson Co., KY. Moved to Ozark, Franklin Co., AR, in 1852 and practiced law there. Editor, Ozark *Southwestern.* Md. Tennessee Bourland; Martha Bullard. 1st lt. Co. C, McRae's AR Bn., July 18, 1861. Adj., McRae's 15th (21st) AR, May 8, 1862. Lt. col., May 30, 1862. Col., Aug. 2, 1862. WIA Corinth Oct. 4, 1862, and POW. Right leg amputated. Exch. March 28, 1863. Rejoined his regiment and POW again at Vicksburg. Again exch. Commanded post of Marshall, TX, thereafter. Postwar Ozark lawyer. Prosecuting attorney, 4th Circuit, 1865–68. Died July 20, 1873, in his Ozark home. Buried Ozark, probably in an unmarked grave in Highland Cemetery.

Border, John Pelham. Born Feb. 19, 1819, Lincolnshire, England. To US in 1823. Lived in NY for a time. Settled in San Augustine, TX, in 1835. Surveyor, merchant, county clerk. Soldier in the Texas Revolution. Md. Catherine Harding (who later married Col. Oran Roberts). Capt., Texas State Troops in 1863. Elected lt. col., Border's TX Cav. Bn., April 9, 1864. Consolidated with Fulcrod's Bn. and increased to a regiment, probably April 1864. Unit mustered into Confederate service Aug. 1, 1864. Elected col., Anderson's/Border's TX Cav., Feb. 27, 1865. Commanded Camp Ford military prison, 1864. Several prisoners charged him with brutality. Surveyor in New Iberia, LA, postwar. Died there June 12, 1873. Buried Protestant Cemetery, New Iberia.

Borland, Solon. Born Aug. 8, 1811, near Suffolk, VA. Reared in Hertford Co., NC. Attd. lectures at UPA Medical College. Grad. Louisville Medical Institute (later U. of Louisville Medical College) in 1841. Physician in NC and Memphis, TN. Newspaper editor in Memphis and Little Rock, AR. Adj. gen. of AR 1844–46. Lt. col. AR Volunteers in Mexican War. US Senate, 1848–53. Ambassador to Nicaragua, 1853–54. Returned to Memphis to edit another newspaper. In April 1861, before Arkansas's secession, he commanded (as ADC to the governor, with the rank of colonel) five companies of militia that seized the army post at Fort Smith. Md. Huldah G. Wright; Eliza Hart; Mary I. Melbourne. Lt. col., 1st (Borland's) Cav. Bn., AR State Troops, 1861. Col., 1st AR Mtd. Volunteers (State Troops). Col., 3d AR Cav. (his state regiment, taken into Confederate service), July 29, 1861. Often absent due to advanced age and "troublesome diarrhea." Not reelected at May 17, 1862, reorganization and discharged May 26, 1862. Returned to his family, then living in Princeton, AR. Moved to TX Sept. 1863 due to ill health and the federal advance. Died Jan. 1, 1864, near Houston. Buried Houston's City Cemetery. Memorial stone in Mt. Holly Cemetery, Little Rock.

Boston, Reuben Beverly. Born April 21, 1834, Fluvanna Co., VA. Attd. UVA. Lawyer in Memphis, TN, 1856–59, then returned to practice in Fluvanna Co. Enlisted Feb. 15, 1862, in Co. F, 3d VA Art. Lt. Co. I, 5th VA Cav., April 28, 1862. Capt., May 2, 1862. Col., June 16, 1864. WIA and POW Aldie. Exch. March 10, 1864. WIA Trevilian Station. MWIA High Bridge near Farmville, April 6, 1865.

Died April 7, the last ANV colonel to be killed in action. Buried in Mrs. Watson's yard near High Bridge; reburied Red Hill Cemetery, Fluvanna Co. Gen. Lomax asserted Boston showed "extraordinary skill and valor on the field."

Bosworth, Abel Ware. Born July 21, 1816, Skawhegan, ME. Reared in Mobile, AL. Moved to New Orleans in 1845. Owner of ice business. City alderman. Militia colonel. Md. Rachel M. Weir. Capt. Co. H, Crescent (LA) Regt., March 5, 1862. Major, March 5, 1862. Col., Oct. 27, 1862. Lost post when regiment consolidated and assigned to staff duties. Commanded post of Brashear City, early 1863. Col., Consolidated Crescent Regt., after Col. Beard's death at Mansfield. Paroled June 4, 1865, Natchitoches. Owned ice company in New Orleans postwar. Bank president. Owned plantation on the Bayou Teche. President of the Crescent Regt. Benevolent Assn. Lost race for mayor in 1882. Died Oct. 11, 1885, at his New Orleans home and buried in New Orleans. A fellow soldier called Bosworth "too impatient and vehement in temperament to get along always, without some stormy episodes."

Boteler, Alexander Robinson. Born May 16, 1815, VA. Grad. Princeton. Lived in Baltimore, MD, then near Shepherdstown, VA (later WVA), prewar. Planter. US Congress 1859–61. Md. Helen M. Stockton. Prominent Whig and Unionist. VADC to Gens. Jackson and Stuart. Aide to Govs. Letcher and Smith of VA. Confederate Congress 1861–62. Lost race for Congress in 1863. Appointed col. and judge of military court, Dept. of Richmond, Nov. 11, 1864. Postwar planter near Shepherdstown. Author. Attorney at US Dept. of Justice in the 1880s. Died May 8, 1892, Shepherdstown, buried Elmwood Cemetery. On his postwar pardon application Boteler said he accepted the colonelcy because he was broke and liable to be conscripted into the reserves. Papers at Duke U.

Botts, Lawson. Born July 25, 1825, Fredericksburg, VA. Grad. VMI. Lawyer in Charlestown prewar. Defense attorney for John Brown after the Harpers Ferry Raid. Officer of vol. militia. Md. Sarah E. B. Ransom. Capt. Co. G (the "Botts Grays"), 2d VA, April 18, 1861. Major, June 12, 1861. Lt. col., Sept. 11, 1861. Col., June 27, 1862. MWIA Groveton, Aug. 28, 1862. Died Sept. 16, 1862, in a private home near Middleburg. Buried Charlestown Zion Episcopal Church. Papers at Duke U.

Bouchelle, Thomas Slater. Born Dec. 2, 1829, Wilkesboro, NC. Attd. Wake Forest U. Physician in Camden Co. prewar. Md. Anne Thompson; Sarah A. Hackett. 2d lt. Co. B, 1st NC, May 16, 1861. 1st lt., April 2, 1862. Capt., July 8, 1862. WIA Antietam. Detailed as recruiting officer in NC's 9th Congressional Dist., Aug. 22, 1863. Retired to Invalid Corps, Feb. 24, 1865. Col., 3d Regt. NC Detailed Men, winter of 1864–65. Camden Co. farmer postwar. Chairman of the county board. Died Oct. 21, 1912, Deland, FL. Buried Oakdale Cemetery,

Deland. One neighbor said Bouchelle was "the best informed man, the best known man, the best loved man in Camden County."

Bounds, Joseph Murphy. Born c. 1822, MO. Moved to McKinney, TX, c. 1845. Farmer. Traveling trader. Hotelkeeper. Lt. in Mexican War. Md. Eliza S. Hurt. Capt. Co. G, 11th TX Cav., Oct. 2, 1861. Lt. col., July 13, 1862. Promoted to col., Jan. 4, 1863. However, due to confusion as to which officers of the regiment had seniority (part of a dispute which lasted the entire war), another officer (George Reeves) took over the 11th and Bounds reverted to his former rank. Murdered Oct. 27, 1863, by Pvt. W. R. Dulaney of the 11th, probably in AL. One (unlikely) story has his murder as part of a Union plot. Buried Pecan Grove Cemetery, McKinney.

Bourland, James G. Born Aug. 11, 1801, Wolfe Creek, Pendleton Dist., SC. Varied prewar career, including slave and horse dealer in TN; planter, trader, surveyor in Cooke Co., TX. State senator. Lt. col. in Mexican War. Indian fighter. Md. Catherine Wells; Nancy S. Barnett. TX commissioner to negotiate with the Five Civilized Tribes, Feb.–May 1861. Commander, 21st Dist. TX militia, June–Dec. 1861. Provost marshal, 21st Dist., 1862. Lt. col. of a battalion 1863. Col., probably March 1, 1864, Bourland's (aka the "Border" Regt.) TX Cav., which was formed by adding to his battalion. "[A] good fighter and a good hater." Helped organize the Gainesville hanging of Unionists in 1862. Lived in seclusion in his Cooke Co. home postwar, farming. He was indicted after the war for murdering the Gainesville prisoners but was acquitted. Died Aug. 20, 1879, Cooke Co. Buried Orlena Cemetery, Cooke Co. Bourland's papers are at the Library of Congress.

Bowen, Henry Smith. Born Aug. 3, 1820, Tazewell Co., VA. Farmer in Tazewell Co. prewar. Md. Elizabeth Black; Mary E. Miller. Col., 188th VA Militia, 1861. Major and commissary in southwest VA, summer of 1862. Col., 22d VA Cav., Aug. 1, 1863. Paroled June 12, 1865, Charleston, WVA. Farmer in Tazewell and Wythe Cos. postwar. Died Nov. 11, 1887, Wythe Co. Buried in a church cemetery north of Wytheville.

Bowen, Robert Esli. Born Sept. 8, 1830, Pickens Dist., SC. Pickens Co. farmer prewar, except for 2 years spent teaching in TX. Md. Martha Oliver. Lt. Co. E, 2d SC Rifles, Oct. 24, 1861. Capt., Dec. 19, 1861. WIA Wauhatchie. Lt. col., Nov. 13, 1863. Col., Jan. 22, 1864. WIA Spotsylvania. Elected to state legislature in 1864, serving while on leave. Appmx. Pickens Co. farmer postwar. State representative and senator. Railroad president. Died Jan. 11, 1909, Fairforest, SC. Buried Pickens Chapel Cemetery, Pickens Co.

Bowen, Wylde Lyde Latham. Born Oct. 22, 1838, Bowen, Grainger Co., TN. Moved to Lake City, FL, in 1860. Orange grove owner and newspaper editor.

Read law. Grad. Mossy Creek Baptist (now Carson-Newman) College in 1861. Md. Mary Jewell in 1877. Major, 4th FL, Aug. 27, 1861. Commanded Confederate forces garrisoning Tampa, FL, fall of 1861. Lt. col., May 16, 1862. Col., Sept. 2, 1862. Won official mention for his gallant conduct at Chickamauga. In 1864 Bowen was assigned to post duty, due to illness. Unsuccessful applicant for judge of a military court. Paroled May 5, 1865. Postwar merchant in Jewell, GA, owning the Jewell Cotton Mills. Died Dec. 14, 1905, Mayfield, near Jewell. Buried Jewell Baptist Church Cemetery.

Bowles, James William. Born May 21, 1837, Louisville, KY. Attd. Yale but left before graduation due to the impending war. Farmer near Louisville prewar. Md. Ann Pope in 1866. 1st lt., KSG, Feb. 2, 1861. 2d lt., CS Regular Army, Sept. 9, 1861. Capt. Co. C, 2d KY Cav., Sept. 21, 1861. Major, Nov. 1862. Lt. col., Jan. 24, 1863. Col., Sept. 9, 1864. WIA and POW at Cynthiana. To Johnson's Island Prison, released June 1865. Real estate agent in Louisville postwar. Retired to Waynesville, NC, in 1903. Died July 16, 1921, Waynesville. Buried Cave Hill Cemetery, Louisville.

Bowles, Pinkney Downie. Born July 7, 1835, Edgefield Dist., SC. Attd. UVA, grad. SCMA. Md. Alice Stearns. To Conecuh Co., AL, in 1859. Lawyer and militia colonel there. Capt. Co. E, 4th AL, April 1, 1861. Major, Aug. 27, 1862. Lt. col., Sept. 30, 1862. Col., Oct. 3, 1862. Arrested by Gen. Law in 1863. Often led Law's brigade in 1864. Postwar lawyer and judge in Evergreen. Gen. in the UCV. Died July 25, 1910, Tampa, FL, while visiting his daughter. Buried Old Historical Cemetery, Evergreen. A wartime newspaper article called Bowles "one of those brave, high-souled good-natured spirits, whom soldiers love and will follow to the death." Numerous sources say Bowles was promoted to gen. in April 1865, to lead a brigade of reservists.

Boyd, Samuel Hill. Born March 11, 1834, Rockingham Co., NC. Merchant in Troublesome, Rockingham Co., prewar. Militia colonel. Unmd. Capt. Co. E, 45th NC, Feb. 27, 1862. Major, Jan. 31, 1863. Lt. col., Feb. 9, 1863. Col., June 26, 1863. WIA Gettysburg. POW Hagerstown, July 4, 1863. Paroled March 3, 1864. KIA Spotsylvania, May 19, 1864, while leading a charge. Buried Wentworth Methodist Cemetery, Rockingham Co.

Boyd, Weir. Born Sept. 14, 1820, Hall Co., GA. Family moved to Lumpkin Co. in 1835. Lawyer in Dahlonega prewar. Methodist preacher. Clerk of the county court. State representative. State senator 1861–63. Indian Wars veteran. Md. Sarah J. Sitton. Pvt. Co. D, 52d GA, March 4, 1862. Col., March 16, 1862. Resigned Nov. 1, 1862, due to typhoid fever. Dahlonega lawyer and preacher postwar. Member of 1865 and 1877 state constitutional conventions. State senator 1888–89. Died Nov. 8, 1893, Dahlonega. Buried Mt. Hope Cemetery,

Dahlonega. A county history called Boyd "always faithful to the right, and fearless against the wrong." Papers at Atlanta Historical Society.

Boyd, William Wade. Born Jan. 1, 1819, Union Dist., SC. Tailor in Marietta and Atlanta, GA, prewar. Officer in vol. militia company. Md. Harriet A. Brem. Col., 19th GA, at its June 11, 1861, organization. Resigned Jan. 12, 1862, due to rheumatism. Atlanta tailor postwar. Deputy Grand Master of the Masons of GA. Died July 9, 1878, Atlanta. Buried Oakland Cemetery, Atlanta.

Boykin, Stephen Madison. Born Dec. 10, 1817, Sumter Dist., SC. Surveyor and farmer in Sumter Dist. prewar. Officer in Mexican War. Md. Anne McLeod; Eliza Arrants; Mary Arrants. Capt. Co. A, 20th SC, Dec. 24, 1861. Major, April 1, 1862. Col., June 2, 1864. WIA Cedar Creek (head) and POW. Released from Fort Delaware Prison July 24, 1865. Kershaw Co. farmer postwar. Died Sept. 25, 1897, SC. Buried Boykin family cemetery, south of Bishopville.

Boyles, William. Born 1818, Mt. Airy, NC. Prewar merchant and lawyer in Mobile. Md. Bridget Dubroca. State representative 1861–63, while serving with the army. Pvt., "Mobile Dragoons," July 30, 1861. Capt., Nov. 18, 1861. Not reelected at 1862 reorganization and discharged. Capt., 15th (aka 1st) AL Partisan Ranger Bn. Major, Aug. 25, 1862. Col., 56th AL Cav. (formed from the 15th), June 8, 1863. Fought in the Atlanta and Carolina Campaigns. Accompanied Pres. Davis on his flight from Richmond. Postwar Mobile lawyer. Died March 29, 1882, Mobile, AL. Buried Little River Baptist Church Cemetery, Mt. Pleasant, AL.

Boylston, Robert Bentham. Born Nov. 22, 1822, Charleston, SC. Grad. U. of SC. Lawyer in Mason, then Winnsboro, SC. James Chesnut noted his "proficiency as a lawyer, his ready capacity for labor." State representative 1852–60, 1864–65. Speaker of the House 1864–65. Md. Susan Cloud. VADC to Gen. Beauregard at Fort Sumter. Lt. col., SC state service, 1861, on staff of Gen. Bonham. Disabled for active service due to asthma. 1st lt. PACS, Aug. 1, 1863. Asst. enrolling officer at Columbia, SC, 1863–64. Col. and judge, military court of Dept. of SC, Nov. 11, 1864. Committed suicide Sept. 4, 1865, Fairfield Co. Buried Sion Presbyterian Church, Winnsboro.

Boynton, James Stoddard. Born May 7, 1833, Henry Co., GA. Monticello lawyer prewar. Md. Fannie Loyall; Susan T. Harris. Pvt. Co. B, 30th GA, Sept. 25, 1861. Sgt. major, 1861. Major, May 13, 1862. Lt. col., Dec. 16, 1862. Col., May 19, 1864. WIA Atlanta. Griffin lawyer postwar. Judge, mayor, state representative. President of the GA State Senate, succeeding to the governorship when Gov. Stephens died. Died Dec. 22, 1902, Griffin. Buried Oak Hill (Griffin City) Cemetery. A fellow colonel called Boynton a "man of peace, he was in the army entirely from a sense of duty."

Brabble, Edmund Crey. Born Jan. 5, 1835, Tyrell Co., NC. Grad. Dartmouth U., 1857, as valedictorian. Teacher in Tyrell Co. in 1860. Capt. Co. L, 1st NC Bn., May 16, 1861. Major, Nov. 29, 1861. Col., 32d NC (formed from the 1st Bn.), March 17, 1862. KIA Spotsylvania, May 10, 1864. Buried Albemarle Cemetery near Columbia, NC. A "strict disciplinarian, yet humane and very considerate."

Bradford, Alsey High. Born Oct. 26, 1822, East Feliciana Parish, LA. Reared in Brownsville, TN. Farmer in Haywood Co. prewar. Md. Mary E. Wilson. Capt. Co. D, 31st TN, Sept. 20, 1861. Col., Oct. 12, 1861. Not reelected at May 1862 reorganization. Dropped May 11, 1862. On staff of Gen. McCown in 1862. Temporarily commanded Hilliard's Legion in East TN, Dec. 1862. Commanded post of Knoxville, 1863. Farmer in Haywood Co. postwar. Brownsville merchant. Died Aug. 6, 1906, Brownsville. Buried Oakwood Cemetery, Brownsville.

Bradford, Charles MacPherson. Born Nov. 10, 1825, Sunbury, PA. Reared in New Orleans and in MS. Attd. USMA. Grad. ULA law school. New Orleans lawyer. Dist. attorney. Lt. in Mexican War. Md. Amelia Dixon. Capt. Co. A, 1st LA Regulars, Jan. 7, 1861. Major, Feb. 6, 1861. Resigned July 22, 1861. Lt. col., 3d LA Bn. (later the 15th LA), Sept. 4, 1861. Court-martialed Jan. 23, 1862, for disrespect to a superior. Sentenced to suspension from command. Resigned June 5, 1862. Major, TX State Troops. Col., Bradford's (aka Mann's) Regt. TX Cav., June 16, 1864. New Orleans lawyer postwar. Died Sept. 26, 1867, New Orleans, of "congestive chill." Probably buried in Hammond, LA. An obituary called him a man "of warm and impetuous temperament." However, a junior officer considered him an immoral drunkard.

Bradford, James Andrew Jackson. Born Jan. 1804, TN. Grad. USMA 1827. Officer in US Army. Commandant of the Fayetteville, NC, Arsenal, 1858–61. Appointed to the NC State Military Board, 1861. Col., 1st NC Art., May 8, 1861. POW Fort Hatteras and paroled. Incapacitated for field duty. Post commander at Greensboro, NC, Feb. 16, 1862, until his death in Fayetteville Sept. 7, 1863. Buried Cross Creek Cemetery, Fayetteville. Bradford had a "fine and cultivated intellect," according to an obituary.

Bradford, William McDermott. Born Feb. 14, 1827, McMinn Co., TN. Lawyer in Athens and Chattanooga prewar. Clerk of Jefferson Co. 1851–54. State representative 1859–61. Md. Eliza K. Inman. Enlisted March 20, 1862. Col., 39th (aka 31st) TN, March 28, 1862. Served in East TN and KY Campaigns. POW Vicksburg and exch. Regiment mounted in the winter of 1863. Served in East TN in 1864. Paroled May 13, 1865, Washington, GA. Chattanooga lawyer postwar. Judge. Died June 12, 1895, Chattanooga. Buried Citizens Cemetery, Chattanooga. An article in *Confederate Veteran* called Bradford "noble, gifted."

Bradfute, William R. Born May 23, 1823, Sumner Co., TN. Capt., TN volunteers in Mexican War. Engaged in "civil pursuits" at McMinnville, TN, 1848–55. Capt., 2d US Cav., 1855–61. Md. Ann E. Bennett; Georgianna Saunders. Capt., CS Regular Army, April 27, 1861. AAG to Gens. Ben McCulloch and Van Dorn. In charge of the artillery of McCulloch's division. Col. of cav., PACS, April 12, 1862. Led a brigade of TX cav. in AR in the fall of 1862. Fell sick and relinquished his command without notifying his superiors, an action that Gen. Hindman did not appreciate. Held minor commands in TX in 1863. Relieved of command Aug. 12, 1863, and ordered to report, in arrest, to the headquarters of the Dept. of TX. Lived in Louisa Co., VA; Nevada; New Mexico; Philadelphia; Limestone Co., TX; and Austin postwar. Wagon hauler for the US army. Auctioneer in Galveston. Stock raiser in TX. Died April 20, 1906, Austin. Buried State Cemetery, Austin. One artillery officer called Bradfute "the most vascillating [*sic*] man I ever saw and as a commander he has my contempt."

Bradley, John M. Born Sept. 17, 1827, Lebanon, TN. Prewar blacksmith in Bradley Co., AR. Lawyer, Methodist minister in Arkadelphia. Md. Louisa M. Hickman. Capt. Co. A, 9th AR (known as the "Preacher's Regiment," because there were 42 ministers in the unit), July 1861. Col., July 20, 1861. Discharged Jan. 12, 1862. Postwar lawyer in Warren, Bradley Co. Judge. Prosecuting attorney for the 9th Circuit 1873–74. Republican who lost race for Congress in 1872. Died March 16, 1887, AR. Buried Old Warren Cemetery. A contemporary newspaper account describes Bradley as an "energetic, selfmade man, brave as caesar and well calculated for a military leader."

Bratton, Hugh Lawson White. Born c. 1837, TN. Merchant in Lafayette, Macon Co., TN, prewar. Md. Mary Joyce Marshall. Pvt. Co. C, 24th TN, Aug. 24, 1861. Sgt. major. Major, May 2, 1862. Lt. col., June 3, 1862. Col., July 29, 1862. MWIA Dec. 31, 1862, Stones River. Died Jan. 4, 1863. Buried on the grounds of the Methodist Church in Murfreesboro. An obituary called Bratton "one of the best and bravest officers in the entire army."

Brazelton, William, Jr. Born July 15, 1831, TN. Farmer and merchant in Jefferson Co. prewar. State representative 1857–61. Md. Maggie Lewis. Lt. col., 2d TN Cav. Bn. (aka 3d, 14th), Aug. 22, 1861. Col., 1st TN Cav., Feb. 17, 1862. Brazelton later wrote that this appointment had been made by mistake. Left regiment in Sept. 1862 to join the staff of Gen. Vaughn. Captured March 7, 1865, New Market, TN, while bearing letters under a flag of truce. Released June 7, 1865. Indicted for treason postwar and for robberies his men committed. Acquitted of the robbery charges and pardoned by the president on the charge of treason. Returned to Jefferson Co. Died Oct. 15, 1869, New Market, while hunting (either an accident, or suicide). Probably buried in a family cemetery in Jefferson Co. One soldier found Brazelton "a splendid officer, brave, kind and much beloved by his men."

Breaux, Gustave Arvilien. Born Dec. 28, 1828, Vermilionville (now Lafayette), LA. Attd. Norwich U. Grad. Harvard Law School, 1850. Attorney in New Orleans prewar. Clerk of the State Senate. Md. Emilie Locke; Josephine Marr. Capt., "Louisiana State Guards," 1861. Col., Sumter Regt., LA Militia (soon to be the 30th LA), March 1, 1862. Dropped Feb. 1863 when the 30th was reduced to a battalion and a full col. no longer needed. Enrolling officer at Lake Charles, LA, 1864–65. Paroled June 16, 1865, Washington, LA. Attorney in New Orleans postwar. State senator. President of the New Orleans Jockey Club. Retired to his sugar plantation in Lafayette Parish. Died Feb. 24, 1910, Oakbourne Plantation, near Lafayette, "honored and loved by all who knew him." Buried St. John's Catholic Church Cemetery, Lafayette. Breaux's wartime diary is at Tulane.

Breckinridge, Robert Jefferson, Jr. Born Sept. 14, 1834, Baltimore, MD. Cousin of Gen. John C. Breckinridge, brother of Col. W. C. P. Breckinridge, and son of a noted Unionist preacher. Attd. Centre College and UVA. Lawyer in Danville and Lexington. In US Coastal Survey. Md. Kate Morrison; Lilla Morrison. Capt., KSG, May 11, 1861. Capt. Co. B, 2d KY, Sept. 5, 1861. Resigned Sept. 21, 1861, upon election to Confederate Congress. Member, KY Secession Convention. Confederate congressman 1862–63. Commissioned col. of cav. Sept. 13, 1864, for a term of 3 months, in order to recruit behind Union lines in KY. POW Woodford Co., KY, Feb. 22, 1865. To Johnson's Island. Released May 22, 1865. Postwar lawyer and judge in Lincoln Co., KY; New York City; and Danville. Died March 13, 1915, Danville. Buried Lexington Cemetery, Lexington, KY. KY Gov. Hawes called him "a gentleman of considerable political intelligence."

Breckinridge, William Campbell Preston. Born Aug. 28, 1837, Baltimore, MD, son of Rev. Robert J. Breckinridge, a prominent Unionist, and cousin of Gen. John C. Breckinridge. Reared in KY. Grad. Centre College and Louisville U. Law School. Lawyer in Lexington, KY, prewar. Md. Lucretia Clay; Issa Desha; Louise Wing. Capt., KSG, May 18, 1861. Col., 9th KY Cav., Dec. 17, 1862. Often led a brigade of KY cav. in the Army of TN. Surrendered at Augusta, GA, May 8, 1865. Lawyer in Lexington postwar. Newspaper editor. US congressman 1885–95. In 1894 he got enmeshed in a nasty breach of promise lawsuit, which ended his political career. Died Nov. 19, 1904, Lexington. Buried Lexington Cemetery. Breckinridge's papers are at the Library of Congress.

Breedlove, Ephriam Bolling. Born 1818, GA. Prewar resident of Tuskegee, AL. Md. Nancy Hart. Capt. Co. H (company originally in 34th AL), 45th AL, March 1, 1862. Major, May 19, 1862. Lt. col., Nov. 4, 1862. WIA at Stones River.

Col., March 25, 1863. Resigned Oct. 28, 1863, due to chronic laryngitis and feeble lungs. Postwar farmer near Tuskegee. Died Oct. 23, 1882, Arredondo, FL.

Brenizer, Addison Gorgas. Born Jan. 19, 1839, Harrisburg, PA. Moved to St. Louis at age 10. Druggist and bookkeeper in St. Louis. Moved to New Orleans in 1860 and clerked there. Md. Frances Gilmer in 1862. Pvt. Co. E, 1st LA Bn., Jan. 23, 1861. Promoted to commissary sgt. Transferred in June 1861, to be chief clerk in the ordnance dept., Richmond, under his cousin, Gen. Josiah Gorgas. Undertook several missions up north in 1861. Appointed capt. in May 1862 and given command of the Charlotte, NC, ordnance depot. Major of artillery, 1863. Commanded Salisbury, NC, arsenal. Elected col., 1st Regt. NC Detailed Men, Oct. 1, 1864. Paroled May 1, 1865, Salisbury. Banker in Columbia, SC, and then Charlotte, NC, postwar. Died April 15, 1918, Charlotte. Buried Elmwood Cemetery, Charlotte. A "thorough accountant . . . a ripe scholar."

Brent, George William. Born Aug. 15, 1821, Alexandria, VA. Grad. UVA. Alexandria lawyer. State legislator. Delegate to VA Secession Convention. Md. Cornelia Wood; Lucy Goode. Major, 17th VA, May 2, 1861. Dropped at April 1862 reorganization. Major AAG to Gen. Beauregard at Shiloh. Lt. col., May 1, 1862. Col., Aug. 8, 1863. Chief of staff to Gens. Beauregard and Bragg. Paroled April 26, 1865, NC. Postwar Alexandria lawyer. Died Jan. 2, 1872, Alexandria, of pneumonia. Buried St. Mary's Cemetery, Alexandria. Brent's papers are at Duke U. and Tulane U. Bragg said of Brent, "in every position he had given me more than satisfaction."

Brent, Joseph Lancaster. Born Nov. 30, 1826, Pomonkey, MD. Grew up in LA. Attd. Georgetown U. Attorney in St. Martinville, LA. Moved to Los Angeles, CA, in the 1850s. Lawyer, state legislator, political leader there. Md. Roselle, daughter of Cong. Duncan Kenner. Arrested in 1861 while sailing back to the South but soon released. Capt. on staff of Gen. Magruder by Feb. 1862. Major of artillery, May 9, 1862. Chief of artillery for Magruder's command in 1862. Chief of artillery, Western Dist. of LA. Commanded the gunboat that sank the Union ironclad *Indianola* in 1863. Col. of art., April 17, 1864. Although no record of the order survives, it is clear Gen. Kirby Smith assigned him to duty as brig. gen. in Oct. 1864. Commanded a brigade of LA Cav. 1864–65. Helped negotiate the surrender of the TMD. Paroled as brig. gen. June 5, 1865. Practiced law postwar in LA and Baltimore. State legislator in LA. Died Nov. 27, 1905, Baltimore, buried Green Mount Cemetery. Brent wrote an invaluable memoir of his early war years.

Brent, Preston. Born May 25, 1833, Pike Co., MS. Attd. WMI. Farmer in Pike Co. prewar. Officer in vol. militia. Md. Frances E. Brent. Major, 1st Regt., MS

"Army of 10,000," Dec. 5, 1861. Capt. Co. K, 38th MS, April 20, 1862. Lt. col., May 16, 1862. Col., Sept. 24, 1862. WIA Vicksburg in face, June 30, 1863, disfiguring him. POW there and paroled. Regiment mounted in 1864. Pike Co. farmer postwar. Died Aug. 12, 1884, Pike Co. Buried Brent Cemetery, near Holmesville, Pike Co.

Brewer, Richard Henry. Born Sept. 22, 1834, Anne Arundel Co., MD. Attd. St. James College. Grad. USMA 1858. Lt., US Army, 1858–61. 1st lt., CS Regular Army, March 16, 1861. AAG to Gen. Polk, Oct.–Dec. 1861. Major, Brewer's AL Cav. Bn., Dec. 1861. Lt. col., March 25, 1862. Col., 8th Confederate Cav. (aka 2d MS and AL Cav., formed in part from Brewer's Bn.), June 1862. He probably was appointed to this rank by Gen. Bragg, prior to any formal election for colonel. Transferred back to staff duty (probably by June 15, 1862, when William B. Wade was appointed colonel) in VA and the West. VADC to Gen. Pender. Capt., ADC to Gen. Wheeler, 1863. Recommended by Gens. Polk and Wheeler for promotion to brig. gen. in 1863. Major of a battalion of the dismounted men of Grumble Jones's brigade at the Battle of Piedmont. MWIA there, died June 25, 1864. Capt. Miller of the 8th found Brewer "a stern, taciturn, strict disciplinarian, remarkably cool and self possessed in battle."

Bringier, Louis Amadee. Born Feb. 4, 1828, LA, of a family said to be the richest landowners in the state. Attd. UVA. Planter at "Hermitage," Ascension Parish, prewar. Surveyor gen. of LA. Md. Stella Tureaud. ADC to Col. John S. Scott, early in war. Lt. col., 7th LA Cav., 1864 (probably April 13). Col., Jan. 7, 1865. Paroled June 6, 1865, Natchitoches. Sugar planter in Ascension Parish and FL postwar. Died Jan. 9, 1897, Tampa, FL. Buried Catholic Cemetery, Donaldsonville, LA. A diehard Confederate who, upon hearing of Lincoln's assassination, told his wife to name their next son "Booth Bringier" after the assassin. Bringier's papers are at LSU. Gens. Richard Taylor, Joseph Brent, and James Trudeau were in-laws.

Brockenbrough, John Mercer. Born Aug. 1, 1830, "Belle Ville" plantation, Richmond Co., VA. Educated at Alexandria Episcopal High School. Grad. VMI. Teacher and farmer in Richmond Co. prewar. Md. Austina Brockenbrough; Kate, sister of Col. Francis Mallory. Col., 40th VA, May 25, 1861. Led Field's Brigade from Antietam to Gettysburg. Resigned Jan. 21, 1864, because a junior officer (H. H. Walker, his lt. col.) was promoted to brig. gen. over him. Col., 2d VA Reserves, Nov. 25, 1864. Teacher in Norfolk and Richmond postwar. Died Aug. 24, 1892, Richmond. Buried Hollywood Cemetery. Brockenbrough was not highly thought of, by subordinates or superiors, the cause of his nonpromotion to permanent brigade command. His brigade behaved badly during Pickett's Charge.

Brockman, Benjamin Thomas. Born Dec. 11, 1831, Greenville Dist., SC. Reared in Greenville. Spartanburg merchant prewar. Unmd. Capt. Co. B, 13th SC, Aug. 31, 1861. Major, June 19, 1862. WIA 2d Manassas. Lt. col., Jan. 6, 1863. Col., June 21, 1863. MWIA in arm and head (the arm had to be amputated) at Spotsylvania, May 12, 1864. Died June 8, 1864, in a Richmond hospital. Buried Hollywood Cemetery.

Brooks, Iverson Lee. Born Feb. 28, 1829, Caswell Co., NC. Attd. Cumberland U. Law School. Prewar lawyer in Brownsville, TN. To Monticello, Drew Co., AR, in 1859. Md. Betty Lee. Sgt. Co. A, 26th AR, March 3, 1862. Capt. Co. G, July 18, 1862. Lt. col., Dec. 6, 1863. Col., April 9, 1864. Postwar lawyer in Drew Co. State legislator. Died Dec. 1876, Monticello. Buried Old Monticello Cemetery.

Brooks, William H. Born Jan. 28, 1838, MI. Reared in Detroit, the son of an army officer. Prewar lawyer in Fayetteville, AR. Capt. Co. E, 1st AR Cav. Bn., 1861. Major, Brooks's (aka 1st) AR Cav. Bn., 1861. Not elected lt. col. when the battalion was increased and reorganized in 1862. Resigned and returned to AR. Col., 34th AR, Aug. 16, 1862. WIA and disabled at Jenkins Ferry. Raised a regiment of cavalry. Transferred to the cavalry in the fall of 1864. Led brigade, 1864–65. Recommended for promotion to general. Postwar Fayetteville lawyer. State legislator. Died March 19, 1869, Fort Smith, of consumption. Buried Oak Grove Cemetery, Fort Smith. One private thought Brooks "the best officer to provide for his men that I have ever been under."

Brooks, William McLin. Born Oct. 15, 1814, Sumter Dist., SC. Attd. U. of SC 1832–33. To Marengo Co., AL, in 1833. Lawyer in Linden, Mobile, and Marion, AL. Judge. Md. Ann E. Terrell. President of AL Secession Convention. Chairman of a committee to provide relief for soldiers' families. Sgt. of Perry Co. militia, 1863. Capt. Co. H, 3d AL Reserves, July 25, 1864. Col., Aug. 16, 1864. Resigned Jan. 1865. Paroled May 26, 1865. Postwar lawyer in Selma, then Birmingham. Died Oct. 26, 1894, Birmingham. Buried Episcopal Cemetery, Marion. An obituary calls him a man of "commanding talents."

Browder, Bartlett Milton. Born c. 1811, LA. Reared in St. Francisville. Attd. Norwich U. Farmer and lawyer in Covington, TN, prewar. Mexican War veteran. Md. Narcissa Hewlett; Sally A. McCraw. Capt. Co. G, 51st TN, 1861 (probably Nov. 4). Col., Jan. 1, 1862. Discharged from the service April 1862. Owned plantation in Carroll Parish, LA, postwar. Died Nov. 27, 1875, at his Carroll Parish home, of dysentery.

Brown, Alexander Jackson. Born Nov. 1, 1835, Madison Co., TN. Attd. UVA. Grad. Cumberland U. Lawyer in Jackson, TN. Lt. col., 55th TN, May 23, 1861. Col., Feb. 14, 1862. POW Island No. 10. Imprisoned at Fort Warren. Exch. Aug. 5, 1862. Resigned Oct. 5, 1863, because of heart disease. Died April 15, 1864.

Buried Riverside Cemetery, Jackson. Gen. McCown's report on Island No. 10 noted Brown's "great zeal and energy."

Brown, Blackburn H. Born Nov. 23, 1828, Maury Co., TN. Grad. U. of Louisville Medical School. Physician in Henderson Co., TN, prewar. Md. Elizabeth Taylor; Sarah B. Hudson. Capt. Co. K, 27th TN, Aug. 17, 1861. Lt. col., Sept. 10, 1861. Col., probably April 6, 1862. WIA Shiloh and soon discharged due to the injuries. Not elected col. at May 15, 1862, reorganization of regiment. Physician in Henderson and Chester Cos. postwar. Died Nov. 28, 1887, at his son-in-law's home near Mifflin, TN. Buried Old Mifflin Cemetery, Chester Co.

Brown, Drury J. Born c. 1813, NC. Merchant, farmer in Hinds and Copiah Cos., MS, prewar. Lawyer. Justice of the peace. County sheriff. Md. Sarah F. Wells; Mrs. Elizabeth Grant. Capt. Co. K, 36th MS, March 7, 1862. Col., March 11, 1862. Defeated for reelection at May 1862 reorganization. Arrested by Reconstruction authorities postwar for failing to pay his taxes. Died Feb. 1868, Copiah Co. Probably buried in an unmarked grave in Grant Cemetery, Copiah Co., where his widow (d. 1867) is buried.

Brown, Hamilton Allen. Born Sept. 25, 1837, Wilkes Co., NC. Attd. Jackson College, UVA, and the US Naval Academy. Farmer in Wilkes Co. prewar. Md. Amelia S. Gwyn. 1st lt. Co. B, 1st NC, June 3, 1861. Detailed to drill recruits. Capt., appointed July 25, 1861, to rank from May 16, 1861. Major, April 21, 1862. Lt. col., July 8, 1862. Col., Dec. 14, 1863. WIA Malvern Hill, Chancellorsville, Mine Run, Spotsylvania (3 times), Opequon Creek, and Cedar Creek. POW Fort Stedman, released July 24, 1865. Farmer postwar. Moved to Columbia, TN, where his family had property, c. 1871. Died April 9, 1917, Richmond, VA. Buried St. Paul's Episcopal Churchyard, Wilkesboro. Brown family papers are at UNC. Gen. James B. Gordon was his half brother.

Brown, John Adams. Born April 13, 1826, MD. Grad. USMA 1846. Officer in US Army, 1846–61, resigning as capt. July 3, 1861. Md. Mildred Holmes. Capt., CS Regular Army, appointed July 19, 1861, to rank from March 16, 1861. Chief of artillery to Gen. Gatlin in NC in 1861. Col. (state rank) commanding Fort Caswell, 1861–62. Major, 1862. Chief of artillery to Gen. Kirby Smith. Lt. col., Jan. 7, 1863. Relieved June 6, 1863. Commanded forts near Mobile, 1864–65. Col., March 18, 1865. Paroled May 10, 1865, Meridian. Lived in Mobile postwar. Schoolteacher. Chief engineer of Mobile 1866–73. Died Oct. 7, 1877, Wilmington, NC. Buried Oakdale Cemetery, Wilmington.

Brown, John Edmunds. Born Aug. 30, 1830, Caswell Co., NC. Attd. Hampden-Sydney College. Attorney in Charlotte, NC. Md. Laura T. Morrison, sister-in-law of Gen. Stonewall Jackson. Lt. Co. D, 7th NC, May 16, 1861. Adj., Aug. 26, 1861. Lt. col., 42d NC, April 22, 1862. Col., Jan. 17, 1864. Paroled Greensboro. Charlotte lawyer postwar. State representative 1872–74. Committed suicide in Charlotte, Jan. 29, 1896. Buried Elmwood Cemetery, Charlotte. An obituary called Brown "a good soldier. He knew no fear" and ascribed his suicide to the lingering effects of a war wound in the head.

Brown, John Thompson. Born Feb. 6, 1835, Petersburg, VA. Grad. UVA. Attorney in Richmond prewar. Md. Mary Martha Southall. Lt., "Richmond Howitzers," April 2, 1861. Capt., May 1861. Major, Sept. 1861. Lt. col., spring of 1862. Col., June 2, 1862. Commanded the reserve artillery of the 2d Corps, ANV. KIA Wilderness, May 6, 1864, by a sharpshooter. He has a memorial stone in Maplewood Cemetery, Charlottesville. One soldier said that "his gentle winning manners won the love of all." A collection of his wartime official papers is at the Museum of the Confederacy.

Brown, John William. Born Nov. 4, 1836, Buckingham Co., VA. Family moved to Rusk Co., TX, in 1850. Prewar farmer. Md. Ella M. Griffin. Sgt. Co. I, 7th TX (a company his father raised), May 18, 1861. Capt., Oct. 7, 1861. POW Fort Donelson. To Johnson's Island Prison. Exch. Sept. 1, 1862. WIA Raymond. Led 7th at Franklin, where he was captured but escaped. Promoted to col., late in war (probably appointed 1865, to rank from Aug. 19, 1864) to head up Granbury's Brigade. Court-martialed Jan. 21, 1865 and cashiered but evidently reinstated. Paroled (as col.) April 24, 1865, Oxford, AL. Lived in Bastrop, LA, postwar, where he worked as a tax assessor and ran a livery stable. Settled in Longview, TX, in 1892. Gregg Co. tax assessor. Died July 9, 1905, Longview, buried Greenwood Cemetery. Gen. Granbury called Brown "enterprising & efficient."

Brown, Joseph Newton. Born Dec. 16, 1832, Anderson, SC. Educated at the classical school in Williamston. Grocer and lawyer in Laurens prewar. Md. Lizzie L. Bruce. Pvt. Co. D, 1st SC (a 6-month unit), Jan. 1861. Capt. Co. E, 14th SC, Aug. 16, 1861. WIA Gaines's Mill (arm) and 2d Manassas. Lt. col., Feb. 20, 1863. WIA Gettysburg. Col., Sept. 17, 1863. POW North Anna, May 23, 1864. Exch. Aug. 3, 1864. Anderson lawyer and bank president postwar. State legislator. Died Jan. 24, 1920, Atlantic City, NJ. Buried Old Silverbrook Cemetery, Anderson. A captain in the 14th claimed that Brown "was wholly devoted to his duty." A book written by a family member contains Brown's wartime letters.

Brown, Reuben R. Born Feb. 3, 1808, Green Co., GA. Came to TX in 1835 to fight in the Texas Revolution. Wounded and taken prisoner in 1836 but escaped. Wealthy Brazoria Co. planter. Md. Jane E. Milton. Lt. col., 13th TX, Oct. 15, 1861. Lt. col., Brown's (12th) TX Cav. Bn., Aug. 8, 1862. Col., 35th (Brown's—often confused with Likens's 35th) TX Cav., Nov. 11, 1863. Postwar farmer in Velasco, Brazoria Co. Died March 2, 1894, Velasco. Buried Peach Point Cemetery, Brazoria Co. On his tombstone is: "His many virtues form the noblest monument to his memory."

Brown, Robert Young. Born Oct. 8, 1841, Copiah Co., MS, son of Gov. Albert G. Brown. Attd. Georgetown U. and UVA. Pvt. Co. H, 18th MS, June 8, 1861. Capt., April 26, 1862. WIA and POW Gettysburg. Exch. March 10, 1864. Major, 6th MS Cav., May 23, 1864. Col., probably July 14, 1864. Paroled Jackson, MS, May 18, 1865. Attorney in New Orleans postwar. Died Oct. 15, 1866, New Orleans. Buried Greenwood Cemetery, Jackson. A more than usually flowery obituary praised Brown's "chivalrous valor" and "knightly bearing."

Brown, Uriah Thomas. Born May 3, 1831, Jackson Co., TN. Physician in Jackson Co. prewar. Md. Belle Galbraith; Cypressa Calvin Brooks. Capt. Co. E, 28th TN, Aug. 11, 1861. Surgeon, 28th TN, 1861–62. Lt. col., March 18, 1862. Col., May 8, 1862. Resigned Aug. 5, 1862. Discharged Dec. 10, 1862, due to pulmonary disease. Physician in Jackson Co. postwar. Murdered March 28, 1870, Flynn's Lick, Jackson Co., while making his rounds, by an unknown assailant. Buried Dry Fork Creek, Jackson Co.

Brown, William Andrew Jackson. Born 1830, Crawford Co., GA. Nephew of Col. Reuben Brown. Attd. UGA. Talbot Co. lawyer prewar. Solicitor general of the circuit. Md. Sarah Shelton; Marie Van Leer. Volunteer at 1st Manassas and slightly wounded there. Capt. Co. G, 10th GA State Troops, Dec. 6, 1861. Capt. Co. H, 59th GA, May 6, 1862. Col., June 16, 1862. WIA (shot through both legs) and POW Gettysburg. Exch. March 10, 1864. WIA in leg 2d Deep Bottom, Aug. 14, 1864. Lawyer in Talbotton, Americus, and Washington, DC, postwar. Active Republican. Collector of Internal Revenue for GA. Died April 2, 1891, Washington. Buried Glenwood Cemetery, Washington. An obituary called "Jack" Brown "a man of generous impulses [with] many friends."

Brown, William Newton. Born Aug. 1, 1826, TN. Reared in Oxford, MS, where his father, a business partner of Pres. Polk, managed Polk's landholdings. Wealthy plantation owner in Bolivar Co., owning a 7,000-acre tract. Officer in Mexican War. Md. Innes Thornton of Greene Co., AL, in 1865. Capt. Co. A, 20th MS, July 10, 1861. Major, July 19, 1861. POW Fort Donelson. Exch. Lt. col., March 12, 1862. POW Vicksburg. Col., Aug. 8, 1863. WIA twice at Franklin, which wounds disabled him from field duty for the remainder of the war. Paroled May 11, 1865, Gainesville. Merchant in Bolivar Co. and in AL postwar. Moved to Victoria, TX, by 1880. Livestock dealer in TX. Died June 18, 1887, Gonzales, TX, where he had moved to improve his health. Buried Masonic Cemetery, Gonzales. Lt. Col. Rorer of the 20th accused Brown of "drunkenness and incompetence" but found it impossible to remove him.

Browne, William Henry. Born Nov. 9, 1838, Tazewell Co., VA. Reared in Jef-fersonville. Attd. Emory & Henry College 1854–55. Attd. USMA 1857–61, re-signing one week after Fort Sumter. Capt. Co. C, 45th VA, May 29, 1861. Col., May 14, 1862. MWIA and POW Piedmont. Died June 8, 1864. Buried Maple-wood Cemetery, North Tazewell.

Broyles, Charles Edward. Born March 26, 1826, Pendleton, SC. Attd. USC. Lawyer in Dalton, GA, prewar. State representative 1859–60. Militia colonel and ADC to his cousin, Gov. Joseph Brown. Md. Lucy Ann Johnson; Nellie E. Arm-strong. Had 17 children from the two marriages. Major, 36th GA, June 12, 1862. POW Vicksburg and paroled. Col., April 28, 1864. Dalton lawyer postwar. State representative 1880–83. Solicitor general, Cherokee Circuit, 1868–72. Moved to CO late in life. Lawyer in Grand Junction and Del Norte. Registrar of US Land Claims in CO. Died Oct. 13, 1906, Antonito, CO. Buried Antonito Cemetery.

Brumby, Arnoldus Vanderhorst. Born Dec. 10, 1809, Sumter Dist., SC. Grad. USMA in 1835. Lt., U S. Army, 1835–36. Fought in Seminole War. Civil engineer in AL, 1836–38. Professor at UAL. Lawyer in AL. Superintendent of GMI. Planter in Cobb Co., GA. Md. Annie E. Wallis. Col., 14th GA, July 17, 1861 (elected in May of 1861). Resigned Nov. 21, 1861. Postwar planter. Lived in At-lanta from 1867. Died April 15, 1887, Cartersville. Buried Oak Hill Cemetery, Cartersville. An officer in the 14th stated Brumby was "drunk often" and in-competent.

Bryan, Guy Morrison. Born Jan. 12, 1821, Herculaneum, Jefferson Co., MO. Nephew of TX founder Stephen Austin. Family moved to TX in 1831. Grad. Kenyon College in Ohio. Lawyer but did not practice. Rancher in Brazoria Co. Fought in TX Revolution and TX-Mexico border wars. State legislator. To Galve-ston in 1857. US congressman 1857–59. Delegate to TX Secession Convention. Md. Laura H. Jack. Major, Sept. 20, 1861. Appointed VADC to Gen. Hebert Oct. 1, 1861. AAG to Gen. Kirby Smith, 1863. Helped organize the TX Cotton Bu-reau and often performed highly confidential tasks for the state government. Col., Feb. 9, 1864, to be judge of Gen. Kirby Smith's military court. Reappoint-ed col., March 23, 1865, to be judge of the military court of the army corps in Texas. Lived in Galveston, Quintana, and Austin postwar. State legislator. Speak-er of TX State House in 1894. Died June 4, 1901, Austin, buried State Cemetery. Pres. Rutherford Hayes, a college classmate and close friend, called Bryan "a real gentleman . . . though not a good scholar."

Buchel, Augustus Carl. Born Oct. 8, 1813, Guntersblum, Hesse, Germany. Attd. military academies in Germany and France. Officer in the Hessian and French armies. Soldier of fortune. Colonel in the Turkish army. Immigrated to TX in 1845. Capt. in Mexican War. Indianola merchant. Collector of customs at

Port Lavaca. Unmd. Appointed col. of TX militia, June 10, 1861, and placed in charge of camps of instruction in the state's 1st military dist. Lt. col., 3d TX, Sept. 4, 1861. Commanded Fort Brown on the Mexican border. Col., 1st TX Cav., May 2, 1863. MWIA Pleasant Hill, while leading a charge. Died April 12 (sources also give April 11 and 15), 1864, Mansfield, LA. Buried State Cemetery, Austin. One observer thought Buchel "the only efficient officer" in south Texas. In 1887 the state legislature laid out a county to be named for Buchel, but the county was never officially formed.

Buck, William Amos. Born Feb. 25, 1830, Reading, PA. Family moved to AL in 1835. Prewar cotton factor in Mobile. Capt. of vol. militia. Md. Margaret Langdon. His militia company occupied Fort Morgan in 1861. Major, "Mobile fire brigade," 1861. Col., 24th AL (formed from the fire brigade), Oct. 15, 1861. WIA at Stones River. Resigned June 2, 1863. Spent rest of war as cotton broker for the government. Postwar cotton factor in Mobile. President of insurance company. Died Oct. 30, 1892, Mobile, buried Magnolia Cemetery.

Bulger, Michael Jefferson. Born Feb. 13, 1806, Richland Dist., SC. Moved to Montgomery, AL, in 1823. Tallapoosa Co. farmer. State legislator. Militia general, served in Creek War. Md. Elizabeth Bozeman. Delegate to AL Secession Convention. Refused to sign ordinance of secession but nonetheless volunteered for the army. Capt. Co. A, 47th AL, March 20, 1862. Major, Aug. 23, 1862. Lt. col., Sept. 13, 1862. Col., July 10, 1863. WIA (twice) at Cedar Mountain. WIA and POW in the assault on Little Round Top. Exchanged March 10, 1864. Retired to the invalid corps Feb. 14, 1865. Postwar farmer and legislator. Unsuccessful candidate for governor of AL. Died Dec. 14, 1900, Dadeville, AL. Buried Dadeville Cemetery. Numerous sources say he was promoted to gen. after his exchange.

Bullock, Edward Courtenay. Born Dec. 7, 1822, Charleston, SC. Attd. College of Charleston. Grad. Harvard 1843. Lawyer and newspaper editor in Eufaula, AL. State senator. Md. Mary Snipes. AL commissioner to FL, 1861. Pvt. "Eufaula Rifles," 1st AL, at Pensacola in early 1861. Col. and IG of AL state forces. Judge advocate on Gen. Bragg's staff. Col., 18th AL, Sept. 4, 1861. "Physically a frail man, and entirely unfitted for the . . . soldier's life." Died Montgomery, AL, of pneumonia Dec. 23, 1861. Buried Fairview (Episcopal) Cemetery, Eufaula. His law partner said Bullock "was the best organized man I ever saw." Bullock Co., AL, is named for him.

Bunn, Henry Gaston. Born June 12, 1838, Rocky Mount, Nash Co., NC. Attd. Davidson College. Family moved to Fayette Co., TN, in 1844, and to Ouachita Co., AR, in 1846. Student when the war started. Md. Louise Holmes; Aralee Conally. 3d lt. Co. A, 4th AR, Aug. 17, 1861. Adj., Nov. 1861. WIA and POW Pea Ridge but soon escaped. Lt. col., May 8, 1862 (elected at reorganization). Col.,

Nov. 4, 1862. WIA Ezra Church. Led brigade at Bentonville. Col., 1st AR Consolidated, April 9, 1865. Postwar lawyer in Camden and El Dorado, AR. State senator 1875–76. Justice, AR Supreme Court, 1893–1904. Died July 17, 1908, El Dorado. Buried Oakland Cemetery, Camden. One soldier praised his "close application to his duties, his affability, his generous good sense and superior educational advantages."

Burbridge, John Quincy. Born May 21, 1830, Pike Co., MO. Attd. St. Louis U. Prewar banker in Louisiana, Pike Co., MO. Militia captain. Gold mined in CA 1849–52. Md. Sarah A. Swink; Matilda Gutsweiler. Capt. Co. B, 1st Inf., 3d Div., MSG. Col., July 3, 1861. Col., 2d Cav., 2d Div., MSG, Oct. 1861. Col., 1st MO Inf. (a temporary name for a new unit later renumbered 2d MO Inf.) at Pea Ridge. Left that unit to raise a cavalry regiment. Col., 4th MO Cav., Nov. 13, 1862. WIA Wilson's Creek and Pea Ridge. POW Brownsville, AR, Aug. 24, 1863. Exch. March 17, 1864. Paroled Shreveport, June 8, 1865. Merchant in St. Louis postwar. Moved to Alton, IL, operating flour mills there. Moved to Jacksonville, FL, in 1882. Railroad president. Mayor of Jacksonville in 1887. Died Tucson, AZ, Nov. 14, 1892. Buried Calvary Cemetery, St. Louis. Recommended for general in 1864 as "a gentleman of strict sobriety, fine judgment and inexhaustible energy."

Burford, Nathaniel Macon. Born June 24, 1824, Smith Co., TN. Attd. Irvine College. Studied law at Lebanon College. Moved to Jefferson, TX, in 1846. To Dallas 2 years later. Lawyer. Dist. attorney. Judge. Md. Mary J. Knight. Pvt., Good's TX Art., June 13, 1861. Col., 19th TX Cav., April 10, 1862. "[A]n affable, genial man . . . not very well beliked" by his men. Resigned June 7, 1864, admitting "I have not the genius, nor talent . . . to make a successful military commander." Resignation enthusiastically accepted by his superiors. Postwar Dallas lawyer. State legislator, judge, speaker of the TX State House. Died May 10, 1898, Dallas. Buried Greenwood Cemetery.

Burgwyn, Henry King, Jr. Born Oct. 3, 1841, Northampton Co., NC. Attd. Burlington College. Grad. UNC and VMI (in 1861). Unmd. Drillmaster (with the other VMI cadets) at Richmond, spring 1861. Commissioned major of NC State Troops, July 5, 1861, and put in charge of a camp of instruction near Raleigh. Lt. col., 26th NC (a regiment he helped drill), Aug. 27, 1861. Col., Aug. 19, 1862. KIA Gettysburg, shot through the lungs July 1, 1863. Buried on the battlefield; reburied Oakwood Cemetery, Raleigh. The youthful Burgwyn was considered brave and brainy but was too strict a disciplinarian to be popular with his men. A biography of Burgwyn was published in 1985.

Burke, Ross Edwin. Born Dec. 20, 1831, Montgomery Co., NY. Bookkeeper in Natchitoches, LA, prewar. Md. Mary Amelia Johnson. Lt. Co. A, 2d LA, May

11, 1861. Capt., Aug. 7, 1861. Major, June 26, 1862. WIA and POW Gettysburg. Exch. May 3, 1864. Promoted to col., May 12, 1864, but never served with regiment after this. Assigned to duty with the VA Reserves in 1864. Dry goods merchant in Natchitoches postwar. Died there July 6, 1877. Buried Catholic Cemetery, Natchitoches.

Burks, Jesse Spinner. Born March 20, 1823, Bedford Co., VA. Attd. Washington College. Grad. VMI. Bedford Co. farmer prewar. State legislator 1853–54. Militia colonel. Md. Elizabeth Otey; Charlotte Thomson; Mrs. Mary T. Claggett. Col., 42d VA, July 1861. Led a brigade, 1861–62. WIA Kernstown and disabled. Resigned July 21, 1862, citing a severe hernia contracted at Kernstown. Bedford Co. farmer postwar. State legislator 1874–77. Died June 15, 1885, Bedford Co. Buried St. Thomas Episcopal Church, Bedford.

Burks, John C. Born Dec. 29, 1834, GA. Moved to Clarksville, TX, in 1846. Attd. Cumberland U. Law School. Prewar Clarksville lawyer. Md. Penelope Donoho; Susan Donoho, his first wife's sister. Capt. Co. E, 11th TX Cav., Oct. 2, 1861. Col., May 8, 1862. MWIA Stones River, Dec. 31, 1862, while leading a charge on a Union battery. He continued to lead his men, holding his hand to the wound to stem the bleeding, until losing consciousness. Died Jan. 4, 1863. Buried Shelbyville, TN; reburied in 1895 in Clarksville Cemetery. The "idol of his regiment"; his last words were, "Forward, boys."

Burnet, William Este. Born July 7, 1833, Harris Co., TX, son of future TX president David Burnet. Attd. KMI. 2d lt., US Army, 1857–61. 1st lt., CS Regular Army, March 16, 1861. Assigned to muster in troops at Grenada, MS. Capt., Burnet's Battery, 1862. Chief of artillery to Gen. Cabell, 1862. Major, Nov. 4, 1862. Col., Aug. 5, 1863. Chief of artillery to Gen. Maury. Commanded artillery in the Mobile defenses, 1863–65. KIA by a sharpshooter March 31, 1865, Spanish Fort. Buried Magnolia Cemetery, Mobile. Maury called Burnet "a man of rare attainments, of extraordinary military capacity . . . the best educated soldier I have ever seen."

Burnett, Henry Cornelius. Born Oct. 5, 1825, Essex Co., VA. Reared in KY. Educated at an academy in Hopkinsville. Lawyer in Cadiz, KY, prewar. US congressman 1855–61. Southern rights spokesman. Md. Mary A. Terry. While in Congress in the spring and summer of 1861, opposed administration war efforts. Called by a hostile newspaper "a big, burly, loud-mouthed fellow who is forever raising points of order." President of the rump KY Secession Convention and commissioner from that convention to the Confederate government. Col., 8th KY, Nov. 1, 1861. Resigned Feb. 3, 1862. Confederate congressman 1861–62. Confederate senator 1862–65. Lawyer in Cadiz postwar. Died there Sept. 28, 1866. Buried East End Cemetery, Cadiz. Burnett never actually led the

8th in the field, being in Congress at the time. He admitted to his lt. col. that he "couldn't command a regiment."

Burnett, John Howell. Born July 8, 1830, Greene Co., TN. Prewar sheriff of Chatooga Co., GA. Moved to Crockett, TX, in 1854. Farmer, merchant, state legislator. Lt. in Mexican War. Md. Catherine Beavers. Elected to State Senate in 1861, serving until 1862. Col., 13th TX Cav., March 1, 1862. Due to illness, transferred to post duty in 1863. Resigned April 22, 1864, due to "chronic gastro entiritis [*sic*]." Returned to Crockett after the war. To Galveston in 1866. Merchant and builder. Bank president. To Houston in 1899. Died June 24, 1901, Summerville, Chatooga Co., GA. Buried Glenwood Cemetery, Houston. In the fall of 1862 Texas's congressmen recommended Burnett for promotion as "a gentleman of the highest respectability."

Burns, Simon Pierce. Born Jan. 1, 1834, Logan Co., OH. Reared in OH and IA. Prewar farmer in Jasper Co., MO, and Collin Co., TX. Texas Ranger. Md. Sarah A. Gibson. Capt. Co. D, 5th Cav., 8th Div., MSG, Aug. 21, 1861. Pvt., Hunter's MO Cav. Bn., July 21, 1862. Major, 8th MO (later redesignated 11th MO), Sept. 1, 1862. Lt. col., Sept. 15, 1862. Col., March 24, 1863. Postwar farmer in Brownwood, TX. State legislator. Helped to prosecute the gunman John Wesley Hardin. Died April 8, 1898, Brown Co., TX. Buried Heflin Cemetery, north of Brownwood. Gen. Jackman called Burns an "excellent [man] . . . none better."

Burt, Erasmus R. Born c. 1820, Edgefield Co., SC. Reared in AL. Physician and farmer in Oktibbeha and Noxubee Cos., MS, prewar. State representative. "Father" of the Mississippi Institute for the Deaf and Dumb. State auditor 1859–61. Capt. of vol. militia. Md. Lucy, sister of Gen. John T. Morgan. Capt. Co. K, 18th MS, April 22, 1861. Col., June 7, 1861. MWIA Ball's Bluff, died Oct. 26, 1861. Buried Greenwood Cemetery, Jackson, MS. His middle name is given as "Arthmala" by a descendant, and it is possible he used the "R" as a phonetic initial for this unusual middle name.

Burt, William Giroud. Born Feb. 11, 1843, Edgefield, SC. Stone cutter in Richland Co. prewar. Md. Mary F. Belcher. Pvt. Co. H, 7th SC, June 1, 1861. Discharged July 28, 1861, due to a hernia. 1st sgt. Co. A, 22d SC, Dec. 1861. 1st lt., March 12, 1863. Lt. col., Aug. 18, 1864, promoted for "valor and skill." Col., appointed Dec. 6, 1864, backdated to rank from July 30, 1864. Appmx. Planter in Bellevue, Bossier Parish, LA, from 1872. Adj. gen., LA National Guard. Died Aug. 29, 1890, at his plantation home, "Utopia." Buried Bellevue Cemetery.

Burtwell, John Robertson Bedford. Born Aug. 15, 1835, Florence, AL. Grad. USMA 1860. Briefly 2d lt., US Army. Md. Matilda Wade. Capt., AL Regular Army,

Jan. 19, 1861. 1st lt., CS Regular Army, March 16, 1861. Adj., 9th AL, July 1, 1861. ADC on staff of Gens. Hardee and Bragg, 1862. Major, 21st Bn. TN Cav., March 16, 1863. Major of artillery, June 2, 1863. Chief of artillery, Hindman's Div. Assigned as inspector of cavalry, Wheeler's cavalry, Oct. 18, 1863. Col. of the newly formed 11th AL Cav. Jan. 14, 1865. Planter and civil engineer in AL postwar. Died Oct. 31, 1873, Florence. Buried Burtwell Cemetery near Florence.

Bush, Louis. Born Dec. 20, 1820, Iberville Parish, LA. Lived in Thibodeaux, Lafourche Parish, prewar. Lawyer. Court Clerk. Deputy Sheriff. State representative 1845–61. Delegate to LA Secession Convention. Md. Josephine Gueno; Celeste Grisham. Capt., "La Fourche Creoles," Sept. 1861. Major, 18th LA, Oct. 5, 1861. Lt. col., April 16, 1862. Declined that rank, due to ill health, and was dismissed May 10, 1862. AAG to Gen. Mouton, 1862–64. Col. of the newly formed 7th LA Cav., April 13, 1864. Appointed col. and chief justice, military court of the TMD, June 6, 1864, but the nomination was later withdrawn. Attorney in Thibodeaux postwar. Moved to New Orleans in 1872. Sugar merchant. President of the New Orleans Board of Trade. State representative 1876–78. Speaker of the LA House 1877–78. Died Aug. 10, 1892, Palmyra, WI. Buried Metairie Cemetery, New Orleans. A "strict disciplinarian, an excellent drill officer, and always had a paternal solicitude for the welfare of the men under his command."

Butler, John Russell. Born Dec. 18, 1823, Shelby Co., KY. Attd. Centre College and U. of Louisville Medical College. Physician in Lexington and Frankfort prewar. ADC to Gen. William O. Butler, his uncle, in the Mexican War. Md. Jane Short. Col., 3d KY Cav., Sept. 2, 1862. Court-martialed (but not convicted) Feb. 1, 1863, for "misbehavior before the enemy." Regiment consolidated with 1st KY Cav. in 1863, and the combined unit is often called the 1st. Sent to Canada in 1864 to work for the release of Confederate prisoners. "Foreman" in Louisville in 1880. Died June 11, 1884, Louisville, of Bright's Disease. Buried Cave Hill Cemetery, Louisville.

Butler, William B. Born April 15, 1831, Greenville, SC. Brother of Gen. M. C. Butler. 2d lt., US Army, 1855–61. Md. Eugenia Ransom. 1st lt., CS Regular Army Engineers, March 16, 1861. Capt. Co. A, 1st SC Regulars (3d SC Art.), Jan. 19, 1861. Lt. col., July 22, 1861. Col., Nov. 8, 1862. Ordered to Richmond in 1864 to supervise Richmond artillery defenses but soon returned to SC. Led brigade in Carolinas Campaign. Insurance agent in Greenville postwar. Librarian of the US House of Representatives. Died Nov. 20, 1910, Greenville. Buried Christ Episcopal Churchyard, Greenville.

Butt, Edgar Mathis. Born c. 1835, Warren Co., GA. Buena Vista lawyer prewar. Md. Mary Mathis. Major, 2d GA, June 1, 1861. Col., April 28, 1862. WIA and disabled (blinded by a shell) at Malvern Hill. Buena Vista lawyer and bank director postwar. Judge. State legislator. Died June 26, 1893, at his Buena Vista home. Buried Buena Vista Cemetery. "[A] nobleman and a good character."

Bynum, William Preston. Born June 16, 1820, Stokes Co., NC. Grad. Davidson U. (valedictorian of the class of 1842). Lawyer in Rutherfordton and Lincolnton prewar. Md. Ann E. Shipp. Lt., "Beatties Ford Rifles," 1861. Lt. col., 2d NC, May 8, 1861. Col., Sept. 17, 1862. Resigned March 21, 1863, to become solicitor of the Lincolnton (7th) Circuit. Solicitor 1863–66, 1868–73. State senator 1866–68. Justice, NC Supreme Court, 1873–79. Moved to Charlotte after 1878. Died there Dec. 30, 1909. Buried Elmwood Cemetery, Charlotte.

Cabell, Henry Coalter. Born Feb. 14, 1820, Richmond. Grad. UVA. Attorney and judge in Richmond prewar. Militia captain. Md. Jane Alston. Capt., "Richmond Fayette Artillery," April 25, 1861. Lt. col., 1st VA Art. (a "paper" organization that never operated as a regiment), Sept. 12, 1861. Col., July 4, 1862. Commanded an artillery battalion in McLaws's division most of the war. Richmond attorney postwar. Director of two railroad companies. Died Jan. 31, 1889, Richmond. Buried Hollywood Cemetery. Gen. E. P. Alexander thought Cabell "a superb soldier."

Cabell, Joseph Robert. Born May 28, 1840, VA. Brother of Gen. W. L. Cabell. Attd. Danville Military Academy. Danville resident prewar. Md. Mary E. Irby. Capt. Co. E (the "Cabell Guards"), 38th VA, May 28, 1861. Major, May 1, 1862. Lt. col., July 3, 1863. Col., Nov. 15, 1863. KIA Chester Station, May 10, 1864. Buried Old Grove St. Cemetery, Danville.

Cage, Duncan Stewart. Born Feb. 2, 1829, MS. Attd. St. Mary's College in Baltimore and U. of Nashville. Owned a sugar plantation in Terrebonne Parish, LA, prewar. Mexican War veteran. Md. Sarah Jane Connell. Capt., "Grivot Guards," early 1862. Lt. col., 26th LA, April 3, 1862. Col., Nov. 10, 1862. Resigned Dec. 30, 1862, due to ill health. VADC to Gen. Kirby Smith in 1863. Appointed col. and judge, military court of the TMD, March 9, 1864, but the appointment was never confirmed. In 1865 he was elected a state representative and served as speaker of the House 1865–67. Died June 20, 1885, Bladon Springs, AL. Buried Magnolia Cemetery, Houma, LA. Cage's successor as colonel called him "the very type of [a] Southern gentleman."

Caldwell, Alexander W. Born Aug. 20, 1838, Henry Co., TN. Farmer in Obion Co. prewar. Md. Mary Ann Walker. Capt. Co. C, 27th TN, Aug. 20, 1861. Lt. col., April 1862. Col., May 15, 1862. Regiment consolidated with 1st TN Jan. 1, 1863, with Caldwell becoming supernumerary. Post commander at Rome and Griffin, GA. Sent to TN in 1864 on a recruiting mission. Paroled c. May 11, 1865,

Memphis. Physician and farmer in Shelby and Obion Cos. postwar. Died Dec. 31, 1911, Troy, TN. Buried Troy Cemetery.

Caldwell, John William. Born Jan. 15, 1837, Russellville, KY. Grew up in Russellville and in TX. Attd. Bethany College and the U. of Louisville. Farmer and clerk. Surveyor in TX. Lawyer after 1858. Md. Sarah J. Barclay. 2d lt., KSG, early 1861. Capt. Co. A, 9th KY, Sept. 27, 1861. Major, 9th KY, Jan. 29, 1862. WIA Shiloh (right arm broken). Lt. col., May 14, 1862. Col., April 22, 1863. WIA Chickamauga (left arm broken and disabled). Captured at Shelbyville, TN, Oct. 7, 1863. Exch. Aug. 3, 1864. On detached service during the Carolinas Campaign. Paroled May 17, 1865, Nashville. Lawyer in Russellville postwar. Judge. US congressman 1877–83. Died July 4, 1903, Russellville, of paralysis. Buried Maple Grove Cemetery, Russellville. Termed "the bravest of the brave" in an obituary.

Caldwell, Josiah Hatcher. Born Sept. 30, 1822, Greene Co., KY. Attd. U. of Louisville Med. School. Prewar physician in Warrensburg, MO. Md. Mariah Anderson. Lt. Co. G, 3d Inf., 8th Div., MSG, June 20, 1861. Resigned Oct. 23, 1861. Appointed to Medical Examining Board of the MSG, 1862. Col. of the new 7th (aka 16th) MO, Dec. 4, 1862. Resigned March 24, 1863, admitting he was deficient in tactics and could do more good as a physician. Postwar physician in Waco, TX. Died Sept. 29, 1896, Waco. Buried Oakwood Cemetery, Waco. Gen. Jackman described him as "one of the bravest and best men I ever knew."

Calhoun, William Ransom. Born July 22, 1827, Charleston, SC. Nephew of Vice Pres. John C. Calhoun. Attd. UVA. Grad. USMA 1850. Lt., US Army, 1850–51. Resigned to become a planter in the Abbeville Dist. Sec. of the US Legation in France, 1857–60. Member of the state Ordnance Board. Unmd. Capt. Co. A, 1st SC Art. Bn., 1861. Lt. col., Aug. 15, 1861. Usually with his old company in VA in 1861 and thus absent from his regiment. Col., 1st SC Art. (formed from the 1st Bn.), March 25, 1862. Submitted resignation Aug. 18, 1862, for "health reasons," and granted a leave of absence. Killed Sept. 5, 1862, near Charleston, in a duel with his subordinate, Alfred Rhett, who succeeded to the colonelcy. Buried Magnolia Cemetery, Charleston. The duel was precipitated by Rhett (drinking in a Charleston tavern) calling Calhoun, with whom he had quarreled, either (depending on the source) a "puppy" or "an unmentionable part of the female anatomy."

Camp, John Lafayette. Born Feb. 20, 1828, near the present-day Birmingham, AL. Grad. UTN. Moved to Gilmer, TX, in 1849. Schoolteacher, lawyer. Md. Mary Ann Ward. Capt., 14th TX Cav., Feb. 15, 1862. Col., May 8, 1862. POW, exch. Oct. 8, 1862. WIA Stones River. WIA and POW Allatoona, GA, Oct. 7, 1864. To Camp Chase prison camp. Moved to San Antonio postwar. Elected to

Congress in 1866 but refused seat. State senator. Judge. US Land commissioner in AZ. Died July 16, 1891, San Antonio, buried Dignowity Cemetery. Camp Co., TX, is named for him.

Campbell, Francis Lightfoot Lee. Born June 10, 1836, Marlboro Dist., SC, son of a US congressman and diplomat. Distant cousin of Robert E. Lee. Reared in Lowndes Co., AL. Attd. USMA. Md. Ellen M. King in 1862. Capt. Co. B, 13th LA, Aug. 10, 1861. WIA Shiloh (shoulder). Major, Dec. 7, 1862. Lt. col., Jan. 11, 1864. Col., Aug. 22, 1864. In Nov. 1864, he asked permission to recruit men from POW camps, explaining that his regiment did not have 100 men for duty. Col., 13th/20th Consolidated. Paroled May 12, 1865, Meridian. "Gentleman" in Flat Rock, NC, postwar. Died Dec. 3, 1874, Lowndes Co. Buried Old Haynesville Cemetery, Haynesville, Lowndes Co.

Campbell, James Alexander. Born May 8, 1832, Beaver Creek, Kershaw Dist., SC. Lawyer in Leake Co., MS, prewar. Judge. Md. Amanda J. Sharkey. Capt. Co. E, 27th MS, April 25, 1861. Major, 1862. Lt. col., Dec. 31, 1862. Col., March 26, 1863. POW Lookout Mountain Nov. 24, 1863, while in charge of the picket line. To Johnson's Island Prison. Died of hepatitis there Feb. 4, 1864. Buried on Johnson's Island. Brother of Col. Josiah A. P. Campbell.

Campbell, John Arthur. Born Oct. 3, 1823, Hall's Bottom, Washington Co., VA. Attd. Emory & Henry, VMI, and UVA. Lawyer in Nashville and Abingdon prewar. State legislator. Antisecessionist. Delegate to VA Secession Convention. Md. Mary Branch. Appointed col., PAVA, June 26, 1861. Col., 48th VA, June 27, 1861. WIA First Winchester (arm, wrist). Resigned Oct. 16, 1862, protesting being passed over for promotion to brigadier general by John R. Jones, a junior officer. Elected judge, serving 1862–65. Judge in Abingdon to 1869. Lawyer. On Board of Trustees of Emory & Henry. Died June 17, 1886, Abingdon. Buried Sinking Springs Cemetery, Abingdon.

Campbell, Josiah Abigail Patterson. Born March 2, 1830, Lancaster, SC. Family moved to Kosciusko, MS, in 1845. Attd. Davidson College. Lawyer. State representative 1851–61. House speaker 1859–61. Md. Eugenia Nash. Confederate Congress, 1861–62. Capt. Co. K, 40th MS, May 3, 1862. Lt. col., May 14, 1862. WIA Corinth. Col., Dec. 16, 1862, to serve on military court of Hardee's Corps. Paroled April 27, 1865, NC. Lawyer in Canton, MS postwar. Chief justice of MS Supreme Court. Died Jan. 10, 1917, Canton, MS. Buried Greenwood Cemetery, Jackson, MS. Some sources give his first middle name as "Adams"; "Abigail" is from a descendant.

Campbell, Reuben Philander. Born April 16, 1818, Iredell Co., NC. Grad. USMA 1840. Lt. and capt., US Army, 1840–61. Often absent from the army on sick leave, due to rheumatism. Mexican War veteran. Col., 7th NC, May 16, 1861.

Distinguished for bravery at the Battle of New Bern. KIA Gaines's Mill, his right arm being shattered by grapeshot while leading a charge. Buried Snow Creek Cemetery, Statesville, Iredell Co. Gen. Branch eulogized Campbell as "brave and honorable as a man and skilful as an officer."

Cantwell, Edward Payne Chrysostom. Born Dec. 22, 1825, Charleston, SC. Grad. Harvard Law School, 1846. Lawyer in Raleigh and Wilmington, NC. Raleigh city attorney. Clerk of NC House. Capt. of vol. militia in Wilmington. Lt., 12th US Inf. in Mexican War. Md. Ellen Denning; Helen Gould. Appointed adj. gen. of NC April 15, 1861. Lt. col., 12th NC May 14, 1861. Not reelected in May 1862 reorganization. ADC to Gen. Clingman, 1862. Lt. col., 4th NC Cav. Sept. 28, 1862. POW at Middleburg, VA, June 19, 1863. Exch. March 10, 1864. Col., Oct. 15, 1864, to be judge of the military court of the 2d Corps, ANV. Postwar lawyer, judge, and state senator in Wilmington, NC. Authored eight books. Taught school in Utica, NY. Professor of law and history at the Georgia Military Academy. Died April 11, 1891, St. Simons Island, GA, while on vacation. Buried Christ Church Cemetery near Frederika, St. Simons Island.

Cantwell, John Lucas Paul. Born Dec. 29, 1828, Charleston, SC. Brother of Col. Edward Cantwell. Reared in Charleston and Columbia. Moved to New Orleans and (in 1851) Wilmington, NC. Drug clerk, then cotton broker, prewar. Mexican War veteran. Militia colonel. Capt., "Wilmington Light Infantry" vol. militia. Md. Catherine Theodesia Blount. Seized Fort Caswell, April 16, 1861, with his militia regiment and commanded the garrison there through July 1861. Then served with his old militia company (now Co. C, 18th NC). Capt. Co. D, 13th NC Art. Bn., Dec. 10, 1861. Col., 51st NC, at April 30, 1862, organization. Resigned Oct. 19, 1862, before charges of intoxication on duty could be brought to trial. Capt. Co. F, 3d NC, Nov. 13, 1863. POW Spotsylvania. One of the "Immortal 600." Released from prison May 26, 1865. Produce broker in Wilmington postwar. Died Dec. 21, 1909, Wilmington. Buried Oakdale Cemetery, Wilmington. His papers are at UNC. According to a physician in the 3d, Cantwell was "one of our best and bravest officers. He was very peculiar though, and such a stickler for army regulations that he was annoying."

Capers, Henry Dickson. Born June 2, 1835, Columbia, SC. Attd. SCMA. Grad. Medical College of SC. Prewar lawyer in Oxford, GA. Md. Mary E. Meade of Oxford. Chief clerk, CS Treasury Dept., 1861–62. Asst. army surgeon, Feb. 13, 1862. On Gen. Magruder's staff. Resigned April 1, 1862. Major, 12th GA Art. Bn. May 29, 1862. Lt. col., Nov. 6, 1862. WIA June 2, 1864, near Cold Harbor in right hip and retired from field duty. Appointed col. and judge of the military court of the Valley Cav. Corps, March 23, 1865. Paroled June 9, 1865. Postwar lawyer in Atlanta, GA, and West Union, SC. Wrote a biography of the Confederate treasury secretary. Died April 18, 1912, Atlanta. Buried Oxford City Cemetery. Brother of Gen. Ellison Capers. Recommended for promotion as "a gentleman of the highest order of sentiment and Christian virtues."

Capers, Richard Legrand. Born March 26, 1820, Sumter Dist., SC. Attd. UAL. Merchant in Homer, Claiborne Parish, LA, prewar. Md. Frances E. Hines. Capt. Co. A, 9th LA, July 7, 1861. Dropped, April 24, 1862. Capt. Co. A, Bayliss's Bn. LA PR, c. June 27, 1862. Major, 3d (Pargoud's) LA Cav., Oct. 1862. Major, 13th Bn. LA PR (formed from 3d Cav.), 1863. Lt. col., April 30, 1863. Col., 5th LA Cav. (formed from the 13th Bn.), c. Feb. 20, 1864. Paroled June 20, 1865, Shreveport. Farmer in Red River Parish postwar. Died April 25, 1893, Arcadia, LA. Buried Arcadia City Cemetery.

Carlton, Charles Hill. Born Dec. 24, 1838, King & Queen Co., VA. Reared in KY. Attd. Cumberland U. Law School. Prewar lawyer in Pine Bluff. Md. Maria Verdier Chapman. Capt. Co. B (the "Jefferson Guards"), 15th AR, July 23, 1861. Major, Nov. 14, 1862. WIA and POW Stones River. Exch. April 29, 1863. Detached in 1863 on recruiting duty in AR. Col., Carlton's AR Cav., Aug. 4, 1864. Postwar lawyer in Chicot Co. State senator 1878–82. Died Aug. 8, 1882, Lake Village, Chicot Co. Buried Lake Village Cemetery.

Carmical, George Hunter. Born Jan. 23, 1842, Newberry Co., SC. Listed as helping his father on the family farm on 1860 census of Coweta Co., GA. Md. Florence Robinson in 1879. Lt. Co. A, 2d GA, May 31, 1861. Capt., Dec. 16, 1861. Major, July 1, 1862. Lt. col., Sept. 1, 1862. Col., Sept. 1, 1862. WIA 2d Manassas; Knoxville; Fussell's Mill. Appmx. Farmer in Coweta Co. postwar. County sheriff. Died Oct. 31, 1929, Newnan. Buried Oak Hill Cemetery, Newnan.

Carpenter, John Nusom. Born June 10, 1825, Pickens Co., AL. Attd. UAL. Lawyer in Carrolton, AL. State legislator. Md. Rosalie Crenshaw. Capt. Co. G, 2d AL Cav., March 8, 1862. Court-martialed Oct. 3, 1862, and temporarily suspended from command. Major, May 27, 1863. Resigned April 2, 1864, but promoted to lt. col. (May 17, 1864) and col. (probably May 18, 1864). Commission merchant in Mobile postwar. Lawyer in Birmingham. Died Dec. 24, 1893, Birmingham. Buried Oak Hill Cemetery, Birmingham. His superior officers called him "highly cultivated by education . . . a perfect gentleman."

Carr, George Watson. Born June 7, 1822, Dundas, Albemarle Co., VA. Grandnephew of Pres. Thomas Jefferson. Attd. UVA. Lawyer in Kanawha Co., VA (now, WVA). Lt., US Army, 1847–48 and 1855–61. Md. Emma Gilmer Watts; Pinnie Laws. Capt., CS Regular Army, March 16, 1861. Served in the Bellona Arsenal and on the staffs of Gens. Wise and Joseph Johnston. Lt. col., 57th VA, Sept. 25, 1861. Col., April 24, 1862. Dropped 2 weeks later (May 7) at reorganization. Capt. and AAIG in southwest VA and under Gen. Bragg. Appointed major and AAIG, Oct. 7, 1863, and ordered to Gen. Breckinridge's staff. Captured Sept. 29, 1864, near Port Republic, VA. To Fort Delaware prison camp. Exch. Feb. 27, 1865. Farmer near Roanoke postwar. Died April 19, 1899, Hawksdale, Roanoke Co. Buried Watts Cemetery, Roanoke; reburied in 1977 in Fairview Cemetery, Roanoke. Gen. Albert Jenkins said Carr was "rather too fond of gun-powder" but "every inch a soldier."

Carrington, Henry Alexander. Born Sept. 13, 1832, Charlotte Co., VA. Grad. VMI and UVA. Richmond lawyer prewar. Militia colonel. Md. Charlotte E. Cullen. Lt. col., 18th VA, May 25, 1861. WIA Seven Pines (shoulder) and 2d Manassas (knee). WIA and POW Gettysburg. Exch. March 3, 1864. Col., July 21, 1864. Paroled April 27, 1865, Burkeville. Clerk of courts in Charlotte Co. postwar. Died Jan. 22, 1885, Richmond. Buried Shockoe Hill Cemetery, Richmond. Gen. Hunton remembered Carrington as "a man of great gallantry and efficiency."

Carroll, Charles Arthur. Born c. 1830, AL (probably Franklin Co.). Lived in Franklin Co. in 1850. Moved to Crawford Co., AR, in 1854. Prewar farmer. Md. Susan Casey. Capt. Co. A, 1st AR Cav., State Troops (a 3-month unit), May 18, 1861. Lt. col., 10th AR Cav. Bn. Col., 1st (Carroll's) AR Cav., Oct. 1862. Led cavalry brigade at Cane Hill. The brigade performed badly there. Arrested Dec. 2, 1862, for drunkenness. Resigned April 12, 1863. Postwar Conway Co. farmer. Moved to Little Rock and died there Feb. 27, 1877. Buried Mt. Holly Cemetery, Little Rock.

Carroll, Charles Montgomery. Born March 18, 1821, Nashville, son of longtime TN Gov. William Carroll and brother of Gen. William H. Carroll. Grad. U. of Nashville, 1838. Farmer near Nashville. Clerk. Moved to Memphis in the 1850s. Asst. postmaster of Memphis in 1860. Officer in vol. militia. Md. Mary J. ——. Col., 15th TN, June 7, 1861. Court-martialed, Oct. 1861, for conduct unbecoming an officer. The 15th straggled badly on a short march, then the soldiers started fighting with each other, and Carroll got into a shouting match with his subordinates. Found guilty and soon transferred to staff duty. Captured Feb. 16/17, 1863, while an inspector on the staff of Gen. Bedford Forrest. Memphis merchant postwar. Died Dec. 9, 1899, Memphis. Buried Elmwood Cemetery.

Carroll, David Williamson. Born March 11, 1816, Baltimore, MD. Attd. St. Mary's College in Baltimore. Moved to Little Rock, AR, in 1836. Moved to Pine Bluff in 1853. Schoolteacher, surveyor, lawyer. State representative 1850–51. Prosecuting Attorney for the Pine Bluff Dist. Md. Melanie Scull. Capt. Co. K, 18th AR, Feb. 22, 1862. Col., April 2, 1862. Resigned Aug. 25, 1862, due to illness ("diarrhea of long standing") and returned to Pine Bluff. Elected to Confederate Congress in 1865. Postwar lawyer in Pine Bluff and Little Rock. Judge. Died June 24, 1905, Little Rock. Buried Calvary Cemetery, Little Rock. A fellow lawyer called Carroll "an able, dignified and most upright judge."

Carter, David Miller. Born Jan. 12, 1830, Fairfield, Hyde Co., NC. Attd. Lovejoy's Academy in Raleigh. Grad. UNC. Lawyer in Washington, Beaufort Co., prewar. Md. Isabella Perry; Mrs. Harriet Benbury. Capt. Co. E, 4th NC, May 16, 1861. WIA Seven Pines (right arm). Lt. col., June 19, 1862. Resigned Dec. 23, 1862, citing his wound. Col. and judge, military court of Jackson's Corps, Dec. 20, 1862. Resigned 1864. State representative 1862–65. Attorney in Washington and (after 1874) Raleigh. Lost race for Congress in 1872. Died Jan. 7, 1879, Baltimore, MD. Buried Oakwood Cemetery, Raleigh. Carter's extensive papers are at UNC.

Carter, George Washington. Born Jan. 1826, Fauquier Co., VA. Prewar Methodist minister in Richmond, VA, teacher and lawyer. Professor at UMS. President of Soule U., Chappell Hill, TX, 1860–61. Noted orator. Md. Ora McIlheny; Virginia Statham. Delegate to TX Secession Convention. In early 1861 he constructed wrought-iron artillery pieces. Appointed col. in Oct. 1861, by the sec. of war, to raise a regiment. He and other Methodist ministers raised 30 companies, the future 21st, 24th, and 25th TX Cav. Col., 21st TX Cav., March 8, 1862. Often led a brigade that Col. W. H. Parsons also claimed to be senior colonel of. The dispute resulted in neither Carter nor Parsons being promoted to brigadier. Sent on a speaking tour of TX in 1863 to drum up support for the war. Paroled June 29, 1865, Houston. Moved to Cameron Parish, LA, postwar. Noted "scalawag" legislator. Speaker of LA House in 1872. US ambassador to Venezuela during the Garfield administration. Writer in Washington, DC; minister in Portsmouth and Lynchburg, VA. Died May 11, 1901, at the Pikesville, MD, Confederate Soldiers' Home. Buried Loudon Park Cemetery, Baltimore. A junior officer called Carter "brave and fearless as a lion," but "dishonest, faithless" with a "fondness for drink."

Carter, James Eppes. Born Oct. 21, 1828, Knox Co., TN. Farmer in Knox Co. prewar. Col. of a militia regiment. Md. Elizabeth Patton. 1st lt. Co. D, 3d TN Cav. Bn., Aug. 8, 1861. Lt. col., 14th TN Cav. Bn., May 12, 1862. Col., 1st (Carter's) TN Cav. (formed from 3d and 14th Bns.), June 9, 1863 (appointed Nov. 14, 1862, upon formation of the 1st). WIA Kernstown, VA, Aug. 1864. Resigned April 17, 1865. Paroled May 7, 1865, Knoxville. Knoxville agent for a New York commercial house postwar. In coal business. UCV general. Superintendent of State Penitentiary. Moved to Calhoun, GA, in 1904, to live with a daughter. Died there Feb. 27, 1905. Buried Old Gray Cemetery, Knoxville.

Carter, James William. Born c. 1830, MS. Half brother of Col. R. P. McKelvaine. Farmer in De Kalb, Kemper Co., MS, prewar. Md. Mary Elizabeth Beville. Capt. Co. K (the "Kemper Legion"), 13th MS, April 13, 1861. Lt. col., April 26, 1862. WIA Malvern Hill. Col., Aug. 12, 1862. KIA Gettysburg, July 2, 1863. Buried Hollywood Cemetery, Richmond, in 1872.

Carter, John C. Born c. 1832, SC. Wealthy prewar Montgomery Co., AL planter. Md. Margaret Shellman. Capt. in an unspecified AL regiment Dec. 13, 1861. Capt. Co. H, 34th AL, April 16, 1862. Slightly WIA Murfreesboro. Lt. col., May 1, 1864. WIA Jonesboro. Col., 24th AL Consolidated, April 10, 1865. Postwar Montgomery Co. farmer. Died Dec. 5, 1880, Montgomery Co. Buried Carter family cemetery, Montgomery Co.

Carter, Nathan William. Born July 18, 1818, Sumner Co., TN. Farmer in Rutherford Co. prewar. Md. Mary Hamilton Thompson. Capt., Carter's Co., Douglas's Bn. TN PR, probably Sept. 1862. This scout company later became Co. A, 21st TN Cav. Col., 21st TN Cav. (more usually known as Carter's or Wheeler's Scouts), upon regiment's organization in Sept. 1864. WIA while leading a charge in an action near Athens, AL, Sept. 24, 1864, which wound disabled him for the rest of the war. Paroled as col. and ADC May 9, 1865, Gainesville, AL. Rutherford Co. farmer postwar. Died Aug. 6, 1886, Rutherford Co. An officer in the 21st called Carter "a famous scout."

Carter, Richard Welby. Born March 11, 1837, Fauquier Co., VA. Attd. VMI. Loudoun Co. farmer prewar. Officer in vol. militia. Md. Sophia DeButts Carter, a cousin. Capt. Co. H, 1st VA Cav., April 27, 1861. Acted as ADC to Gen. G. W. Smith, May 1862. Major, July 24, 1862. Lt. col., c. 1862–63. Col., July 16, 1863. POW Upperville, Dec. 17, 1863. Exch. Aug. 4, 1864. Cashiered for cowardice at Tom's Brook. Captured while at home, Feb. 21, 1865. Released July 19, 1865. Loudoun Co. farmer postwar. Died Dec. 18, 1888, Loudoun Co. Buried in the Carter family cemetery at "Crendel," Loudoun Co. Carter was widely disliked by officers and men, with such comments as "white livered," "a coward," "fat and looked greasy." He and his regiment broke at Tom's Brook, largely causing the Confederate rout there.

Carter, Thomas Henry. Born June 13, 1831, King William Co., VA. Grad. VMI 1849. Attd. UVA. Grad. U. PA Medical School. Intern in Philadelphia hospital, 1852–53. Planter in King William Co. Md. Susan E. Roy. Capt., King William Art., June 1, 1861. Major and chief of artillery, D. H. Hill's Div., Nov. 1, 1862. Lt. col., May 2, 1863. Col., Feb. 27, 1864. Acting chief of artillery for 2d Corps in the Valley Campaign. WIA Opequon Creek. Appmx. Farmed in King William Co. after the war. Railroad commissioner of VA 1873–89. Proctor, UVA. Died June 2, 1908, Romancoke, King William Co. Buried Hollywood Cemetery,

Richmond. Gen. Robert E. Lee said, "Colonel Carter has the finest eye for position of almost any man I know." His wife was a niece of Confederate Sec. of War Seddon. Papers at VAHS.

Cary, Richard Milton. Born Nov. 12, 1821, Pear Tree Hill, Warwick Co., VA. Attd. William & Mary College. Lawyer in Richmond and Hampton prewar. Capt. of vol. militia. Author of a drill manual used early in the war. Md. Anne Dunbar; Lucy Wilson. Ordered with his militia company to Fredericksburg, April 1861. "A fine soldier, strict disciplinarian, and splendid drill master." Col., 30th VA, June 13, 1861. Cary declined to stand for reelection at the April 1862 reorganization. Elected anyway, he refused to accept, opposed in principle to election of officers. Appointed lt. of artillery, June 4, 1862. Capt., March 26, 1863. Major, Sept. 10, 1863. Commanded the Bellona Arsenal and served at arsenals at Macon and Salisbury. Cotton and tobacco merchant in England postwar. Died March 15, 1886, Falmouth Dist., Cornwall, England. Buried Budock Cemetery, near Falmouth.

Cash, Ellerbe Boggan Crawford. Born July 1, 1823, Wadesboro, NC. Attd. USC. Planter in Chesterfield Co., SC, prewar. State legislator. Md. Allen Eunice Ellerbe. Col., 8th SC, March 20, 1861. Dropped at May 1862 reorganization. Col., 2d SC State Reserves, 1862–63. Lawyer and planter in Chesterfield Co. postwar. Lost race for Congress (as a Greenbacker-Republican) in 1882. Died March 10, 1888, at his Chesterfield Co. home, of apoplexy. Buried in a family plot at Cash's Depot, SC, near his home. In the 1880s Cash (a "tall, stalwart fellow . . . red headed, red faced") fought what is said to have been the last formal duel in US history, killing a fellow lawyer. A book (which, for the curious, contains the text of the "Code of Dueling") has been written on that duel. Edward Porter Alexander's memoirs contain a delicious anecdote of Cash at 1st Manassas.

Caskie, Robert Alexander. Born July 12, 1830, Richmond, VA. Attd. UVA. Worked in the family's tobacco business in Richmond prewar. Md. Amanda W. Gregory. Capt. Co. A, 10th VA Cav., May 15, 1861. Major, Aug. 8, 1863. Lt. col., Sept. 11, 1863. WIA Reams Station, Aug. 23, 1864. On limited duty for several months thereafter. Col., probably Feb. 2, 1865, upon J. Lucius Davis's resignation. Appmx. Tobacco merchant in Rocheport, MO, postwar. Died Aug. 28, 1928, at his son's home in Merion, PA. Buried Merion; reburied Hollywood Cemetery. Gen. Jeb Stuart nicknamed him "Old Joshua." Gen. Chambliss thought him efficient and qualified.

Caswell, Theodore Dwight. Born c. 1832, NY. Moved to Augusta, GA, c. 1849. Clerk and grocer there. Md. Lucie Walker. 1st lt. Co. G (the "Baker Volunteers," later Co. A, 4th GA Bn. Sharpshooters, a company he and his business partner helped equip), 3d GA Bn., Sept. 29, 1861. Capt., Dec. 2, 1861. Major, 4th GA Bn. Sharpshooters, March 5, 1863. WIA Chickamauga. Col., 54th GA Consolidated, April 9, 1865. Commission merchant in Augusta postwar. Died Aug. 1, 1887, Asheville, NC, of jaundice. Buried Magnolia Cemetery, Augusta. A soldier in Caswell's battalion found him "an admirable commander. Reared in the peaceful pursuits, on the battlefield he exhibited the most dauntless courage."

Caudill, Benjamin Everage. Born Feb. 11, 1830, Letcher Co., KY. Farmer in Letcher Co. prewar. Md. Martha Asburry. Col., 13th KY Cav., to rank from Sept. 1, 1863 (Gen. Marshall had appointed him col. upon the organization of the regiment, Nov. 2, 1862). POW Gladeville, VA, July 7, 1863. Exch. Aug. 3, 1864. Led the 13th in KY and VA, 1864–65. Farmer and preacher postwar, living in Clay Co. Died Feb. 11, 1889, London, KY. Buried Slate Hill Cemetery, Farriston, KY.

Caudle, John Hiram. Born Nov. 22, 1835, Cherokee Co., AL. Moved to TX by 1850. Merchant in Red River Co. Md. Rosannah Bason; Mary Frances Park. Capt. Co. D, 34th TX Cav. (2d PR), March 7, 1862. Lt. col., Aug. 22, 1863. Col., Aug. 27, 1863. Postwar dry goods merchant and farmer in Red River Co. Minor politician. Moved to Ellis Co. and then Haskell Co. in 1890. Died April 8, 1895, Haskell Co. Buried Pioneer Cemetery, near Graham, Young Co.

Chalmers, Alexander H,. Born June 7, 1839, Holly Springs, MS. Brother of Gen. James Chalmers. Reared in Holly Springs. Merchant in New Orleans prewar. Md. Amelia Perkins in 1866. Major, 1st Cav., 3d Div., MSG, July 28, 1861. Appointed major of cav. June 7, 1862, by Gen. Bragg. Major, Commissary Dept., Jan. 31, 1863. Major, Chalmers MS Cav. Bn., June 1, 1863. Appointed by Gen. Chalmers lt. col., 18th MS Cav. Bn., Oct. 7, 1863. WIA near La Grange, MS, Oct. 1863. Lt. col., Feb. 21, 1865. Col., 18th MS Cav. (formed by consolidation of 18th with 55th MS Cav.), March 16, 1865. Paroled May 12, 1865, Gainesville. Planter postwar in St. Landry Parish, LA, and then AR. Died Dec. 27, 1872, AR. Buried Hernando, MS (probably Hernando Baptist Cemetery). A fellow colonel called Chalmers "a gallant, sober and efficient officer."

Chandler, Green Callier. Born Aug. 24, 1829, Washington Co., AL. Family moved to Lauderdale Co., MS, in 1835. Lawyer in Enterprise, MS, prewar. Farmer, newspaper editor. State representative 1854–55, 1861–62. Md. Martha G. Croft. Capt. Co. D, 8th MS, July 17, 1861. Elected col., April 1862, but another contestant (John C. Wilkinson) challenged and overturned that election on the basis that Chandler gained a plurality, not a majority, of the votes. Wilkinson won the new election in May. Col., 2d Regt., MS State Troops, Sept. 2, 1864. Lawyer in Lauderdale Co. and Corinth, MS, postwar. Scalawag judge. State representative 1870–72. US dist. attorney for northern MS 1878–83. Moved to

Jackson, TN, in 1890. Died April 14, 1905, Jackson. Buried Monte Vista Cemetery, Jackson. His journal, started in 1855, was published in 1953.

Cheek, William Hayes. Born March 18, 1835, Warren Co., NC. Attd. Wake Forest U. Grad. Randolph Macon U. Warrenton lawyer prewar. State representative 1860–61. Officer in vol. militia. Md. Alice M. Jones. Capt. Co. E, 1st NC Cav., May 16, 1861. Lt. col., Sept. 28, 1863. Col., Oct. 17, 1863. WIA Yellow Tavern. POW Burkesville, April 5, 1865. Released July 25, 1865. Lawyer, businessman, planter postwar. Lived in Warrenton; Baltimore, MD; Norfolk, VA; and Henderson, NC. State legislator. Died March 23, 1901, Henderson and buried there, probably in Elmwood Cemetery. Cheek wrote a sketch of the 1st for Clark's "North Carolina Regiments," in which he claimed that Gen. Robert E. Lee recommended him for promotion to general for "special gallantry" at Chamberlain's Run, March 31, 1865. The recommendation came too late for the promotion to be processed.

Chenault, David Waller. Born Feb. 5, 1826, Richmond, KY. Farmer in Madison Co. prewar. Mexican War veteran. Active in local politics. Md. Ann T. Phelps. Col., 11th KY Cav., Sept. 10, 1862. KIA Green River Bridge, July 4, 1863, during Morgan's Ohio Raid. Buried first on the battlefield, later Chenault family cemetery, and finally in Richmond Cemetery.

Chenoweth, James Quilbert. Born Feb. 9, 1841, Louisville, KY. Grad. Asbury U. (now DePauw) in IN in 1860. Resided in Harrison Co. prewar. Studied law in Montgomery, AL. Md. Scota M. Inskeep. Lt., KSG, June 18, 1861. Drillmaster, Bennett's TN Cav. Bn., 1861–62. WIA Shiloh. Major, 1st KY Cav., Sept. 2, 1862. WIA Stones River, Chickamauga. Appointed col., Sept. 6, 1864, and detached from the 1st in order to go behind Union lines in KY and recruit a regiment. Raised Chenoweth's KY Cav., a unit in Gen. Adam Johnson's partisan brigade, and led this regiment to the end of the war. The original appointment was for 3 months only. After it expired Chenoweth was reappointed col. March 13, 1865. Lawyer postwar, in Montgomery, AL; KY; and Bonham, TX. State senator in KY. State representative in TX. Judge. Auditor of the US Treasury 1885–88. Publisher, Bonham *Daily Favorite*. Superintendent of the TX Confederate Home in Austin. Died June 2, 1909, at the Elks home in Bedford, VA. Buried Harrodsburg (KY) City Cemetery. Col. Bennett called him "a gentleman of fine attainments . . . fitted by nature for a military man."

Chester, John. Born May 18, 1827, Jackson, TN. Grad. West TN College and Jefferson Medical College. Physician in Jackson, TN, prewar. Lt., 14th US Inf. in Mexican War. Md. Agatha Taylor. Enlisted as Pvt., Dec. 3, 1861. Lt. col., 51st TN, Jan. 1, 1862. Col., April 22, 1862. 51st and 52d TN consolidated April 1862. Commissioned col. and judge, military court of the Dept of AL, MS, and East

LA, April 6, 1864. Paroled May 9, 1865, Gainesville. Physician in Jackson postwar. Died June 4, 1877, Jackson, of smallpox contracted from a patient. Buried Riverside Cemetery, Jackson. A contemporary found Chester "a man of most amiable traits of character."

Chew, Robert Stanard. Born Oct. 3, 1828, VA. Grad. UVA and Jefferson Medical College. Physician and banker in Fredericksburg. Capt. of vol. militia. Capt. Co. B, 30th VA, April 22, 1861. Lt. col., April 19, 1862. WIA Antietam. Commanded Corse's Brigade late 1863–early 1864. Col., Nov. 5, 1864. Appmx. Returned to Fredericksburg postwar. Clerk of courts. Died Aug. 17, 1886, Fredericksburg. Buried Fredericksburg Confederate Cemetery.

Chisum, Isham Russell. Born Aug. 5, 1818, Marion Co., MS. Moved to TX in 1837. Planter in Rusk Co. and later Rockwell, Kaufman Co. Md. Charlotte Martin. Delegate to TX Secession Convention. Capt. Co. F, 3d TX Cav., June 13, 1861. Resigned May 20, 1862. Lt. col., 2d TX PR, 1862. Col., c. Dec. 14, 1863. Court-martialed in 1865. The record is unclear why, but it may have been due to protesting the regiment's forced conversion to infantry. Resigned April 5, 1865, while the court-martial was pending. Rancher, farmer, and tanner postwar in Kaufman, San Patricio, and Bandera Cos. Died Feb. 1884, Bandera Co. Buried Vanderpool Cemetery.

Christian, William Steptoe. Born Dec. 26, 1830, Middlesex Co., VA. Grad. Columbian College in DC and Jefferson Medical College. Physician in Middlesex Co. prewar. Capt. of vol. militia. Md. Helen E. Steptoe; Alice Goodward. Capt. Co. C, 55th VA, June 2, 1861. Major, May 1, 1862. Lt. col., June 23, 1862. WIA Frayser's Farm (thigh). Col., May 2, 1863. POW Falling Waters, July 14, 1863, during the retreat from Gettysburg. Exch. March 1864. Retired March 14, 1865, to seek a medical post. Returned to his medical practice in Middlesex Co. after the war. Superintendent of county schools. President of Medical Society of VA. Died Dec. 10, 1910, Urbanna. Buried Hewic Plantation Cemetery, Urbanna.

Christie, Daniel Harvey. Born March 28, 1833, Frederick Co., VA. Reared in Loudon Co. Music teacher and merchant in Norfolk, VA. Moved to Henderson, NC, in 1857 and established a military school there. Md. Lizzie Norfleet. Major, 23d NC, July 12, 1861. Col., April 16, 1862. WIA Seven Pines, when his horse was killed and fell on him. WIA Gaines's Mill (leg). MWIA (shot through the lungs) Gettysburg, July 1, 1863. Died July 17, 1863, Winchester, VA. Buried at the Episcopal burial ground, Winchester; reburied postwar Mt. Hebron Cemetery, Winchester.

Churchwell, William Montgomery. Born Feb. 20, 1826, near Knoxville, TN. Attd. Emory & Henry College. Knoxville lawyer. Bank and railroad president.

Special commissioner to Mexico. US congressman 1851–55. Md. Martha Eleanor Deery. Col., 4th (aka 34th) TN, Aug. 5, 1861. Not reelected in April 16, 1862, reorganization. Appointed provost marshal of East TN April 19, 1862. Died Aug. 18, 1862, Knoxville, of typhoid. Buried Old Gray Cemetery, Knoxville. Col. Randal McGavock, his brother-in-law, believed Churchwell squandered his bank's money on his mistress (a New York actress), which caused the bank to fail.

Clack, Calvin Jones. Born 1829, Pulaski, TN. Lawyer in MS and Pulaski prewar. Unmd. 1st lt. Co. A, 3d TN, May 1861. Capt., May 17, 1861. POW Fort Donelson and imprisoned for 7 months. Exch. Sept. 1, 1862. Elected lt. col. at Sept. 26, 1862, reorganization. Col., June 22, 1864, to succeed the deceased Col. C. H. Walker. KIA Jonesboro, Aug. 31, 1864. Buried on the battlefield; reburied Maplewood Cemetery, Pulaski, in 1883. Gen. John C. Brown thought Clack "entirely competent and eminently meritorious."

Clack, Franklin Hulse. Born April 4, 1828, Pensacola, FL. Reared in Norfolk, VA, by his father, a navy capt. Attd. Princeton. Grad. Yale Law School. Moved to New Orleans in 1851 and practiced law there. City attorney prewar. Md. Louise C. Babcock. Lt. Co. D, Confederate Guards Regt., LA Militia, 1861. Capt. Co. A, 12th LA Bn. (aka 16th; Confederate Guards Response Bn.), March 8, 1862. Major, March 8, 1862. Lt. col., Sept. 1862. Col., 33d LA (formed from the 12th Bn.), Oct. 1862. Regiment broken up Nov. 22, 1862, and Clack reverted to battalion command. Lt. col., Consolidated Crescent Regt., c. Nov. 2, 1863 (when the 12th was merged with the Crescent Regt.). MWIA Mansfield, died April 24, 1864. Buried Metairie Cemetery, New Orleans.

Claiborne, Thomas. Born June 20, 1823, Nashville. Lawyer and newspaper editor in Trenton, TN. Officer in US Army 1846–61. Md. Ann A. Maxwell of Nashville, whose family founded Maxwell House Coffee. Capt., CS Regular Army, July 12, 1861. Major, CS Regular Army, backdated to March 16, 1861. Lt. col., 1st KY Bn. in VA, 1861. Staff officer to Gen. Joseph Johnston in VA and to Gen. A. S. Johnston in the West. Appointed by Gen. A. S. Johnston col., 1st (aka 6th) Confederate Cav., April 1, 1862. The appointment was not popular with the soldiers (one soldier tried to kill him), and Claiborne was relieved June 4, 1862. Lt. col., CS Regular Army, May 29, 1863. Chief of cavalry to Gen. Buckner. Col., PACS, with temporary rank, May 7, 1864. Asst. IG of the TMD. Postwar farmer near Nashville. Active in veterans organizations. Died April 23, 1911, Nashville. Buried Mt. Olivet Cemetery. Papers at TN State Library and UNC. Gen. Buckner, under whom Claiborne served, recommended Claiborne, "a fine cavalry officer," for promotion to general.

Claiborne, William Clark. Born Sept. 25, 1819, VA. Wealthy farmer prewar in Pittsylvania Co., VA. Md. Martha J. Haden. Lt. col., 4th NC PR Bn., May 9, 1862. Col., 7th Confederate Cav., May 10, 1862. On Aug. 14, 1863, his officers asked that he be promoted to brig. gen. Three days later, Gen. Martin arrested him. Resigned Sept. 26, 1863, which resignation Martin happily accepted. Postwar farmer in Pittsylvania Co. Died Feb. 3, 1893, Danville, VA. Buried Green Hill Cemetery, Danville. In their recommendation for promotion, Claiborne's officers called him "sober, vigilant and a good officer." However, Martin thought otherwise, and Gen. Whiting suspected Claiborne might be a "scoundrel." Claiborne's brother Thomas was lt. col. 7th VA Cav.

Clark, Benjamin Webster. Born c. 1832, LA. Kenyon College graduate. Prewar planter in West Baton Rouge Parish. Md. Elizabeth Routh Williams. Pvt. Co. F, 4th LA, May 25, 1861. Color sgt., May 25, 1861. Regimental adj., May 19, 1863. Transferred to state service and appointed capt. and AAG to Gov. Allen, Nov. 12, 1863. Lt. col., 1st LA State Guard Bn., 1863. Col., 8th LA Cav. (formed from merging the 1st and 2d Bns.), Oct. 27, 1864. Paroled June 6, 1865, at Natchitoches. Farmed postwar in West Baton Rouge Parish. Died 1885. Buried West Baton Rouge Parish; reburied Baton Rouge in 1905.

Clark, Edward. Born April 1, 1815, New Orleans, LA. His uncle John Clark was Gov. of GA. Reared in GA and AL. Marshall, TX, lawyer prewar. State legislator. Mexican War veteran, TX sec. of state and lt. gov. Md. Lucy Long; Martha M. Evans. When Gov. Houston was forced out of office in 1861 by the Secession Convention for his opposition to secession, Lt. Gov. Clark, his onetime political ally, became governor. Clark narrowly lost election in late 1861 for his own term as governor. Appointed col., 14th TX, Nov. 26, 1861, by Gen. Hebert. Commissioned col., April 16, 1862. WIA at Mansfield and Pleasant Hill; the latter wound, in the leg, kept him on crutches for a year. Fled to Mexico postwar but almost immediately returned to his home in Marshall. Postwar lawyer and businessman. Died in Marshall May 4, 1880. Buried Old Marshall Cemetery. Clark's papers are at UTX. An 1865 newspaper article noted that "his reputation was seriously impaired by too free an indulgence in intoxicating drinks."

Clark, Henry E. Born April 14, 1823, Salem, OH. Reared in OH. Built levees on the Mississippi River. Lived in Memphis, and later Clarkston, MO (a town named for him). Md. Martha——; Josephine——. Capt. and QM, 1st Inf., 1st Div., MSG, June 30, 1861. Lost election for general of the 1st Div. Commissioned col., PACS, Aug. 20, 1862, with authority to raise a regiment. Captured Oct. 26, 1862, at Clarkston while recruiting. Exch. within 2 months and resumed recruiting but decided to let Solomon Kitchen (much more experienced in field duty) take over the new regiment. Paroled Wittsburg, AR, May 25, 1865. Postwar real estate dealer in Cincinnati and Memphis. Died March 25, 1883, Little Rock, AR. Buried Edgar Cemetery, Paris, IL, alongside his father. Clark had three brothers in the Union army.

Clark, James W. Born 1833, Madison Co., AL. Farmer and blacksmith in Madison Co. Overseer in Gibson Co., TN, 1857–60. Then farmed in Jackson Co., AR. Md. Mary S. A. Moon; Mrs. Lavinia Heard Jones. Pvt. Co. A, McCray's AR Inf. Bn., Nov. 2, 1861. Lt., Nov. 2, 1861. Capt., April 16, 1862. Major, 31st AR (formed from McCray's Bn.), July 12, 1862. Sent to AR in 1863 on recruiting service, 1863. Relieved from duty Sept. 1, 1863, when 31st consolidated with 4th AR. Lt. col., 45th AR, 1864. Col., probably Oct. 22, 1864. Paroled at Jacksonport, June 5, 1865. Postwar farmer and stock raiser in Jackson Co. Alive there in 1888. McCray called Clark "one of the most gallant and efficient officers in the Confederate army."

Clark, John Moorman. Born April 27, 1834, Halifax Co., VA. Reared in Paris, TN. Attd. Bethel College. Lawyer and farmer in Paris, TN, prewar. Militia colonel. Md. Anna Porter. Col., 46th TN, Nov. 29, 1861. "A gentleman of pleasant and agreeable manners." POW Island No. 10. Exch. Sept. 30, 1862. Not reelected at Oct. 1862 reorganization. Moved with his family to TX. Said to have joined the 33d TX Cav. in some capacity, though there is no service record for him in a TX unit. Lawyer in Paris postwar. Appointed Indian agent in 1885. Lawyer and agent in Chandler, OK. Died Nov. 6, 1905, Snyder, OK. Buried Fairlawn Cemetery, Snyder.

Clark, Meriwether Lewis. Born Jan. 10, 1809, St. Louis, MO, son of famed explorer William Clark (of Lewis and Clark fame). Grad. USMA 1830. Lt., US Army, 1830–33. Architect in St. Louis. State legislator. Major of MO Art. Bn. in Mexican War. Md. Julie Churchill. Brig. gen., 9th Div., MSG, Oct. 1861. Major of artillery, PACS, Nov. 11, 1861. Col., April 16, 1862. Commanded artillery brigade in Army of MS, 1862. Chief of artillery to Gen. Van Dorn. Transferred to ordnance duty in Richmond, VA. Led Barton's brigade of reservists in the Richmond garrison, 1864–65. POW Amelia Courthouse, April 5, 1865. Postwar taught at KMI in Frankfort, KY. Died Oct. 28, 1881, Frankfort. Buried Bellefontaine Cemetery, St. Louis. One private remembered: "Slow and wedded to routine, he was not a man for emergencies." Family papers are at Missouri Historical Society. Clark's grandson started the Kentucky Derby and named Churchill Downs for his grandmother.

Clark, Whitfield. Born June 24, 1827, Edgefield Dist., SC. Prewar merchant in Barbour Co., AL. Md. Elizabeth Cox; Mary E. Dent. Capt., "Pioneer Guards," 1861. Appointed major, 39th AL, May 15, 1862. Promoted to lt. col. and col.

(probably Oct. 12, 1863). Resigned April 7, 1864, due to chronic rheumatism but resignation revoked. Barbour Co. tax collector in 1864. Retired Nov. 2, 1864. Paroled June 8, 1865, Montgomery. Dry goods and grocery merchant in Clayton, AL, postwar. Died Feb. 14, 1875, Clayton. Buried Clayton Cemetery. One sergeant said Clark was "not wanting in character and courage, but, the truth is, not a military man."

Clark, William Henry. Born Jan. 3, 1827, NC. Attd. Bethany College in VA. Lawyer in Brandon, Rankin Co., MS, prewar. Judge of Probate. Mexican War veteran. Md. Mary McDowell. Lt. Co. D, 6th MS Inf. Bn., May 14, 1862. Major, 46th MS (formed from the 6th Bn.), Dec. 1, 1862. POW Vicksburg. Lt. col., Nov. 26, 1863. Col., March 1, 1864. KIA Allatoona, Oct. 5, 1864, "while gallantly leading the third and last charge." Buried Brandon Cemetery. A sergeant in the 46th called Clark "a small man with a thin voice." Grandfather of US Supreme Court justice Tom Clark.

Clarke, James O. Born March 26, 1825, Augusta, GA. "Master mason" (builder) in Augusta prewar. Mexican War veteran of the 13th US Inf. Officer in vol. militia. Augusta alderman. Md. Sarah——; Mary E. Danforth. Capt. Co. D (his old militia company), 1st (Ramsey's) GA, March 18, 1861. Lt. col., April 3, 1861. Col., Dec. 11 (or 3d), 1861. Regiment mustered out March 18, 1862. Commissioned 2d lt. and drillmaster June 16, 1862, to drill recruits in GA. Promoted to 1st lt., July 17, 1863. Contractor in Augusta postwar. Died there Dec. 6, 1889. Buried Magnolia Cemetery. Clarke's service record is hard to reconcile. It appears he was under arrest in Nov. 1861 and submitted his resignation shortly thereafter, but while the resignation paperwork was being processed Col. Ramsey resigned and Clarke received a postdated commission as colonel. He never led the regiment at that rank.

Clarke, John Graham. Born 1832, VA. Resident of Petersburg prewar. Civil engineer, working on railroads in eastern VA. Md. Lucy Selden Macon. Capt., Confederate Engineer Corps, Feb. 12, 1862. Helped build fortifications near Yorktown. Capt., Engineer Corps of VA, Feb. 15, 1862. Engineer officer in Longstreet's Corps, 1862–63. Major, PACS, May 4, 1863. Lt. col., March 17, 1864. Col. of Engineers, Oct. 19, 1864. Constructed the bridge that allowed the Confederate army to evacuate Savannah. Chief engineer of the Dept. of SC, GA, and FL and of the Army of TN in 1865. Postwar resident of Savannah, GA, then Manchester, VA. Superintendent of Central Railroad of GA. Bridge constructor. Died Sept. 15, 1880, Paterson, NJ, when a runaway train hit him. Buried Hollywood Cemetery, Richmond. E. P. Alexander called him "a fine, clever fellow." Clarke used the middle initial "J" during the war and is indexed in the service records as such.

Clarke, William John. Born Aug. 2, 1819, Raleigh, NC. Grad. UNC, with honors. Lawyer in Raleigh. State Comptroller 1850–55. Lived in San Antonio, TX, 1857–61. Lawyer and railroad president there. Capt. and brevet major, 12th US Inf., in Mexican War. Md. Mary Bayard Devereux (1827–86), noted poet and novelist. Capt., CS Regular Army, 1861. Col., 24th NC, July 18, 1861. WIA Drewry's Bluff, May 15, 1864, in shoulder. POW Dinwiddie Courthouse (captured while returning from sick leave), Feb. 5, 1865. Released July 24, 1865. Often recommended for promotion to general. Lumber mill operator in Johnston Co. postwar. Moved to New Bern in 1886. Lawyer there. State senator. Judge. Newspaper editor in Raleigh. Died Jan. 23, 1886, New Bern. Buried Cedar Grove Cemetery, New Bern. His published war letters reveal a very high opinion of himself and anger that junior officers (notably Matt Ransom) were promoted over him.

Clay, Clement Claiborne. Born Dec. 13, 1816, Huntsville, AL. Grad. UAL and UVA Law School. Lawyer in Huntsville. Newspaper editor. State legislator, judge. US senator 1852–61. Md. Virginia C. Tunstall. In Confederate Senate, 1861–64. Chaired Commerce Committee. Appointed col., April 6, 1864, to be judge of a military court in AL. While still deciding whether to accept the appointment, Pres. Davis (a close friend) sent him to Canada to coordinate Confederate activities there. Arrested for being a coconspirator in Lincoln's assassination but later released. Postwar lawyer in Madison Co., AL. Died Jan. 3, 1882, Madison Co. Buried Maple Hill Cemetery, Huntsville. His widow wrote a famous memoir, *A Belle of the Fifties.*

Clayton, George Wesley. Born June 4, 1841, Asheville, NC. Attd. USMA 1857–61, resigning when NC seceded. Md. M. H. Johnston; Lillie McDowell. Appointed cadet, CS Regular Army, July 18, 1861 (under an often ignored law, no officer's commission could be given to a person under age 21). Lt. in Preston's SC Battery. Commissioned lt. and ADC to Gen. James Martin, July 1, 1862. Resigned Aug. 1, 1862, due to his election as lt. col. 62d NC, July 11, 1862. Col., Aug. 13, 1863. Clayton missed the Cumberland Gap surrender, due to typhoid fever, and led the unsurrendered remnant of the 62d thereafter. Dry goods merchant in Haywood Co. postwar. Died Feb. 22, 1898, Waynesville, NC. Buried Clayton family cemetery, near Asheville. An obituary said Clayton was "[q]uiet and modest in demeanor, fine of purpose, and fixed in principle."

Clifton, William Claiborne. Born March 1, 1834, Kershaw Dist., SC. Attd. USC. Planter in SC and Russell Co., AL. Md. Clara Jones. Capt. Co. E, 39th AL, April 20, 1862. Promoted to major, April 22, 1863. Lt. col., Oct. 12, 1863. WIA severely in battle of Atlanta. Col., Nov. 6, 1864. POW at Nashville, imprisoned at Johnson's Island. Paroled to become an agent forwarding clothes to Confederate prisoners. Postwar civil engineer. Lived in Columbus, GA, Pensacola and Marianna, FL. Died Dec. 18, 1902, Marianna. Buried Linwood Cemetery, Columbus.

Clinch, Duncan Lamont, Jr. Born Nov. 19, 1826, near Pensacola, FL, son of an army general. Reared in Camden Co., GA. Attd. UGA. Grad. UNC. Studied law in Augusta, GA. Wealthy planter in Camden Co. prewar. Capt., 13th US Inf. in Mexican War. Md. Susan A. Hopkins. Capt., May 31, 1861, and VADC to Gen. Lawton. Major, 3d GA Cav. Bn. (Clinch's), Feb. 24, 1862. Lt. col., July 31, 1862. Col., 4th GA Cav. (formed from his battalion), Jan. 16, 1863. WIA at Olustee (in thigh) and in the Atlanta Campaign. POW Dec. 10, 1864, near Savannah. Paroled May 6, 1865, Albany, GA. Camden Co. planter postwar. Died Oct. 28, 1890, Brunswick, GA. Buried Oak Grove Cemetery, Brunswick. Clinch's sister married Union Gen. Robert Anderson of Fort Sumter fame.

Cluke, Leroy Stuart. Born Dec. 30, 1824, Montgomery Co., KY. Commonly known as "Roy" Cluke. Grad. St. Joseph's College. Wealthy farmer in Clark Co. prewar. Mexican War veteran. Traded horses throughout the South. Md. Kate Kerr. Staff officer, KSG, 1861. Col., 8th KY Cav., Sept. 10, 1862. "[E]xtremely bold and tenacious." Captured July 26, 1863, Sabinsville, OH, during Morgan's Ohio Raid. Sent to Johnson's Island Prison. Died there of diphtheria, Dec. 31, 1863. Buried first in a family cemetery in Clark Co.; reinterred in Lexington Cemetery in 1891. A state marker is at the site of his Clark Co. home.

Cobb, John Probert. Born Nov. 23, 1834, Wayne Co., NC. Grad. UNC. Wayne Co. farmer prewar. Md. Sarah E. Whitfield. Lt. Co. H, 2d NC, May 16, 1861. Capt., May 10, 1862. WIA Malvern Hill, Chancellorsville, Cold Harbor. Col., Aug. 30, 1864. WIA (leg amputated) and POW Opequon Creek. Exch. March 1865. Wayne Co. farmer postwar. County clerk. Moved to Tallahassee, FL, in 1883. Died March 13, 1923, Tallahassee. Buried St. John's Episcopal Church, Tallahassee. Brother of Bryan W. Cobb, major, 2d NC.

Cobb, Norvell. Born c. 1824, Buckingham Co., VA. Hotel keeper in Buckingham Co. in 1850 and in Farmville, VA, in 1860. Militia officer. Md. Emma M. Howell. Capt. Co. G, 44th VA, June 1, 1861. Major, May 1, 1862. WIA Chancellorsville. Col., June 16, 1863. WIA Gettysburg. POW May 12, 1864, Spotsylvania. Exch. Aug. 3, 1864. Assigned to conscript duty, Oct.–Nov. 1864. Paroled April 15, 1865, Burkesville. Banker and insurance man in Prince Edward Co. in 1866. Managed hotels in Richmond and in Montgomery Co. Insurance agent in Washington, DC. Manager of the Alum Springs in Rockbridge Co., VA. Died Oct. 8, 1879, Rockbridge Co., accidentally shot while hunting.

Cochran, James Addison. Born Dec. 28, 1828, Augusta Co., VA. Attd. UVA. Farmer in Loch Willow prewar. Lt., "Churchville Cavalry." Md. Elizabeth Brooke; Nancy Crawford. Lt. Co. I, 14th VA Cav., May 13, 1861. Capt., May 15, 1862. Col.,

Feb. 12, 1863. Applied for retirement, Oct. 1864. Court-martialed Jan. 19, 1865, for disobeying orders, found guilty and fined. Augusta Co. farmer postwar. Later Culpeper lawyer, postmaster, newspaper editor. Died there Aug. 17, 1883. Buried Masonic Cemetery, Culpeper.

Cocke, John Benjamin. Born c. 1833, Madison Co., AL. Reared in Monroe Co., MS, and Monroe Co., AR. Lawyer in Clarendon, AR, in 1860. Md. Mahala S. Murrah, Nov. 7, 1861. 2d then 1st lt. Co. A, 15th AR, 1861. Appointed regimental commissary Aug. 27, 1861. Lt. Co. C, 39th (Cocke's) AR, June 29, 1862. Major, Nov. 4, 1862. WIA Helena. Col., Jan. 4, 1864. KIA Jenkins Ferry.

Cockrell, Jeremiah Vardeman. Born May 7, 1832, near Warrensburg, Johnson Co., MO. Attd. Chapel Hill College near Lexington, MO. To CA 1849–53. Prewar farmer in MO. Methodist preacher. Studied law. Md. Jane Douglass; Louisa Mayo. 2d lt. Co. E, 2d Cav., 8th Div., MSG, 1861. Capt. Co. A, 5th MO Inf. Bn., early 1862. Retired at May 24, 1862, reorganization. Col. of a newly raised partisan ranger regiment in western MO, July–Sept. 1862. Led this command at Lone Jack. Elected col. when the regiment originally organized but not reelected when the unit reorganized for Confederate service as the 7th MO. He spent the next year recruiting soldiers in MO and was WIA. In 1864 he accompanied Price's Raid in order to collect his family and take them South. Moved to Sherman, TX, postwar. Lawyer, farmer, and stock raiser. Judge. Chief justice of Grayson Co. US congressman 1893–97. Died March 18, 1915, Abilene, TX. Buried Abilene Municipal Cemetery. Gen. Jackman remembered him as "so true a Confederate, so brave in battle, and with so much goodness of soul." Brother of Gen. Francis M. Cockrell.

Cofer, Martin Hardin. Born April 1, 1832, Elizabethtown, KY. Prewar lawyer in Elizabethtown and (from 1853–56) IL. Newspaper editor. Capt., KSG, 1860–61. Md. Mary Bush. Lt. col., Cofer's KY Inf. Bn., Nov. 1, 1861. WIA severely at Shiloh. Lt. col., 6th KY (formed from his battalion), May 10, 1862. WIA Dec. 29, 1862. Lost race for Confederate Congress in 1863. Col., Sept. 30, 1863. Provost marshal, Army of TN, winter of 1863–64 and from Aug. 30, 1864. During Hood's retreat from Nashville, Cofer organized the crossing of the TN River. Paroled May 1, 1865, Greensboro. Attorney in Elizabethtown postwar. Chief justice, KY Supreme Court. Died in Frankfort May 22, 1881. Buried Elizabethtown Cemetery. A fellow soldier called Cofer "an officer of extraordinary merit. . . . His sense of order was remarkable."

Coffee, John Trousdale. Born Dec. 14, 1816, Smith Co., TN. Moved to MO in 1842. Resided in Springfield and Dade Co. Lawyer, newspaper editor. State senator and representative. Speaker of the MO House 1859–60. Mexican War veteran. Capt., US Army. Md. Eliza Stone; Catherine Hunt; Lavena Weir; Eunice

Vontress. Col., 6th Cav., 8th Div., MSG, probably elected July 4, 1861. Col. of a regiment of newly recruited MO Cav. (later the 6th/11th MO Cav.), 1862. Relieved of command in Nov. 1862 for drunkenness but acquitted on subsequent charges. Appointed col., June 1, 1864, by Gen. Kirby Smith, to raise a regiment of cavalry, but the regiment never fully organized. Signed oath of allegiance in Austin, TX, July 26, 1865. Moved to Georgetown, TX, postwar. Goat rancher. Died May 23, 1890, Brownsville, TX. Buried IOOF Cemetery, Georgetown. Gen. Jackman's memoirs have several amusing anecdotes on Coffee's alcoholism. Jackman asserts that, but for the drinking, the otherwise competent Coffee would have become a major general.

Colbert, Wallace Bruce. Born Nov. 17, 1834, MS. Grad. UAL 1852. Planter in Noxubee and Leake Cos., MS, prewar. Delegate to MS Secession Convention. Pvt. Co. E, 27th MS, April 27, 1861. 1st lt., Aug. 20, 1861. Col., 40th MS, May 14, 1862. Led Hebert's Brigade at Iuka and Corinth. POW Vicksburg. After exchange, led 40th in Atlanta and TN Campaigns. WIA Franklin. KIA Bentonville, March 21, 1865. Buried Oakwood Cemetery, Raleigh, NC.

Colcock, Charles Jones. Born April 30, 1820, Boiling Springs, Barnwell Co., SC. Raised in Charleston by his grandfather. Attd. College of Charleston. Charleston resident prewar. Planter, cotton broker, railroad director. Md. Mary C. Heyward; Lucy F. Horton; Agnes Bostick. 1st lt., "Charleston Mounted Guards," April 1861. Lt. col. of Martin's Regt. SC mounted militia, 1861–62. Capt., "Ashley Dragoons," Feb. 28, 1862. Lt. col., 8th SC Cav. Bn., May 1862. Col., 3d SC Cav. (formed from the 8th Bn.), Aug. 21, 1862. Regiment scattered in garrison along the SC coast for most of the war. Commanded 3d Military Dist. of SC, 1864. Second in command at Honey Hill. Planter in Hampton Co. postwar. Died Oct. 22, 1891, Elmwood Plantation, Hampton Co. Buried Stoney Creek Cemetery, near McPhersonville, Beaufort Co. Late in the war Gen. B. H. Robertson recommended Colcock for brigadier: "Eminently qualified . . . possesses striking military traits—enjoys high social position—is of unexceptionable moral character."

Coleman, Augustus Aurelius. Born May 21, 1826, Camden, SC. Grad. Yale 1844. Prewar lawyer in Sumter Co., AL. Md. Amanda Phares; Mary Stuart. Member, AL Secession Convention. Judge of 7th Judicial Circuit 1858–66. Left bench in 1862 to organize 40th AL. Elected col., 40th AL, May 16, 1862. Resigned April 30, 1863, due to illness ("chronic dysenteria") and returned to the bench. Lived in Greensboro and Birmingham postwar. Lawyer, judge, and state legislator. Died June 5, 1901, Birmingham. Buried Greensboro Cemetery.

Coleman, David. Born Feb. 5, 1824, Buncombe Co., NC. Grad. UNC and US Naval Academy. Midshipman, USN, retiring 1850. Attorney and state senator in

Buncombe Co. prewar. He lost a race for US Congress in 1858 to his cousin, future Gov. Zebulon Vance. Active secessionist. Unmd. Lt., NC State Navy, early 1861, commanding the steamer *Ellis*. Major of a battalion of infantry (later part of the 39th NC), Dec. 10, 1861. Lt. col., Feb. 16, 1862. Col., 39th NC, May 19, 1862, upon the organization of the regiment. Served in the Army of TN. WIA Stones River in leg and disabled. A "tall, slenderly built man of great natural ability" and "surpassing gallantry in the field," although one of his captains found him "drunk all the time." Paroled June 15, 1865, Shreveport. Buncombe Co. lawyer postwar. Delegate to 1875 NC constitutional convention. Died March 5, 1883, Asheville. Buried Riverside Cemetery, Asheville. Coleman was "crushed when the Confederacy failed" and ever after was apt to take long night walks alone, wearing his uniform.

Coleman, Henry Eaton. Born Jan. 5, 1837, Halifax Co., VA. Attd. William & Mary College and VMI. Farmer and civil engineer prewar, in Granville Co., NC. Md. Julia Logan. Capt. Co. B, 12th NC (a company his wealthy uncle equipped), April 26, 1861. Defeated for reelection at May 1, 1862, reorganization. VADC to Gen. Iverson, 1863. Appointed col., 12th NC, to rank from May 4, 1863. WIA Spotsylvania in head. Sent home to recover. While at home in June 1864 helped defend the Staunton River Bridge from Union raiders and received another wound. Returned to 12th in Aug. 1864. Surveyor postwar. Lived in Pittsylvania Co., VA, in 1880. Died June 25, 1890, Halifax Co., VA. Buried "The Oaks," south of Leeds, Halifax Co.

Coleman, Robert Lowry. Born Oct. 8, 1835, Buncombe Co., NC. Brother of Col. David Coleman and cousin of Col./Gov. Zebulon Vance. Farmer and clerk in Buncombe Co. prewar. Md. Victoria Rice. Pvt. Co. E, 1st NC (Bethel), April 24, 1861. Mustered out Nov. 12, 1861. Capt. and asst. commissary, 60th NC, Sept. 10, 1862. Post abolished by Congress July 31, 1863. Major, Commissary of Subsistence, Dist. of Western NC, Sept. 28, 1863. Col., 7th NC Cav., March 2, 1865. Civil engineer postwar, building mills in partnership with his father-in-law. On board of Weaverville College. Farmer in Union Co., SC, in 1880. Died May 27, 1898, Baltimore, where he had gone to Johns Hopkins for medical treatment. Buried Riverside Cemetery, Asheville. A "splendid soldier and a most excellent man."

Coleman, William Osborne. Born Jan. 12, 1837, near Elmira, NY. Lived in Bristol, IN; Baltimore; NY; IL; St. Louis; and Dent Co., MO, prewar. Carpenter and draftsman. Pvt., 2d US Dragoons, 1856–57. Filibusterer. Kansas "border ruffian." Md. Julia C. Jackson. Adj., 1st Inf., 7th Div., MSG, 1861. Col., 4th Cav., 7th Div., 1861. Raised Coleman's MO Cav. in 1862 and elected col. April 3, 1862. Appointed col. by Gen. Hindman June 18, 1862. Arrested July 31, 1862, for refusing to move his regiment out of MO and deprived of command. Partisan/ guerrilla in MO, 1863–64. Released from arrest Jan. 1, 1864. Col., 46th AR Mtd. Inf., 1864, but he relinquished this command to return to MO and recruit another regiment. Paroled Jacksonport, AR, June 1865. Lived in Little Rock, AR; OH; MS; Brownsville, TX; and Miami postwar. Printer in Little Rock. Manufacturer's agent. Farmer in TX. Died June 30, 1921, Dade Co., FL. Buried City Cemetery, Miami. Coleman often wrote of his life, not always with accuracy. Some letters of his are at the AR Historical Commission.

Collins, Charles Read. Born Dec. 7, 1836, PA. Attd. Georgetown U. Grad. USMA 1859. Lt. of engineers, US Army, 1859–61. Resigned June 10, 1861. Md. Susan Augusta Mason. Lt. of artillery, PACS, July 23, 1861. Capt. of Engineers, PACS, commissioned Oct. 7, 1861, to rank from March 16, 1861. Aide to Gens. Field and Smith, 1862. Engineering officer on Gen. Kershaw's staff, early 1863. Major, 15th VA Cav., April 29, 1863. Col., Feb. 28, 1864 (promoted for "valor and skill"). KIA Todd's Tavern, May 7, 1864. Buried St. John's Episcopal Churchyard, King George Court House. Gen. E. P. Alexander (who married a cousin of Collins's wife) said Collins "was superb and admirable, both in person and character, and universally popular."

Collins, Joseph. Born Sept. 12, 1837, New Orleans, LA. Attd. Spring Hill College in Mobile, AL. New Orleans businessman prewar, a partner in a cotton press firm. Md. Mrs. Ellen Minchen Budd; Josephine, sister of Col. T. D. Lewis. Capt. Co. I, 18th LA ("Orleans Cadets"), June 19, 1861. WIA Shiloh. Major, May 10, 1862. Lt. col., July 19, 1862. Col., April 8, 1864. Led Mouton's brigade in 1865. Paroled June 6, 1865, Natchitoches. Postwar worked as a cotton weigher and executive in the cotton business. Member of the New Orleans School Board. Died April 4, 1886, New Orleans. Buried Metairie Cemetery, in the Army of TN tomb. Gen. Polignac thought Collins had "great efficiency [and] excellent military ability."

Colms, Stephen H. Born Oct. 22, 1815, KY. Lawyer in Indianapolis, IN, and Sparta, TN, prewar. Md. Harriet B. Heale. Major, 1st (aka 20th) TN Bn., Jan. 1862. WIA and POW Fort Donelson. WIA Chickamauga. Col., 50th TN Consolidated, Feb. 24, 1864, upon consolidation of the battalion with the 50th. Assigned to post duty at Macon after the fall of Atlanta. Led force in Savannah Campaign. White Co. farmer postwar. Still suffering from war wounds, he committed suicide Dec. 18, 1874, at his home near Crossville, TN. Buried Old Sparta Cemetery. An old history of White County states that Colms "was limited in his literary qualifications but he had a winning personality."

Colquitt, John W. Born Oct. 28, 1840, Columbus, GA. Reared in La Grange, GA. Attd. GMI. Taught school prewar in Monticello, AR. Md. Mollie A. Bond;

Mollie Hudner. 3d lt. Co. I, 1st AR, May 8, 1861. Major, April 1, 1862. WIA Shiloh. Captured at Huntsville, AL, April 9, 1862, while on furlough but escaped the same day. Lt. col., 1862. Col., July 25, 1862. WIA Atlanta, losing his right foot. Disabled. Commanded post of West Point, MS, 1864–65. Retired March 3, 1865. Paroled May 17, 1865, Meridian. Lived in Monticello to 1881, then moved to Little Rock. Teacher. Drew Co. judge. Real estate agent. Pulaski Co. assessor. State land commissioner 1898–1902. Died Sept. 24, 1903, at his Little Rock home. Buried Oakland Cemetery, Little Rock, in his Confederate uniform. An obituary notes Colquitt "was widely known as a scholar and a gentleman." Half brother of Col. Peyton Colquitt.

Colquitt, Peyton Holt. Born Oct. 7, 1831, Campbell Co., GA. Reared in Columbus. Brother of Gen. Alfred Colquitt. Attd. USMA, class of 1853. Editor, Columbus *Standard*. Sec. of the GA Senate. State senator 1857–58. Officer in vol. militia. Md. Julia Hurt. Capt. Co. A, 2d GA Bn., April 20, 1861. Col., 46th GA, March 17, 1862. Commanded Gist's Brigade at the Battle of Jackson. MWIA Chickamauga, Sept. 20, 1863. Died Sept. 21. Buried Linwood Cemetery, Columbus, in 1866. A fellow colonel called Colquitt "one of the most brilliant young men in the commonwealth . . . a splendid physical specimen of a man."

Coltart, John Gordon. Born Jan. 27, 1826, Huntsville, AL. Huntsville bookseller, druggist, and insurance agent. Officer in vol. militia. Capt. Co. E, 3d (Coltart's) AL Bn., April 2, 1861. Lt. col., April 2, 1861. Lt. col., 7th AL (a 12-month unit), May 18, 1861. Col., Jan. 1862. Col., 26th AL, April 16, 1862. Detached because of regimental consolidation in early 1863 and put on conscription duty. Regiment redesignated the 50th, June 6, 1863. WIA Shiloh, Atlanta. Led D. H. Hill's division at Bentonville. Sheriff of Madison Co. 1866–67. Died April 16, 1868, at a lunatic asylum in Tuscaloosa. Buried Maple Hill Cemetery, Huntsville, in 1869.

Colvin, Charles Henry. Born March 25, 1831, Lowndes Co., AL. Prewar farmer in Lowndes Co. Md. Olive Pickett. Capt. Co. I, 1st AL Cav., 1861. Resigned Dec. 8, 1862, "having no command sufficient to justify my remaining in the regiment." Col., 6th AL Cav., May 1, 1863, upon organization of regiment. One of his men called Colvin "a gallant, efficient, and well beloved officer." Served in AL and GA, usually in Clanton's brigade, a unit widely believed to be composed of secret Unionists. Gen. Maury thought if the regiment was placed under Bedford Forrest "it would be useful and after the while will become patriotic, perhaps." Postwar farmer and dry goods merchant in Pike and Bullock Counties. Died Jan. 9, 1893, Woodlawn, AL (now a part of Birmingham). Buried McLaurine-Pickett Cemetery, near Union Springs, AL.

Connally, John Kerr. Born Sept. 3, 1839, Jackson, TN. Reared in Yadkin Co., NC. Attd. US Naval Academy. Md. Alice Thomas. Capt. Co. B, 21st NC, May 12, 1861. Col., 55th NC, May 19, 1862. WIA Gettysburg (arm amputated) and POW. Exch. March 1864. Assigned, due to ill health, to command a brigade of NC Junior Reserves in 1864. Resigned March 7, 1865, in a dispute over his status as a junior reserves officer. Paroled April 26, 1865, Richmond. Minister in Asheville, NC, and VA postwar. Died Jan. 31, 1904, Asheville. Buried Riverside Cemetery, Asheville. Gen. Pender thought Connally "a most conceited fellow."

Conner, Zephanier Turner. Born Jan. 30, 1807, Culpeper Co., VA. Moved to Macon, GA, in the 1830s. Land agent and commission merchant in Macon prewar. Officer in Seminole War and in vol. militia. Md. Louisa Godwin. Pvt. Co. A, 1st GA, March 15, 1861. Lt. col., 12th GA, July 2, 1861. Col., Dec. 3, 1861. Cashiered Nov. 18, 1862, for panicking and incompetence at Front Royal during the Valley Campaign. Farmed near Macon in 1864. Died April 30, 1866, at his home near Macon. Buried Rose Hill Cemetery, Macon. An officer of the 12th called Conner an "arrogant fop," though another soldier noted Conner was "an intelligent and excellent business man." Conner family papers are at the Middle GA Archives, Macon.

Conoley, John Francis. Born May 6, 1811, Robeson Co., NC. Moved to AL in 1833. Dallas Co. merchant, county sheriff, lawyer. Capt. during Creek War. Md. Mary Pitts. Lt. col., 4th Bn. AL Inf. (later 29th AL), Nov. 16, 1861. Col., 29th AL, Dec. 9, 1862. WIA Resaca by cannonball. Involved in defense of Selma while on sick leave in 1865. Paroled Selma May 31, 1865. Postwar judge and lawyer in Selma. Died Feb. 18, 1883, Selma, buried Live Oak Cemetery. Conoley felt aggrieved he was not made the original colonel of the 29th, a regiment he largely raised.

Cook, Edmund C. Born June 18, 1829, TN. Williamson Co. lawyer prewar. State representative 1855–57. Md. Eliza Maury. Capt. Co. D, 32d TN, 1861. Col., Oct. 28, 1861. POW Fort Donelson. To Fort Warren Prison. Exch. July 31, 1862. MWIA Kolb's Farm. Died June 23 (or 28), 1864. Buried Griffin, GA; reburied Rest Haven Cemetery, Franklin, TN. Gen. Bushrod Johnson recommended Cook for brigadier as a "fine organizer and disciplinarian [of] great coolness, skill and gallantry."

Cook, Gustave. Born July 3, 1835, Lowndes Co., AL. Family moved to Richmond, TX, in the 1850s. Prewar lawyer, judge. Md. Eliza Jones. Pvt., 8th TX Cav., enlisted Sept. 7, 1861. Promoted to sgt. Capt. Co. H, Jan. 9, 1862. Major, Feb. 12, 1863. Lt. col., June 25, 1863. Col., 1865 (probably Jan. 14). WIA Shiloh, Farmington, Buck Head Church, Bentonville. Postwar lawyer, state legislator, judge, in Richmond; Houston (from 1870); and San Marcos (from 1892). Died July 27, 1897, San Marcos. Buried San Marcos City Cemetery. Cook modestly admitted after the war that he "could have picked out a hundred men in the ranks of our command better qualified in every respect to command the regiment."

Cook, Joseph Jarvis. Born Dec. 1, 1826, near New Bern, NC. Reared in Pickens Co., AL. Grad. Annapolis, 1847. Midshipman, USN, resigning in 1851. Prewar farmer in Pickens Co. Moved to TX a few months before the war. Md. Melissa Dew. Capt. Co. A, 1st TX Art., July 3, 1861. Major, 3d TX Art. Bn., Sept. 13, 1861. Lt. col., Dec. 7, 1861. Col., 1st TX Art., April 28, 1862. Regiment part of the Galveston garrison for most of the war. Took oath of allegiance Aug. 1, 1865, Columbus, TX. Returned to his AL plantation after the war. Committed suicide Feb. 25, 1869, in Pickens Co. Buried Cook family cemetery, near Cochrane, Pickens Co., AL. A contemporary newspaper called him "a thoroughly educated soldier and accomplished gentleman."

Cooke, James Burch. Born April 1, 1819, Greenville, SC. Reared in McMinn Co., TN. Grad. UTN, 1843. Lawyer in Athens and Chattanooga prewar. State representative, 1851–55, and outspoken Unionist. Md. Doly P. McDermot. Capt. Co. A, 59th TN, Nov. 23, 1861. Col., Aug. 16, 1862. Resigned March 19, 1863, due to chronic diarrhea and liver disease. Refugeed in GA, then arrested in TN in 1864 while coming home to take the oath of allegiance. Lived in Huntsville, AL, 1865–67, then returned to Chattanooga. Lawyer. Justice, TN Supreme Court, 1884–86. Died April 18, 1899, Chattanooga. Buried Citizens Cemetery, Chattanooga.

Corns, James M. Born Dec. 25, 1830, Monmouthshire, Wales. Family came to the US when he was young. Educated in Heidelberg, Germany. Architect in Wayne Co., VA; PA; and OH prewar. Mexican War veteran. Md. Mary Ellen Glasgow; Laura Holland. Capt., "Sandy Rangers" (later merged with the "Fairview Rifle Guards," Co. K, 36th VA), May 28, 1861. Company disbanded Aug. 9, 1861. Col., 8th VA Cav., May 15, 1862. Resigned Feb. 4, 1865, a resignation accepted with delight by his superiors. Took oath of allegiance at Charleston, WVA, March 1, 1865. Imprisoned in the Dry Tortugas immediately after the war for his part in the wartime burning of Chambersburg, PA. Builder in Hallville and Kilgore, TX, postwar. Moved to Shreveport, LA, c. 1890. Died July 11, 1893, Shreveport, drowning in the Red River. Buried Oakland Cemetery, Shreveport. An 1864 inspection report called Corns "a drinking blackguard." Gen. Rosser considered Corns "a very poor officer," though his courage was beyond question.

Corpening, David Jackson. Born July 31, 1819, NC. Known as "Linville Jack" to distinguish him from other Corpening cousins. Farmer on the Linville River in Burke Co., NC, prewar. Md. Jane Horton. Sgt. Co. F, 3d NC Cav., Oct. 7, 1861. QM sgt., Dec. 17, 1861. Discharged June 11, 1862. Appointed AQM, July 28, 1863, to administer the tax in kind in NC's 9th Congressional Dist. Capt., Corpening's Co., NC Senior Reserves, July 13, 1864. Col., 5th NC Senior Reserves, Dec. 5, 1864. Paroled May 29, 1865, Morganton, NC. Burke Co. farmer postwar. Died July 4, 1870. Buried Corpening family cemetery, Morganton.

Corprew, Thomas Jefferson. Born July 4, 1830, Norfolk, VA. Prewar clerk in Norfolk and sheriff. Capt. of vol. militia. Lt. col., 6th VA, May 1, 1861. Col., Dec. 14, 1861. Dropped at May 3, 1862, reorganization. Probably the "Thomas J. Corprew" who was paroled at Appmx. as an agent of the subsistence department. Businessman and railroad executive in Norfolk postwar. City alderman. President of Dismal Swamp Canal Co. Died May 24, 1873, Norfolk. Buried Elmwood Cemetery, Norfolk.

Councell, Edward C. Born c. 1833, MD. Brick mason in Natchez prewar. Lt. Co. D, 16th MS, June 1, 1861. Capt., April 26, 1862. Major, Dec. 20, 1862. Col., May 12, 1864. MWIA and POW Weldon Railroad, Aug. 21, 1864. Died Sept. 10, 1864, at a Union army hospital in Alexandria, VA. Last name also spelled "Council."

Cowan, Robert Harper. Born Aug. 3, 1824, Wilmington, NC. Grad. UNC. Lumber manufacturer in Wilmington prewar. Delegate to NC Secession Convention. Md. Eliza Jane Dickinson. Lt. col., 3d NC, May 16, 1861. Col., 18th NC, April 26, 1862. WIA Seven Pines. Resigned Nov. 11, 1862, due to "congestion of the liver and chronic diarrhea." Elected president of the Wilmington, Charlotte & Rutherford RR in 1864. Railroad president postwar, residing in Wilmington. President of Wilmington Life Ins. Co. State representative 1866–67. Died Nov. 11, 1872, Wilmington, of the lingering effects of his Seven Pines wound. Buried Oakdale Cemetery.

Cowan, Robert Van Buren. Born May 26, 1840, NC. Reared in Statesville. Attd. USMA, resigning April 21, 1861. Capt. Co. A, 33d NC, May 23, 1861. Major, April 25, 1862. Lt. col., Aug. 5, 1862. WIA Chancellorsville (arm). Col., June 18, 1864. Postwar physician in Statesville. Died there March 5, 1877. Buried 4th Creek Presbyterian Church, Statesville. One report has him surrendering at Appmx. Another has him refusing to surrender and riding away.

Cowand, David George. Born March 1, 1835, Bertie Co., NC. Merchant in Washington Co. prewar. Md. Jane Jones. Sgt. Co. A, 32d NC, May 16, 1861. Sgt. major, Oct. 1861. Lt. col., June 18, 1863. Col., May 10, 1864. WIA Spotsylvania (lungs). Led a brigade Dec. 1864–March 1865. Appmx. Merchant in Norfolk and Berkeley, VA, postwar. Died May 2, 1884, Norfolk, of his war wounds. Buried

Oakwood Cemetery, Raleigh. A captain in the brigade thought Cowand lacked "mental capacity" but was likeable and brave. Another soldier found him "modest and gentle as a maiden."

Coward, Asbury. Born Sept. 19, 1835, Berkeley Dist., SC. Grad. SCMA. Co-founder (with future Gen. Micah Jenkins) of King's Mountain Military Academy in Yorkville. Md. Eliza L. Blum. On Gen. D. R. Jones's staff, 1861–62. Capt. and AAG, Aug. 15, 1861. Major, July 11, 1862. Col., 5th SC, Aug. 12, 1862. WIA Wilderness (arm). Appmx. Superintendent of King's Mountain 1866–86. State superintendent of instruction 1882–86. Superintendent of the Citadel from 1890. Died April 28, 1925, Rock Hill, SC. Buried Rock Hill Cemetery. A descendant published Coward's memoirs in 1968. They quote Gen. Robert E. Lee as saying of Coward, "I . . . have always considered him one of the best officers in the army."

Cox, John Threlkeld. Born Dec. 2, 1820, Washington, DC, son of the mayor of Georgetown, DC. Md. Julia Underwood, daughter of a US senator from KY. Moved to Bowling Green, KY. Civil engineer on railroads in KY and TN prewar. Capt., Confederate Engineers, 1861–62. Appointed Dec. 17, 1862 (parts of his confusing service record say Dec. 17, 1863, or June 6, 1863, to rank from Dec. 17, 1862, or May 22, 1863), col., 1st (aka 6th, 12th) Confederate Cav. He led the 1st with great distinction 1863–65, often commanding a brigade. In 1864 he requested promotion to brig. gen. to command a brigade of KY Cav., promising if promoted to cut Sherman's supply lines and (presumably) win the war. Paroled Gainsville May 22, 1865. After the war, his property in ruins, he returned to DC and worked as a detective on the DC police force. Died July 17, 1886, Old Point Comfort, VA. Buried Rock Creek Cemetery, DC. Often included in postwar lists of Confederate generals, though no record of such promotion exists.

Cox, Nicholas Nichols. Born Jan. 6, 1837, Bedford Co., TN. Reared in Seguin, TX. Grad. Cumberland U. Law School, 1858. Lived in AR, TX, and Linden, TN, prewar. Indian fighter on TX frontier. Lawyer in TN. Md. Mary Slayden. Capt. Co. C, 2d TN Cav. Bn., July 9, 1861. Promoted to major July 26, 1861, but left without a command when (in 1862) the battalion was consolidated into 6th TN Cav. Major of a PR battalion that he raised in the fall of 1862. POW Parker's Crossroads, exch. Jan. 1863. Col., 10th TN Cav. (formed from the battalion), upon its Feb. 25, 1863, organization. Resigned Dec. 23, 1863, citing "chronic articular rheumatism and incipient phthesis [sic]." Lawyer and farmer in Franklin, TN, postwar. US Congress 1891–1901. Died May 2, 1912, Franklin. Buried Mt. Hope Cemetery, Franklin.

Crabtree, John Wesley. Born Jan. 20, 1827, TN. Reared in Weakley Co., TN. Family moved to Prairie Co., AR, c. 1845. Prewar farmer in Franklin Co., AR.

Md. Sarah M. Stramler; Clementine Barber. Lt. Co. B, 36th AR, June 18, 1862. Assigned to duty as capt., Sept. 1862. "Displayed the greatest intrepidity" at Helena. Lt. col., 46th AR Mounted Infantry, 1864. Col., 1865. Paroled at Jacksonport, June 1865, as colonel. Postwar farmer in White Co. Died Feb. 14, 1876, Little Rock. Buried Bethesda Cemetery, White Co.

Crandall, Lee. Born May 11, 1832, New Berlin, NY. Prewar merchant in Alexandria, LA. Editor of a Unionist newspaper. Unsuccessful candidate to the Secession Convention. Md. Sophia A. Clark; Hattie Giers. Capt. Co. I, 8th LA (the "Rapides Invincibles"), May 21, 1861. WIA Port Republic. Commissioned major of cav., Feb. 14, 1863, to raise a battalion of cavalry in MO and AR. Col., 47th AR Mounted Infantry, 1864. Led regiment in Price's Raid. WIA and POW Mine Creek, sent to Johnson's Island Prison Camp. Released June 30, 1865. Lived in LA; Morgan Co., AL; and Philadelphia postwar. Newspaper reporter. Published the *National View* in Washington, DC, 1879–84. National secretary of the Greenback Party. Moved to AZ and founded a mining company. Still later returned to DC and worked as a collector for Internal Revenue. Active in UCV. Died Sept. 12, 1926, DC. Buried Arlington National Cemetery. Jeff Thompson recalled that Crandall had a great facility at "spread eagle" (exaggeration).

Craton, Marshall David. Born May 21, 1829, Rutherford Co., NC. Attd. USMA. Physician in Rutherfordton prewar. Md. Margaret Washington. Capt. Co. A, 27th NC, April 15, 1861. Lt. col., 35th NC, Nov. 8, 1861. Resigned April 11, 1862. Col., 50th NC, April 15, 1862. Resigned Dec. 1, 1862, due to diarrhea and dysentery. Goldsboro businessman postwar. Died May 27, 1866. Buried Rutherfordton City Cemetery. One congressman said Craton had "decided intellect, and good habits."

Cravens, Jordan Edgar. Born Nov. 7, 1830, Fredericktown, MO. Reared in Logan Co., AR. Attd. Cane Hill academy. Prewar lawyer in Clarksville, AR. Prospected for gold in CA 1850–51. State representative 1860–61. Md. Emily Batson. On Gov. Rector's staff, early 1861. Volunteer soldier at Wilson's Creek and WIA there. Pvt. Co. C, 17th AR, Nov. 18, 1861. Major, April 24, 1862. Col., 21st AR (formed from the 17th), May 14, 1862. POW Big Black River May 17, 1863. To Johnson's Island. Exch. March 18, 1864. Col., 1st AR Consolidated, in TMD, fall of 1864. Postwar Clarksville lawyer. Judge, state senator, US congressman. Died April 8, 1914, Fort Smith. Buried Oakland Cemetery, Clarksville.

Crawford, Anderson Floyd. Born Jan. 29, 1829, Sparta, GA. Reared in De Soto Parish, LA. Attd. UGA. Planter in LA and Jasper Co., TX. State senator in TX. Md. Elizabeth Aiken. Pvt. Co. G, 13th TX Cav., enlisted March 1, 1862. Lt. col., April 17, 1862. Col., promoted April 22, 1864. Often led a brigade. Called a "worthy officer" by his superior officer. Postwar Jasper Co. farmer. Died Jan. 10, 1867, Keachie, LA, of pneumonia.

Crawford, James. Born Jan. 18, 1807, Winnsboro, SC. To Mobile, AL, in 1827. Commission merchant. Capt. of vol. militia and capt. in Mexican War. Md. Zemula Creswell. Elected capt. "Woodruff Rifles," 1861. Col., 2d AL volunteers (a 90-day militia regiment), July 22, 1861. Regiment organized for Confederate service as the 21st AL, Oct. 13, 1861. Resigned May 1, 1862, due to ill health. Postwar Mobile merchant. Died Sept. 29, 1881, Sweet Springs, MO. Buried Magnolia Cemetery, Mobile.

Crawford, John Hammer. Born July 9, 1814, TN. Prewar Jonesboro resident. Clerk of Washington County Court. Militia officer. Md. Susan Blair; Brunetta J. Earnest. Col., 60th TN, Oct. 1, 1862. POW Vicksburg. Resigned Oct. 25, 1864, citing old age and rheumatism. Farmer in Washington Co. and in Tarrant Co., TX, postwar. Died Jan. 24, 1894, near Fort Worth, TX. Buried Forest Hill Cemetery, Forest Hill, TX.

Crawford, Martin Jenkins. Born March 17, 1820, Jasper Co., GA. Attd. Mercer U. Lawyer in Hamilton and (from 1849) Columbus, GA. Judge. State representative. US congressman 1855–61. Md. Mary C. Crook; Amanda Reese. Confederate commissioner to Pres. Buchanan in 1861. Col., 3d GA Cav., May 28, 1862. POW (along with most of his regiment) at New Haven, KY, Sept. 29, 1862. Paroled. Upon return, court-martialed for allowing his regiment to be surprised and sentenced to 3 months' loss of pay and a reprimand. Resigned March 13, 1863, citing "physical incapacity to discharge the very onerous duties devolving upon a cavalry officer." VADC to Gen. Howell Cobb in the GA Reserves in 1864. Columbus lawyer postwar. Judge of the GA Supreme Court. Died July 23, 1883, Columbus. Buried Linwood Cemetery. Gen. Bragg thought Crawford "intelligent, conscientious and patriotic."

Crawford, William Ayres. Born June 24, 1825, Washington Co., TN. Moved to Saline Co., AR, in 1844. Farmer, county sheriff, state legislator. Mexican War veteran. Md. Sarah Henslee. Lt. Co. E, 1st AR, April 1861. Capt., May 8, 1861. WIA Shiloh. Resigned July 23, 1862. Lt. col., Crawford's Bn. AR Cav., 1862 (perhaps May 18). Col., 1st (Crawford's) AR Cav, Dec. 30, 1863. Led cavalry brigade in 1864. Paroled as col. June 26, 1865. Lived in Saline Co. postwar. Ferry operator. General of state militia in Brooks-Baxter war. Died June 22, 1874, Benton, AR, of lung disease. Buried Lee Cemetery, near Benton. Some Crawford papers are at the AR Historical Commission. An obituary called him one of Arkansas's "truest and very bravest, most devoted sons."

Crawley, William James. Born Nov. 6, 1833, Barnwell Dist., SC. Grad. SCMA. Teacher and farmer in the Barnwell Dist. prewar. Md. Matilda Todd.

Capt. Co. D, Holcombe Legion, Dec. 8, 1861. Lt. col., Dec. 5, 1862. WIA June 29, 1864 (shot through the liver) and disabled. Col., Sept. 28, 1864. Attempted to return to regiment in Feb. 1865 but was unable to perform his duties. Retired to Invalid Corps March 8, 1865. Farmer in Columbia, McDuffie, and Berrien Cos., GA, postwar. McDuffie Co. surveyor, 1893–1900. Died Feb. 8, 1902, near Thomson, GA. Buried Wrightsboro Methodist Church.

Creasman, William Burton. Born 1825, Yancey Co., NC. Farmer and cabinet maker in Yancey Co. prewar. Md. Joyce C. Wheeler. Capt. Co. B, 29th NC, July 3, 1861. Major, June 26, 1862. Lt. col., March 16, 1863. Col., Sept. 8, 1863. Resigned Dec. 29, 1864. Lived near Asheville postwar. Died July 9, 1869, NC. Buried Bethel Baptist Church Cemetery, Buncombe Co.

Crews, Charles Constantine. Born Sept. 3, 1829, Harris Co., GA. Brother of Lt. Col. J. M. Crews, 58th TN. Grad. Castleton Medical College in VT in 1853. Physician in Cuthbert, GA, prewar. Md. Ophelia Smith; Martha Hampton in 1869. Appointed ensign of a company of local cavalry Jan. 10, 1861. Promoted to 2d lt., Oct. 1861. Enlisted in the Confederate army March 4, 1862. Capt. Co. C, 2d GA Cav., May 7, 1862. POW Sept. 30, 1862, Glasgow, KY. Col., Nov. 1, 1862. WIA in the hip in the attack on Dover, TN, Jan. 3, 1863. WIA in the Carolinas Campaign. Often led a brigade of cavalry, 1863–65, in Wheeler's Corps. Particularly distinguished himself during Stoneman's Andersonville Raid. Paroled May 3, 1865, Charlotte, NC. General agent for a railroad, living in Bainbridge, GA, after the war. Moved to TX in the 1870s, then to Hillsboro, NM. Physician. Mine owner in NM. Died Nov. 14, 1887, Hillsboro. Buried Hillsboro Cemetery. Crews is one of three colonels (James Hagan and Moses Hannon being the others) said by Gen. Wheeler, his corps commander, to have been promoted to gen. in 1865.

Crittenden, Robert Flournoy. Born Nov. 5, 1837, Talbot Co., GA. Teacher in Schley Co., GA, in 1860. To Coffee Co., AL. Teacher and lawyer. Md. Frances Reid. 2d lt. Co. F, 33d AL, March 14, 1862. Capt. Co. I, April 1862. Major, April 23, 1862, upon organization of regiment. Lt. col., Aug. 23, 1862. Col., July 21, 1864. POW Franklin. Moved to Randolph Co., GA in 1869. Farmer, merchant, state legislator. Died March 2, 1914, at his home in Shellman. Buried Rehoboth Baptist Church, Randolph Co.

Crockett, Robert Hamilton. Born Feb. 15, 1832, Paris, TN. Grandson of famous frontiersman Davy Crockett. Attd. KMI. Lawyer in Memphis and DeWitt Co., AR. Editor, Memphis *Eagle*. Filibusterer. Md. Sallie Lewis; Mary Lewis. Capt. Co. H (the "Crockett Rifles"), 1st AR, May 19, 1861. Major, 18th AR, April 2, 1862. Lt. col., probably Sept. 1, 1862. Col., Oct. 4, 1862. Second to Gen. Walker in the famous Marmaduke-Walker duel. Provost marshal at Washington, AR,

1865. Postwar lawyer in Arkansas Co. State senator 1885–88. Died Feb. 18, 1902, at his home in Stuttgart, AR. Buried Lone Tree Cemetery, Arkansas Co. A fellow lawyer found Crockett "overflowing with life, redundant with superabundant vitality."

Crook, David Crockett. Born May 27, 1837, TN. Attd. Emory & Henry College. Farmer in Cumberland Co., TN, prewar. Md. Sarah Hanna Turner. Capt. Co. A, 28th TN, Aug. 6, 1861. Elected major at May 8, 1862, reorganization. Lt. col., Oct. 13, 1862. Col., Jan. 2, 1863. Regiment consolidated with 84th TN, March 8, 1863, with Crook lt. col. of the new 28th Consolidated. Col., May 13, 1864. WIA Ezra Church. Farmer in White Co., TN, postwar. Moved to Morgan and later Bullock Cos., AL. Methodist minister in AL. Died March 8, 1891, Bullock Co. Buried Enon Cemetery, Bullock Co.

Cross, David C. Born Aug. 27, 1811, near Winston, NC. Moved to TN in 1835 and to AR in the 1840s. Wealthy planter in Poinsett Co., AR, in 1860, with a net worth of $300,000 and 83,000 acres of land. Md. Mrs. Catherine Duerson. Col., 5th AR, July 27, 1861. Missed Shiloh, being ill with pneumonia. Not reelected at 1862 reorganization. Received medical discharge, May 12, 1862. Lived in Cross Co. (a new county named after him) and Memphis postwar. Farmer and railroad president. Died Aug. 21, 1874, on a visit to Cross Co. Buried at the Wilkins farm, south of Wynne, in Cross Co. An old local history called him a "generous-spirited, influential gentleman of the old school, possessing exalted ideas."

Crossland, Edward. Born June 30, 1827, Hickman Co., KY. Farmer and lawyer in Clinton, Hickman Co., prewar. County sheriff. State representative. Md. Mary Hess. Capt. Co. E, 1st KY (a 12-month unit), April 23, 1861. Major, Dec. 1, 1861. Lt. col., April 19, 1862. Col., 7th KY, May 25, 1862. Regiment mounted in 1864. Led brigade in Forrest's cavalry, with great distinction. WIA Paducah, Tupelo, and Butler's Creek (Nov. 21, 1864). Paroled May 26, 1865, Columbus, MS. Attorney in Mayfield, Graves Co., KY, postwar. Judge. US congressman. Died Sept. 11, 1881, Mayfield. Buried Maplewood Cemetery, Mayfield. The historian of the Orphan Brigade found Crossland "as plain as the proverbial 'old shoe' and an accomplished gentleman."

Crump, Charles Alfred. Born Aug. 16, 1822, Powhatan Co., VA. Attd. VMI. Schoolteacher in Burkeville Junction. Merchant in Burkeville and Richmond. State representative 1859–61. Militia colonel. Md. Mollie Miller. Lt. col., 16th VA, May 1861. Col., 26th VA, July 1861. Dropped at May 13, 1862, reorganization. Rejoined the 16th VA as col., Aug. 28, 1862. KIA 2d Manassas, Aug. 30, 1862, by a bullet through the neck. A "high toned, open hearted Virginian." Buried Haymarket, Prince William Co. Brother of Col. R. P. Crump.

Crump, Richard Philip. Born Jan. 1824, Powhatan Co., VA. Brother of Col. Charles Crump. Attd. USMA. To TX in 1842. Lived at Clarksville and Jefferson. Sheriff, saloon keeper, riverboat owner. Md. Martha Hughes; Cynthia C. Hughes. Major, 1st TX Cav. Bn., Nov. 4, 1861. Not reelected in May 1862 reorganization, despite a reputation for being "brave as a lion." Lt. col., 1st TX PR, c. 1862. Col., Oct. 28, 1864. Paroled June 23, 1865, Marshall. Prominent reconstruction opponent. Arrested for lynching a "loyal league" leader in Jefferson but found not guilty. Died Oct. 14, 1869, Jefferson, buried Oakwood Cemetery.

Crutchfield, Stapleton. Born June 21, 1835, Spring Forest, Spotsylvania Co., VA. Grad. VMI 1855 with first honors. Professor of math and tactics at his alma mater 1855–61. Drilled students at UVA, spring 1861. Capt., PAVA, May 17, 1861. Major of artillery, PAVA, July 1861. Major, 9th VA, July 7, 1861. Major, 58th VA, Oct. 1, 1861. Lt. col., March 1, 1862. Dropped at May 1862 reorganization. Elected col., 16th VA, May 3, 1862, but declined. Appointed col. and chief of artillery, the Valley Dist., May 6, 1862. Chief of artillery for Stonewall Jackson, his friend and colleague at VMI. Lost leg at Chancellorsville. Taught at VMI while recovering. Assigned to duty inspecting seacoast batteries, March 16, 1864. Ordered back to the ANV Jan. 18, 1865. Commanded a brigade of heavy artillery. KIA Sayler's Creek. Buried on the battlefield in an unknown grave. Gen. E. P. Alexander thought Crutchfield "a most excellent officer"; a fellow staff officer found Crutchfield "competent but lazy."

Culberson, David Browning. Born Sept. 29, 1830, Troup Co., GA. Attd. Brownwood Institute in La Grange, GA. Lawyer in Dadeville, AL, 1851–56. Then moved to Upshur Co., TX. Lawyer. State representative 1859–61. Md. Eugenia Kimball. Enlisted as pvt. Lt. col., 18th TX Cav., May 13, 1862. Col., Feb. 23, 1863. Resigned Aug. 10, 1863, due to ill health, which kept him absent from the regiment "nearly all the time." Adj. gen. of TX, 1863–64. State representative 1864–65. Postwar Jefferson, TX, lawyer. US congressman 1875–96. Died May 7, 1900, Jefferson, buried Oakwood Cemetery.

Cullen, Matthew Robinson. Born Nov. 13, 1828, Richmond, VA. Attd. VMI and Georgetown U. Prewar lawyer in Staunton, VA; Chicago; and St. Louis. Active in pro-secessionist "minute men" in St. Louis. Md. Winona Barbour in 1866. Clerk in Confederate War Dept. (due to lameness, he was incapable of field duty) 1862–64. Col., Feb. 9, 1864, to be judge of the military court, TMD. Postwar St. Louis lawyer. Judge. Commissioner for US Circuit Court. Died Feb. 14, 1893, St. Louis, buried Bellefontaine Cemetery. According to an obituary, Cullen earned a "reputation for severity, being universally known as the 'Terrible Judge.'" Another newspaper called him "a profound, energetic and sagacious lawyer."

Cumby, Robert H. Born Aug. 24, 1824 (some sources say 1825), Charlotte Co., VA. Reared in Lafayette Co., MS. Planter in MS and (after 1849) Rusk Co., TX. State representative 1859–61. Md. Nancy Zollicoffer. Formed a company of infantry, May 7, 1861. Capt. Co. B, 3d TX Cav. (his old company, now mounted), June 13, 1861. Showed "great gallantry" at Pea Ridge. Col., May 20, 1862 (elected on regiment's reorganization). Resigned June 12, 1862, due to chronic diarrhea. Appointed major and chief of staff to Gen. Greer, May 2, 1863. Brig. gen., 4th Brigade, TX State Troops, 1864–65. Postwar grocer in Sulphur Springs. Died Nov. 19, 1881, Sulphur Springs. Buried City Cemetery, Sulphur Springs. The town of Cumby, TX, is named after him.

Cumming, John B. Born c. 1823, GA. Town marshal in Macon, GA, prewar. Officer in vol. militia. Sgt. in Mexican War. Md. Sarah A. Cook. Capt. Co. A, 20th GA, May 17, 1861. Lt. col., Sept. 5, 1861. Col., March 7, 1862. Resigned May 29, 1863, due to atrophy of his left leg, and returned to Macon. Col., 5th GA Reserves, June 8, 1864. Paroled April 1865, Macon. Police chief of Macon postwar. Doorkeeper of GA Senate, 1873–77. Died Aug. 4, 1880, at his Macon home. Buried Rose Hill Cemetery. Staff officer McHenry Howard found Cumming "an easy going, reckless fellow, sociable with privates as with his equals in rank, often entertaining us with his cock fighting reminiscences."

Cummings, Arthur Campbell. Born Oct. 1, 1822, near Abingdon, VA. Grad. VMI. Lawyer in Washington Co. Capt. and brevet major, 11th US Inf., in Mexican War. Militia colonel. Md. Elizabeth Preston. Col., 33d VA, July 1, 1861. He led a decisive assault at 1st Manassas, capturing two Union batteries. Dropped at 1862 reorganization, refusing to stand for reelection due to unpopularity with the men (he was too much the disciplinarian) and conflict with Stonewall Jackson. In state legislature 1863–65. Capt., Abingdon Home Guards. Abingdon lawyer, farmer postwar. State representative 1871–73. Died March 19, 1905, at his Abingdon home. Buried Sinking Springs Cemetery, Abingdon. A "very efficient officer."

Cummings, David H. Born April 18, 1818, Washington Co., VA. Attd. UTN. Lawyer in Anderson Co., TN, prewar. Dist. attorney. Wealthy farmer. Lt. col. in Mexican War and WIA at Cerro Gordo. Md. Ann Amelia Preston. Col., 19th TN, June 10, 1861. WIA Shiloh. Not reelected at May 1862 reorganization and dropped as of May 14. Cotton factor in New Orleans postwar, partnering with his brother. Died Dec. 28, 1867, of cholera, on a steamboat on the Red River near Shreveport, LA. Buried in LA; reburied Young-Cummings Cemetery at "Eagle Bend," near Clinton, Anderson Co.

Cummings, Pleasant Wear Harvey. Born Aug. 16, 1836, MO. Prewar merchant in Pineville, McDonald Co., MO. Md. Margaret Gilmer. Capt. Co. D, 6th

Cav., 8th Div., MSG, Sept. 28, 1861. Resigned Dec. 10, 1861. Capt., Cockrell's/ Jackman's regiment of recruits. Major, 16th (aka 7th) MO, Aug. 31, 1862. Lt. col., March 24, 1863. Col., probably May 16, 1865. Paroled as col. in Shreveport, LA, June 1865. Postwar merchant in Shreveport. Died Sept. 8, 1889, Shreveport. Buried Oakland Cemetery, Shreveport. Gen. Jackman called Cummings "one of the bravest men on earth."

Cunningham, Columbus J. L. Born Aug. 11, 1829, GA. Studied law in Tuskegee, AL. Prewar newspaper editor and lawyer in Macon and Pike Cos., AL. Md. Harriet Hamilton. 2d lt. Co. E, 1st AL, March 4, 1862. Resigned July 29, 1862, to take care of his family after his wife had become "partially demented." Major, 57th AL, April 13, 1863. Col., Dec. 26, 1863. WIA Franklin. Postwar lawyer, judge in Union Springs, AL. Editor in Jasper, AL. Later moved to live with his son in Dallas, TX. Died Nov. 10, 1908, Union Springs. Buried Oak Hill Cemetery, Union Springs. Cunningham's service record contains numerous requests for leave to care for his children.

Cunningham, Preston Davidson. Born March 10, 1839, Jackson Co., TN. Attd. Berrit College. Jackson Co. farmer. Md. Mary Sweeney. Pvt. Co. E, 28th TN, enlisting Sept. 28, 1861. Lt. and regimental adj., Sept. 30, 1861. WIA Shiloh. Major, April 9, 1862. Lt. col., May 8, 1862. Col., Oct. 13, 1862. MWIA Stones River, Dec. 31, 1862. Died Jan. 2, 1863. Buried Cunningham cemetery near his home in Jackson Co. A fellow colonel called Cunningham "a gentleman of ability and a most gallant soldier."

Curry, Jabez Lamar Monroe. Born June 5, 1825, Lincoln Co., GA. Grad. UGA. Attd. Law School at Harvard. Prewar lawyer in Talladega Co., AL. State legislator. Pvt. in Mexican War. US congressman 1857–61. Md. Ann A. Bowie; Mary Wortham. Confederate Congress, 1861–63. Defeated for reelection. Lt. col., 5th AL Cav., 1864–65. Appointed col., March 23, 1865, to be judge of military court of Valley Cav. Corps, but Curry was serving in AL at the time and never took this post. Paroled May 16, 1865, Talladega. Postwar he taught at Richmond College, became a Baptist preacher, and helped establish school systems throughout the South. US minister to Spain 1885–88. Authored "Legal Justification of the South in Secession" for the *Confederate Military History.* Died Feb. 12, 1903, Asheville, NC. Buried Hollywood Cemetery, Richmond.

Curtis, William Ezra. Born 1827, GA. "Tinsmith" in Carrollton, Carroll Co., in 1860. County justice. Officer in Mexican War. Md. Mary L. Conyers. Capt. Co. F, 19th GA, June 11, 1861. Lt. col., 41st GA, March 20, 1862. Col., Oct. 31, 1862. POW Vicksburg and paroled. MWIA Feb. 25, 1864, in an action at Mill Creek Gap, GA. Died March 24, 1864, Coweta Co. Buried Carrollton City Cemetery. Curtis's last wish was that he be buried facing north and facing the enemy.

Cutts, Allen Sherrod. Born Dec. 4, 1826, Pulaski Co., GA. Merchant and planter in Americus, GA, prewar. County sheriff. Sgt., US Army, 1846–51. Mexican War veteran. Militia general. Md. Fannie O. Brown. Capt., Sumter Flying Artillery (Co. A, 11th Bn., GA Art.), July 6, 1861. Major, May 22, 1862. Lt. col., May 26, 1862. Col., Feb. 27, 1864, promoted by the sec. of war to command division artillery in the 3d Corps, ANV. Pres. Davis declined to nominate Cutts, finding there was no vacancy for Cutts to fill. Cotton planter near Americus postwar. Mayor of Americus. State legislator. Died March 17, 1896, Americus. Buried Oak Grove Cemetery, Americus. Gen. Pendleton recommended Cutts for promotion because, "although not of polished education," he was "a man of uncommonly strong intellect & character . . . of tried courage & self possession in action."

Daly, John N. Born c. 1832, TN. Reared in Montgomery Co., TN. Grad. Cumberland U., 1851. Prewar lawyer in TN and (from about 1856) Ouachita Co., AR. "[A]n upright man and Mason." Md. Anne W. Carter; Mary Ann McCollum. Pvt. Co. H, 18th AR, March 15, 1862. Capt., March–April 1862. Lt. col., April 2, 1862. Col., Sept. 1, 1862. MWIA Oct. 4, 1862, at the Battle of Corinth and left on the battlefield. Died Oct. 5. Probably buried on the battlefield.

Daniel, Charles Powell. Born Aug. 28, 1839, GA. Farmer in 1860 in Spalding Co., working for his father, a prominent and wealthy planter. Md. Anna E. Blanton. 1st sgt. Co. B ("Griffin Light Guards"), 5th GA, May 10, 1861. Capt., Feb. 20, 1862. Major, May 8, 1862. Col., Dec. 31, 1862. WIA three times at Missionary Ridge. Paroled May 1, 1865, Greensboro. Dry goods merchant in Fayette Co. postwar. Died March 4, 1902, Atlanta, where he had come for treatment of a stomach cancer. Buried Oak Hill (Griffin City) Cemetery.

Daniel, James Jacquelin. Born Aug. 14, 1832, Columbia, SC. Family moved to FL in 1846. Prewar sawmill owner, surveyor, then lawyer in Jacksonville, FL. Pvt. in vol. militia. Md. Emily L'Engle. Pvt., "Jacksonville Light Infantry," Jan. 10, 1861. Capt., "St. Johns Grays" (later Co. G, 2d FL), May 9, 1861. Relieved May 11, 1862, due to illness. Commissioned capt. and QM, Oct. 4, 1862, and assigned to the Conscription Bureau at the Tallahassee camp of instruction. Promoted to major and asst. commandant of the FL conscript camps, Nov. 23, 1863, with headquarters at Madison. Col., 1st FL Reserves, elected Jan. 5, 1865. Led his regiment at Natural Bridge, where he was injured by a runaway horse. Paroled Madison, May 16, 1865. Postwar Jacksonville lawyer, civic leader. Railroad president. Died Oct. 4, 1888, Jacksonville, of yellow fever. Buried Evergreen Cemetery. A death notice called him "everybody's friend."

Dantzler, Olin Miller. Born Jan. 14, 1825, St. Matthews, Orangeburg Dist., SC. Grad. Randolph-Macon College. Orangeburg planter prewar. State legislator 1852–62. Md. Caroline A. Glover; Caroline E. Treutlen. 3d lt. Co. D, 1st (Hagood's) SC (later Co. F, 25th SC), July 20, 1861. 2d lt., Nov. 1861. Resigned Jan. 11, 1862. Lt. col., 20th SC, Jan. 11, 1862. Col., April 29, 1864. KIA June 2, 1864, during a probe of Union lines at Bermuda Hundred. Buried Hollywood Cemetery, Richmond; reburied Tabernacle Methodist Churchyard, St. Matthews. An obituary called Dantzler "a model officer and colonel."

Darnell, Nicholas Henry. Born April 20, 1807, Williamson Co., TN. Prewar lawyer, farmer. State legislator in TN. Moved to San Augustine, TX, in 1838; to Dallas in 1858. TX congressman. Mexican War veteran. Texas Ranger. Md. Isabella Cozart. State House speaker in 1861. Col., 18th TX Cav., March 15, 1862. Resigned Nov. 1864 due to bronchitis. Postwar Tarrant Co. resident. State representative. Doorkeeper of the State House. Prominent Mason. Died July 10, 1885, Fort Worth. Buried Masonic Cemetery, Dallas. In the words of an obituary, Darnell was a "[n]oble patriot, generous friend."

Davidson, Thomas Jefferson. Born c. 1819, TN. Merchant and contractor in Ripley, Tippah Co., MS, prewar and recommended for federal appointment as "honest, capable and faithful." Sheriff. Veteran of Florida and Seminole Wars. Md. Mary Harbin. Capt. and AQM 11th MS, April 27, 1861. Col., 23d MS, Sept. 5, 1861. Led brigade at Fort Donelson, where he was captured. Died April 29, 1862, in the Fort Warren Prison in Boston Harbor, of illness. Buried Hollywood Cemetery, Richmond.

Davidson, William Lee. Born Feb. 10, 1825, "Oak Lawn" plantation, Mecklenburg Co., NC. Attd. Davidson College (which his family had founded). Charlotte merchant prewar. Mexican War veteran. Md. Anne Irvine Pagan in 1870. Capt. Co. D, 7th NC, May 16, 1861. Major, Feb. 24, 1863. Lt. col., May 3, 1863. WIA Chancellorsville. WIA and POW Wilderness. Exch. Aug. 3, 1864. Col., Nov. 28, 1864. Paroled May 15, 1865, Charlotte. Lawyer and clerk for various railroads postwar, living in KY, TN, Lincolnton, NC, Chester and Spartanburg, SC, postwar. Died Aug. 13, 1899, Chester, SC. Buried St. Luke's Episcopal Cemetery, Lincolnton, NC. Davidson's Union captors thought they had captured Gen. Longstreet, whom Davidson strongly resembled.

Davie, James Madison. Born Dec. 13, 1830, Pearson Co., NC. Reared in Madison Co., TN. Grad. Jefferson Medical College in Philadelphia. Prewar physician in TN and White Co., AR. Md. Emma Bowling; Caroline Bowling; Mrs. Sally Thomas Hinson. Capt. Co. A, 36th (aka 28th) AR, June 24, 1862. Major, Nov. 5, 1862. WIA Prairie Grove and Helena. Col., Oct. 24, 1863. Regiment plagued with desertions. Postwar farmer and physician in Beebe, White Co. Died Jan. 25, 1911. Buried Beebe Cemetery.

Davis, Bennett Hillsman. Born Feb. 5, 1832, Somerville, TN. Attd. Centre College, KY. Grad. Hanover College in IN. Brenham, TX, lawyer. Md. Ruth Wilson. Pvt. Co. B, 8th TX Cav., Sept. 17, 1861. Promoted to ordnance sgt. Appointed capt. and acting OO to Gen. Wharton Nov. 18, 1862, but never commissioned as such. Appointed col., March 23, 1865, to serve as judge of the military court of Wharton's Corps. Move to Bryan, TX, in 1866; to El Paso in 1881. Lawyer. Member of 1875 constitutional convention. Died May 20, 1897, El Paso. Buried Evergreen Cemetery, El Paso. An obituary called him "a noble specimen of American manhood."

Davis, Champion Thomas Neal. Born June 16, 1827, Halifax Co., VA. Lawyer in Burke Co., NC, prewar. State senator 1854–56. Moved to Rutherfordton and elected to House of Commons. Whig/Know Nothing Party leader. Md. Mira E. McDowell; Eliza Nixon. Capt. Co. G, 16th NC, May 9, 1861. Col., April 26, 1862. KIA May 31, 1862, Seven Pines. Davis has a memorial stone at Oakdale Cemetery, Wilmington: he may actually be buried in Hollywood Cemetery, Richmond. Lauded in a newspaper obituary as "gallant and glorious."

Davis, James Lucius. Born Jan. 25, 1816, Clarke Co., VA. Grad. USMA 1833. Lt., US Army, 1833–36. Prewar farmer in the Shenandoah Valley and in Henrico Co., VA. Texas Ranger 1839–41. Militia colonel. Md. Frances A. T. Berkeley; Elizabeth Harriet Peck. Col., 46th VA (part of the Wise Legion), June 24, 1861, but he never actually led the regiment, preferring instead to head the cavalry component of the Wise Legion. Authored a cavalry manual for the Confederate army. Lt. col., Wise Legion Cav. (8th VA Cav. Bn.), early 1862. Col., 10th VA Cav. (formed from the 8th Bn.), Sept. 24, 1862. WIA and POW Hagerstown, July 6, 1863. Exch. March 10, 1864. Resigned Feb. 2, 1865, dissatisfied that he had not been promoted to brig. to lead the brigade he had been commanding for months. Superintendent of schools in Buckingham Co. postwar. Died May 11, 1871, Buckingham Co. Buried Emmanuel Episcopal Church, near Richmond, Henrico Co. Known to be both "bold" and "remarkably quiet" under fire.

Davis, John Bunyan. Born May 10, 1826, Fairfield Dist., SC. Attd. Furman Institute and USMA. Studied medicine in Charleston. Physician in Fairfield Dist. prewar. Md. Violet Patterson; Esther Barnwell Fuller. Capt. Co. I, 1st (Gregg's) SC, a 6-month unit, early 1861. Capt. Co. E, 15th SC, Aug. 30, 1861. Col., Jan. 19, 1864. Col., 7th SC Consolidated in April 1865. Paroled May 2, 1865, Greensboro. Physician and Sheriff of Fairfield Co. postwar. Lived briefly in TX. Died Nov. 26, 1899, Monticello, SC. Buried St. John's Episcopal Cemetery, Winnsboro. The brigade historian called Davis "a good disciplinarian, brave, resolute, and an all around good officer."

Davis, Matthew L., Jr. Born Aug. 1829, NC. Reared in Rutherford Co. Grad. USMA 1852. Lt., US Army, 1852–61. 1st lt., CS Regular Army, Aug. 27, 1861. Appointed capt. and AQM, July 11, 1861, and ordered to report to Gen. Beauregard. Major and QM to Gen. G. W. Smith, Oct. 9, 1861. Resigned April 18, 1862. Appointed col., 2d NC Cav., April 12, 1862, to rank from that date. Died of pneumonia at Goldsboro, NC, April 23, 1862, while traveling to join his new regiment.

Davis, Newton Nimrod. Born April 25, 1829, Monroe Co., MS. Prewar farmer in Dale and Pickens Cos., AL. Md. Elizabeth Halbert. Capt. Co. C, 24th AL, Nov. 8, 1861. Major, April 26, 1862. Lt. col., March 25, 1863. Col., June 2, 1863. WIA and POW at Franklin. Postwar farmer in Lowndes Co., MS. Died March 8, 1887, at his Lowndes Co. home. Buried Halbert family cemetery, Lowndes Co. Some of Davis's wartime letters have been published.

Davis, Samuel Boyer. Born Oct. 28, 1826, LA (probably New Orleans). Attd. USMA 1844–45. Lt., 4th LA, and lt., 14th US, in Mexican War. Merchant with the family feed store business in New Orleans. Settled in TX prior to 1861. Md. Mary M. M. Clark; Rhoda C. Milby. AAG, Dist. of Texas, 1861–62. Capt., Davis's TX Battery, Oct. 3, 1861. Major, Davis's Mtd. Bn. (aka 7th TX Inf. Bn.), Oct. 10, 1861. Resigned Dec. 7, 1861, to reassume staff duties. Appointed by Gen. Hebert col., 26th TX Cav. (newly formed from his old battalion.), Feb. 1862. However, members of the regiment insisted on electing their own officers. Faced with this protest, Davis stepped down, and Xavier De Bray (who had succeeded Davis in command of the battalion) was elected. Paroled as capt. Lived in Houston and Galveston postwar. Clerk for a cotton merchant, real estate agent, and bookkeeper. Died Dec. 13, 1885, New Orleans.

Davis, Zimmerman. Born Oct. 8, 1834, Fairfield Dist., SC. Reared in Charleston. Grad. College of Charleston. Cotton merchant in Charleston prewar. Pvt., "Washington Light Infantry," 1860–61. Md. Cornelia McIvor. Lt., "Washington Light Infantry" (part of the Eutaw Bn. in Confederate service), 1861–62. Capt. Co. D, 5th SC Cav., April 12, 1862. AIG on Gen. Butler's staff, 1863–64. Col., 5th SC Cav., Oct. 27, 1864. WIA Lynch's Creek, March 1865. Charleston merchant postwar. Treasurer of the city water works. UCV leader. Died March 30, 1910, Charleston. Buried Magnolia Cemetery.

Davitte, Samuel William. Born c. 1831, SC. Farmer in Paulding Co., GA, and McLennan Co., TX, prewar. Md. Nancy Carnes. Pvt. Co. D, 1st GA Cav., 1862. Regimental QM, with the rank of capt., April 1, 1862. Dropped Oct. 23, 1862. Promoted to major, May 2, 1863, at the special request of Col. Morrison, who noted Davitte's "gallantry in action." Lt. col., April 11, 1864. Col., April 15, 1864.

Resided in Polk Co. postwar. Died Dec. 1898, Paulding Co. Buried Davitte family cemetery, Polk Co.

Dawson, Charles L. Born June 13, 1823 (some sources say 1813, but the above date conforms with census data), Richmond, VA. Physician in Carroll Co., VA. Moved to Centre Point, Sevier Co., AR, in the 1850s. Druggist, Methodist preacher. Militia colonel. Md. Sallie L. Haller. Enlisted as pvt. in 1861. Col., 19th (Dawson's) AR, Nov. 21, 1861. Reelected col., Aug. 13, 1862. The 19th was mostly captured at Arkansas Post. Those not captured remained in AR and consolidated with escapees of the 24th AR to form Dawson's 19th/24th AR. Those captured, after exchange, formed a similar unit in MS. Resigned March 1, 1864, due to ill health (rheumatism, hepatitis, and diarrhea). Moved to Tyler, TX, in 1866. Lawyer, preacher. Died Jan. 11, 1876, Tyler. Probably buried in an unmarked grave in Oakwood Cemetery, Tyler, next to his wife. In 1863 Sen. Charles B. Mitchel urged his promotion to brigadier as "a gentleman of fine general character."

Dawson, Jonathan Smith. Born March 31, 1824, Carroll Co., TN. "Trader" in Henry Co. in 1860. Prewar militia general. Md. Harriet Jane Brown; Sue Gilliam Dunlop. Adj., 46th TN, Nov. 29, 1861. POW Island No. 10. Exch. Sept. 1862. Col., upon Sept. 30, 1862, reorganization. Regiment consolidated with 55th TN, Jan. 1863. Dropped Oct. 21, 1863, as supernumerary. In 1865 he asked for authority to organized fellow supernumerary officers into a unit. Lawyer in Henry Co. postwar. Railroad director. Grandmaster of TN Masons. Died June 26, 1891, at his daughter's home in Erin, TN. Buried Paris City Cemetery.

Dearing, William. Born July 15, 1815, TN. Farmer in Giles and Lawrence Cos. prewar. Militia officer. Md. Rhoda (Smith?). Capt. Co. E, 54th TN, 1861. Col., probably Feb. 6, 1862. 54th consolidated with 48th TN, April 1862. Dropped as supernumerary. Giles Co. farmer postwar. Died Oct. 9, 1871. Buried Smith Cemetery, Giles Co.

Deason, John B. Born July 1, 1824, Trigg Co., KY. Lawyer in Hancock Co., MS, prewar. General collection agent. Officer in vol. militia. Capt. in Mexican War. Delegate to MS Secession Convention. Md. Mary Ann Keller. Capt. Co. G (the "Gainesville Volunteers," his militia company), 3d MS, May 1861. Col., Sept. 25, 1861. Not reelected at March 5, 1862, reorganization. Capt., then major, 3d Bn. MS Cav. Reserves, in Aug. 1864. Lawyer, dist. attorney, and judge postwar, residing in Brookhaven. Died March 29, 1900, Hattiesburg. Buried Rosehill Cemetery, Brookhaven. One soldier of the 3d said Deason "must be a coward and he is very often drunk."

De Blanc, Jean Maximilian Alciabedes. Born Sept. 16, 1821, St. Martinville, LA. Attorney in St. Martinville prewar. Militia colonel. Delegate to LA Secession

Convention. Md. Mathilde Briant. Capt. Co. C, 8th LA, June 19, 1861. Major, Oct. 15, 1862. Lt. col., April 6, 1863. POW Banks Ford, VA, May 4, 1863. Col., July 2, 1863. WIA (arm) at Gettysburg and disabled. Retired to Invalid Corps. Assigned to duty with the LA Reserve forces, Aug. 10, 1864. One of three commissioners to negotiate the surrender of the state in 1865. Attorney in St. Martinville postwar. Reconstruction opponent. Justice, LA Supreme Court, 1877–80. Died St. Martinville Nov. 8, 1883. Buried St. Martin de Tours Catholic Cemetery, St. Martinville. A fellow officer called De Blanc "a perfect gentleman, an excellent officer."

DeBray, Xavier Blanchard. Born Jan. 25, 1818, Schlestadt, France. In French army. To US in 1848. Lived in San Antonio and Austin prewar. Newspaper editor. Teacher. Translator in state land office. Unmd. In early 1861 briefly 1st lt. "Tom Green Rifles" (later Co. B, 4th TX). ADC to Gov. Clark, summer of 1861. Major, 2d TX, Aug. 10, 1861. Lt. col. of Davis's Bn., Dec. 7, 1861. Col., 26th TX Cav. (formed from the battalion), March 17, 1862. Often led a brigade in the Galveston garrison. Assigned to duty as brig. gen. April 13, 1864. Led a brigade of TX Cav. in the Red River Campaign. Settled in Houston and Galveston postwar. Teacher, accountant. Galveston city councilman. Later reassumed his old job as translator in the state land office in Austin. Died Jan. 6, 1895, Austin. Buried State Cemetery. Gen. Kirby Smith considered DeBray "a superior cavalry officer."

De Clouet, Alexander Etienne. Born June 9, 1812, St. Martin's Parish, LA. Grad. Georgetown U. Sugar planter in St. Martin Parish. State representative. State senator. Lost race for governor in 1849. Delegate to LA Secession Convention. Md. Marie Louise de St. Clair. Confederate congressman 1861–62. Col., 26th LA, April 3, 1862. Resigned Nov. 10, 1862, due to age and military inexperience, admitting he only accepted the colonelcy in order to raise the regiment. Later served as VADC to Gen. Mouton in the Red River Campaign. Postwar planter in St. Martin Parish. Died June 26, 1890, Lafayette Parish. Buried St. Martin de Tours Cemetery, St. Martinville. De Clouet's papers are at LSU. De Clouet's lt. col. praised his "[d]ignity, courtesy and courage" but thought De Clouet too old to stand field duty.

Dedman, James Monroe. Born Sept. 11, 1826, Mecklenburg Co., VA. Prewar city marshal of Selma, AL. Md. Mary Scarff. Capt. Co. B, 20th AL, Sept. 16, 1861. Major at an unspecified date. Lt. col., May 28, 1863. Col., Sept. 18, 1863. POW Vicksburg. Paroled Selma May 8, 1865. Postwar hotel keeper and mayor of Selma. Died Feb. 6, 1888, Shelby Springs, AL. Buried Live Oak Cemetery, Selma.

De Marigny, Antoine Jacques Philippe de Mandeville. Born Nov. 21, 1811, New Orleans, LA. Graduate of Saumur, the French military school. Officer in the French army, 1831–34. Returned to LA. New Orleans merchant. Planter. US marshal for East LA. Militia officer. Md. Sophronia, daughter of Gov. Claiborne. Col., 10th LA, July 22, 1861. Resigned July 23, 1862, disgusted with the "favoritism" he thought the War Dept. showed to other officers. Returned to his LA plantations. Broker in New Orleans postwar. Died there June 3, 1890. Buried St. Louis Cemetery No. 1. His name is given many different ways—he was generally known as "Mandeville" Marigny. According to Gen. McLaws, Marigny "sp[oke] English but indifferently well."

DeMorse, Charles. Born Jan. 31, 1816, Leicester, MA, as Charles Denny Morse. His name was garbled as "DeMorse" when he moved to TX in 1835 and he adopted the new spelling. Studied law. Lawyer in Matagorda, TX, 1837–42. Editor, Clarksville *Northern Standard.* Mayor of Clarksville. Major in TX Army. Md. Lodoviska Woolridge. Col., 29th TX Cav., July 20, 1862. Served mostly in North TX and Indian Territory. In 1864 De Morse protested against his troops being commingled with, and sometimes commanded by, Indians. Charged and sentenced to suspension of rank and pay for 6 months. Postwar Clarksville editor. Known as the "Father of the Texas Democratic Press." Active in the Grange. Died Oct. 25, 1887, Clarksville. Buried Clarksville Cemetery.

DeMoss, William Eldridge. Born Oct. 29, 1832, Bellevue, Davidson Co., TN. Attd. WMI. Grad. U. of Nashville Medical School. Physician and farmer in Davidson Co. prewar. Md. Tabitha Allison. 3d lt. Co. A, 20th TN, May 15, 1861. Capt., May 8, 1862. Resigned June 10, 1862, due to scrofula. Capt. Co. A, Napier's Bn. TN Cav., fall of 1862. Major, Feb. 25, 1863. Lt. col., 10th TN Cav. (formed from Napier's Bn.), June 15, 1863. Captured May 13, 1864, Tilton, GA. To Johnson's Island. Col., June 15, 1864 (while in prison). Released from prison May 25, 1865. Davidson Co. farmer postwar. Active in the KKK. Died Feb. 7, 1877, at his Davidson Co. home. Buried DeMoss family cemetery, near Bellevue.

Denis, Jules Charles. Born Oct. 7, 1829, New Orleans, LA. New Orleans merchant prewar. Md. Ann Marshall; Clara A. Creagh. Lt. col., 10th LA, May 1861. Resigned Dec. 28, 1861. Returned to New Orleans and tried to raise a new regiment. Major (appointed Jan. 22, 1864) and provost marshal to Gens. Polk and Stephen D. Lee in MS and to Gen. Maury in Mobile. Headed a battalion of conscripts and active in recruiting. Lt. col., 1st MS Cav. Reserves, Aug. 4, 1864. Col., Sept. 3, 1864. Headed a makeshift reservist brigade in south MS, 1864–65. Commission merchant in New Orleans postwar. Bank president. City police commissioner. Died Nov. 24, 1904, New Orleans. Buried Metairie Cemetery. Gen. Maury thought Denis "an officer of ability and devotion." Some sources mistakenly show Denis as col., 32d LA (Miles Legion).

Derby, Charles Alexander. Born Sept. 12, 1828, Dinwiddie Co., VA. Grad. VMI 1848. Taught at military schools in AL, GA, and TN, including GMI. Clergyman in Dallas Co., AL, in 1860. Md. Clara Hunt; Charlotte Basset. Lt. col., 44th AL, May 16, 1862. WIA 2d Manassas. Col., Sept. 1, 1862. MWIA Antietam, Sept. 17, 1862, at the "Bloody Lane," dying soon after in Union hands. Buried on the battlefield. VMI has some papers of his, which suggest he was "frequently drunk" in the 1850s.

De Rosset, William Lord. Born Oct. 27, 1832, Wilmington, NC. Attd. St. Timothy's Hall, St. James College, and UNC. Commission merchant in his father's firm in Wilmington. Established Clarendon Iron Works. Capt. of vol. militia. Md. Caroline Horatia Nelson; Elizabeth S. Nelson. Major, 3d NC, May 16, 1861. Lt. col., April 26, 1862. Col., July 1, 1862. WIA Antietam (hip and thigh). Resigned March 1863 due to wounds. Assisted his father in blockade running thereafter. Wilmington alderman postwar. Commission merchant. UCV official. Died Aug. 14, 1910, Wilmington. Buried Oakdale Cemetery. De Rosset family papers are at UNC. *Confederate Military History* called him "a gentleman of high character and noble ideals."

De Russy, Lewis Gustavus. Born Dec. 17, 1795, NY, son of a French-born officer in the US Army. Grad. USMA 1813. US Army officer 1813–42. Left the army and settled in LA. Civil engineer. Gen., LA militia. Col. in Mexican War. Md. Elizabeth C. Boerum; Eliza Davenport Russell. Col., 2d LA, May 11, 1861. Resigned July 19, 1861. Appointed major and QM, July 8, 1861. Resigned Dec. 4, 1861. Engineer officer at Columbus, KY, July–Dec. 1861. Later, engineer officer in LA, designing, among other works, Fort De Russy near Marksville. Died Nov. 16, 1864, Grand Encore, LA. Buried Russell (aka De Russy) Cemetery near Natchitoches; reburied in 1999 at Fort De Russy, LA. De Russy's brother and nephew were Union army generals. A lieutenant called him "a good old man" who resigned fearing he might have to face his brother in battle. De Russy was the oldest infantry colonel in the Confederate army and the oldest USMA graduate to serve the South.

De Saussure, William Davie. Born Dec. 12, 1819, Columbia, SC. Attd. USC. Lawyer in Columbia. State legislator. Capt. in Mexican War. Capt., US Army, 1855–61. Md. Mary Louise Ravenal. Capt., 3d Company, 1st SC Regulars, Jan. 19, 1861. Major of SC state cav., Jan. 28, 1861. Capt., CS Regular Army, March 16, 1861. Col., 15th SC, Sept. 9, 1861. KIA Gettysburg July 2, 1863. Buried near the Blackhorse Tavern on the battlefield; reburied in the family plot in 1st Presbyterian Church, Columbia. A very highly thought of officer, the "Bayard of South Carolina," known for his "reckless courage" and "stentorian voice."

Devane, William Stewart. Born March 4, 1828, Newton Co., GA. Attorney in Sampson Co., NC, prewar. Md. Laura Murphy. Pvt., April 1861, for a company later Co. A, 61st NC. Capt. Co. A, Devane's Independent Company, Oct. 9, 1861. Lt. col., 61st NC, Sept. 5, 1862. WIA June 18, 1864, near Petersburg, in shoulder. Col., Oct. 11, 1864. WIA Bentonville (neck) while commanding Clingman's Brigade. Paroled May 2, 1865, Salisbury. Lawyer in New Hanover Co. postwar. Died Feb. 24, 1879, Sampson Co. Buried Oakdale Cemetery, Wilmington. A "competent and worthy officer."

Deyerle, Andrew Jackson. Born April 24, 1823, Montgomery Co., VA. Roanoke Co. farmer in 1860. Md. Jane B. Lewis. Capt. Co. E, 42d VA, June 4, 1861. WIA Cedar Mountain (hip). Col., June 19, 1863. Elected state representative in 1863 and granted leave to attend to his legislative duties. It appears he rarely if ever returned to his regiment. Roanoke Co. farmer postwar. Died June 18, 1907, Elliston, Roanoke Co. Buried East End Cemetery, Salem.

Diamond, George R. Born July 2, 1837, Giles, VA (now WVA). Farmer in Lawrence Co., KY, prewar. Md. Mary Graham. Capt. Co. D, 5th KY, Oct. 26, 1861. Mustered out Oct. 26, 1862. Major, 10th KY Cav., Oct. 9, 1863. Lt. col., Aug. 3, 1864. Col., Oct. 2, 1864. Paroled May 8, 1865, Athens, GA (as lt. col.). Farmer and logger in Lawrence Co. postwar. State legislator. Moved to Scott Co., MO. Died Sandy Woods, Scott Co., MO, Dec. 6, 1919 (dates of birth and death taken from death certificate; other sources give slightly different dates). Buried Hickory Grove Cemetery, Scott Co. Diamond's service record does not show his promotion to colonel, though it records that he was "entitled to be Col. since [Col. Edwin] Trimble's death [on Oct. 2, 1864]" and indirect evidence has him receiving the promotion.

Diamond, James Jackson. Born July 16, 1827, De Kalb Co., GA. Attd. Maryville College in TN. Prewar attorney and legislator in GA. Planter and slave owner in Grayson Co., TX. Secessionist leader. Md. Adeline E. Holmes; Amanda Jordan. Delegate to TX Secession Convention. Capt. "1st TX Regt." (later 11th TX Cav.), May 15, 1861. Lt. col., Oct. 2, 1861. Col., 11th Tex Cav., probably April 16, 1862. Not reelected at May 8, 1862, reorganization, and resigned. Adj. 21st Brigade TX State Troops. Helped organize the "great hanging" of Unionists at Gainesville in 1862. Served in Frontier Regt. Edited the Houston *Dispatch* postwar. Died Oct. 9, 1867, in Houston of yellow fever (which swept away 12 members of his family). Buried Old City Cemetery, Houston. Brother of Lt. Col. W. W. Diamond, 16th TX Cav.

Dickey, James Edwin. Born July 6, 1822, SC. Reared in Calhoun Co., GA. Pachitla farmer. Justice of county court. Md. Mariah Mollette. 1st lt., "Calhoun Repeaters" (a state unit), Aug. 2, 1861. Capt. Co. E (the "Pachitla Guards"), 51st

GA, March 4, 1862. Major, July 2, 1863. POW in Antietam Campaign. Exch. April 1863. Lt. col., Jan. 14, 1864. Col., Nov. 12, 1864. POW Sayler's Creek. State senator 1865–66. Died c. 1876, probably in Calhoun Co.

Dickins, John Robert. Born Jan. 21, 1822, Granville Co., NC. Last name spelled "Dickens" in some sources. Reared in Madison Co., TN. To Panola Co., MS, in 1845. Farmer. State representative 1854–55. Md. Mary Hunt; Fannie Wilborn. Capt. Co. E, 12th MS, Feb. 1861. Major, May 20, 1861. Col., 5th MS, appointed June 29, 1862, by Gen. Bragg. Discharged July 8, 1863, when the appointment was declared illegal and an election ordered. Recruited for MS State Troops in 1864. Postwar Panola Co. farmer. Died Feb. 15, 1887. Buried Rose Hill Cemetery, Sardis. Gen. Chalmers called Dickins "a good soldier and a most excellent officer."

Dickison, John Jackson. Born March 27, 1816, Monroe Co., VA. Reared in SC. Cotton merchant in Georgetown, SC. Adj. gen. of SC militia. Moved to FL in 1856. Planter near Ocala. Md. Mary E. Lester; Mary E. Ling. 1st lt., Marion Light Art., Dec. 12, 1861. Not reelected at April 1862 reorganization. Capt. Co. H, 2d FL Cav., Aug. 21, 1862. Led partisan cavalry forces in East FL opposing Union raids. Won fame as the "Swamp Fox of Florida" for his many successes, including the capture of the gunboat *Columbine* and victories at engagements at Gainesville and Palatka. Promoted to col., April 5, 1865, by the War Dept., but the promotion never reached him. Paroled May 20, 1865, Waldo, FL, as capt. Ocala planter postwar. Reconstruction opponent. State legislator. State adj. gen. UCV official. Died Aug. 23, 1902, Ocala. Buried Evergreen Cemetery, Jacksonville. At least one book and many articles have been written on Dickison. Gen. E. M. Law called him "the hope and defense of the state in the dark days of the Civil War."

Dillon, Edward. Born May 4, 1835, Salem, VA. Educated at New London Academy in Bedford Co., VA. Lt., US Army, 1857–61. Md. Frances Polk, niece of Gen. Leonidas Polk. 1st lt., CS Regular Army, March 16, 1861. On staff of Gens. Ben McCulloch and Van Dorn in TMD. Appointed (by Gen. Van Dorn) major and chief commissary, Army of the West, May 24, 1862. Major, Nov. 3, 1862. In 1863, Gen. Lomax and others tried to get Dillon transferred to Stuart's Cav. Corps, but a suitable position never became vacant, and Dillon returned to MS. Appointed col., 2d MS Cav., July 5, 1863. Commission revoked, spring of 1864, after the officers of the 2d protested the appointment. Assigned to command of dismounted cavalrymen in MS, 1864. Paroled May 16, 1865, Columbus. Resided in Lexington and Indian Rock, VA, postwar. Traffic manager for the James River Canal. President of a company that quarried limestone. Died Aug. 10, 1897, at his Lexington home. Buried Stonewall Jackson Cemetery, Lexington. Gen. Maury and others recommended Dillon for promotion to general, praising him as an "excellent officer."

Dilworth, William Scott. Born May 11, 1822, Camden Co., GA. Grad. Emory U. in 1845. Prewar attorney in Monticello, FL. Planter. Militia officer. State legislator. Delegate to FL Secession Convention. Md. Cornelia Gaulden. Col., 3d FL, Aug. 1, 1861. Served with the FL Brigade in the West. Said to have been a heavy drinker. Often absent from his regiment. Temporarily commanded the Dept. of FL in 1863. Paroled May 10, 1865, Tallahassee. Postwar Monticello attorney. Died July 23, 1869, Monticello, buried Roseland Cemetery.

Dobbins, Archibald Stephenson. Born 1827, Maury Co., TN. Moved to AR c. 1850. Prewar planter near Helena, with other property in MS. Md. Mary Patience Dawson. Raised crops and sold the produce to the army, 1861–62. Appointed col. in 1862 by Gen. Hindman. Served on Hindman's staff. Col., 1st (Dobbins's) AR Cav., 1863. Regiment usually operated in eastern AR on guard/ scout duty. Dobbins led a brigade in the Little Rock Campaign and Price's Raid. Court-martialed for disobeying Gen. Marmaduke's orders during the Little Rock Campaign, after Marmaduke had killed Dobbins's commander in a duel. Found guilty but sentence remitted by Pres. Davis. Praised as "intrepid." Paroled July 13, 1865, Galveston, as a colonel. Settled in New Orleans after the war and became a merchant. Disgusted with Reconstruction, he immigrated to Brazil and tried to establish a mill in the Amazon jungle near Santarem. His family never heard from him after 1869, although he was alive in Rio de Janeiro in 1874, running a hotel. Often termed "general" in postwar writings, Dobbins has a memorial stone at Maple Hill Cemetery, Helena.

Dodson, Eli. Born May 22, 1828, White Co., TN. Reared in Madison Co., AR. Moved to Lead Hill in 1852 and later to Yellville. Farmer, lawyer. Clerk of the circuit court. Md. Rhoda Cantrell; Mary Hastings; Mary Cantrell. Enlisted June 22, 1861, in the 14th (Mitchell's) AR. Lt. col., c. Aug. 22, 1861. Severely WIA in hip at Pea Ridge. Col., May 16, 1862. POW Port Hudson. Resigned May 1862, due to ill health. He later returned to the regiment but again had to resign. State senator 1862–63. Postwar lawyer in Yellville, then later Boone and Marion Cos. State representative 1866. State senator 1872–80. Judge 1880–82, 1892–96. Died Feb. 26, 1921, Kingdom Springs, AR. Buried in a private cemetery on the Purdom farm, Marion Co., AR. A postwar local history calls Dodson "intelligent, trustworthy and efficient."

Donnell, David M. Born c. 1829, Wilson Co., TN. Grad. Cumberland U. in 1847. Prewar teacher. President of Cumberland Presbyterian Female College in McMinnville, Warren Co., TN. Md. Julia M. Johnson. Capt. Co. C, 16th TN, May 28, 1861. Lt. col., May 8, 1862. Col., Feb. 20, 1863. Injured at Chickamauga. Left the 16th in May 1864. Paroled May 10, 1865, Tallahassee. Teacher in Warren and Wilson Cos. postwar. Moved to Suwannee Co., FL, in the 1880s. Died March 29, 1897, Live Oak, FL. Buried Wellborn, FL. A soldier called Donnell "a first class Christian gentleman . . . [but] the war was not a proper place for him."

Doss, Washington Lafayette. Born Jan. 8, 1825, Pickens Co., AL. Farmer in Oktibbeha Co., MS, prewar. Mexican War veteran. Md. Noraline A. Moore. Pvt. Co. G, 14th MS, May 29, 1861. Major, June 4, 1861. POW Fort Donelson. Imprisoned in Fort Warren, exch. Oct. 16, 1862. Lt. col., Oct. 18, 1862. Col., March 16, 1864. Arrested, June 25, 1864, on unspecified charges. Paroled May 14, 1865, Columbus. Farmer near West Point, MS, postwar. Died Jan. 25, 1900, at his West Point home. Buried Greenwood Cemetery, West Point. A fellow prisoner called Doss a "pleasant, clever gentleman."

Douglas, Henry Thompson. Born Sept. 15, 1838, James City Co., VA. Grad. William & Mary College. Prewar civil engineer for US Government. Md. Anne Matilda Roberts. Lt. of engineers, PAVA, May 18, 1861. Worked on the VA Peninsula defenses under Gen. Magruder. Resigned Oct. 10, 1861. Lt., Confederate engineers, Feb. 15, 1862. Capt. and engineering officer to Gen. A. P. Hill, June 9, 1862. Major, May 27, 1863. Appointed chief engineer, TMD, July 6, 1863. Lt. col., 1st Engineer Bn. (a TMD unit), April 1, 1864. Col., Sept. 28, 1864 (appointed by Kirby Smith). Commanded 4th Confederate Engineers, a unit organized c. April 1865. Paroled as col., July 5, 1865. Chief engineer of Baltimore & Ohio Railroad postwar, living in Baltimore, New York City, and Richmond. Brig. gen. in Spanish-American War. Died July 20, 1926, New Kent Co., VA. Buried Hollywood Cemetery, Richmond. Gen. Boggs called Douglas "a splendid specimen of youthful manhood."

Douglass, Henry Lee. Born Jan. 11, 1826, Wilson Co., TN. Farmer in Haywood and Fayette Cos. prewar. Md. Lucy D. Little. Capt. Co. A, 9th TN, May 23, 1861. Col., May 29, 1861. Not reelected at May 1862 reorganization. Farmer in Shelby Co. (near Memphis) postwar. Operated gin and sawmill. State representative 1877–79. Died Dec. 31, 1906, Memphis. Buried Elmwood Cemetery, Memphis.

Douglass, Marcellus. Born Oct. 5, 1820, Thomaston, GA. Grad. UGA. Lawyer in Cuthbert, Randolph Co. Md. Menla Davis. Capt. of a local cavalry company, Feb. 1861. This company disbanded in June 1861 when informed that infantry, not cavalry, was wanted. Capt. Co. E, 13th GA, June 19, 1861. Lt. col., July 8, 1861. Col., Feb. 1, 1862. KIA Antietam. Buried Rosedale Cemetery, Cuthbert. A tribute by the local bar called Douglass "a noble soldier, a gifted lawyer, a warm friend, a valuable citizen."

Douglass, Samuel James. Born Oct. 10, 1812, Petersburg, VA. Attd. William & Mary College and UVA. Prewar lawyer in Petersburg and Tallahassee, FL. US dist. judge in FL. Md. Louisa Kelly; Frances Brown. Appointed col. and judge of the military court of Forney's Corps, Dec. 16, 1862. Judge in Mobile, 1862–65. Paroled Meridian May 9, 1865. Tallahassee lawyer postwar. Justice, FL Supreme Court. Died Nov. 16, 1873, Tallahassee, buried Old City Cemetery.

Dowd, Henry Austin. Born Jan. 5, 1833, NC. Merchant in Edgecombe Co. prewar. Md. Laura Baker. Lt. Co. I, 15th NC, May 22, 1861. Adj., Oct. 7, 1861. Col., April 20, 1862. WIA Malvern Hill. Resigned Feb. 27, 1863, due to wounds. Appointed major and AQM in charge of the NC State Clothing Dept., April 1863. Farmer in Tarboro postwar. Died May 1, 1902. Buried Calvary Episcopal Cemetery, Tarboro. "[A] practical business man."

Dowd, William Francis. Born Dec. 31, 1820, Darlington Dist., SC. Reared in TN. Moved to Monroe Co., MS, in 1841. Lawyer in Aberdeen prewar. Newspaper editor. Very wealthy. Md. Ann W. Brown. Col., 24th MS, Nov. 6, 1861. Resigned Jan. 19, 1864, due to ill health. Appointed col. and judge, military court of northern AL, April 6, 1864. Paroled May 14, 1865, Meridian. Lawyer in Aberdeen postwar. Appointed asst. US attorney, 1871–73, with orders to prosecute KKK outrages. Died Nov. 28, 1878, Aberdeen. Buried Odd Fellows Cemetery, Aberdeen. Said to have taken "special delight in what has been called hair-splitting, and in this particular probably he had no superior in Mississippi."

Dowdell, James Ferguson. Born Nov. 26, 1818, Jasper Co., GA. Grad. Randolph-Macon College. Moved from Greenville, GA, to Chambers Co., AL, in 1846. Lawyer, Methodist minister. US congressman 1853–59. Professor of ancient languages at East Alabama College. Md. Sarah Render. Delegate to AL Secession Convention. Col., 37th AL at May 13, 1862, organization. WIA at Iuka. POW at Vicksburg. Distinguished for "coolness and bravery." Lost race for governor of Alabama in 1863. Retired Aug. 31, 1864, due to ill health. Postwar president of Alabama Female College. Died Sept. 6, 1871, Auburn, AL. Buried City Cemetery, Auburn.

Doyal, Leonard Thompson. Born May 1816, Columbia Co., GA. Lawyer in Henry Co. and Griffin prewar. Judge. Baptist preacher. Officer of vol. militia. Md. Matilda Thompson; Mrs. Elizabeth Eason Brown; Mrs. Ann E. Davis Battle. Capt. Co. D, 2d GA Bn., April 20, 1861. Lost race for Confederate Congress in 1861. Col., 53d GA, May 12, 1862. Often absent due to illness, giving rise to rumors of cowardice. Resigned Oct. 8, 1862. Griffin lawyer postwar. Died July 6, 1874, Griffin. Buried Oak Hill Cemetery, Griffin. An obituary called Doyal a "remarkable man, mentally, physically and socially."

Drake, Jabez Leftwich. Born April 15, 1832, AL (probably Huntsville). Farmer in Leake Co., MS, prewar. Md. Samilda Clearman. 1st lt. "Leake Guards" (Co. E, 27th MS), April 25, 1861. 2d lt. "Leake Rebels," Co. F, 33d MS, March 21, 1862. Major, April 17, 1862. Lt. col., July 16, 1863. Col., Jan. 5, 1864. KIA Peachtree Creek while leading the 33d in a charge. Buried first on the battlefield, later at Oakland Cemetery, Atlanta. Gen. Featherston eulogized Drake as "a gallant and excellent officer," killed while waiving his sword and cheering his men on.

Drake, James Henry. Born June 9, 1822, Newtown, Frederick Co., VA. Plasterer and mechanic in Frederick Co. prewar. Militia officer. Md. Sarah Ann——. Capt. Co. A, 1st VA, April 19, 1861. Appointed regimental commissary. Major, April 22, 1862. Lt. col., April 23, 1863. Col., c. April–May 1863. MWIA Kearneysville, July 16, 1863, shot through the thigh, breast, and shoulder. Died that evening near Shepherdstown. Buried Lutheran Churchyard, Stephens City. Jeb Stuart called Drake "a brave and zealous leader." Papers at Library of Congress.

Drake, Joseph. Born June 14, 1806, KY. Attd. Washington & Lee U. Planter in Carroll Co., MS, prewar. Judge. State legislator. Md. Martha M. Barton. Capt. Co. H, 4th MS, 1861. Col., Aug. 24, 1861. POW Fort Donelson, while leading a brigade. Drake's division commander found him "very gallant, steady and efficient" there. Imprisoned at Fort Warren. Exch. Aug. 27, 1862. Retired (probably Oct. 1, 1862) due to age, after being exchanged. Farmer in Carroll Co. postwar. Died July 9, 1878, on his plantation in Carroll Co. Buried Drake Cemetery, east of McCarley, Carroll Co.

Drew, John Thompson. Born Dec. 25, 1795, GA. Cherokee tribal leader. Fought for the US in the War of 1812. Resided at Webber Falls on the Arkansas River, Indian Territory. Merchant, lawyer, judge. Cherokee senator. Owned several salt works. Capt. of tribal militia. Md. Maria Cody Field (niece of Chief John Ross); Charlotte Gordon Scales. Col., 2d Cherokee MR, Oct. 4, 1861. This unit was composed largely of Ross's faction of the Cherokee Tribe, which was more loyal to its chief than to the South. After the Confederate defeat at Pea Ridge, the regiment dissolved, with most men enlisting in pro-Union Indian units. Drew sat out the rest of the war, selling salt to the Confederacy. Died Aug. 26, 1865, Fort Gibson. Buried on his old home on Bayou Menard near Fort Gibson.

Duckworth, William Lafayette. Born June 29, 1834, Haywood Co., TN. Studied medicine before the war. Militia officer. Md. Timoxena P. Capell in 1867. 2d lt. "Haywood Rangers" (Co. D, 7th TN Cav.), May 23, 1861. Major, June 20, 1862. POW Oxford, MS, Dec. 2, 1862. Exch. March 28, 1863. Lt. col., Jan. 1, 1863. Col., Oct. 8, 1863. Led brigade under Bedford Forrest. Temporarily commanded Jeffrey Forrest's brigade, after that officer's death, with "skill and ability"—

but never given permanent command of the brigade. Bluffed Union City, TN, into surrender, March 24, 1864. Paroled May 12, 1865, Gainesville. Physician in Brownsville postwar, after graduation from the UPA Medical School. Methodist minister. Died Feb. 2, 1915, Brownsville. Buried Oakwood Cemetery, Brownsville.

Duff, James. Born 1828, Perthshire, Scotland. Pvt., then sgt., US Army, 1849–54. Army sutler at Fort Belknap. Merchant in San Antonio. Md. Harriet, daughter of Union Gen. Gabriel Paul. Capt. and lt. col. of improvised force that seized San Antonio in 1861. Brig. gen., 30th Brigade, TX State Troops, early 1862. Resigned May 4, 1862. Capt., Duff's PR Co., May 7, 1862. His troops ambushed and captured German-American Unionists attempting to flee TX. The subsequent execution of the prisoners was called the "Nueces Massacre." Duff, who was not on the scene, has been (unfairly) blamed for the hangings. Major, lt. col., 14th TX Cav. Bn. Col., 33d TX Cav., May 2, 1863. Served in garrison duty in TX. Gen. Hamilton Bee called him "an accomplished soldier . . . indispensable," though a fellow officer thought he was a "specious rascal." Fled to Mexico in 1865. Manager of a British-financed mortgage and investment company in Denver, CO. Promoted irrigation in that state. Later, businessman in London, UK. Died April 16, 1900, Richmond Borough, London.

Duff, William Lewis. Born Aug. 25, 1843, Lafayette Co. MS. Reared in Calhoun Co. Student at UMS in 1861. Lt. Co. K, 17th MS, April 23, 1861. Capt., May 28, 1861. Major, Nov. 1, 1862. WIA Chancellorsville. Officially dropped, Jan. 1, 1864. Lt. col., 19th MS Cav. Bn., late 1863. Col., 8th MS Cav. (formed from 19th Bn.), July 19, 1864. Severely WIA in a skirmish the day before the Battle of Tupelo. Attorney in Memphis postwar. City Recorder. Moved to Eureka, CA, c. 1881. "Landlord" in 1900. Died Feb. 2, 1909, San Francisco. Buried Elmwood Cemetery, Memphis. An 1876 newspaper article called Duff an "excellent young man."

Duke, Richard Thomas Walker. Born June 6, 1822, Albemarle Co., VA. Grad. VMI and UVA. Charlottesville lawyer prewar. Commonwealth attorney 1858–69. Md. Elizabeth S. Eskridge. Capt. Co. B, 19th VA, May 8, 1861. Not reelected at April 1862 reorganization. Col., 46th VA, May 24, 1862. Resigned March 28, 1864. Lt. col., 1st BN. VA Reserves, May 31, 1864. POW Sayler's Creek. Released July 25, 1865. Charlottesville lawyer postwar. US congressman 1870–73. State legislator 1879–80. Died July 2, 1898, Charlottesville. Buried Maplewood Cemetery, Charlottesville. Duke often quarreled with his brigade commander over Duke's frequent requests for leave to take care of his legal duties.

Dulany, Richard Henry. Born Aug. 10, 1820, Loudoun Co., VA. Attd. Dickinson College in PA. Wealthy farmer and stock breeder in Loudoun Co. prewar.

Md. Rebecca Ann Dulany, a cousin. Capt. Co. A, 6th VA Cav., Aug. 1, 1861. Not reelected at reorganization. Lt. col., 7th VA Cav., June 20, 1862. Col., Oct. 30, 1862. WIA Greenland Gap, April 25, 1863 (arm), and Ashland, June 1, 1864 (leg). Suffering from his wounds, he was detailed to court-martial duty in 1864. Col. and judge, military court of the Richmond defenses, March 23, 1865. Paroled May 17, 1865, Winchester. Loudoun Co. farmer postwar. Died Oct. 31, 1906, "Welbourne," Loudoun Co. Buried Sharon Cemetery, Middleburg. A family memoir containing much of Dulany's wartime correspondence was published in 1996.

Dumonteil (de la Grèze), Pierre Felix. Born Dec. 4, 1836, Perigueux, France. Sgt. in French army. Fought in the Crimean War. Immigrated to New Orleans in the late 1850s. Prewar New Orleans merchant. Active in state militia. Md. Susan Robertson in 1862. Major, 2d Special Bn. LA Infantry (a state unit), June 14, 1861. Unit helped form the 10th LA. Major, 10th LA (a unit where French was the language of command), July 22, 1861. Resigned Dec. 31, 1861. Returned to New Orleans. ADC to Gen. Buisson of the LA State Troops. A volunteer with the 13th LA Bn. at Shiloh. Injured at Battle of Baton Rouge, while still serving as a volunteer. Recommissioned major and AAG, Sept. 6, 1862, to command the camp of instruction at Camp Moore, LA. Col., 14th Confederate Cav., July 15, 1863. Ordered arrested Nov. 25, 1863, accused of "illegal pursuits" (looting? trading cotton?). No record of any actual arrest or formal charge. The 14th, a regiment formed largely from reluctant conscripts in southwest MS, did not have a distinguished record. Found physically unfit for duty July 28, 1864, but after some months' leave returned to the army. Returned to New Orleans postwar and ran a restaurant there. Merchant in Turkey before returning to France. Died Aug. 26, 1895, Paris, France. Buried Dammarie-les-Lys, near Paris. Gen. Pemberton thought Dumonteil "brave, energetic and intelligent," but Gen. Joseph Johnston considered him "an unsafe man."

Dungan, Robert Henry. Born Sept. 18, 1834, Smythe Co., VA. Attd. Emory & Henry College. Student in 1860. Taught school after college. Md. Susan Virginia Baker in 1865. Lt. Co. A, 48th VA, May 18, 1861. Capt. Co. D, April 21, 1862. Lt. col., Oct. 16, 1862. Col., May 3, 1863. WIA Cedar Mountain, Chancellorsville, and 2d Kernstown. Led brigade often in 1864. Appmx. Postwar schoolteacher in Chilhowie. Founded the Jonesboro (TN) Male Institute. Died Nov. 6, 1903, Bristol, VA. Buried East End Cemetery, Bristol. A wartime examining board found Dungan "a very efficient officer."

Dunlap, Samuel John Calhoun. Born Dec. 26, 1833, Kershaw, SC. Attd. Wake Forest U. Farmer in Schley Co., GA, in 1860. Md. Mary Jane Ingram; Hennie Ingram. Capt. Co. B, 46th GA, March 4, 1862. WIA Chickamauga (foot). Major,

Jan. 19, 1864. Col., Jan. 19, 1864. WIA Atlanta, Franklin (3 times), the latter wounds disabling him for the rest of the war. Paroled May 1, 1865, Greensboro (while he was at home recuperating). Farmer in Chester Co., SC, postwar. Moved to Bartow Co., FL, in 1886. "Clerk" there in 1900. Died June 11, 1907, Polk Co., FL. Buried Oak Hill Cemetery, Bartow.

Dunlop, Isaac Leroy. Born Sept. 21, 1835, York Dist., SC, of a wealthy planter family. Prewar bookkeeper in Warren, Bradley Co., AR. Md. Elmira C. Franklin in 1862. 1st lt., "Sweeney Riflemen" (later Co. C, 5th AR), Jan. 28, 1861. Capt. Co. D, 9th AR, July 25, 1861. Col., Jan. 12, 1862. Led 9th at Shiloh, where Gen. Bowen complimented Dunlop's "cool courage and self-possession." Died Sept. 9, 1864, near Lovejoy's Station, GA. Probably buried Pat Cleburne Cemetery, Jonesboro, GA.

Dunnington, John William. Born May 8, 1833, Christian Co., KY. Officer in USN 1849–61. Md. Susan G. Booker. 1st lt., CSN, May 2, 1861. Commanded gunboats on the Mississippi River, 1861–62. Commanded batteries on the White River, AR, 1862. Assigned by Gen. Hindman as col. and chief of ordnance. POW Fort Hindman (Arkansas Post), Jan. 12, 1863, while commanding a brigade. Exch. May 5, 1863. Appointed 1st lt., CS Provisional Navy, Jan. 6, 1864. Capt. of blockade runner, 1864. Commanded ironclad *Virginia II* in James River Fleet, 1865. Appointed col. of an improvised regiment of sailors during the evacuation of Richmond. Paroled Greensboro, NC, April 28, 1865. Coal dealer in Columbia, TN, postwar. Died March 10, 1882, near Columbia. Buried Rose Hill Cemetery, Columbia.

Dunovant, Robert Gill Mills. Born May 18, 1821, Chester, SC. Brother of Gen. John Dunovant. First name given as "Richard" in *OR*. Grad. USC. Briefly physician in TX after graduation. Planter in Chester and Edgefield prewar. Lt. col. Palmetto Regt. in Mexican War. Adj. and IG of SC Militia, 1855–61. Delegate to SC Secession Convention. Md. Ellen S. Brooks. Brig. gen., 4th Brigade, SC Militia, at Charleston, Jan. 1861. Brig. gen. of SC State Troops during Fort Sumter bombardment. Resigned his general's commission when his troops were mustered into Confederate service. Col., 12th SC, Sept. 1, 1861. Commanded Fort Beauregard during the attack on Port Royal. Resigned April 2, 1862. State representative 1864–65. Edgefield planter postwar. Died May 12, 1898, Edgefield. Buried Willowbrook Baptist Cemetery, Edgefield. Dunovant wrote a book on the Palmetto Regiment.

Dyer, David. Born Dec. 28, 1823, VA. Farmer in Pittsylvania Co. prewar. Pvt. in Mexican War. Md. Mary L. Davis. Capt. Co. D, 57th VA, June 22, 1861. Major, May 23, 1862. Lt. col., 1862 (probably July 23). Col., July 30, 1862. Resigned Jan. 12, 1863, due to ill health and pressure from his brigade commander, who thought Dyer incompetent. Pittsylvania Co. farmer postwar. Moved to Corsicana, TX, and later Mayesville, SC, later in life. Died May 5, 1899, probably in Mayesville.

Eakin, William Lyle. Born Jan. 25, 1824, Blount Co., TN. Attd. Hiwassee College. Lawyer in Madisonville, Monroe Co., prewar. Md. Jane, sister of Gen. John C. Vaughn. Enlisted as Pvt. Dec. 17, 1861. Major, 1st TN Inf. Bn. (Eakin's), Feb. 1862. Lt. col., 59th TN, April 30, 1862. Col., March 19, 1863. POW Vicksburg and exch. Regiment mounted winter of 1863. POW Piedmont. Imprisoned at Johnson's Island for the rest of the war. Released July 25, 1865. Lawyer and judge in Chattanooga postwar. Died there Oct. 19, 1908. Buried Forest Hills Cemetery, Chattanooga. Eakin had two brothers in the Union army.

Earle, Richard Greene. Born Sept. 4, 1813, Walterborough, SC. To Jacksonville, AL, in the 1840s. Lawyer. Md. Sarah Kelton. Lt. col. in Mexican War. Capt. Co. A, 2d AL Cav., Feb. 24, 1862. Court-martialed for not accepting Maj. Leroy Napier as his commander and imprisoned for several months but eventually acquitted. Col., May 27, 1863. "A skillful officer." KIA May 18, 1864, near Kingston, GA, while leading a charge against the 72d Indiana. Buried in the gardens at "Woodland," north of Kingston. Middle name often given as "Gordon."

Earle, Samuel Girard. Born June 9, 1833, Evergreen, SC. Attd. Bethany College. Moved to Ouachita Co., AR, c. 1858. Prewar farmer and lawyer. Md. Kate P. Hobbs. Capt. Co. G, 3d AR Cav., July 1861. Col., May 17, 1862. Regiment fought dismounted at Corinth. Remounted, winter of 1862. Shot in head and KIA Thompson's Station, March 5, 1863. Buried on the old Lavender place on the battlefield. Van Dorn's florid report of Thompson's Station claimed Earle was "one of the bravest and best officers of our service."

Earp, Cullen Redwine. Born Aug. 8, 1828, Marshall Co., AL. Prewar farmer in Upshur Co., TX. Md. Harriett E. Dunkley. 1st lt. Co. D, 10th TX Cav., Sept. 25, 1861. Lt. col., May 8, 1862. Sent to TX in Nov. 1862 to recruit for regiment. Col., March 20, 1863. Paroled Marshall, TX, July 3, 1865. Died Oct. 11, 1865. Buried Earp Cemetery in western Upshur Co., close to the Wood/Upshur Co. line; reburied Hopewell Cemetery, Upshur Co., 2008.

Ector, Walton B. Born Aug. 24, 1820, Putnam Co., GA. Attd. USMA. Newspaper editor in Columbus in the 1840s. Planter in Meriwether Co., owning 39 slaves in 1860. Officer in Mexican War. Militia general. Md. Elizabeth A. Bray. Capt. Co. B, 13th GA, May 1, 1861. Col., July 8, 1861. Died Jan. 28, 1862, in Greenville, GA, where he'd gone to restore his shattered health. Buried Greenville Cemetery. Brother of Gen. Matthew D. Ector of TX.

Edmonds, Edward Claxton. Born Jan. 21, 1835, Paris, VA. Grad. VMI 1858. Principal of Danville Military Academy. Md. Margaret S. Tutwile. Col., 38th VA,

June 12, 1861. WIA Seven Pines. KIA Pickett's Charge. Buried on the battlefield; probably reburied Hollywood Cemetery, Richmond, in the Confederate section. Edmonds's successor as colonel called him "noble and beloved."

Edmondson, James Howard. Born July 15, 1831, Limestone Co., AL. Reared in Pontotoc Co., MS, and Memphis. Memphis merchant prewar, dealing in hides and leather. Md. Mary E. Titus. Capt. Co. B ("Bluff City Grays," a unit he equipped), 154th TN, May 14, 1861. Appointed (by Gen. Forrest) col., 11th (Holman's) TN Cav., Feb. 25, 1863. Resigned July 22, 1863, when Holman returned from sick leave. In Aug. 1863 he purchased the steamer *Charlotte Clark* to go privateering but instead went into blockade running. Moved to Nassau, the Bahamas, immediately after the war but soon returned to Memphis. Secretary, Carolina Life Insurance Co. Cotton factor. Died Oct. 20, 1884, Memphis, of diphtheria. Buried Elmwood Cemetery. An obituary called Edmondson "a gallant soldier—the same lovable, brave character whether in march, in camp, or in battle."

Edmondson, James Kerr. Born Feb. 11, 1832, near Buena Vista, Rockbridge Co., VA. Attd. Washington College. Clerk of the Lexington City Court prewar. Md. Emily Taylor. Pvt. Co. H, 2d VA, April 18, 1861. Lt., April 18, 1861. Regt. adj., 27th VA, Aug. 27, 1861. Capt., Oct. 7, 1861. Lt. col., July 24, 1862. Col., Nov. 19, 1862. Lost left arm at Chancellorsville. Resigned Dec. 1, 1863. Provost marshal in Lexington, 1863–65. County clerk, 1863–69. Attorney in Lexington postwar. Judge. Mayor of Lexington. State representative 1893–94. Died March 31, 1898. Buried Stonewall Jackson Cemetery, Lexington. Called "one of the ablest and great figures that Lexington has produced."

Edwards, Aaron Cone. Born Nov. 30, 1833, Effingham Co., GA. Prewar farmer. Baptist minister and teacher at Mount Vernon Institute, Washington Co., GA. Md. Martha M. Riddle. Capt. Co. I, 11th GA Bn., 1861. Major, March 22, 1862. Lt. col., 47th GA (formed from the 11th Bn.), May 12, 1862. Court-martialed Aug. 28, 1862, for conduct unbecoming an officer and reprimanded. Col., Aug. 30, 1863. Died April 3, 1868, Effingham Co. Buried Corinth Baptist Church Cemetery, Effingham Co.

Edwards, Jeptha. Born May 10, 1828, Duck Springs, AL. Pvt. in Mexican War. Merchant and planter in De Kalb Co., AL. Md. Margaret Crump. Capt. Co. G, 49th (aka 31st) AL, Dec. 19, 1861. WIA Shiloh. Col., May 8, 1862. Part of the 31st broke at Corinth, through no fault of Edwards, who won praise for his gallantry there. POW Port Hudson. Imprisoned on Johnson's Island for rest of the war. Postwar farmer, postmaster, deputy US marshal in Attalla, AL. Died July 10, 1902, Attalla. Buried Attalla Cemetery.

Edwards, Oliver Evans. Born Nov. 9, 1819, Spartanburg Dist., SC. Reared in Cass Co., GA. Lawyer in Spartanburg prewar. Militia general. State representative 1856–61. Md. Rebecca June Gary. Joined 5th SC as a civilian volunteer in 1861. At 1st Manassas. Col., 13th SC, Sept. 4, 1861. WIA 2d Manassas. MWIA Chancellorsville. Died June 21, 1863, Goldsboro, NC. Buried Oakwood Cemetery, Spartanburg. The brigade historian said Edwards "possessed rare qualities as an officer . . . his great forte was battle."

Elford, Charles James. Born May 11, 1820, Charleston, SC. Greenville lawyer and newspaper editor. Mayor of Greenville 1860–61. Md. Sara Sloan. Appointed Confederate receiver in 1861. Col., 16th SC, Nov. 19, 1861. Resigned April 28, 1862, after failing to be reelected. Col., 3d SC State Reserves (a 6-month unit), Aug. 15, 1862. Died May 20, 1867, Greenville. Buried Springwood (City) Cemetery, Greenville. Gen. N. G. Evans found Elford "faithful and gallant." Elford believed he lost reelection because he was too much of a taskmaster.

Elliott, Benjamin Franklin. Born Aug. 8, 1830, Winchester, VA. Grew up in Madison Mills, VA. Grad. VMI 1851. Moved to CA, then settled near Bates City, MO. In KS-MO border wars. To Lafayette Co. by 1860. Farmer. Md. Susan B. Gibbs. Capt. and drillmaster, 2d Inf., 8th Div., MSG, 1861. Col., Sept. 10, 1861. Resigned Nov. 11, 1861. Pvt. Co. C, 3d Mo. Bn. PACS (later 6th MO), March 2, 1862. WIA at Pea Ridge in face. Discharged June 5, 1862, for disability. Capt. Co. I, 5th (Shelby's) MO Cav., Sept. 10, 1862. Led Shelby's scouting company. Major, 9th (aka 10th Bn., 1st, Elliott's) MO Cav., Sept. 26, 1862. Injured at Prairie Grove while leading a charge, when his horse fell on him. Col., by 1864. Led Shelby's Brigade at Westport. Fled to Mexico after war but soon returned to MO. Farmer in Lafayette Co. Sheriff. Died Aug. 13, 1911, Odessa, MO. Buried Odessa Cemetery. A fellow officer thought Elliott "intelligent, sober, energetic, reliable, skillful."

Ellis, Daniel Hix. Born Aug. 16, 1824, Beaufort Dist., SC. Planter in Beaufort Dist. prewar. State representative 1852–56. Md. Emily Searson. Col., 11th SC, May 3, 1862. Resigned Nov. 27, 1862, a resignation that delighted his superiors. State senator 1862–65. Confederate tax collector for parts of the Beaufort Dist., 1863–64. Died Dec. 13, 1873. Buried Ellis Plantation Cemetery, near Hampton, SC. A soldier in the 11th called Ellis "a good for nothing drunken, fiddling politician."

Elmore, Henry Marshall. Born July 28, 1816, SC. Attd. UAL. Macon Co., AL, planter. Probate judge in Macon Co. Moved to TX in 1854. Farmer in Walker Co. Md. Mrs. Elizabeth F. Harris; Mary De Armond. Enlisted as Pvt., 20th TX (a regiment of older men, raised for coast defense). Elected col., May 14, 1862. Sta-

tioned in Galveston most of the war. One inspector found the 20th "poorly of-
ficered. They have no notions of discipline or military instruction." However,
subsequent inspections found the regiment much improved. Lived in Waverly,
San Jacinto Co., TX, postwar. Lawyer. Died Feb. 21, 1879, Waverly. Buried Old
Waverly Cemetery.

Embry, Benjamin Taylor. Born April 19, 1820, Green Co., KY. Attd. Centre
College. Grad. St. Joseph's College. Prewar lawyer in KY. Then to Memphis; Des
Arc, AR, from 1848; and Pope Co., AR, from 1853. Farmer and merchant in AR.
State representative 1850–51. Md. Sallie M. Taylor. Capt. Co. B, 2d AR MR, July
15, 1861. Lt. col., July 25, 1861. Col., Jan. 26, 1862. Dropped at May 6, 1862, reorganization. Resigned May 2, 1862. State senator 1862–63. Lived in Little Rock
and Atkins, Pope Co., postwar. Lawyer; planter; grocer. State senator 1883–86.
President of the State Senate. Died Jan. 16, 1892, Atkins. Buried Embry family
graveyard at his home in Pope Co. Middle name also given as "Towler."

Erwin, Andrew Eugene. Born Oct. 2, 1833, near Lexington, KY. Called by his
middle name. Grandson of Henry Clay. Attd. KMI. Clerk in a NY collecting
house 1850–51. Clerk for a steamship company in CA, 1851–53. Farmer and
merchant in Independence, Jackson Co., MO, 1854–61. Md. Josephine Russell.
Major, 1st Inf., 8th Div., MSG, Sept. 9, 1861. 1st lt. PACS, Mo. Bn. (later 6th MO),
March 2, 1862. Lt. col., May 15, 1862. Col., 8th MO, Aug. 26, 1862. WIA Pea Ridge
and Corinth. KIA Vicksburg, June 25, 1863, while leading a counterattack. Buried
Vicksburg; reburied Lexington Cemetery, near his grandfather. One soldier in the
6th wrote in his diary that Erwin's "men all loved him like a brother."

Estes, John Baylus. Born June 4, 1835, Anderson Dist., SC. Reared in Hart
and Franklin Cos., GA. Teacher in Jonesboro, GA, prewar. Md. Fannie Bryant.
Capt. Co. D, 44th GA, March 4, 1862. Lt. col., March 17, 1862. Col., June 26,
1862. WIA Mechanicsburg. Resigned May 26, 1863, due to his wounds. Lived in
Gainesville, Hall Co., postwar. Lawyer. State representative 1880–81. Judge.
Died Sept. 16, 1903, Gainesville. Buried Alta Vista Cemetery, Gainesville.

Estes, William Newton. Born Aug. 8, 1831, Fort Payne, De Kalb Co., AL. Prewar farmer near Lebanon, De Kalb Co. Md. Christiane A. McCampbell. Major,
11th AL Cav. Bn., 1862. Lt. col., 3d Confederate Cav. (formed from the 11th Bn.),
Sept. 1, 1862. Col., probably March 26, 1863. KIA at Davis's Ford, on Chickamauga Creek, Sept. 17, 1863. Buried Lebanon Cemetery.

Evans, John Wesley. Born Dec. 24, 1827, Macon, GA. Reared in Bibb Co. Pre-
war lawyer in Bainbridge, Early Co., Murray Co., and Chattanooga. Md. Lucy A.
Beck; Ann Lenoir. Capt. Co. G, 1st GA Regulars, March 18, 1861. Col., 64th GA,
March 26, 1863. WIA Olustee. KIA Battle of the Crater, July 30, 1864. Buried

Blandford Cemetery, Petersburg, in an unmarked grave. "[A]s gallant and amiable a man as ever lived or died."

Evans, Peter Gustavus. Born 1822, Chatham Co., NC. Attd. William & Mary College and UNC. Wealthy planter in Chatham and later Craven Co. Md. Ann Eliza Morehead, daughter of Gov. John Morehead. Capt. Co. E, 3d NC Cav., Oct. 7, 1861. Dropped at April 28, 1862, reorganization. Col., 5th NC Cav., Oct. 1, 1862. MWIA and POW Middleburg, June 21, 1863, while leading a charge. Died July 24, 1863, at a Union hospital in Washington, DC. Buried Rock Creek Cemetery, DC; reburied Presbyterian Cemetery, Greensboro, NC. "A gallant soldier and a good officer."

Ewell, Benjamin Stoddard. Born June 10, 1810, Washington, DC. Elder brother of Lt. Gen. Richard Ewell. Attd. Georgetown U. Grad. USMA 1832. Taught at USMA 1832–36. Professor at Hampden-Sydney, Washington, and William & Mary colleges prewar. Md. Julia McIlvain. Col., 32d VA, July 1, 1861. Dropped at May 1862 reorganization. Appointed col. and AAG, Nov. 24, 1862. AAG on Gen. Joseph Johnston's staff 1862–64. AAG on his brother's staff, 1864. Resigned March 20, 1865, due to disability (varicose veins and diarrhea). President of William & Mary College postwar. Died June 19, 1894, Williamsburg. Buried College Cemetery, Williamsburg. Ewell's papers are at William & Mary College.

Ewing, Andrew. Born June 17, 1813, Nashville, TN. Grad. U. of Nashville. Nashville lawyer. US congressman 1849–51. Trustee of U. of Nashville. Md. Margaret Hines; Rowena Williams. VADC to Gen. Bragg, 1862. Appointed col., Dec. 16, 1862, to become presiding judge of the military court of Polk's Corps. Later judge advocate, Hardee's Corps. Died June 16, 1864, Atlanta. Buried City Cemetery, Nashville.

Fain, John Simpson. Born April 25, 1818, Asheville, NC. Merchant and attorney in Union Co., GA. Officer in Mexican War. Md. Adaline Addington; Malinda Peake; Mira M. Lee. Capt. Co. C, 1st GA Regulars, Feb. 1, 1861. Resigned Sept. 11, 1861. Capt. Co. K, 8th GA State Troops, Nov. 7, 1861. Lt. col., Dec. 14, 1861. Mustered out March 1862. Lt. col. of the inf. bn., Smith's GA Legion, May 24, 1862. Unit transferred to 65th GA, March 1863. Col., 65th GA, March 9, 1863. Resigned June 20, 1863, due to erysipelas of the face. Lawyer in Morgantown, GA, postwar. State representative 1857–59, 1875–76. Moved to Salmon City, ID, around 1878 and then to Smith Co., TX, just prior to his death. Died May 21, 1894, at his son's home near Tyler, TX. Buried Midway Cemetery, near Tyler. Fain's Mexican War pension application contains an extensive narrative of his war service.

Fain, Richard Gammon. Born March 6, 1811, Rogersville, TN. Grad. USMA, 1832. Lt., US Army, resigning in Dec. 1832. Hawkins Co. merchant and banker. Clerk of Hawkins Co. court. Md. Eliza Anderson. Appointed commissary gen. of the TN state army, May 1861. Major and commissary, PACS, Sept. 27, 1861. On Gen. Zollicoffer's staff, 1861–62. Resigned May 31, 1862, having been authorized to raise a regiment. Col., 63d TN, July 30, 1862. Resigned Nov. 3, 1863, due to chronic liver disease. President of Rogersville & Jefferson Railroad. Rogersville farmer postwar. Died Sept. 12, 1878, Mossy Creek, TN. Buried Rogersville Presbyterian Cemetery. A soldier of the 63d stated "Col. Fain was an old man and seldom with us." His wife's wartime diary has been published.

Faison, Paul Fletcher. Born May 4, 1840. Raleigh, NC. Attd. Randolph-Macon College and USMA, resigning from the latter in 1861. Lived in Northampton Co. prewar. Md. Anne Haywood Badger. Capt., NC State Troops, early 1861. Major, 14th NC, May 28, 1861. Defeated for reelection at April 1862 reorganization. Col., 56th NC, July 31, 1862. Court-martialed and acquitted for neglect of duty when the 56th was surprised in 1863. Appmx. Raleigh cotton dealer postwar. Inspector of Indian affairs out west. Died March 3, 1896, in a Shawnee, OK, hotel. Buried Oakwood Cemetery, Raleigh.

Falkner, William Clark. Born July 6, 1825, TN. Resided in Ripley, MS, prewar. Lawyer and railroad builder. Author of three books. Militia general. Officer in Mexican War. Md. Holland Pearce. Capt. Co. F, 2d MS, March 4, 1861. Col., May 10, 1861. WIA 1st Manassas. Dropped at April 1862 reorganization. Col., 7th MS Cav. (aka 1st MS PR), Aug. 1, 1862. The 7th, plagued by desertions and with a poor combat record, essentially dissolved in 1863, leaving Falkner (in his own words) "without employment." Falkner resigned, Oct. 31, 1863, due to "hemorrhoids and indigestion." Lawyer in Ripley postwar. State legislator. Assassinated Nov. 5, 1889, by his former business partner, who was later acquitted of the shooting. Buried Ripley Cemetery. Falkner was great-grandfather of the novelist William Faulkner, who modeled some of his characters after the colonel.

Fannin, James Henry. Born Sept. 19, 1835, La Grange, GA. Attd. UGA. La Grange planter prewar. Construction engineer for the Vicksburg and Shreveport Railroad. Md. Julia Ferrell. Helped raise Co. B, 60th GA, but did not enter service with it. Col., 1st GA Reserves, May 7, 1864. Commandant of the post at Andersonville. POW Fort Tyler in 1865. Troup Co. planter postwar. State legislator. Trustee, UGA. Vice president of the State Agricultural Society. Died Oct. 23, 1909, Savannah. Buried Hillview Cemetery, La Grange. In his 1862 application for appointment as a QM, he was recommended as "a man of intelligence & integrity" who was "physically weak."

Fant, Abner Elkin. Born Feb. 22, 1816, Fairfield Dist., SC. Grad. SC Medical College in 1836. Physician in SC and AL. Moved practice to Noxubee Co., MS, by 1845. Md. Elizabeth O. Starke; Martha Taliaferro. Capt. Co. H, 5th MS, Aug. 30, 1861. Col., Sept. 5, 1861. Honorably discharged June 23, 1862, after the 5th's reorganization. Capt. of a home guard company in 1864. Surgeon, 1st MS Cav. Paroled May 26, 1865, Selma. Physician in West Point, MS, postwar. Newspaper editor. Died Dec. 18, 1883, MS. Buried Amity Baptist Cemetery, Sparta, MS.

Faribault, George Henry. Born c. 1830, NC. Planter in Wake Co. prewar. State representative 1858–59. Md. Rosa Alston. Capt. Co. E, 14th NC, May 1, 1861. Lt. col., 47th NC, March 24, 1862. Col., April 5, 1863. WIA Gettysburg. Resigned Jan. 5, 1865, due to ill health. Farmer in Wake Co. postwar. Moved to San Antonio, TX, in 1885. Admitted to the Austin, TX, Confederate Home in 1894. Died Dec. 16, 1898, San Antonio. Probably buried in an unmarked grave in City Cemetery No. 4, San Antonio, near his wife.

Farinholt, Benjamin Lyons. Born May 26, 1839, near Yorktown, VA. Reared in West Point. Attd. Randolph-Macon College. Barhamsville resident prewar. Md. Leila May Farinholt, a cousin, in 1860. 2d lt. Co. E, 53d VA, July 8, 1861. 1st lt., Sept. 30, 1861. Capt., March 5, 1863. WIA and POW Gettysburg. Escaped from Johnson's Island Prison Feb. 22, 1864. Capt., VA Reserves, May 26, 1864. In charge of an improvised battalion of bridge guards and reservists that protected the Staunton River Brigade against Union cavalry during the Petersburg Campaign. Lt. col., Farinholt's Bn. VA Reserves (formed from his bridge guard), July 18, 1864. Col., 1st VA Reserves, Aug. 12, 1864. Dry goods merchant in Essex Co., Baltimore and West Point postwar. Died Dec. 24, 1919, West Point. Buried Sunny Slope Cemetery, West Point. Middle name also given as "Lines." Papers at VAHS.

Fariss, Robert Clement. Born Feb. 1830, New Canton, VA. Studied medicine. Moved to AL in 1851. Merchant in Montgomery. Capt. of vol. militia company. Md. Catherine Dickenson. Capt., Montgomery "Independent Rifles" (his old militia company, later Co. E, 6th AL), early 1861. Lt. col., 17th AL, Sept. 5, 1861. Col., March 24, 1862. WIA Shiloh. Resigned April 9, 1862, due to his Shiloh wound and hemorrhoids. Recommended by AL congressmen in 1863 for Board of Examiners of Impressment as a "thorough business man of unquestioned integrity." Postwar grocer in Montgomery. Died Nov. 17, 1905, Montgomery. Buried Oakwood Cemetery, Montgomery.

Farquharson, Robert. Born Sept. 14, 1814, Banffshire, Scotland. Came to US with parents in 1827, eventually settling in Fayetteville, Lincoln Co., TN. Merchant, farmer, lawyer. Mayor of Fayetteville. State representative. Militia general. Major in Mexican War. WIA at Cerro Gordo. Md. Sarah Burk. Pvt. Co. F, 41st

TN, Nov. 4, 1861. Col., Nov. 27, 1861. POW Fort Donelson, exch. July 31, 1862. Arrested for intoxication while on duty but acquitted. Retired to Invalid Corps June 3, 1864, suffering from "varicole [swelling] of the left spermatic chord." Paroled May 10, 1865, Meridian. Postwar Chancery Court clerk. Died Sept. 26, 1869, Fayetteville. Buried Rose Hill Cemetery.

Farrell, Michael. Born c. 1838, NY. Noncommissioned officer in the US Army. Left the army to live in St. Louis. Moved to Yalobusha Co., MS, just before the war. Brick mason. Unmd. Drillmaster, 15th MS, 1861. Capt. Co. E., June 7, 1861. Elected lt. col., May 8, 1862. Col., Aug. 1, 1862. Relieved of command by Gen. Rust in Jan. 1863 for commandeering brigade wagons to haul supplies for his regiment but soon reinstated. MWIA Franklin. Multiple wounds, forcing amputation of both legs. Died in a Franklin hospital at "Carnton" Dec. 25, 1864. Buried McGavock Confederate Cemetery, Franklin. Farrell, who spoke with a thick Irish brogue, was considered an expert drillmaster, "fitted by nature for a soldier and to command men." When he settled in the South he had neither connections nor money and rose solely on merit. He normally led his regiment from the front, his back to the enemy, facing his men to check their alignment. Under Farrell's training the 15th won several drill contests against other regiments.

Faulkner, William Wallace. Born c. 1836, Christian Co., KY. Merchant in Woodville, KY, prewar. Md. Ann E. Walden. 1st lt., KSG, April 23, 1861. Capt. of scouts/PR operating in KY and west TN. POW Oct. 16, 1862, near Island No. 10. Escaped while being shipped to Johnson's Island Prison. Authorized March 12, 1863, to raise a battalion of PR. Lt. col. of the battalion 1863. Col., 12th KY Cav., Jan. 28, 1864 (appointed by Gen. Forrest under authority of the president). WIA severely at Tupelo. Killed in Dresden, TN, Feb. 1865, by some AWOL soldiers he was trying to bring back to the army. Buried Herring Cemetery, Ballard Co., KY.

Fauntleroy, Charles Magill. Born Aug. 21, 1822, Warrenton, VA. Educated Warrenton Academy. Officer, USN, 1838–61. Md. Janet Knox; Sally A. Souter; Mary Chambers Elgee. Lt., VA state navy, April 20, 1861. Lt., CSN, June 10, 1861. Commanded battery at Harpers Ferry. Capt. AADC to Gen. Joseph Johnston in 1861. 1st lt., CSS *Nashville*, 1861–62. Col., Sept. 30, 1862 (with temporary rank). AAG and IG to Gen. Johnston 1862–63. Served in naval station, TMD, 1863. Ordered to naval duty in France in late 1863. Took command of the CSS *Rappahannock* in Europe in 1864. On duty with the *Rappahannock,* laid up in France, until the end of the war. Lived in retirement in Rapides Parish, LA (where his 3d wife had family) postwar. Later moved back to Leesburg. Died July 28, 1889, Loudoun Co., VA. Buried Leesburg Presbyterian Cemetery. A fellow staff officer found Fauntleroy "gruff & somewhat selfish."

Featherston, Lucius. Born c. 1834, MS. Nephew of Gen. W. S. Featherston. Reared in Chickasaw Co. Grad. UMS 1854. Prewar lawyer in Clarendon, Monroe Co., AR. Unmd. Major of AR State Troops at Wilson's Creek. Capt. Co. F, 5th AR, July 27, 1861. Col., April 16, 1862 (elected at reorganization). 5th consolidated with 13th AR, July 1863. KIA Chickamauga, Sept. 19, 1863. Buried on the battlefield; reburied postwar in the Confederate Cemetery, Marietta, GA.

Feeney, William A. Born c. 1820, Madison Co., AL. Magistrate and railroad agent in Senatobia, MS, prewar. Md. Bettie Miller. Lt. "Senatobia Invincibles" (Co. I, 9th MS, a 12-month unit), Feb. 4, 1861. Company mustered out March 27, 1862. Capt. Co. B, 42d MS (the reorganized "Invincibles"), May 14, 1862. Major, May 14, 1862. WIA Gettysburg (1st day). Col., Dec. 18, 1863. KIA Wilderness, May 5, 1864. Buried Fredericksburg Confederate Cemetery. A comrade called Feeney "a Christian gentleman in the strictest sense of the term [who] possessed excellent judgment."

Feild, Everard Meade. Born July 18, 1831, Greensville Co., VA. Said to have attd. a military school, probably MD Military Academy. Planter in Greensville Co. prewar. Grocer in Petersburg and in Sussex Co. Capt. of vol. militia. Md. Maria L. Fox. Capt. Co. F, 12th VA, June 6, 1861. Major, Aug. 30, 1862. Lt. col., Oct. 3, 1862. WIA three times, including a wound at Spotsylvania that disabled him. Col., July 30, 1864. Lumber inspector and railroad express agent in Petersburg postwar. Died July 7, 1915, Petersburg. Buried Blandford Cemetery, Petersburg.

Feild, Hume R. Born Sept. 11, 1834, Pulaski, Giles Co., TN. Attd. KMI. Druggist in Giles Co. prewar. Md. Henrietta Cockrill. Capt. Co. K, 1st TN, May 2, 1861. Major, date not specified. Col., May 1, 1862. Regiment consolidated with 27th TN, Jan. 1863, with Feild heading the combined 1st/27th. WIA Kennesaw Mountain. Led Gist's Brigade at Bentonville. Paroled May 1, 1865, Greensboro. Farmer in Union City, TN, postwar. Died June 17, 1921, Union City, of a cerebral hemorrhage. Buried East View Cemetery, Union City. Sam Watkins claimed Feild, a crack shot, killed 21 Yankees by himself during the war and called Feild "the bravest man, I think, I ever knew."

Ferebee, Dennis Dozier. Born Nov. 9, 1815, Currituck Co., NC. Grad. UNC. Camden Co. lawyer and planter prewar. State representative 1846–50. Militia colonel. Delegate to NC Secession Convention. Md. Sarah R. McPherson. Col., 4th NC Cav., Aug. 16, 1862. WIA (foot) Bristoe Station, Oct. 23, 1863. Absent due to wounds 1863–64. Resigned March 24, 1865, to serve on Gov. Vance's staff. Camden Co. farmer and public official postwar. Died April 26, 1884, Camden Co. Buried in a family cemetery in Camden Co. Papers at UNC. One colonel called him "a man of judgment and bravery."

Ferguson, Milton Jameson. Born Feb. 24, 1833, Wayne Co., VA (now WVA). Attorney in Wayne Co. prewar. Md. Martha J. Wellman in 1854. Col., 167th VA Militia, 1861. Captured in July 1861 and released on parole. Exch. Jan.–Feb. 1862. Capt. Co. H, Ferguson's Bn. VA Cav. (later, 16th VA Cav.), Sept. 15, 1862. Col., 16th VA Cav., Jan. 15, 1863. Captured in Wayne Co. Feb. 15, 1864. WIA Opequon Creek. Paroled May 22, 1865, Charleston, WVA. Lawyer and circuit judge in Louisa, KY (Ferguson and other ex-Confederates were barred from practicing law in WVA), postwar. Died April 22, 1881, Louisa. Buried Fairview Cemetery, Wayne Co.

Fisher, Charles Frederick. Born Dec. 26, 1816, Salisbury, NC. Attd. Yale. Planter in Salisbury. Mine owner. Editor of a pro-Calhoun newspaper, the *Western Carolinian*. State senator. President of North Carolina Railroad. Col., 6th NC, May 16, 1861. One soldier found Fisher "noble, true, brave—almost to a fault" and the "best provider" in the army. KIA 1st Manassas, while leading a charge. Buried Old Lutheran Cemetery, Salisbury. Family papers at UNC. Fort Fisher near Wilmington was named for him.

Fisk, Stuart Wilkins. Born Aug. 28, 1820, Natchez, MS. Grad. Yale and Harvard Law School. New Orleans lawyer prewar. Helped manage his family's vast plantation holdings in LA and MS. Unmd. Capt. Co. B (the "Crescent Rifles"), 1st LA Bn. (Dreux's), April 15, 1861. Col., 25th LA, March 23, 1862, a regiment he largely uniformed out of his own pocket. Commanded post of Okolona, MS, July 1862. Col., 16th/25th Consolidated, upon the Nov. 30, 1862, consolidation. Appointed col. and judge, military court of Forney's Corps, Dec. 16, 1862. Before taking this post, he was MWIA Stones River Dec. 31, 1862, during a charge that nearly wiped out his regiment. Died Jan. 1, 1863. Buried near the battlefield, about 1 mile east of Murfreesboro. A contemporary praised Fisk as "[d]evoted to his men . . . fully trusted and deeply regretted."

Fite, John Amenas. Born Feb. 10, 1832, De Kalb Co., TN. Grad, Cumberland U. Prewar Smith Co. lawyer. Md. Mary M. Mitchell. Capt. Co. B, 7th TN, May 20, 1861. Major, May 23, 1862. Lt. col., July 9, 1862. Col., April 8, 1863. WIA Mechanicsville, Cedar Mountain, and Chancellorsville. POW Gettysburg. Imprisoned until 1865. Banker and judge in Smith Co. postwar. State legislator. Adj. gen. of TN. Died Aug. 23, 1925, Lebanon, TN. Buried Old Carthage Cemetery, Carthage. Fite's memoirs are at TSLA.

Fitzgerald, Edward. Born c. 1836, TN, son of US congressman William Fitzgerald. Lawyer in Henry Co., TN, prewar. Md. Martha Hawkins. Capt. Co. F, 154th TN, May 14, 1861. Led a scouting party at the Battle of Belmont that captured 8 prisoners. Major, Oct. 3, 1861. Col., May 10, 1862. KIA Richmond,

KY, Aug. 30, 1862. Fitzgerald's brigade commander at Richmond eulogized his "kind and gentle bearing," diligence, and bravery.

Fitzgerald, William Bushby. Born c. 1822, Washington, DC. Resided in Norfolk prewar. Officer, USN, 1838–61. Md. Clara E. Semmes, cousin of Admiral Raphael Semmes. Lt., VA State Navy, early 1861. Commanded land batteries near Yorktown. Lt., CSN, June 20, 1861. Col. of a projected Confederate artillery regiment, the 1st Light Art., which never formally organized, though the individual companies were raised by April 1862. Died of an "apoplectic spasm" Aug. 9, 1862, Greenville, SC, where he had gone to restore his health. Buried Christ Episcopal Church, Greenville.

Fitzhugh, William F. Born March 12, 1818, Logan Co., KY. When he was a child his family moved to MO, where he grew up. Moved to Melissa, Collin Co., TX, in 1845. Farmed near Melissa. Soldier in Seminole War, Mormon War, Mexican War. Capt., Texas Rangers. Md. Mary Rattan. Capt. Co. B, 16th TX Cav., Feb. 17, 1862. Col., May 8, 1862. Resigned Oct. 1864, due to ill health. Postwar farmer in Melissa, TX. Doorkeeper of State Senate. Killed Oct. 23, 1883, in McKinney, TX, when thrown from a wagon. Buried first Forest Grove Cemetery, near McKinney, subsequently at Fairview Cemetery, Denison.

Fizer, John Calvin. Born May 4, 1835, Dyer Co., TN. Reared by an uncle in Panola Co., MS. Memphis merchant prewar. Md. M. Hayes Dunn in 1866. Lt. Co. H, 17th MS, May 27, 1861. Adj., June 4, 1861. Lt. col., April 26, 1862. WIA Fredericksburg, Gettysburg (3 times), Fort Sanders (lost right arm). Col., Feb. 26, 1864. Retired due to disability, June 12, 1864. Recalled to lead a brigade of GA Reservists in the Carolinas Campaign. Cotton broker and dry goods merchant in Memphis postwar. Died June 14, 1876, Memphis, of the "flux." Buried Elmwood Cemetery, Memphis. Often listed as a Confederate general postwar. A soldier in the 17th said Fizer "is a great favorite with the soldiers." After the war he changed the spelling of his name from "Fiser" to "Fizer," to spell it as it sounded.

Flanagin, Harris. Born Nov. 3, 1817, Roadstone, NJ. Reared in Clermont, PA. To AR in 1837. Prewar teacher and lawyer in Clark Co., AR. State legislator and Whig leader. Delegate to AR Secession Convention. Md. Martha E. Nash. Capt. Co. E, 2d AR MR, July 27, 1861. Col., May 8, 1862. Elected governor of AR Nov. 15, 1862, while still in the army, having been nominated by representatives of all prewar political parties. Gov. of AR 1862–65. VADC to Gen. Holmes at the Battle of Helena. Postwar lawyer in Arkadelphia. Died there Oct. 23, 1874. Buried Rose Hill Cemetery. His diary is at the AR Historical Commission. One brother served in the Union Army.

Fleming, David George. Born April 1832, Columbia, SC. Grad. SCMA. In KS-MO border wars. Civil engineer in Columbia in 1860. Unmd. Lt. Co. B, 1st SC Art., Jan. 1861. Capt., Jan. 1, 1862. WIA Battery Wagner Aug. 20, 1863. Col., 22d SC, June 2, 1864. He was appointed from outside the regiment on the recommendation of the 22d's officers, two of whom were his brothers. KIA in the Crater explosion, July 30, 1864. Body never found. A memorial stone for Col. Fleming is in Oakwood Cemetery, Spartanburg. Gen. Elliott found Fleming "reliable, but you must not crowd him with ideas."

Fletcher, James Henry. Born March 25, 1839, Stewart Co., TN. Moved to Little Rock c. 1859. Deputy sheriff of Pulaski Co. prewar. Md. Mary Williams; Nellie Taylor. 1st lt. Co. F, 1st AR, May 29, 1861. Drillmaster under Gen. Polk in early 1862. Pvt. Co. A, 20th AR (King's), Feb. 17, 1862. Major, April 9, 1862. Lt. col., July 7, 1862. Col., probably Oct. 4, 1862, though his service record contains no mention of the promotion. Resigned Jan. 5, 1863, due to ill health and the fact that the regiment had been reduced to 75 men. Purchased supplies in TX for the army for the remainder of the war. Lived in Stewart Co., TN, 1865–67; Sykestown, MO, 1867–85; then Little Rock. Farmer, miller, merchant. Died June 6, 1906, Little Rock. Buried Oakland Cemetery, Little Rock.

Flournoy, George M. Born Nov. 20, 1832, Louisville, GA. Attd. UGA. Grad. in law from UAL. Prewar Austin, TX, attorney. State attorney general. Secessionist leader. Md. Eugenia Haralson; Virginia L. Holman. Delegate to TX Secession Convention, coauthoring the declaration of causes for secession. Appointed col., Oct. 18, 1861, by Gen. Hebert, to raise a regiment. Raised the 16th TX, of which he was (on April 25, 1862) commissioned col. The TX congressional delegation recommended him for promotion to brigadier, citing his "marked abilities" and his often leading a brigade in Walker's Texas Div. Detailed to court-martial duty, 1865. Fled to Mexico postwar, where he served in Maximilian's army. Returned to TX and practiced law in Galveston. Moved to CA in the 1870s. Lawyer in San Francisco. Died Sept. 18, 1889, San Francisco. Buried Mt. Calvary Cemetery, San Francisco; reburied Holy Cross Cemetery, Colma, CA.

Flournoy, Peter Creed. Born Sept. 15, 1828, Chesterfield Co., VA. Attd. UVA and U. of MD Medical School. Prewar physician in Amelia Co., VA, and later Linneus, MO. Sgt. VA volunteers in Mexican War. Md. Mary Jeter. Major, 3d Inf., 3d Div., MSG, Sept. 20, 1861. Capt. Co. K, 2d MO, Jan. 16, 1862. Court-martialed and found guilty of fighting with his sergeant. Col., July 20, 1863. POW Vicksburg. Led Cockrell's MO Brigade in late 1864. POW Fort Blakely. Paroled May 16, 1865, Meridian. Physician postwar in KS and Linneus. Died March 2, 1891, Linneus. Buried Old Linneus Cemetery. A fellow officer called Flournoy "incomparable in battle."

Flournoy, Thomas Stanhope. Born Dec. 15, 1811, Prince Edward Co., VA. Grad. Hampden-Sydney College. Lawyer in Halifax, VA, prewar. US congressman 1847–49. Delegate to VA Secession Convention. Md. Susan A. Love; Mildred H. Coles. Capt. Co. G, 6th VA Cav., Aug. 19, 1861. Major, April 15, 1862. Col., July 16, 1862. Resigned Oct. 15, 1862, citing a "domestic affliction" (probably the illness of a young daughter). Lost race for governor of VA in 1863. Lawyer in Danville postwar. Died March 12, 1883, on his estate in Halifax Co. Buried in a family cemetery on his estate. Flournoy's "power of swaying a crowd from the stump was second only to his effectiveness before a jury."

Floweree, Charles Conway. Born Oct. 26, 1842, Salem, Fauquier Co., VA. Reared in Independence, MO. Cadet at VMI when the war began. Md. Jennie Wilson in 1867. Drillmaster (with other cadets) in Richmond, spring 1861. Lt. Co. K, 7th VA, May 1861. Appointed adj., 7th VA, Oct. 7, 1861. Major, April 27, 1862. WIA Williamsburg. Arrested Feb. 19, 1863, in Richmond for intoxication while on duty. Sentenced to be cashiered, but sentence remitted. Lt. col., June 3, 1862. WIA 2d Manassas (thigh). Col., July 21, 1863. POW Sayler's Creek. Released July 28, 1865. Moved to Vicksburg, MS, in 1866. Lawyer, banker, postmaster. President of Vicksburg Ice Co. Active in establishing the Vicksburg National Military Park. Died Sept. 16, 1929, at "Floweree," his home in Vicksburg. Buried Cedar Hill Cemetery, Vicksburg. One soldier called Floweree "the most immodest obscene profane low flung blackguard on this earth." Brother of Lt. Col. D. W. Floweree, MSG.

Floyd, Richard Ferdinand. Born July 7, 1810, Fairfield Plantation, Camden Co., GA. County sheriff. Capt. GA Volunteers in Seminole War. Moved to St. Augustine, FL, prior to 1850. Draftsman. Planter in St. Augustine and St. John's Co. Md. Mary Ann Chevalier. Col., FL State Troops, and ADC to Gov. Milton, 1861. Appointed brig. gen. and commander in chief FL State Troops, Nov. 29, 1861. Commanded state forces garrisoning Apalachicola. Col., 8th FL, July 15, 1862. Resigned Oct. 2, 1862, due to illness. Postwar insurance agent in Clay Co., FL. Died June 27, 1870, Green Cove Springs. Buried Hickory Grove Cemetery, Green Cove Springs. A favorite to Gov. Milton, who called him "the only gentleman in Florida occupying a distinguished position whose reputation has never been assailed." Uncle of Col. C. R. F. Hopkins.

Flynt, Guilford Griffin. Born Oct. 4, 1829, Culloden, GA. Farmer in Newton Co., MS, prewar. Md. Eliza Mapp; Patience Adams. Capt. Co. B, 8th MS, May 11, 1861. Col., Aug. 31, 1861. Resigned April 22, 1862. Farmer in Monroe Co., GA, postwar. Died Feb. 24, 1903, Culloden. Buried Culloden Cemetery. Col. Chandler of the 8th thought Flynt was "a fine man personally, but lacked the indispensable qualities of a commanding officer—leadership, initiative, magnetism and fortitude."

Folk, George Nathaniel. Born Feb. 18, 1831, Isle of Wight Co., VA. Attd. William & Mary College. Prewar lawyer in VA, Charlotte, NC, and Boone, NC. State representative 1856–57, 1860–61. Md. Elizabeth A. Councill. Capt. Co. D, 1st NC Cav., May 16, 1861. Resigned May 9, 1862. Lt. col., 7th NC Cav. Bn., June 18, 1862. Col., 6th NC Cav. (formed from the 7th Bn.), Aug. 3, 1863. WIA Chickamauga and Pea Vine Church. POW near Kinston, June 22, 1864. One of the "Immortal 600." Exch. Dec. 15, 1864. Paroled May 26, 1865, Salisbury. Law teacher in Boone, Lenoir, and Caldwell Cos. postwar. State senator 1876–77. Died May 14, 1896, Lenoir. Buried Bellavue Cemetery, Lenoir. Folk had trouble with his regiment, many members of which were closet Unionists and "Sunshine Patriots."

Folsom, Robert Warren. Born Aug. 28, 1835, Savannah, GA. Reared in Twiggs Co. Physician in Wilkerson Co. prewar. Unmd. Capt. Co. B, 14th GA, July 9, 1861. Major, Aug. 1, 1861. Lt. col., Sept. 1, 1861. WIA Mechanicsville. Col., Oct. 23, 1862. Repeatedly cited for gallantry and good conduct. MWIA Wilderness, May 6, 1864, while leading a counterattack. Died May 24, 1864, Richmond. Buried Hollywood Cemetery. According to an old county history, Folsom was a "born leader and a rigid disciplinarian."

Folsom, Sampson. Born June 14, 1820, Oktibbeha Co., MS. Choctaw tribal leader and member of a prominent mixed-blood family. Merchant in Moose Prairie, the Choctaw Nation, prewar. Md. Susan Catherine Colbert. Col., 1st Choctaw Cav., spring 1862. Unit served in the Indian Territory for about a year and was then reorganized. Folsom does not appear to have led the regiment after reorganization. Postwar he often represented his tribe in Washington. Died Jan. 1872 near Doaksville, Indian Territory. He is often confused with his cousin, Lt. Col. Simpson Folsom, who took over the reorganized regiment.

Fontaine, Clement Royster. Born Aug. 2, 1831, Buckingham Co., VA. Attd. Hampden-Sydney College and UVA. Farmer in Buckingham Co. prewar. Md. Mary Strange. Lt. Co. A, 57th VA, May 29, 1861. Capt., April 24, 1862. Major, Feb. 4, 1863. WIA Pickett's Charge. Col., July 5, 1863. Paroled May 3, 1865, Columbia, VA. Farmer in Wytheville postwar. Died April 8, 1906, Wythe Co. Buried East End Cemetery, Wytheville. A soldier in the 57th wrote that Fontaine did not possess "great interlectual [sic] endowments."

Forbes, William Archibald. Born May 31, 1824, Richmond, VA. Grad. VMI. Professor of mathematics at VMI, 1844–46. Professor at WMI, 1847–48. Teacher and later president of Masonic College (later Stewart College) in Clarksville, TN. Md. Sarah Bryce; Mrs. Mary E. Brunson Garland. Capt. of engineers, TN state army, May 16, 1861. Capt. Co. A, 14th TN (organized mainly from his students), 1861. Col., June 6, 1861. WIA Gaines's Mill. MWIA 2d Manassas, Aug. 30, 1862. Died Sept. 2, 1862. Buried on the battlefield; reburied Shockoe Cemetery, Richmond, in 1866.

Ford, John Salmon. Born May 26, 1815, Greenville Dist., SC. Moved to TN. To TX in 1836. Physician, newspaper editor, state senator. Mexican War veteran, where his letters notifying families of soldiers' deaths, ending with "Rest In Peace," gave him the nickname "Rip." Headed the TX Rangers in the 1850s. Noted fighter of Indians and border bandits. Md. Louisa Swisher; Mary Davis; Adeline N. Smith. Delegate to TX Secession Convention. The convention put him in charge of the expedition to force the surrender of US Army posts in the Rio Grande Valley, electing him colonel of a mounted rifle regiment March 19, 1861. Col., 2d TX MR, May 18, 1861. Helped guard the Mexican border. Appointed chief of conscription in TX in 1862. In 1863 he was again sent to the Mexican Border, to raise a force and clear the Rio Grande Valley of bandits and Unionists. Commanded Western Sub-District of TX in 1865. His forces won the last battle of the Civil War, at Palmito Ranch, a month after Appomattox. Paroled July 18, 1865. Settled in Brownsville postwar. Mayor, editor, state senator, author. Died Nov. 3, 1897, San Antonio. Buried Confederate Cemetery, San Antonio. One observer called the colorful Ford "the most inveterate gambler and the hardest swearer I have ever met." Several books have been written about this multifaceted man.

Forno, Henry. Born Nov. 5, 1806, Charleston, SC. New Orleans resident. Agent for railroad. City police chief. Mexican War veteran. Militia colonel. Md. Mariah Ketchum. Lt. col., 5th LA, May 10, 1861. Col., July 31, 1862. WIA 2d Manassas. Retired April 29, 1864. Put in charge of the brigade-sized Andersonville prison garrison and later commanded prison camps in GA. Killed July 31, 1866, in a locomotive explosion at Amite, LA. Buried Girod St. Cemetery, New Orleans. The date of birth given above, from a census return, differs from one given in other sources (b. c. 1797, LA). An 1864 inspection report describes Forno as "active, intelligent, energetic, and zealous."

Forrest, Jeffrey Edward. Born June 10, 1838, Tippah Co., MS. Reared by his older brother, future Gen. Nathan Bedford Forrest, in De Soto Co. and Memphis. Slave trader in Vicksburg, MS, prewar. Md. Sallie Dyche of Aberdeen, MS, during the war. Pvt. Co. D, 7th TN Cav., 1861. 2d lt. Co. C, Forrest's TN Cav., June 1861. Capt., March 11, 1862. Resigned June 17, 1862. Major, 13th (aka 8th) TN Cav., late 1862. Col., Forrest's AL Cav. Regt., 1863. WIA severely at Bear's Creek, AL, Oct. 26, 1863. Captured and paroled there. Led brigade under his brother in 1864. KIA Feb. 22, 1864, near Okolona, MS, shot while leading the pursuit of Sooy Smith's Union cavalry. Buried Odd Fellows Cemetery, Aberdeen; reburied Elmwood Cemetery, Memphis, in 1868. Jeffrey was doted upon by his older brother, who lavished his wealth on Jeffrey's education and of all the brothers considered Jeffrey's military ability to be closest to his own.

Forsberg, Ludwig August. Born Jan. 13, 1832, Stockholm, Sweden. Attd. Stockholm School of Engineering. Engineer lt. in the Swedish army. Moved to the US in 1855 to work as a civil engineer, settling in Charleston, SC. Worked on the US Capitol Building. Md. Mrs. Mollie Otey. Volunteer topographical engineer at Charleston, April 1861. Lt. of Infantry, PACS, Nov. 11, 1861. On Gen. Floyd's staff. Helped drill 51st VA. Cited for bravery at Fort Donelson. Lt. col., 51st VA, May 26, 1862. Col., July 8, 1863. WIA Opequon Creek (right hand). POW Waynesboro. Released July 24, 1865. Civil engineer in Lynchburg postwar. Died July 15, 1910, Lynchburg. Buried Presbyterian Cemetery, Lynchburg. Papers (including his memoir of the war) at Washington & Lee U. Forsberg was the highest ranking Swedish-born Confederate.

Forsyth, Charles Meigs. Born c. 1836, AL. Attd. GMI. Lt. in vol. militia. Prewar clerk in Mobile. Md. Laura Sprague. 2d lt., CS Regular Army (appointed from DC), April 26, 1861. 3d lt. Co. A, 3d AL, April 28, 1861. Regimental adj., April 28, 1861. Major, Aug. 15, 1861. Lt. col., May 31, 1862. Col., Aug. 20, 1863. Injured at Gettysburg, WIA at Spotsylvania. Court-martialed Oct. 21, 1864, and suspended from command, a sentence remitted by Pres. Davis due to Forsyth's past "gallantry and efficiency." Postwar editor of the *Mobile Register,* which his father owned. Wrote a short history of the 3d AL. Died March 13, 1872, in Mobile, of a self-inflicted gunshot wound. Buried Magnolia Cemetery, Mobile.

Foster, Thomas Jefferson. Born July 11, 1809, Huntsville, AL. Grad. U. of Nashville 1827. Planter and manufacturer in Lauderdale and Lawrence Cos. Md. Virginia Watkins; Ann Hood; Mrs. Longstraw. In 1861 the governor chose Foster to raise a regiment. He raised Foster's Regiment (later the 27th AL), but when the regiment officially organized, another officer (A. A. Hughes) was elected colonel instead. His compiled service record shows him as major, Foster's Regiment, in 1862, officially dropped Feb. 5, 1863. Elected to 1st and 2d Confederate Congress. "Of courtly bearing . . . fine conversational talent." Elected to US Congress after the war but not seated. Postwar planter in Lawrence Co. Died Feb. 12, 1887, Lawrence Co. Buried Florence.

Foster, William Green. Born Dec. 18, 1831, GA. Floyd Co. farmer prewar. Md. Sarah Adeline Mayo. Junior 2d lt. Co. C, 8th GA State Troops, Nov. 28, 1861. 2d lt., Dec. 20, 1861. Mustered out May 1, 1862. 1st lt. Co. F, Smith's Legion Inf. Bn., May 6, 1862. Capt., July 1, 1862. Unit became Co. D, 65th GA, March 1863.

WIA Franklin in the arm. Col., 65th GA, Feb. 4, 1865. Floyd Co. farmer postwar. State representative 1882–83. Died Oct. 22, 1892, Floyd Co. Buried Brush Arbor Baptist Church, Floyd Co. In 1864 an examining board certified Foster's "admirable good sense."

Franklin, Cyrus F. Born Aug. 8, 1823, Highland Co., OH, of VA-born parents. Mexican War veteran of an Ohio regiment. Prewar attorney in Ottumwa, IA, and Schuyler Co., MO. State legislator. "Intensely pro-slavery." Md. Maria Fernour. Capt., 2d Div., MSG, 1861. Col., 4th Cav., 2d Div., MSG, Aug.–Nov. 1861. Lt. col., 2d Northeast MO Cav. (a regiment of recruits), 1862. Col., 1862. Regiment largely dispersed by Union forces in 1862, the survivors going to form Josiah Caldwell's new 7th MO in 1863. Franklin is listed as colonel of this unit, which was soon merged into the 16th MO. Rest of war record obscure, although in 1863 he did report to Pres. Davis on affairs in MO. Postwar attorney in Memphis, TN, and Springfield, MO. Died Jan. 17, 1885, Osceola, MO. Buried Osceola Cemetery. An Iowan remembered him as "tall, angular, restless, furtive and peculiar."

Frederick, Andrew David. Born Jan. 14, 1818, Orangeburg Dist., SC. Orangeburg physician prewar. Mexican War veteran. State representative 1860–62 and 1864. Md. Louise Felder. Capt. Co. A, Lamar's Art. Bn., Nov. 19, 1861. Lt. col., 1st SC Art., May 7, 1862. Col., 2d SC Art., Oct. 17, 1862. Orangeburg physician postwar. Died Nov. 23, 1888, Orangeburg Co. Buried Paul Felder Cemetery near Orangeburg.

Freeman, Thomas Jones. Born July 19, 1827, Gibson Co., TN. Lawyer in Trenton prewar. Md. Martha Rains. Col., 22d TN, Aug. 10, 1861. WIA Shiloh and caught typhoid while recovering. Not reelected at May 11, 1862, reorganization. Appointed col., Dec. 23, 1862, to raise a regiment in West TN, but his recruiting efforts never brought in enough men, and the appointment expired. On Gen. Forrest's staff, 1864. Brownsville lawyer postwar. Justice, TN Supreme Court. Moved to TX c. 1890 for health reasons. Died Sept. 16, 1891, Dallas. Buried Oakland Cemetery, Trenton. A fellow lawyer called Freeman "the walking encyclopedia."

Freeman, Thomas Roe. Born Feb. 22, 1829, Scott Co., MO. Lived in Dent and Crawford Cos. prewar. Blacksmith, livestock trader, lawyer. Md. Mary Lamb; Mrs. Olive Fuller Spangler. Lt., Wingo's Dent Co. Cav. Co., MSG, 1861. Col., 6th Inf., 7th Div., MSG. POW Feb. 14, 1862, Crane Creek, MO. To Alton, IL, Prison Camp. Exch. Sept. 23, 1862. Major, 12th MO Cav. Bn., Jan. 26, 1864. Col., Freeman's MO Cav. (formed from the 12th Bn.), Jan. 26, 1864. Led a brigade of raw recruits in Price's 1864 Raid. Paroled Jacksonport, AR, June 5, 1865. Postwar lawyer in Jacksonport; Shannon Co.; Rolla; and Newton Co., MO. Prosecuting attorney of Newton Co. Owned a farm near Waddill. Died Feb. 28, 1893, at his daughter's home in Tiff City, MO. Buried Neosho IOOF Cemetery. John N. Edwards called Freeman's 1864 brigade a "brave brigade truly, but better than none, without doubt."

French, James Milton. Born Sept. 14, 1834, Bland Co., VA. Reared in Gladeville, Wise Co. Prewar attorney in Wytheville. Md. Rhoda Henderson. Lt. Co. A, 51st VA, July 16, 1861. Dropped May 26, 1862. Major, 63d VA, May 24, 1862. Captured April 15, 1863, in KY, while recruiting for a projected "65th VA" that never got off the ground. Exch. Col., April 4, 1864. WIA Kolb's Farm. POW Dec. 5, 1864, near Lavergne, TN. Sent to Camp Chase. Paroled July 25, 1865. Lawyer in Mercer Co., WVA, postwar. Later moved to San Diego, CA. Died Jan. 3, 1916, San Diego. Buried Mt. Hope Cemetery, San Diego. A private in the 63d said French "was a better talker than he was a military strategist."

French, William Henderson. Born 1812, Giles Co., VA. Realtor in Princeton (now part of WVA) prewar. Landowner with extensive holdings in Mercer Co. County sheriff. State representative 1844–45. State senator 1848–51. Md. Sarah Steele. Capt. Co. D, 8th VA Cav. (later Co. A, 17th VA Cav.), July 31, 1861. Col., 17th VA Cav., Jan. 28, 1863. Court-martialed Feb. 2, 1864, and reprimanded. Resigned Sept. 3, 1864. Farmed in Mercer Co., WVA, postwar. Died there July 16, 1872. Buried Shumate family cemetery, near his home.

Fristoe, Edward T. Born Dec. 16, 1830 (some sources give 1827 and 1829), Rappahannock Co., VA. Grad. VMI 1849. Attd. UVA and Columbian College in DC. Prof. of Mathematics at Columbian College 1855–60. Prof. of Mathematics at U. of MO 1860–62. Md. Julia Laub. Capt., Boone Co. Home Guards, 3d Div., MSG, April 24, 1861. Left school Feb. 25, 1862, to join the Confederate army. Capt., PACS, AAG in Price's Army, fall of 1862. Col., Fristoe's MO Cav., July 5, 1864. Led this regiment of recruits in Price's 1864 Raid. Paroled Jacksonport June 6, 1865. Returned to teaching at Columbian College in DC postwar. Prof. of Chemistry at the National College of Pharmacy. Died July 30, 1892, Washington. Buried Oak Hill Cemetery, Washington. John N. Edwards called Fristoe "a truly deserving and intelligent officer."

Fulkerson, Abraham. Born May 13, 1834, Washington Co., VA. Grad. VMI 1857. Teacher in Rogersville, TN, prewar. Md. Selina Johnson. Capt. Co. K, 19th TN, May 22, 1861. Major, June 11, 1861. Not reelected at May 10, 1862, reorganization. Lt. col., 63d TN, July 20, 1862. WIA Chickamauga. Col., Nov. 9, 1863. POW Petersburg, June 17, 1864. One of the "Immortal 600." Released from prison July 21, 1865. Lawyer in Bristol, VA, postwar. Longtime state legislator. US congressman 1881–83. Died Dec. 17, 1902, Bristol. Buried East Hill Cemetery. Fulkerson was one of six brothers in the Confederate army, three of whom became field officers.

Fulkerson, Samuel Vance. Born Oct. 31, 1822, Washington Co., VA. Reared in Grainger Co., TN. Lawyer in Estillville prewar. Judge in Abingdon. Officer in Mexican War. Unmd. Col., 37th VA, May 28, 1861. Often led a brigade. A "great favorite" of Stonewall Jackson. MWIA Gaines's Mill, died June 28 at a field hospital. Buried Sinking Springs Cemetery, Abingdon. Papers at UTX. Brother of Col. Abraham Fulkerson, 63d TN.

Fuller, Charles Alexander. Born Aug. 22, 1814, Dorchester, MA. Grad. USMA 1834. US Army officer 1834–37. Resigned and became a civil engineer, working on improving the navigation on the lower Mississippi River near New Orleans. Md. Charlotte A. Fullerton. Lt. col., 1st LA Heavy Art., April 15, 1861. Col., Aug. 14, 1861. Commanded Fort Macomb, LA, late 1861. Chief of heavy artillery, Dept. of MS and East LA, 1862–63. POW Vicksburg and paroled. Commanded an artillery brigade in the Mobile garrison, 1864–65. Paroled May 13, 1865, Meridian. Engineer in Louisville, KY, and Appleton, WI, postwar, working for the government in improving the Fox River. Died Dec. 16, 1890, Appleton. Buried Riverside Cemetery, Appleton. An obituary praised Fuller as "a man of more than ordinary intelligence . . . a large hearted man."

Fulton, Alfred S. Born Sept. 9, 1824, Fayetteville, TN. Fayetteville resident prewar. Officer in TN militia and in Mexican War. Pvt., 8th TN, May 19, 1861. Col., May 27, 1861. Discharged, Feb. 22, 1862. Lincoln Co. farmer postwar. Died Nov. 2, 1879, Lincoln Co. Buried Rose Hill Cemetery, Fayetteville. A contemporary newspaper article called Fulton "gallant and competent." Brother of Col. John S. Fulton.

Fulton, John S. Born March 31, 1828, Fayetteville, TN. Attd. Georgetown U. Lawyer in Lincoln Co. prewar. Pvt. Co. F, 44th TN, March 27, 1862. Capt., April 14, 1862. WIA Stones River. Major, April 19, 1863. Col., May 5, 1864. Led Bushrod Johnson's brigade at Chickamauga and around Petersburg. MWIA by a shell burst June 30, 1864, Petersburg, died July 4. Buried First Presbyterian Church Cemetery, Fayetteville. A sgt. in the 44th remembered Fulton as "loved by comrades and respected by officers."

Funk, John Henry Stover. Born June 28, 1837, Winchester, VA. Grad. Winchester Medical College in 1860. Marion Co. physician prewar. Capt. of vol. militia. Capt. Co. A (the "Marion rifles," his prewar militia unit), 5th VA, April 28, 1861. Lt. col., April 21, 1862. Col., Aug. 29, 1862. MWIA Opequon Creek. Died Sept. 21, 1864, at his father's home in Winchester. Buried Mt. Hebron Cemetery, Winchester.

Funsten, David. Born Oct. 14, 1819, Clarke Co., VA. Grad. Princeton. Lawyer in Alexandria, VA. State representative 1844–46. Md. Susan E. Meade. Lt. col., 11th VA, May 16, 1861. Col., May 23, 1862. WIA Seven Pines (foot). Resigned due to this wound Sept. 24, 1863. Confederate Congressman 1863–65. Died April 6, 1866, near Alexandria, of pneumonia brought on by his war wound. Buried Ivy Hill Cemetery, Alexandria. Papers at UNC and VAHS. Brother of Col. Oliver Funsten.

Funsten, Oliver Ridgeway, Sr. Born April 15, 1817, White Post, Clarke Co., VA. Grad. UVA and Jefferson Medical College. Physician in Clarke Co. prewar. State senator 1852–58. Md. Mary C. Meade; May Bowen. Capt. and ADC at Harpers Ferry, May 1861. Major, 7th VA Cav., July 17, 1861. Lt. col., 17th VA Cav. Bn., Oct. 14, 1862. Col., 11th VA Cav. (formed from the 17th Bn.), July 23, 1863. WIA Wilderness. Resigned Feb. 21, 1865, due to lumbago. Clarke Co. farmer postwar. Died July 14, 1871, at "Highlands," Clarke Co. Buried Meade Memorial Cemetery, White Post. A very large man who carried a very large saber, Funsten served as Turner Ashby's second in command during the Valley Campaign. Stonewall Jackson's criticism of the cavalry's performance led both Ashby and Funsten to submit their resignations.

Gadberry, James M. Born c. 1818, NC. Tinworker, lawyer in Union Co., SC. State legislator. Owned plantations in SC and TX. Mexican War veteran. Delegate to Secession Convention. Capt. Co. E, 1st (Gregg's) SC (a 6-month unit), Feb. 1861. Pvt. Co. B, 18th SC, Dec. 17, 1861. Col., Jan. 2, 1862. KIA 2d Manassas, Aug. 30, 1862. Buried Presbyterian Churchyard, Union Co., SC. In his report of 2d Manassas, Gen. Evans eulogized Gadberry's "dauntless conduct and unflinching courage."

Gaillard, Peter Charles. Born Dec. 29, 1812, Charleston, SC. Middle name often given as "Cheves." Attd. USC. Grad. USMA. Lt., US Army, 1835–38. Cotton factor in Charleston, 1838–61. Md. Anne L. Snowden. Capt., "Phoenix Riflemen" in Charleston, Feb. 1861. Lt. col., 17th SC Militia, Nov. 9, 1861. Major, Charleston Bn., April 5, 1862. Lt. col., April 1862. WIA Secessionville. WIA Battery Wagner (lost hand). Col., 27th SC (formed from the Charleston Bn.), Oct. 3, 1863. On sick leave from June 8, 1864, and detailed to command the post of Weldon, NC. Retired to Invalid Corps March 6, 1865. Cotton factor in Charleston postwar. Mayor of Charleston 1865–68. County treasurer 1877–79. Died Jan. 11, 1889, Charleston. Buried Magnolia Cemetery. An obituary cites Gaillard's "spotless integrity and unbending will." Gen. Hagood said Gaillard "was every inch a soldier."

Gaither, Beal. Born Aug. 22, 1833, TN. Prewar farmer in Carroll Co., AR. Md. Adeline F. Clark. Capt. Co. D, 27th AR, Feb. 15, 1862. POW Carroll Co., April 4,

1863. Exch. July 24, 1863. Major, April 21, 1863. Col., Nov. 27, 1863. The 27th and Shaver's 38th were consolidated in the spring of 1864, with Shaver taking over the consolidated regiment and Gaither as lt. col. Paroled June 8, 1865. Postwar Boone Co. farmer. Moved to OR in 1887 to become the Indian agent at the Siletz Reservation. Lived in OR and WA thereafter. Died July 8, 1915, Kalama, Cowlitz Co., WA. Buried Kalama IOOF Cemetery. One soldier called Gaither "a much respected officer."

Galloway, Morton Gilmour. Born c. 1836, MD. Family moved to Pulaski Co., AR, soon after. Attd. WMI. Farm manager in Pulaski Co. in 1860. Lt. in vol. militia. Md. Ann K. Walton. Capt. Co. F, 1st AR MR, June 14, 1861. POW at Pea Ridge. Exch. Sept. 1862. WIA Stones River in arm. Lt. col., probably March 5, 1864. Col., sometime in 1864–65. WIA Ezra Church. Led Reynolds's AR Brigade at Bentonville. Postwar farmer in Pulaski Co. Died Oct. 11, 1873, on his plantation. Buried Mt. Holly Cemetery, Little Rock.

Galloway, Thomas Spraggins, Jr. Born June 18, 1840, "Mon Vue," Rockingham Co., NC. Attd. UNC. Grad. VMI in 1861. Lawyer in Eagle Falls, NC, prewar. Md. Minerva Allison Greenlea. Drillmaster in Richmond, spring 1861. Major, 22d NC, July 11, 1861. WIA Seven Pines. Defeated for reelection at May 1862 reorganization. Pvt. Co. H, 45th NC, March 7, 1863. Capt., backdated to Feb. 27, 1863. WIA Gettysburg. Col., 22d NC, Sept. 21, 1863. Appmx. Lawyer in Rockingham Co. in 1870. Lawyer and planter in Somerville, TN, after 1870. Died May 23, 1903, Somerville. Buried Old Episcopal Church Cemetery, Arlington, Shelby Co., TN.

Gantt, Edward W. Born March 17, 1829, Maury Co., TN. Reared in Williamsport, AR. Prewar lawyer. Moved to Washington, AR, in the 1850s. Lawyer there. Dist. prosecuting attorney. Elected to US Congress in 1860 as a Hindman ally and ultrasecessionist but never took his seat. Md. Margaret Reid of Tulip, AR, sister of Col. Thomas J. Reid. Col., 12th AR, July 29, 1861. Led brigade at Island No. 10. Acting brig. gen. of the garrison. POW there, exch. Aug. 1862. Never reassigned to command. Gantt turned Unionist in 1863 (some say in disappointment at not being promoted) and issued public calls for the South to surrender. Postwar lawyer in Tulip and Little Rock. State prosecutor. Supervisor of the Freedmen's Bureau for Southwest AR. Codified Arkansas's laws. Died June 10, 1874, Little Rock. Buried Webb-Smith Cemetery (the Methodist Churchyard), Tulip. Gantt was a smooth talker of undoubted energy and doubtful morals, "a full share of native talent, warm hearted, impulsive—very profane." Brother of Lt. Col. George Gantt, 9th TN Cav. Bn. Middle name probably "Williams."

Gantt, Frederick Hay. Born Oct. 10, 1833, SC. Attd. SCMA. Lawyer in Colleton Co. prewar. Unmd. Lt. Co. K, 11th SC, Sept. 7, 1861. Lt. col., May 3, 1862. Col., Nov. 27, 1862. Paroled May 18, 1865, Augusta. Barnwell Co. lawyer postwar. Solicitor, 2d Dist., 1876–85. Died Nov. 10, 1885, at his Barnwell home. Buried Boiling Springs Presbyterian Church Cemetery. Gen. Hagood considered Gantt "a good drill officer."

Gantt, Henry. Born 1831, Albemarle Co., VA. Attd. VMI. Farmer in Scottsville prewar. Militia officer. Md. Pattie Eppes. Capt., "Scottsville Guard" (later Co. C, 19th VA), April 1861. Major, 19th VA, May 17, 1861. Lt. col., April 29, 1862. WIA 2d Manassas. Col., Sept. 14, 1862. WIA Gettysburg, during Pickett's Charge. Often absent because of his wounds thereafter. Paroled April 1865 at Columbia, VA. Albemarle Co. farmer postwar. Died Oct. 4, 1884, while on a trip to White Sulphur Springs in Buckingham Co. Buried on his estate, "Valmont," near Scottsville. Several sources give him a middle name of "Perkins."

Garland, Hugh Alfred, Jr. Born Feb. 13, 1837, Boydton, Mecklenburg Co., VA. Attd. UVA 1854–55 and St. Louis U. Prewar lawyer in St. Louis. Capt. of vol. militia. Capt. Co. F, 2d Regt. Missouri Militia at Camp Jackson in 1861. Capt. Co. F, 1st MO (PACS), Aug. 24, 1861. Major, elected May 8, 1862, to rank from April 4. Lt. col., Aug. 9, 1862. WIA Champion Hill. POW Vicksburg, and later exch. Col., 1st/4th MO (Consolidated), May 30, 1864. KIA Franklin. Buried Bellefontaine Cemetery, St. Louis.

Garland, Robert Rice. Born May 11, 1821, Lovington, Nelson Co., VA. US army officer 1847–61. Md. Elizabeth Wolfe. Capt., CS Regular Army, March 16, 1861. Col., 6th TX, Sept. 3, 1861. Commanded brigade at Arkansas Post, where he was captured. After exchange (April 29, 1863), he had a hard time getting back into the war, as he was in part blamed for the Arkansas Post surrender. Paroled in AL June 3, 1865. Lived near Lynchburg, VA, postwar, as a retired officer. Died June 13, 1870, at his sister's home in Lynchburg, of tuberculosis contracted while in a Northern prison. Buried Presbyterian Cemetery, Lynchburg. Opinion on Garland was mixed. A fellow colonel called him "attentive, industrious, sober & efficient," but others thought he was "a perfect martinet" with a "want of firmness."

Garnett, Thomas Stuart. Born April 19, 1825, Westmoreland Co., VA. Attd. VMI 1840–41. Received a medical degree from UVA in 1845. Physician in Caroline, New Kent, and Westmoreland Cos. prewar. Westmoreland Co. judge. Militia colonel. Officer in Mexican War and twice wounded there. Md. Emma L. Baber. Capt., "Lee's Light Horse," Co. C, 9th VA Cav., May 25, 1861. Lt. col., 48th VA, June 27, 1861. WIA Cedar Mountain (thigh). Col., Oct. 16, 1862. MWIA Chancellorsville, May 3, 1863, shot through the throat while leading the

Stonewall Brigade. Died the next day. Buried Hollywood Cemetery, Richmond; reburied first in a Garnett family cemetery and finally in the Baber family burial ground, King George Co. War letters at Virginia State Library.

Garrett, Thomas Miles. Born June 13, 1830, Hertford Co., NC. Grad. UNC. Lawyer in Murfreesboro, Bertie Co., prewar. Unmd. Capt. Co. F, 5th NC, May 16, 1861. Arrested, Dec. 23, 1861, for submitting a false report and refusing to obey orders but cleared. WIA and POW Williamsburg. Elected to State Senate in 1862 while a POW. Released Aug. 1862. WIA Antietam (foot). Col., Jan. 16, 1863. WIA Chancellorsville (leg). KIA Spotsylvania, May 12, 1864. A fellow colonel called Garrett "a man of fine talent, excellent judgment and most unflinching courage." College diary at UNC.

Gates, Elijah P. Born Dec. 17, 1827, Lancaster, Garrard Co., KY. Reared in KY, he left to join the CA gold rush. He then moved to MO, settling in Livingston and later Buchanan Cos. Hemp farmer. Md. Maria Stamper. Capt., MSG, May 14, 1861. Lt. col., 1st Cav., 5th Div., MSG, Sept. 23, 1861. Resigned Jan. 17, 1862. Col., 1st MO Cav. (PACS), Dec. 30, 1861. POW at Big Black River Bridge in 1863 but escaped 3 days later. WIA Lost Mountain. WIA in both arms at Franklin, while leading a charge. Arm amputated. Captured while in a field hospital but escaped from the train taking him north. Led the MO Brigade in the 1865 Mobile Campaign. POW Fort Blakely. Postwar he returned to St. Joseph, Buchanan Co. Farmer, businessman, county sheriff. State treasurer. Died March 4, 1915, St. Joseph. Buried Mt. Mora Cemetery, St. Joseph. A staff officer thought Gates "a plain honest man and a good officer."

Gause, Lucien Cotesworth. Born Dec. 25, 1836, near Wilmington, NC. Attd. UVA. Grad. Cumberland U. Law School. Prewar lawyer in Jacksonport, AR. Md. Virginia Ann Page. 1st lt. Co. G, 1st AR, May 8, 1861. Lt. and adj., 32d AR, June 11, 1862. Major, Aug. 6, 1862. Col., Dec. 9, 1862. Often led a brigade in TMD. Paroled June 14, 1865, Shreveport. Postwar lawyer in Jacksonport. State representative 1866–67. US congressman 1875–79. Died Nov. 5, 1880, Jacksonport, of consumption. Buried in a private graveyard near Jacksonport.

Gause, William Randall. Born May 30, 1831, Chester Co., PA. Reared in IN. Prospected for gold in CA 1849–54. Returned to IN, then moved to Gentry Co., MO. Lawyer. Md. Amanda Louthen. Capt. Co. A, 2d Inf., 4th Div., MSG, June 3, 1861. Major, Sept. 8, 1861. Capt. Co. B, 3d MO (PACS), Jan. 1, 1862. Lt. col., May 8, 1862. Col., Nov. 16, 1862. Badly WIA at Corinth and Vicksburg. POW Vicksburg. Regiment consolidated with 5th MO after exchange. Gause, now a supernumerary, commanded the post of Mobile, March–June 1864. He later commanded militia in VA, then was transferred to the TMD. Returned to MO postwar. Lawyer in Jackson, MS, 1866–70. Lawyer in Fort Worth, TX, thereafter. Died Nov. 26, 1882, Fort Worth, buried Oakwood Cemetery.

Gayle, Bristor Brown. Born April 19, 1839, Portsmouth, VA. Grad. VA Military and Collegiate Institute. Prewar teacher in Somerville, AL. Unmd. Capt. Co. H, 12th AL, July 8, 1861. Col., June 1, 1862. KIA South Mountain, Sept. 14, 1862. Buried Washington Confederate Cemetery, Hagerstown, MD; reburied Cedar Grove Cemetery, Portsmouth.

Gee, James Madison. Born March 5, 1813, SC. Reared in SC and Talladega, AL. Ferry operator. Capt. AL volunteers in Mexican War. To Camden, AR, in 1852. Merchant there. Md. Angeline Weatherly. Lt. col., 3d AR Cav., July 29, 1861. Resigned Sept. 1861. Col., 15th AR (Gee-Johnson's), at its Jan. 2, 1862, organization. POW Fort Donelson. Imprisoned at Fort Warren. Exch. Sept. 1862. Not reelected on Oct. 16, 1862, when the regiment was reorganized and consolidated. Died Oct. 2, 1869, Camden. Buried Oakland Cemetery, Camden.

George, James Zachariah. Born Oct. 20, 1826, Monroe Co., GA. Family moved to MS in 1834, eventually settling in Carrollton. Lawyer in Carroll Co. prewar. State Supreme Court reporter. Mexican War veteran. Delegate to MS Secession Convention. Md. Elizabeth Young. Lt. Co. C, 20th MS, April 19, 1861. Capt., July 15, 1861. POW Fort Donelson. Exch. Sept. 1862. Brig. gen., MS State Troops, 1862–63. Col., 5th MS Cav., Oct. 30, 1863. POW in an attack on Collierville, TN, Nov. 3, 1863. Imprisoned on Johnson's Island for the rest of the war. Lawyer in Carrollton postwar. Chief justice of the MS Supreme Court. US senator 1880–97. Nationally known "Bourbon" Democrat. Died Aug. 14, 1897, Mississippi City, MS. Buried Evergreen Cemetery, Carrollton.

Gerard, Aristide. Born c. 1830, Bordeaux, France. In French army. Immigrated to New Orleans in the 1850s. Prewar newspaper editor. Inspector in custom house. Prominent duelist. Md. Caroline Lauve. Lt., "Governor's Guards" (Co. F, 13th LA), 1861. Lt. col., 13th LA, Sept. 10, 1861. WIA Farmington. Court-martialed in July 1863 for disobeying orders to evacuate and blow up Fort De Russy but acquitted. Col., Jan. 11, 1864. Dropped by a board of examiners Aug. 22, 1864. Postwar civil engineer and merchant in New Orleans. Inventor, with three patents. Died in New Orleans Aug. 26, 1890. Probably buried St. Louis Cemetery #3.

Gholston, James S. Born Aug. 1812, Madison Co., GA. Farmer in Danielsville prewar. State senator 1857–58. Justice, Madison Co. Court, 1856–61. Delegate to GA Secession Convention. Md. Mary Daniel; Jane Harris; Mary Allie Tatum. Capt. Co. A, 16th GA, July 11, 1861. Major, Feb. 1, 1862. Lt. col., Aug. 31, 1863. Col., Nov. 29, 1863. Retired to Invalid Corps Aug. 24, 1864, due to chronic bronchitis and diarrhea. Paroled May 8, 1865, Athens. State senator and judge in Madison Co. postwar. Moved to Shelby Co., TX, by 1872. Hotelkeeper there. Died March 14, 1892, Centre, TX. Buried Fairview Cemetery, Centre. A GA Supreme Court decision contains the particularly messy details of the divorce from his second wife.

Gibbons, Simeon Beauford. Born May 25, 1825, Page Co., VA. Grad. VMI. Teacher at a military school in MD. Merchant and civil engineer in Harrisonburg, VA. Capt. of vol. militia. Md. Frances Shacklett. Col., 10th VA, July 1, 1861. KIA McDowell. Buried Woodbine Cemetery, Harrisonburg. Col. S. V. Fulkerson called Gibbons "one of the best men I ever saw."

Gibbs, George Couper. Born April 7, 1822, St. Simons Island, GA. Cousin of the famous painter James McNeill Whistler. Reared in FL. Officer in Mexican War. Clerk in New Orleans in 1850. Later, planter in St. Augustine, FL. Md. Julia Williams. Capt. of volunteers who seized Fort Marion, FL, Jan. 1861, under orders from the governor. Capt., CS Regular Army, May 20, 1861. Major, Jan. 1, 1862. Commandant of Salisbury, NC, POW Camp, 1862. Col., 42d NC (made up of units that had been serving as prison guards), April 22, 1862. Often ill (fever and a facial ulcer), which caused him to be absent from the regiment. Resigned Jan. 7, 1864, due to illness. Col., 2d GA Reserves, 1864. Commanded post of Andersonville (but not the prison camp itself) and Macon POW Camp. Paroled June 16, 1865, Washington, DC. Gibbs returned to St. Augustine after the war, dying there June 14, 1872. Buried Evergreen Cemetery, St. Augustine. Sometimes listed as a Confederate general, for his command of a brigade of GA Reservists in 1864. The Andersonville prisoners thought Gibbs a humane captor.

Gibson, Jonathan Catlett. Born July 28, 1833, Culpeper, VA. Grad. UVA. Attorney in New York City and Culpeper prewar. Md. Mary Shackelford. Capt. Co. K, 49th VA, June 8, 1861. Lt. col., May 1, 1862. WIA Seven Pines, Seven Days, 2d Manassas, Antietam, Fredericksburg. Col., Jan. 31, 1863. WIA and disabled Bethesda Church. Culpeper lawyer and state legislator postwar. US attorney. Died Jan. 29, 1907, Culpeper. Buried Fairview Cemetery, Culpeper. In all, Gibson was wounded eleven times during the war.

Gibson, William. Born March 10, 1822, Warren Co., GA. Lawyer in Warrenton and (from 1856) Augusta. Judge. State senator 1857–58, 1861–63. State representative 1869–60. Md. Martha M. Rogers; Ora Hardaway; Fannie Johnson. Pvt. Co. C, 48th GA, March 3, 1862. Col., March 4, 1862. WIA Malvern Hill, 2d Manassas, Antietam. WIA and POW Gettysburg. Resigned Nov. 12, 1864. State senator 1865–66. President of the GA Senate. Augusta lawyer and judge. Died April 5, 1893, Warren Co. Buried Magnolia Cemetery, Augusta. His corps commander thought Gibson "entirely unfitted" for brigade command. Moxley Sorrel (who was promoted above Gibson to take over the brigade) called him "a very brave officer, repeatedly wounded, but without discipline or organization."

Gilchrist, James Graham. Born Oct. 20, 1814, Richmond Co., NC. Attd. Princeton and USC. Lowndes Co., AL farmer, lawyer, state legislator. Md. Elizabeth Briggs; Elizabeth McGehee. Delegate to AL Secession Convention. Capt. Co. I, 45th AL, March 13, 1862. Lt. col., May 19, 1862. Col., 1862. Resigned March 25, 1863, due to age. Postwar farmer in Montgomery Co. Died May 18, 1890, Montgomery. Buried Oakwood Cemetery, Montgomery; reburied McGehee Cemetery near Montgomery. A contemporary called him "well educated, and a Southern gentleman in every feeling of his nature."

Giles, James. Born June 2, 1831, Danville, VA. Grad. VMI 1851. Teacher, surveyor, and civil engineer in Portsmouth, NC, and GA prewar. Capt. of vol. militia. Md. Anna M. W. Riddick; Harriet Riddick. Major, 29th VA, Nov. 4, 1861. Lt. col., May 13, 1862. Col., April 10, 1863. POW Five Forks. Released June 6, 1865. Teacher and civil engineer in Brandon, MS; NM; and Dallas, TX, postwar. Died March 7, 1887, Hall Co., TX. Buried Oakwood Cemetery, Austin. An 1864 inspection report declared that Giles displayed "total indifference" to his duties and was "completely inept."

Giles, John Robert Russell. Born c. 1833, SC, son of a wealthy Union Co., SC, planter. Union Co. farmer in 1860. 1st lt. Co. D, 5th SC, April 13, 1861. Capt., May 25, 1861. Col., April 23, 1862. KIA Seven Pines, May 31, 1862. Gen. Longstreet called Giles a "valuable" officer.

Gilham, William. Born Jan. 13, 1818, Vincennes, IN. Grad. USMA 1840. Lt., US Army, 1840–46. Professor at VMI. Author of a book on drill and tactics used extensively by the Confederate army. Md. Cordelia A. Hayden. Commanded a camp of instruction in Richmond, spring 1861. Col., PAVA, April 1861. Col., 21st VA, July 1861. Led a brigade in the Romney Campaign. After that campaign Stonewall Jackson (always a hard man to satisfy) preferred charges against Gilham, an old colleague, for moving too slowly. Ordered back to his teaching post at VMI, Jan. 20, 1862. Dropped April 21, 1862. Professor at VMI postwar. Chemist with a fertilizer company in Richmond. Died Nov. 16, 1872, at his brother's house in Brandon, VT. Buried Stonewall Jackson Cemetery, Lexington. One VMI cadet wrote that Gilham, unlike Jackson an excellent teacher, "commanded our profound respect, admiration, and love."

Gill, William G. Born Nov. 1825, NJ. Appointed to USMA from Reading, PA. Grad. USMA 1848. Lt., US Army, 1848–61. Capt. Co. D, 1st GA Regulars, Feb. 1861. Capt. of artillery, CS Regular Army, March 16, 1861. OO in Savannah. Assigned to command Augusta, GA, arsenal, Aug. 3, 1861. Lt. col., fall 1861. OO in Dept. of SC, GA, and FL, winter of 1861. Col. (with temporary rank), April 3, 1861. Chief OO, Army of MS. Died June 7, 1862, Tupelo, MS.

Gillespie, Clayton Crawford. Born Jan. 18, 1822, Franklin Co., GA. Prewar Methodist minister in Galveston, TX and LA. Editor, Texas *Christian Advocate;* New Orleans *Christian Advocate.* Md. Julia A. Lewis; Caroline Stuart; Anne Preston. Col., 25th TX Cav., June 1, 1862. POW Arkansas Post. Exch. April 29, 1863. Col., 17/18/24/25 Consolidated TX Cav., Dismounted, in 1863. Relieved in 1863 and returned home. Commanded post of Hempstead, TX, 1864–65. Paroled June 22, 1865, Houston. Postwar resumed his ministry. Editor, Houston *Telegraph* and San Antonio *Express.* Died Dec. 26, 1876, Austin. Buried Oakwood Cemetery, Austin. A naval officer called Gillespie "a genial pleasant fellow." Another contemporary called him "a strong and forcible writer but rather a poor editor."

Gillespie, David Adams. Born Aug. 17, 1837, Danville, KY. Attd. Centre College. Prewar schoolteacher in Vermillion, LA; Grand Gulf, TX; and Batesville, AR. Md. 2d lt. Co. G, 7th AR, June 16, 1861. 1st lt., July 26, 1861. AAAG of regt. Col., May 14, 1862. On recruiting service, Jan.–Feb. 1863. WIA (wrist) Chickamauga. Died Oct. 25, 1863, in a hospital in Forsyth, GA, of disease and wounds. Buried Forsyth City Cemetery. An obituary claimed "as a man all loved him."

Gillespie, James Wendell. Born Aug. 9, 1819, Rhea Co., TN. Grad. U. of Nashville Medical School. Physician and merchant in Rhea Co. prewar. State representative 1859–61. Mexican War veteran. Md. Nancy Brazelton, sister of Col. William Brazelton. Asst. IG of TN State Troops, May 1861. Pvt. Co. B, 43d TN (5th East TN Volunteers), Dec. 10, 1861. Col., 43d TN, Dec. 14, 1861. Commanded post of Knoxville, TN, in early 1862. POW Vicksburg and paroled. Regiment mounted in Dec. 1863. Escorted Pres. Davis on his flight south after the fall of Richmond. Paroled May 1, 1865, Washington, GA. Died Oct. 10, 1874, Washington, Rhea Co. Buried Mynatt Cemetery, Rhea Co. Gillespie's nephew was a Union army general.

Gillum, Henry. Born Dec. 7, 1832, Pascagoula, MS. Reared in Jackson Co., MS. Prewar builder/architect and cotton merchant in New Orleans. Md. Virginia Duffield. Capt. Co. H, 14th LA, July 1, 1861. Shot in the head Dec. 1861, losing sight in his right eye. Resigned June 12, 1862, due to his wound and after a dispute with his regimental commander. Authorized in 1863 to raise a battalion in MS and LA. Authorized Jan. 11, 1864, to raise a regiment in MS behind enemy lines and started organizing stray cavalry companies and reservist units. Col., Gillum's Cav., probably in 1865, though it is unclear whether the unit ever actually formed. Paroled May 18, 1865, Grenada, as col. Postwar partner in a

New Orleans firm specializing in Texas land claims. Moved to TX in order to claim his wife's inherited landholdings. Later lived in Asheville, NC, and New York City. Died March 24, 1907, at the Hotel San Remo in New York City. Temporarily buried New York City; reburied 1909 Zion Episcopal Church Cemetery, Charles Town, WVA. One LA congressman called Gillum "an energetic & reliable gentleman."

Gilmer, John Alexander, Jr. Born April 22, 1838, NC. Son of a US congressman and nephew of Gen. Jeremy Gilmer. Attd. UNC. Greensboro lawyer prewar. Md. Sallie Lindsay in 1864. Lt. Co. B, 27th NC, April 20, 1861. Adj., Nov. 1861. Major, Jan. 6, 1862. Lt. col., Nov. 1, 1862. Col., Dec. 5, 1862. WIA Fredericksburg (leg) and Bristoe Station. Commanded Salisbury POW Camp in 1864. Retired Jan. 11, 1865, to Invalid Corps. Attorney in Guilford Co. postwar. State legislator. Justice, NC Supreme Court. Died March 17, 1892, Greensboro. Buried Green Hill Cemetery, Greensboro.

Gilmore, Jerome Bonaparte. Born 1827, Jefferson Co., KY. Moved to Shreveport, LA, in 1849. "Gun smith." Served in Seminole Wars. Md. Emma Fraim. Capt. Co. F, 3d LA, May 17, 1861. Lt. col., May 8, 1862. WIA (five flesh wounds) and POW Iuka. Exch. Oct. 1862. Col., Nov. 5, 1862. POW Vicksburg. Resigned Aug. 20, 1863, due to a paralyzed left arm caused by his Iuka wounds. Postwar cotton buyer in Shreveport. Mayor of Shreveport 1869–71. Died May 7, 1900, Shreveport. Buried Greenwood Cemetery. Major Tunnard of the 3d called Gilmore "indefatigable—untiring . . . with a temperament that flashed up like gunpowder."

Giltner, Henry Lyter. Born June 5, 1829, Carrollton, KY. Attd. Hanover College in IN. Owned ferry in Carrollton prewar. County sheriff. Md. Martha R. Young. Capt., KSG, June 15, 1861. Capt. and ADC to Gen. Humphrey Marshall, 1861. Member, KY Secession Convention. Capt. Co. F, 4th KY Cav., Sept. 2, 1862. Col., Oct. 6, 1862. Led brigade in VA and KY, 1864–65. Surrendered at Mt. Sterling April 29, 1865. Farmer in Carrollton postwar. Owned marble business. Died Aug. 19, 1892, Murfreesboro, TN. Buried IOOF Cemetery, Carrollton. A fellow staff officer called Giltner "cool, firm as adamant law & sure as the step of death."

Gist, Joseph Fincher. Born Oct. 11, 1818, Union Dist., SC. Brother of Gen. States R. Gist. Attd. USC. Lawyer and planter in Union, SC, prewar. Judge. State representative 1846–48. State senator 1858–60. Militia general. Unmd. Major, 15th SC, Sept. 10, 1861. Lt. col., Oct. 19, 1861. Col., July 2, 1863. WIA Chickamauga. Resigned Jan. 5, 1864, due to disability. Union Co. lawyer postwar. Probate judge. County treasurer. Died Oct. 6, 1890, Union. Buried Fair Forest Cemetery, Union Co.

Glenn, David Chalmers. Born c. 1824, NC. Lived in NC; TN; Holly Springs, Jackson, and Harrison Co., MS. Lawyer. Attorney general of MS (elected at age 25!). Md. Patience B. Wilkinson. Delegate to MS Secession Convention. 2d lt. Co. A, 1st MS, May 1861. Dropped Sept. 4, 1861. Elected 1st lt. Co. A, 34th MS, but declined. Appointed col. and judge of military court of A. P. Hill's Corps, July 18, 1863. Allowed to resign, Oct. 14, 1864, rather than face charges he had "been disgracefully drunk" and "made a public exhibit of himself." Ordered to report to Gen. Richard Taylor, in AL, Oct. 14, 1864. Resigned Dec. 3, 1864. Paroled May 13, 1865, Meridian. Postwar lawyer in Mississippi City. Died Sept. 19, 1868, Okolona, MS. "He was a thorough lawyer, a brilliant logician, and a most eloquent advocate."

Glenn, Jesse A. Born Dec. 21, 1833, Gwinnett Co., GA. Reared in Chatooga Co. Lawyer, teacher, judge in Summerville. Moved to Dalton in 1858. Md. Eliza Crook. Capt. Co. H, 2d GA, April 20, 1861. Col., 36th GA, April 24 (or July 12), 1862. WIA and POW Vicksburg. Paroled. Court-martialed for financial misdealings and dismissed from the service Jan. 23, 1864. Later, applied to raise a brigade of cavalry from reserve forces in GA. Dalton lawyer postwar. State representative. Postmaster. Died March 20, 1904, Dalton. Buried West Hill Cemetery, Dalton. Gen. Stevenson found Glenn "energetic, efficient, and faithful."

Glenn, John Edward. Born Nov. 29, 1828, Newberry, SC. Lived in Columbia, SC; GA; and Prairie Co., AR, prewar. Lawyer. Md. Anna Eddins; Rebecca Trippe. Major, 1st AR (State Troops), 1861. Major, 15th AR (formed from the 1st). Lt. col., 36th AR, 1862. Col., Nov. 5, 1862. Resigned Sept. 15, 1863, due to ill health (wounds and an ulcerated leg). Commanded post of Washington, AR. Captured March 29, 1864, Ashley Co., AR. Released Nov. 29, 1864, on his claim that he was a civilian. Twice wounded during war. Paroled Marshall, TX, July 15, 1865. Postwar lawyer in Howard Co., AR. Died Nov. 20, 1905, at the soldiers' home in Jacksonville, FL. Buried Old City Cemetery, Jacksonville. Gen. McRae called Glenn "one of the best officers in the service."

Glover, Thomas Jamison. Born July 30, 1830, Orangeburg, SC. Grad. USC. Orangeburg lawyer prewar. State representative in 1860. Md. Elizabeth T. Whitner. Lt. col., 1st (Hagood's) SC, Jan. 8, 1861. Col., July 12, 1862. MWIA 2d Manassas. Died Aug. 31, 1862, VA. Buried Orangeburg Presbyterian Church Cemetery. Nephew of Col. D. F. Jamieson. Gen. Hagood remembered that Glover's "worth was conspicuous and endeared him much to his men."

Gober, Daniel C. Born March 3, 1828, De Kalb Co., GA. Attd. U. of Louisville Medical College. Physician in Fayette Co., TN. Moved to Opelousas, LA, c. 1851, and practiced there. Md. Rosella Compton McDavitt. Capt., "Big Cane Rifles" (Co. K, 16th LA), Sept. 11, 1861. Major, 16th LA, Sept. 26, 1861. Col., May 8,

1862. Detached April 17, 1864. Col., Gober's Regt. Mounted Infantry, June 1864. Regiment (an improvised one) disbanded winter of 1864–65, and Gober took over command of John S. Scott's Cav. Brigade. Commanded Dist. of Southwest MS and East LA in May 1865. Physician in Frankfort, KY, postwar. Died Oct. 13, 1889, Frankfort. Buried Elmwood Cemetery, Memphis. A soldier in the 16th found Gober "a perfect gentleman, a better man than officer," and Col. John S. Scott found him "a man of intelligence and of military bearing."

Godwin, David Jeremiah. Born 1829, Suffolk, VA. Portsmouth lawyer prewar. Militia major. Md. Lucrece P. Wilson; Eliza S. Wingfield. Lt. col., 14th VA, May 17, 1861. Defeated for reelection at May 1862 reorganization. Lt. col., 9th VA, May 20, 1862. Col., May 24, 1862. WIA Seven Pines. Resigned Oct. 30, 1862, due to wounds and a riding injury. Posted in 1863 to conscript duty in eastern VA. Raised a cavalry battalion, which did outpost duty on the lower Rappahannock. Postwar lawyer and judge in Norfolk. Lost race for Congress in 1869. Moved to Washington, DC., in 1889 to work at the General Land Office. Died Jan. 19, 1890, at his DC home. Buried Cedar Grove Cemetery, Portsmouth. A "man of fine literary and legal attainments."

Gonzales, Ambrosio Jose. Born Oct. 3, 1818, Matanzas, Cuba, and baptized Ambrosio Jose Candido Gonzalez (he changed the "z" to "s" after he left Cuba) Rufin. Attd. a semimilitary prep school in NY. Grad. U. of Havana. Professor at schools in Havana. Exiled himself to US in 1848. Adj. gen. in Cuban revolutionary army—called "general" thereafter. Filibusterer. Part-time translator for US State Dept. Md. Harriet Elliott, a South Carolina heiress. AIG to Gen. Beauregard (a classmate of his at school in NY; the two looked so alike they were often confused for each other) at Charleston, April 1861. Lt. col., SC state service, appointed May 1861. Appointed major and AAG, PACS, Aug. 27, 1861, but declined the appointment and remained in state service. Lt. col., PACS, June 4, 1862. Col., Aug. 14, 1862. Chief of artillery, Dept. of SC, GA and FL, 1862–65. Chief of artillery, Army of TN, 1865. Paroled April 30, 1865, Greensboro. Returned to SC after the war. Charleston merchant, mill owner, planter. Went broke. After that lived in Cuba, Baltimore, Washington, and New York City, earning a scanty living as a teacher and translator. Died July 31, 1893, New York City. Buried Woodlawn Cemetery, the Bronx. Gen. Hardee praised Gonzales's "thorough and practical knowledge of artillery." A biography of Gonzales was published in 2003.

Good, John Jay. Born July 12, 1827, Columbus, MS. Attd. Cumberland U. Law School. Moved to AL, then (in 1851) Dallas. Lawyer. Gen. AL militia. Capt. in vol. militia. Md. Susan A. Floyd. Capt., Good's TX Art. Battery, June 10, 1861. Served in Army of the West. Resigned May 10, 1862, and returned to Dallas. Col.

and judge of military court of Pemberton's army, Dec. 16, 1862. Paroled May 9, 1865, Meridian. Postwar Dallas lawyer. Judge. Mayor of Dallas. Died Sept. 17, 1882, El Paso. Buried Odd Fellows Cemetery, Dallas. His wartime letters have been published.

Goode, Charles Thomas. Born Oct. 26, 1835, Upson Co., GA. Grad. UGA 1853. Prewar lawyer in Thomaston, GA. Md. Cornelia Warren. Capt., "Houston Volunteers," 1861. Major, 11th GA, July 2, 1861. Resigned Jan. 20, 1862. Major, 19th GA Cav. Bn., Oct. 14, 1862. Col., 10th Confederate Cav. (formed from the 19th Bn.), Dec. 27, 1862. WIA Chickamauga. Retired June 20, 1864. Postwar lawyer in Americus. State legislator. Died Jan. 15, 1875, Americus. Buried Evergreen Cemetery, Perry, GA. A contemporary called Goode the "Silver Tongued Orator."

Goode, Edmond. Born May 4, 1825, Bedford Co., VA. Grad. VMI 1846. Teacher at New London Academy prewar. Farmer in Bedford Co. Md. Ann M. McGhee. 1st lt. Co. C, 25th VA, May 15, 1861. Appointed adj. 4 days later. Capt., 1861. Col., 58th VA, Sept. 27, 1861. Died March 8, 1862, at his Bedford Co. home, of pneumonia. Buried Longwood Cemetery, Bedford Co. A family book calls him "a modest, unobtrusive gentleman."

Goode, Edmund James. Born July 17, 1822, Chesterfield Co., VA. Attd. Reedy Spring Academy. Moved to Monticello, MS, in 1847. Lawyer in Brookhaven, Lawrence Co., MS, in 1860. Prominent Mason. Md. Sarah D. Stone. Capt. Co. G, 7th MS ("Goode Rifles"), 1861. Col., Sept. 23, 1861. Resigned in 1862, probably April 24. Lost race for judgeship in 1863. Appointed in 1865 to a MS state board for the education of soldiers' children. Lawyer and real estate dealer in MS, LA, and later Des Moines, IA, postwar. Died June 22, 1901, Brooklyn, NY. Buried Woodland Cemetery, Des Moines. His first name is often given as "Enos" or, less often, "Elias." The above name is from a family history and census data.

Goode, John Thomas. Born July 21, 1835, Boydton, Mecklenburg Co., VA. Attd. VMI. Lt., US Army, 1855–61. Md. Sarah C. Buford; Carrie C. Sturdivant; Bessie M. Morton. Capt. of artillery, CS Regular Army, March 16, 1861. Major, 34th VA, Oct. 3, 1861. Lt. col., April 1862. Col., May 15, 1862. Often led Wise's Brigade. WIA three times in war. Appmx. Tobacco farmer in Mecklenburg Co. postwar. State legislator, 1891–92. Died April 13, 1916, Chase City, VA. Buried St. James Church, Boydton.

Goode, Thomas Francis. Born June 28, 1825, Roanoke Co., VA. Lawyer in Mecklenburg Co. prewar. Lost race for Congress in 1859. Delegate to VA Secession Convention. Md. Rosa C. Chambers. Capt. Co. A, 3d VA Cav., May 14, 1861. Major, c. Oct. 1861. Lt. col., Oct. 4, 1861. Col., April 26, 1862. Resigned Nov. 18,

1862, due to ill health. State representative 1863–64. Attorney in Mecklenburg Co. postwar. Businessman. Proprietor of the Buffalo Lithia Springs. Died Jan. 6, 1905, Boydton. Buried Boydton Presbyterian Church Cemetery.

Goodlett, Spartan David. Born April 20, 1831, Greenville, SC. Editor, Greenville *Patriot*, prewar. Attorney. Md. Mary Lyles. Pvt., —— SC, April 1861. Lt. col., 22d SC, Jan. 29, 1862. Col., May 15, 1862. Gen. "Shanks" Evans brought charges against him for misconduct in the battle of Kinston. One of Evans's staff officers gave Goodlett an order that Goodlett refused to obey. Goodlett believed the order a mistake and voiced the opinion that the staff officer, and Evans, must have been drunk to have given it. The trial record contains lengthy testimony as to Goodlett's courage and coolness and how the order (to cross a river in the face of a victorious enemy) was madness. Cashiered by court-martial April 28, 1864, on the Kinston charges. Lawyer in Pickens and Greenville postwar. Died May 16, 1874, Pickens. Buried Springwood Cemetery, Greenville Co.

Goodner, John Fite. Born July 6, 1822, Carthage, TN. Farmer in De Kalb Co., TN, prewar. Mexican War veteran. Md. Nancy Floyd. Capt. Co. A, 7th TN, May 20, 1861. Lt. col., May 27, 1861. Col., May 23, 1862. Resigned April 8, 1863, due to ill health. Died Aug. 4, 1870, Alexandria, TN. Buried Eastview Cemetery, Alexandria. Goodner's war letters have been published.

Goodwin, Edward. Born Sept. 7, 1830, Aberdeen, MS. Grad. La Grange College, AL, 1851. Teacher in Aberdeen. Professor of languages at his alma mater. Wrote a novel and farmed. Md. Ann King. Lt. col., 35th AL, March 12, 1862. Col., Nov. 12, 1862. Died Sept. 25, 1863, Columbus, MS. Buried Odd Fellows Cemetery, Aberdeen; reburied King Cemetery, near La Grange. A student remembered him as a "conscientious and successful teacher" with "reckless courage."

Goodwyn, William Sabb. Born Aug. 11, 1825, at "Totnes," SC. Attd. USC. Richland Dist., SC, planter and legislator. Planter in Macon Co., AL. Md. Celestine Raoul. Outspoken secessionist. Capt. Co. K, 45th AL, March 15, 1862. Col., May 19, 1862. Resigned Nov. 4, 1862 due to "diarrhea," "debilitation," and hemorrhaging lungs. Postwar planter in Macon Co. Died Nov. 5, 1868, at "Elba," his home in Macon Co. Buried in the family cemetery at Elba.

Gordon, Anderson. Born Feb. 13, 1820, Maury Co., TN. Reared in AL. To Lewisburg, Conway Co., AR, in 1839. Store clerk; grocer; farmer; postmaster. State representative 1854–55. Md. Lydia Griffin. Capt. Co. B, Gordon's 4th AR Cav., June 14, 1862. Major, May 28, 1863. Lt. col., Oct. 26, 1863. Col., Dec. 15, 1863. WIA in leg in attack on Pine Bluff in 1863, which crippled him for life. WIA (arm) during Price's Raid. Lewisburg merchant postwar. Postmaster. Militia gen. Died Feb. 13, 1893, Morrilton, AR. Probably buried in the old Gordon burying ground north of Morrilton. One veteran asserted, "No braver, cooler officer ever fought and bled for Dixie."

Gordon, Benjamin Franklin. Born May 18, 1826, Henry Co., TN. Family moved to Lafayette Co., MO, in 1831. Merchant in Waverly, MO, owning a drug store. Pvt. in Mexican War. Md. Sarah Henton. 3d lt. Co. D, 2d Inf., 8th Div., MSG, June 19, 1861. Capt. and adj., June 19, 1861. WIA Wilson's Creek. Elected lt. col., 5th MO Cav. (PACS), Sept. 12, 1862. Col., Dec. 15, 1863. One of Jo Shelby's favorite subordinates, frequently praised in battle reports. Often led Shelby's Brigade. Assigned to duty as brig. gen., May 16, 1865, by Gen. Kirby Smith. Fled to Mexico with Shelby in 1865 but returned to MO. Died Sept. 22, 1866, Waverly, buried Waverly Cemetery.

Gordon, George Anderson. Born Sept. 26, 1830, Savannah, GA. Grad. Yale. Savannah lawyer prewar. US Dist. attorney 1856–57. State representative 1857–59. State senator 1861–63. Officer in vol. militia. Md. Caroline B. Steenbergen; Ellen C. Beirne. Capt. "Phoenix Riflemen," 1st GA, May 30, 1861. The company was never officially attached to the 1st and was reorganized into three companies that formed the nucleus of the 13th GA Bn. Major, 13th GA Bn., April 26, 1862. Col., 63d GA (formed from the 13th Bn.), Dec. 23, 1862. VADC to Gen. McLaws at the siege of Savannah. Lawyer in Huntsville, AL, postwar. Died there Oct. 5, 1872. Buried Maple Hill Cemetery, Huntsville.

Gordon, James. Born Dec. 6, 1833, Monroe Co., MS, son of a Scottish immigrant. Reared in Pontotoc Co. Attd. St. Thomas's Hall and LaGrange College. Grad. UMS in 1855. Prewar planter, owning 500 slaves and $1.6 million in property. Said to be the richest man in MS prewar. State representative 1857–61. Md. Virginia Wiley, niece of Interior Sec. Jacob Thompson. Capt. "Chickasaw Rangers" (later Co. B, Jeff Davis Legion, a company he spent $32,000 equipping), Aug. 20, 1861. Lt. col., Gordon's MS Cav. Bn., May 12, 1862. Col., 2d MS Cav. (formed from his battalion), 1862. However, this promotion was challenged (see J. L. McCarty) and eventually overturned, and Gordon resigned Aug. 27, 1863, in the hopes of ending the dispute. In 1864 Pres. Davis sent Gordon to Europe to purchase a privateer. He returned in Jan. 1865 but was captured in Wilmington, NC, by Union troops. The next month he escaped from a prison ship at Old Point Comfort and fled to Canada to join Jacob Thompson. He met John Wilkes Booth in Montreal and was later charged as an associate in the plot to assassinate Pres. Lincoln. Planter in Pontotoc Co. (Okolona) postwar. Celebrated as an exemplar of the old-fashioned gentleman planter. Wrote articles for various magazines under the pseudonym "Pious Jeems." Three-term state legislator. US senator 1909–10. Died Nov. 28, 1912, Okolona. Buried Odd Fellows Cemetery, Okolona.

Gordon, William Westmore. Born Aug. 1, 1831, Essex Co., VA. Grad. VMI and UVA. Teacher at VMI. Worked for the US coast survey. Lawyer in Lewisburg. Md. Frances B. Brockenbrough in 1857. Said to have been appointed capt. of a cavalry company in early 1861, but before taking this position he was, on May 30, 1861, elected col., 27th VA. Gordon resigned due to ill health and poor eyesight (he had suffered from poor eyesight throughout his life), Oct. 14, 1861. Another source has him affiliated with the Confederate Signal Corps until war's end. Lawyer in New Kent Co., 1865–71, then moved his family and practice to Richmond. Died Dec. 5, 1892, at his Richmond home. Buried Hollywood Cemetery.

Gore, Mounce Lauderdale. Born July 16, 1840, Jackson Co., TN. Jackson Co. farmer prewar. Md. Susan Cassety in 1868. Pvt. Co. K, 8th TN, May 14, 1861. Discharged Sept. 17, 1861, due to typhoid fever. Capt. Co. G, 13th TN Cav. (Dibrell's), Aug. 26, 1862. Promoted to col. March 1865 but never received his commission. Farmer and merchant in Gainesboro, Jackson Co., postwar. Circuit court clerk. Died June 18, 1909, Jackson Co. Buried Gore family cemetery near his home. An obituary calls Gore a "man of conspicuous courage." Sen. Al Gore is a distant relative.

Gould, Nicholas C. Born c. 1835, RI. First name may actually have been Nehemiah. Prewar attorney and merchant in Gouldsboro, TX, then Clarksville. Md. Virginia E. Harris. Capt., "Clarksville Light Infantry," Texas State Troops, June 15, 1861. Capt. Co. D, Forrest's TN Cav. (later Co. D, 23d TX Cav.), Sept. 13, 1861. After the fall of Fort Donelson, sent to TX to recruit. Col., 23d TX Cav. May 2, 1862. Served in TMD. Died Aug. 20, 1866. Buried Clarksville Baptist Cemetery. Gen. Henry McCulloch had no confidence in "Our man Gould, who drinks, swaggers, and talks big . . . has neither the brains nor prudence enough for a county court lawyer, when sober, and none when he is not."

Goulding, Edwin Ross. Born July 26, 1821, Oglethorpe Co., GA. In lumber business prewar, in Talbot Co. Seminole and Mexican Wars veteran. Md. Sarah Searcy Owen; Jane E. Bryan. Capt. Co. E ("Talbot Guards"), 9th GA, June 11, 1861. Col., June 11, 1861. Died April 4, 1862, Orange Courthouse, VA, of disease. Buried Old Ephesus Presbyterian Church, Woodland, GA.

Grace, William. Born c. 1830, Ireland. Came to US shortly before the war. Contractor on the Nashville and Northwestern RR. Capt. Co. B, 10th TN, Sept. 1, 1861. Major, Jan. 26, 1862. POW Fort Donelson. A tall man (6 foot 4), nicknamed "Battling Billie" by his men. Lt. col., Nov. 6, 1862. Col., May 12, 1863.

MWIA Jonesboro (shot in the stomach), died Sept. 1, 1864. Buried near the battlefield; reburied in 1889 in Mt. Olivet Cemetery, Nashville.

Graham, Malcolm Daniel. Born July 6, 1827, Autauga Co., AL. Attd. Transylvania U. Lawyer in Wetumpka, then Montgomery, AL. To Henderson, TX, in 1855. State senator 1857–59. State attorney general. 1859–61. Md. Amelia C. Ready; Sarah Cornelia Bethea. Delegate to TX Secession Convention. Confederate congressman 1861–63. Defeated for reelection by Col. John R. Baylor. Appointed col. and judge of the military court of TMD, Feb. 19, 1864. Captured at Natchez, MS, April 17, 1864. Exchanged. Reappointed col., March 23, 1865, to be chief judge of the military court of the Texas Corps, TMD. Lawyer in Montgomery, AL, postwar. Died Oct. 8, 1878, Montgomery, buried Oakwood Cemetery. Middle name given as "Duncan" in some sources; "Daniel" is from his tombstone.

Graham, Robert Fladger. Born Nov. 12, 1833, Marion, SC. Attd. Mt. Zion Institute and USC. Attorney in Marion prewar. Md. Harriet Harllee. 1st lt. Co. K, 1st SC (6-month State Troops), 1861. Col., 21st SC (the 2d Regt., Harllee Legion), Jan. 26, 1862. WIA Port Walthall Junction. Paroled May 1, 1865, Greensboro. Marion lawyer and judge postwar. State representative 1862–64 and 1864–66. Died Nov. 5, 1874, Charleston, of yellow fever. Buried Old Town Cemetery, Marion. A book on the Harllee family contains many of Graham's wartime letters. The family remembered him as "large in stature, strong in body."

Grammar, John, Jr. Born June 1, 1833, Locust Grove, Dinwiddie Co., VA. Reared in Brunswick and later Halifax Cos. Attd. UVA. Grad. NYU Medical College. Physician in NY and Halifax Courthouse prewar. Capt. of the "Halifax Blues," vol. militia. Unmd. Capt. Co. A, 53d VA, April 24, 1861. Major, May 22, 1862. WIA Seven Pines (arm). Lt. col., Aug. 29, 1862. Col., Jan. 6, 1863. Resigned March 5, 1863, due to ill health and "a chronic state of disagreement" with his brigade commander, Lewis Armistead. Thereafter surgeon with the 26th VA Bn. and the 62d VA. Halifax Courthouse physician postwar. Died March 27, 1900, Halifax Co. Buried St. John's Episcopal Church Cemetery, Halifax.

Gray, Peter W (middle initial stands for nothing). Born Dec. 12, 1819, Fredericksburg, VA. To TX in 1838. Houston lawyer. Capt. in TX army. State legislator. Judge, 1854–61. Delegate to TX Secession Convention. Confederate Congress, 1861–63. VADC to Gen. Magruder at Battle of Galveston. Fiscal agent for TMD, 1864. Commissioned col. and judge of military court, TMD, Jan. 9, 1864. Declined appointment Feb. 18, 1864. Postwar Houston lawyer. Briefly justice, TX Supreme Court. Died Oct. 3, 1874, Houston. Buried Glenwood Cemetery, Houston. Gov. Roberts of TX called Gray "the very best district judge that ever sat upon the Texas Bench." Sister md. Gen. C. W. Sears; brother Edward Fairfax Gray was lt. col. 3d TX.

Graybill, Tully. Born June 2, 1821, Hancock Co., GA. Physician in Sandersville, Washington Co., prewar. Md. Annabella Tucker. Capt. Co. A (the "Irish Guards"), 28th GA, Sept. 10, 1861. Major, May 3, 1862. POW Seven Pines, exch. Sept. 1, 1862. WIA Antietam. Col., Nov. 3, 1862. Sandersville physician postwar. Died Oct. 2, 1883, Washington Co. Buried Graybill-Tucker family cemetery, Oconee, Washington Co. A local newspaper remembered that "in the late war he won the hearts and confidence of his comrades in arms."

Grayson, William Powhatan Bolling. Born Sept. 9, 1810, Greenup Co., KY. Cousin of Gen. John C. Breckinridge. Wealthy farmer in Henderson Co. prewar. Md. Susan Dixon. Commissioned col., Oct. 10, 1864, under an act of Congress, to raise a regiment behind enemy lines in KY. The record gives no reason why Congress, at this late date, sent Grayson, rather than an experienced officer, on such a difficult mission. Captured in Hardinsburg, KY, while recruiting, Jan. 24, 1865. Imprisoned at Johnson's Island, released July 25, 1865. Died 1872. Buried Fernwood Cemetery, Henderson Co. His brief service record is as col., 13th KY Cav., but his regiment never formally organized. The Unionist gov. of KY, on Grayson's postwar pardon application, called him "more sinned against than sinning."

Green, Francis Marion. Born Nov. 7, 1823, Fauquier Co., VA. Lawyer in Oxford, MS, prewar. Md. Susan Webb. Capt. Co. G, 11th MS, Feb. 23, 1861. Major, Oct. 3, 1861. Col., appointed May 12, 1863, to rank from Sept. 25, 1862. WIA Gettysburg. The Senate did not confirm the appointment until three days after his death. Reappointed col., May 4, 1864, to rank from Feb. 19, 1864. The Senate balked at confirming Green because it felt that W. B. Lowry was entitled to the colonelcy. Lowry was senior capt. to Green under the original 12 months enlistment in 1861. However, Green's company voluntarily reenlisted for the war, whereas Lowry's company reorganized under the 1862 conscript law. As Pres. Davis interpreted the law, Green thereby retained his 1861 date of commission, whereas Lowry's dated from the 1862 reorganization and reelection. The Senate acted upon an earlier War Dept. order saying Lowry was senior. MWIA Spotsylvania, May 10, 1864, died May 15, 1864, near Spotsylvania. Buried Sharon Cemetery, Middleburg, VA. Green's war letters are at Mississippi Dept. of Archives and History.

Green, John Alexander. Born April 2, 1821, Winchester, TN. Attd. Lebanon College, TN. Lawyer. Moved to La Grange, TX, in 1845. Mexican War veteran. Dist. attorney 1846–52. Md. Catherine E. West. Delegate to TX Secession Convention. Capt. AAG on staff of Gen. Tom Green, his brother. Acting provost marshal to Gen. Wharton, April 1864. Appointed col., March 23, 1865, to serve as chief judge of the military court of Wharton's Corps. Postwar lawyer in Austin and San Antonio. Died July 7, 1899, San Antonio. Buried City Cemetery No. 4, San Antonio.

Green, John Uriah. Born May 7, 1829, Madison Co., AL. Reared in Covington, Tipton Co., TN, and TX. Grad. Centre College. Physician and farmer in Covington, prewar. Md. Mary Jane Sanford; Sallie Ann Green. Lt. Co. B, 6th TN Cav. Bn. (later 7th TN Cav.), May 31, 1861. Capt. Co. C, 12th TN Cav., Oct. 18, 1862. Lt. col., Feb. 14, 1863. On April 1, 1863, the soldiers of the 12th (which was raised in West TN behind Union lines) were ordered to disband and reassemble in MS. Captured April 9, 1863, near Memphis. He and fellow prisoners seized the ship that was transporting them to the North and escaped. Col., Dec. 1, 1863. Court-martialed and cashiered Oct. 4, 1864, for disobeying the order placing Col. Ed Rucker in command of the brigade. Resigned Oct. 18, 1864. Covington farmer postwar. Editor, *Tipton Record.* Died April 12, 1906, Covington. Buried Mt. Carmel Cemetery, Tipton Co.

Green, Peter V. Born c. 1837, Rutherford Co., NC. Prewar lawyer in Bradley Co., AR. 3d lt. Co. C, 5th AR, 1861. Capt., June 28, 1861. Major, April 16, 1862. Lt. col., 5th/13th AR, Sept. 19, 1863. Col., July 22, 1864. Led Govan's Brigade at Bentonville. A soldier in his regiment called "Peavine" Green and his brother "pleasant men, both of them, and of reckless courage, but gamblers and dissipated." Moved to be with his parents in Rusk Co., TX, after the war. Murdered near Millville, TX, March 1869, by a gang of negroes he had, while on a "bender," insulted. Green's brother helped lynch the murderers and was himself jailed for his crime of revenge.

Green, William Edwin. Born Feb. 5, 1827, "Greenwood," Charlotte Co., VA. Grad. Hampden-Sydney College and UVA. Wealthy farmer in Charlotte Co. prewar. Owned a plantation in MS. Md. Jennie E. Boylan. Capt. Co. I, 56th VA, July 18, 1861. Major, Sept. 17, 1861. Lt. col., July 31, 1863. Col., June 13, 1864. Farmer and lawyer in Charlotte Co. postwar. Died Dec. 12, 1891, "Greenwood."

Greene, George Colton. Born July 7, 1833, SC. Known by his middle name. Early life unknown. Moved to St. Louis in the 1850s. Wealthy merchant. Active secessionist. Headed the "minute man" movement in St. Louis. Unmd. Drillmaster, MSG, 1861. Dispatched by Gov. Jackson to seek help from the Confederate govt. Col. and AAG, 7th Div., MSG, Oct. 28, 1861. Commanded the 7th Div. (reformed as Confederate volunteers) at Pea Ridge. Col., 3d MO Cav., Nov. 4, 1862. Often led Marmaduke's Brigade in TMD. Court-martialed in 1864 for disobeying orders to turn over his regiment's mules to the government but acquitted. Recommended for promotion to general in 1865. Paroled Houston, TX,

June 27, 1865. Moved to Memphis after the war. Life insurance agent, banker, and civic leader. Very wealthy. Helped to establish the Memphis Public Library. Died Sept. 23, 1900, Memphis. Buried Elmwood Cemetery. Gen. Duke said of him that "no braver or better officer ever drew a sword." His reminiscences of 1861–62 have been published. Often called "general" postwar.

Gregg, Edward Pearsall. Born Nov. 27, 1833, Courtland, AL. Attd. La Grange College. Moved to Houston Co., TX, in 1852. Prewar lawyer in Houston Co., Fairfield, and McKinney. Md. Lucy Goree. Lt. col., 16th TX Cav., April 16, 1862. Col., probably in Oct. 1864. WIA Milliken's Bend. POW Pleasant Hill. Lawyer and judge postwar in Marshall and Sherman, TX. Died March 13, 1894. Buried West Hill Cemetery, Sherman. Brother of Gen. John Gregg.

Gregg, Nathan. Born Aug. 5, 1835, Sullivan Co., TN. Farmer and carpenter in Sullivan Co. prewar. Md. Catherine Morrell. 2d lt. Co. B, 19th TN, May 25, 1861. 1st lt., Jan. 4, 1862. WIA Shiloh. Resigned April 20, 1862, due to that wound. Lt. col., 60th TN, Oct. 1, 1862. POW Big Black River Bridge. To Johnson's Island. Exch. late in the war. Regiment mounted in the winter of 1863. Col., Oct. 25, 1864. Sullivan Co. farmer postwar. State legislator. County sheriff. Died July 15, 1894, Sullivan Co. Buried New Bethel Presbyterian Church. Gen. Vaughn called Gregg "gallant, efficient and meritorious."

Griffin, Joel Robert. Born c. 1836, SC. Reared in Macon and Oglethorpe, GA. Attd. GMI. Macon lawyer in 1860. Capt. of vol. militia company, the "Macon Guards." Md. Mrs. Mary E. (King) Slapper. Capt. Co. E, 3d GA, April 27, 1861. Major, 1st GA Bn. PR, June 18, 1862. Lt. col., 15th GA Bn. PR, July 1, 1862. Col., 62d GA, Aug. 1, 1862. Regiment reformed into the 8th GA Cav., July 11, 1864. Heavily criticized for his actions during the Siege of Petersburg. Superintendent at Andersonville prison site, 1865. Lawyer and newspaper publisher in Houston Co. postwar. State representative 1871–72, elected as a "Radical" Republican. Moved to Nashville, TN, after his wife's death in 1874 and practiced law there. Died c. 1895, Nashville. Probably buried in Joelton, near Nashville.

Griffin, Thomas Milton. Born Jan. 7, 1816, GA. Planter in Coweta Co., GA, and Madison Co., MS, prewar. Gen. in GA militia. Md. Sarah Colbert. Lt. col., 18th MS, June 7, 1861. WIA Malvern Hill. Col., Nov. 18, 1862. WIA Gettysburg. Retired due to wounds Nov. 18, 1864. Commanded post of Newnan, GA, during the Atlanta Campaign. Farmer in Madison Co. postwar. State representative 1865–67. Died Oct. 2, 1878, in MS, of yellow fever. Buried Cayuga, MS, Methodist Church.

Griffith, John. Born Aug. 1, 1831, Colleton Dist., SC. Lived in SC and Lauderdale Co., MS prewar. To Sebastian Co., AR, in 1858. Prewar planter. Md. Catherine Weaver Weldon. Capt. Co. E, 3d AR State Troops, 1861. At Wilson's

Creek. Lt. col., 17th AR, Dec. 17, 1861. Col., April 16, 1862. Led 11th/17th AR (mounted) in 1863. Often led a brigade of cavalry in south MS, 184–65. Captured the tinclad USS *Petral* in 1864. Paroled May 13, 1865, Jackson. Returned to his ruined plantation after the war. Reconstruction opponent, organizing armed resistance to federal authorities. Fled to TX in 1868 after his brother was killed by federal militia. Farmer in Taylor and Kimble Cos. Killed March 7, 1889, near his home, by two neighbors. Buried Copperas Cemetery, Kimble Co. Gen. Cabell called him "a brave and daring man." Known to his men as the "lustful Turk," for reasons that can only be speculated.

Griggs, George King. Born Sept. 12, 1839, Henry Co., VA. Attd. VMI. Merchant in Pittsylvania Co. in 1860. Md. Sallie Boyd; Alice Boatwright. Capt. Co. K, 38th VA, June 2, 1861. WIA Seven Pines (head) and Antietam. Major, July 3, 1863. WIA Gettysburg (thigh). Lt. col., Nov. 15, 1863. Col., May 16, 1864. WIA Drewry's Bluff. Led brigade at Appmx. Danville businessman postwar. Superintendent, Danville & Western Railroad. Died Oct. 15, 1914, Danville. Buried Greenhill Cemetery, Danville. Griggs's wartime diary is printed in Southern Historical Society Papers.

Grigsby, Andrew Jackson. Born Nov. 2, 1819, Rockbridge Co., VA. Brother of Col. J. Warren Grigsby. Attd. USMA and Washington College. Rockbridge Co. farmer prewar. Mexican War veteran (in a MO unit). Md. Edith S. Howell. Major, 27th VA, June 12, 1861. Lt. col., Oct. 14, 1861. Col., May 28, 1862. WIA Malvern Hill. Often led Stonewall Brigade. Resigned Nov. 19, 1862, because Jackson promoted a junior officer (E. F. Paxton) over him to command the brigade. Spent the remainder of the war organizing militia in the Valley. Farmer near Lexington postwar. Died Dec. 23, 1895, Stony Point, VA, of pneumonia. Buried Goss family cemetery near Stony Point. The officers of the Stonewall Brigade urged Jackson to appoint Grigsby brigadier. But Jackson allegedly blocked the promotion because Grigsby had a habit of cursing, a habit that (in Jackson's mind) outweighed Grigsby's courage, popularity, and war record.

Grigsby, John Warren. Born Sept. 11, 1818, Rockbridge Co., VA. Brother of Col. A. J. Grigsby of the 27th VA. Attd. William & Mary College and UVA. Newspaper editor in Rockbridge Co. US consul at Bordeaux, France, 1841–49. Lawyer in New Orleans. Farmer in Lincoln Co., KY. Md. Susan Shelby. Staff officer, KSG, 1861. Col., 6th KY Cav., Sept. 2, 1862. WIA Milton, TN, March 20, 1863. Often led a cavalry brigade in Wheeler's Corps. Appointed IG of Cav., Army of TN, 1864. Appointed chief of staff to Gen. Wheeler, 1865. Paroled May 1865. Lived in Lincoln Co. and Danville postwar. Attorney. State representative 1875–77. Died Jan. 12, 1877, Lexington, KY. Buried Lexington Cemetery. The "brave, determined, fearless, enterprising" Grigsby was often listed postwar as a

Confederate general, but he was paroled a colonel. Grigsby-Shelby papers are at the Filson Club.

Grinstead, Hiram Lane. Born 1829, Lexington, KY. Grad. Transylvania U. Law School. Prewar lawyer in Lexington. Lawyer and judge in Cameron Co. and later Jefferson, TX. Came to Camden, AR, in 1859 and practiced law there. Md. Catherine A. Goodwin. Col., 33d AR, July 11, 1862. Led his regiment with "gallantry and zeal" at Prairie Grove and the Little Rock Campaign. Led Tappan's Brigade at Pleasant Hill. KIA Jenkins Ferry. Buried Oakland Cemetery, Camden. Gen. Tappan eulogized Grinstead as "a brave and gallant officer . . . a good and useful citizen."

Grivot, Maurice Claude. Born Feb. 14, 1814, Baton Rouge, LA. Prewar New Orleans lawyer. Capt. in Mexican War. Md. Jeanne E. Bion. Adj. gen. of LA 1855–63. Appointed col. and chief judge of the military court of Buckner's Corps March 23, 1865. Died March 5, 1875, New Orleans, buried Girod St. Cemetery. Gen. Buckner commended Grivot "as a gentleman of legal ability, of intelligence and great firmness and integrity of character."

Groner, Virginius Despaux. Born Sept. 7, 1836, Norfolk, VA. Grad. Norfolk Military Academy. Lawyer and newspaper editor in Norfolk. Fought Indians in TX. Md. (in 1867) Katherine, daughter of Supreme Court justice John Campbell. Capt. and AAG, March 16, 1861. Helped organize troops arriving in Richmond. According to one report, given a cavalry command in southeast VA in the spring of 1862. Col., 61st VA, Oct. 1, 1862. Court-martialed Feb. 1, 1863, and reprimanded. WIA Spotsylvania. Appmx. Shipping magnate in Norfolk postwar. Owner "Groner's Wharf" in that city. Died Nov. 25, 1903, Norfolk. Buried Cedar Grove Cemetery, Norfolk. One veteran remembered that Groner was "a strict disciplinarian and an accomplished tactician."

Gurley, Edward Jeremiah. Born June 7, 1827, Franklin Co., AL. Attd. La Grange College. Lawyer in Tuscumbia, AL. Moved to Waco, TX, in 1852, to practice law with his brother-in-law. Md. Annie Blocker; Virginia Alexander. Col., 30th TX Cav. (aka 1st TX PR) June 2, 1862. Often led Gano's brigade in the Indian Territory and AR. Called "brave, gentle and kind" by one veteran. Postwar Waco lawyer, planter. State legislator. Died July 4, 1914, Waco. Buried Oakwood Cemetery.

Hagan, James. Born June 17, 1822, Co. Tyrone, Ireland. Reared in Philadelphia, PA. Wealthy merchant in New Orleans and Mobile, AL. Plantation owner. Capt., 3d US Dragoons in Mexican War. Md. Bettie Oliver, a celebrated AL "belle." Capt., "Mobile Dragoons," early 1861. Major, 1st MS Cav., Oct. 29, 1861. Col., 3d AL Cav. July 1, 1862. WIA 3 times. Resigned Nov. 28, 1863, but resignation revoked May 12, 1864. Led brigade 1864–65. Paroled May 9, 1865,

Meridian. Gen. Wheeler called him "a most thorough soldier and able commander," but his alcoholism delayed his promotion. Postwar held minor governmental posts in Mobile. Died Nov. 6, 1901, Mobile, buried Magnolia Cemetery, Mobile. Promoted to brig. in the last days of the war, but the promotion was never confirmed and the paperwork was lost in the fall of Richmond.

Hagood, James Robert. Born Nov. 26 (gravestone says Nov. 15), 1844, Barnwell Dist., SC. Student at SCMA when the war started. Pvt. Co. C, 1st (Hagood's) SC, summer 1862. Sgt. major, Aug. 1862. Adj., Nov. 6, 1862. Capt. Co. K, Jan. 2, 1863. Col., Nov. 16, 1863, at age 18, promoted over four senior captains for "distinguished skill and valor." Died Nov. 15, 1870, Columbia, as a result of a train wreck. Buried Short Staple Cemetery, Barnwell Co. Hagood, the brother of Gen. Johnson Hagood, was the youngest full colonel in the Confederate Army. His unpublished war memoir is at USC.

Hale, Smith D. Born c. 1827, TN. Prewar attorney and judge in Huntsville, AL. Md. Sarah E. Pynchon. Col., 49th AL, Jan. 30, 1862, but resigned almost immediately (May 1862). In 1863 he applied for a post as enrolling officer, admitting he was "unfit for camp duty." Postwar lawyer in Perry Co. (where he'd moved during the war). Died after 1873. One source has him buried in Citizens Cemetery, Marietta, GA (his wife's hometown), but a record of that cemetery's gravestones does not reflect this.

Hall, Bolling, Jr. Born Sept. 17, 1837, GA. Grew up in Robinson Springs, AL. Grad. UAL 1858. Attd. UVA. Unmd. Prewar clerk of Montgomery, AL, city court. Pvt. Co. G, 6th AL, June 2, 1861. Corp., July 28, 1861. Discharged Feb. 10, 1862. Capt. Co. E ("Fitzpatrick Blues"), 2d Bn. Hilliard's Legion, March 16, 1862. Lt. col., June 25, 1862. Col., 59th AL (formed from the 2d Bn.), Nov. 25, 1863. WIA Chickamauga; lost leg at Drewry's Bluff May 16, 1864. Paroled Augusta, GA, May 18, 1865. Died Feb. 3, 1866, near Montgomery, of his war wounds. Buried Hall family cemetery at "Ellerslie," Elmore Co. A "gentleman of sober, steady habits, and generous, gallant and brave." The AL Archives have a collection of family letters.

Hall, Edward Dudley. Born Sept. 7, 1823, Wilmington, NC. Educated at Donaldson Academy. Turpentine distiller in Wilmington prewar. State legislator 1846–47. County sheriff 1852–60. Md. Susan Hill Lane; Sallie Landon Green. Capt. Co. H, 3d NC Art., May 16, 1861. Major, 7th NC, Aug. 17, 1861. Col., 46th NC, April 4, 1862. Resigned Dec. 31, 1863, due to disability and to his election as county sherrif. State senator 1864–67. Wilmington police chief and mayor postwar. Gen. in UCV. Died June 11, 1896, Wilmington. Buried Oakdale Cemetery. "[A] brave man, and good disciplinarian."

Hall, Josephus Marion. Born Oct. 15, 1828, Eutaw, AL. Attd. Cumberland U. Law School. Prewar lawyer in Greene and Clarke Cos., AL. Md. Eliza Erin; Lida E. Hamill. Capt. Co. A, 5th AL, May 6, 1861. Lt. col., April 27, 1862. Col., July 17, 1862. Lost right arm at Spotsylvania. Retired Nov. 29, 1864. Moved to Marshall, TX, in 1871. Lawyer and judge in Marshall and Cleburne. Mayor of Marshall. Died Feb. 6, 1915, at his daughter's home in Comanche, TX. Buried Cleburne Cemetery. A subordinate wrote in his diary, "Col. Hall is so much afraid of Genl. Rodes that he renders himself perfectly ridiculous. . . . He is laughed at by every man in his regiment."

Hall, Matthew Robert. Born March 15, 1836, Warren Co., GA. Grad. NYU Medical School, 1857. Physician in Warrenton prewar. Md. Fannie I. Latimer. Capt. Co. B, 48th GA, March 4, 1862. Major, July 17, 1863. Lt. col., Dec. 24, 1863. WIA Wilderness. Col., Nov. 12, 1864. Detailed to Danville, VA, at the time of Lee's surrender. Paroled Augusta, GA. Warrenton physician postwar. State legislator, farmer. Died Jan. 28, 1905, at his home in Warrenton. Buried Warrenton City Cemetery.

Hall, Winchester. Born Nov. 12, 1819, Louisville, KY. Lawyer in Thibodeaux, LA. Hardware dealer in Chicago, IL. Md. Ruth M. Carr. Capt. Co. I, 26th LA, March 15, 1862. Major, April 3, 1862. Lt. col., Nov. 10, 1862. Col., Dec. 30, 1862. "[V]ery unpopular in the regiment." WIA and POW Vicksburg. Appointed col. and judge, military court of S. D. Lee's Corps, April 6, 1864, but since he hadn't yet been formally exchanged, the appointment was recalled and he rejoined his regiment. Led Thomas's Brigade in LA in 1865. Paroled June 3, 1865, Alexandria. Lawyer in LA, Chicago, IL, and Pocomoke City, MD, postwar. Died Dec. 10, 1909, Pocomoke City. Buried Metairie Cemetery, New Orleans. Hall wrote an engaging history of the 26th and books on the theory of education.

Ham, Joseph Hutchinson. Born June 6, 1838, Hampton, VA. Attd. Cary Institute. Grad. VMI. Civil engineer prewar. Living in Hampton in 1860. Md. Anna Gambol. 2d lt., PAVA, May 23, 1861. Assigned to 16th VA as drillmaster. Capt. Co. F, 16th VA, Aug. 17, 1861. Lt. col., May 3, 1862. Praised for "conspicuous gallantry" at Malvern Hill. Col., Aug. 30, 1862. WIA 2d Manassas (hip), May and Oct. 1864. Often absent due to wounds. Lived in Hampton and Morrison postwar. Teacher. Clerk of court. Died April 26, 1912, at his home in Morrison. Buried Emmanuel Episcopal Church near Morrison.

Ham, Thomas Wiley. Born c. 1828, TN (per census—family sources say Lauderdale Co., AL). Educated at Euclid Academy in Tishomingo Co., MS. Farmer there. Md. Eliet Jane Bellew. Capt., Ham's Co., MS State Cav. (later Co. B, Ham's Regt.), Jan. 26, 1863. Major, 16th (aka 1st) Bn. MS Cav. State Troops, May 18, 1863. Col., Ham's MS Cav., May 4, 1864 (the date the regiment was transferred to Confederate service). MWIA Ezra Church, died July 30, 1864. Probably buried Oakland Cemetery, Atlanta. Gen. Gholson found Ham "a good officer."

Hamilton, Daniel Heyward, Sr. Born May 2, 1816, Callawassie Island, SC, son of a governor of SC. Attd. UVA. Politician. US marshal for SC, appointed 1858. Charleston resident prewar. Mexican War veteran. Md. Rebecca Middleton. Major, 1st (Gregg's, a 6-month unit) SC, Jan. 7, 1861. Regiment reorganized and entered Confederate service July 1861 with Hamilton as lt. col. Col., Dec. 14, 1861. Permanently detached from the regiment Aug. 27, 1863, when he was appointed an enrolling officer. Resigned Jan. 4, 1864. Died Dec. 29, 1868, Morristown, NJ. A fellow colonel said the admittedly brave Hamilton did not have the confidence of the brigade, since he had "never shown any capacity."

Hampton, George James. Born c. 1827, AL (or TN). Prewar sheriff of Victoria Co., TX. Capt., Texas Rangers, 1859–60. Md. L. Yeary. In 1861 the county sent him to Mexico to purchase arms. Capt. Co. C, 4th TX Cav. (the "Victoria Invincibles"), Sept. 11, 1861. Major, March 8, 1862. Lt. col., April 14, 1863. Col., appointed April 14, 1865, to rank from Oct. 28, 1864. WIA Valverde and Mansfield. No parole record. Farmer in De Soto and Claiborne Parishes, LA, postwar. Died c. 1889. One soldier remembered Hampton as "a staunch disciplinarian . . . and brave, even to a fault, on the battlefield."

Hancock, Ezekiel Wheeler. Born July 2, 1817, Rockingham Co., NC. Farmer in Rockingham Co. prewar. County clerk, surveyor, treasurer. Mexican War veteran. Md. Mary Allen. 2d lt., 13th NC, May 3, 1861. Defeated for reelection at reorganization, April 26, 1862. Pvt., Williams's Co., NC Senior Reserves, June 18, 1864. Lt. col., 7th NC Senior Reserves, Nov. 28, 1864. Col., Jan. 28, 1865. Paroled May 11, 1865. Rockingham Co. farmer postwar. Died there Feb. 12, 1887. Buried Wentworth United Methodist Church Cemetery.

Hannon, Moses Wright. Born Dec. 14, 1827, Baldwin Co., GA. Moved to Montgomery, AL, in 1847. Montgomery merchant. Lived 8 years in CA. Md. Caroline Mastin. Capt. Co. B, 1st AL Cav., 1861. Lt. col., Dec. 3, 1861. Col., 53d AL PR (which he raised), Nov. 5, 1862. Resigned in Dec. 1863, but resignation revoked the next month. Led brigade 1864–65, often winning the praise of his superiors. WIA Monroe's Crossroads, disabled rest of war. Postwar lived in Montgomery, New Orleans, then Freestone Co. and Oakwood, TX. Merchant and planter. Died June 3, 1897, Oakwood. Buried Oakwood Cemetery. Many sources state he was promoted to brig. in 1865.

Hardcastle, Aaron Bascom. Born July 5, 1836, Caroline Co., MD. Grad. USMA. Lt., US Army, 1855–61. Md. Alice Hatch. 1st lt., CS Regular Army, Sept.

19, 1861. Capt., postdated to rank from March 16, 1861. Mustering officer in Vicksburg. Major, 3d MS Inf. Bn., Nov. 16, 1861. WIA Shiloh. Col., 33d (later, 45th) MS, April 18, 1862. Leg badly broken in KY Campaign. Disabled for field duty and assigned to post command at Dalton, GA. In 1864 the regimental organization was declared illegal, and Hardcastle reverted to lt. col. Assigned (as capt., CS Regular Army) to ordnance duty in AL. Appointed col. and judge, military court of Wheeler's Corps, March 23, 1865, but he never was able to report for this duty. Captured April 3, 1865, Tuscaloosa, AL, while commanding that post. Farmer and miller postwar at Easton, MD. Died Feb. 10, 1915, Easton. Buried Spring Hill Cemetery, Easton. Col. John B. Sale said Hardcastle was "an accomplished Christian soldier [with] a deliberate well balanced mind."

Hardeman, Peter. Born May 28, 1831, Rutherford Co., TN. Family moved to TX in 1835, eventually settling in Travis Co. Prewar plantation owner. Md. Nancy C. Keese. Capt. Co. A, 2d TX MR, May 23, 1861. Helped to capture 700 regular army soldiers near Fort Fillmore, NM, in 1861. Lt. col., Dec. 16, 1861. Col., 1st TX Cav., AZ Brigade, Feb. 13, 1863. His health broke down, but he returned to the army the next year and served until war's end. In 1869 he took his family and immigrated to Brazil. Hardeman helped establish the "Americana" colony of ex-Confederates ("os Confederados") near Sao Paolo. Farmed there. Died May 18, 1882, Americana. Buried Campo Cemetery, five miles from Americana. One private complained that Hardeman "treats us more like slaves than anything else."

Hardeman, Thomas, Jr. Born Jan. 12, 1825, Eatonton, GA. Grad. Emory U. Lawyer, merchant, and state legislator in Macon. US congressman 1859–61. Officer in vol. militia. Md. Jane S. Lumsden. Capt. Co. C, 2d GA Bn., April 20, 1861. Major, May 15, 1861. Col., 45th GA, March 15, 1862. WIA Frayser's Farm, severely. Resigned Oct. 13, 1862, because of that wound. Elected to GA House of Representatives in 1863, where he served as House speaker. AAG of the GA Militia Div., 1864. Postwar cotton merchant in Macon. Speaker of the GA State House 1874–76. US congressman 1883–85. Known as "Georgia's peerless orator." Died March 6, 1891, Macon. Buried Rose Hill Cemetery.

Hardin, Thomas Joseph. Born July 27, 1829, Monroe Co., KY. Reared in Marshall Co., MS. Farmer in Marshall Co. prewar. Capt. Co. I, 19th MS, May 25, 1861. Major, May 5, 1863. Lt. col., July 17, 1863. Col., Jan. 20, 1864. KIA Spotsylvania, May 12, 1864. Buried Spotsylvania Confederate Cemetery. A memorial stone for him is at Hill Crest Cemetery, Holly Springs, MS.

Hardy, Washington Morrison. Born Feb. 9, 1835, NC. Buncombe Co. lawyer prewar. Militia colonel. Md. Mary Erwin; Rebecca Wilson Carson. 1st lt. Co. E, 1st (Bethel) NC, April 27, 1861. Mustered out Nov. 12, 1861. Capt., "Hardy's

Light Artillery" (later Co. A, 60th NC), 6th NC Bn., Jan. 27, 1862. Major, 60th NC, Feb. 21, 1863. Col., May 14, 1863. Often on furlough due to ill health. Led (more accurately, misled) an improvised brigade at Bentonville. Asheville lawyer postwar. Librarian of the NC State House in 1879. Died March 29, 1880, Spartanburg, SC. Buried Episcopal Church of the Advent Cemetery, Spartanburg. Esteemed "for his bravery and kind-heartedness," Hardy fell off his horse at Bentonville while botching an attack and was relieved of command.

Hardy, William Richard. Born July 27, 1831, GA. Teacher in Columbia Co., AR, prewar. Md. Elizabeth Doss; Margaret E. Smith. 1st lt. Co. A, 24th AR, 1862. Major, 1862. Lt. col., Nov. 23, 1862. Most of regiment captured at Arkansas Post. The remainder stayed in the TMD and were merged with the 19th AR. Col., 19th/24th, probably March 1, 1864. Postwar schoolteacher in Ouachita Co. State senator briefly in 1891. Died Jan. 23, 1891, Buena Vista, Ouachita Co. Buried Riddick Cemetery, near Camden. "Frail in constitution" but "a gallant soldier."

Harkie, Cyrus Brown. Born c. 1832, Mecklenburg Co., NC. Reared in Cobb Co., GA. Grad. GMI with high honors. Civil engineer and attorney in Randolph Co. prewar. Capt. Co. H, 1st GA State Troops, Sept. 26, 1861. Col., Oct. 9, 1861. Arrested Oct. 28, 1861, for commandeering tents without authority. Arrested in 1862 for allowing liquor in camp and for granting unauthorized passes. Found guilty and sentenced to suspension from command. Regiment disbanded April/May 1862. Elected col., 55th GA, May 17, 1862, a regiment that included 300 men of his old unit. Court-martialed in Jan. 1863 and dismissed from the service. Harkie was accused of profiteering from captured property and habitual neglect of duty. His officers demanded his resignation, and his men forced him to perform humiliating tasks for their amusement. Restored to rank through political influence and allowed to resign Sept. 23, 1864. Returned to Randolph Co. Railroad surveyor. Died Dec. 25, 1869, near Cuthbert, in an apparent suicide but possible murder. A modern author sums up Harkie as "an unscrupulous ne'er-do-well."

Harman, Asher Waterman. Born Jan. 24, 1830, Waynesboro, VA. Operated a stage line in Staunton prewar. Md. Virginia Callaghan. Capt. Co. G, 5th VA, April 28, 1861. Major, Feb. 1862. QM of post at Staunton in 1862. Col., 12th VA Cav., June 21, 1862. WIA Brandy Station. POW near Harpers Ferry July 14, 1863. Released c. Feb. 1865. Paroled April 30, 1865, Staunton. Railroad executive in Staunton postwar. Died April 9, 1895, Richmond. Buried Thornrose Cemetery, Staunton. Brother of Cols. Michael and William Harman.

Harman, Bledsoe Desha. Born c. 1828, Georgetown, KY. Reared in Scott Co., KY. Farmer there and in Memphis, TN. Mexican War veteran. Md. Mary Jane Coffin. Authorized in Jan. 1862 to recruit a regiment from the Memphis area.

The companies he raised were siphoned off into (or eventually joined) other regiments, and his unit never formally organized, though some companies attempted to organize the regiment, and there is a service record for "Harman's Regiment." Commanded post of Grenada, MS, in 1862, as col. No record of service after 1863. Filed for postwar pardon as col., PACS. Died Aug. 20, 1882, Washington, DC. Buried Congressional Cemetery, Washington. Gen. Ruggles praised him as "distinguished for his zeal, influence in our cause, and ability."

Harman, Michael Garber. Born Aug. 22, 1823, Staunton, VA. Hotel keeper in Staunton prewar. Helped operate a stagecoach line. Md. Caroline V. Stevenson. Major and QM, PAVA, April 1861. Nominated major and QM, PACS, June 28, 1861. Elected capt. Co. H, 34th VA, in 1861 but declined. Lt. col., 52d VA, Aug. 19, 1861. Col., May 1, 1862. WIA McDowell (arm). Retired June 6, 1863, due to disability. QM in Staunton, 1863–65. Exonerated on charges of impropriety as QM. Returned to Staunton after the war. Stage line operator. President of the Valley Railroad. Died Dec. 18, 1877, on a train in Richmond. Buried Thornrose Cemetery, Staunton.

Harman, William Henry. Born Feb. 17, 1828, Waynesboro, VA. Lawyer in Augusta Co. prewar. Commonwealth attorney. Mexican War veteran. Md. Margaret S. Garver. Brigadier general, 13th Brigade, VA Militia in 1861. Helped to seize Harpers Ferry. Lt. col., 5th VA, May 7, 1861. Col., Sept. 11, 1861. Dropped at April 1862 reorganization. VADC to Gen. Edward Johnson, 1862. Appointed AAAG Feb. 19, 1864. Led a regiment of reservists at Piedmont and in the 1864–65 Valley Campaign. KIA Waynesboro. Buried Thornrose Cemetery, Staunton.

Harper, Kenton. Born 1801, Chambersburg, PA. Moved to Staunton, VA, c. 1820. Editor, Staunton *Spectator*. Farmer. Mayor of Staunton. State representative. Capt. in Mexican War and military governor in northern Mexico. Md. Eleanor Calhoun. Major gen., 5th Div., VA Militia, in early 1861. Harper's militia seized Harpers Ferry (named after a distant cousin) April 18, 1861. Col., 5th VA, May 7, 1861. Resigned Sept. 1861 to be with his dying wife. Col. of a temporary regiment of reserves at the Battle of Piedmont in 1864. Died Dec. 25, 1867, at his home ("Glen Allen") in Augusta Co. Buried Thornrose Cemetery, Staunton. A "born soldier . . . [of] energy, skill and sagacity." Papers at UNC.

Harper, Robert Withers. Born July 21, 1833, Marlboro, MD. Attd. Georgetown U. Lawyer in MD. Moved to Little Rock, AR, in 1856. Prewar lawyer there. Bought cotton plantation in Conway Co. State legislator. Md. Laura Cox. Major, 1st AR MR, June 6, 1861. Col., April 14, 1862. KIA by a cannonball at Chickamauga, Sept. 20, 1863. Gen. McNair recommended him for promotion in Dec. 1862 saying, "There is not a more efficient officer in the service, possessing a good military education [Harper had been in the cadet program at Georgetown] and besides a most excellent disciplinarian."

Harrell, John Mortimer. Born Dec. 14, 1828, Gates Co., NC. Grad. U. of Nashville 1847. Farmer, lawyer prewar in Nashville and Little Rock. Prospected in CA for a while. US Dist. attorney 1859–60. Md. Kate Ferris. Appointed state solicitor general in 1861. Pvt. in the militia force that seized Fort Smith, AR, in April 1861. VADC to Gen. Holmes at 1st Manassas and to Gen. Breckinridge in 1862. Adj. gen. of Monroe's AR Cav. Brigade at Cane Hill. Raised a battalion of AR cavalry in 1863. Lt. col., Harrell's (aka 17th) Bn., April 30, 1864. Unit consolidated with Crawford's Regt. Often led a brigade in 1864–65. Said to have been promoted to col. in 1865. Paroled June 22, 1865, at Houston, as lt. col. Postwar lawyer in Little Rock, Pine Bluff, and Hot Springs. Militia general. Died July 4, 1907, San Antonio, TX. Buried Hollywood Cemetery, Hot Springs. Harrell wrote the Arkansas volume of *Confederate Military History,* in which his claim to have been promoted to full col. appears. A wartime newspaper, reporting on a cotton card fraud, referred to Harrell (the fraud victim) as "a sort of easy, good for nothing fellow named Harrell, commonly called Lord Mortimer."

Harris, Charles Jenkins. Born Nov. 26, 1833, Milledgeville, GA. Attd. Oglethorpe U., then studied law under his father. Macon lawyer prewar. Md. Mary C. Wiley. Capt. Co. K, 59th GA, May 15, 1862. Major, June 16, 1862. Lt. col., Dec. 22, 1862. Resigned July 10, 1863. Col., 3d GA Reserves, May 17, 1864. Resigned Nov. 5, 1864. Lawyer, judge in Macon postwar. State representative 1877–78. Died Jan. 22, 1893, Macon. Buried Rose Hill Cemetery, Macon. Gen. W. M. Browne considered Harris well intentioned but "entirely incompetent to the task" of raising the GA Reserves. Harris's papers are at Duke U.

Harris, David Bullock. Born Sept. 28, 1814, Louisa Co., VA. Grad. USMA 1833. Lt., US Army, 1833–35. Tobacco farmer in Goochland Co. Civil engineer. Md. Louisa Knight. Capt. VA engineers, May 2, 1861. Engineer on Gen. Beauregard's staff, 1861. Capt., PACS, Feb. 15, 1862. Major, Oct. 3, 1862. Lt. col., May 5, 1863. Col., Oct. 8, 1863. Planned the defenses of Island No. 10, Vicksburg, Charleston, and Petersburg. Chief engineer, Dept. of SC, GA, and FL. Died Oct. 10, 1864, Summerville, SC, of yellow fever. Buried Hollywood Cemetery, Richmond. Gen. Beauregard, his superior officer and close friend, praised Harris as "the only officer in his command who never made a mistake."

Harris, James Alpheus Skidmore. Born Aug. 29, 1832, Rockingham Co., NC. Known by his middle name of Skidmore. Gold miner in Cherokee Co., GA. Operated copper mines near Canton. Md. Anne Donalson. Lt. Co. F, 2d GA, April 18, 1861. Lt. col., May 14, 1861. WIA Antietam. Col., 43d GA, March 20, 1863.

MWIA Champion Hill, died May 17, 1863. Buried on the battlefield; reburied First Methodist Church, Canton.

Harris, Merry B. Born 1829, Copiah Co., MS. Lawyer in Gallatin, MS, prewar. Md. Eveline Allen; Hettie Bullock. Capt., "Pettus Rifles" (Co. D, 12th MS), March 11, 1861. WIA Seven Pines, Chancellorsville. Lt. col., 1863 (probably April 2). Col., March 19, 1864. WIA Weldon Railroad, June 24, 1864, shot in the head by a sharpshooter. Returned home on sick leave. Died Aug. 30, 1865, Columbus, KY, of brain fever brought on by his wounds. Probably buried Bullock Cemetery, near Columbus. Some Harris letters are at the U. of So. MS.

Harris, Sampson Watkins. Born March 18, 1838, Wetumpka, AL. Grad. UGA. Lawyer in Lexington and Athens prewar. Md. Lucy W. Todd. Lt. Co. K, 6th GA, May 28, 1861. Capt., Nov. 1, 1862. WIA (left leg broken) Olustee. Lt. col., July 7, 1864. Col., Feb. 14, 1865. WIA twice at Bentonville. Lawyer in Carrollton postwar. Judge, 1881–1903. Adj. gen. of GA, 1903–7. Died May 31, 1912, Carrollton. Buried Pinewood Cemetery, West Point, GA.

Harrison, Archibald Taylor. Born Oct. 28, 1829, Goochland Co., VA. Attd. VMI. Prewar farmer. Md. Mary M. Orgain. Lt. col., 30th VA, June 13, 1861. Col., April 19, 1862. Absent frequently due to a fractured shoulder blade, suffered when thrown by his horse. Retired Nov. 5, 1864, citing his injury, diarrhea, and "extreme general debility." Paroled July 21, 1865, Richmond. Farmer in Prince George Co. postwar. Moved to Richmond, where he died May 5, 1889. Buried Shockoe Hill Cemetery, Richmond.

Harrison, Francis Eugene. Born April 3, 1826, Andersonville, SC. Attd. UVA. Planter in Anderson Dist. prewar. Md. Anna E. Ross; Mary Eunice Perrin; Elizabeth Perrin Cotchran. Capt. Co. D, 1st SC Rifles, July 20, 1861. WIA Gaines's Mill. Major, Nov. 12, 1862. Lt. col., March 25, 1863. Col., May 5, 1863. Retired to Invalid Corps April 8, 1864. Andersonville merchant postwar. Built a cotton mill. Died Nov. 16, 1878, Andersonville. Buried in family graveyard in Andersonville Baptist Church; reburied Roberts Churchyard, 1959. Papers at UNC. An obituary calls him "kind and gentle . . . a pure, christian and noble gentleman."

Harrison, George Paul, Jr. Born March 19, 1841, near Savannah, son of George P. Harrison Sr., general of GA State Troops during the war. Grad. GMI 1861. Md. Fannie M. Drake. Lt. and adj., 1st GA Regulars, April 8, 1861 (while still in school). Col., 5th GA State Troops, June 23, 1861. Col., 32d GA, May 15, 1862. WIA at the Siege of Charleston and at Olustee. Commanded Florence, SC, prison, 1864. Led a brigade in the Carolinas Campaign and repeatedly praised by superiors. Often stated (for example, in *Confederate Military History*) to have been promoted to brig. gen. in 1865. Lawyer and planter in Opelika, AL, postwar. State senator 1878–84, 1900–1904. US congressman 1894–96. Gen. in UCV. Died July 17, 1922, Opelika. Buried Rosemere Cemetery, Opelika.

Harrison, Isaac F. Born Nov. 21, 1818, Jefferson Co., MS. Grad. St. Joseph College in KY. Wealthy planter in Natchez, MS, and Tensas Parish, LA, prewar. Capt. of a vol. militia company, the "Tensas Cavalry." Md. Sarah Frances Gibson, cousin of Gen. Randall Gibson. Capt., "Tensas Cavalry" (Co. A, Wirt Adams's 1st MS Cav.), Aug. 29, 1861. Major, Aug. 15, 1862. Resigned upon transfer to TMD. Major, 15th LA Cav. Bn., c. Jan. 1863. Lt. col., July 8, 1863. Col., 3d LA Cav. (formed from the 15th Bn.), Nov. 1863. Led a cavalry brigade in north LA, 1864–65. Paroled June 6, 1865. Moved to Honduras after the war and engaged in railroad development. Returning to the US, he lived in New Orleans; Natchez; Fort Worth; El Paso; and back to Fort Worth. Real estate dealer in Fort Worth, with interests in mines. Died Aug. 17, 1890, Fort Worth. Buried Pioneer Cemetery, Fort Worth. Nicknamed "Black" Harrison, to distinguish him from Col. William "Red" Harrison. A private called Harrison "a fearless man, a born soldier, [but] not a tactician. Said he brought his men out to fight and not to drill."

Harrison, Isham, Jr. Born March 3, 1821, Jefferson Co., AL. Two brothers were Confederate generals; twin brother Richard Harrison was col. 43d MS. Grad. Transylvania U. Law School. Lawyer in Columbus, MS, prewar. Dist. attorney. Judge. Md. Julia R. Whitfield. Major, 13th MS, May 23, 1861. Dropped at April 1862 reorganization. Unsuccessfully sought appointment to a military court. Col., 6th MS Cav., Dec. 24, 1863. KIA Tupelo. Buried Friendship Cemetery, Columbus. Eulogized as a "gallant, dashing, brave commander."

Harrison, Julien. Born Feb. 6, 1827, Richmond, VA. Attd. William & Mary College and UVA. Wealthy farmer at "Elk Hill," Goochland Co. prewar. Capt., "Goochland Light Dragoons," vol. militia. Md. Lavinia Heth (sister to Gen. Henry Heth); Lillie Johnston. Lt. col., 6th VA Cav., Sept. 11, 1861. Col., April 15, 1862. Resigned July 28, 1862, due to hemorrhoids but reappointed Sept. 19, 1863. WIA Oct. 11, 1863, Brandy Station. Found unfit for field duty Jan. 15, 1864. Retired March 6, 1865. Appointed col. and judge, Military Court of the Richmond defenses, March 23, 1865. Farmed at "Elk Hill" postwar. Then moved to Richmond to become a tobacco and warehouse inspector. Accidentally shot and killed himself July 17, 1877, Richmond. Buried Hollywood Cemetery. An obituary called him "gallant" and "universally beloved." Brother of Col. Randolph Harrison.

Harrison, Randolph. Born Feb. 12, 1831, Richmond, VA. Attd. William & Mary College, UVA, and Princeton. Grad. UPA Medical School. Planter in Goochland Co. prewar. Md. Elizabeth Williamson. Capt. Co. H, 46th VA, May 19, 1862. Lt. col., May 24, 1862. Col., March 28, 1864. WIA Petersburg, June 15, 1864, in neck. Returned to duty Oct. 27, 1864. POW Oct. 27, 1864, near Petersburg. Released June 13, 1865. Physician in Williamsburg postwar. Died June 14, 1894, Williamsburg. Buried Bruton Parish Churchyard, Williamsburg.

Harrison, Richard. Born March 3, 1821, Jefferson Co., AL. Brother of Col. Isham Harrison and Gens. Tom and James Harrison. Grad. Transylvania U. Physician and planter in Aberdeen, MS, prewar. State senator 1858–61. Md. Mary Ragsdale; Mollie Tompkins; Emma Buck. 1st lt. Co. C, 43d MS, April 1, 1861. Major, May 15, 1862. Lt. col., Oct. 4, 1862. Col., Nov. 10, 1862. POW Vicksburg and paroled. Led Adams's MS Brigade in 1865 and often included in postwar lists of Confederate generals. Paroled Meridian, May 16, 1865. Moved to Waco, TX, in 1866. Physician and planter. Died Nov. 1, 1876, at his residence southeast of Waco. Buried First Street Cemetery, Waco.

Harrison, Samuel R. Born 1819, MS. Reared in Wilkinson Co., MS. 1st lt. in Mexican War. Prewar lawyer in Wilkinson Co. and New Orleans. Md. Jennie M. Chinn. Lt. Co. I, 1st LA (the "Orleans Light Guards"), April 25, 1861. Major, Oct. 10, 1861. Appointed major and brigade commissary, Nov. 1, 1861. Col., 1st LA, April 28, 1862. Resigned June 8, 1862. Major commissary for Joseph Davis's Brigade for remainder of war. Killed himself April 21, 1867, in Plaquemines Parish. Buried Springfield Plantation, West Feliciana Parish.

Harrison, William. Born March 4, 1829, Twiggs Co., GA. Prewar farmer in Quitman Co. Moved to Bossier Parish, LA, c. 1859. Md. Eugenia Crawford. Capt., "Bossier Cavalry," April 6, 1862. This company served in Wimberly's LA Cav. Squadron, in the 18th TN Cav. Bn., and in the 2d KY Cav. Harrison returned to LA in the spring of 1863. Lt. col., Harrison's LA Cav. Bn., Dec. 1863. Col., 6th LA Cav. (formed from the battalion), winter of 1864–65. Paroled June 12, 1865, Shreveport. Returned to his Quitman Co. farm postwar. Lawyer (which he had studied before the war but never practiced). Longtime state legislator. Moved to Evergreen, AL, in 1893 and a few years later to Caddo Parish, LA. Died Sept. 13, 1914, Lewis, GA. Buried Harrison family cemetery, Quitman Co. Harrison was nicknamed "Red" because of his whiskers.

Hart, Benjamin Rufus. Born April 7, 1834, Ramer, AL. Prewar Montgomery Co., AL, planter. Capt. Co. K, 22d AL, Oct. 6, 1861. Major, Dec. 15, 1862. Lt. col., Sept. 20, 1863. Col., Dec. 15, 1863. WIA Shiloh, Chickamauga. KIA July 28, 1864, Ezra Church, near Atlanta, shot once while leading a charge and a second time when being helped off the field. Body fell into Union hands and presumably was buried on the field. "A pure patriot and a gallant soldier."

Hart, John R. Born c. 1831, NC. Farmer and minister in Sardis, Floyd Co., GA. Md. Agnes ——. Capt. Co. G ("Sardis Volunteers," a unit largely made up of his parishioners), 21st GA, May 9, 1861. Capt. Co. G, Smith's GA Legion Cav.,

May 8, 1862. Lt. col., July 12, 1862. Col., 6th GA Cav., March 6, 1863. WIA July 21, 1864, near Atlanta. Paroled May 3, 1865, Charlotte. Arrested by federal authorities in 1865 on charges that his men murdered 2 federal prisoners but released. "Drummer" for an Atlanta newspaper, in Rome, GA, and in Morgan Co. postwar. Attorney in Upson Co. Died June 1, 1878, Floyd Co. Buried Myrtle Hill Cemetery, Rome. Col. J. C. Nisbet thought Hart "a gallant soldier, a dashing cavalryman, if he did 'love licker' and would at times imbibe too freely."

Hart, Robert A. Born c. 1837, Ireland. Bookkeeper in Memphis, TN, in 1860. Major, AAG on Gen. Hindman's staff in AR, 1862. Lt. col., 30th AR, Aug. 18, 1862. Col., Nov. 12, 1862. MWIA at Helena, struck by a shell in the right leg. Died in a Union hospital in Memphis Aug. 6, 1863. Buried Elmwood Cemetery, Memphis.

Harvie, Edwin James. Born Feb. 1, 1835, Amelia Co., VA. Attd. VMI. Lt., US Army, 1855–61. Capt., CS Regular Army, March 16, 1861. Capt. and QM to Taliaferro and Wise, 1861. Capt. AIG to Gen. Joseph Johnston. Lt. col., May 20, 1862. AIG to Gens. Johnston and Robert E. Lee. Col., March 31, 1863. Paroled May 2, 1865, NC. Postwar lived in Richmond, then Washington, DC. Employed by the US pension bureau. Later involved with compiling OR. Died July 11, 1911, Washington. Buried Hollywood Cemetery, Richmond. Gen. Johnston recommended Harvie for promotion to general as "an officer of rare merit, full of courage, truth, zeal & fidelity."

Haskell, Alexander Cheves. Born Sept. 22, 1839, Abbeville Dist., SC. Grad. USC just prior to the war. Md. Rebecca Singleton; Alice V. Alexander, sister of Gen. E. P. Alexander. Pvt. Co. D, 1st SC (Gregg's), Jan. 1861. Adj., Feb. 1861. Brevet 2d lt., July 1861. Lt. and ADC to Maxcy Gregg, Dec. 14, 1861. Capt. and AAG, Jan. 18, 1862. Lt. col., 7th SC Cav., April 20, 1864. Col., June (1?), 1864. WIA Fredericksburg, Chancellorsville, Metadequin Creek (May 30, 1864), Darbytown Road. The latter wound, a shot to the head, disabled him for 6 months and caused him to temporarily lose his memory and power of speech. Appmx. Abbeville teacher, lawyer postwar. President of two railroads. State representative 1865–66. Died April 13, 1910, Columbia. Buried Elmwood Cemetery, Columbia. Mary Chesnut observed Haskell "has all human perfections except that he stammers fearfully in speech." Subject of a biography.

Hatch, Lemuel Durant. Born Feb. 22, 1841, Greensboro, AL. Attd. Princeton prior to the war. Md. Willie McRae; Willie Adams. 2d lt. Co. B, 4th AL Bn. (later 29th AL), Sept. 22, 1861. Lt. and adj., 29th AL, Oct. 1, 1861. Major, Hatch's Bn., AL LDT, winter of 1863. Lt. col., 8th AL Cav. (formed from his battalion), April 26, 1864. Col., 1864 (probably April 26), though Gen. Polk appointed another officer (Charles P. Ball) to be colonel. Hatch's subsequent capture ended the command dispute. WIA in foot and POW Lafayette, GA, June 26, 1864. Imprisoned at Johnson's Island rest of war. Postwar farmer in Hale Co., AL. Died Feb. 17, 1905, Perdido Beach, FL. Buried St. John's Cemetery, Pensacola.

Hatch, Lewis Melvin. Born Nov. 28, 1815, Salem, NH. Moved to Charleston, SC, in 1833. Partner with his brother in a NY-based merchandise house. Owned farm near Charleston. Seminole War veteran. Capt. of vol. militia. Md. Emily E. Bell. QMG of SC, 1861. AQM under Gen. Beauregard, Aug. 1861. Raised a coast defense battalion that later became the 23d SC. Col., 23d SC, Nov. 11, 1861. Resigned April 1862. Returned to SC and remained in state service in an unspecified role. Farmed near Charleston postwar. Moved to Buncombe Co., NC, by 1880. Manufacturer and farmer there. Managed a rent and collection agency. Died Jan. 12, 1897, Asheville, NC. Buried Magnolia Cemetery, Charleston. Wartime letters and papers at UNC. An obituary eulogized Hatch as "a very soldierly man, an expert swordsman, and very active in his habits."

Hately, John Carroll. Born 1823, GA. Appointed to USMA in 1842 but failed the entrance exam. Lt., GA volunteers, in Mexican War. Prewar lawyer in Alachua Co. and later Jasper, Hamilton Co., FL. Planter. Treasurer of Hamilton Co. Md. Zenobia Frink. Col., 5th FL, April 8, 1862. WIA Antietam (shot through both thighs at the "Bloody Lane") and furloughed. Resigned due to wounds July 6, 1863. He returned home to resume his law practice and planting, though making a later attempt at reinstatement. Postwar "scalawag." Murdered Aug. 9, 1869, by William Daugherty. Buried Evergreen Cemetery, Jasper.

Hawkins, Edwin Robert. Born Feb. 21, 1831, Macon Co., NC. Grad. Augusta (GA) Medical College. Physician in GA. Moved to Titus Co., TX, in 1858. Md. Arelia J. Wynne. Capt. Co. A, 27th TX Cav. (company originally in 2d AR MR), Aug. 13, 1861. Lt. col., 27th (aka Whitfield's Legion), April 16, 1862. Col., May 9, 1863. Resigned Nov. 23, 1864, in order to return to TX and raise troops. Never wounded, though clothes pierced 11 times by bullets. Postwar physician in Titus Co. and Greenville. Died Jan. 8, 1904, Greenville. Buried East Mount Cemetery, Greenville.

Hawkins, Hiram. Born Sept. 9, 1826, Bath Co., KY. Farmer in Bath Co. prewar. Merchant. Owned a sheep ranch in TX. State senator. Militia colonel. Capt., KSG. Md. Mary Workman; Mrs. Louisiana A. Boykin. Commanded camp of recruits in Prestonsburg, KY, Sept. 1861. Capt. Co. C, 5th KY, Oct. 21, 1861. Major, Jan. 17, 1862. Lt. col., April 18, 1862. Col., Nov. 14, 1862. WIA Atlanta. Moved to Eufaula, AL (his wife's home), after the war. Farmer. State legislator. President of Union Female College. Active in the Granger movement. Died July 27, 1913, Eufaula, of paralysis. Buried Fairview Cemetery, Eufaula. A fellow officer stated Hawkins's men "loved him."

Hawkins, William Stewart. Born Oct. 2, 1837, Triana, Madison Co., AL. Attd. WMI/U. of Nashville; Bethany College; Cumberland U. Christian minister. Studied law in Nashville prewar. Md. Georgiana Turner. 2d lt. Co. C, 11th TN Cav. Bn. Major, 6th TN Cav. Lt. col., partisans. Appointed col. of Gen. Wheeler's Scouts, 1863. POW Jan. 10, 1864, Hickman Co., KY. Sent to Camp Chase. Wrote popular poetry while in prison. Released after the war. Returned to his Nashville home and resumed his law studies. Died Nov. 7, 1865, Nashville, of rheumatism. Nephew of Gen. A. P. Stewart. A comrade called him "[b]right-hearted and brilliant."

Hawpe, Trezevant Calhoun. Born Sept. 16, 1820, Franklin Co., GA. Lived in GA, KY, and TN before moving to TX in 1846. Dallas Co. rancher, merchant. County sheriff and county coroner. Md. Electa A. Underwood. Enlisted April 1862, Dallas. Col., 31st TX Cav., May 14, 1862. The 31st was dismounted in Nov. 1862. Resigned Nov. 11, 1862, due to ill health and dissatisfaction over the dismounting. Hawpe returned to Dallas and engaged in hauling supplies for the army. Stabbed to death Aug. 14, 1863, on the Dallas Co. Courthouse steps, by a friend he was arguing with. Buried Pioneer Memorial Cemetery, Dallas.

Hays, Upton. Born March 29, 1832, Callaway Co., MO. Grandson of frontiersman Daniel Boone. Resided in Jackson Co., MO, prewar. Managed wagon trains heading to the southwest. Owned a freighting company. Md. Margaret Watts. Capt. Co. E, 1st Cav., 8th Div., MSG, 1861. Lt. col., Dec. 23 (or 31), 1861. Col., Hays's Jackson Co. Regt. (aka 12th), MO Cav., Aug. 1862. KIA near Newtonia, MO, Sept. 12, 1862, shot while scouting. Buried near Newtonia; reburied Forest Hill Cemetery, Kansas City, in 1871. Papers at KS Historical Society. John N. Edwards called Hays "[b]rave, daring, devoted, and intelligent."

Hays, William Jordan. Born c. 1832, TN. Farmer in Wilson Co., TN, prewar. Md. Mary (Weatherly?); Sarah Kirby. His war record prior to 1864 cannot be traced for certain. Capt. of a battalion of cavalry operating in TN, 1864. Col., 28th TN Cav., a regiment formed from his battalion in late 1864/early 1865. Paroled May 16, 1865, Chattanooga, as col. Farmer in Wilson Co. postwar. Moved to Waco and later Ellis Co., TX, in the 1870s. Died Dec. 24, 1882, Ellis Co. Hays is perhaps the most obscure Confederate colonel, in both his life and his service. He went by his middle name of "Jordan."

Haywood, Edward Graham. Born c. 1830, NC, son of US senator William Haywood. Attd. St. James College, MD. Raleigh lawyer prewar. State representative 1859–60. Md. Margaret Henry, his cousin. Lt. col., 7th NC, May 16, 1861. Col., June 27, 1862. WIA 2d Manassas, Chancellorsville, Wilderness. Cashiered for drunkenness, Dec. 26, 1863. Retired to Invalid Corps Nov. 28, 1864, due to partial blindness caused by his wounds. Raleigh attorney postwar. Died there

July 18, 1887, of heart disease. Buried Oakwood Cemetery, Raleigh. Called in an obituary "one of the finest intellects the state of North Carolina has ever produced."

Head, John Waller. Born Nov. 2, 1822, Castalian Springs, Sumner Co., TN. Sumner Co. lawyer prewar. State representative 1855–57. Reporter for the State Supreme Court 1858–62. Attorney general 1859–62. Md. Evelyn Brooks. Col., 30th TN, Oct. 22, 1861. POW Fort Donelson. Exch. Sept. 1862. Not reelected at Sept. 29, 1862, reorganization. Sumner Co. lawyer postwar. Elected to US Congress in 1874 but never served, dying Nov. 9, 1874, in Sumner Co. Buried Gallatin City Cemetery. A "great orator and lawyer."

Heard, Samuel Smith. Born June 4, 1807, GA. Lived in Morehouse Parish, LA, and Hinds Co., MS, prewar. Wealthy planter, worth over $200,000 in 1860. Gen. MS militia. Md. Elizabeth Matthews; Sallie Nixon. Col., 17th LA, Sept. 29, 1861. Dropped, May 23, 1862. Deemed "too indulgent" to his men, though "esteemed." Spent rest of war in the commissary department and as VADC to Gen. Ruggles. Postwar planter in Morehouse Parish and Raymond, MS. Died between March 20 and May 3, 1887, Hinds Co., MS. Buried Raymond Town Cemetery.

Hedgepeth, Isaac Newton. Born 1820, Maury Co., TN. Lived in Doniphan, MO, prewar. Sawmill owner, lawyer, farmer. State senator. Md. Margaret Reeves; Elizabeth Brandaway. Lt. Co. A, 3d Inf., 1st Div., MSG, June 22, 1861. Capt. and adj., July 5, 1861. Lt. col., Aug. 1, 1861. Resigned Jan. 8, 1862. Capt. of what eventually became Co. K, 6th MO, Jan. 9, 1862. His company helped man the Confederate warships at the Battle of Memphis. Major of bn., July 2, 1862. Lt. col., July 12, 1862. Lt. col., 6th MO, Aug. 26, 1862. WIA (right leg) and POW Corinth. Disabled by wounds. Col., June 25, 1863. When the 6th was consolidated with the 2d MO, Hedgepeth, already disabled, retired. Returned to MO postwar, then moved to Prairie Co., AR. Died Jan. 1, 1878, at his Prairie Co. home. Buried Oak Grove Cemetery, near Des Arc, AR. An obituary calls him "a pure man, a brave soldier, and a conscientious officer." Hedgepeth's daughter married Col. Willis Ponder.

Hedrick, John Jackson. Born c. 1825, Wilmington, NC. Clerk, then dry goods merchant, in Wilmington prewar. Md. Sarah Elizabeth Beery. On Jan. 9, 1861, his vol. militia company seized Fort Caswell near Wilmington, an action Gov. Ellis repudiated, the state not yet having seceded. Enlisted April 16, 1861. Capt. Co. C (the "Cape Fear Light Artillery"), 2d NC Art., June 17, 1861. Major, Feb. 27, 1862. Col., 3d NC Art., Oct. 4, 1863. Commanded Fort Holmes in the Wilmington defenses. Hospitalized in March 1865, for a wound in the left thigh suffered at the Battle of Kinston. Dry goods merchant in Wilmington postwar. Died there June 24, 1894. Buried Oakdale Cemetery, Wilmington.

Heiman, Adolphus. Born April 17, 1809, Potsdam, Prussia. Studied architecture, engineering, and stone masonry in Prussia under the famous Alexander Von Humboldt. To America c. 1834. Architect and engineer in Nashville. Officer in Mexican War. Unmd. Capt. and AAG, TN State Army, May 18, 1861. Engineer officer for the state of TN, early 1861, helping to build Forts Henry and Donelson along the TN River. Col., 10th TN (an Irish-American unit), May 29, 1861. Led brigade at Forts Henry and Donelson. POW Fort Donelson. To Fort Warren. Exch. Sept. 1862. Died Nov. 16, 1862, at Jackson, MS. Buried Mt. Olivet Cemetery, Nashville. Known to his men as "Uncle Dolph," Heiman spoke with a thick German accent and tended to swear in German when aroused. Pvt. Sam Mitchell thought Heiman "a soldier in everything it takes to make one, brave, kind and gentle." Heiman's promotion to brigadier was in the works when he died.

Heiskell, Carrick White. Born July 25, 1836, Ebenezer, TN. Attd. UTN. Grad. Maryville College. Teacher and lawyer in Rogersville, TN, prewar. Md. Eliza Netherland. 1st lt. Co. K, 19th TN, May 22, 1861. Capt., June 10, 1861. Major, April 15, 1863. WIA Chickamauga in foot. Lt. col., Nov. 25, 1863. Col., July 22, 1864. Led Strahl's Brigade in Hood's TN Campaign. Attorney and judge in Memphis postwar. City attorney. Died July 29, 1923, Memphis. Buried Elmwood Cemetery. A fellow soldier said Heiskell had an "active and impetuous nature."

Helvenston, Alexander Humboldt. Born Feb. 6, 1836, Macon Co., GA. Attd. GMI. Md. Tallulah Walker. Pvt. Co. G, 16th AL, July 8, 1861. Capt., Aug. 6, 1861. Major, Aug. 15, 1861. Lt. col., Aug. 14, 1862. Col., June 17, 1863. "A man of unflinching courage, a good officer and a tried disciplinarian." WIA Shiloh, Perryville, Stones River. Often absent due to wounds. Resigned March 26, 1864, due to a spinal injury caused by a fall from his horse. Later applied for post duty. Gainesville, AL, farmer postwar. Moved to Sumter Co., FL, in 1875. Citrus grower there. To Lake City, FL, after 1900. Died May 9, 1912, Columbia Co., FL. Buried Oak Lawn Cemetery, Lake City.

Henagan, John Williford. Born Nov. 11, 1822, Marlboro Dist., SC. Educated at academies in Bennettsville and Parnassus. Farmer in Marlboro Dist. County sheriff. State legislator. Militia general. Unmd. Lt. col., 8th SC, April 13, 1861. Col., May 13, 1862. WIA South Mountain. Often led brigade in 1864. POW near Winchester, VA, Sept. 13, 1864. To Johnson's Island Prison. Died of pneumonia April 26, 1865, Johnson's Island and buried there. The brigade historian thought Henagan "always at his post and ready to go forward."

Henderson, Charles C. Born c. 1832, Ouachita Parish, LA. Reared in Morehouse Parish, LA. Planter and lawyer there. Lawyer in Pensacola, FL, in 1860. Md. Mary Guice; Elizabeth Tharp. Capt., "Morton Confederates," a FL company that became Co. C, 40th TN, Sept. 13, 1861. Lt. col., 40th TN (later renamed 5th Confederate, with companies from FL, AR, and AL), Nov. 11, 1861. Col., March 11, 1862. "Tyrranical [*sic*] and unpopular with his command." POW Island No. 10. Exch. Nov. 8, 1862. Regiment disbanded at this time, and the companies were assigned to units from their respective states. POW Vicksburg and paroled. On conscript duty in FL 1863–64. Lawyer in Shreveport, LA, postwar. Died July 30, 1886, Shreveport. Buried Oakland Cemetery, Shreveport, in an unmarked grave.

Henderson, James L. Born Nov. 12, 1813, Warrenton, VA. Entered USN in 1828, rising to commander by 1861. Md. Sarah L. Williamson. Commodore, CSN, March 26, 1861. Commanded land-based naval batteries near Yorktown, 1861. Ordered to take charge of an arsenal in Mobile, AL, Jan. 1862. Capt., OO to Gen. Samuel Jones, April 1862. Col., PACS (with temporary rank), Dec. 12, 1862. Spent remainder of war on court-martial duty in Richmond. Farmer in Princess Anne Co., VA, postwar. Died Dec. 20, 1875, Charlestown, WVA. Buried Cedar Grove Cemetery, Norfolk. A fellow naval officer considered Henderson "one of the most capable and energetic officers in the Navy."

Henderson, Robert Johnson. Born Nov. 12, 1822, Newton Co., GA. Grad. UGA. Planter, mill owner, lawyer, judge in Covington. State representative 1859–60. Md. Laura E. Wood. Col., 42d GA, March 20, 1862. POW Vicksburg and exch. WIA Resaca. Called "one of the bravest soldiers Georgia ever sent out" and "remarkably expert in managing his command." Led Cummings's Brigade at Bentonville in a charge that saved the army. Gen. Joseph Johnston promoted Henderson to brig. gen. on the battlefield, but he was never legally commissioned by the government. Mill owner and planter in Covington postwar. Died Feb. 3, 1891, at his daughter's home in Atlanta. Buried Southview Cemetery, Covington.

Hennen, William Davison. Born March 25, 1823, New Orleans, LA. Attd. Yale. Lived in St. Tammany Parish, then New Orleans. Lawyer. Wrote digest of LA laws. Lt. in Mexican War. Md. Margaret I. Coddington. Appointed "special commissioner" in 1863 to investigate the status of prisoners in the Dept. of East Tennessee. Appointed col., March 24, 1865, to be judge advocate in TMD. Postwar lawyer in New Orleans and New York City. Died May 16, 1883, New York City, buried Woodlawn Cemetery. John Bell Hood married Hennen's niece.

Henningsen, Charles Frederick. Born Feb. 21, 1815, Brussels, Belgium. Lived in England during his early life. Soldier of fortune in Spain and Hungary. Came to America in 1851. Gen. with William Walker's Nicaraguan filibusterers. New York City resident in 1860. Md. Willamina B. Connelly. Pvt. in a Burke Co., GA, company, early 1861. Col., 59th VA (2d Regt., Wise's Legion), Aug. 1, 1861.

Often directed the artillery of Wise's Brigade. Resigned Nov. 5, 1862, just prior to the regiment's reorganization. Spent the remainder of the war calling Pres. Davis "an ass" and grumbling about how junior officers had been promoted over him. Lived in retirement, impoverished, in Washington, DC, postwar, until his death on June 14, 1877. Buried Congressional Cemetery. Henningsen, "of scholarly attainments," wrote six books and spoke five languages fluently. He probably had more prewar military experience than any other Confederate colonel.

Henry, Samuel. Born July 17, 1825, Sevier Co., TN. Attd. USMA 1846–48. Prewar farmer/merchant in Gunter's Landing, AL. Md. Charity E. Fennell. Capt. Co. K, 9th AL, July 1861. Lt. col., July 3, 1861. Col., Oct. 21, 1861. Arrested for cowardice for his actions at the Battle of Williamsburg. Cashiered, March 19, 1863. Said in some sources to have been Capt. Co. F, 8th AL Cav., late in war, although no service record has been found. Gadsden, AL, merchant postwar. Died March 20, 1893, Gadsden. Buried Forrest Cemetery, Gadsden.

Herbert, Arthur. Born July 27, 1829, "Carlyle House," Alexandria, VA. Reared in Loudoun Co. Banker in Alexandria prewar. Capt., "Alexandria Rifles," vol. militia. Md. Alice Goode Gregory. Capt. Co. H, 17th VA, April 17, 1861. Major, April 27, 1862. WIA Seven Pines (foot). Lt. col., Nov. 1, 1862. Col., July 8, 1864. Led Corse's Brigade at Appomattox. Banker in Alexandria postwar. Resided and farmed near Falls Church. Died Feb. 23, 1919, Alexandria. Buried Ivy Hill Cemetery. Herbert's place of birth and the bank he founded are Alexandria landmarks.

Herbert, Hilary Abner. Born March 12, 1824, Laurens, SC. Attd. UAL and UVA. Lawyer in Greenville, AL. Md. Ella B. Smith. Capt. Co. F, 8th AL, May 20, 1861. Major, March 20, 1862. Lt. col., June 16, 1862. Col., Nov. 2, 1864. Retired due to wounds, Nov. 2, 1864. He had often commanded the 8th as lt. col. and was retired as col. in recognition of his gallantry in action. WIA Wilderness. Postwar lawyer in Greenville, Montgomery, and Washington, DC. US congressman 1877–93. Sec. of the Navy 1893–97. Wrote several books. Died March 5, 1919, Tampa, FL. Buried Oakwood Cemetery, Montgomery. His ms. memoirs are at UNC.

Herbert, Philemon Thomas. Born Nov. 1, 1825, Pine Apple, AL. Attd. UAL, being suspended after stabbing a fellow student. Lawyer in TX; Mariposa Co., CA; and (from 1859) El Paso, TX. US congressman (from CA) 1855–57. His political career there was halted after he killed a waiter during a brawl in a DC hotel. In Mexican War. Strong secessionist. Delegate to TX Secession Convention. Appointed in 1861 Texas's commissioner to the AZ Territory. Lt. col., Herbert's Bn. TX Cav., 1862. On staff of Gen. Sibley. Lt. col., 7th TX Cav., May 16, 1863. Col., sometime in 1864 (probably March 17). Service record is very sketchy. Often absent due to sickness. Severely WIA Mansfield. Died July 23, 1864, Kingston, LA, of his Mansfield wounds. Buried Evergreen Cemetery, Kingston.

Herndon, Thomas Hord. Born July 1, 1828, Erie, AL. Attd. La Grange College and Harvard. Grad. UAL in 1847. Prewar newspaper editor and lawyer in Eutaw, Mobile, and Greene Co. State representative. Delegate to AL Secession Convention. Md. Mary Alexander. Major, 36th AL, May 13, 1862. Lt. col., March 14, 1863. Severely WIA at Chickamauga and Atlanta. Col., Dec. 13, 1864. Often on sick leave 1864–65. In 1864 he tendered his resignation, citing ill health and a regiment "not large enough to make three good companies." Paroled May 10, 1865, Meridian. Mobile lawyer postwar. US congressman 1879–83. Died March 28, 1883, Mobile. Buried Magnolia Cemetery. A "lawyer of superior attainments." In a letter he admits, "I would never do for colonel of a regiment. I cannot divest myself of sympathy for the men."

Herrick, Charles Henry. Born June 3, 1833, Nelson, Portage Co., OH. Resided in Cleveland, OH; Joliet, IL; and New Orleans, prewar. Md. Eliza Janes Grant in Cleveland in 1855. Capt. Co. E, 23d LA, Dec. 5, 1861. Appointed QM, 1st LA Heavy Art., April 26, 1862. Col., 23d LA, May 25, 1862. MWIA in the first assault on Vicksburg, May 19, 1863, while serving as chief of artillery for Hebert's Brigade. Died May 22 of his wounds. Probably buried in an unmarked grave in Cedar Hill Cemetery, Vicksburg.

Herron, Andrew Stewart. Born Oct. 27, 1823, Nashville, TN. Prewar lawyer in Baton Rouge. Banker. Sec. of state of LA. Delegate to LA Secession Convention. Md. Ann M. Beale. Capt. Co. B, 7th LA, June 7, 1861. In ANV 1861–63. Appointed col., Jan. 24, 1863, to be judge of military court in Mobile. Helped organize reservists in that city. Paroled May 9, 1865, Meridian. Postwar Baton Rouge lawyer. Elected attorney general of LA in 1865. Col. of a regiment of Louisianans and government employees in the Mobile garrison, March 1865. Elected to US Congress in 1882 but died Nov. 27, 1882, in Baton Rouge before he could take his seat. Buried Magnolia Cemetery, Baton Rouge. An obituary said that, "as a lawyer, he stood high, both for learning and integrity."

Heyward, William Cruger. Born July 29, 1808, NY. Grad. USMA. Lt., US Army, 1830–32. Rice planter in Colleton Dist., SC. Unmd. Appointed capt., CS Regular Army, May 24, 1861, but declined. Appointed col., 11th (aka 9th) SC, July 1861. Dropped at May 3, 1862, reorganization. Later served as sgt. in the local militia. Died Sept. 1, 1863, Charleston. Buried St. Michael's Episcopal Church, Charleston. One soldier in the 11th deplored the loss of Heyward, "our good old colonel, who all . . . loved and admired" and the election of D. H. Ellis, a "whippyswamp politician."

Higginbotham, John Carlton. Born Nov. 11, 1842, Amherst Co., VA. Attd. Lynchburg College and received military training there. Unmd. Capt. Co. A, 25th VA, May 27, 1861. Major, May 11, 1862. WIA McDowell (leg) and 2d Manassas (thigh). Lt. col., Oct. 8, 1862. Col., Jan. 28, 1863. WIA Gettysburg. KIA Spotsylvania, May 10, 1864. Buried Spotsylvania Confederate Cemetery. Said to have been wounded seven times during the war.

Higley, John Hunt. Born Dec. 4, 1830, Pensacola, FL. Prewar merchant in Mobile, AL. Sgt. of vol. militia. Md. Lily Marshall. 2d lt. Co. A, 3d AL, April 23, 1861. Resigned Oct. 8, 1861. Elected sheriff of Mobile Co. in late 1861. Col., 2d AL Militia, March–May 1862. Lt. col., 40th AL June 5, 1862. Col., April 30, 1863. POW Vicksburg. "Brave and skillful." Often led a brigade in the Atlanta Campaign and was recommended for brigadier by numerous superior officers. Paroled Montgomery, AL May 18, 1865. Postwar Mobile cotton factor and insurance businessman. Died Feb. 7, 1889, Mobile. Buried Magnolia Cemetery. An obituary says that "every man was his friend."

Hill, Albert Potts. Born Feb. 15, 1819, York Dist., SC. Grad. USC, 1837. Lawyer in Canton, MS. Newspaper editor. Sgt. in Mexican War. Delegate to MS Secession Convention. Md. Margaret A. Love. 2d lt. Co. C, 18th MS, June 7, 1861. Capt., July 28, 1861. Elected lt. col., 1st Regt., MS State Troops (a 60-day unit), Dec. 5, 1861, but declined the commission. WIA Leesburg. Resigned April 26, 1862. Capt. Co. D, Wirt Adams's MS Cav., 1862. Resigned Dec. 10, 1862, upon appointment to judgeship. Col. and judge of the military court of Longstreet's Corps, Dec. 16, 1862. Lost race for Confederate Congress in 1863. Paroled May 10, 1865, Meridian. Died Oct. 15, 1868, Canton. Buried in an unmarked grave in Canton City Cemetery. Brother of Gen. D. H. Hill.

Hill, John Fry. Born Aug. 29, 1822, Perry Co., TN. Family moved to AR in 1829. Prewar merchant and tailor in Clarksville. Johnson Co. sheriff 1858–64. Lt. in Mexican War. Md. Hannah E. Bradshaw; Emeline T. Gray. Capt. of a militia company that garrisoned Fort Smith, early 1861. Pvt. Co. C, 16th AR, Oct. 7, 1861. Capt., Oct. 29, 1861. Col., Dec. 4, 1861. Not reelected. Resigned May 3, 1862. Raised a battalion of cavalry in 1863, which soon was increased to become the 7th AR Cav. Col., 7th AR Cav., July 15, 1863. Badly WIA at Pilot Knob, disabling his arm for life. WIA Westport. Postwar merchant in Clarksville. State senator 1879–82. Died Feb. 3, 1882, Johnson Co. Buried Oakland Cemetery, Clarksville.

Hill, Munson Rufus. Born May 4, 1821, Monroe Co., NY. Moved to Dyersburg, TN, in 1839. To Trenton, TN, in 1849. Lawyer. State senator 1849–53. Md. Elizabeth Hale. Col., 47th TN, Dec. 16, 1861. Resigned Jan. 5, 1863, due to "remittant [sic] fever" and gastroenteritis. Lost race for Confederate Congress in

1863. Memphis lawyer postwar. Died Oct. 24, 1867, Memphis, of yellow fever. Buried Oakland Cemetery, Trenton. A "man of decision, of great industry, and unyielding determination."

Hill, Robert Clinton. Born July 28, 1833, Iredell Co., NC. Reared in Iredell Co. Grad. USMA 1855. Lt., US Army, 1855–61. Lt., CS Regular Army, March 16, 1861. On staff duty at 1st Manassas. Major and AAG to Gen. Toombs, Aug. 1861. AAG to Gen. Branch, Nov. 1861. Col., 48th NC, April 9, 1862. Died Dec. 4, 1863, NC, of neuralgia. Buried Old Bethany Presbyterian Church, Iredell Co. Hill was known as "Crazy Hill" in the old army, due to his excitable manner. A soldier in the 48th found him "a very fine military man, very strict and much beloved by his men," but often absent due to ill health.

Hilliard, Henry Washington. Born Aug. 4, 1808, Fayetteville, NC. Grad. USC, 1826. Lived in Athens, GA, and Tuscaloosa and Montgomery, AL. Professor of literature at UAL. Methodist preacher. Lawyer in Montgomery. State legislator. Militia colonel. US minister to Belgium. US congressman 1845–51. Whig leader in AL. Antisecessionist. Md. Mary Bedell; Eliza G. Mayes. Confederate commissioner to TN, 1861. Col., Hilliard's Legion, April 24, 1862. Led the Legion (a 5-battalion unit) in the East TN Campaign of 1862. Resigned Dec. 1, 1862, to take care of personal affairs and because he had not been promoted to brig. "Military genius was not one of the brilliant parts . . . of this many-sided man." Lived in Augusta, Columbus, and Atlanta, GA, postwar. Lawyer, author. US minister to Brazil 1877–81. Died Dec. 17, 1892, Atlanta. Buried Oakwood Cemetery, Montgomery. Hilliard published his famous reminiscences, *Politics and Pen Pictures at Home and Abroad,* in 1892.

Hinsdale, John Wetmore. Born Feb. 4, 1843, Buffalo, NY. Family moved to Raleigh a few months after his birth. Attd. Starr's Military Academy in NY and UNC. Student when the war broke out. Md. Ellen Devereux. Lt. and ADC to Gen. Theophilus H. Holmes, his uncle, July 27, 1861. AAG to Gens. Pettigrew, Pender, and Holmes. IG to Gen. Price. Col., 3d NC Junior Reserves, Jan. 3, 1865. Paroled May 2, 1865, NC. Attd. Columbia U. Law School postwar. Lawyer in Fayetteville and (from 1875) Raleigh. President of the NC Bar Assn. Died Sept. 15, 1921, at his Raleigh home. Buried Oakwood Cemetery, Raleigh. His wife's papers are at UNC.

Hinton, James William. Born March 3, 1827, Pasquotank Co., NC. Lawyer and merchant in Elizabeth City prewar. County clerk. Md. Susan Pool. Capt. Co. A ("Hinton Guards"), 8th NC, May 16, 1861. POW Roanoke Island and paroled. Major, Oct. 25, 1862. Lt. col., Feb. 20, 1863. Col., 68th NC (a regiment organized for state service only), July 8, 1863. Captured Dec. 12, 1864, near Hamilton, NC, while spending the night in a private house. Released July 21, 1865. Lawyer in

Norfolk, VA, postwar. Died Jan. 23, 1875, Norfolk. Buried Elmwood Cemetery, Norfolk, in a grave unmarked until 1998. An obituary stated, "As a soldier he was brave and generous, winning the devotion of his own men."

Hobbs, James Harvey. Born Aug. 16, 1829, Nelson Co., KY. Prewar lawyer in Benton Co., AR. Bentonville merchant. Clerk of the State House. State swamp land commissioner. Md. Mary Greenwood, daughter of congressman Alfred B. Greenwood. Capt. Co. A, 15th (Northwest) AR, July 15, 1861. Lt. col., Dec. 3, 1861. Col., May 20, 1862. Resigned Aug. 22, 1862, due to ill health (frailness). Family tradition has him staying on with his regiment after the resignation and being killed at the Battle of Corinth. The service record does not confirm or deny this, though other evidence (an 1866 probate of his estate) suggests that he died around this time.

Hobby, Alfred Marmaduke. Born 1836, Macon, GA. Grew up in GA and Tallahassee, FL. To Refugio Co., TX, in 1857. Merchant. State legislator. Knights of the Golden Circle organizer. Md. Mrs. Gertrude Menard c. 1867. Delegate to TX Secession Convention. Major, 8th TX Bn., May 14, 1862. Col., 8th TX, Feb. 20, 1863. The 8th spent the war as part of the Galveston garrison. Paroled July 5, 1865, Houston. Postwar merchant in Galveston and San Lorenzo, NM. Author of prose and poetry. "[A] man of culture, with understanding singularly comprehensive." Died Feb. 5, 1881, Silver City, NM. Buried Georgetown Cemetery, Grant Co., NM, in an unmarked grave; probably reburied Fort Bliss Cemetery.

Hobson, Anson W. Born April 14, 1825, Athens, GA. Grad. Jefferson Medical College in Philadelphia. Prewar physician in Camden, AR. Editor, Camden *States Rights Eagle*, a Unionist organ. Delegate to AR Secession Convention. Unmd. Capt. Co. H, 3d AR Cav., July 29, 1861. Major at 1862 reorganization. Lt. col., May 26, 1862. WIA Corinth. Col., March 6, 1863. WIA at Franklin, TN, during Wheeler's Raid. Broke his leg during the retreat from Nashville, prompting the troops to nickname him "legs." Paroled Chesterville, SC, May 5, 1865. Camden physician postwar. Moved to Hope in 1876 and to Washington, AR, in 1880. Editor, Camden *Constitutional Eagle* and other newspapers. Outspoken foe of Reconstruction. State legislator. Elected to US Congress in 1866 but not seated. Died Feb. 9, 1882, Washington. Buried Rose Hill Cemetery, Hope. A fellow convention delegate noted Hobson "seldom said much, but prompt in understanding any question."

Hobson, Edwin Lafayette. Born Oct. 13, 1835, Greensboro, AL. Attd. UVA. Greensboro farmer. Capt. of "Greensboro Light Artillery." Md. Frances, daughter of Gen. J. R. Anderson. Capt. Co. I, 5th AL, April 13, 1861. Lt. col., July 15, 1862. Col., Nov. 29, 1864. WIA Chancellorsville (thigh) and Spotsylvania (right arm, May 10). Often led Battle's brigade. Official at Tredegar Iron Works (his father-in-law's company) in Richmond postwar. Farmed in Goochland Co. Died Nov. 9, 1901, Richmond. Buried Hollywood Cemetery. Gen. Battle called him "the flower of chivalry and the soul of honor."

Hodge, Benjamin Lewis. Born c. 1824, TN. Prewar resident of Shreveport, LA. Farmer, lawyer, shopkeeper. Delegate to LA Secession Convention. Md. Caledonia Cash. Capt. Co. G, Sept. 19, 1861. Col., Nov. 11, 1861. Resigned July 15, 1862, due to failing health. Lost race for governor of LA in 1863. Appointed col. and presiding judge, military court of the TMD, Feb. 19, 1864. Elected to the Confederate Congress March 1864. Died in office in Richmond Aug. 12, 1864. Buried Oakland Cemetery, Shreveport, in an unmarked grave. A contemporary newspaper found Hodge "well known as one of the most brilliant men in North Louisiana."

Hodges, James Gregory. Born Dec. 28, 1829 (some sources say 1828), Portsmouth, VA. Attd. Portsmouth Literary, Scientific and Military Academy. Attd. UPA Medical School 1850–51. Portsmouth physician prewar. Mayor, 1856–57. Militia colonel. Md. Sallie Wilson. On April 20, 1861, his militia regiment seized the Norfolk Navy Yard. Col., 14th VA, May 17, 1861. WIA Malvern Hill by an exploding shell. KIA Gettysburg, during Pickett's Charge. Buried Cedar Grove Cemetery, Portsmouth. A contemporary called Hodges "ardently patriotic . . . his whole being, convictions and feelings were with the Confederate cause."

Hodges, Wesley C. Born April 20, 1821, Washington, GA. Attd. Emory U. Cotton merchant in Columbus prewar. Novelist. Mexican War veteran. Unmd. Lt. Co. G, 2d GA, April 16, 1861. Lt. col., 17th GA, Aug. 9, 1862. Col., Jan. 4, 1863. WIA Wilderness (arm disabled) and absent thereafter. Cotton broker in Columbus postwar. Died Sept. 19, 1874, Columbus. Buried Linwood Cemetery. An obituary calls Hodges a "gentleman and brave soldier."

Hodgson, Joseph, Jr. Born Jan. 18, 1838, Fluvanna Co., VA. Attd. UVA. Grad. Princeton. Lawyer in Kansas City in 1860. Moved to AL just before the war. Montgomery lawyer. Md. Florence Holt. Commissioned 1st lt. Co. C, 18th AL, Aug. 30, 1861. Resigned Nov. 27, 1861. Lt. Co. G, 1st AL Cav., late 1861. Capt., Dec. 15, 1861. Tendered his resignation March 6, 1862, in order to take command of a privateer. POW 1862; exchanged Nov. 15, 1862. Resigned March 2, 1863. Col., 7th AL Cav., July 22, 1863. Paroled May 14, 1865, Gainesville, AL. Postwar editor in Montgomery, Mobile, and New Orleans. Author. AL state superintendent of education. Register of Chancery in Mobile. Died April 24, 1913, Mobile. Buried Magnolia Cemetery, Mobile.

Hoffman, John Stringer. Born June 25, 1821, Weston, VA. Clarksburg lawyer prewar. State representative 1859–61. Sgt. Co. C, 31st VA, May 21, 1861. Major,

Dec. 14, 1861. Col., May 1, 1862. WIA Feb. 5, 1865. Clarksburg lawyer postwar. Justice, WVA Supreme Court. Died Nov. 18, 1887, Clarksburg. Buried IOOF Cemetery, Clarksburg. According to a soldier in the 31st, Hoffman was "a hard, brave fighter, but a dull and slow man, unsuited to command."

Hoffmann, Gustav V. Born Nov. 10, 1817, Stuhmbei, Prussia, Germany. In Prussian Army. Immigrated to TX, where he became a leader in the German community. New Braunfels farmer, mayor. Capt. Co. B, 7th TX Cav., Oct. 8, 1861. Major, Nov. 5, 1862. WIA Fort Butler (neck) June 28, 1863. Lt. col., April 14, 1864. Col., 1864 (probably July 23). Paroled Sept. 11, 1865, San Antonio. Returned to his New Braunfels farm after the war. State legislator. Later moved to San Antonio. Died there March 10, 1889. Buried Comal Cemetery, New Braunfels.

Hoge, Edward Foster. Born Jan. 16, 1840, Lafayette, Walker Co., GA. Grad. Oglethorpe U. Lawyer in Walker Co. prewar. Md. Julia Clayton, of a prominent GA family, in 1866. Lt. Co. G (the "Lafayette Volunteers" of Lafayette), 9th GA, June 12, 1861. Capt., Aug. 28, 1861. WIA Gettysburg. Lt. col., Aug. 17, 1863. Col., March 1, 1864. Lawyer in Atlanta postwar. Editor, Atlanta *Journal*. State representative 1871–76, 1882–83. Died Aug. 10, 1885, Mount Airy, GA. Buried Oakland Cemetery, Atlanta. A death notice called Hoge "impressive in conversation and affable to all, high or low."

Hoke, John Franklin. Born May 8, 1820, Lincoln Co., NC. Uncle of Gen. Robert Hoke. Grad. UNC. Lincolnton lawyer. State senator 1850–56. State representative 1860. Capt. 12th US Inf. in Mexican War. Md. Catherine Wilson Alexander. Adj. gen. of NC, with the rank of brig. gen. in early 1861. Col., 23d NC, July 15, 1861. Not reelected at May 10, 1862, reorganization. Elected to State Senate. Col., 1st NC Senior Reserves, Sept. 7, 1864. Attorney in Lincolnton postwar. State legislator. Died Oct. 27, 1888, Lincolnton. Buried St. Paul's Episcopal Church Cemetery, Lincolnton. An "upright, honorable and cultivated gentleman."

Hoke, William James. Born Oct. 5, 1825, Lincolnton, NC. Brother of Col. J. F. Hoke. Merchant in Lincolnton prewar. Capt. of volunteer militia. County clerk. Md. Georgianna T. Sumner. Capt. Co. K, 1st (Bethel) NC, April 25, 1861. Col., 38th NC, Jan. 17, 1862. WIA Gettysburg (leg). Often led a brigade. Returned to Invalid Corps June 18, 1864. Adj. and IG NC Reserves. Commanded post of Charlotte, NC, from Aug. 1864. Commanded a brigade of reserves at Salisbury, 1865. Lincolnton merchant and town clerk postwar. Died Oct. 11, 1870, Columbia, SC. Buried St. Paul's Episcopal Church Cemetery, Lincolnton. The often critical Gen. Pender called the well-liked Hoke "the greatest old granny."

Holcombe, Edward Paddleford. Born Nov. 2, 1833, Augusta, GA. Lowndes Co., AL farmer. Md. Elizabeth Johnson; Caroline M. Murray. Capt. Co. A, 17th AL, Sept. 5, 1861. Lt. col., April 25, 1862. WIA Resaca. Col., 17th AL Consolidated, April 20, 1865. Paroled Greensboro, NC, May 1, 1865. Planter in Lowndes Co. and in Harrisburg, TX, postwar. Died Dec. 24, 1880, Burkville Depot, AL. Buried Oakview Cemetery, Lowndesboro, AL.

Holder, William Dunbar. Born March 6, 1824, Madison Co., KY. Planter in Pontotoc Co., MS, prewar. US marshal. State legislator. Md. Catherine T. Bowles. Capt. Co. C, 17th MS, June 1, 1861. Col., April 26, 1862. WIA Malvern Hill, which kept him from field duty for 8 months. WIA Gettysburg (groin). Resigned Feb. 26, 1864. Confederate congressman 1864–65. Farmer in Pontotoc and Lafayette Cos. postwar. Insurance adjuster in Memphis. MS state auditor 1896–1900. Gen. in the UCV. Died April 26, 1900, Jackson, MS. Buried Greenwood Cemetery, Jackson.

Holland, Orlando Stinson. Born Oct. 6, 1826, Thomaston, Upson Co., GA. Attd. UGA 1840–42. Newspaper editor in Enterprise, Clarke Co., MS, prewar. Md. Rebecca Parker; Lucy P. Freeman. 1st lt. Co. A, 37th MS, March 6, 1862. Pvt. Co. D (the "Enterprise Tigers"), 37th MS, March 7, 1862. Lt. col., April 28, 1862. Col., Oct. 4, 1862. POW Vicksburg and exchanged. In 1864 another colonel was promoted to command Sears's MS Brigade, an action that caused discontent among the officers and a transfer of the 37th to Cantey's Brigade. Paroled May 2, 1865, Greensboro. Newspaper editor in Columbus, GA, postwar. Murdered March 30, 1875, in the streets of Columbus, by a part-time policeman. Buried Linwood Cemetery, Columbus. An obituary called him "a high-toned, honorable gentleman."

Holliday, Frederick William Mackey. Born Feb. 22, 1828, Winchester, VA. Grad. Yale and UVA Law School. Attorney in Frederick Co. prewar. Commonwealth attorney. Md. Hannah Taylor; Caroline Stuart. Capt. Co. D, 33d VA, May 10, 1861. Major, April 22, 1862. WIA Cedar Mountain, losing his right arm. Lt. col., Nov. 15, 1862. Col., Feb. 1, 1863. Retired to Invalid Corps, March 21, 1864. Confederate congressman 1863–65. Attorney in Winchester postwar. Governor of VA 1877–81. Died May 29, 1899, Winchester. Buried Mt. Hebron Cemetery, Winchester. Papers at Duke U.

Holman, Daniel Wilson. Born Oct. 2, 1832, Mulberry, TN. Grad. Union College. Lawyer in Lincoln Co. prewar. Md. Fannie Landers. Major, 1st TN (Provisional Army), April 27, 1861. Not reelected at April 1862 reorganization. Major, Holman's Bn. TN PR, Oct. 13, 1862. WIA in hip in attack on Fort Donelson, Jan. 13, 1863. Appointed (by Gen. Forrest) lt. col., 11th TN Cav. (formed from his battalion), Feb. 25, 1863, an appointment resented by the company officer, who wanted to elect the field officers. Col., July 22, 1863. Paroled May 11, 1865, Gainesville. Fayetteville lawyer postwar. Died Sept. 22, 1885, Fayetteville, from the effect of typhoid fever. Buried Rose Hill Cemetery, Fayetteville. Brother of Lt. Col. James Holman, 1st TN.

Holt, Bolling Hall. Born Nov. 10, 1840, GA. Attd. UGA. Resident of Columbus prewar, living with his father, a prominent judge. Pvt. Co. G, 2d GA, April 16, 1861. Major, 35th GA, Oct. 14, 1861. Lt. col., June 1, 1862. Col., Nov. 1, 1862. Court-martialed March 25, 1863, and fined. Appmx. Died Sept. 25, 1867, Wynnton, GA. Buried Linwood Cemetery, Columbus.

Holt, Gustavus Adolphus Christian. Born March 2, 1840, Salem, KY. Grad. U. of Louisville Law School in 1859. Lawyer in Murray, Calloway Co., KY, prewar. Md. Inez Berry. Inspector, KSG, early 1861. 1st lt. Co. H, 3d KY, 1861. Capt., July 22, 1861. WIA Jackson, MS, which caused his right hand and arm to be paralyzed. Lt. col., Aug. 30, 1863. Col., March 25, 1864. Lawyer in KY and Memphis, TN, postwar. State senator. Speaker of the KY Senate. Lt. gov. Died June 1, 1910, Memphis. Buried Forest Hill Cemetery, Memphis. A 1931 history of Calloway Co. remembers Holt as "idolized by his men."

Holt, Willis Cox. Born c. 1830, Talbot Co., GA. Druggist in Putnam Co. in 1850. Talbot Co. farmer and lawyer prewar. Md. Susan Bird Bussey. Capt. Co. C, 10th GA, May 18, 1861. Major, Aug. 4, 1862. Lt. col., Aug. 29, 1862. WIA Crampton's Gap. Col., May 19, 1864. MWIA Cedar Creek. Died Nov. 18, 1864, near the battlefield. Buried Massanutten Cemetery, Woodstock, VA.

Hooker, Charles Edward. Born April 9, 1825, Union, SC. Attd. Randolph-Macon College; grad. Harvard Law School. Lawyer in Jackson, MS. Dist. attorney. State legislator. Md. Fannie Sharkey. Lt. Co. A, 1st MS Light Art., March 22, 1862. WIA (lost arm) and POW Vicksburg. Col. and judge of military court of Polk's command, Sept. 6, 1863. Paroled Meridian May 10, 1865. Elected attorney general of MS in 1865 but removed by occupation authorities. Jackson lawyer. US congressman 1875–83, 1887–95, 1901–3. Died Jan. 8, 1914, Jackson, buried Greenwood Cemetery. Known as the "silver-tongued orator of Mississippi." Wrote the MS volume of *Confederate Military History.*

Hooper, James C. Born Oct. 27, 1824, Jackson Co., AL. Lived prewar in GA; De Kalb Co., AL; and Dade Co., MO. Farmer. Mexican War veteran. Md. Lavinia H. Spurgeon. Capt. Co. D, 5th Inf., 8th Div., MSG, Aug. 22, 1861. Resigned Dec. 28, 1861. Elected lt. col., Coffee's Southwest MO Cav. Regt. (aka 6th), Nov. 9, 1862. Col., at an unknown date but late in the war, possibly to rank from Col. Smith's death at Newtonia Oct. 28, 1864. WIA at Dardanelle, AR, during Price's 1864 Raid. Paroled Shreveport, June 1, 1865, as col. of Hooper's MO Cav. Postwar farmer in Dade Co.; Giles Co., TN; Falkner Co., AR; and Pineville, McDonald Co., MO. Died Jan. 27, 1898, Pineville. Buried Pineville Cemetery. Praised as a "clever gentleman" and an "excellent officer."

Hooper, Thomas William. Born Jan. 7, 1840, Cassville, GA. Attd. the US Naval Academy. Md. Martha Trippe. Adj., 4th GA Bn. (later 21st GA), July 20, 1861. Major, 21st GA, Sept. 27, 1861. Lt. col., March 30, 1862. WIA Gaines's Mill. Led the regiment the numerous times his colonel (John T. Mercer) was either drunk or under arrest. Col., April 18, 1864. POW Opequon Creek. Released from Fort Delaware July 24, 1865. Lawyer in Atlanta and Cartersville postwar. Moved to Clarendon, AR, in the 1870s. Attorney and judge there. Died July 13, 1886, Little Rock. Probably buried Shady Grove Cemetery, near Clarendon. Hooper's brother John W. was major, 19th GA.

Hopkins, Charles Rinaldo Floyd. Born Dec. 1, 1824, Camden Co., GA. Grad. Annapolis 1847. Officer, USN, 1847–51. Civil engineer in St. Augustine, FL. Md. Frances Humphreys. Major, 1st FL Bn., Feb. 12, 1861. Lt. col., May 1862. WIA in arm and thigh at Olustee. Col., 10th FL (formed from the 1st Bn.), June 11, 1864. Appmx. Postwar civil engineer in Duval Co. Died Jan. 17, 1898, Jacksonville. Buried Old City Cemetery, Jacksonville. Nephew of Col. R. F. Floyd.

Hopkins, Edward Stevens. Born Feb. 11, 1809, Bellville, GA. Reared in Camden Co., GA. Moved to Jacksonville, FL, by 1850. Wealthy planter. State senator 1855–56. Seminole War veteran. Lost race for governor in 1860, running as an antisecessionist. Md. Mary E. Dufour. Col., 4th FL, Aug. 27, 1861. Commanded the garrison at Apalachicola. Criticized for insobriety, bad military judgment, and failing to keep discipline. Defeated for reelection May 10, 1862. Postwar Jacksonville grocer. Mayor of Jacksonville 1868–70. Collector of customs. Died Sept. 28, 1887, Jacksonville. Buried Evergreen Cemetery, Jacksonville.

Hopkins, Warren Montgomery. Born June 1, 1839, Powhatan Co., VA. Farmer in Washington Co. Teacher at Abingdon Male Academy. Md. Mary H. Baltzell. Corporal, then sgt. Co. D, 1st VA Cav., enlisting April 1861. 1st lt. and regimental adj., Oct. 3, 1861. ADC to Gen. W. E. Jones, 1862. Appointed major and commissary, Jones's Brigade, Dec. 22, 1863. Served on Jones's staff until Jones's death at Piedmont. Col., 25th VA Cav., Dec. 31, 1864. Miller in Abingdon postwar. Died Dec. 9, 1875. Buried Sinking Springs Cemetery, Abingdon. One staff officer described Hopkins as a "modest, intelligent man, no doubt a fine officer."

Howard, James Ross. Born Sept. 22, 1822, Dinwiddie Co., VA. Reared in LA. Attd. St. Michael's College in LA and studied in Paris, France. Civil engineer. Pvt. in Mexican War. Active in Knights of the Golden Circle. Major of a cavalry battalion, 1862. Lt. col., 11th AL Cav. Bn., Aug. 9, 1862. Col., 3d Confederate Cav. (formed from the 11th Bn.), Sept. 1, 1862. WIA Stones River, which wound disabled him from field duty. Resigned March 26, 1863. AADC to Gen. M. J. Wright, 1863. Appointed col. and judge, military court of Wheeler's Corps, March 23, 1865. Postwar he wrote for the London *Times.* Soldier of fortune. Served in the Carlist Wars in Spain. Returned to US in 1875. Civil engineer in DC. Indian agent. Died Nov. 22, 1892, Washington, DC, at the home of his old commander Gen. Wright, with whom he'd been living. Buried Glennwood Cemetery, Washington. "Few men possessed, or deserved, a wider circle of friends."

Howell, Edward Alexander. Born March 22, 1839, Martin Co., NC. Cousin of Col. Vannoy Manning of the 3d AR. Reared in Hardeman Co., TN. Moved to Prairie Co., AR. Prewar merchant, county surveyor. Md. Harriet Todd; Martha Pierce. Enlisted June 10, 1861, in Co. G, 5th AR, the "Brownsville Rifles." Corp., June 10, 1861. 1st lt., Aug. 7, 1861. Capt., May 1862. WIA and POW at Perryville. Major, 5th/13th AR, Sept. 19, 1863. Lt. col., July 22, 1864. Col., 1st AR Consolidated (1st, 2d, 5th, 13th, 15th, 24th AR), April 9, 1865. Paroled April 29, 1865, at Greensboro, NC. Postwar Drew Co. farmer. Died Feb. 22, 1872, Drew Co. Buried Harrell family cemetery, near Selma, Drew Co.

Hubbard, Richard Bennett, Jr. Born Nov. 1, 1832, Walton Co., GA. Attd. Mercer U., UVA, and Harvard Law School. Moved to Tyler, TX, in 1853 and practiced law there. Prewar state legislator and US Dist. attorney for West TX. Md. Eliza Hudson; Janie Roberts. Lt. col., 5th TX Bn., April 15, 1862. Col., 22d TX (formed from the 5th Bn.), June 17, 1862. Applied in 1863 for an appointment as judge of a military court but withdrew that application to remain in the field. WIA Jenkins Ferry. Lawyer in Tyler postwar. Lt. gov. 1873–76. Gov. 1876–79. US minister to Japan. Known as the "Demosthenes of Texas" for his eloquence. Died July 12, 1901, Tyler, buried Oakwood Cemetery. One private grumbled that Hubbard was "mean in every respect."

Huger, Daniel Elliott. Born Nov. 30, 1836, Camden, SC. Reared in St. Mary's Parish, LA. Attd. WMI. Prewar merchant in Mobile, AL. Md. Hattie, daughter of Gen. Jones Withers. Pvt., "Mobile Cadets." Sgt. Co. A, 3d AL, April 23, 1861. Appointed major, VA state forces, and detached to be ADC to Gen. Withers, May 18, 1861. AAG to Gen. Withers, 1861–64. Col., 62d AL (1st AL Reserves), Aug. 10, 1864. Paroled Meridian, May 1865. Postwar cotton broker in Mobile. Died Feb. 5, 1904, Mobile, buried Magnolia Cemetery.

Huger, Frank. Born Sept. 29, 1837, Fortress Monroe, VA. Grad. USMA 1860. Lt., US Army, 1860–61. Md. Julia Trible. Lt., CS Regular Army, March 16, 1861. Capt., Huger's VA Battery (Norfolk Light Art.), June 12, 1861. Lt. of artillery, Nov. 13, 1861. ADC to his father (Gen. Benjamin Huger), 1862. Major of artillery, May 2, 1863. Second in command of Porter Alexander's Art. Bn. Lt. col., Feb. 27, 1864. Col., Feb. 18, 1865. POW Sayler's Creek. Lived in Lynchburg postwar. Superintendent of several railroads. Died Roanoke, VA, June 11, 1897. Buried Spring Hill Cemetery, Lynchburg. Porter Alexander called Huger "glorious . . . never shirked a care or danger or grumbled over a hardship in all his life."

Huggins, James Howard. Born Aug. 7, 1828, Macon Co., NC. Farmer and merchant in Union Co., GA, prewar. Delegate to GA Secession Convention, voting against secession. Md. Mary Jones. Capt. Co. B, 23d GA, Aug. 31, 1861. Major, Aug. 16, 1862. WIA South Mountain in both legs. Lt. col., Sept. 17, 1862. Col., Dec. 15, 1863. Resigned Aug. 13, 1864. Dry goods merchant in Athens and in Hall Co. postwar. Died March 1, 1900, Lula. Buried Oconee Hill Cemetery, Athens.

Hughes, Adolphus Alexander. Born April 28, 1818, AL. Franklin Co. farmer, county sheriff, state representative. Md. Sarah —— (d. 1847); Mary Beacham. Col., 27th AL, Jan. 28, 1862. POW at Fort Donelson, released July 21, 1862. Died Nov. 2, 1862, Magnolia, MS. Buried Old Burleson Cemetery, Franklin Co.

Hughes, Henry. Born April 17, 1823 (year of birth per gravestone; some sources give an 1819 date of birth), Port Gibson, MS. Grad. Oakland College. Lawyer in Port Gibson prewar. Sociologist and author of *Southern Sociology.* Unmd. Pvt., "Port Gibson Riflemen," 1861. Capt. Co. H ("Claiborne Guards"), 12th MS, March 14, 1861. Col., Nov. 13, 1861. Not reelected at April 1862 reorganization, in part because of dissatisfaction with his rigid discipline. Returned to MS to raise a PR battalion. Died Oct. 3, 1862, Port Gibson, of disease contracted while in the VA army. Buried Wintergreen Cemetery, Port Gibson. A postwar history called him "a most remarkable man" intellectually.

Hughes, John Mason. Born c. 1834, TN. Last name often spelled "Hughs." Hotel keeper in Livingston, Overton Co., TN prewar. Md. Sarah Gerling; Alice J. Mallory. Lt. Co. D, 25th TN, Aug. 1, 1861. Major, summer of 1862. Col., July 21, 1862. WIA Stones River. Led partisans in TN in 1863, while recuperating. 25th transferred to ANV in 1864. Resigned March 17, 1865, saying the 25th was down to 20 privates and had been consolidated with other units. Prior to this, Hughes had been found incompetent by a board of examiners, a finding heartily endorsed by his superiors. Farmed and ran a saddle shop in Lincoln, Moore, and Rutherford Cos., TN, postwar. Whiskey distiller in Lynchburg, mentoring the legendary Jack Daniel, and later federal whiskey tax collector. Died c. 1896–1900, TN. A soldier in the 25th praised Hughes as "gallant, faithful, and effective . . . a stout, active, athletic man, and one of the best marksmen in the Confederate army."

Hughes, John Taylor. Born July 25, 1817, near Versailles, KY. Reared in MO. Grad. Bonne Femme College. Lived in Howard, Chariton, and Clinton Cos. pre-war. Teacher. State legislator. Militia colonel. Author of a nationally famous book on his Mexican War experiences. Md. Mary L. Carpenter. Capt. Co. K, 1st Inf., 4th Div., MSG, May 25, 1861. Col., June 21, 1861. WIA siege of Lexington. On recruiting duty in MO, winter of 1861–62. As colonel, led a battalion of Confederate Volunteers at Pea Ridge. Accompanied Sterling Price into MS in 1862 but sent back to MO to recruit. KIA leading an attack on Independence, MO, Aug. 11, 1862. Buried Woodlawn Cemetery, Independence. Remembered by a Unionist as "the most ambitious and daring officer in Price's army." Often called "general" in various accounts, perhaps because he commanded the 4th Div. (which would normally require a general's rank), or because of an unofficial promotion by Gen. Price.

Hughes, William Edgar. Born March 15, 1840, Morgan Co., IL. Attd. Illinois College in Jacksonville, IL. Moved to KS in 1859. To TX in 1860. Sheepherder. Cowboy. Md. Anna Clifton Peete in 1867. Pvt. Co. O, 1st Inf., 8th Div., MSG, 1861. Corporal, Good's TX Battery, 1862–64. Capt. on the staff of Gen. B. J. Hill, 1864. Involved with organizing conscripts, guerrilla bands, deserters, etc., in TN and north AL into PACS units. Praised by Hill for "cool courage and gallantry." Elected col., "16th Confederate Cav.," c. March 1, 1865. Paroled as col. "10th" Confederate Cav. at Memphis, May 1865. Very successful postwar career. Lawyer in Weatherford, TX. Livestock trader. Bank president in Dallas. Bank president and president of a cattle company in St. Louis. Moved to Denver in 1891. Became very wealthy, with business and cattle interests throughout the West. Died July 29, 1918, Denver. Buried Fairmount Cemetery, Denver. Hughes's memoir, *The Journal of a Grandfather,* gives the details of his career as colonel and the name of the unit. He said the muster rolls were sent to the War Dept. but were lost in the fall of Richmond. There is no official record of such a unit being raised, although evidence in *OR* hints at its existence, and Hughes is always referred to as "colonel" postwar. Under the law in 1865, an election to colonel, without further action by the authorities, would not have been sufficient to legally make an officer a PACS colonel.

Hulme, Isaac Newton. Born Sept. 26, 1826, Williamson Co., TN. Perry Co. merchant prewar. Md. Mary Jane Clayton. Capt. Co. G ("Perry County Blues"), 42d TN, Nov. 9, 1861. POW Fort Donelson. Exchanged. Lt. col., Oct. 9, 1862. Col., Aug. 25, 1863. WIA Franklin. Williamson Co. farmer postwar. Died June 3, 1873, Williamson Co. Buried Hulme Cemetery, Williamson Co.

Hundley, Daniel Robinson. Born Dec. 12, 1832, Madison Co., AL. Attd. Bacon College; UVA; Harvard Law School. Lawyer in Huntsville, AL. Settled in

Chicago, IL, in 1856, to manage his father-in-law's real estate there. He abandoned large properties in Chicago in order to fight for the South. Md. Mary Ann Hundley, a cousin. Capt. Co. D, 2d Confederate, 1861–62. Col., 31st AL, April 1862. WIA Port Gibson. POW Big Shanty, GA, June 15, 1864, sent to Johnson's Island prison. Released July 1865. A sgt. in the 31st called him "the best manager in the world." Postwar lawyer, author, newspaper editor in Huntsville. Wrote *Prison Echoes of the Great Rebellion*, a narrative of his time at Johnson's Island. Died Dec. 27, 1899, Mooresville, AL. Buried Maple Hill Cemetery, Huntsville. Brother William was lt. col. 12th AL Cav. War diary at UNC.

Hunt, Archibald Anderson. Born c. 1825, Baldwin Co., GA. Lawyer in Baker Co. and Albany, GA, prewar. Schoolteacher in Mobile, AL. Md. Martha A. Thomas. Traveled to KY with some friends in 1861 and captured a Union steamer there. Col., 2d GA PR (aka 13th GA Cav.), elected c. May 25, 1862, at organization. It appears that there were only 8 companies present and voting at this election, not the required 10, and the "regiment" was later downgraded to a battalion (the 16th GA Cav. Bn.). MWIA July 7, 1862 (accidentally shot by his own men), while leading a charge at Tompkinsville, KY. Died July 25, 1862. An obituary called him "idolized by his regiment."

Hunt, Isaac Foster. Born Nov. 16, 1833, Newberry Dist., SC. Attd. SCMA. Newberry merchant prewar. Md. Harriet Austin. Pvt. Co. B, 1st SC (Gregg's; a 6-month unit), early 1861. Capt. Co. D, 13th SC, Aug. 23, 1861. Major, Jan. 6, 1863. Lt. col., June 21, 1863. Col., June 8, 1864. WIA Gaines's Mill, Fredericksburg, and Fussell's Mill. Appmx. Cotton merchant in Charleston postwar. Moved to Greenville in 1878. President of an insurance company. Died April 13, 1900, Greenville. Buried Rosemont Cemetery, Newberry.

Hunt, James P. Born c. 1834, SC. Reared in Greenville Co. Prewar lawyer in New River Co., FL. Capt. Co. F, 4th FL, May 23, 1861. Col., May 12, 1862. Arrested July 1, 1862, for halting his regiment while on the march and allowing his men to cook food. Died Sept. 3, 1862, of disease, at Chattanooga, TN. Buried New River Co.

Hunt, Theodore Gaillard. Born Oct. 23, 1805, Charleston, SC. Grad. from the Law Dept. of Columbia College in NY. Lawyer in Charleston. Moved to New Orleans, LA, in 1830. Judge. State representative 1837–53. US congressman 1853–55. Lt. col. in Mexican War. Md. Cornelia V. Nicholson. Col., 5th LA, May 10, 1861. Resigned July 31, 1862. Later served as LA state adj. gen. Attorney in New Orleans postwar. Died there Nov. 1, 1893. Buried Metairie Cemetery. Gen. McLaws considered Hunt "an old gentleman of independent manners" with "a considerable opinion of his influence, and of his ability both as a soldier and a member of society."

Hunt, Thomas Hart. Born Jan. 2, 1815, Lexington, KY. Uncle of Gen. John Hunt Morgan. Merchant in Lexington and (from 1848) Louisville. Major, then col., KSG, 1860–61. Md. Mary Tilford. In the spring of 1861, as col. 2d Regt. KSG, established a KSG camp of instruction near Louisville. Col., 9th KY, Oct. 1, 1861. WIA Baton Rouge. Resigned April 22, 1863, "impelled by a sense of duty to his family." Lived in Augusta, GA, the remainder of the war. Merchant in New Orleans postwar. Sec. of the World's Fair Exposition. Died May 6, 1884, New Orleans. Buried in the Hunt-Morgan Lot, Lexington Cemetery. Hunt, with a "superior natural intellect" (the historian of the Orphan Brigade said "he knew every man in the regiment by name"), often won praise from his superiors and, if he had stayed in the army, would soon have been promoted to general.

Hunt, Zimri. Born Oct. 7, 1820, Greensboro, NC. Lawyer in Belleville, TX. State legislator. Md. Frances L. Springfield. Capt. Co. F, 16th TX, March 29, 1862. Detailed for court-martial duty in TMD in 1863. WIA Red River Campaign. Assigned to duty as AAG to Gen. Forney, Dec. 1864. Appointed col. and judge, military court of Buckner's Corps, March 23, 1865. Postwar lawyer, alderman, and judge in Dallas. Called "the Nestor of Texas lawyers." Died Jan. 22, 1883, Dallas, buried Greenwood Cemetery.

Hunter, DeWitt Clinton. Born Aug. 2, 1830, Manchester, Morgan Co., IL. Prewar miner in NV and CA. Attorney in Nevada, MO, a town he named. Vernon Co. clerk. Militia officer. Md. Katherine Blake; Mary Watts. Col., 7th Cav., 8th Div., MSG, July 10, 1861. Resigned Dec. 12, 1861. Col., Hunter's MO Cav. (aka 2d, 8th MO), 1862. Resigned March 24, 1863. Col., Hunter's MO Cav., a new regiment he raised in 1864. WIA Lone Jack and Marks Mill. Lawyer in Nevada, MO, postwar. Moved to Oklahoma in the 1880s. Died Oct. 3, 1904, Checotah, OK. Buried Deepwood Cemetery, Nevada, MO. A fellow officer thought Hunter panicked at Lone Jack but afterward performed well.

Hunter, Fountain Winston. Born Jan. 19, 1820, Sumter Dist., SC. Planter in Lowndes Co. and Montgomery, AL. Mexican War veteran. Md. Caledonia T. Harrison. Capt., "Metropolitan Guards" of Montgomery (Co. F, 3d AL), April 26, 1861. Resigned Nov. 1861. Col., 2d AL Cav., May 1, 1862. Court-martialed for conduct unbecoming an officer (striking a subordinate) and dismissed April 4, 1863. Farmed near Montgomery postwar. Died June 17, 1891, Montgomery. Buried Oakwood Cemetery.

Hunter, Samuel Eugene. Born 1832, Chester or York Dist., SC. Attd. WMI. Prewar attorney in Clinton, LA. Md. Stella Bradley Taylor. Capt., "Hunter Rifles," May 25, 1861. Major, 4th LA, May 25, 1861. Lt. col., March 21, 1862. Col., Jan. 19, 1863. Captured near Franklin, TN, Dec. 17, 1864. To Johnson's Island prison. Released July 25, 1865. Postwar Clinton lawyer. Died June 19, 1870, Clinton, of congestive chills. Buried Rosehill Cemetery, Clinton. A junior officer said Hunter was "probably a good man and capable soldier, but he was not popular." A court of inquiry cleared Hunter of charges of cowardice at the battles of Shiloh and Baton Rouge. Hunter family papers are at LSU.

Hunter, William L. Born c. 1826, VA. His mother was a cousin of Pres. Polk. Reared in Moulton, AL. Prewar merchant in Knox Co., TN, and Washington Co., VA. Part owner of the Abingdon, VA, salt works. Capt. Co. A, 63d VA, March 31, 1862. Resigned Feb. 17, 1863. Appointed provost marshal of Abingdon. Appointed col., "1st Chickasaw Infantry," to rank from Sept. 25, 1863. This was a unit being raised in the Indian Territory. The Chickasaws requested Hunter's appointment on the recommendation of Hunter's old friend and fellow townsman David Hubbard, Confederate agent to the Indian tribes. However, the 1st never formally organized, and the Confederate Senate rejected the appointment Feb. 17, 1864. Hunter disappears from all records after this.

Hurst, David Wiley. Born July 10, 1819, Summit, Pike Co., MS. Attd. Oakland College. Lawyer in Amite Co. prewar. State representative 1848–50. Delegate to MS Secession Convention, voting against secession. Md. Sarah G. Tillotson. Capt. Co. K, 33d MS, March 1, 1862. Col., April 17, 1862. Severely WIA Corinth. Elected in Oct. 1863 to state High Court of Errors. Resigned his commission Jan. 5, 1864, to take up his judicial duties. Postwar Pike Co. lawyer and judge. Died July 10, 1882, Summit. Buried Woodlawn Cemetery, Summit. A county history called Hurst "a man of great ability . . . full of sarcastic wit."

Hurt, Charles Stuart. Born Feb. 2, 1836, VA. Reared in Petersburg, VA. Attd. VMI. Professor of mathematics in TX, MS, and TN prewar. Studied law in Florence, AL, in 1860. Md. Mrs. Margaret A. Fowler. Drillmaster in Florence, early 1861. Capt. Co. D, 9th TN, May 24, 1861. Lt. col., May 29, 1861. Col., May 7, 1862. Led consolidated 6th/9th for much of the war. Repeatedly praised by his superiors for "a dashing gallantry, combined with an aptitude for command," and "efficiency." Led brigade in 1865. Paroled May 1, 1865, Greensboro. Planter in Panola Co., MS, postwar. Died Aug. 26, 1885, Panola Co. Buried Chapeltown Cemetery, near Batesville, Panola Co.

Hutcherson, Thomas. Born Nov. 2, 1817, Pittsylvania Co., VA. Farmer in Cherokee Co., GA, prewar. Md. Susan Dickerson. Col., 23d GA, Aug. 31, 1861. Resigned June 12, 1862, due to chronic rheumatism. Farmer in Cherokee Co. postwar. Died Sept. 7, 1901. Buried Hutcherson Cemetery, Cherokee Co.

Hutchins, Andrew Jackson. Born Aug. 17, 1838, Gwinnett Co., GA. Attd. WMI/U. of Nashville. Md. Sarah Jennie Word. Major, 19th GA, May 1, 1861. Lt. col., June 26, 1862. Col., Jan. 12, 1863. Commended for "spirit and energy" at

Chancellorsville. Resigned Aug. 20, 1863, due to a "nervous disability" the examining surgeon blamed on "habits which he is unable to abandon in the army and which unfit him for the discharge of the duties of his office." Two days later Hutchins attempted to revoke this resignation, hinting that he resigned under threat of charges involving an unspecified "moral disgrace." Appointed capt. and ACS, Dec. 3, 1863. Assigned to post duty at Rome, GA, with GA State Guard, Jan. 4, 1864. On Gen. Iverson's staff, 1863–65. Lawyer in Cumming, GA, and Iuka, MS, postwar. Died Feb. 10, 1872, Iuka. Buried Oak Grove Cemetery, Iuka. Brother of Lt. Col. Nathan Hutchins, 3d GA.

Hutchison, Augustus Simpson. Born May 9, 1837, Laurens Co., SC. Grad. SCMA 1859. Prewar teacher in Nashville, Hempstead (later Howard) Co., AR. Md. Ella Ozella Hankins; Susan V. Purdom. Pvt., "Davis Blues," Co. F, 5th AR State Troops, June 18, 1861. Capt., June/July 1861. Enlisted in Co. C, 19th AR, Oct. 19, 1861. Adj., 19th AR, Nov. 21, 1861. Major, 1862. Lt. col., Aug. 13, 1862. POW Arkansas Post. Exch. April 29, 1863. The exchanged prisoners of the 19th and 24th AR on the east side of the Mississippi River were consolidated into one unit in MS. Col., 19th AR, at an unknown date. According to his grandson, he was elected col. shortly before the war ended. WIA (shot in left arm) Battle of Atlanta. Furloughed home to recover and never rejoined regiment. Lived in Howard Co. postwar. Farmer, teacher, 4-term county sheriff. Died Jan. 5, 1912, Nashville. Buried Nashville Cemetery.

Hyams, Samuel Myers. Born Nov. 16, 1840, Natchitoches, LA. Attd. WMI and LSU. Living with his father in Natchitoches in 1860. Md. Alice M. Waddell. 3d lt. Co. D, 3d LA (of which his father was lt. col.), May 17, 1861. Regimental adj., July 1861. Appointed lt. col., 2d MO Cav., by the War Dept., in 1864. When Hyams reported to the 2d, the men protested and in a subsequent election voted in another officer. Hyams's appointment was later declared illegal. Col., 1st MS PR (aka 7th MS Cav.), assigned temporarily (by Gen. Chalmers) May 19, 1864. Court-martialed, Dec. 5, 1864, for disobeying orders and cashiered. Postwar planter in Natchitoches Parish. Died July 17, 1882, Natchitoches. Buried American Cemetery, Natchitoches.

Hyman, Joseph Henry. Born March 24, 1835, Tarboro, NC. Grad. UNC. Wealthy Edgecombe Co. farmer prewar. Md. Milly Staton; Sally Polk Rayner. Capt. Co. G, 13th NC, May 1, 1861. Major, Oct. 15, 1862. Lt. col., March 2, 1863. Col., June 13, 1863. WIA Gettysburg (right arch). Commanded Scales's Brigade at Appomattox. Moved to MS postwar. Real estate broker in Stephenville, TX, in 1880. Died Feb. 6, 1901, Stephenville, TX. Buried Oakwood Cemetery, Fort Worth. "[A] true and gallant officer."

Imboden, George William. Born June 25, 1836, Augusta Co. VA. Brother of Gen. John D. Imboden. Educated at Staunton Academy. Staunton attorney prewar. Militia captain. Md. Mary Frances Tyree; Angia M. Dickinson. 4th lt., Staunton Art. (his brother's company), April 17, 1861. 3d lt., Sept. 28, 1861. Not reelected at April 1862 reorganization. Capt. Co. A, 62d VA, July 3, 1862. Major, Sept. 9, 1862. Col., 18th VA Cav., Dec. 15, 1862. WIA Gordonsville (face). Paroled July 15, 1865, Waynesboro. Settled in Crittenden Co., KY, in 1866 but returned to VA in 1869. Lawyer in Ansted, WVA, from 1870. President of county court. Mayor of Ansted. State legislator. Manager, Fayette Coal Co. Died Jan. 8, 1922, Ansted. Buried West Lake Cemetery, Ansted.

Inge, William Murphy. Born Feb. 22, 1832, Greene Co., AL. Attd. USMA. Lawyer in Corinth, MS, prewar. Md. Flora Augusta Evans. Capt., 9th MS, at Pensacola in early 1861. Resigned due to boredom. Capt., AAG, Dec. 10, 1861. On staff of Gens. Griffith and Clark, 1861–62. Major, AAG, Gen. Barksdale's staff, 1862. Major, Inge's (12th) MS Cav. Bn., Feb. 4, 1863. Col., 10th MS Cav., Jan. 17, 1865. Lawyer in Corinth postwar. State representative and speaker of the MS House. Died Nov. 26, 1900, Corinth. Buried Henry Cemetery, near Corinth. An obituary praised him as "one of the brainiest and most prominent, well-known and influential men of the state."

Ives, Joseph Christmas. Born Dec. 25, 1829, New York City. Attd. Yale. Grad. USMA 1852. Engineer officer, US Army, 1852–61. Explored the Grand Canyon. Briefly in charge of building the Washington Monument. Md. Cora Semmes, sister of Sen. Thomas Semmes of LA. Capt., CS Regular Army, March 16, 1861. Chief engineer on Robert E. Lee's staff in SC, 1861. Col. and aide to Pres. Davis, April 19, 1862. Known as "Miss Nancy" to the Davis staff because he was "too pretty for a man." Rumored to be an alcoholic and (falsely) a Union spy. Left the US after the war to visit Europe and the Caribbean. Returned to live in New York. Died Nov. 12, 1868, New York City, of alcoholism. Probably buried Evergreens Cemetery, Brooklyn.

Ives, Samuel Spencer. Born Aug. 15, 1835, Masonville, AL. Lauderdale Co. farmer. Overseer in Franklin Co. in 1860. Md. Amanda Mitchell; Mary Kennedy. Lt. Co. I, 9th AL, June 18, 1861. Capt. Co. A, 35th AL, March 12, 1862. Major, May 8, 1862. Lt. col., Nov. 12, 1862. Col., 1863 (probably Sept. 25). WIA Baton Rouge. WIA and disabled at Franklin. Postwar Lauderdale Co. (Florence) farmer, county sheriff, US marshal. Died March 22, 1917, Lauderdale Co., AL. Buried Florence Cemetery.

Jackman, Sidney Drake. Born March 7, 1826, Jessamine Co., KY. Reared in Howard Co., MO. Prewar teacher and farmer in Papinville, Bates Co., MO. Officer in a home guard company during the KS-MO border wars. Md. Martha R.

Slavin; Mrs. Cass Kyle Gaines. Capt. of a home guard company, 1861–62. Col. of MO Confederate recruits at Lone Jack. Col., 7th (aka 16th) MO, Sept. 1862, but resigned the next month after the regiment was dismounted. Noted "guerrilla" in MO 1863–64. Col., Jackman's MO Cav., 1864. Led a brigade of MO Cav. in Price's 1864 Raid. Twice WIA during the war. Assigned to duty as brig. gen. by Gen. Kirby Smith, May 16, 1865. Fled to Mexico postwar but soon returned and settled near Kyle, Hays Co., TX. Farmer. State legislator. US marshal for West Texas. Died June 2, 1886, at his Hays Co. Ranch. Buried Kyle Cemetery. Jackman, "a stern, able and devoted soldier," left a fascinating memoir of his war experiences that was published in 1997.

Jackson, Andrew, III. Born April 4, 1834, at "The Hermitage," Pres. Andrew Jackson's home near Nashville, son of Andrew Jackson Jr., the president's nephew and adopted son. Attd. WMI and KMI. Grad. USMA. Lt., US Army, 1858–61. Md. Amy A. Rich. 1st lt., CS Regular Army, March 16, 1861. Capt., company number 4, Art. Corps of TN, May 13, 1861. Capt. Co. F, 1st TN Heavy Art., Aug. 5, 1861. Stationed at Columbus and Island No. 10, 1861–62. Col., May 10, 1862. POW Vicksburg. Exch. Stationed at Fort Morgan, near Mobile. POW there. Released June 5, 1865. Farmer in Davidson Co., TN, postwar. IRS agent in Nashville, Cincinnati, and Knoxville. Died Dec. 17, 1906, at his West Knoxville home. Buried at The Hermitage. A "man of genial disposition, and firmness of character."

Jackson, George. Born Jan. 25, 1833, Clarksburg, VA. Grad. USMA 1856. Lt., US Army, 1856–61. 1st lt., CS Regular Army, March 16, 1861. Major, Oct. 21, 1861. Led squadron of cavalry in 1861 WVA campaigns. Briefly Major, 14th VA Cav. (appointed Sept. 5, 1862), the unit into which his squadron had been absorbed. On Gen. Beverly Robertson's staff, Dec. 1862. Commissioned col., Oct. 4, 1863, and ordered to report to Gen. Whiting in Wilmington, NC. Post commandant at Wilmington in 1865. Paroled May 13, 1865, as col. Lived in Parkersburg, WVA, postwar. In mineral oil business. Died May 27, 1883, Parkersburg, buried Riverview Cemetery. Brother of Gen. William L. Jackson. A diarist in 1861 stated that Jackson "drinks hard."

Jackson, James. Born Oct. 18, 1819, Jefferson Co., GA. Grad. UGA 1837. Lawyer in Monroe and Athens, GA, prewar. State legislator. Judge. US congressman 1857–61. Md. Ada Mitchell; Mrs. Mary Schoolfield. Appointed col. and judge of the military court of Jackson's Corps Dec. 16, 1862. Resigned Oct. 5, 1863. Postwar lived in Macon and Atlanta. Justice, GA Supreme Court, 1875–79; chief justice 1879–87. Died Jan. 13, 1887, Atlanta. Buried Rose Hill Cemetery, Macon. One contemporary noted "his private virtues eclipsed . . . his public distinctions."

Jackson, James. Born April 21, 1822, Nashville, TN. Privately educated. Planter near Florence, AL. Md. Elizabeth Perkins. Pvt. Co. H, 4th AL, April 28, 1861. WIA at 1st Manassas and discharged Aug. 6, 1861. Lt. col., 27th AL, Jan. 28, 1862. POW Fort Donelson, imprisoned 7 months. Col., Nov. 2, 1862. Lost arm at Kennesaw Mountain June 18, 1864, and missed the rest of the Atlanta and TN Campaigns. Led Loring's Div. at Bentonville. Postwar planter in Lauderdale Co. Died Aug. 14, 1879, Florence. Buried at his home; reburied Cypress Cemetery at "The Forks," Lauderdale Co.

Jackson, James Washington. Born Sept. 28, 1831, GA. Reared in Meriwether Co., GA. Attd. GA Military Academy and medical school in New York City. Lafayette, AL, physician. Md. Jennie Cloud. Capt. Co. A, 7th AL, March 1861. Resigned Oct. 1861 due to ill health. Lt. col., 47th AL, May 22, 1862. Col., Aug. 11, 1862. WIA in arm at Antietam while leading brigade. Collapsed from fatigue and illness in the attack on Little Round Top. Resigned July 10, 1863, as questions surfaced about his conduct at Gettysburg (some thought his collapse had more to do with cowardice than illness). He recuperated at his father's plantation in Greenville, GA. Died there July 1, 1865. Buried Greenville City Cemetery.

Jacquess, John A. Born Feb. 14, 1830, Alexandria, KY. Attd. St. Gabriel's College in Vincennes, IN. New Orleans attorney prewar. Merchant. State legislator. Lt. in Mexican War. Militia captain. Filibusterer with William Walker. Md. Eliza Simpson. Capt. Co. D, 1st LA Regulars, April 15, 1861. Major, July 23, 1861. Lt. col., Sept. 10, 1861. Col., May 23, 1862. Cashiered and dismissed Feb. 13, 1863, for misbehavior at Stones River (leaving his regiment on the day of the battle without proper authorization). Capt. Taylor Beattie wrote that Jacquess "deserted his regiment and colors." VADC to Gen. Gardner at Port Hudson. POW there, exch. Aug. 3, 1864, at Charleston. Returned to New Orleans after the war but soon settled in Mobile. Cotton broker there. Moved to Bosque Co., TX. Sheep raiser in Bosque Co. Died May 1, 1888, Bosque Co. Buried Oakwood Cemetery, Waco, TX, in an unmarked grave. A contemporary history called Jacquess a man of "strong force of character and undoubted integrity."

Jamison, David Flavel. Born Dec. 14, 1810, Orangeburg Dist., SC. Attd. USC. Orangeburg lawyer and planter. State legislator. Militia general. Md. Elizabeth Rumph. President of SC Secession Convention. Appointed sec. of war of SC, Jan. 13, 1861. Appointed col. and judge of military court of Beauregard's Corps, Dec. 16, 1862. President of military court, Dept. of SC, GA, and FL. Died Sept. 14, 1864, Charleston, SC, of yellow fever. Buried Old Presbyterian Churchyard, Orangeburg. Jamison's daughter married Gen. Micah Jenkins.

Jayne, Joseph McAfee. Born c. 1823, Covington Co., MS. Planter in Rankin Co., MS, prewar. Chairman of State Democratic party. Md. Melissa McRae. Capt. Co. A, 18th MS, June 7, 1861. WIA Ball's Bluff. Col., 48th MS, Jan. 17, 1863. WIA Chancellorsville. POW Sayler's Creek, released June 18, 1865. Bank cashier in Rankin Col. postwar. Moved to Greenville, MS, by 1880. Died April 12, 1885, near Brandon. Buried Greenville Cemetery. Jayne's plantation papers are at Duke U. A fellow soldier called Jayne "as modest as a woman, as brave as a lion, and as fine a type of the old, antebellum gentleman as could be found."

Jeans, Beal Green. Born Jan. 13, 1826, Mt. Sterling, KY. Pvt., 2d KY, in Mexican War. Prewar farmer in Jackson and Johnson Cos., MO. Md. Mary E. Renick. Lt. Co. A, 3d Inf., 8th Div., MSG, June 14, 1861. Resigned Sept. 23, 1861. Lt. col., Hays's Jackson Co. Regt. (12th MO Cav.), 1862. Col., Sept. 13, 1862. Resigned due to wounds, late in 1863. WIA while recruiting behind Union lines in Jackson Co., March 20, 1864. Postwar Jackson Co. farmer. To Benton Co., AR, in the 1880s, then to Adair, OK. Died Oct. 25, 1904, Adair. Buried Adair Cemetery.

Jeffers, William Lafayette. Born Sept. 25, 1827, Gallipolis, OH. Grew up in Mason Co., VA. To Jackson, Cape Girardeau Co., MO. Pvt. in US Army 1846–52. Prewar saddler in Bollinger Co., MO. Md. Eliza Abernathy; Ellen Ramsey; Emily M. Hargraves. Capt. Co. A, 2d Cav., 1st Div., MSG, June 15, 1861. Lt. col., Aug. 2, 1861. Resigned Sept. 15, 1861. Capt. of a company briefly (c. June 1862) in Matlock's Regt., AR Cav., later Co. B, 3d MO Cav. Col., 8th MO Cav., Dec. 11, 1862. POW Mine Creek. Paroled at Johnson's Island July 25, 1865. Postwar hotel keeper in Dexter, Stoddard Co., and Clarkton. Moved to Corpus Christi, TX, late in life for health reasons. Died Feb. 21, 1903, Corpus Christi. Buried Jackson Cemetery. John N. Edwards called Jeffers "a gallant and skillful soldier."

Jenifer, Walter Hanson. Born Aug. 21, 1823, St. Mary's Co., MD. Attd. USMA. Officer in US Army 1847–48, 1855–61. Merchant in CA 1848–55. Celebrated horse trainer. Invented the Jenifer Saddle, widely used during the war. Arrested by the governor of Pennsylvania at the start of the war on suspicion of communicating with the enemy. Capt., CS Regular Army, March 16, 1861. Lt. col. of a cav. bn. at 1st Manassas. Col., PACS, Sept. 24, 1861. Assigned to command 8th VA Cav., Jan. 1862. Dropped in May 1862 reorganization. Commandant, post of Selma, AL, 1863. Inspector of cavalry on Gen. Maury's staff, 1864. Postwar merchant in Baltimore. From 1870–75 served as officer in the Egyptian Army. Died April 9, 1878, Richmond, VA, where he had gone for an operation. Buried Shockoe Cemetery, Richmond. A staff officer remembered "Jenifer was worthless as an officer—a great dandy but small man." Another officer thought Jenifer's horses showed more sense than their trainer.

Johnson, Abda. Born Oct. 8, 1826, Elbert Co., GA. Reared in Cassville. Grad. UGA with 1st honors. Cassville lawyer prewar. State representative 1852–56. Md. Frances E. Trippe. Capt. Co. I, 40th GA, March 4, 1862. Col., March 19, 1862. WIA and POW Vicksburg. Exch. Surrendered at Greensboro April 26, 1865. Cartersville lawyer postwar. Trustee of UGA. Member, 1877 state constitutional convention. Died July 10, 1881, Cartersville. Buried Cartersville City Cemetery. A junior officer asserted Johnson was "remarkably unpopular" with his men because "he usually gets drunk when the enemy is near." His brother Jefferson Johnson was major, 18th GA.

Johnson, Albert W. Born Aug. 21, 1830, Great Crossings, Scott Co., KY. Relative of Vice Pres. Richard M. Johnson and US senator Robert W. Johnson of AR. Prewar cotton planter in Phillips Co., AR. Wealthy slave owner. Md. Helena Loftin. Capt. in 1861 of a company later in the 13th AR. Col., Johnson's (aka 39th) AR Infantry, when the regiment was organized in the summer of 1862. Resigned Nov. 6, 1862. Appointed to military court in TMD, Feb. 9, 1864, but declined appointment. Lived postwar in Phillips Co.; Staunton, VA; Evansville, IN; Louisville; Indianapolis; and New York City. Farmer. Chief of police in Louisville. Owned street car companies in Indianapolis and New York City. Died Nov. 6, 1895, at his son's home in Euclid, OH. Buried Greenwood Cemetery, Brooklyn. His son, Tom L. Johnson, became mayor of Cleveland, OH.

Johnson, Benjamin Whitfield. Born July 23, 1835, Upson Co., GA. Family moved to Camden, AR, in 1849. Grad. U. of Louisville School of Law in 1856. Prewar Camden lawyer. Md. Nannie Hawkins; Lizzie Sherman. Pvt., then 1st lt. and adj., 15th AR, 1861. WIA and POW Fort Donelson. Exch. fall of 1862. Elected col., Oct. 16, 1862, of the reorganized 15th. WIA and POW Port Hudson. Imprisoned at Johnson's Island for the remainder of the war. Postwar lawyer in Calhoun Co., then Camden. State representative 1875–76. Dist. attorney, 1876–80. Died May 17, 1907, Camden. Buried Oakland Cemetery, Camden. Called "universally popular" by a postwar newspaper.

Johnson, Henry Poston. Born Aug. 6, 1823, MO. Prewar cotton merchant in Hempstead Co., AR, and New Orleans. Unmd. A "large man . . . and a high-minded gentleman." Capt. Co. B, 20th AR, March 1, 1862. Elected col. at May 13, 1862, reorganization. KIA Corinth, Oct. 4, 1862, shot from his horse by the 56th IL during a charge. Buried on the battlefield.

Johnson, James A. Washington. Born Oct. 13, 1823, GA. Known as "Wash" Johnson. Attd. Miami U. Lawyer in Dalton prewar. Solicitor general, Cherokee Circuit. Md. Mary Jane McGhee. Lt. col., 10th GA State Troops, Feb. 18, 1862. Col., 34th GA, May 17, 1862. POW Vicksburg. Paroled. WIA Missionary Ridge.

Dalton lawyer postwar. State senator 1865–66. Committed suicide Sept. 9, 1885, Dalton. Buried West Hill Cemetery, Dalton.

Johnson, James Theodore. Born March 31, 1836, Catawba Co., NC. Attd. Rutherford College. Grad. UPA Medical School in 1861. Burke Co. physician. Md. Susan C. Warlick. Lt. Co. K, 35th NC, Oct. 15, 1861. Capt., Nov. 28, 1861. WIA Malvern Hill. Major, Dec. 14, 1862. WIA near Bermuda Hundred, May 1864, in the leg. Col., June 18, 1864. POW Dinwiddie Courthouse, April 1, 1865. Released June 19, 1865. Physician in Hickory, NC, postwar. Died Dec. 24, 1914, Hickory. Buried Oakwood Cemetery, Hickory.

Johnson, John Evans. Born Sept. 16, 1815, Chesterfield Co., VA. Attd. USMA. Planter in Chesterfield Co. prewar. Owned tobacco factory in Richmond. Noted architect, designing plantation homes of great elegance. Md. Adelia H. Armistead; Mary M. Swift. Major, VA State Troops, May 2, 1861. Cavalry instructor at a camp at Ashland. Relieved Nov. 5, 1861. Lt. col., 1st Bn. VA Cav. Col., 9th VA Cav. (formed from the 1st Bn.), Jan. 1862. Dropped at April 1862 reorganization. VADC to Gen. Ewell, 1863. Moved to New York City postwar to live with his son. Died there May 31, 1870. Buried Greenwood Cemetery, Brooklyn. A staff officer called Johnson "quick, active & brave—with as many bristles as a porcupine." A biography of Johnson, focusing on his career as an architect, was published in 1983. Uncle of Gen. John Pegram and brother of Lt. Col. Marmaduke Johnson.

Johnson, Middleton Tate. Born April 13, 1809, Spartanburg Dist., SC. Grew up in Franklin Co., GA, and Marshall Co., AL. State legislator in AL. To Shelby Co., TX, in 1840. Later lived in Tarrant Co. Planter. TX congressman. Indian fighter. Lost races for governor in 1851, 1853, 1855, and 1857. Capt. in Mexican War. Md. Vienna Parker; Mary Louise Givens. Delegate to TX Secession Convention. In Nov. 1861 the War Dept. asked Johnson to raise a brigade of cavalry for 12 months service, with the promise of a brigadiership if he did. He raised 5 regiments, the 14th through 18th TX Cav. Col., 14th TX Cav., Feb. 5, 1862. He declined reelection as col., believing (mistakenly) that he would soon be promoted to gen., though Gen. Hindman claimed that Johnson, who was "awful" and "never with his command," resigned at Hindman's request. Johnson later supervised a program to export cotton and import war supplies. Postwar state legislator. Died May 13, 1866, near Austin, while returning home from a session of the legislature. Buried State Cemetery; reburied in a family cemetery south of Arlington, TX. Johnson Co., TX, is named for him.

Johnson, Robert Adams. Born May 3, 1817, near Lexington, KY. Nephew of Vice Pres. Richard M. Johnson and cousin to many other prominent politicians in KY and AR. Grad. UVA 1839. Commission merchant in Louisville and New

Orleans prewar. Attorney in Vicksburg, MS. Md. Cornelia Ruffin; Mrs. Lucy Johnson; Ellen McMahon. Lt. col., 2d KY, July 12, 1861. Col., July 16, 1861. WIA Shiloh. Resigned Oct. 19, 1863, due to dysentery. Appointed col. and judge, military court of the Texas Corps, TMD, March 23, 1865. He lived in retirement postwar in Louisville and (after 1880) Knoxville. Prominent horse breeder and racer. Died March 15, 1886, Knoxville. Buried Lexington Cemetery. Private Jackman of the Orphan Brigade found Johnson "a clever brave man but utterly ignorant of military tactics." Johnson and his family owned plantations in Washington Co., MS, before and after the war, and he is sometimes said to have been buried there.

Johnson, William Arthur. Born Sept. 26, 1827, Lauderdale Co., AL. Steamboat pilot and owner on the Tennessee River. Md. Kate Barton. Operated steamboat 1861–62. Scouted for the army. Major, 4th AL Cav., Oct. 21, 1862. Lt. col., April 23, 1863. Col., Aug. 3, 1863. Often led brigade under Bedford Forrest, who noted that "Hell could not stop him." WIA Pulaski, TN. Paroled May 4, 1865, Citronelle, AL. Lived in Tuscumbia, AL, postwar. Cotton broker and planter. Died June 4, 1891, Tuscumbia. Buried Oakwood Cemetery.

Johnston, Robert. Born July 3, 1830, Richmond, VA. Grad. USMA 1850. Lt., US Army, 1850–61. Md. Catherine S. Van Rensselaer. Capt., CS Regular Army, March 16, 1861. Major on the staff of Gen. Robert E. Lee, April 1861. Lt. col., PAVA, May 10, 1861. Col., 3d VA Cav., June 20, 1861. Dropped at May 1862 reorganization. Capt. AAG on the staff of Gen. Pickett (his cousin) 1862–63. Educator at Deveaux College in NY postwar. Died July 8, 1902, Geneva, NY. Buried Albany Rural Cemetery, near Albany, NY. Johnston's letterbook is in the Museum of the Confederacy.

Johnston, Thomas Henry. Born Dec. 17, 1832, Adair Co., KY. Attd. Centre College. Lawyer in Hernando, MS, prewar. Md. Annie Jeter. Pvt. Co. D (the "De Soto Grays"), 1st MS, Aug. 27, 1861. Major, Sept. 9, 1861. POW Fort Donelson. Exch. WIA (knocked out by an exploding shell) and POW Port Hudson. One of the "Immortal 600." Again exch. Lt. col. at an unspecified date. Col., Nov. 26, 1863. Lawyer in Hernando and in Tate Co. postwar. State legislator. Died Jan. 29, 1907, Coldwater, MS. Buried Hernando Baptist Cemetery. A fellow soldier called Johnston "a modest, rather effeminate young man . . . always a favorite with the men."

Johnston, William Preston. Born Jan. 5, 1831, Louisville, KY. Son of Gen. A. S. Johnston. Attd. WMI and Yale. Prewar Louisville lawyer. Md. Rose Duncan. Major, 2d KY, July 16, 1861. Lt. col., 1st KY, Oct. 14, 1861. Col., April 19, 1862, to serve as Pres. Davis's aide. Johnston made several inspection trips during the war, essentially serving as Davis's informant on conditions in the West.

To Canada postwar. Returning to US, taught at Washington & Lee U. President of LSU and Tulane. Authored many historical articles and a biography of his father. Died July 16, 1899, Lexington, VA. Buried Cave Hill Cemetery, Louisville. Johnston passionately, if not always accurately, defended his father's reputation in his postwar writings.

Jones, Alexander Caldwell. Born 1830, near Moundsville, VA (now WVA). Grad. VMI 1850. Moved to Iowa, then St. Paul, MN. Lawyer, judge, farm implement dealer. Adj. gen. of MN 1858–60. Md. Ellen Clemens. Major, 44th VA, June 14, 1861. Detached to lead partisan units in northwest VA. Lt. col., May 1, 1862. WIA Gaines's Mill. Assigned to duty in adj. gen.'s office 1862–63. Resigned June 16, 1863. Transferred to TX. Col. and chief of staff to Gens. Slaughter, Walker, and Magruder. Commanded a district in TX. To Mexico briefly in 1865. Editor of newspaper in DC. US consul in Japan and China. Died Jan. 13, 1898, Chunking, China. A few Jones papers are at VAHS. It appears that, in 1865, Gen. Kirby Smith promoted Jones to brig., and he was paroled July 24, 1865, at that rank.

Jones, Allen Cadwalader. Born Nov. 7, 1811, Everetts, Martin Co., NC. Grad. UNC. Greene Co., AL, planter and state senator. Capt., "Greensboro Guards" vol. militia. Md. Catherine Ervin. Led the "Guards" in the occupation of Fort Morgan, Jan.–Feb. 1861. Lt. col., 5th AL, May 11, 1861. Col., Nov. 20, 1861. Dropped at April 27, 1862, reorganization. Postwar Greensboro planter. Died Jan. 6, 1894. Buried Greensboro Cemetery. Major Campbell Brown thought Jones a "good officer."

Jones, Buehring Hampden. Born May 12, 1823, Clifton, Kanawha Co., VA (later WVA). Lawyer, teacher, newspaper editor in Palmyra, MO, prewar. State representative in 1858. Md. Letitia Smythie. Returned to VA upon the outbreak of the war. Capt. Co. C (the "Dixie Rifles"), 60th VA, June 26, 1861. Lt. col., April 27, 1862. Col., Aug. 6, 1862. POW Piedmont. Released from Johnson's Island Prison July 19, 1865. Lawyer in Lewisburg, WVA, postwar. Died March 18, 1872, Charleston, WVA, while serving as secretary of a state convention. Buried Old Stone Churchyard, Lewisburg. Jones wrote a book during his time in Yankee prison, *Prison Prose and Poetry,* published in 1868. An obituary states, "as a soldier, he had but few equals."

Jones, Bush. Born May 12, 1836, Perry Co., AL. Attd. UAL and Cumberland U. Law School. Uniontown, AL, lawyer. Md. Carrie Evans. Pvt. Co. D, 4th AL, April 25, 1861. Lt., Aug. 2, 1861. Lt. Co. L, 18th AL (aka 9th AL Bn.), Dec. 1861. Capt., July 31, 1862. Lt. col., 9th Bn., April 16, 1862. Col., 58th AL (formed from 9th Bn.), July 25, 1863. Often led Holtzclaw's brigade during Atlanta Campaign. Gen. Manigault called him "one of the noblest fellows I ever saw." Paroled

Meridian, 1865. Lawyer in Uniontown postwar. Probate judge 1865–68. Died Sept. 27, 1872, Uniontown. Buried Rosemont Cemetery, Uniontown.

Jones, Cadwallader. Born Aug. 17, 1813, Halifax, NC. Grad. UNC. Lawyer in Hillsboro and Wilmington. State representative 1840–42, 1848–51. Moved to Rock Hill, SC, in 1856. Md. Anne Iredell. Capt. Co. H, 12th SC, Aug. 13, 1861. Major, Aug. 30, 1861. Lt. col., April 2, 1862. Col., Sept. 27, 1862. Resigned Feb. 27, 1863, due to ill health. State senator 1864–65. Farmer in Yorkville and Columbia. Died Dec. 1, 1899, Columbia. Buried Elmwood Cemetery, Columbia.

Jones, Daniel Webster. Born Dec. 15, 1839, Bowie Co., TX. Reared in Hempstead Co., AR. Law student at the start of the war. Md. Margaret P. Hadley. 1st lt. Co. A, 3d AR State Troops, 1861. Capt. Co. A, 20th AR, Feb. 26, 1862. Major, July 7, 1862. Severely WIA at Corinth (shot through the heart on the second day) and left for dead. Captured there. Col., Jan. 5, 1863. POW Vicksburg. After exchange, his regiment was mounted and operated in AR. Court-martialed for retiring from the field at the battle of Mark's Mills but acquitted. Postwar lawyer in Washington, AR. Prosecuting attorney. Attorney general of AR 1885–89. State representative 1891–92, 1915–16. Governor 1896–1900. Died Dec. 25, 1918, Little Rock. Buried Oakland Cemetery, Little Rock.

Jones, Dudley William. Born 1840, Lamar Co., TX. Grew up in Mt. Pleasant, Titus Co. Attd. Maury Institute. Pvt. Co. I (the "Titus Grays"), 9th TX Cav, 1861. 1st lt. and adj., Oct. 14, 1861, the adjutancy position becoming vacant when the soldiers hung the officeholder for bigamy and abolitionist leanings. Lt. col., May 26, 1862. Col., March 30, 1863. Led Ross's TX Cav. Brigade in 1865. Paroled May 13, 1865, Jackson. Houston lawyer postwar. Owned a Houston newspaper. Delegate to state constitutional convention of 1866. Died Aug. 14, 1868, Houston. Buried Houston, probably in an unmarked grave in Old City Cemetery. Called "the Boy Colonel."

Jones, Egbert J. Born Feb. 22, 1818, Limestone Co., AL. Attd. UVA. City attorney of Huntsville. State legislator. Capt., 13th US Inf. during Mexican War. Md. Mary Echols. Capt. Co. E, 4th AL, April 26, 1861. Col., May 7, 1861. MWIA in both hips at 1st Manassas. Died Sept. 2, 1861, Orange Courthouse, VA. Buried Graham Cemetery, Orange; reburied Maple Hill Cemetery, Huntsville. A postwar historian called "his temperament . . . phlegmatic."

Jones, Erwin Patton. Born Feb. 20, 1814, Laurens, SC. Attd. UGA. Grad. UVA. Lawyer in Greenville prewar. State legislator. Militia colonel. Briefly a farmer in GA. Md. Georgianna Earle. Enlisted April 9, 1861. Lt. col., 2d SC, May 16, 1861. Col., Feb. 15, 1862. Dropped at May 13, 1862, reorganization. Spent the remainder of the war seeking a post in a military court. Greenville lawyer postwar. Died Aug. 26, 1883, White Oak, Polk Co., NC. Buried White Oak. An obituary calls Jones "decidedly popular."

Jones, George H. Born c. 1838, GA. Reared in Warren and Glasscock Cos. Justice, Glasscock Co. Court, prewar. Major, GA militia in 1861. Capt. Co. B, 22d GA, Sept. 3, 1861. Col., Nov. 14, 1863. WIA and POW Gettysburg. Exch. March 22, 1865. Probably died shortly after the war.

Jones, George Washington. Born Sept. 5, 1828, Marion Co., AL. Moved to Bastrop, TX, in 1848. Prewar lawyer, dist. attorney. Md. Ledora Mullen. Capt., "Bastrop Guards," 1861. Reenlisted as pvt. March 22, 1862. Lt. col., 17th TX, June 9, 1862. POW Pleasant Hill. Exch. April 20, 1864. Col., probably July 27, 1864. Practiced law in Bastrop postwar. Lt. gov. of TX, 1866–67. US congressman 1879–87. Died July 11, 1903, Bastrop. Buried Fairview Cemetery. A fellow soldier called Jones "the grandest man I ever saw both in battle and in camp."

Jones, Hamilton Chamberlain, Jr. Born Nov. 3, 1837, near Salisbury, NC. Grad. UNC. Salisbury lawyer prewar. Officer in vol. militia. Md. Connie Meyers. Capt. Co. K, 5th NC, May 16, 1861. WIA Williamsburg. Lt. col., 57th NC, July 17, 1862. POW Rappahannock Station, Nov. 7, 1863. Exch. Feb. 20, 1865. Col., Feb. 1865. WIA Fort Stedman. Paroled May 12, 1865, Salisbury. Attorney postwar. Moved to Charlotte in 1867. Editor, Charlotte *News*. State senator 1869–71. US dist. attorney 1885–89. Died Aug. 23, 1904, Wilmington, NC, on a visit to a hospital there. Buried Elmwood Cemetery, Charlotte.

Jones, Hilary Pollard. Born July 13, 1833, Fluvanna Co., VA. Attd. UVA. Taught at Hanover Academy near Taylorsville, VA, prewar. Md. Claudia H. Marshall. Lt., Morris (VA) Art., Aug. 1861. Capt., Feb. 1862. Major of artillery, May 28, 1862. Lt. col., March 2, 1863. Acting chief of artillery, 2d Corps, after Chancellorsville. Col., Feb. 7, 1864. Chief of artillery, Dept. of NC and Southern VA, 1864. Chief of artillery, Anderson's Corps, 1864. Appmx. Principal of Hanover Academy postwar. Died Jan. 1, 1913, Washington, DC. Buried Leeds Episcopal Church Cemetery, Hume, VA.

Jones, James. Born Oct. 3, 1805, Edgefield Co., SC. Grad. USC. Edgefield lawyer prewar. Chairman of the Board of Visitors of SCMA. Owned a cotton mill. Seminole War veteran. Md. Catherine L. Creyon. Col., 14th SC, Sept. 9, 1861. Resigned April 11, 1862, feeling slighted that a junior officer (S. R. Gist) had been promoted ahead of him. QM gen. of SC thereafter. Manufacturer. Died Oct. 19 (per gravestone: other sources have Oct. 20), 1865. Buried Jones Private Cemetery, Edgefield Co. A lt. in the 14th called Jones "one of the most wicked men I ever saw."

Jones, James Fitzgerald. Born Sept. 10, 1822, near Winchester, VA. Attd. William & Mary College and UVA. Moved to Fauquier Co. Lawyer. Rich planter and slaveholder. Md. Annie Lewis Marshall. Ran the Marshall-Jones family farms, 1861–62. Removed to Staunton, VA, when the Union armies neared. Capt., Nitre and Mining Bureau, June 3, 1863. Commanded Bureau activities near Staunton. Col., 1st VA LDT (a unit organized around Richmond from the staff of the Nitre Bureau), Oct. 2, 1863. Appointed major in the Nitre and Mining Corps, to rank from June 15, 1864. Returned to his farm, "Oak Hill," the Marshall family seat in Fauquier Co., after the war. Murdered Oct. 9, 1866, Fauquier Co., by a man he had denounced for being a wartime stay-at-home. Buried Emmanuel Episcopal Church near "Oak Hill." S. Bassett French said Jones "was highly esteemed for his probity." Brother of Major Francis B. Jones, 2d VA.

Jones, James Henry. Born Sept. 13, 1830, Shelby Co., AL. Reared in Talladega Co. Moved to Henderson, TX, c. 1851. Prewar lawyer. Md. Eliza Hall. Capt. Co. B, 11th TX, Feb. 26, 1862. Lt. col., June 23, 1862. Col., Oct. 19, 1864. Paroled July 11, 1865, Marshall, TX. Postwar Henderson lawyer. US congressman 1883–87. Died March 22, 1904, Henderson, buried New City (aka Graham-Hall) Cemetery. "[A]n elegant gentleman, of graceful manners, and a fluent speaker."

Jones, John Abraham. Born Dec. 6, 1821, Baldwin Co., GA. Attd. Georgetown U. and Emory U. Lawyer and politician in Columbus. Officer in Mexican War. Known as "Little Jack." Md. Mary Louise Leonard. Capt. Co. I, 20th GA, May 23, 1861. Major, Aug. 30, 1861. Lt. col., April 3, 1862. Attempted but failed to raise a sharpshooter battalion during the summer of 1862. Col., May 29, 1863. KIA Gettysburg, July 2, 1863. He has a memorial stone at Linwood Cemetery, Columbus, his remains having been lost at sea. Middle name also given as "Augustus."

Jones, John G. Born c. 1835, Person Co., NC. Attd. Wake Forest U. Baptist minister in Person Co. prewar. Unmd. Capt. Co. E, 35th NC, Oct. 29, 1861. Major, April 15, 1862. Lt. col., July 1, 1862. Col., June 15, 1863. KIA June 17, 1864, near Petersburg. Recommended for promotion to brig. as "a man of education and considerable refinement . . . cool and collected in battle."

Jones, Joseph Pickett. Born May 8, 1833, Wadesboro, NC. Middle name given as "Peck" in USMA records. Attd. USMA 1849–50. Grad. UNC. Lawyer in Anson Co., NC. Lt., US Army, 1856–61. Md. Victoria C. Moreno, sister-in-law of Sen. Stephen Mallory. 1st lt., CS Regular Army, March 16, 1861. Capt. AAG to Gen. Bragg. Lt. col., 5th NC, May 16, 1861. Resigned Oct. 24, 1861. Temporarily assigned to duty as col., 17th AL, April 13, 1862, to July 3, 1862. AIG, Army of Tennessee, late 1862. On Gen. Bragg's staff, 1862–65, spending the last two years as a roving inspector. Fled to Mexico after the war and served as an officer in Maximilian's army. Returned to US in 1867. Lawyer in Monticello and Pensacola, FL, postwar. Mayor of Pensacola 1875–77. Died March 4, 1895, Pensacola. Buried St. Michael's Cemetery, Pensacola. A congressman, in recommending Jones for promotion, cited his "great zeal and efficiency" and "high military talent." Gen. Bragg (a hard man to please) thought Jones had "no superior" as a regimental commander.

Jones, Richard Washington. Born Feb. 22, 1821, VA. Attd. Emory & Henry College and USMA. Grad. UPA Medical College. Innkeeper in Smyth Co., VA. Physician in Penhook, LA, prewar. Capt. of AL Volunteers in Mexican War. Md. Cornelia Thurman; Alice R. Mitchell. Capt. Co. I, 14th LA, May 20, 1861. Lt. col., 1861 (probably Sept. 13, when the 14th was mustered in). Col., Feb. 19, 1862. Resigned after Fredericksburg (predated to Aug. 15, 1862), due to ill health and anger over not being promoted. Physician in Hawkins Co., TN, postwar. Died Jan. 11, 1886, Church Hill, Hawkins Co. Buried Old Presbyterian Cemetery, Rogersville. Although Jones was praised as a "capable officer" and recommended for promotion to brig., his absence at the Battle of Fredericksburg led to his being eased out of the colonelcy.

Jones, Robert Harris. Born Sept. 22, 1828, Elbert Co., GA. Methodist minister, tanner, and carriage manufacturer in AL, Hart Co., GA, and Cartersville, GA, prewar. Md. Lucintha E. Cotton. Raised the "Fireside Defenders" (later Co. G, 22d GA), early 1861. Col., 22d GA, Aug. 31, 1861. WIA Seven Pines and Malvern Hill. WIA Antietam in head and stomach. Resigned because of these wounds April 22, 1863. Minister and carriage manufacturer in Cartersville postwar. Died Sept. 1, 1897 (not 1899, as given in some sources), Cartersville. Buried Oak Hill Cemetery, Cartersville. "Too strict for his own good."

Jones, Robert Tignall. Born Oct. 8, 1815, Mecklenburg Co., VA. Grad. USMA 1837. Lt., US Army, 1837–38. Planter in Perry Co., AL. President of Cahaba & Marion Railroad. Md. Lucy M. Jones (a cousin); Mary I. Seawell. Declined appointment as brig. gen. AL State Troops, 1861. Commanded artillery at Fort Morgan, early 1861. Col., 12th AL, July 17, 1861. Accepted the colonelcy of the 20th AL in Sept. 1861 but soon returned to the 12th. KIA Seven Pines, May 31, 1862, shot in the chest while leading an attack. Jones was "a man of sound judgment, inflexible will, lofty sense of honor, upright character," according to a contemporary history.

Jones, Theophilus Allan. Born Oct. 23, 1832, VA. Grew up in Rogersville, TN. Attd. UVA. Prewar attorney in Florence, AL. Capt. and QM, 7th AL, May 4, 1861. Resigned Sept. 13, 1861. Capt. Co. E, 27th AL, Dec. 24, 1861. Major, 3d MS Bn. (later 45th MS), April 16, 1862. Plagued by ill health. On staff of Gen. S. D.

Lee 1863–64. Appointed col. and judge, military court of S. D. Lee's Corps, April 6, 1864. Florence lawyer postwar. Died there Oct. 18, 1872, buried Florence Cemetery. An obituary said Jones "never was known to have the illwill of a single human being." However, a cousin became disgusted with Jones's "constant electioneering for [army] position."

Jones, Thomas Marshall. Born March 11, 1832, Elizabeth City Co., VA. Grad. USMA 1853. Lt., US Army, 1853–61. Md. Mary Cowan London. Capt., CS Regular Army, April 4, 1861. Commissary officer on Gen. Bragg's staff at Pensacola in 1861. Col., 27th MS, Jan. 14, 1862. Assigned to duty by Gen. Bragg as brig. gen., April 21, 1862. Commanded the much-criticized evacuation of Pensacola. Led brigade at Perryville. WIA Stones River, resigned Feb. 27, 1863. Commanded Fort Caswell, NC, part of the Wilmington defenses, in 1864. Postwar schoolteacher in Fauquier Co., VA. Professor at the U. of MD. Teacher to Indian tribes in WY, NM, OK, and AZ. Died March 31, 1913, Prescott, AZ. Buried Masonic Cemetery, Prescott. A renowned educator and scholar, whom friends thought unfitted for a military career. He retired with a wound very early in the Battle of Stones River; many (including his men and his superior officers) thought he used the wound as an excuse to shirk his duty. He resigned under this cloud and was never given field command again. In fairness to Jones, it should be noted that he had been repeatedly praised for gallantry at Pensacola, and his wound, thought slight, appears to have disabled him for some time. Brother-in-law of Gen. John D. Barry.

Jones, Warner Paul. Born Oct. 20, 1829, VA. Lawyer in Obion Co., TN, in 1860. Md. Louise Paxton. In 1861, while KY was still neutral, Jones raised a company of Tennesseans that crossed the Mississippi River and became capt. Co. G, 1st Inf., 1st Div., MSG. Capt. Co. G, 33d TN, Sept. 22, 1861. Lt. col., Nov. 19, 1861. Col., May 8, 1862. Regiment assigned to post duty in 1863, and Jones requested transfer to active duty with Forrest's cavalry. KIA June 30, 1864, near Marietta, GA, by a sharpshooter. Gen. A. P. Stewart called Jones a "true man" of "dash," "coolness, courage."

Jones, Waters Burras. Born Dec. 31, 1825, Greenville Dist., SC. Sheriff of Troup Co., GA, prewar. Editor, La Grange *Reporter*. Md. Elizabeth Miller. Capt. Co. B, 4th GA Bn. (soon to become 60th GA), July 17, 1861. Major, 60th GA, Aug. 17, 1863. WIA Wilderness. Promoted to col. late in the war. Col. 60th/61st GA at Appomattox. Editor/printer in La Grange postwar. State fertilizer inspector. Died May 28, 1898, La Grange. Buried Hillview Cemetery.

Jordan, John Thomas. Born Nov. 9, 1839, Washington Co., GA. Grad. UGA. Lawyer in Washington Co. prewar. Md. Mrs. Elizabeth Rives Arnold. Pvt. Co. E, 1st GA, March 18, 1861. Discharged, July 20, 1861. Lt. Co. C, 49th GA, March 4,

1862. Capt., July 31, 1862. Lt. col., Feb. 23, 1864. Col., March 24, 1864. WIA April 2, 1865, Petersburg. Hancock Co. lawyer and legislator postwar. Mayor of Sparta. Died March 10, 1895, Sparta. Buried Sparta City Cemetery.

Jordan, John Vaughn. Born Oct. 12, 1831, SC, son of the British consul to Charleston. Reared in PA. Appointed to USMA from PA but did not graduate. Druggist in New Bern, NC, prewar. Md. Julia Lane. Col., 31st NC, Sept. 19, 1861. POW Roanoke Island. Exch. Sept. 1862. WIA May 16, 1864, near Petersburg. Resigned Nov. 5, 1864. Druggist in New Bern postwar. Died Sept. 5, 1895, New Bern. Buried Cedar Grove Cemetery, New Bern. "A faithful officer and fine disciplinarian."

Josey, John E. Born 1831, Marengo Co., AL. Reared in Oktibbeha Co., MS. Attd. UMS. Grad. Nashville Medical College. Prewar physician in Osceola, AR. Md. Clementine J. Borum in 1864. 1st lt. Co. E, 15th AR, July 23, 1861. Major, April 14, 1862. Lt. col., Nov. 14, 1862. Col., Dec. 17, 1862. Regiment broken up and consolidated with other units in 1863. Josey returned to AR and began recruiting. Wounded and captured in a skirmish on the St. Francis River, AR, Feb. 14, 1864. Imprisoned in Camp Chase. Paroled June 15, 1865, Memphis. Returned to Mississippi Co., AR, postwar. Died Oct. 31, 1866, Osceola. Buried Elmwood Cemetery, Memphis. An obituary called him a "true friend, a noble hero and patriot."

Judge, Thomas James. Born Nov. 1, 1815, Richland Dist., SC. Lived in Greenville and Hayneville, AL. Editor, Greenville *Whig*. State legislator. Lawyer. Twice a losing candidate for Congress. Md. Kate Herbert. Volunteer pvt. at Pensacola, 1861. Col., 14th AL, July 19, 1861. Resigned July 10, 1862, due to a leg fracture suffered in a Feb. 1862 railroad accident. Col. and presiding judge of the military court of Forney's Corps, Dec. 16, 1862. Helped organize reservists in Mobile in Aug. 1864. Paroled Meridian May 9, 1865. Greenville lawyer postwar. Justice, AL Supreme Court. Died March 3, 1876, at his Greenville home. Buried Pioneer Cemetery, Greenville.

Keeble, Richard Hudson. Born March 1831, TN. Reared in Rutherford Co. Grad. Cumberland U. Law School in 1853. Lawyer in Murfreesboro prewar. Md. Harriet Amelia Clayton in 1860. Lt. Co. K, 23d TN, Aug. 22, 1861. Lt. col., probably in May 1862. Col., Dec. 16, 1862. KIA Petersburg, VA, June 30, 1864. Buried Hollywood Cemetery, Richmond; reburied Evergreen Cemetery, Murfreesboro.

Keen, Elisha Ford. Born July 25, 1825, Pittsylvania Co., VA. Danville tobacconist prewar. State representative 1857–61. Md. Mary Anne Perkins. Major, Keen's Bn. VA Infantry, c. July 1861. Major, 57th VA, formed from his battalion Sept. 23, 1861. Lt. col., April 24, 1862. Col., May 7, 1862. Resigned July 31, 1862,

due to a "frail and feeble constitution." Partner in a firm that manufactured car-
bines for the Confederate army. State senator 1863–67. Tobacco manufacturer
in Danville postwar. Died Dec. 8, 1868, VA. Buried in a family cemetery west of
Danville. His granddaughter was the famous Lady Astor.

Keitt, Lawrence Massillon. Born Oct. 4, 1824, Orangeburg Dist., SC. Grad.
USC. Orangeburg lawyer. State legislator. US congressman 1853–56, 1856–60.
Delegate to SC Secession Convention. Prominent secessionist. Md. Susanna
Sparks. Confederate congressman 1861. Col., 20th SC, Jan. 11, 1862. Served on
the SC coast, 1862–64. Ordered to join Lee's Army in 1864. MWIA Cold Har-
bor, June 1, 1864, while leading a brigade in his first battle. Died June 4, 1864,
Richmond. Buried West End Cemetery, near St. Matthews, SC. Mary Chesnut
found Keitt "immensely clever and original." Papers at Duke U.

Kellar, Andrew Jackson. Born Aug. 17, 1835, Covington, KY. Attd. Miami U.
in Ohio. Studied law in New Orleans. Lawyer in Memphis and in Somerville,
TN. Md. Margaret Chambers. Capt. Co. D, 4th TN, May 15, 1861. Lt. col., April
24, 1862. Col., July 28, 1863. Served as AIG, Dept. of AL, MS, and East LA, 1863–
64. Reassigned to 4th TN in Sept. 1864. Led brigade at Nashville. Lawyer and
owner of the Memphis *Avalanche* postwar. Lost race for Congress in 1872. Mine
owner in Empire, KY. Moved to Hot Springs, SD, in 1893. Lawyer and state senator there. Died July 28, 1907, Hot Springs. Buried Evergreen Cemetery, Hot
Springs. A Douglas Democrat before the war, a Republican postwar, who la-
bored hard to reconcile the South to Reconstruction. Keller's obituary called
him "a gentleman at all times, a good Christian man, an excellent neighbor."

Kelley, David Campbell. Born Dec. 25, 1833, Wilson Co., TN. Grad. Cumberland U. and U. of Nashville Medical School. Pastor of a church in Huntsville,
AL, prewar. Missionary in China. Md. Amanda M. Harris; Mary Owen Campbell; Mrs. Mary E. Knight. Capt. Co. F, Forrest's (3d) TN Cav., July 1861. Major,
date unspecified. Lt. col., April 3, 1862. Lt. col., 26th TN Cav. Bn. Col., Forrest's
TN Cav., 1864. Captured in Madison Co., AL, Nov. 1864 and released that same
evening. Paroled May 11, 1865, Gainesville. Pastor of various churches in TN
postwar. Trustee of Vanderbilt U. Died May 15, 1909, Nashville. Buried Mt.
Olivet Cemetery. Kelley was known as "Forrest's fighting preacher," "as brave a
man as ever smelled gunpowder."

Kellogg, Henry Clay. Born Dec. 20, 1829, Jackson Co., GA. Farmer in Coal
Mountain, Forsyth Co., in 1860. Clerk of the US Mint at Dahlonega. Md. Ophe-
lia Troup Anglin. Capt. Co. E, 43d GA, March 4, 1862. Major, March 20, 1862.
Lt. col., probably May 17, 1863; col., Dec. 18, 1863. WIA New Hope Church. Led
Stovall's Brigade at Bentonville. Farmer in Forsyth Co. and Canton postwar.

Elected to legislature in 1870 but not seated by the Reconstruction authorities. Died July 16, 1889, Canton. Buried Ebenezer Cemetery, Forsyth Co.

Kelly, Henry Brooke. Born Oct. 3, 1823, Huntsville, AL, son of a US senator. Reared in New Orleans. Attd. St. Louis U. Lawyer in New Orleans and later in Alexandria, LA, prewar. State legislator. Lt., US Army, 1847–48, 1855–61. Md. Marie Louise Morgan; Adeline Taylor McNeill. 1st lt., CS Regular Army, Aug. 27, 1861. Col., 8th LA, June 10, 1861. Often absent due to stomach ailments. Appointed col. and judge, military court of Pemberton's Corps, April 6, 1863. Lawyer in New Orleans postwar. Judge 1885–94. Died June 16, 1894, New Orleans. Buried Metairie Cemetery. Kelly wrote a short but valued book on the Battle of Port Republic.

Kenan, Daniel Lafayette. Born March 23, 1825, Duplin Co., NC. Family moved to Quincy, Gadsden Co., FL, in 1831. Carriage maker and wheelwright. State representative. Md. Martha Gregory; Virginia Nathans. 1st sgt. Co. A, 6th FL, March 12, 1862. Major, April 18, 1862. Lt. col., Nov. 16, 1863. Col., May 28, 1864. WIA at Jonesboro, losing 2 fingers. Lost leg at Bentonville. Paroled May 7, 1865, Charlotte, NC. Returned to Quincy postwar. County assessor. State senator 1865–66. Died Feb. 1, 1884, Quincy. Buried Western Cemetery, Quincy. An enlisted man, speaking of the officers of the 6th, wrote home that Kenan "is a fine man, the rest are not fit to tote guts to a bear."

Kenan, Thomas Stephens. Born Feb. 12, 1838, Duplin Co., NC. Attd. Central Military Institute of Selma, AL. Attd. Wake Forest U. Grad. UNC. Kenansville lawyer prewar. Md. Sallie Dortch. Capt. Co. C, 12th NC, April 15, 1861. Capt. Co. A, 43d NC, March 6, 1862. Lt. col., March 20, 1862. Col., April 21, 1862. WIA (thigh) at Gettysburg and captured July 4 on the retreat from Gettysburg. Paroled March 14, 1865, but never exchanged. Kenansville lawyer postwar. Mayor of Wilson. State representative 1865–68. State attorney general. Died Dec. 12, 1911, Raleigh. Buried Oakwood Cemetery, Raleigh.

Kennedy, John B. G. Born c. 1822, LA. New Orleans resident. Prewar watchmaker/jeweler. Capt. in Mexican War. Militia captain. Md. Adeline Quave. Capt. in the commissary department, LA militia, April 30, 1861. Resigned Aug. 14, 1861. Lt. col. "Jackson Regiment," LA militia, 1861. Lt. col., 5th LA Inf. Bn. (formed from his militia unit), Oct. 22, 1861. Col., 21st LA (formed from the 5th Bn.), Feb. 9, 1862. Part of the 21st was captured at Island No. 10. After exchange, the unit's numbers were so low Gen. Bragg ordered that it be disbanded. The 21st was reorganized and consolidated Sept. 23, 1862, and Kennedy lost his job. Moved to Tuskegee, AL, and farmed there. Appointed agent for the QM dept., March 11, 1864. Owned a lamp store in New Orleans postwar. Moved to Augusta, GA. Died Nov. 26, 1869, Montgomery, AL. A letter in his service record calls Kennedy "a notorious thief and imposter of the basest kind, void of all principal [*sic*] and integrity."

Kennon, Richard Ewing. Born Dec. 24, 1839, Fort Gaines, GA. Attd. UGA and UVA. Lawyer in Harris Co. prewar. Md. Dorliska White; Ann McAllister. Capt. Co. H, 17th GA, Aug. 15, 1861. Resigned May 23, 1862. Capt. Co. C, 3d GA Cav., May 1, 1862. Lt. col., 1862. POW New Haven, KY, Sept. 29, 1862. Col., March 13, 1863. Resigned July 31, 1863, due to dysentery. Postwar lawyer and state legislator. Mayor of Fort Gaines. Died May 7, 1894, Fort Gaines. Buried New Park Cemetery, Fort Gaines.

Kent, James. Born Jan. 8, 1830, Petersburg, VA. Attd. UPA Medical College; grad. William & Mary College. Druggist in New Orleans. Physician in Selma, AL. Md. Mary Grey. Capt. Co. D, 8th AL, May 10, 1861. Resigned Nov. 8, 1861. Col., 44th AL May 12, 1862. Resigned Sept. 1, 1862, due to heart trouble. Physician in Selma and Birmingham postwar. State legislator 1880–81. Died May 22, 1881, Birmingham. Buried Live Oak Cemetery, Selma. An obituary notes he was "universally esteemed."

Ketchum, Charles Thomas. Born Dec. 24, 1815, Augusta, GA. Attd. Columbia College. Cotton planter in Augusta. Grocer in Mobile, AL. Md. Emily Sims; Kate Ewing. Capt. Co. B, 38th AL, 1862. Col., May 15, 1862. Resigned Nov. 13, 1863. Planter in Washington Co., AL, postwar. Died Dec. 22, 1875, Washington Co. Buried Magnolia Cemetery, Mobile.

Key, John Cotlett Garrett. Born Feb. 25, 1817, Edgefield Dist., SC. Prewar lawyer in SC; Belview, LA; and Gonzales, TX. Organized company in 1860 to fight border bandits. Md. Martha B. Harmon; Ann Ardis. Raised company in early 1861 to help seize San Antonio. Capt. Co. A, 4th TX, July 11, 1861. Major, March 3, 1862. Lt. col., June 27, 1862. Col., July 10, 1862. WIA Gaines's Mill and Gettysburg. Retired April 29, 1864, due to ill health. Died Jan. 7, 1868, Gonzales. Buried Masonic Cemetery, Gonzales.

Kilpatrick, Franklin Whitner. Born Sept. 30, 1837, Pendleton Dist., SC. Attd. UVA. Pickens Dist. planter prewar. Pvt., 1st SC (State Troops), early 1861. Capt. Co. E, 4th SC, June 7, 1861. Capt. Co. B, Palmetto Sharpshooters, April 14, 1862. Major, July 22, 1862. Appointed col. to rank from Aug. 12, 1862, but declined. Col., 1st SC (Hagood's), Jan. 31, 1863, appointed from outside the regiment on the application of the 1st's officer. KIA Wauhatchie, Oct. 28, 1863. Buried Taylor Cemetery, Anderson, SC. Gen. Hagood called Kilpatrick "gallant and meritorious."

King, George Washington. Born May 10, 1825, Coahoma Co., MS. Left a substantial inheritance by his father, which he lost by trusting others to manage it. Overseer in Warrenton Co., MS (a close neighbor of Jefferson Davis when living there) in 1850. Saved a little and bought a plantation in Pulaski Co., AR. Md. Delia Sailor; Frances Somerville. Capt. Co. C, 13th Regt., AR Militia, early 1861. In April 1861 King led his vol. militia company, the "Little Rock Grays," on an expedition to occupy Fort Smith. 1st lt. Co. F, 1st AR MR, summer of 1861. Col. of a state regiment, later the 22d AR, at its Aug. 1861 organization. Capt. Co. I, 22d (aka 20th) AR, Feb. 26, 1862. Col., April 9, 1862. Not reelected upon reorganization. Postwar farmer in Dallas and Jefferson Cos. Died May 5, 1877, Redfield, AR. Buried Red Bluff Cemetery, east of Redfield.

King, Henry Clay. Born July 29, 1831, Burkesville, KY. Attd. UAL. Prewar lawyer in Paducah, KY, and Memphis. Md. Sarah Haughton; Maria J. Dallum. Capt. Co. K, 21st TN (a KY company later transferred to King's Bn.), June 13, 1861. Appointed major, King's Bn. KY Cav., April 5, 1862 (he had been in command of this battalion, as major, prior to this). Elected col., 1st (aka 6th, 12th) Confederate Cav., Sept. 24, 1862. POW Shelbyville, TN, June 27, 1863. Imprisoned for 18 months. After exch., in March 1865, sent from Richmond to the TMD on a secret mission. Postwar lawyer in Memphis. In 1891 he murdered fellow lawyer David Poston, in one of the most notorious murders in Memphis history. King had fallen in love with the widow of Gen. Pillow, abandoning his wife and family. Poston made insulting comments on the relationship, whereupon King shot him. Tried and sentenced to the State Penitentiary at Nashville. Died in prison, of stomach cancer, Dec. 10, 1903. Buried Calvary Cemetery, Nashville. Union Gen. David Stanley called King "one of the bravest and most fearless men" he had ever known.

King, James Pleasant. Born Sept. 30, 1832, Decatur, AL. Reared in Madison Co., AL. Prewar Madison Co. farmer. Md. Jennie Wilson. 1st lt., Brown's Co., Carroll's Regt., AR State Troops, 1861. Capt. Co. B., 35th (aka Rector's 1st) AR, June 18, 1862. Major, July 11, 1862. Col., Sept. 14, 1862. Often absent due to illness. Postwar dry goods merchant, farmer (owning 7,000 acres), mill owner in Franklin Co., AR. Very wealthy. Died Sept. 1, 1897, Mulberry, AR. Buried King Cemetery, Mulberry.

King, Joseph Horace. Born Jan. 5, 1837, Decatur, AL. Decatur merchant. Unmd. Capt. Co. E, 9th AL, June 4, 1861. Major, June 5, 1861. Col., March 19, 1863. WIA Frayser's Farm and Gettysburg. Court-martialed Feb. 10, 1864, and suspended temporarily from command. Often led Perry's brigade 1864–65. The regiment's surgeon remembered his "perfect coolness and obstinate courage . . . He loved a good soldier with all his heart, but was too severe on a poor one." He missed the surrender at Appomattox, being absent on recruiting duties. Decatur merchant postwar. Died March 10, 1874, Decatur, and is buried there.

King, Wilburn Hill. Born June 10, 1839, Cullodenville, GA. Studied law and medicine in Americus, GA. Moved to Cass Co., TX. Clerk in store in Warrensburg, MO. Md. Lucy Furman. 1st lt. Co. E, 3d Infantry, 8th Div., MSG, May 1, 1861. Capt., June 21, 1861. WIA Wilson's Creek and returned to TX. Pvt. Co. B, 18th TX, 1862. Drillmaster. Major, May 13, 1862. Lt. col., Feb. 25, 1863. Col., Aug. 10, 1863. WIA Mansfield. Assigned to duty as brig. gen., April 16, 1864, to rank from April 8. Led a brigade and later Walker's Div., 1864–65. Immediately after the war he fled to Mexico, then established a sugar plantation in Central America. Returning to TX, he practiced law in Jefferson and Sulphur Springs. State legislator. Mayor of Sulphur Springs. Adj. gen. of TX 1881–91. Died Dec. 12, 1910, Sulphur Springs. Buried Oakwood Cemetery, Corsicana. King's memoirs of the war have been published.

King, William Hugh Means. Born May 28, 1832, near Madison, Morgan Co., GA. Grad. Emory U. and UGA, 1853, first in class. Prewar lawyer in Columbus, Hamilton, and Bainbridge, GA. Mayor of Bainbridge 1860–61. Md. Jane Varner; Elizabeth Gordon. Capt. Co. H, 5th GA, May 11, 1861. Aide to Gen. Richard Anderson at Pensacola, 1861. Major and brigade QM, April 24, 1862. Resigned Nov. 7, 1862. Appointed col. of cavalry Feb. 1863 by Gen. Bragg, to collect unattached cavalry companies and form them into a regiment under King's command. But the regiment never formed, and King served on Gen. Wheeler's staff the rest of the war. WIA Feb. 26, 1864. Lived in Muscogee Co., GA, Tuskegee and Evergreen, AL, postwar. Lawyer. Principal of Evergreen Academy. Mayor of Evergreen. Died June 5, 1914, Evergreen. Buried Old Historic Cemetery, Evergreen. Called "an elegant-looking man, tall, and always well dressed."

Kinnard, Motey. Born c. 1790, GA or AL, a mixed-blood Creek. Last name variously spelled Kennard, Kinnaird, and Canard; first name variously Motty, Mooty, Moody or Moty. May have served with his father Col. Noble Kinnard, in Creek Removal War of 1817–18, allied with US forces. Removed to the Indian Territory in 1829. Chief of the Lower Creeks 1857–63. Principal Chief of the Creeks, 1859–61. Led the Creeks into an alliance with the Confederacy. Appointed col., with titular rank only, April 4, 1864, by virtue of a secret clause in the treaty of alliance the Confederacy made with the Creek Nation. The treaty provided Kinnard would receive the rank and pay of a Confederate colonel of cavalry for life and a rifle. Kinnard died in the Indian Territory near the end of the war, or soon thereafter. Chief Grayson called Kinnard "a man of extraordinary physical stature" (nearly seven feet tall) who "possessed no fitness for the office" of chief.

Kirkpatrick, Milton Leander. Born Aug. 6, 1830, GA. Reared in Montgomery, AL. Prewar Montgomery merchant. Md. Louisa Josephine Moore;

Frances M. Barnes. Lt. "Montgomery Independent Rifles" (Co. E, 6th AL), April 25, 1861. Capt., Dec. 24, 1861. Dropped at 1862 reorganization. Capt. Co. H, 51st AL PR, Sept. 2, 1862. Lt. col., Aug. 12, 1863. Col., Nov. 16, 1863. Paroled Charlotte May 3, 1865. Postwar farmer in Montgomery Co. Involved in railroad promotion. Moved to Highland Home, Crenshaw Co. late in life. Died there Feb. 28, 1892. Buried Fair Prospect Cemetery, north of Highland Home.

Kitchen, Solomon George. Born c. 1820, Roane Co., TN. Moved to Stoddard Co., MO, in 1836. Surveyor. Lawyer. State senator. Judge of county court. President of the Cairo and Fulton Railroad. Md. Martha A. Giboney; Mary Richardson. Capt. Co. C, 2d Cav., 1st Div., MSG, June 15, 1861. Major, Aug. 1, 1861. Lt. col., Sept. 17, 1861. Resigned Dec. 24, 1861. Capt. Co. B, 2d MO Cav, Jan. 26, 1862. Resigned Oct. 16, 1862. Lt. col., Clark's MO Bn., April 9, 1863. Col., 7th MO Cav. (formed from Clark's Bn.), July 9, 1863. WIA Westport. Paroled May 25, 1865, Wittsburg, AR. Postwar lawyer in Bloomfield, Dexter, St. Louis, and Kirkwood, MO. Died April 19, 1891, Kirkwood, MO. Buried Oak Ridge Cemetery, Kirkwood.

Lamar, Charles Augustus Lafayette. Born April 1, 1824, Savannah, GA, the godson of Revolutionary War hero Lafayette. Savannah merchant and alderman prewar. Railroad executive. In vol. militia. Md. Caroline A. Nicholl. Capt., "Savannah Mounted Rifles," April 1861. Col., 26th GA, Oct. 10, 1861, a unit reorganized as the 7th GA Bn. on Nov. 2, 1861 (and later as the 61st GA), with Lamar as lt. col. Resigned as lt. col., March 12, 1862. In 1864 Gov. Brown appointed Lamar a state agent to export state-controlled cotton. In 1865 VADC to Gen. Howell Cobb, head of the GA Reserves. KIA Columbus, GA, April 16, 1865, during the Union attack on that town. Buried Linwood Cemetery, Columbus; reburied Laurel Grove Cemetery, Savannah, in 1866. Lamar is best known as an ardent exponent of reopening the slave trade. In 1858 he was arrested and convicted of operating a slave ship. Papers at Emory U.

Lamar, John Hill. Born c. 1840, GA. Reared in Bibb Co., GA. Attd. UGA and Oglethorpe U. Planter near Macon. Md. Jane A. Carter. Pvt. Co. B, 2d GA Bn., April 20, 1861. Major, 61st GA, Oct. 11, 1861. Lt. col., March 15, 1862. Col., June 1, 1862. WIA Fredericksburg (lost a finger). KIA Monocacy, shot from his horse while leading a charge. Buried Rose Hill Cemetery, Macon. Gen. John B. Gordon thought Lamar "a most promising young officer."

Lamar, Lucius Mirabeau. Born June 25, 1834, Pineville, Bibb Co., GA. Grad. UGA. Wealthy Bibb Co. planter in 1860. Capt., "Macon Guards" vol. militia. Md. Mary Frances Rawls. Capt. Co. C, 8th GA, April 15, 1861. Slightly WIA at 1st Manassas. Major, Sept. 12, 1861. Lt. col., Dec. 24, 1861. Col., Jan. 28, 1862. WIA and POW Garnett's Farm but recaptured the next day. Resigned Dec. 1862. Appointed col. and judge, military court of Beauregard's Corps, Dec. 20, 1862. Pulaski Co. planter postwar. US marshal. State senator 1882–83. Died Feb. 25, 1889, Macon. Buried Rose Hill Cemetery, Macon. One soldier in the 8th called Lamar "the handsomest man in the army . . . and as clever and brave as he was handsome."

Lamar, Lucius Quintus Cincinnatus. Born Sept. 17, 1825, Eatonton, GA. Reared in Covington, GA. Grad. Emory U. Planter and lawyer prewar, in Covington and Macon. State legislator in GA. Professor at UMS, Oxford, MS. Lawyer in Holly Springs, MS. US congressman 1857–61. Delegate to MS Secession Convention and author of that state's ordinance of secession. Md. Virginia Longstreet (cousin of Gen. Longstreet); Henrietta Dean. Lt. col., 19th MS, June 11, 1861. Col., May 5, 1862. Resigned Nov. 24, 1862, citing vertigo and apoplexy. Appointed Confederate commissioner to Russia, Nov. 19, 1862. The Senate never confirmed the appointment, and Lamar returned to the South in 1864. Commissioned col. and judge of the military court, A. P. Hill's Corps, Dec. 3, 1864. Appmx. Postwar lawyer and professor of law at the UMS. A leading voice for sectional reconciliation after the war. US congressman 1873–77. US senator 1877–84. Sec. of the Interior, 1885–88. Justice, US Supreme Court, 1888–93. Died Jan. 23, 1893, Vineville, GA, while returning home to MS. Buried St. Peter's Cemetery, Oxford. Brother of Col. T. B. Lamar.

Lamar, Thomas Gresham. Born May 28, 1826, Edgefield, SC. Attd. SCMA. Edgefield planter. Elected state representative in 1860. Md. Mary Whatley; Sarah Dunbar. Lt. col. of State Troops during the bombardment of Fort Sumter. Capt., 2d SC Art. Bn., Oct. 10, 1861. Promoted to major and lt. col. at unspecified dates. Col., 2d SC Art. (formed from the 2d Bn.). WIA Secessionville while defending a fort named after him. Considered the hero of that battle. Died Oct. 17, 1862, of malaria, in a Charleston hotel. Buried Lamar family cemetery, Hamburg, SC. An obituary notes Lamar's "fearless determination and honesty of purpose."

Lamar, Thompson Bird. Born Jan. 27, 1828, Oxford, GA. Grad. Jefferson Medical College. Brother of Col. Lucius Q. C. Lamar. Prewar planter in Jefferson Co., FL. Very wealthy. State legislator. Delegate to FL Secession Convention. Md. Sarah B. Bailey. Capt. Co. I, 1st FL, April 5, 1861. Honorably discharged, Jan. 30, 1862. Elected lt. col., 5th FL, April 8, 1862. WIA Antietam. AAG to Gen. Joseph Johnston, 1862–63. Col., July 6, 1863. WIA Wilderness, May 6, 1864, in the left hand and leg. KIA near Petersburg, Aug. 30, 1864. "Highly cultivated in mind . . . [A] perfect gentleman."

Lamb, Jonathan J. Born Dec. 14, 1833, TN. Attd. Cumberland U. Law School. Lawyer in Paris, Henry Co., prewar. State representative 1857–59. Pvt. Co. C, 5th TN, July 16, 1861. Major, May 6, 1862. Col., Dec. 27, 1862. Detached to Conscript Bureau, Feb. 5, 1863, when regiment consolidated with 4th TN. Returned to 4th/5th for Atlanta Campaign. MWIA by a sharpshooter May 28, 1864, Ellsbury Ridge, GA. Died the next day. Buried City Cemetery, Paris. Eulogized as "one of our bravest and best officers."

Lamb, William Harvey. Born Sept. 27, 1835, Norfolk, VA. Attd. Norfolk Academy and Rappahannock Military Academy. Attd. William & Mary College. Editor, Norfolk *Argus* (a newspaper his influential father owned) before the war. Officer in vol. militia. Md. Sarah Anne Chaffee. Capt. Co. C, 6th VA, April 18, 1861. Major and QM, Dept. of Cape Fear, Sept. 24, 1861. Col., 2d NC Art. (36th NC), Sept. 19, 1862. Built Fort Fisher and commanded that fort. WIA and POW in the capture of Fort Fisher in Jan. 1865. Bank president and mayor of Norfolk postwar. Died there March 23, 1909. Buried Elmwood Cemetery, Norfolk. Lamb's article on Fort Fisher appears in *Battles and Leaders*. Diary at William & Mary College.

Lampkin, Alexander Woods. Born Nov. 3, 1815, Madison Co., AL. Prewar merchant in Columbus, MS, and Mobile. Md. Margaret Barnett. Major, 2d AL Militia. Lt. col., 2d AL Militia, 1862. Capt. Co. A, 1st Mobile Inf. LDT (aka 1st Mobile Volunteers), July 20, 1863. Col., Aug. 28, 1863. Unit served in the Mobile defenses 1863–65. Postwar cotton factor in Mobile. Later farmed in Oktibbeha Co., MS. Died April 10, 1890, Starkville, MS. Buried Odd Fellows Cemetery, Starkville.

Lampley, Charles Harris D. Born Aug. 22, 1833, NC. Went by his middle name of "Harris." Prewar merchant in Louisville, AL. Pvt., "Eufaula Rifles" (Co. B, 1st AL), 1861. Capt. Co. A, 45th AL, Feb. 18, 1862. Major, Nov. 4, 1862. Lt. col., March 25, 1863. Col., Oct. 28, 1863. WIA in shoulder and POW at Battle of Atlanta, died Aug. 24, 1864, at a Union hospital in Marietta, GA. Buried City Cemetery, Louisville. "Prompt, energetic, decisive, brave." Lampley died of chagrin over being captured, according to the Union colonel who captured him. However, an eyewitness disputes the oft-repeated story of his capture and death.

Landry, Joseph Octave. Born June 15, 1835, Ascension Parish, LA. Prewar planter in Ascension and St. Landry Parishes. Sugar broker in New Orleans. Md. Sophia Kennedy. Commanded militia battalion 1861–62. Lt. col., 29th LA, May 3, 1862. POW Vicksburg. Lt. col., 22d LA Consolidated (formed from the Vicksburg parolees of the LA regiments in the Vicksburg garrison), Jan. 26, 1864. Col., Feb. 4, 1864. Transferred to TMD May 26, 1864. Paroled June 24, 1865, Washington, LA. Resided in New Orleans postwar. Warehouseman. City comptroller and administrator of commerce. Died Oct. 1, 1889, New Orleans. Buried St. Louis Cemetery No. 2. A contemporary called him "over six feet in stature, robust and red faced in proportion, physically one of the most powerful men in the state."

Lane, Andrew Jackson. Born June 6, 1822, VA, but grew up in GA. Wealthy planter in Hancock Co., GA, prewar, owning a 1,500-acre plantation east of Sparta. Md. Frances Brooking. Capt. Co. I, 49th GA, March 4, 1862. Col., March 22, 1862. WIA Seven Pines and Mechanicsville (elbow shattered). Resigned May 8, 1863. Moved to his property in Macon postwar. Railroad president. State legislator. Died Jan. 2, 1886, at his son-in-law's home in Sparta, GA. Buried Rose Hill Cemetery, Macon. "Just, upright, honorable and public-spirited."

Lane, John Randolph. Born July 4, 1835, Chatham Co., NC. Farmer and merchant in Chatham Co. prewar. Md. Mary E. Siler. Corp. Co. G, 26th NC, June 10, 1861. Capt., Sept. 2, 1861. Lt. col., Aug. 19, 1862. Col., July 1, 1863. WIA Gettysburg (neck and head), Wilderness (thigh), and Reams Station (breast). In a Danville hospital at the time the ANV surrendered at Appomattox. Paroled May 2, 1865, Greensboro. Chatham Co. merchant postwar. Operated cotton gin and gristmill. Died Dec. 31, 1908, Ore Hill, NC. Buried Brush Creek Baptist Church, near his Chatham Co. home. Soldiers remembered his "unbounded patience, forbearance, kindness, sagacity and presence of mind." He sported a full beard his entire life to conceal his Gettysburg wound. Papers at UNC.

Lang, David. Born May 9, 1838, Camden Co., GA. Grad. GMI 1857. Surveyor. Moved to Suwanee Co., FL, just prior to the war. Md. Mary Campbell. Pvt. Co. H, 1st FL, April 2, 1861. 2d sgt., May 10, 1861. 1st sgt., Oct. 1, 1861. Mustered out April 6, 1862. Capt. Co. C, 8th FL, May 10, 1862. WIA Antietam. Col., Oct. 2, 1862. Badly wounded in head at Fredericksburg, the day before the main battle. Often led the ANV's FL Brigade, due to Gen. Perry's illnesses, but (for reasons not apparent to historians) never given permanent command of the brigade. Led brigade at Gettysburg and Appomattox. Postwar store clerk in Suwanee. Civil engineer. Cashier of the FL State Hospital. State adj. gen. Private secretary to governor. Died Dec. 13, 1917, Tallahassee. Buried Old City Cemetery, Tallahassee. Lang's war letters have been published.

Langhorne, Maurice Scaisbrooke. Born March 27, 1823, Cumberland Co., VA. Reared in Lynchburg. Tobacco merchant in Lynchburg prewar. Capt. of vol. militia. Md. Anne Maria Rodes; Elizabeth G. Means; Ann S. Langhorne. Capt. Co. A, 11th VA, April 22, 1861. WIA Seven Pines. Major, Aug. 21, 1861. Lt. col., May 7, 1862. Col., Sept. 24, 1863. Detailed to post duty at Lynchburg, due to his wound. Retired Dec. 20, 1864. On engineering duty at Richmond and Lynchburg in 1865. Paroled April 15, 1865, Lynchburg. Insurance agent and tobacco manufacturer in Lynchburg postwar. Died there March 27, 1908, buried Spring Hill Cemetery.

Lanier, Thomas C. Born 1823, York Co., SC. To Pickens Co., AL, in 1840. Wealthy farmer and county commissioner. Md. Sarah Cureton. Capt. Co. B, 2d AL, April 1, 1861. Lt. col., 42d AL, May 26, 1862. Col., probably 1863. WIA Corinth, Selma. POW Vicksburg. WIA New Hope Church, Selma. Operated orange groves near Leesburg, FL, postwar. Died Nov. 26, 1891, near Leesburg. Buried Lone Oak Cemetery, Leesburg.

Lankford, Augustus Rufus. Born Nov. 7, 1823, Humphreys Co., TN. Farmer in Waverly, TN. Town constable. Pvt. 3d US Inf. in Mexican War. Md. Amelia Taylor; Mary Wyly. 1st lt. Co. D, 2d AL, April 1, 1861. Capt., Aug. 31, 1861. Capt. 38th AL, March 17, 1862. Lt. col., May 15, 1862. POW near Lavergne, TN, Oct. 7, 1862. Paroled 2 days later. Col., Nov. 13, 1863. WIA Rocky Face, Feb. 1864. POW Resaca May 15, 1864, while carrying his regiment's colors, his Union captors "deeming him too brave to be shot." Imprisoned at Johnson's Island, exchanged Feb. 20, 1865. Paroled May 11, 1865. Postwar farmer in Waverly. Died Sept. 27, 1887. Buried Wyly Cemetery, Humphreys Co.

Lawrence, Robert Josiah. Born 1825, AL. Grew up in La Grange, AL. Clerk in Mobile in 1850. Moved to Shubata, Clarke Co., MS, in the 1850s. Mexican War veteran. Md. Mary Ledyard. Capt. Co. A, 14th MS, March 28, 1861. POW Fort Donelson. Exch. Sept. 1862. Major, Oct. 18, 1862. Lt. col., March 16, 1864. Col., 14th MS Consolidated, April 9, 1865. Resided in Clarke Co. postwar. Died Aug. 20, 1887, Shubata. Buried Magnolia Cemetery, Mobile.

Lawther, Robert Ralston. Born Jan. 21, 1836, Warren Co., PA. Prewar store clerk in Newburg, NY, and Muscatine, IA. Grocer in Jefferson City, MO. Md. Ellen E. Hoopes. VADC to Gen. A. E. Steen, MSG, 1861. Col., 1st Cav., 6th Div., MSG, 1861. Major, 1st MO Cav., Dec. 31, 1861. Authorized June 2, 1862, to raise a regiment of PR. Commissioned col. of cav., May 28, 1862, under this authorization. Captured near Batesville, AR, while recruiting. Taken to Gratiot St. Prison and later exchanged. Col., 10th MO Cav., Dec. 12, 1863. Resigned Feb. 27, 1865, due to ill health (hepatitis, prostration, and "phthistosis pulmonalis"). Paroled June 20, 1865, Galveston. He tried to return to PA after the war, but a delegation of local citizens requested that he depart. Postwar farmer/grocer in Galveston, Brenham, and Dallas, TX. Dallas alderman. Died Oct. 1, 1911, Dallas. Buried Oakland Cemetery, Dallas. Gen. Fagan regarded Lawther as a "gallant and competent officer."

Lawton, Winburn Joseph. Born Sept. 30, 1817, Beaufort Dist., SC. Wealthy planter in Dougherty Co., GA, prewar. Railroad builder. Officer in vol. militia. State senator 1847–48, 1855–56. Md. Harriet Jaudon; Sarah Lewis. Capt. Co. B ("Dougherty Hussars"), Cobb's Legion, Aug. 10, 1861. Col., 2d GA Cav., May 7, 1862. Resigned in the middle of the 1862 KY Campaign (accepted Oct. 22,

1862), to take care of his family. Lived in Macon, GA, and Jacksonville, FL, postwar. Merchant, factor, banker, railroad promoter, house builder. Died Sept. 6, 1884, Macon. Buried Rose Hill Cemetery, Macon. The ever-critical Tom Cobb thought Lawton "won't fight" and considered him a "hypocritical dog" for resigning his captaincy. Gen. Alexander Lawton was a cousin.

Lay, Benjamin Dudley. Born c. 1830, MO. Physician in Paducah and Henderson, KY, prewar. Md. Pauline ——; Nannie Carlos. Pvt., then sgt., 3d KY, enlisting July 5, 1861. Appointed asst. surgeon, PACS, March 5, 1862, serving first with the 45th MS, then as a general surgeon. Received permission in Jan. 1864 to recruit a regiment within Union lines in MS. Col., Lay's MS Cav. (aka 20th Confederate Cav.), April 23, 1864. The unit remained a mere skeleton (his volunteers were conscripted before they could join up with him) and was consolidated with other units in Feb. 1865. Insurance agent and physician postwar in Atlanta, in Mobile, and in Grenada, MS. Noted duelist, who claimed to have acted as principal or second in 42 "affairs of honor." Alive in 1880 in Mobile. Died Aug. 1881. Buried Catholic Cemetery, Mobile.

Lay, John Fitzhugh. Born Nov. 2, 1826, Richmond, VA. Attd. UVA. Prewar lawyer and judge in Powhatan Co. Md. Caroline McCaw. Lt., Powhatan Cav. Troop vol. militia, enlisted April 15, 1861. Unit assigned to Gen. Beauregard's HQ. Capt. Co. E, 4th VA Cav., July 1, 1861. Resigned April 29, 1862. Capt. and AAG to Gen. Beauregard, April 29, 1862. Appointed (by Beauregard) col., 6th (aka 1st) Confederate Cav., c. June 4, 1862. Did not get elected col. in Sept. 1862 when regiment formally organized and returned to his staff duties. Major, Dec. 4, 1863. AAIG to Gens. Jones and Hardee, 1863–65. Inspector of Cav., Dept. of SC, GA, and FL. Associated with the Life Insurance Co. of Virginia postwar. Moved to FL to raise oranges but returned to Richmond when his health failed. Died April 16, 1900, Richmond. Buried Shockoe Cemetery, Richmond. An obituary called Lay "a man of scholarly attainments, a gentleman of the old school, and a man of the truest character." His elder brothers were Bishop Henry Lay and Lt. Col. George W. Lay.

Layton, Pierre Soule. Born Jan. 18, 1839, Charleston, SC. Grad. SCMA. Moved to Rankin Co., MS, to become superintendent of the Brandon State Military School. Md. Mary W. Reber; Mary Douglas; Almedia Lewis. AAG 2d brigade, MS State Troops, 1861. Lt. col., 4th MS, Aug. 24, 1861. Col., Oct. 1, 1862. Often absent due to illness. Resigned July 16, 1863, due to lung hemorrhages and bronchitis. Staff officer with the MS State Troops, 1864. Postwar "agent" in Rankin, Lauderdale, and Wayne Cos. Civil engineer. Committed suicide April 2, 1906, Andalusia, AL. Buried Mt. Zion Cemetery, Buckatunna, Wayne Co. Gen. S. D. Lee found Layton "perfectly reliable."

Lea, Benjamin James. Born Jan. 1, 1833, Caswell Co., NC. Attd. Wake Forest U. Lawyer in Brownsville, Haywood Co., TN, prewar. State representative 1859–61. Md. Mary C. Currie. Appointed asst. QM, TN Provisional Army, June 21, 1861. Col., 52d TN, Jan. 1862. Honorably discharged April 23, 1862, when regiment consolidated with 51st TN. Commanded post of Huntsville, AL, in 1863. In 1865 the War Dept. declared the consolidation illegal and Lea was recommissioned col. to rank from April 27, 1863. Brownsville lawyer postwar. State senator. State attorney general 1878–86. Justice, TN Supreme Court. Died March 15, 1894, Brownsville. Buried Oakwood Cemetery, Brownsville. According to a death notice, Lea had "a big brain and a big heart."

Lea, John Willis. Born Sept. 18, 1838, Leasburg, NC. Reared in Caswell Co. and Holly Springs, MS. Attd. USMA, resigning in 1861. Md. Maggie Goodrich Durfey; Mrs. Kate Wilson. 2d lt., CS Regular Army, March 16, 1861. Capt. Co. I, 5th NC, May 16, 1861. Lt. col., Feb. 2, 1862. WIA (leg) and POW Williamsburg. Exch. Nov. 1862. WIA Chancellorsville (head) and Opequon Creek. Col., May 12, 1864. Commanded R. D. Johnston's Brigade in 1865. Appmx. Went into the lumber business with his brother-in-law in Williamsburg, VA, postwar. Episcopal minister in Coalburg and St. Albans, WVA. Died May 15, 1884, Shadwell, VA. Buried Teay's Cemetery, St. Albans. A "very intelligent officer," nicknamed "Gimlet" at West Point because of his long, lean build. His best friend at West Point, future Union general George Custer, was best man at Lea's 1862 wedding in Williamsburg, when Lea was still a Union prisoner.

Ledbetter, Daniel Alexander. Born July 18, 1828, near Pendleton, SC. Millwright in Townville prewar. Militia colonel. Md. Elizabeth E. Vandiver. Capt. Co. A, 1st SC Rifles, 1861. Major, July 23, 1861. Lt. col., Jan. 29, 1862. Col., Aug. 29, 1862. MWIA 2d Manassas. Died Sept. 1, 1862, VA. Buried Bushy Park Farm, on Route 676, Prince William Co., VA. A junior officer said Ledbetter was "much esteemed for conscientiousness, vigilance and courage."

Lee, Charles Cochrane. Born Feb. 2, 1834, Charleston, SC, son of Col. Stephen Lee. Grad. USMA 1856. Lt., US Army, 1856–59. Teacher at NC Military Institute in Charlotte, 1859–61. Md. Anna Fripp. Sent by the state of NC to purchase military supplies in the North, Jan. 1861. 1st lt., CS Regular Army, Dec. 1, 1861. Lt. col., 1st (Bethel) NC, a 6-month unit, May 11, 1861. Col., Sept. 1, 1861. Mustered out Nov. 12/13, 1861. Col., 37th NC, Nov. 20, 1861. KIA Frayser's Farm by a cannonball. Buried Elmwood Cemetery, Charlotte. Lee "was as brave as a lion and gentle as a lamb."

Lee, George Washington. Born Sept. 25, 1831, De Kalb Co., GA. Sawmill owner in De Kalb Co. and Atlanta. Major in state militia. Sgt. in vol. militia. Md. Nancy Dean. Capt. Co. D, 1st GA Confederate, March 25, 1861. Resigned Aug.

6, 1861. Pvt. Co. M, 38th GA, Sept. 26, 1861. Lt. col., Oct. 11, 1861. Col., Feb. 18, 1862. Resigned July 14, 1862, due to tuberculosis. Capt. and provost marshal of Atlanta, July 15, 1862. Major, June 30, 1863. Resigned June 3, 1864. Major in the state service, May 2, 1863. Lt. col., 3d GA State Guard Bn. (the Atlanta Fire Bn.), a 6-month unit raised in Aug. 1863. Lt. col., 25th GA Cav. Bn. (provost guard). Lee was post commander in Atlanta for most of the war. Lived in Conyers, Cartersville, and Rome postwar. Railroad engineer. Inventor. Owned iron works. Died April 3, 1879, Rome. Buried Myrtle Hill Cemetery, Rome. Gen. Bragg thought Lee illiterate and a swindler of company funds while captain. The former charge, at least, is demonstrably untrue—Lee's correspondence in his service record is impeccable. Gov. Brown said Lee "proved to be a faithful, energetic, and in every way acceptable officer" as post commander.

Lee, Richard Henry. Born Aug. 24, 1821, Alexandria, VA. Distant cousin of Robert E. Lee. Reared in Alexandria and Washington, DC. Prewar lawyer in Charlestown, VA. Commonwealth attorney for Jefferson Co. Md. Evelyn Boyd Page. Lt. Co. G, 2d VA, April 18, 1861. WIA Kernstown. Col. and presiding judge, military court of Jackson's Corps, Dec. 16, 1862. POW Sept. 22, 1863, Orange Co., VA. Exch. Jan. 29, 1864. Paroled April 19, 1865, Winchester. Postwar lawyer in Millwood, VA. Judge. Died June 18, 1902, "Grafton," Clarke Co., VA. Buried Old Chapel Cemetery, Millwood.

Lee, Roswell Walter. Born Aug. 12, 1810, Hamden, CT, son of a US Army colonel. Reared in Springfield, MA. Attd. Norwich U. Grad. USMA 1833. Lt., US Army, 1833–38. Dismissed for "signing false certificates." Settled in Fannin Co., TX. County clerk, surveyor, militia colonel. Md. Susannah Jackson. Lt. and ADC to Col. Douglas Cooper, 1861. WIA Chusto Talasah. 2d lt. Co. E, 1st Choctaw and Chickasaw, 1862. Transferred to Gen. Hindman's staff, Nov. 1862. Major, acting chief of ordnance, 1st Corps, TMD, late 1862. Capt. and ADC to Hindman, Dec. 28, 1862. Assigned to Lee's TX Battery, c. May 1863. Asst. superintendent of Indian affairs. Promoted to col. Aug. 21, 1864. Commanding post of Fort Arbuckle, Indian Territory, in 1865. Paroled July 7, 1865, as col. Died Dec. 20, 1873, Bonham, TX. Buried Pioneer's Rest Cemetery, Fort Worth. His promotion to colonel probably came via appointment by Gen. Kirby Smith. A man of great talents, who would have risen far "but for his love of strong drink."

Lee, Stephen. Born June 7, 1801, Charleston, SC. Father of Col. C. C. Lee and uncle of Gen. Stephen D. Lee. Attd. USMA. Teacher at SCMA and at a boys school in Asheville, NC, prewar. Md. Caroline Lee; Mrs. Sarah Morrison. Col., 16th NC, June 17, 1861 (also elected col., 15th NC, on that date). Resigned Feb. 13, 1862, due to old age, diarrhea, and swelling of the legs. Capt. of a company of LDT (the "Silver Grays") in NC late in the war. Tobacco farmer in Buncombe

Co. postwar. Died Aug. 2, 1879, Asheville. Buried Riverside Cemetery, Asheville. Lee fathered 14 children, including 9 sons who served in the Confederate army. A soldier in the 16th praised Lee as "a strict disciplinarian."

Lemoyne, George W. Born c. 1815, VA. May have fought in the Texas Revolution. Moved to Conway Co., AR. Later to Dardanelle, AR. Teacher. Lawyer. State representative and senator. Md. Penelope Walton. Capt. of a company of the 17th AR, 1861. Elected col., 17th AR, upon Aug. 1861 organization. Commissioned col. to rank from Jan. 3, 1862. Resigned probably in 1862, though Lemoyne's skimpy service record does not give any date. Postwar lawyer in Dardanelle. Died July 27, 1867, of pneumonia, at his Dardanelle home. Probably buried in an unmarked grave at Bearley Cemetery, Dardanelle, where his wife and family are buried. An obituary asserted that "his life obtained the admiration of all who knew him."

Leovy, Henry Jefferson. Born May 17, 1826, Augusta, GA. Family moved to New Orleans in 1832. Studied law in KY and at ULA. New Orleans lawyer. "Energetic and brilliant" editor of the New Orleans *Delta*. Enlisted for Mexican War. Md. Elizabeth A. Monroe. Leovy, an associate of Horace Hunley, helped finance the CSS *Hunley*. After the fall of New Orleans, he went to TX and was involved in the cotton trade. Appointed in 1864 special Confederate commissioner to investigate charges of disloyalty in southwest VA. Appointed col. and judge, military court of the Dept. of Southwest VA, Dec. 26, 1864. After the fall of Richmond he joined Pres. Davis and his old friend Judah Benjamin in their flight south. Postwar lawyer in New Orleans. City attorney. Died Oct. 3, 1902, at his New Orleans home. Buried Live Oak Cemetery, Pass Christian, MS.

Lester, James Dunovan. Born Sept. 4, 1829, Newberry Co., SC. Reared in Yalobusha and Lafayette Cos., MS. Lafayette Co. physician prewar. Md. Josephine Oliver. Capt. Co. K, 22d MS, July 1, 1861. Col., Nov. 12, 1862. WIA July 14, 1863. Service record is very skimpy. Farmed in Lafayette Co. postwar. Died June 26, 1879. Buried St. Peter's Cemetery, Oxford.

Lester, Richard Paul. Born Nov. 30, 1832, Lawrenceville, GA. Reared in Cummings. Prewar attorney in Cummings. Md. Mary Jane Waddell. Capt. Co. E (the "Lester Volunteers"), 14th GA, July 4, 1861. Major, Nov. 8, 1862. Lt. col., May 10, 1863. Col., May 8, 1864. Appmx. Cummings lawyer postwar. Moved to Covington c. 1901. Died Nov. 29, 1902, at his son's home in Midway, GA. Buried Southview Cemetery, Covington. An obituary says Lester "was highly esteemed and beloved by everyone who knew him."

Letcher, Samuel Houston. Born Feb. 23, 1828, Rockbridge Co., VA. Brother of wartime Gov. John Letcher. Attd. Washington College. Attorney in Lexington prewar. Unmd. Capt. Co. B, 5th VA, April 1861. Capt., PAVA, May 7, 1861. Lt. col., 58th VA, Oct. 13, 1861. Col., May 1, 1862. Resigned Oct. 30, 1862, due to ill health. Newspaper editor in Lexington postwar. Died there Nov. 10, 1868. Buried Stonewall Jackson Cemetery, Lexington. "A brave soldier, an able editor, a true and loyal friend."

Levy, William Mallory. Born Oct. 31, 1827, Isle of Wight Co., VA. Grad. William & Mary College. Attorney in Norfolk, VA. Lt. in Mexican War. To Natchitoches, LA, in 1852. Practiced law there. Militia major. State representative 1859–61. Md. Catherine E. Bausch. Capt. Co. A, 2d LA, May 11, 1861. Col., July 19, 1861. Dropped at May 1, 1862, reorganization. AAG to Gen. Richard Taylor, appointed July 31, 1862. Lt. col. and AIG to Taylor, fall 1864. He was the sole officer to accompany Taylor at the final surrender of Taylor's command. Paroled May 10, 1865, Meridian. Postwar Natchitoches lawyer. US congressman 1875–77. Justice, LA Supreme Court, 1880–82. Died Aug. 14, 1882, Saratoga, NY. Buried American Cemetery, Natchitoches. Levy was a favorite officer of Gens. Magruder and Taylor. Gen. Howell Cobb thought Levy's failure to win re-election "a public calamity."

Lewis, Joseph C. Born April 3, 1816, Charleston, SC. Prewar merchant in Yazoo City, MS. Moved to New Orleans in the 1850s. Commission merchant and cotton factor there. Md. Mary Ann Hays, sister of Gen. Harry Hays. Lt. col., 25th LA, March 20, 1862. 25th consolidated with 16th LA, Nov. 30, 1862. Col. of the consolidated regiment, Dec. 31, 1862. On recruiting duty throughout much of 1863. KIA Jonesboro, Aug. 31, 1864. Probably buried Jonesboro's Confederate Cemetery. Gen. Gibson thought Lewis "a zealous, brave, and intelligent officer."

Lewis, Levin Major. Born Jan. 6, 1832, Baltimore, MD. Reared in Dorchester Co. Attd. MD Military Institute and Wesleyan U. in CT. Methodist minister in Liberty, MO. Principal of Plattsburg College. Md. Margaret Barrow. Capt., "Washington Guards," 3d Inf., 5th Div., MSG, 1861. Col., 3d Inf., 5th Div., MSG, summer 1861; resigned Nov. 1861. Capt. Co. A, 7th MO, June 18, 1862. WIA Lone Jack. Major, 1862. Lt. col., Dec. 4, 1862. Col., March 24, 1863. WIA and POW Helena. Exch. Sept. 1864. Declined an appointment to the Confederate Senate. Led brigade in TMD. Assigned to duty as brig. gen., May 16, 1865. Led the fight against surrender of the TMD. Postwar Methodist minister in Shreveport, Galveston, St. Louis, Waxahachie, Dallas. President of Marvin College in Waxahachie. Died May 28, 1886, Los Angeles, CA, where he had gone for his health. Buried Greenwood Cemetery, Dallas. A profound scholar, "popular and attractive, humorous and magnetic."

Lewis, Robert Nicholas. Born Jan. 11, 1836, Scottsville, VA. Reared in Nashville, TN. Wealthy planter in Bolivar Co., MS, prewar. Md. Margaret Watt;

Emma Frayser. Major, 34th TN, Aug. 5, 1861. Lt. col., April 16, 1862. WIA Chickamauga. Col., Oct. 2, 1863. Resigned Feb. 27, 1865, because of wounds. Owner of cotton press in New Orleans postwar. Died March 31, 1886, Philadelphia, PA. Buried New Orleans.

Lewis, Trevanion Dudley. Born c. 1836, LA. Clerk in Baton Rouge, age 24, on 1860 census. Md. Estelle E. DeRussy. Lt. Co. A, 8th LA, June 19, 1861. Regimental adj., 1861–62. Major, May 7, 1862. WIA Antietam. Lt. col., Oct. 15, 1862. Col., April 6, 1863. POW at Fredericksburg, May 4, 1863. Paroled 2 weeks later and exch. KIA Gettysburg, July 2, 1863. Buried on the battlefield; probably reburied postwar in Hollywood Cemetery, Richmond. An obituary called Lewis a "modest and unobtrusive gentleman." Lewis's father came from Ohio, and he had numerous relatives in the Union army.

Liddell, Philip Franklin. Born April 25, 1824, GA. Parents moved to MS in the 1830s. Resided in Choctaw Co., MS. State representative 1854–55. Officer in Mexican War. Carroll Co. lawyer in 1860. Unmd. Capt. Co. K, 11th MS, Feb. 26, 1861. Appointed AAG, Army of MS, March 12, 1861. Lt. col., May 4, 1861. Col., April 21, 1862. MWIA Antietam, Sept. 16, 1862, in skirmishing the day before the main battle. Died Sept. 25, 1862, at the home of Pastor Andrews, in Shepherdstown, VA. Buried Evergreen Cemetery, Carrolton, MS. Gen. Longstreet considered Liddell "an officer of great merit, modesty, and promise."

Lightfoot, Charles Edward. Born April 18, 1834, Culpeper Co., VA. Grad. VMI. Teacher at Culpeper Military Institute and Hillsboro (NC) Military Academy prewar. Md. Georgianna Chapin. Capt. of artillery at Fort Macon, NC, in state service, early 1861. Major, 6th NC, May 16, 1861. WIA 1st Manassas. Lt. col., July 11, 1861. Briefly commanded the 5th AL Bn. in 1862. Col., 22d NC, March 29, 1862. POW Seven Pines. Sent to Fort Delaware. Exch. Aug. 5, 1862. While in prison, Lightfoot lost reelection at the 22d's June 13, 1862, reorganization. Lt. col. of art., Aug. 18, 1862. Commanded a battalion of artillery in the Richmond defenses the remainder of the war. Paroled April 24, 1865, Richmond. Professor at Bethel Military Academy in Culpeper postwar. Died July 3, 1887 (not 1878, as given in some sources), Culpeper. Buried Masonic Cemetery north of Culpeper. Gen. Pender thought Lightfoot a good drill officer and assistant but "an ass."

Lightfoot, James Newell. Born Aug. 14, 1839, Blakely, GA. Family moved to Henry Co., AL in 1849. Clerk in Abbeville. Md. Mrs. Mary Gordon McAllister. 2d lt. Co. A, 6th AL (the "Henry Grays"), May 11, 1861. Capt., Nov. 30, 1861. Lt. col., May 30, 1862. Col., May 7, 1863. WIA Seven Pines, Antietam, Gettysburg, Spotsylvania. Retired to Invalid Corps March 11, 1865. Farmed in Henry Co. postwar. Cotton broker in Savannah, GA, and Eufaula, AL. Died Sept. 18, 1885,

Eufaula. Buried Abbeville City Cemetery. The wartime letters of the Lightfoot brothers have been published.

Likens, James Benjamin. Born c. 1830, Morgan Co., GA. Prewar lawyer in Rusk and Jefferson Cos., TX. Mexican War veteran. Md. Salina A. Cameron. Capt., "Sabine Guards," TX militia, in 1861. Organized a mixed battalion in late 1861, under orders from Gen. Hebert, which was later Likens's Inf. Bn. Major, 6th (Likens's) Inf. Bn., 1862. Major, then lt. col., Likens's TX Cav. Bn., at unknown dates. Col., 35th TX Cav. (formed from his battalion), Oct. 23, 1863. Paroled, Sabine Pass, July 12, 1865. Postwar lawyer in Jefferson Co., Galveston and Houston. State legislator. Died Sept. 18, 1878, Houston. Buried Glenwood Cemetery, Houston. A Confederate congressman called him "a noble fellow when sober but a dreadful nuisance when intoxicated."

Lillard, John Mason. Born May 14, 1827, Rhea (later Meigs) Co., TN. Grad. UPA and U. of Nashville Medical Schools. Physician and lawyer in Decatur, Meigs Co., prewar. State representative 1853–55. Mexican War veteran. Md. Mary Jane Thomas. 1st lt. Co. B, 26th TN, June 14, 1861. Capt., June 14, 1861. Col., Sept. 6, 1861. WIA and POW Fort Donelson. Exch. MWIA Chickamauga, Sept. 19, 1863. Died the next day. Buried first on the battlefield, later in the Upper Goodfield Baptist Churchyard, Meigs Co. Brother of Col. N. J. Lillard. Lillard family papers are at TSLA.

Lillard, Newton Jackson. Born April 18, 1832, Cocke Co., TN. Merchant and farmer in Decatur, Meigs Co., TN, prewar. County clerk 1858–60. Mexican War veteran. Md. Elma Caroline Worth. Enlisted May 2, 1861. Capt. Co. I, June 1, 1861. Lt. col., May 14, 1862. Col., Sept. 17, 1862. POW Vicksburg and paroled. Regiment mounted, late 1863. Meigs Co. dry goods merchant, farmer postwar. Circuit Court clerk. Died Oct. 22, 1905, Decatur. Buried Decatur Cemetery. Brother of Col. J. M. Lillard.

Lindsay, Andrew Jackson. Born Dec. 1820, Limestone Co., AL. Attd. USMA. Capt., US Army, 1848–61. Md. Jane Delany. Major, CS Regular Army, Sept. 14, 1861. Capt. on staff of Gen. A. S. Johnston. Col., 1st MS Cav., April 2, 1862. WIA Shiloh. Not reelected at the reorganization that summer. Paroled June 1865. Farmer near St. Louis, MO, postwar. Died June 3, 1895, St. Louis. Buried Calvary Cemetery, St. Louis. Lindsay's lt. col. found him "a very reticent, but agreeable, gentleman" who "seemed to have no energy, and devolved on me very largely the duties he ought to have performed. His chief pleasure and only occupation . . . was in playing solitaire."

Lipscomb, Thomas Jefferson. Born March 27, 1833, Asheville Dist., SC. Attd. UVA. Grad. SC Medical College and Jefferson Medical College. Shortly after graduation he was called home to manage his father's plantation. Planter in Laurens and Newberry prewar. Md. Hattie Harrington. Lt. Co. B, 3d SC, April 14, 1861. ADC to Gens. Bonham (his uncle) and Kershaw, 1861–62. Raised a cavalry company and resigned as lt., May 4, 1862. Capt. Co. G, 2d SC Cav., June 20, 1862. Major, Aug. 22, 1862. Lt. col., June 10, 1863. Col., Sept. 1, 1863. Cotton merchant in Newberry postwar. Moved to Columbia in 1878. Head of the state penitentiary. Mayor of Columbia. Died Nov. 4, 1908, Columbia. Buried Rosemont Cemetery, Newberry. Col. John L. Black found Lipscomb "would never learn Red Tape."

Little, Francis Hamilton. Born c. 1839, GA. Grad. UGA, 1861. Lawyer in Lafayette, GA. Unmd. Lt. Co. G, 11th GA, July 3, 1861. Major, July 11, 1862. Col., Nov. 8, 1862 (by election). WIA Gettysburg and Reams Station. Called "dashing" by a wartime newspaperman. Led G. T. Anderson's brigade late in the war. Returned to GA postwar. Elected to US Congress in 1867 but not seated. Died May 17, 1868, at his father's home in Walker Co., GA. Believed to be buried on his father's farm in an unmarked grave.

Littlefield, Asahel. Born Dec. 24, 1811, Spartanburg, SC. Farmer in Cass (later Gordon) Co., GA, prewar. Md. Elizabeth Miller; Mary Bradley Stanton. Lt. col., 8th GA Inf. Bn., spring 1862. Elected col., 33d GA (organized Nov. 1861 as the 30th), Nov. 1861. However, only seven companies voted in the election. The needed three additional companies never joined, and the regiment was disbanded. Gordon Co. farmer and mill operator postwar. Died Dec. 24, 1882, Gordon Co. Buried Hayes Cemetery, near Folsom, Bartow Co.

Livingston, Henry James. Born July 27, 1833, near Prattville, AL. Prewar Prattville lawyer. Md. Eleanor Stewart. Pvt. Co. H, 3d AL Cav., May 2, 1861. Discharged due to disability May 20, 1862. Lt. col., 7th AL Cav., July 22, 1863. In Jan. 1864 he requested authority to organize a regiment of cavalry out of unattached companies. Col., 8th AL Cav., March 14, 1864, assigned to duty by order of Gen. Polk. Resumed his Prattville law practice postwar. Delegate to 1875 AL constitutional convention. Died Sept. 13, 1907, Prattville. Buried Oak Hill Cemetery, Prattville. "[A] gallant officer."

Livingston, James William. Born Aug. 12, 1832, Abbeville Dist., SC. Grad. USC. Lawyer in Abbeville. Moved to Pendleton Dist. in 1858. Planter there. Md. Clara Kilpatrick, sister of Col. F. W. Kilpatrick. Capt. Co. A, 1st SC Rifles, July 20, 1861. Major, Jan. 29, 1862. Col., Sept. 1, 1862. "Fainted from heat" at Antietam. Resigned Nov. 12, 1862, due to ill health. Lawyer postwar. Moved to Seneca in 1874. Newspaper editor. State senator 1876–80. Died Aug. 25, 1886, Seneca. Buried Old Stone Church, Pendleton Co.

Locke, Matthew Francis. Born July 10, 1824, Rutherford Co., TN. Reared in Marshall Co., MS. Prewar farmer. Moved to Upshur Co., TX, in 1850. Mexican War veteran. Speaker of TX State House. Delegate to TX Secession Convention. Md. Elizabeth Buie; Narcissa Montgomery. TX state col. and ADC, to head the camps of instruction in the 6th Militia Dist., June 10, 1861. Col., 10th TX Cav., Sept. 25, 1861. Resigned March 20, 1863, due to ill health (hepatitis). Moved to Van Buren, AR, postwar. Editor, farmer, and miller in Alma, AR. AR state commissioner of agriculture. Moved to El Paso, TX, in 1909. Died June 4, 1911, El Paso. Buried Concordia Cemetery, El Paso. John H. Reagan called him "a man of high character & strict integrity." Other sources give middle name as "Franklin" and "Fielding."

Lockett, Samuel Henry. Born July 7, 1837, Mecklenburg Co., VA. Family moved to AL in 1853. Attd. Howard College. Grad. USMA 1859 (2d in class). Md. Cornelia Clarke. Lt. of engineers, US Army, 1859–61. Capt., CS Regular Army, March 16, 1861. Engineer officer. Chief engineer, Dept. of MS and East LA, 1862–63. Helped lay out Vicksburg defenses. Major, Jan. 1, 1863. Lt. col., Nov. 13, 1863. Col., Aug. 18, 1864. Chief engineer, Dept. of AL, MS, and LA. Paroled May 10, 1865, Meridian. Postwar he was a professor at East TN. U. and LSU. Colonel in the Egyptian Army. Railroad contractor in Chile. Died Oct. 12, 1891, Bogota, Colombia. His papers are at UNC.

Lofton, John T. Born Nov. 11, 1827, GA. Grad. UGA. Lawyer in Elberton and Lexington prewar. Md. Lizzie Johnson. Capt. Co. K, 6th GA, May 28, 1861. Col., Sept. 17, 1862. KIA Jan. 15, 1865, at Sugar Loaf, north of Fort Fisher, NC. Buried Elmhurst Cemetery, Elberton. A junior officer called Lofton "one of the bravest officers that ever unsheathed a sword. Gifted with a powerful mind and most convincing eloquence." Sources give varying dates of his death. The above date comes from a witness and a contemporary newspaper article.

Logan, John Leroy. Born Feb. 14, 1833, near Greenwood, SC. Reared in Abbeville, MS. Briefly a druggist in Holly Springs, MS. Moved to Camden, AR, in 1854. Prewar druggist and merchant. Md. Mary Jane Danforth. Capt. Co. G, 11th AR, July 21, 1861. Gen. Polk, on Nov. 5, 1861, authorized Logan to raise a battalion or regiment. He raised a battalion, but some new companies were brought in and, in a subsequent election for regimental colonel, elected another officer. Logan protested the legality of the election but eventually returned to the 11th. POW Island No. 10. Exch. Sept. 1862 (declared exchanged Nov. 8, 1862). Col., Sept. 30, 1862. Regiment consolidated with 17th AR, March 31, 1863. 11th/17th served as mounted infantry in the Port Hudson Campaign. Transferred to TMD, winter of 1863. Led a regiment of cavalry (made up largely of paroled/exchanged members of his old 11th), 1864–65. Paroled Marshall,

TX, June 23, 1865. Moved to New Orleans in 1869. Merchant there. Died Nov. 1, 1871, New Orleans, of yellow fever. Buried Girod St. Cemetery, New Orleans.

Logwood, Thomas Henry. Born March 2, 1829, Fayette Co., TN. Memphis lawyer prewar. Militia colonel. Capt. of vol. militia. Md. Kate Weakley; Mary Driver. Capt., "Memphis Light Dragoons," May 1861. Lt. col., 6th TN Cav. Bn., Sept. 1861. Resigned April 1, 1862, in order to recruit a regiment of lancers. However, when he found out the members of the 6th couldn't transfer to the proposed new unit, he asked to be reinstated. Resignation revoked May 2, 1862. Col., 16th TN Cav. (raised behind Union lines in West TN), Aug. 27, 1863. When the regiment came out of TN, it was consolidated with the 15th TN Cav. Lt. col., 15th TN Cav. Consolidated. Col., Aug. 21, 1864. Memphis lawyer and judge postwar. Newspaper editor. Lived in Austin, TX, briefly. Died May 2, 1884, Florence, AL. Buried Elmwood Cemetery, Memphis. A fellow lawyer found him "a social, genial, liberal-hearted man . . . [but] not a severe student."

Lomax, Tennent. Born Sept. 20, 1820, Abbeville, SC. Grad. Randolph-Macon College. Lawyer in Eufaula, AL. Editor, Columbus, GA, *Times*. Planter near Montgomery, AL. Capt. in Mexican War. Md. Sophie Shorter; Mrs. Carrie Billingslea Shorter. Col., 2d AL (state vol. militia) at Pensacola, early 1861. Lt. col., 3d AL, April 28, 1861. Col., July 31, 1861. KIA Seven Pines, June 1, 1862. Buried Oakwood Cemetery, Montgomery. According to Gen. Battle, "In peace, as well as in war, he commanded universal respect and confidence."

Long, James A. Born Dec. 10, 1825, probably in Robertson Co., TN. Robertson Co. schoolteacher, farmer prewar. Capt. Co. F, 11th TN, May 12, 1861. Major, Dec. 14, 1863. Lt. col., Dec, 14, 1863. Col., probably Aug. 15, 1864. MWIA Jonesboro during a Sept. 1, 1864, counterattack. Died Sept. 17, 1864, Forsyth, GA. Buried Forsyth City Cemetery; reburied Long Cemetery, Robertson Co.

Loomis, John Quincy. Born c. 1826, SC. Lawyer in Wetumpka, AL. Sgt. in Mexican War and capt. of vol. militia. Md. Mary Henry. Capt., "Wetumpka Light Guards" at Pensacola, April–May 1861. Capt. Co. E, 1st Bn. AL Art., Feb. 23, 1861. Lt. col., 1st (Loomis's) AL Bn., Sept. 17, 1861. Col., 25th AL, Jan. 28, 1862. WIA Shiloh and Stones River. A "high reputation in the army as tactician and disciplinarian." Often led brigade. Resigned Sept. 14, 1863, due to rheumatism. Died Dec. 1869, AL. Buried Wetumpka City Cemetery, in an unmarked grave.

Looney, Robert Fain. Born Aug. 5, 1824, Maury Co., TN. Attd. Jackson College in TN. Lawyer in Columbia and (from 1852) Memphis. Prominent Whig and Unionist, said to have delivered the last Union speech given in Memphis prior to the war. Md. Louisa Crofford. Capt. "Gayoso Guards," 22d TN, June 13, 1861. His company transferred to 38th TN upon that regiment's organization, as company "B." Col., 38th TN, Oct. 26, 1861. Not reelected at May 1862 reorganization. Dropped May 10, 1862. Taken prisoner March 11, 1863, in West TN, while recruiting for the army. Later exchanged. Memphis lawyer and businessman postwar. Died Nov. 19, 1899, Memphis. Buried Elmwood Cemetery. Brother-in-law of Gen. Preston Smith. Tennessee's congressmen recommended "Bob" Looney for promotion for his "gallantry & usefulness in camp and in the field."

Love, Robert Gustavus Adolphus. Born Jan. 4, 1827, Waynesville, NC. Attd. Washington College. Farmer in Waynesville prewar. Mine owner. State representative 1848–54. Militia colonel. Unmd. Capt. Co. I, 16th NC, May 4, 1861. Lt. col., June 17, 1861. Defeated for reelection at April 28, 1862, reorganization. Col., 62d NC, July 11, 1862. Captured and paroled Dec. 30, 1862, near Zollicoffer, TN, seized by Union cavalry while riding a train. Often ill and absent, including the day in 1863 when the 62d was captured at Cumberland Gap. Resigned Aug. 13, 1863, due to "physical debility" ("attacks of something very like epilepsy"). Owned a copper mine in GA postwar. Died May 24, 1880, near Waynesville. Buried Green Hill Cemetery, Waynesville. A "man of first class ability," according to a member of the 62d. Gen. C. W. Frazer, the commander at Cumberland Gap, thought otherwise, saying the regiment was "badly disciplined and badly drilled" and that Love, after his resignation, "became an open advocate of reunion in his county." The latter charge, at least, cannot be confirmed. Brother-in-law of Col. W. H. Thomas.

Lowe, John Hollinger. Born May 5, 1833, Stewart Co., GA. Prewar Chattahoochee Co. farmer. Md. Lucy Haynes. Capt. Co. G, 31st GA, Nov. 10, 1861. Major, May 13, 1862. WIA 2d Winchester. Lt. col., Aug. 19, 1863. Col., May 19, 1864. Led Evans's Brigade at Appomattox. Farmer in Stewart and Chattahoochee Cos. postwar. State legislator. Superintendent Stewart Co. schools. Moved to Buena Vista, GA, in 1884 and owned a store there. Returned to Stewart Co. and became a cotton broker. Died May 30, 1911, Buena Vista. Buried Buena Vista Cemetery. Gen. Evans found Lowe an "excellent disciplinarian." Lowe was charged with cowardice at Monocacy but acquitted.

Lowe, Samuel D. Born c. 1829, NC. Merchant in Lincoln and Catawba Cos. prewar. Md. Laura E. Houston. Lt. Co. C, 28th NC, Aug. 13, 1861. Capt., Sept. 26, 1861. Major, April 12, 1862. POW Hanover Courthouse. Exch. Sept. 20, 1862. Lt. col., June 11, 1862 (while in prison). Col., Nov. 1, 1862. WIA Gettysburg. Retired to Invalid Corps July 8, 1864, due to "general debility." Commanded post of Asheville, NC, after that. Postwar merchant in Iron Station, Lincoln Co.; TX; GA. Died May 30, 1891, Buena Vista, VA, while visiting his daughter. Buried Lincoln Co. Lowe's accession to the colonelcy was "very much regretted" by many in the 28th.

Lowrance, William Lee Joshua. Born July 26, 1836, Mooresville, NC. Attd. Davidson College. Teacher in Memphis, TN, and Lebanon, MS, prewar, returning to NC when the war started. Md. Cordelia Stuart. Lt. Co. D, 34th NC, Sept. 9, 1861. Capt., Oct. 25, 1861. WIA Gaines's Mill. Col., Feb. 10, 1863. Often led a brigade 1864–65. Merchant and state senator in Oxford, MS, postwar. Moved to TX in 1880. Minister of the Oak Cliff Presbyterian Church, Oak Cliff (now part of Dallas), TX. Died March 24, 1916, Forestville, TX. Buried Oak Cliff Cemetery.

Lowry, William Benjamin. Born Sept. 3, 1843, near Crawfordsville, MS. Reared in SC and Columbus, MS. Attd. King's Mountain Military Academy and UMS. Md. Mary Agnes Crosby. Capt. Co. A, 11th MS, April 26, 1861. Major, Sept. 17, 1862. Lt. col., Sept. 26, 1862. Appointed col. to rank from Sept. 25, 1862, but this appointment was rescinded by Pres. Davis May 12, 1863. Davis had decided that another officer merited the colonelcy under the law (see F. M. Green bio. for the details). WIA in face at Seven Pines, which led to his resignation Dec. 1, 1864. Paroled July 5, 1865, Millican, TX. Newspaper editor in Johnson Co., TX, postwar. City marshal of Cleburne, TX. Died Nov. 26, 1880, near Cleburne, after being shot in a gunfight. Buried Cleburne City Cemetery. A fellow student described Lowry as a tall man, slenderly built, "courteous and refined."

Lowry, William L. Born Feb. 26, 1831, Chesterfield Co., SC. Brother of Gen. Robert Lowry. Physician in Jasper Co., MS prewar. Md. Sallie Flowers. Capt. Co. K, 2d MS State Cav., Jan. 10, 1863. Lt. col., April 16, 1863. Col., May 1, 1864, when the regiment was transferred to PACS service. Regiment consolidated Feb. 18, 1865, with Lowry becoming a supernumerary. Paroled May 21, 1865, Citronelle. Physician in Scott Co., MS, postwar. Murdered Feb. 18, 1879, on a steamboat near Johnsonville, MS, by a lawyer with whom he had argued. Buried Brandon City Cemetery.

Lowther, Alexander Allen. Born Nov. 29, 1826, Jones Co., GA. Russell Co., AL, farmer. Pvt. in Mexican War. Md. Mary C. Schaaf. Capt. Co. A, 15th AL, July 26, 1861. Major, Jan. 25, 1862, appointed by Col. Cantey. Resigned July 12, 1862, citing ill health and fatigue, but resignation later revoked. Often absent. Arrested Sept. 5, 1862, for allowing straggling but never prosecuted. Col., promoted June 9, 1864, to rank from April 28, 1863. WIA Cold Harbor and Fussell's Mill. Appmx. Postwar farmer in Lee Co., AL. Died Sept. 4, 1889, Lee Co. Buried Linwood Cemetery, Columbus, GA. Fellow officers denounced Lowther as a cowardly incompetent. William C. Oates, who usually led the regiment in Lowther's absence, disputed both Lowther's appointment as major and his promotion to colonel.

Lubbock, Francis Richard. Born Oct. 16, 1815, Beaufort, SC. Educated at private schools. Clerk at Charleston and Hamburg, SC. Druggist and jeweler in New Orleans. To Houston, TX, in 1837. Merchant. Lt. gov. of TX, 1857–59. Md. Adele F. Baron; Sarah Black; Lou Scott. Gov. of TX 1861–63. Lt. col. AAG to Gen. Magruder, 1863–64. Appointed col. and ADC to Pres. Davis, June 14, 1864. Captured with the president May 10, 1865, GA. Postwar merchant in Houston and Galveston. State treasurer. Died June 22, 1905, Austin, buried State Cemetery. Author of a noted memoir.

Lubbock, Thomas Saltus. Born Nov. 29, 1817, Charleston, SC. Brother of Col. Francis R. Lubbock. Lived in New Orleans before moving to TX in 1836. Cotton factor. Veteran of the TX Revolution. Houston businessman. Md. Sarah A. Smith. Delegate to TX Secession Convention. A volunteer scout and aide in VA in the summer of 1861. Lt. col., 8th TX Cav. ("Terry's Texas Rangers"), Sept. 23, 1861. Col., Jan. 8, 1862. Died the next day in Nashville of typhoid fever. Buried Glenwood Cemetery, Houston. At least three different dates in Jan. 1862 are given as his date of death. The above date is from his gravestone and service record.

Luckett, Philip Noland. Born 1824, Augusta Co., VA. Grew up in Ohio. Attd. USMA and U. of Louisville Medical College. Moved to Corpus Christi, TX, in 1847. Physician. An outspoken secessionist, despite (or perhaps because of) his being reared in the North. Unmd. Delegate to TX Secession Convention. Appointed commissioner in Feb. 1861 to negotiate the surrender of US forces in TX. Briefly QM gen. and commissary gen. of TX, 1861. Col., 3d TX, Sept. 4, 1861. Acting brig. gen. in TX in 1863. Often absent from regiment on post duty. In 1863 the 3d, then in garrison at Galveston, mutinied over bad food and pay. Fled to Mexico in 1865. Returned to US and was arrested for his role in seizing federal property in 1861. Later arrested in New Orleans on another charge. Died May 21, 1869, New Orleans. Buried Spring Grove Cemetery, Cincinnati, Ohio. An English observer noted "he was a very pleasant fellow, though a thirsty one, but was entirely ignorant of military matters."

Lumpkin, Samuel P. Born Dec. 5, 1833, Oglethorpe Co., GA. Grad. Jefferson Medical College. Physician in Clarke Co. prewar. Unmd. Capt. Co. C, 44th GA, March 4, 1862. Lt. col., June 28, 1862. WIA Malvern Hill, Chancellorsville. Col., May 26, 1863. WIA 1st day of Gettysburg, losing his leg. Captured at Williamsport during the retreat from Gettysburg. Died Sept. 11, 1863, Hagerstown, MD. Buried Rosehill Cemetery, Hagerstown, in the Confederate section. A fellow soldier said, "There was no better, braver or cooler officer."

Lyles, Oliver Perry. Born Nov. 27, 1828, TN. Family moved to Crittenden Co., AR, by 1841. Clerk on boat. Lawyer. Judge. County clerk 1850–58. State representative 1858–59. Md. Jane McClung. Ordnance sgt. in the "Crittenden Rangers," AR State Troops, June 3–July 29, 1861. Discharged because he refused a transfer to the PACS. Capt. Co. D, 23d AR, March 1, 1862. Elected col. upon reorganization, Sept. 10, 1862. POW Port Hudson. Exch. April 23, 1864. Postwar lawyer in Crittenden Co., then Memphis. State senator 1866–67. Elected to US Congress but not seated. Died April 17, 1893, Memphis. Buried Elmwood Cemetery, Memphis. A strong disciplinarian, unpopular with his soldiers. A fellow lawyer thought Lyles "a rare gem of the first water . . . and as brave a soldier as ever led men in battle."

Lynn, David Andrew. Born c. 1825, TN. Farmer in Montgomery Co. prewar. Md. Sarah Margaret Geraldine Lockhart. Capt. Co. F, 49th TN, Dec. 2, 1861. Major, Dec. 26, 1861. POW Fort Donelson. Exch. Col., June 30, 1863. Resigned Aug. 26, 1863, because the regiment had no confidence in him. Gen. Maxey, his brigade commander, endorsed the resignation, finding Lynn faithful, brave, and patriotic but indecisive and inexperienced. Farmer and tobacco inspector postwar, in Montgomery Co. and (from 1872) Ballard Co., KY. Alive in 1883.

Lyon, Richard. Born c. 1813, MD. Prewar lawyer in Montgomery, AL, and Camden, AR. Veteran of Seminole War. Md. Mary A. Keely. Elected col., 6th AR, June 5, 1861. Accepted in Confederate service July 26, 1861. Killed in KY Oct. 10, 1861, when his horse fell over a precipice and into the Tennessee River, breaking Lyon's back. Buried in a family cemetery near El Dorado, AR. Future explorer Henry Morton Stanley, a pvt. in the 6th, remembered Lyon as "purely and simply a soldier."

Lythgoe, Augustus Jackson. Born Feb. 6, 1830, Aiken, SC. Attd. SCMA. Railroad engineer on the Blue Ridge Railroad. Merchant in Abbeville. 3d lt., "Abbeville Minute Men," at Fort Sumter, Feb. 1861. Md. Margaret Weir. 1st lt. Co. G, 19th SC. Capt. Lt. col., Jan. 3, 1862. Col., May 19, 1862. KIA Stones River, Dec. 31, 1862. Buried Evergreen Cemetery, Murfreesboro. "[A] gallant soldier and a capable officer."

Mabry, Hinchie Parham. Born Oct. 27, 1829, Laurel Hill, Carroll Co., GA. Attd. UTN. Moved to Jefferson, TX, in 1851. Lawyer, merchant. State legislator. Md. Abbie Heywood. Capt. Co. B, 3d Tex Cav. (the "Dead Shot Rangers"), June 13, 1861. WIA during a scouting trip in MO. Lt. col., May 8, 1862. Col., June 12, 1862. WIA Iuka (ankle) and POW. Exch. Oct. 1862. Led brigade of MS Cav., often under Bedford Forrest, 1864–65. Ordered to TMD in March 1865. Paroled Shreveport, LA, June 22, 1865. Postwar lawyer and judge in Jefferson and Fort Worth. Died March 21, 1884, Sherman, after he had accidentally shot himself in the foot. Buried Oakwood Cemetery, Jefferson. Often called "general" postwar (he is termed "general" in a late war roster in the *OR*) and praised as "a man of a high sense of honor, and firm as the Rock of Gibraltar."

MacFarlane, Archibald A. Born c. 1835, Scotland. Reared in Savannah, GA, where his father, a clergyman, had settled. Moved to St. Louis, MO, where he worked in a plumbing business. Md. Sarah Baldwin in 1864. Lt. of a militia company captured at Camp Jackson in 1861. Capt. and adj., 2d Inf. Regt., 7th Div., MSG, July 10, 1861. Col., Sept. 4, 1861. Mustered out Dec. 26, 1861. Major, MacFarlane's MO Inf. Bn., April 5, 1862. Col., 4th MO (formed from his battalion), April 28, 1862. WIA Corinth (in head). Col., consolidated 1/4 MO, Nov. 1862, but never took command due to his Corinth wounds. Post commander at Gainesville, AL; Canton, MS; and Jackson, MS. Paroled May 12, 1865, Jackson. Charged postwar with executing Black prisoners while commanding at Jackson. MacFarlane strongly denied the charges, which were later dropped. Moved to Canton, MS (where his wife was from), postwar. Merchant. Died in 1881 in Wisconsin, according to a family history, but more probably died in MS. Lt. Col. Bevier called MacFarlane "a talented and most gallant officer."

MacMahon, James John. Born Dec. 10, 1825, Annahilla, Co. Tyrone, Ireland. Immigrated to Canada in 1844. Came to New York in 1848. Studied at Union Theological Seminary in NY. Presbyterian minister in Richmond, VA, 1853–58. Minister in Washington and Marion Cos., VA, 1859–62. Editor of a Presbyterian newspaper. Noted evangelist. Md. Mary M. Allison; Lizzie Gurnee. Chaplain, 51st VA, 1861. Major, ADC to Gen. Floyd (a close friend), 1861–62. Col., 63d VA, May 24, 1862. Relieved of command by Gen. Buckner Sept. 13, 1863, for not enforcing discipline. Resigned April 4, 1864, citing asthma. MacMahon's letter of resignation explained that, as a minister, he tried to control his men by using moral persuasion rather than by orders and that he wished to become a military chaplain. Presbyterian minister in Haverstraw and Stony Point, NY, postwar. Died Nov. 4, 1912, West Haverstraw, NY. Buried Mt. Repose Cemetery, Haverstraw.

Maddox, Robert Flournoy. Born Jan. 3, 1829, Putnam Co., GA. Moved to La Grange, Troup Co., in 1858. Merchant. County sheriff and treasurer. Moved to Atlanta just prior to the war. Md. Nannie J. Reynolds. Capt. Co. K ("Fulton County Guards"), 42d GA, March 4, 1862. Lt. col., March 20, 1862. Resigned in 1863. Col., 2d GA Reserves, May 9, 1864. Atlanta merchant and banker postwar. Elected state representative in 1865. City councilman. Died June 6, 1899, Atlanta, buried Oakland Cemetery.

Madison, George T. Born c. 1830, NY. Mexican War veteran. Settled in NM Territory. Filibusterer. Sheriff, hotel owner, rancher, and merchant in San Piedro. Pvt., San Elizara spy company, 1861. 1st lt., "Brigands" spy company,

March 21, 1862. POW (probably at Glorieta); paroled April 5, 1862. Capt., "Madison's Spy Company," April 21, 1862. Lt. col., 3d AZ Cav., Nov. 16, 1862. WIA Donaldsonville, LA, June 28, 1863. Col., probably June 28, 1863, to succeed Col. Phillips. Paroled as col., June 1, 1865. In cattle business in North Texas postwar. One story (which sounds suspiciously similar to what provably happened to Col. Jacob Biffle) has him shot and mortally wounded Dec. 1876 by a man named Walters, dying 9–10 days later in Henrietta, TX. Another possibility is that he died in AR in 1868.

Magevney, Michael, Jr. Born c. 1835, Co. Fermagh, Ireland. Schoolteacher in Ireland. Immigrated to the US in 1854. Memphis bookkeeper prewar. Officer in vol. militia. Md. Ellen Murphy. Capt. Co. C, 154th TN, May 14, 1861. Lt. col., May 3, 1862. Col., Aug. 30, 1862. 154th consolidated with 13th TN in March 1863. Commanded post of Okolona, MS, in 1863. Led 13/154th in Atlanta Campaign. WIA Franklin. POW Nashville, Dec. 16, 1864. To Johnson's Island. Released May 22, 1865. Merchant in Memphis postwar. Became rich but soon lost his fortune. Died Sept. 21, 1883, Memphis, of alcoholism. Buried Elmwood Cemetery; reburied Calvary Cemetery in 1887. An obituary praised him as "a man of remarkable coolness and courage . . . of extensive reading, fine culture, and delicate sensibilities."

Magill, William Joseph. Born March 10, 1827, Charleston, SC. Grad. SCMA. Marietta, GA, lawyer. Commandant of GMI. Mexican War veteran. Md. Mary Parcival. 1st lt., "Kennesaw Dragoons," 1861. Capt. Co. A, 1st GA Regulars, Feb. 1, 1861. Lt. col., June 8, 1861. Col., Feb. 6, 1862. WIA Antietam (lost arm). Retired Aug. 3, 1864. Commanded post of Athens, GA, in 1864. Ran insurance business in Atlanta postwar. Moved to Jacksonville, FL, in 1876. Orange grower there. Died Sept. 17, 1890, Jacksonville. Buried Evergreen Cemetery, Jacksonville. "A gallant soldier, a fine citizen, and a first rate business man."

Magruder, John Bowie. Born Nov. 24, 1839, Scottsville, VA. Attd. Albemarle Military Academy. Grad. UVA in 1860. Teacher at Nelson's academy in Culpeper. Attd. VMI for a short time in 1861 to learn tactics. Capt. Co. H, 57th VA, July 22, 1861. Major, 1862 (probably July 23). Lt. col., July 31, 1862. Col., Jan. 12, 1863. MWIA Pickett's Charge. Died July 5, 1863, in a Union army hospital. Magruder's remains were sent south by fraternity brothers and buried at "Glenmore," Albemarle Co. His war letters are at Virginia State Library.

Mallett, Peter. Born May 24, 1825, Fayetteville, NC. Privately tutored. Prewar commission merchant in New York City. Member of the famous 7th Regt. NY vol. militia. Md. Annabella Gibbs; Susan Pixley Dean. Capt. Co. C, 3d NC, May 16, 1861. Major and AAG to Gen. Holmes, May 21, 1862. Commandant of conscripts in NC. Praised for his efficiency. Appointed col., Nov. 13, 1862, but appointment not confirmed by Congress, and he reverted to his rank of major. WIA at battle of Kinston in Dec. 1862, while commanding a temporary regiment of conscripts. Commanded post of Raleigh, NC, in 1864. Postwar merchant in New York City, Wilmington, and Fayetteville. Died Nov. 27, 1907, Wilmington, while visiting his daughter. Buried Oakdale Cemetery, Wilmington. Papers at UNC.

Mallory, Francis. Born May 2, 1833, Norfolk, VA. Attd. Hampton Academy. Grad. VMI. Civil engineer on the Norfolk and Petersburg Railroad 1853–56. Lt., US Army, 1856–61. Unmd. 1st lt., CS Regular Army, March 16, 1861. Col., 55th VA, Sept. 12, 1861. KIA Chancellorsville, May 2, 1863. Buried first on the battlefield, later in Hollywood Cemetery, and eventually in Elmwood Cemetery, Norfolk. Mallory's "good conduct" earned "the most unwavering confidence" of his men.

Malone, Frederick James. Born June 22, 1826, Limestone Co., AL. Attd. Oxford College, MS, leaving school to volunteer for the Mexican War. Prospected for gold in CA 1849–50. Then moved to Lavaca Co., TX. Cattle rancher. To Goliad Co. in 1861. Md. Abbie Humphries. Capt. of a company of TX State Troops, Aug. 6, 1861. 1st lt. Co. C, 31st Tex Cav., April 5, 1862. Major, May 14, 1862. Col., Sept. 26, 1864. Postwar cattle rancher in Rockport and later Bee Co. Bee Co. commissioner. Died Dec. 5, 1891, Beeville. Buried Evergreen Cemetery, Beeville. A contemporary called Malone "charitable well nigh to a fault."

Malone, James Chappell, Jr. Born May 21, 1837, Athens, AL. Attd. UVA and Cumberland U. Law School. Lawyer in Athens and Nashville. Md. Eva Williams. 2d lt. Co. A, 1st TN, Aug. 1, 1861. Not reelected in 1862 and discharged. Major, 14th AL Cav. Bn., 1862. Lt. col., Sept. 16, 1862. WIA 3 times during war. Col., 9th AL Cav., Sept. 5, 1864. Paroled Jackson, MS, July 1865. Postwar lawyer in Nashville. Died Sept. 11, 1908, near Nashville. Buried Mt. Olivet Cemetery, Nashville.

Mangham, Samuel Watson. Born Sept. 21, 1830, Zebulon, GA. Reared in Columbus. Clerk in Pike Co. in 1850. Moved to Griffin after that. Officer in vol. militia. Md. Pope Reeves; Harriet L. Reeves. Capt. Co. B, 5th GA, May 10, 1861. Col., Feb. 1, 1862. Resigned May 12, 1862, due to disability. Later militia colonel and lt. col. 6th GA State Guard. Insurance agent in Griffin postwar. Died Jan. 5, 1888, Griffin. Buried Oak Hill Cemetery, Griffin. Brother of Col. T. W. Mangham.

Mangham, Thomas Woodward. Born Nov. 1836, Columbus, GA. Brother of Col. S. W. Mangham. Lived in Griffin to 1857, then moved to Macon. Railroad conductor, bank clerk. Md. Ida Winship in 1865. 4th sgt. Co. B, 2d GA, April 20,

1861. 1st lt. and adj., 30th GA, Nov. 1861. Lt. col., Oct. 14, 1862. Col., April 2, 1863. WIA and disabled at Chickamauga. Retired to Invalid Corps April 23, 1864. Bank cashier at Macon postwar. Died Nov. 7, 1873, Macon, buried Rose Hill Cemetery.

Mann, Walter Leman. Born Dec. 16, 1838, Holmes Co., MS. Reared in Corpus Christi, TX. Attd. UVA. Studied medicine in New Orleans 1859–60. Prewar Galveston lawyer. Md. Lida M. McMarris. Capt., Nueces Co. militia, 1861. 1st lt. Co. F, 1st TX Cav, May 14, 1862. Detached July 2, 1863, to staff duty. 1st lt. and AAG to Gen. H. Bee, 1863–64. Authorized Jan. 16, 1864, to raise a battalion of cavalry. Lt. col., Bradford's (aka Mann's) TX Cav. (formed in part from his battalion), June 16, 1864. Col., spring 1865. Paroled June 22, 1865, Houston, as col. Galveston lawyer postwar. Died July 11, 1875, Galveston. Buried Episcopal Cemetery, Galveston. Gen. Bee called Mann "an officer of great promise—ambitious—honorably and universally known and esteemed in western Texas."

Manning, Vannoy Hartog. Born July 26, 1839, Edgecombe (or Wake) Co., NC. Family moved to MS in 1841. Attd. WMI/U. of Nashville. Prewar lawyer in Hamburg, AR. Md. Mary Z. Wallace. Capt. Co. K, 3d AR, May 20, 1861. Major, July 9, 1861. Col., March 11, 1862. WIA Antietam (while leading a brigade) and Gettysburg. WIA (right thigh) and POW at Wilderness, May 6, 1864. Imprisoned at Fort Delaware. One of the "Immortal 600." Released from prison July 24, 1865. Postwar lawyer in Holly Springs, MS. US congressman 1877–83. Practiced law in Washington, DC, thereafter. Died Nov. 3, 1892, Branchville, MD. Buried Glenwood Cemetery, DC. In 1863 Gen. Longstreet recommended Manning for promotion as "one of the most active and capable officers of his rank." Cousin of Col. E. A. Howell of AR.

Manning, William Richard. Born 1817, Telfair Co., GA. Planter in Coffee and Lowndes Cos., GA. Justice of the peace. Militia general. Md. Virginia E. Ashley. Col., 50th GA, March 22, 1862. WIA South Mountain. Resigned July 31, 1863, due to wounds. Valdosta farmer postwar. Delegate to 1865 state constitutional convention. Died Oct. 11, 1871, Valdosta. Buried Sunset Cemetery, Valdosta.

Marks, Albert Smith. Born Oct. 16, 1836, Daviess Co., KY. Self-educated. Planter/lawyer in Winchester, TN, prewar. Md. Novella Davis. Capt. Co. E, 17th TN, May 20, 1861. Major, April 1862. Col., June 15, 1862. Charged with conduct unbecoming an officer, for telling a guard the provost marshal could "go to Hell." WIA Stones River, losing his leg. Retired from field duty. Appointed col. and judge, military court of Forrest's Corps, April 6, 1864. Lawyer and farmer in Winchester postwar. Judge. Gov. of TN 1880–82. Died Nov. 4, 1891, Nashville. Buried Winchester City Cemetery. Gen. Hardee recommended Marks for the military court post as "a lawyer of distinguished merit . . . high character as a soldier."

Marks, Leon Dawson. Born 1829, Bayou Sara, West Feliciana Parish, LA. Moved to Shreveport in the 1850s. Grad. ULA law school. Prominent attorney and newspaper editor. Briefly US attorney for the Western Dist. of LA. Mexican War veteran. Delegate to LA Secession Convention. Md. Amelia Jordan, a relative of Mrs. Ulysses S. Grant. 2d lt., "Shreveport Grays," Co. D, 1st Bn. (Dreux's) LA Volunteers, April 20, 1861. Col., 27th LA, April 19, 1862. MWIA in the head June 28, 1863, at Vicksburg, by an exploding shell. Captured and paroled there, he returned to Shreveport, where he died Sept. 23, 1863. Buried Oakland Cemetery, Shreveport. An obituary found him "an enthusiastic soldier, chivalrous and daring." Nephew of Col. S. F. Marks, 11th LA, and one of 6 Confederate colonels of Jewish descent.

Marks, Samuel Fleming. Born Dec. 20, 1804, Louisville, GA. Uncle of Col. Leon D. Marks. Grew up near St. Francisville, LA. Attorney. Wounded in Seminole War. Col. in Mexican War. Active politician, serving in the State Senate and as state auditor. Lost race for governor in 1859. New Orleans postmaster 1856–61. Md. Mary E. Worthington; Leodicia Aubun. Col., 11th LA, Aug. 9, 1861. Led a brigade at Belmont and in the Island No. 10 garrison, winning praise from Gens. Polk and Pillow for his leadership. WIA Shiloh. Regiment disbanded, by order of Gen. Bragg, June 1862. Lived in Brashear and Morgan City postwar. Apothecary. Mayor of Morgan City 1867–69. Died Oct. 11, 1871, Morgan City. Buried Willow Grove Cemetery, Berwick. Bragg's order was later acknowledged to be illegal and unnecessary, but by that time it was too late to reconstitute the regiment.

Marrast, John Calhoun. Born Jan. 23, 1825, Greensboro, AL. Attd. Spring Hill College and Georgetown U. Mobile merchant. 1st lt. 13th US Inf. in Mexican War. Md. Harriet E. Winters. 1st lt. Co. K, 3d AL, April 24, 1861. Resigned Aug. 13, 1861. Promoted to capt. and detached to recruit. Lt. col., 22d AL, Oct. 25, 1861. Col., Dec. 13, 1862. Resigned due to rheumatism Aug. 9, 1863. Died of paralysis Dec. 14, 1863, Mobile. Buried Mobile Co.; reburied Marrast family cemetery, Tuscaloosa.

Marshall, James Keith. Born April 17, 1839, Fauquier Co., VA. Grad. VMI in 1860. Teacher in Edenton, NC, prewar. Unmd. Capt. Co. M, 1st (Bethel) NC, April 29, 1861. Mustered out with regiment. Nov. 1861. Col., 52d NC, April 23, 1862. Killed in Pickett's Charge, while leading a brigade. Buried on the battlefield; probably reburied postwar in Hollywood Cemetery, Richmond. According to one soldier Marshall had "a remarkable aptitude for military affairs."

Marshall, Jehu Foster. Born Aug. 28, 1817, SC. Grad. USC. Abbeville lawyer. Wealthy planter. State senator 1848–62. Officer in Mexican War. Md. Elizabeth Ann De Brull. Lt. col. 1st SC Rifles, July 20, 1861. Col., Jan. 29, 1862. KIA 2d Manassas, Aug. 29, 1862. Buried Trinity Episcopal Churchyard, Abbeville. A fellow officer termed Marshall "a man of acute intelligence, great tact, of affable and cordial address."

Marshall, John F. Born c. 1823, Charlotte Co., VA. Prominent editor of the Jackson, MS, *Southern Reformer* and *Mississippean*. To Austin, TX, in 1854. Editor, Austin *State Gazette*. Lawyer. Chairman of the state Democratic Party. Avid secessionist. Advocated reopening the slave trade, an extreme stance that helped defeat Marshall's candidate for gov. of TX in 1859. Md. Ann P. Newman. Appointed lt. col., 4th TX, Oct. 2, 1861, by his old friend Jefferson Davis. The appointment was unpopular with the soldiers of the regiment, who thought that Marshall used his connections to get the job. Col., March 3, 1862. Shot in the head and instantly killed while leading a charge at Gaines's Mill. Buried Hollywood Cemetery, Richmond. The scholarly Marshall was, according to an old friend, "esteemed as a brave man, and admired as an eminent civilian, an able editor." However, the rough-and-tumble soldiers in the 4th resented his appointment and tried to get him to resign.

Martin, David Bell. Born Dec. 28, 1830, Sumner Co., TN. Moved in the 1850s to Rusk, TX. Merchant in Rusk. Md. Sue Wiggins. Brig. gen., 10th Brigade, TX State Troops, from early 1862. Enrolling officer in northeast TX. Appointed major in 1864 and put in charge of the camp of instruction for the Northern Sub-District of TX. Appointed col. and commandant of conscripts, Dist. of TX, May 2, 1864. Paroled Marshall, TX, July 6, 1865, as col. Postwar merchant in Shreveport, LA. Died Aug. 26, 1894, Shreveport. Buried Old Oakland Cemetery, Shreveport.

Martin, John Donelson. Born Aug. 18, 1830, Davidson Co., TN. Grandnephew of Pres. Andrew Jackson. Grad. UPA Medical College in 1852. Physician in Memphis prewar, owning a plantation in MS. Mexican War veteran. Md. Rosalie Adelia White. Capt. Co. E, 154th TN, 1861. Major, May 8, 1861. Col., 25th MS (2d Confederate), Aug. 10, 1861. Regiment disbanded May 8, 1862. Led a brigade in the Army of the West in 1862 as acting brig. gen. KIA Corinth, Oct. 3, 1862. Buried first in MS, later in Elmwood Cemetery, Memphis. Martin, who "possessed rare talents and untiring energy," was a special favorite of Gen. Price.

Martin, John Marshall. Born March 18, 1832, Edgefield Dist., SC. Grad. SCMA 1852. Prewar planter. Moved to Ocala, FL, in 1856. Md. Willie Wellborn; Sallie B. Waldo. Capt., Marion Light Art., Dec. 12, 1861. WIA severely at Battle of Richmond, KY. Resigned March 17, 1863. Confederate congressman 1863.

Refused to run for reelection. Lt. col., 6th FL Bn., Sept. 5, 1863. Col., 9th FL (formed from 6th Bn.), April 28, 1864. Furloughed in Dec. 1864 and never rejoined unit. Postwar orange grower in Ocala Co. Died Aug. 10, 1921, Ocala. Buried Greenwood Cemetery, Ocala.

Martin, Leonidas M. Born July 22, 1823, Madison Co., AL. An uncle was Gov. of AL. Reared in AL, TN, KY, MS. Clerk, merchant. Attorney in CA. Tavern owner in McKinney, TX. US consul at Mazatlan, Mexico, 1855–56. Pvt., TX volunteers in Mexican War. Md. Eliza F. White. Enlisted June 22, 1861, in a state unit that later became the 11th TX Cav. Lt., Throckmorton's Co., 6th TX Cav. (a 12-month unit), 1861. Capt. Co. K, 10th Bn. TX Cav., July 5, 1862. Major, Oct. 1862. Col., 5th TX PR (formed from the 10th Bn.), Feb. 6, 1863. Served in north TX and the Indian Territory. Appointed enrolling officer for the Northern Sub-District of TX, Oct. 1863. Arrested in 1864 for refusing to serve under an Indian officer (Col. Tandy Walker). Returned to McKinney after the war. Tavern owner. Active Methodist layman. Moved to Dallas in the 1870s and owned a home-furnishing store there. Died March 2, 1904, Oak Cliff, TX (now a part of Dallas). Buried Oak Cliff Cemetery.

Martin, Mathias. Born June 18, 1812, Bedford Co., TN. Attd. U. of Nashville. Bedford Co. farmer and lawyer. Mexican War veteran. Md. Sarah Williams; Elizabeth Martin. Elected major gen. of TN Militia in 1861. Capt. Co. D, 23d TN, July 15, 1861. Col., July 31, 1861. WIA Shiloh. Not reelected at May 1862 reorganization. Said to have served with Gen. Clanton the remainder of the war. Lawyer in Manchester and Tullahoma postwar. Died Jan. 11, 1892, Maury Co. Buried Zion Presbyterian Churchyard, Ashwood, Maury Co., TN. In 1861 his officers charged Martin with drunkenness, deficiency in tactics, and inability to drill the regiment.

Martin, Robert Maxwell. Born Jan. 10, 1840, Greenville, KY. Worked on his father's farm prewar. Md. Caroline Wardlaw. Scout for Forrest's Cav., 1861–62. Lt. col., 10th KY Cav., Aug. 13, 1862. Col., at some unrecorded date. Served with Gen. Adam Johnson in partisan operations in KY behind Union lines. WIA McMinnville, TN, April 19, 1863. WIA Mt. Sterling in 1864. After recovering, sent to Canada on clandestine operations. Involved in the Confederate scheme to burn New York City, 1864. Paroled Augusta, GA, May 26, 1865. Martin was held in New York City 1865–66 on arson charges stemming from the 1864 scheme. Tobacco warehouseman in Evansville, IN, 1866–74. Warehouse inspector in Brooklyn, 1874–87. Tobacco broker in Louisville after that. Made and lost several fortunes after the war. Died Jan. 9, 1901, New York City, where he had gone for treatment of his lung disease. Buried Greenwood Cemetery,

Brooklyn; reburied Cave Hill Cemetery, Louisville. Gen. Duke found Martin "a man of extraordinary dash and resolution."

Martin, William Francis. Born July 3, 1821, Pasquotank Co., NC. Attd. UNC. Attorney in Elizabeth City prewar. Lost race for US Congress in 1851. Md. Elizabeth McMarine. Capt. Co. L, 17th NC, May 4, 1861. Col., July 27, 1861. POW Fort Hatteras (along with most of his regiment), Aug. 29, 1861. Exch. Feb. 1862. Appointed col., May 16, 1862, of the reorganized 17th, the original 17th having lost many men in the Fort Hatteras surrender. Present through 1865. Attorney in Elizabeth City postwar. Died Jan. 12, 1880, Elizabeth City, of apoplexy. Buried Episcopal Cemetery, Elizabeth City.

Martin, William Joseph. Born Dec. 11, 1830, Richmond, VA. Grad. UVA. Professor of chemistry at UNC and Washington (PA) College prewar. Md. Susan A. McCoy; Letitia Costin. Capt. Co. C, 28th NC, Sept. 2, 1861. Major, 11th NC, April 28, 1862. Lt. col., May 6, 1862. WIA Bristoe Station (head and arm). Col., April 27, 1864. WIA Jones Farm (thigh). Appmx. Professor at UNC, at Davidson College, and in TN postwar. Vice president of Davidson College. Died March 23, 1896, at his home near Davidson. Buried Davidson College Cemetery, Mecklenburg Co., NC. Papers are at Davidson. A fellow professor called Martin "responsive to every noble impulse and to every call of service."

Marye, Morton. Born Sept. 1, 1831, at "Brompton," near Fredericksburg, VA. Educated at Fredericksburg Classical and Mathematical Academy. Merchant in Alexandria prewar. Capt. of vol. militia. Md. Caroline Homassel Voss. Capt. Co. A, 17th VA, April 17, 1861. Lt. col., April 27, 1862. POW Frayser's Farm, exch. July 31, 1862. WIA 2d Manassas, losing his leg. Col., Nov. 1, 1862. Retired due to disability July 8, 1864. Served on courts of inquiry the remainder of the war. Merchant in Memphis, TN; Baltimore, MD; and Alexandria postwar. Clerk of courts in Alexandria 1870–83. VA state auditor 1884–1910. Died Dec. 22, 1910, Richmond. Buried Hollywood Cemetery. One soldier found Marye "of a highly nervous temperament, but in action he was the coolest man I ever saw. Nature molded him for a soldier." Marye's boyhood home, "Brompton," is in the middle of the Fredericksburg battlefield, and Marye's Heights is named for his family.

Mason, Arthur Pendleton. Born Dec. 11, 1835, Alexandria, VA. Attd. UVA. Planter in Alexandria and Richmond. Planter/lawyer in Auburn, AR, prewar. Md. Mary Ellen Campbell, daughter of Supreme Court justice John Campbell. Lt. Co. E, 6th AR, June 5, 1861. Transferred to Gen. Joseph Johnston's staff. Capt. and AAG to Johnston, March 1, 1862. Capt., AAG to Gen. Robert E. Lee, 1862. Major, Dec. 2, 1862. Rejoined Gen. Johnston's staff for the Vicksburg and Atlanta Campaigns. Appointed col., 2d MS Cav., Jan. 2, 1864. Pres. Davis declined to nominate Mason, and the appointment was later voided. On staff duty to the end of the war. Lt. col., AAG, Nov. 12, 1864. Merchant in New Orleans postwar. Died April 22, 1893, Moriss Park, Westchester, NY. Buried Green Mount Cemetery, Baltimore. John M. Barbour called Mason "a gentleman of superior talents."

Matheny, William Grimsley. Born Sept. 9, 1824, Roane Co., TN. Prewar farmer in Jackson Co., TN, and Evening Shade, AR. Pvt. TN Volunteers in Mexican War. Sgt., 14th US Inf. Md. Louisa F. Terry. Capt. Co. F, 14th AR (later Co. B, 21st AR), Sept. 23, 1861. Lt. col., 21st AR, May 14, 1862. WIA Corinth. Court-martialed March 5, 1863, and reprimanded. POW Big Black River Bridge. Exch. Feb. 17, 1865. Promoted to col. late in the war, probably to succeed Cravens when Cravens became col. of a consolidated regiment. Service record does not show this promotion. Returned to Evening Shade postwar. Farmer, county judge. State legislator. Died June 24, 1906, at his home south of Evening Shade. Buried Mt. Carmel Cemetery, near Sidney, AR. A death notice calls him "universally liked."

Mathews, James Davant. Born Aug. 27, 1827, GA. Grad. Mercer U. Lexington lawyer prewar. Md. Dolly A. Chappell; Mary Cox; Sarah E. Mitchell. Capt. Co. E, 38th GA, Sept. 29, 1861. Major, June 1862. Severely WIA in the legs Gaines's Mill, the wounds crippling him and preventing further active service (but not, seemingly, further promotion). Lt. col., July 15, 1862. Col., Dec. 13, 1862. Retired to Invalid Corps Oct. 31, 1864. State representative 1864–65. Lexington lawyer postwar. Elected to US Congress in 1865 but not seated. Delegate to 1865 and 1877 state constitutional conventions. Died Aug. 2, 1878, White Sulphur Springs, GA. Buried Lexington Presbyterian Church Cemetery. A diarist in the 38th accused Mathews of continual insubordination (quarreling with Col. G. W. Lee) that undermined the efficiency and discipline of the regiment.

Matlock, Charles H. Born c. 1831, TN, probably Franklin Co. Reared in De Soto Co., MS. Studied medicine in Memphis. Prewar physician in Augusta, Jackson Co., AR. Md. Catherine Kirkwood. Raised a company of State Troops in early 1861. Capt. Co. F, 1st AR MR, June 9, 1861. Lt. col., June 16, 1861. Dropped at May 1862 reorganization. Lt. col. of a battalion of cavalry, June 11, 1862. Battalion dismounted July 18, 1862, and reinforced with five companies of conscripts to form the 32d AR Inf. Col., Aug. 16, 1862. Resigned Nov. 10, 1862, suffering from chronic enteritis. Captured at Woodruff, AR, Aug. 31, 1863, while recruiting. To Johnson's Island POW Camp. Died there Dec. 9, 1864. Buried Johnson's Island Cemetery. Remains sent to Memphis for reburial.

Maury, Henry. Born 1827, VA. Known as "Harry." To Mobile in 1848. Prewar merchant, ship owner, city marshal, filibuster. Cousin of Gen. Dabney Maury. Unmd. Capt., AL Regular Army, Jan. 19, 1861. Capt., 1st AL Art., 1861. Col., 2d AL, guarding Fort Morgan, April 26, 1861. Arrested for drunkenness but charges later dropped. Resigned 1862. Lt. col., 32d AL, May 2, 1862. WIA Stones River and Jackson. POW Oct. 7, 1862, near Lavergne, TN, paroled two days later. Col., 15th Confederate Cav., Sept. 24, 1863. Court-martialed again in 1865 for drunkenness but acquitted. Paroled May 12, 1865, Gainesville. Died Feb. 22, 1869, Mobile, from his war wounds. Buried Magnolia Cemetery, Mobile. "Nature stamped him a genius . . . with all the eccentricities and drawbacks that belong to it."

Maxwell, George Troup. Born Aug. 6, 1827, Bryan Co., GA. Reared in Liberty Co., GA. Attd. the medical school of NYU. Prewar physician, planter in Tallahassee, FL. Surgeon at the marine hospital in Key West, 1857–59. Md. Hetty A. Jones; Martha E. Maxwell; Mrs. Elizabeth C. Butler. Sgt. Co. I, 1st FL, April 17, 1861. Discharged July 29, 1861. Lt. col., 1st FL Cav., Jan. 1, 1862. Col., Nov. 4, 1862. POW Missionary Ridge, imprisoned at Johnson's Island until March 14, 1865. Paroled May 25, 1865, Tallahassee. Postwar physician in Tallahassee, Fernandina, Jacksonville, FL; DE; and Atlanta, GA. State representative 1865–66. Died Sept. 2, 1897, at his daughter's home in Jacksonville. Buried in an unmarked grave in Old City Cemetery (where many family members are buried). His lt. col. found him "very handsome and a good soldier. But gaseous [verbally] exceedingly."

May, Andrew Jackson. Born Jan. 28, 1829, Prestonsburg, KY. Lawyer in Prestonsburg prewar. Md. Matilda Davidson; Nell Davidson. Capt. Co. A, 5th KY, Oct. 21, 1861. Lt. col., Nov. 17, 1861. Col., April 18, 1862. Resigned Nov. 14, 1862, due to ill health. Col., 14th KY Cav., Aug. 6, 1863. Resigned July 4, 1864, due to bladder inflammation and went to live in Jeffersonville, VA. Commanded LDTs in southwest VA in 1864. Commissary agent in Tazewell Co., VA, in 1865. Lawyer in Tazewell, VA, postwar. Died May 3, 1903, Tazewell Co. Buried Jeffersonville Cemetery.

Mayo, Joseph, Jr. Born Feb. 5, 1834, Westmoreland Co., VA. Grad. VMI. Lawyer in Westmoreland Co. Teacher at VMI. Newspaper editor in Richmond and Petersburg. Md. Mary Armistead Taylor. Major, 3d VA, May 3, 1861. Lt. col., Nov. 6, 1861. Col., April 27, 1862. Court-martialed April 30, 1863, and reprimanded. WIA Antietam and Gettysburg. Led Terry's Brigade at Five Forks. Paroled April 25, 1865, Richmond. Farmer in Westmoreland Co. postwar. State treasurer, 1872–74. Vice president, Southern Historical Society. Died April 11,

1898, at "Auburn," Westmoreland Co. Buried Yeocomico Church, Westmoreland Co. Brother of Col. R. M. Mayo.

Mayo, Robert Murphy. Born April 28, 1836, Westmoreland Co., VA. Attd. William & Mary College and VMI. Studied law at Washington College. Prewar lawyer. Taught at VMI 1856–58. Then taught math at Mt. Pleasant Military Academy in NY. Md. Lucy Claybrook. Major, 47th VA, May 8, 1861. Col., May 1, 1862. WIA Seven Days (arm) and 2d Manassas (hand). Court-martialed Aug. 31, 1863, for drunkenness on duty during the retreat from Gettysburg but retained rank and command. Often led brigade, 1864–65. Paroled April 27, 1865, Ashland. Westmoreland Co. lawyer postwar. State representative 1881–82, 1885–88. US congressman 1883–84. Died March 29, 1896, at his Westmoreland Co. home. Buried Yeocomico Church, Westmoreland Co.

Mayson, James Hamilton. Born June 6, 1833, MS. Grad. UMS 1852. Lawyer in Marion Co., MS. Delegate to MS Secession Convention. Md. Mary L. Pittman. Capt. Co. D, 7th MS, May 4, 1861. Lt. col., Sept. 24, 1861. Col., April 24, 1862. Not reelected at reorganization and discharged May 21, 1862. Member, 1865 MS constitutional convention. Died Oct. 8, 1869, Marion Co. Buried Greenwood Cemetery, Jackson. A soldier in the 7th called "little Col. Mayson" "as brave a man as ever went into battle."

McAfee, Leroy Mangum. Born Dec. 17, 1837, NC. Attd. UNC. Attorney in Shelby, Cleveland Co., pre- and postwar. Md. Hattie Cameron; Agnes Adelaide Williams. Major, 49th NC, April 12, 1862. Lt. col., June 19, 1862. Col., Nov. 1, 1862. WIA Drewry's Bluff, Fort Stedman, and Five Forks. Elected to state legislature from Cleveland Co. in 1870. KKK leader. Died Sept. 23, 1873, Yorkville, SC. Buried Rose Hill Cemetery, Yorkville. McAfee's nephew wrote the book on which the landmark movie *Birth of a Nation* was based, allegedly modeling the lead character on Col. McAfee.

McAlexander, Edward Asbury. Born March 2, 1833, AL. Grad. La Grange College. Lauderdale Co. physician. Md. Elizabeth J. Koger; Sarah A. Koger. 1st lt. Co. C, 27th AL, Dec. 25, 1861. Major, Jan. 30, 1862. POW at Fort Donelson. Lt. col., June 30, 1862. Commanded post of Cherokee, AL, during Hood's TN Campaign. Col., 27th AL Consolidated, April 9, 1865. Paroled Greensboro, May 1, 1865. State representative 1865–67. Died Oct. 13, 1870, Lauderdale Co. Buried Florence Cemetery, Florence, AL.

McAnerney, John, Jr. Born Aug. 10, 1838, Providence, RI. Resided in New Orleans from 1850. In wholesale and retail iron business prewar. Md. Ellen M. Marshall. Sgt. Co. F, 3d AL, April 28, 1861. 1st lt., May 1, 1862. WIA Gaines's Mill, losing the use of his right arm. Resigned Dec. 13, 1862, due to this disability. Capt. Co. B, 3d VA Bn. LDT (formed from employees of government departments in Richmond), June 18, 1863. WIA at Green's Farm during the Dahlgren-Kilpatrick Raid. Lt. col., April 20, 1864. Col., 3d VA LDT (formed from the 3d Bn.), Sept. 23, 1864. Paroled May 5, 1865, Chester, SC. Owner of a New York City railroad supply firm postwar. President of Seventh National Bank. Died March 22, 1928, at his home in New York City. Buried Holy Cemetery, Jersey City, NJ. McAnerney was hailed as the "savior of Richmond" for his actions in repulsing the Dahlgren Raid.

McBee, Joshua Thompson. Born Jan. 20, 1832, MS. Attd. UMS. Planter in Holmes Co. prewar. Md. Mary Dalton Harbour. Capt. Co. A, 8th MS Cav., Jan. 4, 1862. Major, May 10, 1863. Col., April 1, 1865. Paroled May 12, 1865, Gainesville. Farmer in Holmes Co. postwar. Died Oct. 24, 1881. A wartime examining board found McBee had a "superior" knowledge of tactics, was courageous and sober.

McBlair, Charles Henry. Born Dec. 24, 1808, Baltimore, MD. USN 1823–61, rising to the rank of commander. At the start of the war second in command of the Washington Navy Yard. Md. Fanny Duncan. Commander, VA Navy, early 1861. Commander, CSN, March 26, 1861. Temporarily capt. of artillery. Col., PACS, Jan. 12, 1862, to be the chief of artillery, Dept. of Middle and East FL. Commanded batteries at Fernandina, FL. Soon transferred back to the navy. Commanded warships on the Mississippi River, at Mobile and Charleston. Paroled April 28, 1865. Lived in Baltimore and Washington, DC, postwar. Adj. gen. of MD 1871–74. Died Nov. 15, 1890, Washington. Probably buried Congressional Cemetery, DC, where his wife is buried. A distinguished linguist, "one of the most accomplished officers of the old navy"; his command of the (then unfinished) ironclad *Arkansas* drew criticism from younger officers.

McBride, Andrew Jackson. Born Sept. 29, 1836, Fayetteville, GA. Jonesboro lawyer prewar. Md. Malinda Carroll; Frances Johnson. Lt. Co. E, 10th GA, May 20, 1861. Capt., Oct. 16, 1861. WIA Crampton's Gap; Wilderness; Cold Harbor. Invalided home. Col., Feb. 20, 1865. Atlanta crockery manufacturer and retailer postwar. City councilman. Authored numerous articles on his war experiences for the Atlanta *Journal.* Died March 4, 1922, Atlanta. Buried Oakland Cemetery. A soldier of the 10th noted McBride's "indomitable courage and confidence." His papers are at Duke U. and the Atlanta Historical Society.

McCarty, John Lee. Born Dec. 28, 1815, Rhea Co., TN. Farmer in AL and Pontotoc Co., MS, prewar. Railroad agent. Veteran of Seminole War. Md. Martha Ann Thompson; Annie J. Bailey. Capt. Co. E ("Mooresville Blues"), Gordon's Bn. (soon to be 2d MS Cav.), April 1, 1862. Col., elected Aug. 4, 1862. The legality of this election was disputed by James Gordon, the lt. col. of the battalion from which the 2d had been formed, who maintained the law didn't allow for an election at this stage and that McCarty's election had never been recognized by the government. Gordon also averred that McCarty was "the most utterly worthless and incompetent officer in the Regt." An examining board found for McCarty. McCarty was arrested in July 1862 on trivial charges (McCarty blamed Gordon for this). Although the charges were dismissed, McCarty was not released from arrest (the court findings having been lost) until Jan. 1864. Resigned May 30, 1864. Farmer in Lee Co., MS; Cherokee and Ellis Cos., TX, postwar. Died April 12, 1899, Ennis, TX. Buried IOOF Myrtle Cemetery, Ennis, Ellis Co.

McCarver, John Stanhope. Born Jan. 30, 1820, Lincoln Co., NC. Family moved to Lincoln Co., TN, in 1832. Attd. Franklin Academy. Prewar teacher and Methodist minister in AR. Lived in Batesville, Napoleon, Harrison, Lacy, Bentonville, and Fayetteville. Principal of the Bluff Springs Academy in 1853. Md. Eliza Ann Clark. Elected col. (McCarver's) 14th AR, Sept. 18, 1861. Commanded post of Pocahontas, AR, winter of 1861. Unit never fully formed and in 1862 was broken up, its members being transferred to the 21st AR. Resigned in 1863 and moved to TX. Postwar minister at various places in TX, including Corsicana, Mexia, Gatesville, South Belton, and Leander. Died Feb. 12, 1895, Paint Rock, Concho Co., TX. Buried Paint Rock Cemetery. An obituary noted his "marked physical courage" and "extraordinary weight [which] made it difficult for him to get about."

McConnell, Joseph Thornton. Born 1829, GA. Lawyer in Ringgold in 1860. State representative. Delegate to GA Secession Convention. Md. Adelia M. Lane. 1st lt. Co. G, 1st GA (State Troops), Oct. 8, 1861. Resigned Dec. 11, 1861. Col., 39th GA, March 20, 1862. WIA Champion Hill. MWIA Missionary Ridge, shot through the head near the Tunnel. Died Dec. 1, 1863, at Ringgold. Buried Macedonia Methodist Church Cemetery, Chatooga Co. Gen. Cumming eulogized McConnell as "a most gallant and meritorious soldier."

McCord, Henry Junius. Born Sept. 1835 near Columbia, SC. Prewar grocer and machinist in Greenwood, Sebastian Co., AR. Md. Margaret Emma Hood; Mary J. Barnes. 1st lt., 3d AR State Troops, 1861. WIA Wilson's Creek. 1st lt. Co. C, 17th AR, Nov. 12, 1861. Capt. Co. A, 35th (aka 22d) AR, June 12, 1862. Major, Aug. 12, 1862. Lt. col., Sept. 14, 1862. Col., Dec. 2, 1863. Postwar farmer in Sebastian Co. Died there, or just west in Leflore Co., Indian Territory, Jan. 1894.

McCord, James Ebenezer. Born July 4, 1834, Abbeville, SC. Reared in Abbeville and Pontotoc Co., MS. To Henderson, TX, in 1853. Merchant, surveyor. Texas Ranger. Md. Sarah E. Mooney. Appointed by governor on Jan. 29, 1862, major of the Frontier Regt. (aka McCord's 46th TX Cav.), a state unit formed to guard the western frontier. Lt. col., summer of 1862. Col., Feb. 11,

1863. Regiment transferred to Confederate service March 1, 1864, and served briefly on the Gulf Coast. Rancher in Henderson postwar. Moved to Coleman in 1879. Bank president. Died Dec. 23, 1914, Coleman, buried Coleman Cemetery.

McCown, James C. Born March 21, 1817, Kanawha Co., VA. Moved to Henry Co., MO, in 1840. To Warrensburg, MO, in 1845. Farmer. County clerk. Enrolling clerk of state legislature. Md. Caroline T. Burgess. Capt., 8th Div., MSG, early 1861. Lt. col., 2d Cav. Regt., 8th Div., MSG, June 29, 1861. Col., Oct. 23, 1861. Pvt., Waddell's Co., 1st MO Inf. Bn., PACS. Lt. col., McCown's Bn., March 23, 1862. Col., 5th MO Cav., Sept. 1, 1862. WIA Corinth. POW Vicksburg. POW at Fort Blakely, 1865. Led Cockrell's Brigade. Died July 5, 1867, near Warrensburg, of typhoid. Buried Warrensburg Cemetery. A tribute in a local newspaper called him "a good citizen, a kind parent, and a gentle confiding husband."

McCray, Thomas Hamilton. Born 1828, Washington Co., TN. Lived prewar in Washington Co., TN; GA; Little Rock, AR; Tellico, TX; and Wittsburg, AR. Mill owner in AR. Manufacturer in TX. Md. Angeline Galbreath; Nannie Hamilton. Lt. and adj., 5th AR, 1861. Mustering officer for Gen. Hardee in northeast AR. Major, McCray's AR Bn. (which he raised), Jan. 25, 1862. Lt. col., April 2, 1862. Col., 31st AR (formed from the battalion), May 2, 1862. Led brigade, with great credit, in the 1862 KY Campaign. Regiment consolidated in 1863, and McCray returned to AR. Organized a brigade of cavalry in AR in 1864, which he led during Price's Raid. Paroled at Jacksonport, AR, June 1865. Wittsburg farmer postwar. Became traveling salesman, based in Chicago. Died Oct. 19, 1891, Chicago. Buried Dunning Cemetery, Chicago. Opinion on McCray was mixed: Gen. Kirby Smith recommended him for promotion to general for his leadership at the battle of Richmond, but John N. Edwards considered him unenterprising. It appears Col. Dandridge McRae received, by mistake, the general's commission intended for McCray.

McCreary, Comillus Wycliffe. Born June 1836, Williston, SC. Grad. SCMA. Professor at Aiken Military Academy in SC prewar. Unmd. Capt. Co. A, 1st SC (Gregg's), July 13, 1861. Major, July 1, 1862. Col., Jan. 4, 1864. WIA Spotsylvania, Jones Farm, and Pegram House. KIA Hatcher's Run, March 31, 1865. Buried Williston Cemetery. Called "gallant" in Perrin's report of Gettysburg.

McCulloch, Robert A. Born Nov. 23, 1820, Albemarle Co., VA. Family moved to MO in 1835. Prewar farmer in Cooper Co. Prospected for gold in CA 1849–53. Md. Louisa George. Capt. Co. G, 1st Cav., 6th Div., MSG, May 1861. Lt. col., June 30, 1861. Col., Oct. 14, 1861. Resigned March 3, 1862. Lt. col., 4th MO Cav. Bn., April 27, 1862. Col., 2d MO Cav., Aug. 17, 1862. Led a brigade in Bedford Forrest's cavalry off and on 1863–65. Known as "Black Bob" to distinguish himself from his cousin, Lt. Col. "Red Bob" McCulloch. WIA Tupelo and Harrisburg, MS. One of Forrest's favorite subordinates, often recommended for promotion. Postwar farmer near Boonville. County collector and sheriff. Died Sept. 4, 1905, Boonville. Buried Walnut Grove Cemetery, Boonville. Gen. Chalmers said McCulloch "has no equal as a brigade commander of cavalry."

McCullough, James. Born Feb. 20, 1824, Greenville, SC. Planter in Greenville Dist. prewar. Horse raiser. Md. Keziah J. Sullivan. Lt. col., 16th SC, Nov. 27, 1861. Col., April 29, 1862. In State House 1862–64. Resigned Feb. 2, 1865, due to ill health and concern over his family. Farmer and merchant in Greenville postwar. Died Oct. 1, 1892, near Greenville. Buried on the McCullough plantation, near Princeton. Nicknamed "old beeswax" by his men.

McCurtain, Jackson Frazier. Born March 4, 1830, Tukuawa, Choctaw Co., MS. Of a prominent mixed-blood Choctaw family. Reared in the Indian Territory. Attd. Spencer Academy. Resided near Red Oak, Indian Territory, prewar. Member of tribal council. Md. Marie Riley; Jane Austin. Capt. Co. G, 1st Choctaw Cav., July 22, 1861. Lt. col., 1st Choctaw Cav. Bn., 1862. Col., 3d Choctaw Cav., 1864. President of the Choctaw Senate 1866–80. Principal chief, 1880–84. Died Nov. 14, 1885, at his home in Tuskahoma. Buried Old Choctaw Cemetery, Tuskahoma. A wartime inspector found McCurtain "zealous, diligent, and attentive to his duties . . . sober."

McDaniel, Charles Addison. Born Nov. 27, 1830, De Kalb Co., GA. Grad. Emory College with 1st honors. Methodist minister. Founder and president of Bowden College in Carroll Co. Md. Victoria Haines. Capt. Co. B, Cobb's Legion Inf., July 30, 1861. Col., 41st GA, March 17, 1862. MWIA Perryville. Died Oct. 18, 1862, of his wounds, at a hospital in Harrodsburg, KY. Buried Bowden Methodist Protestant Church Cemetery in 1872. Gen. Maney asserted the South "lost neither a truer soldier nor a more amiable and admirable gentleman . . . than Colonel Charles A. McDaniel."

McDaniel, Coleman Adams. Born Nov. 13, 1823, Lincoln Co., TN. Fayetteville farmer. State representative 1847–49. Went to CA in the gold rush. State legislator there. Returned to TN c. 1857. Militia officer. Lieutenant in Mexican War. Md. Margaret Buchanan. 1st lt., Spencer's TN Cav., Nov. 1861. Col., 44th TN, Dec. 16, 1861. WIA Shiloh. 44th consolidated with 55th April 18, 1862, and McDaniel ("whose health was wretched") became supernumerary. Forage agent thereafter. Fayetteville farmer postwar. Died July 15, 1896, Lincoln Co. Buried McDaniel Cemetery near Boonshill, Lincoln Co.

McDonald, Angus William, Sr. Born Feb. 14, 1799, Winchester, VA. Grad. USMA 1817. Lt., US Army, 1817–19. Moved to MO, becoming partner in a fur trading company. Lawyer in Romney, VA, 1825–44, 1847–61. Md. Anne Naylor; Cornelia Peake (whom he married in 1847 during a three-year sojourn in Hannibal, MO). VADC to Stonewall Jackson, May 1861, with the rank of militia colonel. Col., 7th VA Cav., June 5, 1861. Disabled by rheumatism. Relieved of command, Nov. 1861. Post commander at Winchester and Lexington. POW July 13, 1864, Rockbridge Co. Released Nov. 15, 1864. Appointed Nov. 28, 1864, to command the post of Staunton. Died Dec. 1, 1864, Richmond, from epilepsy and from his time spent in prison. Buried Hollywood Cemetery, Richmond. Pres. Davis considered McDonald "one of the greatest heroes of the war." His wife's wartime diary has been published.

McDonald, Emmet. Born 1837, Steubenville, OH. Family moved to St. Louis in the 1850s. Prewar lawyer. Sgt. in the MO militia in the 1860 Southwest Expedition. Unmd. Capt. of a vol. militia company, captured at Camp Jackson. He refused his parole, claiming that as a member of a legally assembled state militia unit he could not be imprisoned as a Confederate. He sued to void his parole and won. ADC to Col. Weightman and Gen. Price in the MSG. Capt., St. Louis Light Art., organized as an MSG battery in the fall of 1861, transferred to PACS in 1862. Col., McDonald's MO Cav., raised in AR in mid-1862. KIA Hartsville, MO, Jan. 11, 1863. Buried 1865 in Bellefontaine Cemetery, St. Louis. One young soldier called McDonald "my ideal of a soldier. His long black hair reached his shoulders, and his skin was as fair and fresh as a girl's." McDonald vowed not to cut his hair until the Confederacy won, and thus he could be recognized at long distances by friend and foe.

McDowell, James Charles Sheffield. Born Feb. 6, 1831, Burke Co., NC. Attd. Davidson College. Farmer in Burke Co. prewar. Md. Julia Manly. Lt. Co. G, 1st (Bethel) NC (a 6-month regiment), April 25, 1861. Capt. Co. G, 54th NC, March 21, 1862. Lt. col., May 16, 1862. Col., Sept. 7, 1862. MWIA Chancellorsville (head), May 4, 1863. Died May 9, 1863, in a hospital near Fredericksburg. Buried Raleigh City Cemetery. An obituary claims, "A braver or more gallant soldier, or more disinterested patriot, never fell on the field of battle."

McDowell, John A. Born June 20, 1826, NC. Businessman in Bladen Co. prewar, managing the family plantation and dealing in naval stores. Major, 1st NC, May 16, 1861. Lt. col., April 21, 1862. WIA Mechanicsville. Col., July 8, 1862. Resigned Dec. 14, 1863. Bladen Co. farmer postwar. Died Jan. 11, 1899, Bladen Co., of a heart attack. Buried in a family cemetery in Bladen Co. Confederate congressman Thomas McDowell was his brother; Col. T. J. Purdie was a cousin.

McDowell, Joseph Alburton. Born Nov. 20, 1821, NC. Attd. College of Charleston Medical School. Physician in Warm Springs, Madison Co., prewar. State legislator. Delegate to NC Secession Convention. Md. Julia Patton. Capt.,

2d Company, 6th (McDowell's) NC Bn., April 5, 1862. Major, May 1862. Lt. col., Aug. 1, 1862. Col., 60th NC (formed from the 6th Bn.), Oct. 8, 1862. Resigned April 22, 1863, citing hemorrhoids. Asheville physician postwar. Died March 10, 1875, Asheville. Buried Riverside Cemetery, Asheville. The regiment broke at Stones River, and McDowell was heavily criticized for his leadership. One junior officer wrote of McDowell, "He has never once attempted to drill his Regt. & I think takes very little interest in it. . . . [He is] entirely unfit for his position." His brother William was lt. col. of the 60th.

McElroy, John Smith. Born Feb. 28, 1835, Yancey Co., NC, son of John W. McElroy, a brigadier general of NC State Troops during the war. Gen. R. B. Vance md. his sister. Lawyer in Yancey and Madison Cos. prewar. Md. Mary Josephine Carter. Capt. Co. C, 16th NC, May 16, 1861. Elected lt. col., April 26, 1862. Col., June 1, 1862. "[U]niversally trusted by his men." WIA Chancellorsville (mouth). Resigned Dec. 8, 1863. Madison Co. lawyer and state senator postwar. Died June 3, 1919, Madison Co. Buried near his home; reburied West Memorial Cemetery, Weaverville.

McElroy, Kennon. Born c. 1840, MS. Attd. UMS, class of 1861, while residing in Marion, Lauderdale Co., MS. Lauderdale Co. farmer. Capt. Co. G, 13th MS, March 30, 1861. Major, April 26, 1862. Lt. col., Aug. 12, 1862. WIA Antietam, Gettysburg. Col., July 3, 1863. KIA in the assault on Fort Sanders, Knoxville, Nov. 29, 1863. Probably buried Confederate/Bethel Cemetery, Knoxville, along with the other Confederate dead in this assault. Gen. Humphreys called McElroy's loss "irreparable."

McGavock, Randal William. Born Aug. 10, 1826, Nashville, TN. Grad. U. of Nashville and Harvard Law School. Nashville lawyer. Mayor of Nashville 1858–59. Author of a book on his European travels. Capt. in vol. militia. Md. Seraphina Deery. Capt. Co. H ("Sons of Erin," an Irish unit), 10th TN, May 9, 1861. Lt. col., May 29, 1861. POW Fort Donelson. Imprisoned at Fort Warren. Exch. Aug. 1862. Col., Nov. 16, 1862. KIA Raymond. Buried Dickerson family graveyard in Columbus, MS; reburied postwar in Mt. Olivet Cemetery, Nashville. A soldier called McGavock "a clean, strong, brave man, a noble soldier, a loyal friend." His entertaining and informative diary has been published.

McGehee, James H. Born c. 1835, TN. Farmed in Crittenden Co., AR, before the war. Md. Catherine ——. Pvt., "Crittenden Rangers" (Co. C, 6th AR Cav. Bn., and later Co. A, 2d AR Cav.), July 29, 1861. Capt. Co. A, 2d AR Cav., probably May 15, 1862. Transferred to Co. I, 30th AR, as capt., c. Aug. 1862. Transferred to Chrisman's AR Cav. Bn., Sept. 29, 1862. Capt. of a guerrilla band near Memphis, winter of 1862–63. Captured the Union steamboats *Hercules* and *Musselman* near Memphis, Feb. 17, 1863. Col., McGehee's (44th) AR Cav., 1864.

In Price's Raid. WIA Westport and Mine Run. Paroled at Wittsburg, AR, May 25, 1865. Retail dealer in St. Francis Co. in 1870. Thought by collateral descendants to have moved west after this.

McGlashan, Peter Alexander Selkirk. Born May 19, 1830, Edinburgh, Scotland. Immigrated to Savannah, GA, in 1848. Saddle maker in Savannah and Thomasville, GA, prewar. To CA during the gold rush. Filibusterer with William Walker in Nicaragua. Md. Ann Willis Seixas. Pvt. Co. E, 29th GA, Aug. 1861. Promoted to sgt. but soon returned home. Lt. Co. E, 50th GA, March 4, 1862. Capt., Oct. 1, 1862. Col., July 31, 1863. WIA Cedar Creek in both thighs. Repeatedly praised by his superiors, especially for his capture of the federal skirmish line at Fussell's Mill. POW Sayler's Creek. Released July 25, 1865. Ran saddle and harness shop in Thomasville postwar. Elected mayor. Moved to Savannah in 1885. City plumbing inspector and saddle shop owner. Gen. in the UCV. Died June 13, 1908, of a heart attack while swimming near Savannah. Buried Laurel Grove Cemetery, Savannah. Often included in postwar lists of Confederate generals, but there is no evidence he actually received the promotion.

McGuire, John Pleasant. Born June 23, 1833, Lincoln Co., TN. Millville merchant prewar. Md. Rachel J. Alsup. 3d lt. Co. I, 32d TN, Oct. 19, 1861. POW Fort Donelson. Exch. Sept. 1, 1862. Major, Sept. 19, 1862. WIA Chickamauga, New Hope Church, and near Marietta. Col., Aug. 11, 1864. Regiment consolidated in 1865, and McGuire became supernumerary. Grocer and commission merchant in Pulaski and Nashville postwar. Died Oct. 12, 1888, Nashville. Buried Mt. Olivet Cemetery, Nashville. Gen. Brown regarded McGuire as "one of the very best officers in the army."

McGuirk, John. Born June 24, 1827, NY. Druggist in Holly Springs, MS, prewar. Md. Louisa Mahaffy. AAG, Army of MS (State Troops), 1861. Capt. Co. B, 17th MS, May 8, 1861. Lt. col., June 6, 1861. Dropped at May 1862 reorganization. VADC to Gen. Wheeler, Oct. 1862. Appointed col., 3d MS Cav. (State Troops), June 9, 1863. Col., 3d MS Cav., upon its transfer to Confederate service May 1, 1864. Paroled May 12, 1865, Gainesville. Lawyer and hotel operator in Holly Springs postwar. Died Oct. 16, 1871. Buried Hill Crest Cemetery, Holly Springs.

McIntosh, Chillicothe ("Chilly"). Born c. 1800, Coweta, GA. Three-fourths blood Creek and leader of the Lower Creeks. Moved to the Indian Territory 1828. Farmer. Interpreter for the government. Baptist minister. Major of Indian volunteers fighting with the US Army in the Creek wars. Md. Leah Porter. Lt. col., 1st Creek Cav. Bn., Sept. 1861. "Behaved with great coolness and courage" at battle of Old Fort Wayne. Col., 2d Creek Cav., late 1862–early 1863. Resigned prior to war's end. Farmer near Fame, Indian Territory, postwar. Died Oct. 2, 1875, on his farm. Buried near his home. Half brother of Col. D. N. McIntosh.

McIntosh, Daniel Newman. Born Sept. 20, 1822, Indian Springs, GA. Attd. Smith Institute in TN. Clerk of the Creek Council and member of the Creek Supreme Court. Rich planter and slave owner in the Indian Territory. Baptist minister. Md. Elsie Otterlifter; Jane Ward; Winnie Canard. Capt., 1st Creek Cav., Aug. 8, 1861. Lt. col., 1861. Col., Aug. 12, 1861. Often led a brigade in the Indian Territory. Postwar farmer and stockraiser near Fame, Indian Territory. Member, Creek House of Representatives, 1887–91. Died April 10, 1896, on his farm near Fame. Buried Fame Cemetery.

McIntosh, David Gregg. Born March 16, 1836, Society Hill, Darlington Dist., SC. Grad. USC 1855. Prewar Darlington lawyer and planter. Lt. in vol. militia. Md. Virginia, sister of Gen. John Pegram, in 1865. 1st lt. "Darlington Guards" (Co. B, Gregg's 1st SC, a 6-month unit), Jan. 3, 1861. Capt. Co. D, 1st SC (Gregg's), July 29, 1861. Capt., Pee Dee (SC) Art. (the former Co. D), March 1862. Major of artillery March 2, 1863. Commanded artillery battalion in A. P. Hill's Corps. Lt. col., Feb. 27, 1864. WIA Aug. 18, 1864, near Petersburg. Col., Feb. 18, 1865. Acting chief of artillery, 2d Corps, at war's end. Postwar lawyer in Towson, MD. Pres. of the MD Bar Assn. Died Oct. 6, 1916, Towson. Buried Hollywood Cemetery, Richmond. McIntosh's papers are at VAHS.

McIntosh, William McPherson. Born Feb. 14, 1815, GA, son of a Scots immigrant. Elbert Co. lawyer and planter, owning 56 slaves in 1860. State representative 1846–47. State senator 1855–56. Md. Maria L. Allen. Major, 15th GA, July 15, 1861. Lt. col., Dec. 21, 1861. Col., March 29, 1862. MWIA Garnett's Farm, June 27, 1862. Leg amputated. Died June 29, Richmond. Buried Heardmont Cemetery, Elbert Co. "A born gentleman . . . the soul of honor." Papers at GDAH.

McKelvaine, Robert Public. Born Nov. 2, 1838, Kemper Co., MS. Attd. UMS. Md. Mary Elizabeth Naylor. Capt. Co. I, 24th MS, June 27, 1861. Lt. col., Nov. 16, 1861. Col., Jan. 19, 1864. WIA Perryville (leg), Chickamauga (shot in cheek), and Ezra Church (severely in left shoulder). Died Jan. 17, 1868, at his Kemper Co. home. Buried Union Methodist Church Cemetery, DeKalb, MS.

McKenzie, George Washington. Born Feb. 7, 1818, Forsyth Co., GA. Farmer and hog drover in Meigs Co., TN, prewar. Militia officer. Officer in Mexican War. Md. Susan Keenum. Capt. Co. B, 1st (Rogers's) TN Cav., Nov. 1, 1861. Lt. col., 13th TN Cav. Bn., May 24, 1862. Col., 5th TN Cav., Dec. 19, 1862. Meigs Co. farmer, hog drover, and storekeeper postwar. Died Nov. 11, 1907, Decatur, TN. Buried Goodfield Cemetery, Decatur. An obituary praised McKenzie's "kindheartedness and integrity."

McKethan, Hector McAlister. Born Sept. 15, 1834, Fayetteville, NC. Worked in his father's carriage making business prewar. Lt. in vol. militia. Unmd. 3d lt. Co. H, 1st (Bethel) NC, April 17, 1861. Mustered out Nov. 1861. Capt. Co. I, 51st NC, March 19, 1862. Major, April 30, 1862. Lt. col., probably Oct. 19, 1862. Col., Jan. 19, 1863. Court-martialed Feb. 21, 1864, and reprimanded. WIA Petersburg June 17, 1864. Transferred to hospitals in NC. Carriage maker in Fayetteville postwar. Died Nov. 6, 1881, at his Fayetteville home. Buried Cross Creek Cemetery No. 2, Fayetteville. Nicknamed "Old Hec" by his men, "he did not know what fear was."

McKinney, Robert M. Born Feb. 12, 1835, Lynchburg, VA. Grad. VMI. Professor at NC Military Institute in Charlotte prewar. Capt. Co. A, 6th NC, May 16, 1861. Col., 15th NC, June 24, 1861. KIA in a skirmish at Lee's Mill, VA, April 16, 1862, shot through the forehead while "gallantly" leading a charge. Buried Lynchburg Presbyterian Cemetery.

McKinstrey, Alexander. Born March 7, 1822, Augusta, GA. Family moved to Mobile soon after. Drug store clerk, lawyer, Mobile alderman, judge. Col. of militia. Md. Virginia Dade. Col. 32d AL, April 18, 1862. Assigned to command Post of Chattanooga, Sept. 21, 1862. Often on military court duty, 1862–64. Commissioned col. of cav., April 6, 1864, to serve as presiding judge of the Military Court of Forrest's Corps. Paroled Gainesville May 9, 1865. Postwar Mobile lawyer, state legislator, lt. gov. of AL. Died Oct. 9, 1879, Mobile, buried Magnolia Cemetery.

McKoin, James Litton. Born Aug. 6, 1797, Stokes Co., TN. Moved to Gallatin, Sumner Co., TN c. 1820. Cabinetmaker. Mayor of Gallatin. State senator 1847–49. Officer in Seminole War. Md. Frances Wade. Col., 55th TN, c. Jan. 30, 1862. Unit lost heavily at Shiloh and was consolidated with the 44th April 18, 1862. McKoin resigned shortly afterward due to ill health and old age. Died July 1, 1877, at his daughter's home in Blount Co. Buried City Cemetery, Gallatin. Gen. Zollicoffer described McKoin as "voluble . . . competent and noble-spirited."

McKoy, Allmand Alexander. Born Oct. 11, 1825, Clinton, NC. Attd. UNC. Clinton lawyer prewar. State senator 1858–59. Md. Lydia A. Howard. Col., 24th Regt. NC Militia, from Feb. 15, 1861. Receiver for the Confederate govt. under the Sequestration law. Lt. col., 27th Bn. NC Home Guards, 1863–64. Col., 8th NC Senior Reserves (formed from the senior reserves of the 3d and 4th congressional districts), Dec. 22, 1864. Lawyer in Clinton postwar. Judge, Superior Court, 1874–85. Lost race for US Congress in 1868. Died Nov. 11, 1885, Clinton. Buried Clinton Cemetery.

McLain, Robert. Born May 5, 1814, VA. Tailor in Knoxville, TN. Presbyterian minister in Grenada and Wayne Co., MS. State senator 1859–62. Md. Elizabeth Hooker; Laura Brown. Chaplain, 37th MS. Pvt. Co. B, 37th MS, March 8, 1862. Col., April 28, 1862. MWIA Corinth, Oct. 4, 1862, while leading a brigade, when a shell tore into his leg. Died in Corinth the next day, after an amputation. Buried Enterprise Cemetery, Clarke Co., MS. His last words were, "Tell them I fell in defense of a just cause."

McLean, Angus D. Born 1836, FL. Father was speaker of the State Senate. Reared in Walton Co., FL. Attd. Knox Hill Academy. Grad. Cumberland U. Law School, 1859. Prewar lawyer in Milton, FL. Capt. Co. H, 6th FL, April 2, 1862. Lt. col., April 14, 1862. Col., Nov. 16, 1863. KIA May 28, 1864, Dallas, GA, shot in the head while mounting the breastworks to lead a charge. Buried on the battlefield. A cousin called McLean "a noble young soldier."

McLemore, William Sugars. Born Feb. 1, 1830, Spring Hill, TN. Attd. Cumberland U. Lawyer in Franklin, TN, prewar. Md. Anne Louise Wharton. 1st lt. Co. F, 4th TN Cav., Oct. 30, 1861. Capt., at an unspecified date. During Forrest's 1862 West Tennessee raid McLemore failed to detect a Union advance, resulting in Forrest's near capture. Major, March 1863. Col., Feb. 23, 1864. Led Dibrell's Brigade at Bentonville. Took oath of allegiance at Nashville, May 31, 1865. Lawyer and judge in Franklin postwar. Died Aug. 7, 1908, Murfreesboro. Buried Rest Haven Cemetery, Franklin. In 1864, an examining board recommended him for promotion as "gallant and meritorious."

McLeod, Hugh. Born Aug. 1, 1814, New York City. Grew up in Macon, GA. Grad. USMA, 1835. Lt., US Army, 1835–36, resigning his commission to fight in the TX Revolution. Adj. gen. of TX and brig. gen. of the TX Army. He led the Texan Santa Fe expedition in 1841, which proved a disaster. He and his men were captured by Mexican forces and imprisoned. San Antonio lawyer. State legislator. Lost race for US Congress in 1851. Railroad executive. Md. Rebecca J. Lamar, cousin of TX Pres. Mirabeau Lamar. As lt. col. of TX State Troops helped capture the federal garrisons in South TX in 1861. Major, 1st TX, Aug. 20, 1861. Lt. col., Sept. 2, 1861. Col., Oct. 21, 1861. Died Jan. 2, 1862, Dumfries, VA, of pneumonia. Buried State Cemetery, Austin. A "fat, jovial man," personally popular but never fully trusted by the people of TX after the Santa Fe fiasco.

McLin, John Blair. Born Feb. 7, 1820, Little Limestone, Carter Co., TN. Jonesboro, Washington Co., lawyer prewar. Md. Catherine Earnest; Mrs. Margaret Naff. Capt. Co. G, 1st TN Cav. (Rogers's), Oct. 21, 1861. Major, probably Jan. 7, 1862. Col., May 24, 1862. Regiment reduced to a battalion in Aug. 1862. McLin was relieved from duty Aug. 12, 1862, due to the effects of a bullet wound in the lung (suffered in a skirmish) and the reduction of the regiment. Carter Co. lawyer postwar. Died May 5, 1877, Little Limestone, of the lingering effects of his wartime wound. Buried Old Salem Cemetery, Washington Co.

McMaster, Fitz William. Born March 26, 1826, Winnsboro, SC. Grad. USC. Columbia lawyer prewar. Treasurer of his alma mater. Md. Mary J. McFie. Fought at 1st Manassas as Pvt. Lt. col., 17th SC, Dec. 18, 1861. WIA 2d Manassas. Col., Sept. 1, 1862. WIA Antietam. In 1864 Gen. "Shanks" Evans brought charges against McMaster, ostensibly for misconduct at the battle of Kinston but in reality because McMaster had asked that the brigade be transferred away from Evans. The court found that Evans had maliciously prosecuted McMaster. Commanded Elliott's Brigade at the Battle of the Crater. In SC legislature 1864–65. POW Fort Stedman, released July 24, 1865. Columbia lawyer postwar. State representative 1884–86. State senator 1886–90. Mayor of Columbia 1890–92. Died Sept. 10, 1899, Mars Hill, NC. Buried 1st Presbyterian Churchyard, Columbia. Papers at South Caroliniana Library. A soldier in the 17th found McMaster "a man respected and loved by every man in the Regiment." However, Gen. Elliott thought McMaster a hypocrite and probably a coward.

McMillan, Robert. Born Jan. 7, 1805, Antrim, Ireland. Grocer and dry goods merchant in Elbert Co., GA, prewar. State senator 1855–56. Md. Ruth Ann Banks. Col., 24th GA, Aug. 30, 1861. Lost a race in 1863 for Confederate Congress. Resigned Jan. 9, 1864. Col., 4th GA Militia, in Atlanta Campaign. Died May 6, 1868, Clarksville. Buried Old Cemetery, Clarksville. Gen. McLaws considered McMillan "zealous" and "gallant" but "quite ignorant of his duties." Said to have paid for his regiment's uniforms. McMillan's son was a major in the 24th.

McMurray, James Addison. Born c. 1825, Sumner Co., TN. Grad. U. of Nashville. Lawyer in Gallatin and Nashville prewar. Unmd. 1st lt. Co. B, 20th TN, May 20, 1861. Lt. col., 34th (aka 4th) TN, Aug. 5, 1861. Col., April 16, 1862. MWIA Chickamauga. Died Oct. 2, 1863, at the Marietta, GA., Confederate hospital. Buried Confederate Cemetery, Marietta. A visiting chaplain called McMurray "no Christian and a man of very few words." Gen. Maney (his prewar law partner) eulogized McMurray as "a gentleman of the noblest qualities and an officer of fine abilities." Said (like several other officers) to have been promoted to brig. gen. on his deathbed.

McMurry, Lipscomb Pemberton. Born July 9, 1816, Smith Co., TN. Farmer and merchant in Smith and Gibson Cos. prewar. Capt. in Mexican War. Md. Eugenia Wilson. Capt. Co. H, 22d TN, June 19, 1861. Major, Nov. 14, 1861. Col., probably May 12, 1862. 22d consolidated with 12th, June 16, 1862. Lt. col., 12th/22d TN Consolidated. Farmer in Gibson Co. postwar. Chairman of the Gibson Co. Court. Active Granger. Died July 22, 1881, Gibson Co. Buried Oakland Cemetery, Trenton, TN.

McNeely, James A. Born April 1, 1820, Rowan Co., NC. Druggist in Craighead Co., AR, prewar. Deputy county clerk. Elder in the Episcopal Church. Md.

Margaret Morrison; Jane McCoy. Elected major, 13th AR, April 1, 1861. Elected col., April 16, 1862. WIA Shiloh in right arm and hip. Resigned May 27, 1862, citing wounds, poor health, and the fact that he had been elected in his absence "and greatly contrary to my wish." Moved to Stoddard Co., MO, in 1868. To Alma, Crawford Co., AR, in 1877. Merchant. Druggist. Mayor of Alma. Died April 7, 1896. Buried Alma City Cemetery. One private called McNeely a "modest, plain, unobtrusive man . . . large, elderly, grave, slow-walking."

McNeill, Archibald James. Born 1836, AL. Reared in Marshall Co., MS. Attd. UMS. Prewar planter in Carroll Parish, LA. Md. Nancy Hall Wilson in 1865. Capt., "Brierfield Rebels," Sept. 1, 1861, a LA cavalry company that was attached to the 1st AR Cav. Bn. as Co. D (later A). Major, April 21, 1862. Col., 30th AR, June 18, 1862. Resigned Nov. 12, 1862, due to ill health. Lt. col., McNeill's (aka 19th) LA Cav. Bn., Nov. 7, 1863. Col., 4th LA Cav. (formed from the 19th Bn.), c. Jan. 1864. Paroled June 6, 1865, Natchitoches. Moved to Ellis Co., TX, postwar. Farmer there and in Dallas Co. On May 31, 1883, near Mesquite, despondent over his brother's recent death and his own addiction to morphine, he committed suicide. Buried Pleasant Mound Cemetery, Dallas.

McNeill, Henry Cameron. Born Feb. 22, 1833, Natchez, MS. Family moved to Colorado Co., TX, in 1835. Attd. KMI; WMI. Grad. USMA 1857. Lt., US Army, 1857–61. Md. Margaret L. Murray, niece of Col. T. S. Anderson. 1st lt., CS Regular Army, March 16, 1861. Lt. col., 5th TX Cav., Aug. 9, 1861. He captured Pino's New Mexico Regt. during Sibley's Campaign and otherwise distinguished himself during the war. Col., May 20, 1863. Paroled June 28, 1865, Houston. Postwar planter in Eagle Lake, TX. Died Nov. 1876, Columbus, TX. Probably buried Lakeview Cemetery, Eagle Lake, in an unmarked grave. Gen. Green thought McNeill possessed "all the qualifications necessary to a proper discharge of the duties incumbent on a Brigade Commander."

McNeill, James Hipkins. Born May 23, 1825, Cumberland Co., NC. Reared in Pittsboro. Attd. UNC, Yale, Delaware College, Union Theological Seminary, and Presbyterian Theological Seminary. Presbyterian clergyman. Sec. of the American Bible Society. Resided in Elizabeth, NJ, the society's headquarters, prewar. Md. Kate Chamberlain. Capt. Co. A, 5th NC Cav., June 19, 1862. Major, Oct. 26, 1862. WIA Middleburg. Col., Nov. 24, 1864. Editor, *North Carolina Presbyterian*, 1861–65. KIA Chamberlain's Run, March 31, 1865. Buried Cross Creek Cemetery, Fayetteville.

McPheeters, Gabriel P. Born Dec. 19, 1831, Natchez, MS. Grad. USC, 1850. Grad. ULA law school. Prewar lawyer in MS and New Orleans. Ordnance sgt., "Crescent Rifles," May 1861. Lt. col., Crescent Regt., LA militia, 1861. Lt. col. when Crescent Regt. (aka 24th LA) transferred to Confederate service, March 6,

1862. Col., July 28, 1862. KIA at the Battle of Thibodeaux, Oct. 27, 1862. Buried on the battlefield. Memorial marker to him in Natchez City Cemetery.

McRae, Duncan Kirkland. Born Aug. 16, 1820, Fayetteville, NC. Attd. UNC and William & Mary College. Fayetteville attorney. State legislator. US consul gen. in Paris. Lost race for governor in 1858. Md. Louise V. Henry. Col., 5th NC, May 16, 1861. WIA South Mountain. Resigned Nov. 13, 1862, ostensibly for "failing health," but more because he had been passed over for promotion. Sent to Europe by the state of NC to purchase supplies. Editor, Raleigh *Confederate*, 1864–65. Attorney in Wilmington; IL; and NY postwar. Died Feb. 12, 1888, Brooklyn. Buried Woodlawn Cemetery, New York City. A fellow lawyer found McRae "a pleasant, genial gentleman." His brother Alexander McRae, an officer in the US Army, was KIA Valverde.

McRae, John Henry Duncan. Born Feb. 15, 1831, Walton Co., GA. Teacher in Jackson Co. prewar. Md. Ann E. Jackson; Susan J. Newton; Mary A. Pennington. Capt. Co. F, 16th GA, July 19, 1861. Lost race for the legislature in 1863. Col., probably Aug. 24, 1864. POW Sayler's Creek, released June 19, 1865. Methodist minister in FL postwar. Died Nov. 5, 1911, Jacksonville, FL. Buried Evergreen Cemetery, Jacksonville.

McSpadden, Samuel King. Born Nov. 12, 1823, Warren Co., TN. Apprenticed to a saddle maker when young. To Cherokee Co., AL, in 1842. Tanyard worker, lawyer, state senator, general of militia. Md. Charlotte Garrett. Major, 19th AL, Sept. 4, 1861. Lt. col., Aug. 16, 1862. Col., Oct. 30, 1862. POW Resaca May 14, 1864, captive at Johnson's Island rest of war. Postwar lawyer and judge in Center, AL. Died May 3, 1896, Center. Buried Garrett Cemetery near Center. In 1864 AL's governor recommended McSpadden for promotion as "a gallant and courageous soldier."

Mead, Lemuel Green. Born Jan. 8, 1830, Paint Rock, AL. Prewar lawyer in Huntsville and Paint Rock. Md. Susan Daniel; Mary F. Kimbrough. Capt. Co. C, 50th (26th) AL, Sept. 30, 1861. Resigned July 1, 1862, about the time Union troops invaded his north Alabama home grounds. Organized a company of PR to operate behind enemy lines. Major, 25th Bn. AL Cav., Jan. 1864. By Feb. 1865 Mead had raised 19 companies and captured 900 Union soldiers. Gov. Watts wished Mead promoted to brig. to command these men, calling him "a man of high character and intelligence." Authorized on March 1, 1865, to reorganize his men into a regiment. Promoted to col. by Feb. 1865, but when and by what authority is not clear. In May 1865 Mead refused demands for his surrender. Declared an outlaw, he held out in the mountains of TN until Sept. 1865, when he took the oath of allegiance. Postwar lawyer in Scottsboro, AL. Active in politics. Killed Jan. 14, 1878, Gurley, AL, in a dispute with a sharecropper. The killer, who emptied both barrels of a shotgun into Mead, was later tried and found not guilty by reason of self-defense. Buried Old Paint Rock Cemetery.

Means, John Hugh. Born Aug. 18, 1812, Fairfield Dist., SC. Grad. USC. Planter in Fairfield Dist. State representative 1844–45. Governor of SC 1850–52. Delegate to SC Secession Convention. Md. Susan R. Stark. Col., 17th SC, Dec. 18, 1861. MWIA 2d Manassas, Aug. 30, 1862. Died two days later. Buried Haymarket, near the battlefield; reburied 1st Presbyterian Churchyard, Columbia. Sen. James Hammond called Means "a very respectable country gentleman of very moderate parts and cultivation." The elderly and infirm Means joined the army only because he wanted to share the dangers of those fighting for the secession he had long advocated.

Meares, William Gaston. Born March 19, 1821, Wilmington, NC. Attd. USMA. Lawyer and commission merchant in Wilmington. Capt. of AR volunteers in Mexican War. Md. Catherine de Rosset. Col., 3d NC, May 16, 1861. KIA Malvern Hill. Buried Oakdale Cemetery, Wilmington. According to a fellow officer, "no more cool, brave, and able officer lived."

Mellon, Thomas Armour. Born Nov. 13, 1826, MS. Wealthy cotton planter near Bolton, MS, prewar. Mexican War veteran. Md. Frances C. Liddell. Capt. Co. E, 3d MS, Aug. 9, 1861. Major, Oct. 1, 1861. Lt. col., Jan. 20, 1862. Col., April 16, 1862. WIA Peachtree Creek in head and resigned. Gen. of MS State Troops, late in war. Paroled May 10, 1865, Meridian. Commission merchant in Bolton's Depot, MS, postwar. Died May 15, 1873. Buried Raymond Town Cemetery.

Mercer, John Thomas. Born Feb. 7, 1830, Crawfordville, GA. Attd. Mercer U. and Columbian College in DC. Grad. USMA 1854. Lt., US Army, 1854–61. Unmd. Appointed 1st lt. Co. A, 2d GA Regulars (a regiment that was never formed), Feb. 1861. Lt., CS Regular Army, April 27, 1861. Lt. col., 4th GA Inf. Bn., July 19, 1861. Col., 21st GA, Sept. 27, 1861. Mercer, "tall, handsome, . . . brave," had trouble with "booze." He passed out, drunk, at Gaines's Mill. Arrested and court-martialed but got off with only a reprimand. Very unpopular with the regiment, which wanted to get rid of him. KIA Plymouth, NC, April 18, 1864. Buried Calvary Episcopal Churchyard, Tarboro, NC.

Merrick, Thomas Dwight. Born May 23, 1814, Brimfield, MA. Prewar commission merchant in Little Rock. Mayor of Little Rock. Militia general. Md. Ann Adams. Col., 10th AR, July 27, 1861. Not a success as regimental commander. Merrick accused his company commanders of laziness and lax discipline. They, in turn, filed charges against him of "conduct unbecoming an officer," inebriation, and abusing the troops. WIA Shiloh (thigh broken). Not reelected at May 8, 1862, reorganization. Merrick spent the rest of the war angling for promotion to general. Died March 18, 1866, Little Rock. Buried Mt. Holly Cemetery.

Messick, Otis M. Born June 16, 1837, Louisville, KY. Sherman, TX, physician. Sgt. in the US Army. Md. Susan Hathaway; Regina Gomez. Lt. and adj., 11th TX Cav, Oct. 2, 1861. Relieved Dec. 9, 1861, when the legality of his appointment was questioned. Major, elected May 26, 1862, but this election was challenged based on the fact he was not legally a member of the regiment. A mess was made of promotions in this regiment (see Bounds, Burks, Diamond, Reeves). Lt. col. at unknown date but probably (and unofficially) Oct. 27, 1863. Provost marshal on Gen. Wheeler's staff, 1864–65. Nominated for col. Feb. 28, 1865, but nomination rejected by the senate March 16, 1865. Paroled Salisbury, NC, May 2, 1865, as col. Fled to Tuxpan, Mexico, postwar, as he was wanted in Texas for some shootings. US vice-consul in Tuxpan. Died in Mexico c. 1883–93. Gen. Wheeler called Messick "a brave officer and a good tactician." However, there was "a deep-seated prejudice in the regiment against him."

Miles, William Raphael. Born March 25, 1817, Nelson Co., KY. Attd. St. Joseph's College in KY. Prewar lawyer in Yazoo Co., MS, and New Orleans. Planter in MS. Merchant in New Orleans. MS state legislator. Delegate to LA Secession Convention. Md. Fanny Mayrant; Mary B. White. In 1861 Miles, along with other New Orleans merchants, financed a privateer. Col., Miles Legion (which he largely financed), May 16, 1862. Led a brigade in the Port Hudson garrison. POW there, exch. Oct. 11, 1864. Commanded post of Choctaw Bluffs, AL, in 1865. Paroled May 17, 1865. Postwar lawyer and planter in Yazoo City, Moved to Holmes Co. in 1894. Died Jan. 1, 1900, near "Mileston," Holmes Co. Buried Catholic (now Glenwood) Cemetery, Yazoo City. It was said of Miles, a very popular person, that even his political opponents found it hard to vote against him.

Miller, George McDuffie. Born Aug. 2, 1830, SC. Farmer in Abbeville Dist. prewar. Md. Virginia Griffin. Capt. Co. G, 1st SC Rifles, July 20, 1861. Major, March 25, 1863. Lt. col., May 4, 1863. WIA Chancellorsville. Col., April 7, 1864. POW April 3, 1865, released July 25, 1865. Farmer in Ninety Six, Abbeville Dist. postwar. UCV official. Died July 12, 1899, Ninety Six. Buried Presbyterian Church Cemetery, Ninety Six. An obituary called Miller "a gallant and fearless officer."

Miller, Horace H. Born March 15, 1826, KY. Lawyer in Vicksburg, MS, prewar. Publisher. US chargé d'affaires in Bolivia. Sgt. major in Mexican War. Md. Sarah Rogan. Capt., "Vicksburg Sharpshooters" (later Co. E, 12th MS), Jan. 10, 1861, helping to block the MS River. Brig. gen. of militia in 1861, fortifying Vicksburg. AAG, MS state army, 1861. Lt. col., 20th MS, Feb. 15, 1862. Col. of the new 9th MS Cav., Aug. 20, 1863. Reappointed col., Dec. 21, 1864. Under arrest in 1865. Vicksburg lawyer and judge postwar. Died Jan. 26, 1877, Vicksburg.

Buried Cedar Hill Cemetery, Vicksburg. An 1864 inspection report charged that Miller's regiment was illegally constituted, that Miller himself was "a mere political favorite" who "had been picked over old soldiers." Other documents hint Miller engaged in illegal cotton trading.

Miller, Hugh Reid. Born May 12, 1812, Abbeville Dist., SC. Grad. USC. Moved to Pontotoc Co., MS, in 1835. Lawyer, judge, state legislator prewar. Organized the "Pontotoc Minute Men," a vol. militia company in 1860. Delegate to MS Secession Convention. Md. Susan Gray Walton. Capt. Co. G, 2d MS (his old militia company), May 3, 1861. At 1st Manassas. Lost election for colonel of the 2d in April 1862. Discharged from company April 23, 1862, and returned to MS. Col., 42d MS, May 14, 1862. MWIA Gettysburg during Pickett's Charge. Died July 19, 1863, in a private home in Gettysburg. Buried in Hollywood Cemetery, Richmond, in the vault of "Mr. Davies"; reburied postwar Odd Fellows Cemetery, Aberdeen, MS. A "true, devoted and fearless leader."

Miller, John Lucas. Born Sept. 5, 1829, York Dist., SC. Grad. Davidson College. Yorkville lawyer prewar. Editor, Yorkville *Enquirer*. State representative 1860–61. Md. Mary Green Sadler. Capt. Co. B, 12th SC, Aug. 13, 1861. WIA Gaines's Mill and Antietam. Major, Sept. 27, 1862. Lt. col., Feb. 9, 1863. Col., Feb. 27, 1863. MWIA Wilderness, May 5, 1864; died May 6, 1864. Buried Hollywood Cemetery, Richmond. A cousin of Confederate diarist Mary Chesnut, noted for his "affable and courteous deportment."

Miller, Thomas C. H. Born c. 1807, Cabarrus Co., NC. Farmer in Marshall Co, TN, prewar. State representative 1843–45. Seminole War veteran. Capt. Co. F, 17th TN, 1861. Lt. col., July 11, 1861. Col., May 18, 1862. Resigned June 24, 1862. Gen. Hardee gratefully endorsed the resignation request, calling Miller "ignorant . . . and utterly unfit for command." Capt. Co. C, 11th TN Cav., Sept. 19, 1862. Paroled May 1, 1865, Gainesville. Died July 15, 1869. Buried Wilson-Cole Cemetery, Chapel Hill, Marshall Co.

Millican, William Terrell. Born Jan. 7, 1823, Jefferson, GA. Attd. UGA. Jackson Co. lawyer prewar. Militia general. Md. Lucinda E. Weld. Capt. Co. B, 15th GA, July 14, 1861. Lt. col., May 1, 1862. Col., July 22, 1862. KIA Antietam. Buried Hagerstown Confederate Cemetery.

Mills, Roger Quarles. Born March 30, 1832, Todd Co., KY. Moved to TX, in 1849. Corsicana lawyer. State representative 1859–60. Md. Caroline R. Jones. Lt. col., 10th TX Cav., Oct. 21, 1861. Col., Sept. 12, 1862. POW Arkansas Post, exch. April 1863. Regiment consolidated with the 6th and 15th TX Cav. in 1863. WIA Missionary Ridge and Atlanta. Often in brigade command. Corsicana lawyer postwar. US congressman 1873–92. Chairman of the House Ways & Means

Committee. US Senate 1892–99. Eloquent orator. Died Sept. 2, 1911, Corsicana, buried Oakwood Cemetery. A county in OK is named for him.

Minter, John Abner. Born Nov. 29, 1835, Henry Co., VA. To Coffee Co., AL, in 1859. Dale Co. merchant in 1860. Md. Eliza Ziegler in 1857; Minnie Buford in 1893. Capt. Co. H, 40th TN, Sept. 4, 1861. Major, Nov. 11, 1861. POW Island No. 10. Lt. col., Oct. 9, 1862. Requested local duty Dec. 15, 1863, citing chronic inflammation of the bowels. Lt. col., 54th AL, March 5, 1864. Col., March 5, 1864. Tobacco merchant in Memphis in 1867. Later a Baptist minister in Northeast MO. Owned store in Lewis Co. Died April 16, 1909, at the Baptist hospital in St. Louis, MO. Buried Forest Grove Cemetery, Canton, MO. Gen. Baker thought him "excellent" but "rather a diffident man." Gen. Clayton praised him as a "valuable and experienced officer."

Mitchell, Addison. Born Oct. 1811, NC. Reared in Rutherford Co., TN. Farmer in Rutherford Co. prewar. Md. Maryanne Hodges. Capt. Co. E, 45th TN, Nov. 28, 1861. Col., Dec. 1861. Not reelected at May 1862 reorganization. Died 1862, Iuka, MS.

Mitchell, Charles Samuel. Born Feb. 25, 1840, Franklin Co., VA. Reared in Saline Co., MO. Attd. Arcadia College and Central College. Studied law in St. Louis. Md. Julia Sevier Rector, daughter of AR gov. Henry Rector; Fannie Rector. Enlisted May 10, 1861, in the "Saline Jackson Guard," 1st Inf, 6th Div., MSG, as 2d sgt. Appointed lt. and adj., 2d Inf, 6th Div MSG Sept. 3, 1861. Resigned Sept. 15, 1861. Lt. col., 8th MO, Oct. 19, 1862. Col., appointed Jan. 16, 1863, to rank from Aug. 8, 1862. A strict disciplinarian, unpopular with the regiment. Led MO brigade at Pleasant Hill and throughout 1864–65. Paroled Shreveport, June 7, 1865. Moved to Dallas, TX, postwar. Hardware merchant. Active in UCV. Died June 14, 1910, Fort Worth. Buried Oakwood Cemetery, Fort Worth. A postwar biographer called him "the embodiment of courtesy and elegance."

Mitchell, Julius Caesar Bonaparte. Born 1819, GA. Wealthy planter in Montgomery Co., AL. Md. Jane Murdock; Rebecca Murdock. Delegate to AL Secession Convention. Lt. col., 13th AL, July 19, 1861. Resigned Nov. 27, 1861. Col., 34th AL, 1862 (probably April 16), a regiment he largely equipped with his own money. A good provider for his men but "entirely unfitted for active service" due to infirmity. In late 1863, being unfit for field duty, sent to conscript bureau. Commanded post of Fort Valley, GA, in 1864. Postwar planter, railroad executive. Died Oct. 4, 1869, Mt. Meigs, AL. Buried Mitchell Cemetery, Mt. Meigs.

Mitchell, William Christmas. Born Jan. 23, 1807, Sparta, TN. Prewar farmer in Carroll Co., AR. County clerk. Longtime state senator. Lost several children in the famous Mountain Meadows Massacre. Md. Nancy Dunlap. Capt., (Mitchell's) 14th AR, Aug. 1861. Elected col. at regiment's organization on Aug. 22, 1861. POW Pea Ridge. Paroled May 23, 1862. Released in 1863 due to ill health. Died June 2, 1863, at his home in Lead Hill, Carroll (today Boone) Co. Buried Cedar Hill Cemetery near Lead Hill. One friend claimed Mitchell "was endowed with plenty of wit and humor and enjoyed all the fun loving jokes he could pass off on his friends."

Mitchell, William Dixon. Born Jan. 8, 1839, Thomas Co., GA. Grad. UGA 1860. Thomas Co. lawyer prewar. Md. Emma S. Williams. Capt. Co. H, 29th GA, Oct. 1, 1861. Lt. col., May 10, 1862. WIA Chickamauga. Col., Jan. 19, 1864. POW Nashville. Released from Johnson's Island July 1865. Thomasville lawyer postwar. State representative 1865–66. Judge, 1878–92. Died Oct. 17, 1892, Thomasville. Buried Laurel Hill Cemetery. A "conscientious officer," according to a fellow colonel.

Monaghan, William. Born c. 1817, Ireland. Prewar notary in New Orleans. Capt. in Mexican War. Md. Sarah Mitchell. Capt. Co. F, 6th LA, June 4, 1861. POW at Strasburg, VA, June 2, 1862. Exch. June 5, 1862. WIA Chantilly. Lt. col., Sept. 17, 1862. Col., probably Nov. 7, 1862. Led Hays's and Hoke's brigades in the Mine Run Campaign. KIA Aug. 25, 1864, in an action at Shepherdstown, WVA. Buried Elmwood Cemetery, Shepherdstown.

Monroe, James Cade. Born 1837, Marion Co., SC. Attd. SCMA and Kings Mountain Military Academy. Attd. college in Baltimore. Moved to Arkadelphia, AR, in the 1850s. Clerk in store there. Unmd. Capt., "Clark County Volunteers," early 1861. Lt. col., 1st AR, May 8, 1861. Resigned in 1862. Lt. col., 1st AR Cav., 1862. Col., Oct. 25, 1862. Led a cavalry brigade in the Prairie Grove Campaign. Led a brigade in Price's 1864 Raid. WIA at Pilot Knob and disabled. Known as the "Ragged Colonel of the Rawhides" because he dressed as poorly as his men. Went to Mexico at war's end and purchased a farm near San Luis Potosí. Murdered there Sept. 1866: the two stories his family have are that he was either murdered by a robber or killed while trying to protect his foreman from attack.

Montague, Edgar Burwell. Born Aug. 2, 1832, Essex Co., VA. Attd. VMI and William & Mary College. Lawyer and merchant in Middlesex and King and Queen Cos. prewar. Md. Virginia Eubank. Major, Montague's VA Inf. Bn., c. May 1861. Unit temporarily attached to the 32d VA in 1861. Lt. col., 53d VA (formed from his battalion), Nov. 9, 1861. Col., 32d VA, May 21, 1862. "[A] splendid man and officer," according to his brigade commander. Paroled April 24, 1865, Richmond. Lawyer and merchant in King and Queen Co. postwar. Judge. Died there Feb. 21, 1885. Buried Inglewood, Middlesex Co. Montague was great-grandfather of the wife of Marine Corps legend "Chesty" Puller.

Moody, Daniel N. Born c. 1823, CT. Owned a jewelry and watch store in Vicksburg, MS, prewar. Lt. in vol. militia company. Md. Mary Eloise Maury Butts. Capt. Co. A, 21st MS, May 15, 1861. Major, Nov. 2, 1861. Lt. col., July 2, 1863. Col., Oct. 28, 1863. WIA three times during war, losing a heel from a wound at Malvern Hill. Paroled May 15, 1865, Jackson, MS. Printer and cotton factor postwar, in Vicksburg and later in Issaquena Co. Died Sept. 26, 1895, Issaquena Co. Buried Cedar Hill Cemetery, Vicksburg.

Moody, William Lewis. Born May 19, 1828, Essex Co., VA. Attd. UVA. Lived in Chesterfield Co., VA, and New Orleans, before moving to Galveston, TX, in 1852. Lawyer. Galveston merchant. Fairfield, Freestone Co., lawyer. Md. Pherabe E. Bradley. Capt. Co. G, 7th TX, July 25, 1861. Major, Feb. 15, 1862. POW Fort Donelson. Lt. col., Aug. 29, 1862. WIA and disabled (partially paralyzed leg) at Raymond. Assigned to post duty in Austin thereafter. Promoted to col., Aug. 19, 1864 (to rank from Feb. 29, 1864), and resigned the same day due to disability. He moved to Galveston in 1866. Cotton factor and banker. Very wealthy. State legislator. Died July 17, 1920, Galveston. Buried in the Moody family burial grounds in Chesterfield Co., VA. The Moody Foundation has funded parks and other public improvements in Galveston.

Moore, Alexander Duncan. Born May 19, 1836, New Hanover Co., NC. Reared in Wilmington. Cadet at USMA in 1861. Lt., Wilmington Light Art., March 16, 1861. Capt., May 16, 1861. Col., 66th NC, Aug. 3, 1863. KIA Cold Harbor by a sharpshooter. One captain called Moore "a noble, brilliant, gallant young officer."

Moore, Alfred Cleon. Born Dec. 12, 1805, Patrick Co., VA. Reared in Surry Co., NC. Attd. UNC. Surry Co. attorney. NC State representative 1829–31. Moved to Wythe Co., VA, in 1831. Prewar farmer. Militia colonel. Md. Ann Frances Kent. Appointed col., VA State Troops, May 25, 1861. Col., 29th VA, Nov. 4, 1861. Gen. Humphrey Marshall arrested Moore in Dec. 1861 for being a lax disciplinarian (especially ironic, considering Marshall was a lax disciplinarian also) but later dropped the charges. Resigned April 8, 1863, due to "advanced age" and "failing health." Commanded reserve forces in Wythe Co. late in the war. Wytheville farmer postwar. Died March 16, 1890, Wythe Co. Buried McGavock Cemetery, Fort Chiswell, Wythe Co. Three of Moore's sons also served in the 29th. Moore's courage at Middle Creek won praise, and he remained popular enough that he was recommended for promotion to general in 1864, long after he had resigned.

Moore, George Fleming. Born July 17, 1822, Elbert Co., GA. Attd. UGA and UVA. Prewar lawyer in GA; AL; Crockett, TX; Austin; Nacogdoches. Md. Susan Spyker. Pvt. Co. A, 17th TX Cav., Feb. 1, 1862. Col., elected March 15, 1862. Relieved from duty May 24, 1862. Justice, TX Supreme Court, 1862–66. While on the court he upheld the right of the Confederate Congress to conscript men into the army. Chief justice 1866–67. Removed from office by Reconstruction authorities and resumed his Austin law practice. Again justice, TX Supreme Court, 1874–78. Chief justice, 1878–81. Died Aug. 30, 1883, Washington, DC. Buried Oakwood Cemetery, Austin. Called a "Cato of Integrity," "gentle as a child."

Moore, John Courtney. Born Aug. 18, 1834, Pulaski, TN. Reared in St. Louis, MO. Attd. UMO. Prewar lawyer. Prospected for gold in CO. First mayor of Denver, CO. Md. Pauline Harris. Pvt., McDonald's St. Louis Battery. Sgt., Jan. 8, 1862. Elected capt. in 1862 but resigned. Lt. Co. E, Shaler's 27th AR, Aug. 28, 1862. Appointed lt. and AAG on Marmaduke's staff March 20, 1863. Major, Aug. 31, 1864. Judge advocate of Dist. of AR. Appointed col., in 1865, by Gen. Kirby Smith, to raise troops in north AR. War ended before he could organize a regiment. Fled to Mexico in 1865. Returned to MO in 1866, settling in Kansas City. Lawyer. Editor, Kansas City *Times.* Editor, Pueblo (CO) *Press.* Wrote the MO volume of *Confederate Military History.* Died Oct. 27, 1915, at his son's home in Excelsior Springs, Clay Co., MO. Buried Elmwood Cemetery, Kansas City. Gen. Marmaduke recommended Moore for colonel as a "talented, experienced man & soldier."

Moore, John Edmund. Born Sept. 25, 1815, Rutherford Co., TN. Brother of Col. Sydenham Moore. Grad. UAL. Lawyer in Huntsville and Florence, AL. Judge. State legislator. Md. Letitia Watson. Candidate for governor of AL, 1861. Assigned to duty as judge advocate July 5, 1862. Appointed col. to rank from Dec. 16, 1862, to be presiding judge of the military court of Hardee's Corps. It is unclear in his service record whether he accepted or declined the appointment. Died May 3, 1865, Richmond, VA. Buried Hollywood Cemetery, Richmond.

Moore, John Vinro. Born c. 1826, SC, son of a prominent clergyman. Lawyer, teacher, and newspaper editor in Anderson, SC, prewar. Mayor of Anderson. State representative 1860–61. Md. Elizabeth Robinson. Capt. Co. F, 2d SC Rifles, Oct. 29, 1861. Col., May 12, 1862. MWIA 2d Manassas. Died Sept. 3, 1862, VA. Buried Haymarket, VA.

Moore, Robert Hughes. Born May 26, 1809, Clark Co., GA. Attd. classes at UGA. Owned gold mine near Dahlonega, Lumpkin Co. Farmer and hotel owner in Floyd Co. State legislator. Md. Mary Ann Kennon; Lucindy Morrison. Capt., Inf. Bn., Smith's GA Legion, May 6, 1862. Major, July 1, 1862. Unit became 65th GA, March 1863. Lt. col., April 28, 1863. Col., June 20, 1863. Gold miner in Lumpkin Co. postwar. Died Sept. 6, 1890, Dahlonega. Buried Mt. Hope Cemetery, Dahlonega.

Moore, Samuel Preston. Born Sept. 16, 1813, Charleston, SC. Grad. SC Medical College, 1834. Physician in Little Rock, AR, 1834–35. US Army Surgeon 1835–61, eventually rising to the rank of major. Md. Susannah Pearson. Named surgeon general of the Confederacy, with the rank of colonel, CS Regular Army, June 1861, and commissioned to rank from March 16, 1861. Held that position the entire war. Generally credited with being an able and innovative administrator, very brusque and a stern "old army" disciplinarian. Congress passed a law to make the surgeon general a substantive general, but Pres. Davis vetoed the legislation on grounds unrelated to Moore. Postwar physician in Richmond, VA. Died May 31, 1889, Richmond, buried Hollywood Cemetery.

Moore, Sydenham. Born May 25, 1817, Rutherford Co., TN. Attd. UAL 1833–36. Greensboro, AL, lawyer, judge. Capt. in Mexican War. US congressman 1857–61. Md. Amanda Hobson. Col., 11th AL, June 11, 1861. MWIA (shot in knee and spine) at Seven Pines, died Aug. 20, 1862, Richmond. Buried Hollywood Cemetery, Richmond; reburied Greensboro Cemetery. Gen. Edward O'Neal and Col. Edward Hobson were brothers-in-law of Moore. Moore's Mexican War journal has been published.

Moore, Walter Raleigh. Born May 9, 1832, Warsaw, Duplin Co., NC. Prewar merchant in Lake City, Columbia Co., FL. Md. Elizabeth Peeples. Capt. Co. C (the "Columbia Rifles"), 2d FL, May 22, 1861. Major, May 31, 1862. Lt. col., 1863. Col., July 12, 1864. WIA Seven Pines (throat) and Chancellorsville. WIA (thigh) and POW Gettysburg. Exch. Oct. 11, 1864. Appmx. Postwar farmer in Columbia Co. Died Oct. 9, 1898, Wellborn, Suwannee Co. Buried Huntsville Methodist Church Cemetery, Lake City.

Moore, William Hudson. Born Sept. 14, 1829, AL (probably Lamar Co.). Attd. Georgetown U. Farmer in Aberdeen, MS, prewar. Md. Sarah A. Timms; Eliza A. Brooks. Capt. Co. I, 11th MS, Feb. 20, 1861. Col., May 4, 1861. Wounded himself in the foot with an accidental shot, the day after 1st Manassas. Invalided home and resigned April 4, 1862. Col., 43d MS, May 21, 1862. MWIA Corinth, Oct. 4, 1862. Died Nov. 9, 1862, Corinth. Buried Taylor Cemetery, near Aberdeen.

Moore, William Lawson. Born May 5, 1830, Mulbery, Lincoln Co., TN. Merchant in Harrodsburg, KY, and Mulberry, prewar. Md. Louise Neet. Capt. Co. H, 8th TN, May 18, 1861. Lt. col., May 27, 1862. Col., July 21, 1862. KIA Stones River, Dec. 31, 1862. A fellow soldier found Moore a "kind officer, a brave soldier, and a Christian gentleman."

Moore, William M. Born Sept. 30, 1837, Cynthiana, KY. Grew up in Canton, Lewis Co., MO. Grad. UMO. Canton farmer. Md. Fannie Garnett; Rosa Fry. Pvt.

Co. B, 1st Cav., 2d Div., MSG, 1861. Promoted to adj. WIA Lexington. Lt. col.,
early 1862. Capt. Co. A, 10th MO, Sept. 1, 1862. Lt. col., Dec. 7, 1862. Col., Dec.
2, 1863. WIA Helena and Jenkins Ferry. Often led a brigade. Paroled Shreveport,
June 8, 1865. Postwar farmer in Lewis Co. Sheriff. State legislator. Returned to
Cynthiana in 1884. Bank president and city councilman. State representative
1889–92. Speaker of the KY House, 1891–92. Died Dec. 25, 1927, at his Cynthiana home. Buried Battle Grove Cemetery, Cynthiana. An obituary called him
"a most interesting conversationalist, with a remarkable memory."

Moragne, William Caine. Born March 15, 1818, Abbeville Dist., SC. Educated in Germany. Grad. USC. Edgefield lawyer, newspaper editor, scholar. Officer in Mexican War. Md. Emma Butler. ADC to Gen. Bonham at 1st Manassas,
with his militia rank of colonel. Col., 19th SC (a regiment he organized), Jan. 3,
1862. Resigned March 14, 1862, due to ill health. Returned to his Edgefield home
and died there Oct. 5, 1862. Buried Willowbrook Baptist Cemetery, Edgefield.

Morehead, James Turner, Jr. Born May 28, 1838, Greensboro, NC. Grad.
UNC. Lawyer in Guilford Co. prewar. Unmd. 2d lt. Co. B, 27th NC, April 20,
1861. 1st lt., Oct. 15, 1861. Defeated for reelection. Capt. Co. C, 45th NC, April
1862. Lt. col., May 6, 1862. WIA Gettysburg. Col., July 19, 1864. WIA Fisher's
Hill (leg). POW near Petersburg, March 25, 1865. Released June 7, 1865. Greensboro lawyer postwar. State senator 1865–66, 1871–74, 1883–84. State Senate
president and acting lt. gov. Died April 1, 1919, Greensboro. Buried Presbyterian Cemetery, Greensboro. His papers (694 items) are at Duke U.

Morehead, John Henry. Born Dec. 11, 1833, Guilford Co., NC. Brother of
Col. James T. Morehead. Attd. UNC. Grad. Princeton. Merchant in St. Joseph,
MO, prewar. Md. Susan Lindsay. Capt. Co. E, 2d NC, May 16, 1861. Lt. col., 45th
NC, April 3, 1862. Col., Sept. 30, 1862. Died of typhoid June 26, 1863, at Mar-
tinsburg, VA. Buried Presbyterian Cemetery, Greensboro. A "noble and gener-
ous hearted man," according to one soldier.

Morehead, Joseph Clayton. Born 1828, Butler Co., KY, son of a US senator.
Attd. USMA. Lt. in Mexican War. Lawyer in CA. State legislator. Commanded
an expedition sent to fight the Yuma Indians. However, during that expedition
he illegally confiscated supplies, and a warrant for his arrest was issued. Filibusterer in Mexico in the 1850s. Returned to KY, practicing law in Cloverport,
then settled in Jackson, MS. Md. Nancy Hamilton; Sallie Thomas. In early 1861
Morehead applied for a captaincy in the CS Regular Army. Appointed col. in
1861 by the provisional gov. of KY to raise a regiment. Authorized by Confederate military authorities on April 24, 1862, to recruit a PR regiment. Captured
June 17, 1862, Hernando, MS. Exch. June 22, 1863. VADC to Gen. Helm. Authorized to collect his recruits (who had in the meantime joined other units).

Died Nov. 20, 1863, in a hospital in Troy, AL. Buried Oakwood Cemetery, Montgomery, AL. His very confusing service record is listed under Morehead's KY PR Regt., though the unit was never formally organized, and Morehead's claims of recruiting success were greatly exaggerated.

Moreland, Micajah D. Born 1822, TN. Farmer in TN and later Tishomingo Co., MS. Lt. in Mexican War. Md. Eliza L. Fry. Capt. Co. E, 17th MS (the "Burnsville Blues"), 1861. Court-martialed Jan. 13, 1862, and temporarily suspended from command. Resigned July 19, 1862, to raise a cavalry company. Capt. of a company, organized Sept. 7, 1862, later Co. C, Roddey's 4th AL Cav. (and still later Co. G, Moreland's MS Cav. Bn.). Major, Moreland's Bn., Aug. 1, 1863. Lt. col., Jan. 20, 1864. Col., Moreland's MS Cav. (formed from his battalion) 1864. His regiment was composed largely of reservists and was not highly thought of. Died Oct. 3, 1867, Memphis, TN.

Morgan, Asa Stokely. Born Nov. 13, 1825, Macon, GA. Moved to Union Co., AR, in 1843. Prewar planter and merchant. Md. Lida Wright; Pattie McRae. Capt. Co. A, 1st (Fagan's) AR, May 17, 1861. ADC to Fagan at Shiloh. Dropped May 8, 1862. Morgan returned to AR to raise troops. Lt. col., Morgan's Bn., probably June 14, 1862. Appointed col., 26th AR, July 23, 1862. Led 26th at Prairie Grove. The legality of the appointment was subsequently challenged, and when an election was ordered Morgan declined to be a candidate. Inspector of field transportation in TMD, 1864–65. Farmer in Union Co. and later Camden postwar. State legislator. Died Feb. 25, 1909, Camden. Buried Mt. Holly Cemetery, Mt. Holly, Union Co. Recommended in 1864 for a staff position as "a gentleman of great intelligence, high integrity and first rate business capacity." The AR History Commission has some of Morgan's letters.

Morgan, Charles Leroy. Born Aug. 24, 1840, Bastrop Co., TX. Attd. Bastrop Military Institute. Md. Mary Duval. 1st lt. Co. D, 8th TX Cav., Sept. 7, 1861. Resigned Dec. 11, 1861, due to disability. Major, 18th TX Cav., March 15, 1862. Lt. col. of a battalion (Morgan's) of TX Cav., fall of 1863. Unit operated with Parsons's Brigade in the Red River Campaign of 1864. Unit increased to a regiment in March 1865 by the addition of a company. Appointed col. at this time. Paroled July 1865 in Houston. Postwar grocer in Bastrop and Hill Cos. Died March 11, 1924, Ballinger, TX. Buried Coleman Cemetery, Coleman. A "dashing young officer." Richmond fell before Morgan's promotion to col. could be acted upon, and he was paroled a lt. col.

Morgan, Richard Curd. Born Sept. 13, 1836, KY. Brother of Gen. John Hunt Morgan. Attd. KMI. Worked in the family's general merchandise business in Lexington prewar. Adj., KSG, Jan. 5, 1861. Md. Alice Bright. Capt., PACS, March 23, 1862. On A. P. Hill's staff (Hill was his brother-in-law). Major, AAG, May 26,

1862. On March 24, 1863, Morgan was authorized to recruit a regiment of cavalry and to receive a colonel's commission to date from the completion of the muster rolls. Transferred to his brother's staff. POW July 19, 1863, during the Ohio Raid. Exch. Aug. 3, 1864, as col., Morgan's KY Cav. Regt. (sometimes called the 14th KY Cav.). Assigned to his brother's staff again. Col., 2d Special Bn., in Basil Duke's Brigade, late 1864. Captured again, Dec. 1864. To Johnson's Island Prison. Hemp dealer in Lexington postwar. Died Sept. 28, 1918, Lexington. Buried Lexington Cemetery. Gen. Pender thought Morgan "weak," an assessment backed up by his numerous transfers.

Morgan, Robert Jarrell. Born March 25, 1836, La Grange, GA. Grad. UGA. Lawyer in La Grange. Moved to Memphis in 1859. Md. Mary H. Battle; Martha Fort. Col., 36th TN, Feb. 26, 1862. The unit (largely raised in East TN) had a reputation for disloyalty, and Morgan took command reluctantly. It suffered so many desertions that it could not be reorganized successfully. Morgan was not reelected at the May 1862 attempted reorganization. On staff of Gen. Polk, 1862–64. Thereafter a member of a court of claims. Memphis lawyer postwar. City attorney, judge. Died July 23, 1899, Aberdeen, MS. Buried Elmwood Cemetery, Memphis. A fellow soldier remembered Morgan as "strong intellectually and physically and a fine speaker."

Morgan, Thomas Jefferson. Born Dec. 18, 1827, near Hamburg, SC. Family moved to Batesville, Independence Co., AR, in 1832. Prewar Independence Co. farmer. Mexican War veteran. Md. Sarah E. Allen. Capt. Co. D, 8th AR, July 18, 1861. 8th and 7th AR were consolidated May 7, 1862, and Morgan became a supernumerary officer. Returned to AR. Capt. Co. C, 8th (aka 2d, 5th, Morgan's) AR Cav., July 2, 1863. Col., Dec. 24, 1863. Paroled Jacksonport, AR, June 5, 1865. Postwar farmer in Independence Co. State representative 1875–76. Died July 21, 1906. Buried in a private cemetery near McHue, AR. One lt. called Morgan "not a business or military man like Col. Newton, but much more beliked by men and officers."

Morgan, William Augustine. Born March 30, 1831, Fairfax Co., VA. Reared in Jefferson Co. Farmer in Jefferson Co. prewar. Md. Anna J. Smith. Capt. Co. F, 1st VA Cav., April 18, 1861. Major, Oct. 2, 1862. WIA near Gettysburg, July 4, 1863. Lt. col., July 16, 1863. Col., Dec. 7, 1864. Led Payne's Brigade at Appomattox and escaped before the surrender. Paroled April 21, 1865, Winchester. Jefferson Co. farmer postwar. Deputy sheriff. Died Feb. 14, 1899, near Shepherdstown, WVA. Buried Elmwood Cemetery, Shepherdstown. One trooper said of the much-admired Morgan, "a braver and better man never drew sword in the defense of any cause."

Morris, John Dabney. Born Jan. 28, 1813, Taylor's Creek, Hanover Co., VA. Attd. UVA. To San Antonio, TX, in 1837. Lawyer, legislator there. Lt. col. in TX army during its wars with Mexico. Moved to Christian Co., KY, in 1844, to run a farm. Md. Margaret L. Meriwether. In late 1861 appointed by the Confederate government to sequester the deposits of KY banks. Enlisted as pvt., 1st KY Cav., 1862. VADC to Gen. John S. Williams 1862–63. Lost race for the Confederate Congress in 1864. Served (as a volunteer) with the 28th VA in the Wilderness Campaign. Appointed col., PACS, Sept. 13, 1864, to raise a regiment in KY, the commission to be issued if he raised it within 3 months. Captured in KY in 1865 while recruiting. The Union troops put him in chains and threatened to shoot him as a spy, but after protests by the Confederate govt. he was treated as a POW and exchanged. Farmer and lawyer in Hopkinsville, Christian Co., postwar. Newspaper owner. Died July 30, 1896, Hopkinsville. A relative noted that Morris "led a wild and roving life."

Morrison, Charles H. Born c. 1820, LA. Prewar attorney in Monroe, LA. Deputy sheriff of Ouachita Parish. Registrar of the state land office. Wealthy planter, worth $190,000 in 1860. Speaker of the LA State House in 1861. Md. Fannie Farmer. Capt., then lt. col., Morrison's (aka 6th) LA Inf. Bn., May 14, 1862. Col., 31st LA (formed from the 6th Bn.), June 11, 1862. Paroled June 10, 1865, Monroe. Postwar plantation owner near Monroe. Died Oct. 18, 1876, Delhi, LA, of pneumonia. An obituary pays tribute to "Col. Morrison's native talent, his industry, energy and unflagging pursuit of a purpose."

Morrison, James J. Born Oct. 31, 1829, Hopkinsville, KY. Attd. UGA. Moved to Cedartown, GA, in 1850. Planter. Served in US Army in Mexican War. Md. Athey Jones; Hattie Cox. Major, 4th GA Bn., July 19, 1861. Lt. col., 21st GA, Sept. 27, 1861. Resigned March 30, 1862. Acting lt. col., 1st GA Cav., 1862. Col., May 21, 1862. WIA Chickamauga. Resigned April 15, 1864, due to ill health. Merchant in Atlanta and Decatur postwar. Owned a hotel at Stone Mountain and a farm in Morgan Co. Died Sept. 3, 1910, Eastman, GA. Buried Woodlawn Cemetery, Eastman. Gen. Bragg complimented Morrison for his "dash and daring."

Morton, Richard. Born 1835, Richmond, VA. Attd. Hampden-Sydney College. Prewar civil engineer in VA and Brazil. Md. Mary Green. 1st lt. of engineers, Nov. 19, 1861. Capt., April 18, 1862. Major, May 28, 1863. Asst. superintendent of Nitre and Mining Bureau. Lt. col., June 15, 1864. Col. and chief of the bureau, Feb. 17, 1865. Lived in Richmond briefly postwar. To Baltimore in 1869. Partner in company dealing in railroad and engineering supplies. Died June 25, 1898, at his Baltimore home. Buried St. Thomas's Churchyard Cemetery, Garrison Forest, Baltimore Co.

Mosby, John Singleton. Born Dec. 6, 1833, Powhatan Co., VA. Reared in Albemarle Co. Attd. UVA. Lawyer in Howardsville, Albemarle Co., and Bristol, VA, prewar. Md. Pauline Clark in 1857. Enlisted in April 1861 in the Washington MR (Co. D, 1st VA Cav.). 1st lt. and adj., 1st VA Cav., Feb.–April 1862. Scouted for Gen. Jeb Stuart. Captured July 1862. Soon exchanged. Detached in Jan. 1863 to organize and command guerrilla forces in northern VA. Capt., March 15, 1863. Major, March 26, 1863. Lt. col., 43d VA Cav. Bn., Jan. 21, 1864. Col., Mosby's Regt. VA Cav., Dec. 7, 1864. Known as the "Gray Ghost" for his almost incredible exploits leading raids against Union outposts. Parts of VA became known as "Mosby's Confederacy." He disbanded his men after Appomattox and remained a fugitive until being arrested in Jan. 1866. His wife then obtained from Gen. Grant a special pardon for him. Attorney in Warrenton and San Francisco postwar. US consul in Hong Kong. Died May 30, 1916, Washington, DC. Buried Warrenton Cemetery, Warrenton, VA. Mosby's papers are at the Museum of the Confederacy and UVA. His reminiscences were published in 1917. A TV series based (loosely) on his wartime exploits aired in the 1950s.

Moss, Adolphus A. Born 1819, Davidson Co., NC. Farmer and merchant in Davidson Co. prewar. Md. Louisa Caroline Eccles. 2d lt. Co. A, 21st NC, May 8, 1861. 1st lt., July 3, 1861. Declined to stand for reelection at April 1862 reorganization. Lt. col., Sept. 29, 1864, of a battalion of reservists. Col., 6th NC Senior Reserves (formed from his battalion), Dec. 3, 1864. The 6th guarded prisoners at Salisbury, NC, and helped arrest deserters in western NC. Merchant in Davie Co. postwar. Died Dec. 28, 1880, Mocksville, NC. Buried Joppa Cemetery, near Mocksville.

Moss, James W. Born Oct. 1822, Greensburg, KY. Capt. in Mexican War. Trader in livestock and produce in Greensburg and later Columbus, KY. Capt. Co. A, 2d KY, July 5, 1861. POW Fort Donelson. Exch. Sept. 1862. Major, Dec. 1, 1862. Lt. col., Sept. 20, 1863. Col., Oct. 19, 1863. MWIA Jonesboro, Aug. 31, 1864 (arm shattered), and POW. Died Sept. 19, 1864, Marietta, GA, while in Union hands. Buried Marietta; reburied State Cemetery, Frankfort, KY, in 1888. A stern, quiet man, said by a fellow soldier to be "wholly insensible to fear as though he knew himself invulnerable."

Mott, Christopher Haynes. Born June 22, 1826, Livingston Co., KY. Attd. St. Thomas's Hall and Transylvania U. Lawyer in Holly Springs, MS. Law partner with L. Q. C. Lamar. Judge. State representative 1850–51. Officer in Mexican War. Md. Sally Govan. Brig. gen., MS State Troops, 1861. Soon resigned to become col., 19th MS, on June 11, 1861. KIA Williamsburg. Buried Hollywood Cemetery, Richmond; reburied 1867 in Hill Crest Cemetery, Holly Springs. Gen. Longstreet called him "gallant," and Lamar said "a nobler man never lived."

Muldrow, Henry Lowndes. Born Feb. 8, 1837, near Tibbes Station, Clay Co., MS. Reared in Starkville. Grad. UMS. Starkville lawyer prewar. Md. Eliza D. Ervin. Pvt. Co. C, 14th MS, May 30, 1861. POW Fort Donelson, exch. Sept. 1862. 3d lt., Sept. 25, 1862. 2d lt., Aug. 20, 1863. Organized a company of scouts. Capt. of a state company, later Co. H, 11th MS Cav., Sept. 7, 1863. Major, Nov. 20, 1863. Lt. col., 11th MS Cav., Dec. 23, 1863. Promoted to col., March 20, 1865, the promotion coming so late that it is not reflected in his service record. Attorney, planter, bank president in Starkville postwar. Dist. attorney, 1869–71. State representative 1876–77. US congressman 1877–85. 1st asst. sec. of the interior 1885–89. Chancellor 1899–1905. Died March 1, 1905, Starkville. Buried Odd Fellows Cemetery, Starkville.

Mullins, John Bailey. Born Dec. 1829, TN. Grad. USMA, 1854. Lt., US Army, 1854–61. Md. Emily Garrison, 1861. 1st lt., CS Regular Army, April 27, 1861. Capt., to rank from March 16, 1861. Slated to be major, 5th VA Cav., in 1861, but the regiment did not organize until later. Major, 19th MS, Dec. 11, 1861. Lt. col., May 5, 1862. WIA in abdomen during Seven Days. Col., Nov. 24, 1862. Resigned July 1864 due to his wounds. Farmer in Norfolk Co., VA, postwar. Died Oct. 3, 1891. Buried Elmwood Cemetery, Norfolk.

Munford, Edward W. Born Oct. 16, 1820, Lincoln Co., KY. Privately studied law. Lawyer in Clarksville, TN, and later Memphis. Owned plantation in AL. Md. Amelia Watkins; Mrs. Mary E. Gardner. Major, VADC, on Gen. A. S. Johnston's staff, 1861–62. Due to rheumatism, he had to leave the army. On Gen. Hardee's staff in 1864. Appointed col. and judge, military court of S. D. Lee's Corps, Jan. 9, 1865. Paroled Meridian, May 9, 1865. Lived in Memphis and McMinnville, TN, postwar. President of insurance company. Died Nov. 4, 1887. Buried Riverside Cemetery, McMinnville. Sen. Phelan called him "a perfect gentleman—a fine lawyer—of unimpeachable morals."

Munford, Thomas Taylor. Born March 28, 1831, Richmond, VA. Grad. VMI. Planter and railroad executive in Lynchburg prewar. Md. Elizabeth H. Taylor; Emma Tayloe. Lt. col., 2d VA Cav., May 8, 1861. Col., April 25, 1862. Often led Fitzhugh Lee's brigade. WIA 2d Manassas and Cold Harbor. Court-martialed late in the war because he hadn't gotten his men to volunteer for a raid, but cleared. Best evidence indicates Munford was appointed (by unknown authority) brig. gen., April 1, 1865, the promotion being received six days later. Commanded Fitz Lee's cavalry division in the Appomattox Campaign at that rank. Paroled April 20, 1865, Lynchburg. Cotton planter in Lynchburg and Uniontown, AL, postwar. Vice president, Lynchburg Iron & Mining Co. Sec. of the Southern Historical Society. Frequent contributor to historical publications. Died Feb. 27, 1918, Uniontown. Buried Spring Hill Cemetery, Lynchburg. Papers (invaluable for any historian of Stuart's Cavalry) at Duke U. Gen. Early described Munford as "a nice gentleman, but not remarkably brilliant intellectually." On his postwar application for presidential pardon Munford stated he had never received a general's commission but in later years always asserted he had. Munford did not get along with Jeb Stuart, a factor that delayed the promotion his services and seniority otherwise entitled him to.

Murchison, Kenneth McKenzie. Born Feb. 18, 1831, Fayetteville, NC. Grad. UNC. Merchant in Fayetteville, Wilmington, and New York City prewar. Md. Katherine Williams. Lt. Co. C, 8th NC, May 16, 1861. Capt. Co. C, 54th NC, March 22, 1862. Major, May 16, 1862. Lt. col., Sept. 7, 1862. Col., May 8, 1863. POW Rappahannock Station, VA, Nov. 7, 1863. Released July 25, 1865. Financier in New York City and Wilmington postwar. Died June 3, 1904, Baltimore, MD. Buried Oakdale Cemetery, Wilmington. An "example of splendid physical manhood."

Murphy, Virgil S. Born June 27, 1837, SC. Montgomery, AL, lawyer. Lt. in vol. militia. Md. Nellie Gindrat. 2d lt. Co. F, 3d AL, 1861. Major, 17th AL, Sept. 5, 1861. Col., April 25, 1862. POW Franklin, released June 23, 1865. Died May 1, 1890, Montgomery, of typhoid, buried Oakwood Cemetery. His obituary notes he was "the most splendid looking officer . . . in the Western Army." Wartime diary at UNC.

Murray, John Edward. Born March 1843, Fauquier Co., VA. Reared Pine Bluff, AR, where his father, a judge, had moved. Attd. USMA 1860–61. Drilled recruits in AR, early 1861. Pvt. Co. B, 15th AR, July 23, 1861. Sgt. major, Aug. 20, 1861. Lt. col., 5th AR, Dec. 20, 1861. A favorite of Gen. Cleburne, "particularly distinguished for skill and gallantry" at Chickamauga and elsewhere. Philip D. Stephenson thought Murray "looked reckless but was not . . . he was but a boy— yet every inch a man." Col., 5th/13th AR, Sept. 19, 1863. MWIA Atlanta, July 22, 1864. Died on the battlefield the next day. Buried Cool Spring Cemetery near Atlanta; reburied Mt. Holly Cemetery, Little Rock, in 1867. It is said that his commission as general reached the army the day after his death.

Murray, John Perry. Born July 14, 1830, Gainesboro, Jackson Co., TN. Lawyer and judge in Jackson Co. prewar. Md. Evelyn Elizabeth Eaton. Enlisted Sept. 12, 1861. Col., 28th TN, Sept. 28, 1861. WIA Shiloh. Declined reelection to enter the cavalry service. Col., Murray's (aka 4th) TN Cav., Aug. 1862 to Jan. 23, 1863, when the unit was disbanded. Confederate congressman 1863–65. Gainesboro lawyer postwar. Died Dec. 21, 1895, Gainesboro. Buried in a family cemetery on his estate in Gainesboro. His successor as colonel said of Murray, "A more faithful and qualified officer never served."

Musser, Richard H. Born Feb. 6, 1829, Claysville, Harrison Co., KY. Reared in Cynthiana, KY. To Brunswick, Chariton Co., MO, in 1848. Prewar store clerk, lawyer, judge, editor. Unmd. Lt. col. and judge advocate, 3d Div., MSG, June 23, 1861. Lt. col., Musser's MO Inf. Bn., 1862. Lt. col., 9th MO (formed from his battalion), Jan. 22, 1863. Tried for disobeying orders to detail men to an artillery unit but acquitted. Col., Jan. 1, 1864. Attorney for Gen. Sterling Price at Price's court-martial. Postwar lawyer and businessman in St. Louis and Brunswick. Wrote several articles on his wartime experiences. Died Nov. 24, 1898, St. Joseph, MO. Buried Elliott Grove Cemetery, Brunswick. John N. Edwards called Musser "a scholar of extensive erudition . . . versatile in the cabinet and in the field."

Myers, Abram Charles. Born May 14, 1811, Georgetown, SC. Grad. USMA 1833. US Army officer 1833–61. Brevetted lt. col. for Mexican War service. Md. Marion, daughter of Gen. David Twiggs. Appointed QM gen. of LA, Feb. 1861. Appointed lt. col., CS Regular Army, and QM gen., March 29, 1861, to rank from March 16th. Col., Feb. 15, 1862. Myers ably performed the impossible task of supplying the Confederate armies with uniforms and equipment. In 1863 his supporters in Congress passed legislation upgrading the rank of the QM gen. to brig. gen., intending that Myers be promoted. Pres. Davis approved the legislation but appointed Gen. A. R. Lawton to the "new" post. Rumor attributed Pres. Davis's action to Myers's wife calling the dark-complexioned Mrs. Davis a "squaw." A disappointed Myers resigned Aug. 10, 1863. Lived postwar in GA; Europe; MD; and Washington, DC. Died June 20, 1889, Washington. Buried St. Paul's Church Cemetery, Alexandria, VA.

Myers, John Jacob. Born Oct. 5, 1821, Lincoln Co., MO. Farmer in MO. Lt. in Mexican War. Accompanied John C. Frémont in his explorations, and mined gold in CA. To Caldwell Co., TX, in 1852. Farmer and stock raiser. Md. Sarah E. Hudspeth; Elizabeth Skaggs. Capt. Co. B, 26th TX Cav., July 1, 1861. Major, Dec. 7, 1861. Lt. col., April 15, 1862. Col., April 8, 1864. Returned to his Lockhart farm after the war. Drove cattle to Salt Lake City and Abilene. Said to have driven the first herd of TX cattle into Abilene. Attacked by robbers in Omaha, while returning from a cattle drive. After returning home, he died Dec. 10, 1874, poisoned by the chloroform the robbers used on him. Buried Lockhart Cemetery.

Nadenbousch, John Quincy Adams. Born Oct. 31, 1824, Hampshire Co. VA. Carpenter, miller. Prewar mayor of Martinsburg. Capt. of vol. militia. Md. Hester J. Miller. Capt. Co. D, 2d VA, April 18, 1861. WIA 2d Manassas (groin). Col., Sept. 16, 1862. WIA Chancellorsville. Resigned due to disability Feb. 19, 1864. Commanded post of Staunton, 1863–64. Operated a flour mill and distillery in Martinsburg postwar. Died Sept. 13, 1892, Martinsburg, of paralysis. Buried Old

Norbourne Cemetery, Martinsburg. Nadenbousch's papers are at Duke U., UVA, and the Museum of the Confederacy.

Nance, James Drayton. Born Oct. 10, 1837, Newberry, SC. Grad. SCMA. Newberry lawyer prewar. Unmd. Capt. Co. E, 3d SC, April 14, 1861. Col., May 14, 1862. WIA Fredericksburg. KIA Wilderness, May 6, 1864. Buried Rosemont Cemetery, Newberry. A junior officer called Nance "the best all round soldier in Kershaw's Brigade." Papers at USC.

Neal, James Henry. Born Oct. 21, 1835, Macon, GA. Reared in Pike Co. Attd. UGA. Lawyer in Atlanta, GA, prewar. Capt. Co. B, 19th GA, June 11, 1861. Major, June 26, 1862. Lt. col., Jan. 12, 1863. Col., Aug. 20, 1863. KIA Kinston, NC, March 8, 1865. Buried on the battlefield; reburied Oakland Cemetery, Atlanta.

Neely, James Jackson. Born 1816, Maury Co., TN. Brother of Col. Rufus P. Neely. Attd. U. of Louisville Medical College. Physician in Bolivar, Hardeman Co., TN, prewar. County official. Md. Fanny Stephens, sister of Col. W. H. Stephens. Capt. Co. B (the "Hardeman Avengers"), 6th TN Cav. Bn., June 1861. Unit consolidated in April 1862. Left a supernumerary, Neely returned to west TN and recruited a regiment. Col., 14th TN Cav., July 1, 1863. Led brigade in Forrest's Corps in 1864. In Aug. 1864 a junior colonel (Edmond Rucker) was placed in command of the brigade. Neely and the other colonels protested. Cashiered for disobeying orders, Oct. 4, 1864. Postwar physician in Bolivar. County sheriff. Died Nov. 1894, Bolivar. Buried Polk Cemetery, Bolivar. A soldier called Neely "a faithful, brave and efficient commander."

Neely, Rufus Polk. Born Nov. 26, 1808, Spring Hill, Maury Co., TN. Cousin of Pres. Polk. Moved to Hardeman Co. in 1823. Railroad president. Militia general. County clerk. State representative 1839–41. Seminole War veteran. Md. Elizabeth Lea. Capt., "Pillow Guards," 1861. Col., 4th TN, May 15, 1861. Court-martialed in 1861 for drunkenness and neglect of duty. Successfully defended himself, not by denying the charges but by asserting the actions occurred before his regiment was mustered into Confederate service. In 1862 Gen. Beauregard suspended Neely from command. Resigned May 13, 1862. No further field service but aided in recruiting. Captured Aug. 11, 1862, Bolivar, TN. Exch. Sept. 25, 1863. Postwar newspaper editor. President of the Memphis and Knoxville Railroad. Died Aug. 10, 1901, Bolivar. Buried Polk Cemetery, Bolivar.

Neff, John Francis. Born Sept. 5, 1834, near Rude's Hill in the Shenandoah Valley, VA. Grad. VMI. Lawyer in New Orleans and Memphis prewar. Lt. and adj., 33d VA, early 1861. Col., April 22, 1862. Placed under arrest in the summer of 1862, probably in connection with the resentment the Stonewall Brigade felt when Charles Winder, an outsider, was placed in command of the brigade. Released just prior to 2d Manassas. KIA Groveton, Aug. 28, 1862. Buried Cedar Grove Church Cemetery, Rude's Hill. One story has it that Neff was a Dunkard who went to war against the wishes of his pacifist family.

Neil, James H. Born May 27, 1827, Bedford Co., TN. Bedford Co. attorney prewar. Mexican War veteran. Md. Jane Greer Whitney. Capt. Co. E, 23d TN, July 1, 1861. Lt. col., July 31, 1861. Col., May 1862. WIA Shiloh, which wound disabled him from field duty. Commissioned col. and judge, military court of Gen. Kirby Smith, Dec. 20, 1862. Shelbyville attorney postwar. Clerk of court. State representative 1869–71. Died Oct. 21, 1903, Shelbyville. Buried Willow Mount Cemetery, Shelbyville.

Neill, George Gilbreath Falls. Born Aug. 10, 1810, TN (probably Wilson Co.). Reared in Robertson Co., TN. Wealthy lawyer and planter in Carroll Co., MS, prewar. State representative 1850–52; state senator 1857–62. Mexican War veteran. Md. Caroline Hart; Helen Humphries. Col., 30th MS, April 12, 1862. Resigned June 6, 1863, due to ill health. Appointed Confederate tax collector for MS. Carroll Co. farmer postwar. Died April 27, 1877. Buried Evergreen Cemetery, Carrollton. Cong. Barksdale recommended Neill for collector as "a man of superior capacity."

Nelson, Andrew McCampbell. Born March 2, 1830, White Co., TN. Lawyer and judge in Carroll Co., MS, prewar. Md. Laura Caldwell. Capt. Co. A, 42d MS, May 14, 1862. Lt. col., Dec. 18, 1863. Col., May 5, 1864. WIA Wilderness. POW Hatcher's Run, April 2, 1865. Released from prison June 18, 1865. Lawyer in Carroll Co. postwar. Private sec. and adj. gen. to Gov. Stone. Died Oct. 2, 1883, Winona, MS. Buried Oakwood Cemetery, Winona. "A gentleman of high culture."

Nelson, Noel Ligon. Born c. 1830, Walton Co., GA. Prewar farmer in Claiborne Parish, LA. Md. Emma Moragne. 1st lt. Co. L, 12th LA, Aug. 13, 1861. Capt., Jan. 9, 1862. Major, May 11, 1862. Lt. col., Jan. 5, 1863. Col., May 10, 1864. MWIA Franklin, Nov. 30, 1864, having both of his legs crushed by a cannon shot. Died that evening in the Carnton field hospital. Buried McGavock Confederate Cemetery, Franklin. The Carter House Museum at Franklin has a heartrending letter describing his last moments.

Nelson, William. Born Dec. 19, 1808 (per his tombstone—one source has Dec. 14, 1808), Yorktown, VA, of a prominent and well-connected VA family. Farmer in Hanover Co. prewar. State representative 1857–58. Unmd. Capt., Hanover Light Art., April 1861. Unit mustered into state service May 21, 1861. Dropped at April 20, 1862, reorganization, because he was too severe a disciplinarian. Major of artillery, May 26, 1862. Lt. col., March 3, 1863. Col., Feb. 18,

1865. Commanded an artillery battalion in the ANV's II Corps. Hanover Co. farmer postwar. Died April 17, 1892, "Oakland," Hanover Co. Buried Fork Episcopal Church, Hanover Co.

Nethercutt, John Hawkins. Born c. 1824, NC. Middle name also given as "Hussey." Farmer in Duplin and Jones Cos. prewar. Jones Co. sheriff. Md. Zilpha Quinn; Susan Dixon. 1st lt. Co. I, 27th NC, June 17, 1861. Not reelected at reorganization. Capt. Co. A, 8th NC Bn. PR, April 29, 1862. Major, Aug. 23, 1862. Lt. col., 66th NC (formed from the 8th Bn.), Aug. 3, 1863. Deserters from his unit were involved in the infamous Kinston hanging. Col., June 3, 1864. WIA near Petersburg, VA, June 18, 1864, in the face, by a shell. Commanded a brigade of NC junior reserves at Bentonville. Paroled Greensboro. Murdered Dec. 8, 1867, in his home. The murderers (associated with the Carpetbagger regime) were acquitted in a rigged trial but hung by the local citizens. Buried Trenton Cemetery. Nethercutt was considered "plain, blunt, but every inch a soldier."

Newman, Tazewell Waller. Born March 27, 1827, Harrisonburg, VA. Reared in Knox Co., TN. Grad. UTN. Franklin Co. bricklayer in 1860. State representative 1855–59. Officer in Mexican War. Md. Sarah Buchanan. Col., 17th TN, June 11, 1861. Not reelected at reorganization. Major, 23d TN Inf. Bn., Nov. 29, 1862. WIA Chickamauga. Unit consolidated with the 45th TN, Nov. 1863. Newman, a supernumerary, was on detached service the remainder of the war. Died Oct. 2, 1868, Winchester, TN, of his war wounds. Buried Winchester.

Newsom, John Francis. Born Sept. 16, 1827, Madison Co., TN. Farmer in Madison Co. prewar. Md. Susan Epperson; Margaret E. Smith. Capt. Co. F, 6th TN, May 15, 1861. WIA Shiloh. Resigned April 12, 1862. Authorized by Gen. Pillow to raise a regiment within federal lines. Captured in 1862 and exchanged. Organized Newsom's TN Cav. at Jackson, TN, July 27, 1863. Col., 18th TN Cav., May 11, 1864. WIA Tupelo. Captured after the battle of Nashville but escaped while en route north. Sawmill owner in Jackson, TN, postwar. Died Dec. 11, 1884, Henderson, Chester Co. Buried Riverside Cemetery, Jackson.

Newton, Robert Crittenden. Born June 2, 1840, Little Rock, AR. Attd. WMI. Prewar lawyer in Little Rock. Capt., "Pulaski Light Artillery," a vol. militia unit. Md. Cassie Reider in 1866. 1st lt. Co. F, 18th AR, July 27, 1861. Capt. Co. F, 3d Confederate (formerly the 18th AR), Dec. 4, 1861. Dropped March 15, 1862. Capt. and AAG, Dec. 1, 1861. AAG to Gens. Hindman and Holmes, 1861–62. Appointed col. and chief of staff by Gen. Hindman, June 1, 1862. Hindman's chief of staff, 1862–63. Appointed col., 5th (aka 8th) AR Cav., by Gen. Holmes April 12, 1863, but the appointment was later acknowledged illegal. Turned over command to Thomas Morgan, Dec. 24, 1863, when regiment renumbered (as Morgan's 2d). Col., 3d AR State Cav., Sept. 5, 1864. Regiment transferred to

Confederate service and renamed the 10th AR Cav., Oct. 31, 1864. Led a cavalry brigade in the TMD. Postwar lawyer in Little Rock. Militia general. State legislator. Briefly state treasurer in 1874. Died June 5, 1887, Little Rock. Buried Calvary Cemetery, Little Rock.

Nichols, Ebenezer B. Born Oct. 12, 1815, Cooperstown, NY. Broker in New
York City. Moved to Houston in 1838. Settled in Galveston in 1850. Wealthy cotton merchant. Grand Master of TX Masons. Veteran of TX Wars. Gen. in state
militia. Delegate to TX Secession Convention. Md. Margaret Clayton Stone. In
March 1861 Nichols commanded the state forces that seized Fort Brown near
the Mexican border. Col., 9th TX (a 6-month unit), Oct. 1, 1861. Commanded
Sub-District of Galveston in late 1861–early 1862. After the 9th disbanded,
Nichols served as a volunteer aide to Gen. Magruder. Postwar merchant, banker
in Galveston. Died Nov. 30, 1872, Galveston. Buried Galveston Episcopal Cemetery.

Nisbet, James Cooper. Born Sept. 26, 1839, Macon, GA. Reared in Macon.
Grad. Oglethorpe U. Farmer in Dade Co. prewar. Md. Mary E. Young; Louise
Bailey. Capt. Co. H, 21st GA, July 2, 1861. WIA Gaines's Mill and Antietam. Resigned to raise a regiment. Col., 66th GA, Oct. 8, 1863. POW Atlanta July 22,
1864. Imprisoned for the rest of the war. Returned to Dade Co. farm after the
war. State representative 1868–70. Sec. to 1877 GA constitutional convention.
Worked for Acme Kitchen Furniture Co. in Chattanooga and moved there in
1902. Died there May 20, 1917. Buried Confederate Cemetery, Chattanooga.
Nisbet wrote a much-cited memoir, *Four Years on the Firing Line.*

Nixon, George Henry. Born Oct. 9, 1822, Maury Co., TN. Lawyer in
Lawrenceburg. Registrar of US Land Office in Brownville, NE, 1857–61. Officer in Mexican War. Md. Sarah Busby. Major, 23d TN, July 31, 1861. Not reelected at May 1862 reorganization. Col., 48th TN, April 7, 1862. Severely WIA
at Richmond. Lost race for Confederate Congress in 1863. Dropped July 22,
1864, when his regiment was consolidated with Voorhies's 48th. Col., 22d (aka
20th, Nixon's) TN Cav., 1864. Practiced law in Lawrenceburg postwar. Judge.
Died July 4, 1887, Lawrenceburg. Buried Old City Cemetery, Lawrenceburg.

Norris, William. Born Dec. 6, 1820, Baltimore Co., MD. Grad. Yale 1840.
Lawyer in New Orleans 1840–49. Judge advocate, USN, 1849–51. Moved to
Reistertown, MD (near Baltimore), in 1851. President of Baltimore Mechanical
Bakery. Md. Ellen Hobson. On July 28, 1861, he was authorized to set up a sig-
nal system on the Yorktown Peninsula. Capt., Gen. Magruder's staff, 1862. Com-
missioned major, Oct. 8, 1862. Headed the Confederate Signal Corps 1862–64.
Also chief of the Confederate intelligence bureau in Richmond. Appointed col.,
April 25, 1865 (2 weeks after Appomattox, at a time when the Confederate gov-

ernment was dissolving), to head the prisoner exchange program. Postwar farmer in Reistertown. Died at his Reistertown home Dec. 29, 1896. Buried All Saints Episcopal Church Cemetery, Reistertown. Porter Alexander called Norris "an excellent man." Papers at UVA.

Norris, William Henry. Born Oct. 27, 1810, Baltimore, MD. Grad. Yale 1829. Prewar Baltimore lawyer. Md. Mary Ellen Owen. Active secessionist. Imprisoned early in the war at Fort McHenry for aiding the Confederacy. Released, and went south in June 1862. Appointed col. and judge of the military court of Jones's Corps, Dec. 16, 1862. Postwar lawyer in Baltimore. City councilor. Died Jan. 31, 1890, Baltimore. Judah Benjamin, a college friend, recommended Norris for appointment as "an accomplished lawyer" with "large experience in court-martial."

Norwood, Alexander Scott. Born c. 1826, LA. Farmer in East Feliciana Parish prewar. Parish sheriff. Md. Catherine Andrews. 2d lt. Co. A (the "Skipwith Guards"), 27th LA, March 1, 1862. Capt., appointed March 29, 1862, to rank from Feb. 6, 1862. Major, Nov. 12, 1862. WIA and POW Vicksburg. Paroled and exchanged. Col., appointed May 26, 1864, to rank from Sept. 23, 1862. Paroled June 8, 1865, Shreveport. Resided in Clinton, LA, postwar. Local agent for a New Orleans–based firm of cotton factors. Died March 9, 1869, at his home in East Feliciana Parish. Buried Major Doughty Cemetery, near Felixville.

Norwood, Isaiah Theophilus. Born July 26, 1827, East Feliciana Parish, LA. Attd. Centenary College. Prewar Avoyelles Parish planter. State legislator. Md. Mary M. McIntyre. Major, 2d LA, May 1861. Col., elected at May 2, 1862, reorganization. MWIA Malvern Hill. Died in Richmond July 16, 1862. Buried Hollywood Cemetery. Comrades praised him for his "mildness, kindness, generosity, frankness and calm equanimity." His last words to his men were, "Don't stop, boys, but press on until the hill is ours."

Nuckols, Joseph Preyer. Born April 28, 1826, Barren Co., KY. Deputy sheriff in Glasgow, Barren Co., prewar. Capt., KSG. Md. Malinda Carr; Caron Donaldson. Capt. Co. A, 4th KY, Sept. 13, 1861. Major, April 7, 1862. Lt. col., Dec. 8, 1862. Col., Feb. 28, 1863. WIA Shiloh, Stones River, Chickamauga. Retired c. Feb. 1864 because of his wounds. Commanded post of Aberdeen, MS, in late 1864. Paroled May 15, 1865, Meridian. County clerk postwar. State representative. State adj. gen. Died Aug. 30, 1896, Glasgow. Buried Glasgow Cemetery. His uniform coat, showing his Chickamauga wound, still exists.

Oates, William Calvin. Born Nov. 30, 1833, Pike Co., AL. Teacher, carpenter, and house painter FL, LA, TX, and finally in Abbeville, AL. Studied law and edited an Abbeville newspaper. Md. Sarah Toney. Capt. Co. G, 15th AL, July 26, 1861.

Appointed col. to rank from April 28, 1863, but never confirmed, because the former lt. col. (A. A. Lowther) revoked his resignation and claimed the colonelcy on the basis of seniority. Major, appointed June 9, 1864, to rank from April 28, 1863. As col., led the 15th in the famous attack on Little Round Top. WIA Brown's Ferry. Temporarily major (and acting col.) 48th AL June–Aug. 1864. Arm shattered at Fussell's Mill, Aug. 16, 1864. Lt. col., Dec. 7, 1864. Appointed col. of cav. March 23, 1865, to serve on military court of Wheeler's Corps. Abbeville lawyer postwar. State legislator 1870–72, US congressman 1880–94, governor of AL 1894–96. Brig. gen. US Volunteers in Spanish American War. Died Sept. 9, 1910, Montgomery, AL, buried Oakwood Cemetery. Authored a highly regarded book on the war. One soldier of the 15th thought Oates "too aggressive and ambitious but he . . . did not require his men to charge where he was unwilling to share the common danger."

Oatis, Martin Augustus. Born April 2, 1833, Hancock Co., MS. Reared in Monticello and Brookhaven, MS. Grad. UMS (with honors) and Cumberland U. Law School. Lawyer in Brookhaven in 1860. Moved to Cleburne, TX, just prior to the war. Md. Helen Teunisson; Mrs. Nancy Hooker Smith. 1st lt. Co. A, 22d MS, April 27, 1861. Capt., Dec. 24, 1861. Major, March 9, 1864. WIA Shiloh, Baton Rouge, and Peachtree Creek. Led regiment there and at Nashville. Led Featherston's Brigade at Bentonville. Col., 22d MS Consolidated, April 19, 1865. Paroled May 1, 1865, Greensboro. Lawyer in Brookhaven and (from 1870) Cleburne postwar. Probate judge. Died Jan. 26, 1895, TX. Buried Cleburne Cemetery.

Ochiltree, William Beck. Born Oct. 18, 1811, Fayetteville, NC. Reared in NC, FL, and AL. Practiced law in AL. To Nacogdoches, TX, in 1839. Marshall, TX, lawyer. Treasurer of Republic of TX. Judge. State legislator. Md. Mary L. Smith; Noraline Kennard; Atala Hitchkiss. Delegate to TX Secession Convention. Confederate Congress, 1861–62. Col., 18th TX, May 13, 1862. Resigned Feb. 23, 1863, due to ill health. Settled in Jefferson, TX, postwar. Died Dec. 27, 1867, Jefferson. Buried Oakwood Cemetery, Jefferson. Major W. H. King of the 18th thought Ochiltree an "old fellow . . . pot bellied and pompous." Ochiltree Co., TX, is named for him.

Ogden, Frederick Nash. Born Jan. 25, 1837, Baton Rouge, LA. Moved to New Orleans in 1855 to live with his uncles. Prewar clerk for a New Orleans cotton factor. Md. Laura B. Jackson. Pvt. Co. B, 1st LA Inf. Bn., April 13, 1861. Color sgt., June 14, 1861. Major, 8th LA Art. Bn., April 15, 1862. POW Vicksburg. Exch. Major, 9th LA Bn. PR, March 1864. Lt. col., Ogden's Cav. Bn., June 6, 1864. Col., Ogden's LA Cav. Regt. (formed from the battalion), Jan. 1865. Paroled Gainesville May 12, 1865. Postwar merchant in New Orleans. Commanded the "White

League" trying to overthrow Reconstruction rule. Unsuccessful candidate for governor in 1879 and 1883. Died May 25, 1886, New Orleans. Buried Metairie Cemetery. An Ogden family history calls him "distinguished for military capacity and headlong daring."

Oglesby, Landon Ware. Born Nov. 22, 1833, Overton Co., TN. Dry goods merchant in Jackson Co. prewar. Large landowner. Md. Martha M. Fowler. Appointed asst. QM, Provisional Army of TN, June 28, 1861. Capt. and QM, 8th TN (a unit he largely uniformed), July 19, 1861. Col., May 8, 1862. Rejected by a board of examiners as unqualified and incompetent. Resigned June 10, 1862, and returned home. Moved to Collin Co., TX, postwar. Merchant, farmer, grist mill owner in Plano. County tax collector. Died Jan. 16, 1887, at "Honeysuckle Hill," his Plano home (one story has it he committed suicide after arrearages were found in his tax collections). Buried Plano Mutual Cemetery.

Oliver, James McCarty. Born May 12, 1831, Elbert Co., GA. Reared in Chambers Co., AL. Grad. Oglethorpe U. Prewar merchant, later lawyer, in Dadeville, AL. Md. Matilda Allen; Catherine Carter of Perry, GA. Capt. Co. K, 47th AL, April 29, 1862. Elected col. at May 22, 1862, organization of regiment. Resigned Aug. 11, 1862, citing chronic liver disease. However, his lt. col. wrote that Oliver had resigned because he wasn't "fond of the smell of . . . gun powder." Postwar lawyer in Dadeville and Lafayette, AL. Died Aug. 23, 1896, Perry, after falling and hitting his head on an outhouse. Buried Evergreen Cemetery, Perry.

Olmstead, Charles Hart. Born April 2, 1837, Savannah, GA. Grad. GMI. Cashier in a mercantile house in Savannah prewar. Md. Florence Williams. Adj., 1st GA, when it seized Fort Pulaski in early 1861. Major, 1st GA, May 27, 1861. Col., Dec. 26, 1861. Commanded Fort Pulaski in 1862. POW there. Exch. Sept. 20, 1862. Unit transferred to Army of TN in 1864. Led Mercer's Brigade late in war. WIA Atlanta. Paroled May 1, 1865, Greensboro. Savannah merchant and banker postwar. Died Aug. 17, 1926, Savannah. Buried Laurel Grove Cemetery. Olmstead was heavily criticized for surrendering Fort Pulaski, and Gen. Cleburne found him "not efficient" as a brigade commander. Olmstead's wartime reminiscences have been published.

O'Neil, John G. Born Feb. 1841, Co. Kerry, Ireland. Farmer in Humphreys Co., TN, prewar. Md. postwar, perhaps Nancy Drusilla Jackson of KY. Capt. Co. A, 10th TN, Sept. 1, 1861. "A gentleman of reflection and unflinching determination." Major, May 12, 1863. WIA Resaca. Lt. col., Sept. 17, 1864. Col., Sept. 27, 1864. Recruited Irish-born Union army prisoners for the Confederate army. POW Bentonville. Paroled May 1, 1865, Greensboro. Nothing certain is known of his postwar career, though he probably lived in KY and St. Louis. Died c. 1874–1880.

Orr, James Lawrence. Born May 12, 1822, Craytonville, SC. Grad. UVA. Anderson lawyer. Editor, Anderson *Gazette*. State representative 1844–47. US congressman 1849–59. Speaker of the US House 1857–59. Delegate to SC Secession Convention. Md. Mary Jane Marshall, sister of Col. J. F. Marshall. Col., 1st SC Rifles ("Orr's Rifles"), July 20, 1861. Resigned Feb. 1, 1862, upon election to the Confederate Senate. Senator 1862–65. Chairman of the Senate Committee on Foreign Affairs. Gov. of SC, 1865–68. Judge, 1868–70. US minister to Russia (appointed by Pres. Grant), 1872–73. Died May 5, 1873, St. Petersburg, Russia. Buried Presbyterian Cemetery, Anderson. Mary Chesnut thought Orr was "always a Union man," a belief supported by Orr's postwar affiliation with the Republicans. Brother of Col. Jehu A. Orr. Papers at USC.

Orr, Jehu Amaziah. Born April 10, 1828, Anderson Dist., SC. Brother of Col. James L. Orr. Family moved to MS in 1843. Grad. Princeton, 1849. Lawyer in Pontotoc Co. prewar. Dist. attorney. State legislator. Delegate to MS Secession Convention. Md. Lizzie Gates; Cornelia Vandegraff. Confederate congressman 1861–62. Lt. col., Orr's MS Inf. Bn., Jan. 31, 1862. Col., 31st MS, April 9, 1862. Resigned March 11, 1864, due to ill health. VADC to Gens. Forrest and Lee at Tupelo. Confederate congressman 1864–65. Lawyer and judge in Columbus postwar. Died March 9, 1921, Columbus. Buried Friendship Cemetery, Columbus. Orr's service record contains numerous testimonials from his superiors as to his ability.

Osborne, Edwin Augustus Young. Born May 6, 1837, Moulton, AL. Reared in AL, Jefferson Co., AR, and Hill Co., TX, eventually moving in with relatives in Iredell Co., NC. Attd. Statesville Military Academy in Iredell Co. Md. Fannie Moore. 2d lt. Co. C, 4th NC, May 16, 1861. Capt., May 16, 1861. Major, Dec. 23, 1861. WIA Seven Pines (thigh). WIA and POW Antietam. Exch. Dec. 1862. WIA Spotsylvania (hand—two fingers amputated). Lt. col., May 19, 1864. Col., July 18, 1864. Retired to Invalid Corps April 1, 1865. Lawyer in Charlotte postwar. Clerk of the superior court. Episcopal minister in Henderson Co. Minister and superintendent of an orphanage in Charlotte. Served as chaplain, 2d NC, in Spanish-American War. Died Oct. 12, 1926, Charlotte. Buried Elmwood Cemetery, Charlotte. "Greatly loved and respected."

Otey, Kirkwood. Born Oct. 19, 1829, Lynchburg, VA. Grad. VMI. Attd. UVA. Banker in Lynchburg prewar. Militia officer. Md. Lucy D. Norvell. Lt. Co. G, 11th VA, April 23, 1861. Capt., May 9, 1861. Cashiered for drunkenness on duty, April 1863. Major, May 23, 1862. WIA Gettysburg. Lt. col., Sept. 24, 1863. WIA Drewry's Bluff. Col., Dec. 20, 1864. Assigned to duty in Lynchburg April 1, 1865, to recruit Negro troops. Paroled April 15, 1865, Lynchburg. Lynchburg insurance agent postwar. City auditor. Died June 1, 1897, Lynchburg. Buried Spring Hill Cemetery, Lynchburg.

Ould, Robert. Born Jan. 31, 1820, Georgetown, DC. Attd. Jefferson College in PA. Grad. Columbian College in DC and William & Mary College. Prewar lawyer in DC. Dist. attorney. Prosecuted congressman and future Union general Dan Sickles for murder in one celebrated case. Militia general. Md. Sarah Turpin; Mrs. Madge Dorsey Handy. Appointed asst. sec. of war, Jan. 1862. Resigned April 1, 1862. Appointed Confederate commissioner of exchange, with the rank of col., July 1862. Judge advocate, court-martial duty in Richmond, 1863–65. Indicted and imprisoned for treason after the war on the charge of misappropriating funds belonging to Union prisoners but soon released. Richmond lawyer postwar. State legislator. Railroad president. Died Dec. 15, 1882, Richmond, buried Hollywood Cemetery. An obituary said he "was ever the soul of honor, and was always brilliant."

Owen, Thomas Howerton. Born June 11, 1833, Halifax Co., VA. Grad. VMI 1856. Farmer in South Boston. Civil engineer. Capt. of vol. militia. Md. Elizabeth A. Williams in 1861. Lt. Co. C, 3d VA Cav., Aug. 16, 1861. Capt., Dec. 16, 1861. Lt. col., Oct. 21, 1862. Col., Nov. 18, 1862. "As gallant as possible" but not "calm and un-excited in battle." Court-martialed April 29, 1864, and temporarily suspended from command. WIA Spotsylvania (hand). Civil engineer, schoolteacher, and farmer in South Boston postwar. Died May 8, 1894, Halifax Co. Probably buried in an unmarked grave in Oak Ridge Cemetery, South Boston, along with his wife. Owen's original promotion to col. was messed up; he had to be reappointed in 1865.

Owens, John Crowder. Born March 19, 1830, Mathews Co., VA. Reared in Portsmouth. Pharmacist. Capt. of the Portsmouth Rifle Company, vol. militia. Carpenter. Md. Mary A. Foster. Capt. Co. G, 9th VA (his old militia company), April 20, 1861. Major, May 24, 1862. WIA Aug. 1862, Warrenton Springs. Col., Oct. 30, 1862. MWIA Pickett's Charge. Died July 4, 1863, in the Pickett's Div. field hospital along Marsh Creek, near Gettysburg. Buried by Marsh Creek; reburied postwar Oakwood Cemetery, Portsmouth.

Owens, Robert Armstrong. Born Nov. 28, 1831, Stewart Co., TN. Farmer in Henry Co. prewar. Md. Malinda Wimberly. Capt. Co. I, 46th TN, Nov. 29, 1861. POW Island No. 10. Exch. Sept. 1862. Lt. col., Sept. 30, 1862. WIA Jackson, MS, May 13, 1863, disabling his arm for life. Col., Oct. 21, 1863. WIA Ezra Church. Retired due to disability. Henry Co. farmer postwar. Justice of the peace. Died Nov. 5, 1906, Henry Co. Buried Williams Cemetery, Henry Co. One soldier called Owens "a very efficient officer . . . a fine disciplinarian."

Owens, William Allison. Born Sept. 19, 1833, Charlotte, NC. Grad. UNC. Lawyer. Mayor of Charlotte. Md. Alice B. Caldwell. Lt. Co. B, 1st (Bethel) NC, April 16, 1861. Capt., Sept. 28, 1861. Major, 34th NC, Jan. 28, 1862. Lt. col., 11th

NC, March 31, 1862. Col., 53d NC, May 6, 1862. WIA Spotsylvania (side and head). MWIA Snicker's Ford, VA, July 18, 1864. Died there the next day. Buried Old Stone Church near Berryville; reburied Old Settlers' Cemetery, Charlotte. A "good officer, brave, humane, social, popular with both men and officers."

Page, Powhatan Robertson. Born June 29, 1821, Gloucester Co., VA. Gloucester Co. farmer prewar. 1st lt., US Army, in Mexican War. Capt. of vol. militia. Md. Lizzie Scollay. Lt. col., 26th VA, May 1861. Col., May 13, 1862. KIA June 17, 1864, shot through the body near Battery 16, Petersburg. Buried Blandford Cemetery, Petersburg. The chaplain of the 26th called Page "beloved . . . a noble officer and a proven patriot."

Page, Thomas Jefferson. Born Jan. 4, 1808, "Shelley," Gloucester Co., VA. Officer, USN, 1827–61. Md. Benjamina Price. Commander, CSN, June 10, 1861. Commanded batteries at Gloucester Point, VA, May 1862. Col., PACS, June 12, 1862. Commanded batteries at Drewry's Bluff, 1862–63. Commissioned capt. CSN, May 13, 1863. Sent to Europe to purchase warships. Commanded CSS *Stonewall* in 1865. Cattle ranched in Argentina postwar (where he had conducted explorations for the navy prewar). Moved to London. Retired to Florence and Rome, Italy. Died Oct. 25, 1899, Rome. Buried Protestant Cemetery, Rome. His son Thomas Jr. was a major of artillery. An obituary says "a more courageous officer never trod the deck of a vessel."

Palmer, John Boynton. Born Oct. 13, 1826, Plattsburg, Clinton Co., NY, son of a local politician and US congressman. Moved to Detroit, MI, where his older brother had set up a law practice. Detroit merchant. Moved to Western NC between 1857 and 1860. Wealthy farmer in Watauga Co. Unsuccessful antisecession candidate to the NC Secession Convention. Md. Frances Marvin Kirby, first cousin to Gen. E. Kirby Smith. Capt., "Mitchell Rangers," Dec. 11, 1861. Attempted to recruit the "Palmer Legion" in the spring and summer of 1862. Lt. col., 5th NC PR Bn. (the cavalry companies he raised for the legion), May 13, 1862. Col., 58th NC (the infantry companies he raised), July 29, 1862. WIA Chickamauga. Regiment consolidated with 60th NC in Nov. 1863, and Palmer was relieved of duty. Commanded Dist. of Western NC, Nov. 18, 1863, to Dec. 1864. Commanded a brigade in that district, Dec. 1864–May 1865. Paroled May 8, 1865, Athens, GA. Settled in Columbia, SC, postwar. President of railroad. Bank president. Retired to Winter Park, FL. Died Dec. 10, 1893, Winter Park, FL. Buried Elmwood Cemetery, Columbia. Gov. Vance found Palmer "a good bureau officer" but not a good field commander. He owned considerable property in Detroit during the war and had several close relatives in the Union army.

Pargoud, John Frank (Jean Francois). Born Nov. 18, 1828, Monroe, LA. Educated in France and served in French Army. Moved back to LA to manage the vast properties of his relatives, part of which he inherited. Wealthy planter (worth $800,000 in 1870) in Ouachita Parish prewar. Md. Amanda Storer. Capt. "Ouachita Rangers," LA militia, April 21, 1861. Lt. and ADC. to Gen. Blanchard, 1862. Col., 3d LA Cav. (Pargoud's) at Oct. 1862 organization of regiment. Gen. Richard Taylor relieved him of command Jan. 16, 1863, for disobeying orders to stop a Union raid and broke up the regiment. Taylor subsequently found Gen. Blanchard more to blame for the fiasco and praised Pargoud as "possessing ability and soldierly qualities." Postwar planter in Ouachita Parish. Moved to New Britain, CT, c. 1876–80. Died March 4, 1908, New Britain. Buried Fairview Cemetery, New Britain. Journalist Kate Stone found Pargoud "young and splendid looking" in 1862, as the local girls swooned over him.

Parham, William Allen. Born c. 1830, VA. Planter in Sussex Co. Md. Hannah Turnbull of Warrenton, NC. Lt. Co. A, 41st VA, May 24, 1861. Capt., early 1862. Lt. col., May 3, 1862. WIA Malvern Hill in his right side. Col., July 25, 1862. WIA Antietam. Left the army in 1863 due to his wounds and was assigned to provost duty at Weldon, NC. Lost race for Confederate Congress in 1863. Retired to Invalid Corps March 31, 1865. Died July 2, 1866, Warrenton. A "generous, brave, high-spirited gentleman."

Parker, Francis Marion. Born Sept. 21, 1827, Nash Co., NC. Educated at Lovejoy's Military Academy in Raleigh. Halifax Co. planter prewar. Officer in the "Enfield Blues" vol. militia company. Militia colonel. Md. Sarah Phillips. Lt. Co. I (the "Enfield Blues"), 1st (Bethel) NC, April 19, 1861. Capt., Sept. 1, 1861. Col., 30th NC, Oct. 7, 1861. WIA Antietam (head), Gettysburg (face), Spotsylvania (abdomen). Incapacitated by this last wound. In 1864 the NC legislature recommended him for promotion, but Parker ("a brave, cool, and excellent officer") admitted he was too feeble to serve as general. Retired to Invalid Corps Jan. 17, 1865. Commanded post of Greensboro, NC, in 1865. Farmer in Enfield, Halifax Co., postwar. Died Jan. 18, 1905, Enfield. Buried Calvary Episcopal Cemetery, Tarboro. His wartime letters were published as *To Drive the Enemy from Southern Soil.*

Parks, Marcus A. Born Oct. 9, 1831, NC. Wilkesboro farmer prewar. Md. Mary Lenoir Hickerson in 1865. 1st lt. Co. B, 1st NC, May 16, 1861. Resigned April 12, 1862. Capt. Co. F, 52d NC, March 14, 1862. Major, April 18, 1862. Lt. col., April 25, 1862. WIA (leg and arm) at Gettysburg and POW. Not exch. until March 1865. Col., appointed while in prison, to rank probably from July 3, 1863. Farmer in Wilkes Co.; CA; Augusta, AR; and Muscogee, OK, postwar. Died April 5, 1897, OK. Buried Enid Cemetery, Enid, OK.

Parrish, Henry Tucker. Born Sept. 14, 1829, Newington, Cumberland Co., VA. Grad. VMI. Attd. UVA. Farmville lawyer prewar. Militia captain. Md. Virginia C. Ragland. Lt. Co. K, 3d VA Cav., early 1861. Major, 16th VA, May 16, 1861. Lt. col., May 17, 1861. Col., Jan. 6, 1862. Failed reelection at May 3, 1862, reorganization. Parrish contested the election results, got briefly reinstated, but was again dropped eight days later. Provost marshal in Farmville but removed for not holding a valid commission. VADC to Gen. Colston. Made several applications for appointment to a military court. Lawyer in Appomattox Co. postwar. Judge. On VMI Board. Moved to Roanoke in 1888. Died Feb. 15, 1913, Roanoke. Buried Fairview Cemetery, Roanoke.

Parsons, William Henry. Born April 2, 1826, NJ. Reared in Montgomery, AL, where his father operated a shoe factory. Attd. Emory U., leaving to join the US Army and fight in the Mexican War. Settled in TX after this war. Farmer. Editor, Tyler *Telegraph* and Waco *Southwest*. Active in politics. Noted stump speaker and secessionist. Md. Louisa Dennard. Appointed col. and ADC of TX militia, June 10, 1861, to head up the camp of instruction in Texas's 9th militia dist. Commissioned July 1861 to raise a 12-month cavalry regiment for state service. Col., 12th TX Cav., Oct. 28, 1861. Led a brigade of Texas cavalry in AR in 1862 and in the Red River Campaign. Parsons and G. W. Carter, another col. in the brigade, had a warlong dispute over who was the brigade's senior col. and entitled to promotion. Parsons claimed seniority from the date of his state commission—Carter countered that Parsons's seniority should count from Oct. 28, 1861, when his regiment was mustered into Confederate service. The dispute resulted in neither being promoted. Became a "scalawag" Republican after the war. Gen. in TX state militia. TX state senator 1870–71. State commissioner of immigration. Customs official in Norfolk, VA. Dabbled in health fads and radical politics. Also lived in Baltimore, New York City, and Chicago. Died Oct. 2, 1907, Chicago. Buried Mt. Hope Cemetery, Hastings-on-Hudson, NY. One soldier averred that "Col. P. . . . is more popular with his Regiment than any Colonel in America. The longer I am out with him [the] better I like him." His younger brother Albert, a Socialist agitator, was executed for murder for his part in the Haymarket Riot in Chicago.

Pate, Henry Clay. Born April 21, 1832, Bedford Co., VA. Attd. UVA. Lived in Louisville and Cincinnati. Lawyer and newspaper editor in MO. Militia officer. "Border ruffian" in the KS troubles. Returned to VA to edit a newspaper in Petersburg. Md. Susan Thomas. Capt., "Petersburg Rangers" (later Co. D, 5th VA Cav.), June 5, 1861. Lt. col., 2d VA Cav. Bn., May 1862. Lt. col., 5th VA Cav. (formed from the 2d Bn.), June 24, 1862. WIA Aldie. Col., Sept. 28, 1863. KIA Yellow Tavern. Buried on the battlefield; reburied Hollywood Cemetery. Pate had a long feud with the oft-critical Gen. Rosser, who charged Pate was "totally inefficient, and lacks every qualification of an officer." However, the regiment thought highly of him.

Patterson, Josiah. Born April 14, 1837, Somerville, Morgan Co., AL. Attd. Somerville Academy. Morgan Co. lawyer prewar. Md. Josephine Rice. 1st lt. Co. C, 1st AL Cav. (later Co. D, 5th AL Cav.), late 1861. Capt., 1862. Col., 5th AL Cav., appointed by Gen. Roddey Dec. 15, 1862. Often led Roddey's cavalry brigade. Briefly captured at Battle of Selma in 1865 but soon escaped. Paroled May 19, 1865. Postwar lawyer in Somerville and Florence. To Memphis, TN, in 1872. US congressman 1891–97. Died Feb. 12, 1904, Memphis. Buried Forest Hill Cemetery, Memphis. Patterson's son was also a US congressman.

Patterson, William Kerr. Born Oct. 22, 1823, TN (probably Sumner Co.). Attd. Wirt College in Sumner Co. Lawyer in Sumner Co. and later Jacksonport, AR. State representative 1854–55. Prosecuting attorney of AR's 3d Circuit, 1856–60. Md. Samuella J. Ridley. Col., 8th AR, July 6, 1861. Resigned April 30, 1862. Tried to raise troops in northeast AR in 1863. Appointed col. of a military court, Dist. of AR, Sept. 1864. Postwar Jacksonport lawyer. Trustee of Arkansas College in Batesville. To Rutherford Co., TN, in 1876. Farmer there. Died 1911 in TN. Probably buried in an unmarked grave in Patterson Cemetery, Rutherford Co.

Patton, George Smith. Born June 26, 1833, Fredericksburg, VA. One of four brothers to become Confederate colonels. Reared in Richmond. Grad. VMI 1856. Lawyer in Charleston, VA (now WVA), prewar. Capt. of vol. militia. Md. Susan T. Glassell. Capt. Co. H, 22d VA, May 22, 1861. Lt. col., July 7, 1861. WIA Scary Creek in shoulder, July 17, 1861. Left on the battlefield and captured. Declared exchanged March 1862, although there was some confusion as to his exact parole status and date of exchange. Col., Nov. 23, 1861. WIA in the stomach May 10, 1862, Giles Court House. Often led Echols's Brigade. MWIA Opequon Creek. Died Sept. 25, 1864, at the home of John J. Williams in Winchester. Buried Stonewall Cemetery, Winchester. Grandfather of Gen. George S. Patton of WWII fame. An officer in the 22d thought Patton "a very competent officer and strict disciplinarian."

Patton, Isaac Williams. Born Feb. 4, 1828, Fredericksburg, VA. Brother of Cols. George, John, and Waller Patton of VA. Educated at Fairfax Institute near Alexandria. Studied law with his father. Lt., US Army, 1847–55. Moved to New Orleans in 1857. Owned cotton and sugar plantations prewar. Md. Frances E. Merritt. Capt. Co. F, 22d LA (an infantry regiment but trained to handle heavy artillery), Dec. 31, 1861. Appointed major and brigade QM, March 9, 1862. Declined the appointment July 4, 1862. Elected col., 22d LA, May 15, 1862. Commanded the batteries at Snyder's Bluff, near Vicksburg. WIA (hip) May 20, 1863. POW Vicksburg. Exch. Col. 22d LA Consolidated, Jan. 26, 1864. Served in the Mobile garrison 1864–65. Recommended several times for promotion to general. Paroled May 9, 1865, Meridian. Commission agent in New Orleans postwar. State Adj. gen. 1877–78. Mayor of New Orleans 1878–80. City treasurer. Died Feb. 9, 1890, New Orleans. Buried Lafayette Cemetery No. 2.

Patton, John Mercer, Jr. Born May 9, 1826, Spring Farm, Culpeper Co., VA. Reared in Richmond by his father, a prominent politician. Grad. VMI. Richmond lawyer prewar. Md. Sarah L. Taylor; Lucy A. Crump. Major, commanding state forces at Jamestown Island, April 1861. Lt. col., 21st VA, June 1861. Col., April 21, 1862. Resigned Aug. 8, 1862, ostensibly due to "impaired health" ("disorders of the stomach, bowels & liver") but more probably in protest over a junior being appointed over him. Commissioned col. and judge, military court of G. W. Smith's command, Dec. 16, 1862. Later a judge in the ANV's IId Corps court. Appmx. Richmond lawyer postwar. Wrote several books on the law. Died Nov. 24, 1898 (not Oct. 9, as given in most sources), Ashland, VA. Buried Shockoe Cemetery, Richmond. Papers at VAHS. One unimpressed private called Patton "a pigeon-headed fellow."

Patton, Waller Tazewell. Born July 15, 1835, Fredericksburg, VA. Grad. VMI. Taught at his alma mater 1852–56. Attorney in Culpeper. Capt. of vol. militia. Unmd. Capt. Co. B, 13th VA, April 17, 1861. Major, 7th VA, July 1, 1861. Lt. col., April 27, 1862. Col., June 3, 1862. WIA 2d Manassas (hand). Elected to the State Senate in 1863 but chose to remain with the army. MWIA Pickett's Charge. Died July 21, 1863, at a Union hospital in Gettysburg. Buried in Baltimore; reburied Stonewall Cemetery, Winchester, in 1876.

Payne, Robert Newton. Born Jan. 4, 1834 (or Jan. 14, 1832), TN. Carpenter in Obion Co. TN, prewar. Md. Cally Miles; Belle F. Smith. 2d lt. Co. D, 33d TN, Sept. 9, 1861. 1st lt., April 3, 1862. Major, May 8, 1862. Col., July 22, 1864. Paroled May 1, 1865, Greensboro. Carpenter and lumber dealer in Haywood and Carroll Cos. postwar. Died July 15, 1892, Carroll Co. Buried Oak Hill Cemetery, Huntingdon. Gen. Strahl thought Payne "an excellent officer."

Peebles, William Hubbard. Born May 4, 1837, Henry Co., GA. Physician in Henry Co. prewar. Md. Eliza Ann Weems. Capt. Co. A, 44th GA, March 4, 1862. Surgeon, 44th, July 1862. Major, March 4, 1863. Lt. col., May 26, 1863. Col., Sept. 11, 1863. POW Spotsylvania. Exch. Aug. 3, 1864. WIA Opequon Creek. Postwar physician in Hampton. State legislator. Died Oct. 1, 1885, Hampton. Buried Hampton City Cemetery. A contemporary notes Peebles "was loved and respected by his men."

Pegram, William Ransom Johnson. Born June 29, 1841, Richmond, VA. Brother of Gen. John Pegram. Attd. UVA. Prewar law student. Member of vol. militia company. Unmd. Lt. and drillmaster, Purcell (VA) Art., May 1861. Capt.,

April 1862. Major, March 2, 1863. Commanded battalion of artillery in A. P. Hill's Corps. Lt. col., Feb. 27, 1864. Col., Feb. 18, 1865. KIA Five Forks. Buried Hollywood Cemetery, Richmond. Nicknamed "specs" and "our boy colonel." A private called Pegram "a shining example of the influence a good officer has over his men." War letters at VAHS.

Pegues, Christopher Claudius. Born Aug. 3, 1823, Chesterfield Dist., SC. Grad. USC, 1842. Moved to Cahaba, AL, that year. Lawyer there. Capt. of the "Cahaba Rifles" in Jan. 1861. Md. Caroline A. Coleman. Capt. Co. G (the "Cahaba Rifles"), 5th AL, April 10, 1861. Col., April 27, 1862. MWIA Gaines's Mill, while leading a charge. Died in a Richmond hospital July 15, 1862. Buried Hollywood Cemetery. Gen. D. H. Hill called him a "noble Christian commander."

Pendleton, Edmund. Born Sept. 29, 1823, Amherst Co., VA. Grad. VMI 1842. Prewar lawyer in Buchanan Co., VA, and Cincinnati, OH. Moved to New Orleans just prior to the war. Md. Cornelia M. Morgan. Major, 3d LA Bn., Sept. 9, 1861. Lt. col., 15th LA (formed from the 3d Bn.), June 5, 1862. POW July 28, 1862, during Seven Days. Exch. Aug. 5, 1862. WIA Antietam (ankle). Col., Oct. 14, 1862. WIA Chancellorsville (hand). Usually absent in 1863–64 due to his wounds. Appmx. Resided in Lexington, VA, postwar. Attorney. On VMI Board. State senator 1869–71. Died July 26, 1899, Lexington. Buried Stonewall Jackson Cemetery, Lexington. "[N]ot highly considered" for promotion by Gen. Lee.

Penn, Davidson Bradfute. Born May 13, 1836, Lynchburg, VA. Family moved to Richmond, then to New Orleans. Attd. Spring Hill College. Grad. VMI and UVA. Cotton merchant and lawyer in New Orleans. Md. Marie Allain. Capt. Co. D, 7th LA, May 27, 1861. Major, May 28, 1862. Lt. col., June 12, 1862. WIA Gaines's Mill (shoulder). Col., July 25, 1862. WIA Antietam (leg). POW at Chancellorsville and at Rappahannock Station. To Johnson's Island Prison. Released Feb. 2, 1865, to await exchange. Paroled May 12, 1865, Athens, GA. Merchant in New Orleans postwar. City Recorder of Conveyances. Adj. gen. of LA. Lt. gov. 1872–74 and a key figure in the LA election riots. Planter in Tensas Parish. Died Nov. 15, 1902, New Orleans. Buried Live Oak Cemetery, Pass Christian, MS. An obituary says Penn was "a man of strong and attractive personality."

Penn, John Edmund. Born July 3, 1837, Patrick Co., VA. Attd. Randolph-Macon College and UVA. Patrick Co. lawyer prewar. Md. Alice Grant Hoge in 1866. Capt. Co. H, 42d VA, May 22, 1861. Appointed major, lt. col., col., all to rank from Aug. 9, 1862. Lost his leg at Antietam and captured there. Exch. Nov. 1862. Resigned Feb. 24, 1863, due to disability. Lawyer in Patrick Co. postwar. Moved to Roanoke in 1882. Died there Sept. 27, 1895. Buried City Cemetery, Roanoke. His gravestone reads "In Life a Soldier of the Confederacy, In Death a Soldier of the Cross."

Perkins, Caleb J. Born Dec. 13, 1829, Clark Co., KY. Prewar farmer in Randolph Co., MO. Md. Mary ——. Capt., Randolph County Co., 5th Inf., 3d Div., MSG, 1861. Major, Sept. 24, 1861. Led a cavalry battalion at Pea Ridge. Lt. col., 11th MO Cav. Col., Perkins's MO Cav., a regiment he raised in 1864. WIA Glasgow, MO, Sept. 23, 1864, during Price's Raid. Regiment dismounted that winter and reduced to a battalion. Paroled, Alexandria, June 7, 1865, as lt. col. Perkins's MO Inf. Bn. Randolph Co. farmer postwar. Died Feb. 27, 1901, at Prairie Hill, MO, of the "grippe." Buried Old Prairie Hill Cemetery, Chariton Co.

Perrin, James Monroe. Born June 8, 1822, Abbeville Dist., SC. Grad. USC. Abbeville attorney prewar. Sgt., Palmetto Regt. in Mexican War. Lt., 12th US Inf., in Mexican War. Md. Mary, sister of Col. A. M. Smith; Kitty Tillman. Capt., "Abbeville Volunteers" (Co. D, Gregg's 1st SC, a 6-month unit), Feb. 1861. Capt. Co. B, 1st SC Rifles, July 20, 1861. State representative 1862–63. Lt. col., Sept. 1, 1862. Col., Nov. 12, 1862. MWIA Chancellorsville, May 3, 1863. Died May 5, 1863, VA. Buried Upper Long Cane Presbyterian Church, Abbeville. A soldier called Perrin "the soul of his regiment."

Perrin, Robert Oliver. Born Nov. 3, 1823, Abbeville, SC. Brother of Gen. Abner Perrin. Lived in Pickens Co., AL, and Kemper Co., MS, prewar. Physician and farmer. Md. Elizabeth Spencer; Mary Collier. Capt. "Southern Guards" (eventually Co. C, Jeff Davis Legion), a company he formed in Kemper Co. in Dec. 1860. Company entered state service in March 1861 and was mustered in Confederate service Aug. 17, 1861. Resigned April 1862, due to disability. Capt., Perrin's Co., MS State Cav., May 26, 1863. Lt. col., Perrin's Bn. MS State Cav., July 15, 1863. Col., 11th MS Cav., to rank from Dec. 23, 1863, the date the unit transferred to Confederate service. Resigned March 20, 1865. Paroled May 14, 1865, Meridian. Resided in Greene Co., AL, postwar. President of an agricultural association. Died Oct. 8, 1878. Buried Eutaw Cemetery, Eutaw, AL. A staff officer wrote, "Col. Perrin stands very high with his men & with the officers under whom he is placed."

Perry, Madison Starke. Born 1814, Lancaster Dist., SC. Attd. USC. Moved to Alachua Co., FL, in the 1830s. Planter. State representative. State senator. Governor, 1857–61. Md. Martha P. Starke, a cousin. Col., 7th FL, July 3, 1862. Resigned June 2, 1863, due to illness. Died March 7, 1865, on his plantation in Gainesville, FL. Buried Oak Ridge Cemetery, Alachua Co. His successor in office found Perry "a man of strong prejudices, without very extraordinary intellectual abilities."

Persons, Alexander William. Born c. 1837, GA. Attd. GMI and Cumberland U. Law School. Lawyer in Fort Valley prewar. Md. Susan Malone. Brigade Inspector of GA militia, in May 1861. Lt. col., 7th GA (State Troops), Nov. 23, 1861.

Lt. col., 55th GA, May 17, 1862. Promoted to col., probably Jan.–Feb. 1863, *vice* the unlamented C. B. Harkie, who muddied the promotion waters by being reinstated. The 55th was largely captured at Cumberland Gap in 1863. Persons, who was on furlough at the time, led the remnant thereafter. Assigned to command the post of Andersonville, GA, Feb. 26, 1864, perhaps in an effort to resolve the command dispute in the 55th. Macon lawyer postwar. Died Feb. 21, 1872, Americus, GA. Buried Oak Grove Cemetery, Americus. Called by one Andersonville prisoner "a good looking and mild mannered officer."

Peters, William Elisha. Born Aug. 18, 1829, Bedford Co., VA. Grad. Emory & Henry College and UVA. Resided in Washington Co. prewar. Professor at Emory & Henry. Spent 3 years studying languages at the U. of Berlin in Germany. Md. Margaret Sheffey; Mary Sheffey. 1st lt., "Smyth Dragoons" (later Co. A, 8th VA Cav), July 21, 1861. Capt., AAG (state rank?) to Gen. Floyd, Aug. 19, 1861. Lt. col., 45th VA, Nov. 14, 1861. Col., Jan. 6, 1862. Dropped at May 1862 reorganization. Col., 2d VA State Line, June 3, 1862. Unit disbanded Feb. 28, 1863. Col., 21st VA Cav. (formed from the disbanded soldiers of the VA State Line), Aug. 21, 1863. WIA Moorefield Aug. 7, 1864. Arrested by Gen. McCauseland for disobeying orders to burn Chambersburg, PA, but the charges were later dropped. State senator 1863–64, serving while recuperating for his wounds. Taught at Emory & Henry and UVA postwar. Died March 22, 1906, Charlottesville. Buried Sheffey family cemetery, Marion. A eulogy called him "a man of iron resolution and imperturbable courage"; an inspector called him "a gentleman, but ignorant of military duty."

Phelan, James. Born Oct. 11, 1821, Huntsville, AL. Huntsville newspaper editor. State printer of AL. To Aberdeen, MS, in 1849. Lawyer. State senator 1861–62. Md. Eliza Jones Moore. Confederate senator 1861–63. Defeated for reelection. Appointed col. and chief judge, military court of S. D. Lee's Corps, April 6, 1864. Postwar Memphis lawyer. Died May 17, 1873, Memphis. Buried Odd Fellows Cemetery, Aberdeen. His son of the same name was a US congressman.

Phillips, Charles Duval. Born Oct. 12, 1835, Asheville, NC. Attd. UGA. Marietta lawyer prewar. Md. Sarah E. Smith; Ella Combs. Pvt. Co. A, 52d GA, March 4, 1862. Lt. col., March 16, 1862. Col., Nov. 16, 1862. WIA and POW Champion Hill. Exch. in 1865. On recruiting service in GA thereafter. Marietta lawyer postwar. State representative 1878–79. Died Jan. 23, 1912, Marietta. Buried Citizens Cemetery, Marietta. Brother of Col. William Phillips. "[A]n advocate of decided power," according to a fellow lawyer.

Phillips, James Jasper. Born Jan. 23, 1832, VA. Reared in Suffolk. Grad. VMI. Taught at VMI. Principal, Chuckatuck Military Academy. Md. Lou Emma Betts. Capt. Co. F, 9th VA, May 18, 1861. Major, June 1862. Lt. col., July 1, 1863. WIA

Pickett's Charge (hit by grapeshot in the left breast). Col., July 4, 1863. Declined promotion to brigadier. POW Sayler's Creek. Released July 25, 1865. Owner of a packing and canning business in Norfolk and New York City postwar. President of New York City Board of Trade. Died Feb. 11, 1908, New York City. Buried Cedar Hill Cemetery, Suffolk. Phillips, the uncle of Sallie Corbell Pickett, "was possessed of great personal magnetism."

Phillips, Jefferson Curle. Born Sept. 30, 1821, Elizabeth City Co., VA. Farmer in Hampton prewar. Md. Caroline E. Sinclair. Capt. Co. F, 3d VA Cav., May 14, 1861. Major, Oct. 4, 1861. Lt. col., 13th VA Cav., July 12, 1862. WIA Brandy Station. Found guilty, June 1863, of being AWOL and reprimanded. Col., Dec. 19, 1863. WIA June 1, 1864, Ashland (head). Resigned Feb. 11, 1865. Hampton farmer postwar. Died June 6, 1910, near Hampton. Buried at "the Old Phillips Farm, near Fort Worth St." Brother of Col. Joseph Phillips of TX.

Phillips, Joseph. Born Oct. 10, 1831, Elizabeth City, VA. Prewar farmer, sawmill owner, livery stable owner in Elizabeth City. Md. Mary T. Morrow. Enlisted May 14, 1861, as pvt. Co. B, 3d VA Cav. Promoted to the staff. ADC to Gens. Magruder and Hood, 1861–62. 2d lt., CS Regular Army, Oct. 12, 1861. Capt. of Cav., PACS, Oct. 14, 1862. Col., 3d TX Cav. (AZ Brigade), Feb. 11, 1863. Unpopular with the men because he was a non-Texan and a strict disciplinarian. KIA in the attack on Fort Butler, near Donaldsonville, LA, June 28, 1863, and buried there. A memorial stone to him is in St. John's Churchyard, Hampton, VA. A neighbor recalled that Phillips was "the fightin'est man that ever lived."

Phillips, Pleasant Jackson. Born July 3, 1819, Harris Co., GA. Banker in Columbus. Planter. Major in the state militia. Md. Laura Osborne. Col., 31st GA, Nov. 19, 1861. Resigned May 13, 1862, having failed to get reelected at reorganization. Appointed brig. gen. of militia July 7, 1862. Appointed col. of the reorganized militia in 1863. Brig. gen. 2d Brigade, GA Militia, during the Atlanta Campaign. He commanded the militia in their disastrous attack at Griswoldville. Although accused of intoxication in that battle, it is probable Phillips was merely incompetent. Banker in Columbus postwar. Died Oct. 12, 1876, Wynnton. Buried Linwood Cemetery, Columbus.

Phillips, Seaborn Moses. Born Aug. 3, 1822, Marion Co., MS. Lawyer in Yazoo City, MS, prewar. Newspaper editor. Mexican War veteran. Md. Emily C. Walker. Capt. Co. I, 10th MS, March 2, 1861. Col., April 11, 1861. Died in camp, near Pensacola, May 23, 1861, of "congestive fever." Buried Greenwood Cemetery, Jackson, MS.

Phillips, William. Born July 8, 1824, Asheville, NC. Reared in Habersham Co., GA. Attd. UGA. Marietta lawyer. Solicitor, Blue Ridge Circuit. Capt. of vol.

militia. Md. Catherine Mongin Smith; Mary Waterman. Appointed brig. gen., 4th Brigade, GA State Troops, in 1861, by his political ally Gov. Brown, who wrote lengthy letters to Pres. Davis trying to get Phillips the rank of Confederate general. Col., Phillips Legion, Aug. 2, 1861. Resigned Feb. 13, 1862, due to paralysis and recurrent typhoid. He eventually lost sight in one eye due to the illness. Managed the Marietta Paper Mills the rest of the war. Major, 9th Cav. Bn., GA State Guard, 1864. Lawyer and farmer in Marietta postwar. Railroad developer. State representative 1877–78. Died Sept. 24, 1908, at his Marietta home. Buried Citizens Cemetery, Marietta. Brother of Col. C. D. Phillips. It was said he was "as true to his men as a man could be."

Phinizy, Charles Henry. Born Jan. 16, 1835, Augusta, GA. Grad. UGA 1853. Said to have taken engineering courses at West Point. Railroad engineer and clerk in Augusta prewar. Md. Mary Yancey. 1st lt. Co. B, 10th GA, May 18, 1861. Capt., July 19, 1861. Capt. and AAG to Gen. Cumming, Oct. 30, 1862. POW Vicksburg and paroled. Col., 39th GA Consolidated, April 9, 1865. Cotton broker in Augusta postwar. President of the Georgia Railroad. Died April 28, 1898, Augusta. Buried Magnolia Cemetery.

Phipps, Richard Wright. Born Oct. 11, 1833, Marshall Co., TN. Reared in Oxford, MS. Grad. UMS, 1852 (valedictorian); attd. Cumberland U. Law School. Oxford lawyer prewar. Md. Mary D. Lennard in 1885. Lt. Co. F, 19th MS, June 7, 1861. Capt., Jan. 1863. Major, Oct. 8, 1863. Lt. col., Jan. 20, 1864. Col., May 12, 1864. Appmx. State legislator in MS postwar. Moved to FL in 1884. Farmer in Manatee Co., FL. Died Oct. 21, 1912, Terra Ceia, FL. Buried Myrtle Hill Cemetery, Tampa, FL.

Pickens, Samuel Bonneau. Born July 13, 1839, Pendleton Dist., SC. Grad. SCMA. Md. Anna Ingraham. Lt., CS Regular Army, March 16, 1861. Adj., 12th AL, 1861. Appointed lt. col., 12th AL, June 1, 1862. Col., Sept. 14, 1862. WIA South Mountain, Chancellorsville, Spotsylvania (in shoulder, May 10, 1864), Opequon Creek. Paroled at Farmville, VA, 1865. Railroad agent in Charleston, SC, postwar. Died Sept. 17, 1891, Charleston. Buried St. Paul's Episcopal Church, Charleston. An obituary termed him "an honest, conscientious Christian gentleman." A cousin found him "a very gallant fellow & an excellent officer."

Pickett, Alexander Corbin. Born April 11, 1821, on the family plantation in Limestone Co., AL. Brother of Col. Richard Pickett, 10th AL Cav. Sgt. of AL Volunteers in Mexican War. Prewar lawyer in Whitesburg and Jacksonport, AR. Capt. Co. G, 1st AR, May 19, 1861. Dropped at reorganization. Appointed major, 10th MO, 1862. Col., Dec. 7, 1862. Relieved by an election, Dec. 2, 1863. Postwar lawyer in Augusta, AR. Judge of the Jackson Co. Circuit Court. Died Jan. 17, 1883, Augusta. Buried Augusta Cemetery.

Pickett, Edward, Jr. Born Aug. 3, 1826, AL (probably Huntsville). Reared in Hinds Co., MS. Said in some sources to have attd. KMI, but there is no record of his being there. Attd. Centenary College. Editor of newspapers in Jackson, Natchez, and Vicksburg, MS, prewar. Clerk of the MS State House. Lawyer in Memphis and editor of the Memphis *Appeal.* Col. of militia. Md. Cornelia Brown. Col., 21st TN, July 9, 1861. Slightly WIA (hand) and had horse shot from under him at Belmont. On March 31, 1862, a Union raiding party surprised the 21st in its camp. An embarrassed Pickett was discharged, though later investigations cleared him of wrongdoing. 21st Regt. consolidated with the 2d TN, July 21, 1862, with Pickett becoming supernumerary. Temporarily VADC to Gen. Price, 1862. Spent the rest of the war seeking another position and objecting to the legality of the consolidation. Commanded post of Milledgeville, GA, from Dec. 1864. Lawyer in Memphis postwar. Died c. 1876. In 1862 Gov. Harris recommended Pickett, a noted orator, as "a gentleman of character, a lawyer of business capacity and very much desirous to continue in the service."

Pickett, Richard Orrick. Born Aug. 22, 1814, Fauquier Co., VA. To AL in 1829. In Creek War. Lawyer in Limestone and Lawrence Cos. Judge. State legislator. Adj. gen. of AL. Md. Fannie Boggs. Capt. Co. H, 35th AL, March 12, 1862. POW Corinth, exchanged one week later. Major, Pickett's Bn. AL Cav. late 1863. Col., 10th AL Cav. Sept. 22, 1864. Postwar lawyer in Florence and Leighton, AL. State legislator. Died Nov. 23, 1898, Leighton. Buried Florence Cemetery. Brother of Col. A. C. Pickett.

Pinckard, Lucius. Born Aug. 4, 1841, AL. Tuskegee resident. Student (and cadet) at the UAL in 1861. Md. Fannie L. Graves, 1865. Adj. 14th AL, Nov. 16, 1861. Lt. col., July 18, 1862. Col., Oct. 3, 1862. WIA Salem Church. WIA (right arm, disabling it) and POW Gettysburg, exchanged late 1864. Postwar planter and sheriff of Macon Co., AL. To Atlanta in 1886. Insurance agent there. Died Sept. 11, 1909, Allegheny, PA. Buried Westview Cemetery, Atlanta.

Pinson, Richard Alexander. Born April 26, 1829, Lincoln Co., TN. Family moved to Pontotoc Co., MS, in 1834. Merchant in Pontotoc Co. State representative 1858–60. Md. Sina Duke. Capt. Co. K, 1st MS Cav., 1861. Col., June 10, 1862. Twice wounded in war. Often recommended for promotion to general. POW Selma, AL, April 2, 1865. Paroled May 16, 1865, Columbus. Elected to the US Congress in 1865 (from MS) but not seated. Lived in Mobile 1866–68. To Memphis in 1868. Merchant there, in partnership with Col. J. C. Fizer. President of the Memphis Chamber of Commerce. Died May 17, 1873, Memphis, of cholera. Buried Elmwood Cemetery, Memphis. A fellow officer remembered

Pinson as "one of the best of all the cavalry colonels in the service. A man who knew no fear, who shirked no duty, who sought no soft places."

Pitman, Robert William. Born July 18, 1835, Fayette Co., TN. Attd. Trinity U. Grad. U. of Nashville. Professor at WMI/U. of Nashville prewar. Md. Mary E. C. Rives. Capt. Co. H, 13th TN, June 4, 1861. WIA Shiloh (thigh). Lt. col., March 3, 1863. Col., Nov. 18, 1863. AAIG on Bedford Forrest's staff, 1864–65. Paroled May 20, 1865, Memphis. Professor of natural sciences at Trinity U. postwar. Moved to TX c. 1877, settling in Denton eventually. Died May 15, 1900, at the Nashville Confederate Veterans' Home. Buried IOOF Cemetery, Denton.

Pitts, Fountain Elliott. Born July 4, 1808, Georgetown, KY. Methodist minister in TN and KY prewar. Noted preacher. Md. Martha Britt; Sarah Vaughn. Chaplain, 11th TN. Col., 61st TN, Oct. 10, 1862. Resigned Feb. 15, 1864. Resignation revoked the next month. Retired Aug. 1, 1864. Paroled May 12, 1865, Thomasville, GA. Settled in Brazil postwar but soon returned to the US. Pastor in TN and KY. Died May 22, 1874, near Louisville, KY. Buried Mt. Olivet Cemetery, Nashville. Sen. Henry of TN, endorsing Pitts's application for promotion to brigadier, said Pitts "has the same angry and fanatical zeal that made Oliver Cromwell the most renowned warrior of his age . . . he is quite at his old trade [of preaching], the transition being so slight that his change of position is scarcely perceptible."

Player, Samuel Thomas. Born c. 1817, GA, as Samuel Thomas Fleetwood. Orphaned at an early age and taken in by a family named Player. Changed his name to Player in 1837. Lawyer, teacher, farmer in Irwinton, Wilkinson Co., GA, prewar. Md. Nancy Ann Freeman. Capt. Co. A, 49th GA, March 4, 1862. Major, Sept. 9, 1862. Lt. col., May 8, 1863. Col., June 9, 1863. Resigned March 24, 1864, having been elected to the GA Legislature. Wilkinson Co. farmer in 1870. Farmer and miller in Thomasville in 1880. Died May 28, 1884, Thomas Co.

Pleasants, Joseph C. Born April 14, 1817, Louisa Co., VA. Moved to AR in 1844. Prewar farmer in Phillips Co., then Arkansas Co. Md. Minerva Phillips. ADC to Gen. Hardee, 1861. Col., 37th AR (aka 29th), June 6, 1862. MWIA in leg at Prairie Grove. Died Dec. 21, 1862, Van Buren, AR. Buried Arkansas Co. An obituary called Pleasants "cool, calm, fearless and self-possessed."

Poage, Thomas. Born Jan. 1, 1825, near Staunton, VA. Pulaski Co. lawyer prewar. Md. Mary A. Vermillion. Capt. Co. I, 50th VA, June 25, 1861. Col., May 25, 1862. KIA Jan. 30, 1863, Kelly's Store, VA, by a shell. Buried Newbern Cemetery, Pulaski Co. A private wrote Poage "was a good colonel and good to his men."

Polk, Cadwallader Long. Born Oct. 16, 1837, Columbia, TN. Brother of Gen. Lucius Polk. Attd. WMI. Grad. UNC. Prewar Helena, AR, planter. Md. Caroline

Lowry in 1864. 2d lt. Co. H, 1st TN, May 9, 1861. Resigned May 1, 1862. Lt. col., 39th AR, Nov. 4, 1862. WIA and POW Prairie Grove. Col., April 30, 1864. Post-war farmer near Helena. Died there July 9, 1921. Buried Maple Hill Cemetery, Helena.

Polk, Trusten. Born May 29, 1811, Sussex, DE. Grad. Yale 1831. Lawyer. To St. Louis in 1835. St. Louis city counselor. Prominent Methodist. Elected governor of MO in 1856. Elected to the US Senate in 1857 by the legislature after only a few days in office as governor, a move widely denounced as opportunistic. Strongly pro-Southern but not an active secessionist. Md. Elizabeth Skinner. Formally expelled from the Senate, Jan. 10, 1862, for being a Southern sympathizer. Col. and presiding judge of Gen. Holmes's military court in AR, Dec. 16, 1862. POW Bolivar, MS, Sept. 19, 1863. To Johnson's Island. Paroled Nov. 26, 1863. Relieved Aug. 2, 1864. Fled to Mexico at war's end but soon returned. Post-war St. Louis lawyer. Died April 16, 1876, St. Louis, buried Bellefontaine Cemetery. Papers, including 1865 diary, at UNC.

Pond, Preston, Jr. Born Sept. 9, 1823, Hinsdale, NH. Reared in LA. Attd. Centenary College. Lawyer and planter in Jackson, East Feliciana Parish. Militia colonel. State representative. Ran for US Congress in 1856 but lost. Md. Emelie Cooper; Adelaide A. Woodward. IG of 3d LA militia division, April 3, 1861. Col., 16th LA, Sept. 26, 1861. Led a brigade at Shiloh. Resigned May 8, 1862, after failing to be reelected. Led a unit of PR near Baton Rouge in 1862. Died June 15, 1864, LA. Buried Jackson Cemetery.

Ponder, Willis Miles. Born Oct. 12, 1823, Bon Acqua, Hickman Co., TN. To Doniphan, Ripley Co., MO, in 1843. Farmer, sawmill owner, grain and livestock broker. Ripley Co. Clerk. Md. Mary J. Kittrell; Susan E. Hedgepeth (daughter of Col. Isaac Hedgepeth); Mary A. Montgomery. Sgt., then capt., 3d Inf., 1st Div., MSG, early 1861. Major, July 8, 1861. Resigned Jan. 8, 1862. Capt. of what was to become Co. A, 9th MO, Jan. 8, 1862. Lt. col., 9th (White's) MO, Oct. 22, 1862. Col., 12th MO (as the 9th was renumbered), April 22, 1863. POW April 18, 1864, at Cotton Plant, AR. To Johnson's Island. Exch. Jan. 23, 1865. Paroled Shreveport June 9, 1865. Moved to Lawrence Co., AR, postwar. Farmer, merchant, sawmill owner. State legislator. Died April 9, 1904, Walnut Ridge, Lawrence Co. Buried Lawrence Memorial Gardens, Walnut Ridge. A contemporary recalled, "He had great powers of persuasion, and was gifted in the art of conversation. He was respected and well liked."

Pool, Stephen Decatur. Born March 25, 1819, Elizabeth City, NC. Lived in Elizabeth City and Beaufort prewar. Newspaper editor. Principal of an academy. Md. Caroline S. Lockwood. Capt. Co. H (the "Old Topsail Riflemen"), 1st NC

Art. (10th NC), May 16, 1861. Lt. col., Oct. 1, 1862. Col., Sept. 7, 1863. State representative 1864–65. Chief of artillery to Gen. L. S. Baker in Dept. of NC in 1865. Editor in New Bern postwar. Published *Our Living and Our Dead,* a veterans magazine. NC superintendent of public instruction 1872–74. Moved to New Orleans in 1877 and to Osyka, MS (to escape a yellow fever epidemic), in 1887. Died Dec. 21, 1901, Osyka, MS. Buried Osyka Cemetery.

Pool, Thomas W. Born Aug. 27, 1831, Perry Co., AL. Grew up in Union Co., AR. Moved to Claiborne Parish, LA, in 1851. Teacher, then merchant, in Vienna, LA, prewar. Md. Elizabeth Wilder. Capt. Co. I, 28th LA. Major, May 14, 1862. Col., April 15, 1864. "All his men had entire confidence in him." Paroled June 14, 1865, Monroe, LA. Postwar merchant in Homer, LA. State commissioner of immigration. Died July 25, 1896, Homer. Buried Old Homer Cemetery.

Porter, George Camp. Born Nov. 15, 1835, Fayette Co., TN. Grad. KMI. Lawyer in Memphis and in Haywood Co. prewar. Md. Susan Madison. Capt. Co. A, 6th TN, May 21, 1861. Major, May 23, 1861. Col., May 6, 1862. 6th consolidated with 9th in early 1863. Detached to Conscript Bureau for a time. Led 6th/9th, and often Maney's Brigade, in the Atlanta Campaign. Resigned Sept. 9, 1864. Lauderdale Co. lawyer postwar. Member, 1870 state constitutional convention. State senator 1871–73. State representative 1877–79. Moved to Nashville in 1895. Superintendent of state capitol. Died Sept. 20, 1919, Nashville. Buried Brownsville, TN.

Porter, John Crump. Born Feb. 2, 1827, Raccoon Ford, Orange Co., VA. Grad. VMI. Teacher and farmer in Culpeper Co. prewar. Md. Elizabeth Payne Green. Capt. Co. C, 7th VA, April 30, 1861. Resigned March 25, 1862. Col., 3d VA Art., March 6, 1862. Regiment (a paper organization) broken up May 1862. Enrolling officer, 8th congressional district of VA, 1862–64. Enlisted Oct. 10, 1864, as a private in Mosby's command. Paroled April 22, 1865, Winchester. Culpeper Co. farmer postwar. Died Oct. 4, 1903, Culpeper Co.

Porter, Joseph Chrisman. Born Sept. 12, 1819, Jessamine Co., KY. Attd. Marion College in Philadelphia, MO. Prewar farmer in Lewis Co., MO. Md. Mary Ann Marshall. Capt. Co. K, 1st Cav., 2d Div., MSG, 1861. Lt. col., June 1861. WIA Lexington. Col., Dec. 3, 1861. Commanded 2d Div., MSG. Resigned March 19, 1862. Traveled to his north MO home in 1862 to recruit troops for the Confederacy behind Union lines. Raised several thousand men and fought several engagements with Union troops. Col., 1st Northeast MO Cav., Aug. 4, 1862. Unit dispersed while trying to reach Confederate lines. Appointed (in late 1862) to command a brigade in Marmaduke's Cavalry Div. MWIA in the attack on Hartsville, MO, Jan. 11, 1863. Died Feb. 19, 1863, near Batesville, AR, while en route to a Little Rock hospital. Buried near Little Rock. John N. Edwards thought Porter an "excellent officer."

Porterfield, George Alexander. Born Nov. 24, 1822, Berkeley Co., VA. Grad. VMI 1844. Farmer in Jefferson Co. Officer in Mexican War. Md. Emily C. Terrill. Col. and IG of militia at Harpers Ferry, 1861. Col., 25th VA, May 4, 1861. Ordered to organize forces in northwest VA. Most of his recruits were captured or dispersed at Philippi. Chief of ordnance of Gen. Loring's army, Aug. 9, 1861. Assigned to brigade command, April 21, 1862. Dropped May 1, 1862, when he failed to get reelected at reorganization. Captured and paroled, June 1862. Banker in Charlestown postwar. Died Feb. 27, 1919, Martinsburg, WVA. Buried Greenhill Cemetery, Martinsburg. Porterfield wrote an article for SHSP of his 1861–62 experiences.

Portis, John Wesley. Born Sept. 9, 1818, Nash Co., NC. Attd. UVA. Lawyer and planter in Suggsville, AL, and (1838–41) Houston, TX. State legislator 1843–44. Trustee of UAL 1844–58. Md. Rebecca Rivers. Lost a race for Confederate Congress in 1861. Lt. Co. D, 2d AL (a 12-month unit, later 42d), April 1, 1861. Elected col., 42d, May 16, 1862. WIA Corinth. POW Vicksburg. Resigned March 1864. Paroled Citronelle June 2, 1865. Practiced law in Suggsville postwar. Died April 1, 1902, Suggsville. Buried Portis Cemetery, Suggsville.

Portlock, Edward Edwards, Jr. Born March 10, 1840, Portsmouth, VA. Attd. Norfolk Military Academy. Bookkeeper for his father, a Norfolk auctioneer, in 1860. Md. Nannie M. Bridges. 2d lt., CS Regular Army, Nov. 1, 1861. Clerk in War Dept. Capt. and AAG to Gen. Roane, 1862. Elected col., 24th AR, June 6, 1862. Commanded post of St. Charles, AR, winter of 1862–63. POW at Arkansas Post. Exch. April 29, 1863. Appointed col. and IG of the Indian Territory, Aug. 22, 1864. Relieved from this duty Feb. 24, 1865, and assigned to training duty in FL. Paroled May 12, 1865, Tallahassee. Returned to VA postwar. Auditor for Norfolk & Petersburg (later Norfolk & Western) Railroad, living in Lynchburg and Roanoke. Died April 10, 1887, Roanoke, of pneumonia. Buried Blandford Cemetery, Petersburg. An obituary calls Portlock "a brave soldier, a true man, a faithful friend."

Powel, Samuel Jackson. Born Sept. 27, 1821, Hawkins Co., TN. Attd. Washington College. Rogersville lawyer prewar. State representative 1849–51. Officer in Mexican War. Md. Mary E. Armstrong. Capt. Co. K, 29th TN, July 19, 1861. Col., Sept. 30, 1861. WIA Mill Springs. Led brigade at Perryville. Resigned Nov. 5, 1862, due to his wounds. Lawyer in Hernando, MS, postwar. Judge. State legislator. Died July 10, 1902, Hernando. Buried Old Presbyterian Cemetery, Rogersville.

Powell, Robert Michael. Born Sept. 23, 1826, Montgomery, AL. Moved to TX in 1848. Montgomery Co. lawyer, farmer. Md. Elizabeth Wood; Elizabeth Grace. Appointed col. of militia, June 10, 1861, to command the camp of instruction in Texas's 4th military dist. Capt. Co. D, 5th TX, Aug. 2, 1861. Major, Aug. 22, 1862. Lt. col., Aug 30, 1862. Col., Nov. 1, 1862. WIA and POW at Gettysburg, July 2, 1862. Released from military prison Feb. 2, 1865. Took over Hood's TX Brigade, as senior colonel, after exchange. Cotton broker in Baltimore, MD, postwar. Moved to St. Louis, MO, late in life to live with his son. Died Jan. 15, 1916, St. Louis. Buried Calvary Cemetery, St. Louis. Chaplain Davis lauded Powell's "brave spirit and gentlemanly bearing." Powell strongly resembled Gen. Longstreet, so much so that when he was captured at Gettysburg his captors thought they had captured Longstreet.

Powell, William Llewellyn. Born March 6, 1826, Leesburg, VA. Officer, USN, 1841–61. Dismissed April 20, 1861. 1st lt., CSN, June 11, 1861. Fitted out warships in Richmond. Resigned Nov. 25, 1861. Appointed capt. of artillery, CS Regular Army, Nov. 16, 1861. Col., PACS, Nov. 24, 1861. Commanded forts in Mobile Bay. Often led brigade in the Dept. of the Gulf. Died Sept. 25, 1863, Mobile. Buried Magnolia Cemetery, Mobile. Gen. Maury thought him "an excellent officer."

Powers, Frank P. Born c. 1836, Ireland. Resided in Beaumont, TX, prewar. "Laborer" in 1860. Md. Mary T. Valleau. Capt. of a company of TX State Troops, the "Jefferson Dragoons," raised around Beaumont in 1861, that occupied Fort Brown near the Rio Grande. Resigned to join Gen. Ben McCulloch's staff. WIA Pea Ridge. Chosen Col., 14th AR, in May 1862 by the officers of the regiment but never received a commission as colonel. Led the 14th at Iuka and Corinth. Regt. consolidated at Port Hudson in 1863. Gen. Gardner then made Powers chief of cavalry for his district. Organized Powers's Regt. of Cav., 1864, in east LA and southeast MS. Postwar he owned a hotel in Jackson, LA. Tax collector for East Feliciana Parish. Violent opponent of Reconstruction, in one instance heading an armed force to break up a Negro meeting. Lumberman in TX and railroad promoter in MS. Alive in 1886 but disappears after that. Dead by 1900. Col. John Griffith called him "an able, efficient, and gallant officer." A private called him "not a very great soldier, but was a daring sort of fellow."

Pressley, James Fowler. Born Aug. 30, 1835, Williamsburg Dist., SC. Grad. SCMA and Charleston Medical College. Williamsburg physician prewar. Md. Emma Wilson. Lt. col., 10th SC, May 31, 1861. Col., April 26, 1863. Arrested during the Atlanta Campaign for failing to turn over his Black servants to become army cooks. WIA (shattered shoulder) and disabled at the Battle of Atlanta. Elected state representative in 1865. Postwar physician in SC; Cynthiana, KY.

Militia general in SC. Moved to Suisun, CA, in 1869. Physician in Suisun and San Jose, CA. Died Feb. 13, 1878, in a San Francisco hospital, of tuberculosis. Buried Fairfield City Cemetery in CA. A contemporary diarist called Pressley "a noble and brave spirit."

Preston, James Francis. Born Nov. 8, 1813, Montgomery Co., VA. Attd. Washington U. and USMA. Wealthy planter in Montgomery Co. State representative 1852–53. Officer in Mexican War. Md. Sarah Ann Caperton. Col., 75th VA Militia, early 1861. Col., PAVA, April 25, 1861. Col., 4th VA, c. July 1, 1861. WIA 1st Manassas. Led Stonewall Brigade, Nov. 1861. Suffered from rheumatism. Died Jan. 20, 1862, at his Montgomery Co. home. Buried Preston Cemetery at "Smithfield" Plantation, near Blacksburg.

Preston, Robert Taylor. Born May 26, 1809, Lexington, VA. Brother of Col. J. F. Preston. Wealthy farmer in Montgomery Co. prewar. Militia colonel. Md. Mary Hart. Col. of state forces (PAVA), on duty at Lynchburg, May 1861. Col., 28th VA, July 1, 1861. Dropped at April 29, 1862, reorganization. Col., 5th VA State Line, Aug. 23, 1862. Resigned 1863. Lt. col., 4th VA Reserves, Aug. 27, 1864. Elected col. Sept. 30, 1864. Led his reserves at the Battle of Saltville. Paroled April 30, 1865, Greensboro. Montgomery Co. farmer postwar. Died June 20, 1880, Montgomery Co. Buried Preston Cemetery at "Smithfield" Plantation, near Blacksburg. In 1861 Preston's company officers called upon him to resign, charging he was ignorant of anything military. Preston's papers are at VA Tech. John S. Wise's *End of an Era* contains many anecdotes of Preston.

Price, Felix L. (initial also given as "A." and "M."). Born c. 1835, Butts Co., GA. Reared in Jackson, Butts Co. Attd. Georgetown U. and Atlanta Medical College. Butts Co. farmer. Md. Mary Eugenia McCalla. Capt. Co. I, 14th GA, July 12, 1861. Major, July 17, 1861. Lt. col., Aug. 18, 1861. Col., Dec. 9, 1861. WIA Cedar Mountain. Resigned Oct. 23, 1862, due to disability. Mill keeper in Butts Co. postwar. Physician in Atlanta, Macon, and Pine Barren, FL. Died March 13, 1900, Pine Barren. Buried Pine Barren Cemetery. In Nov. 1861 Price was charged with "drunkenness and improper conduct towards a lady." A letter from a soldier in the 14th calls Price "that miserable contemptable [*sic*] low flung, low life vagabond" who was too drunk to drill the regiment.

Pridemore, Auburn Lorenzo. Born June 27, 1837, near Purchase, Scott Co., VA. Reared and worked on the family farm in Scott Co. Schoolteacher. Md. Caledonia J. Hill; Lucy E. Crockett; Sallie R. Neal. Capt. Co. C, 21st VA Inf. Bn., Aug. 1861. Major, 1862. Lt. col. 64th VA (formed from the 21st Bn.), Dec. 14, 1862. Col., Feb. 5, 1864. The 64th was mounted in 1863 and is often called the 64th Cav. in the records. Arrested March 15, 1865, for disobeying orders. Paroled by Union forces at Cumberland Gap, April 1865. Studied law postwar. Attorney in

Jonesville. State senator 1871–75. US congressman 1877–79. Died May 17, 1900, at his Jonesville home. Buried Hill Cemetery, Jonesville. One staff officer wrote in his journal that Pridemore "has been a nuisance, and a clever fellow withal, but no soldier."

Pritchard, James Avery. Born Dec. 25, 1816, Bourbon Co., KY. Prewar farmer in KY and (from 1852) Carroll Co., MO. Prospected for gold in CA 1849–51. State legislator 1858–60. Capt. in Mexican War. Md. Mathilda Williamson. Capt. Co. E, 1st Inf., 4th Div., MSG, June 19, 1861. Lt. col., June 22, 1861. WIA Wilson's Creek. Lt. col., 3d MO, Jan. 16, 1862. Col., May 8, 1862. MWIA Corinth, Oct. 4, 1862. Died Oct. 20 (service record says Nov. 6, but a comrade's diary, an obituary, and his widow's Mexican War pension application fix the Oct. 20 date), 1862, Coffeeville, MS. Buried in an unmarked grave near Coffeeville. His last order was "Boys, do your duty!" Pritchard's prewar diary has been published.

Provence, David. Born Nov. 25, 1827, Jefferson Co., KY. Prewar planter and attorney. Lt. of IN Volunteers in Mexican War. Active in filibustering in the Caribbean. Planter at "Strother," near Winnsboro, SC. Md. Elizabeth Hall. Lt. col., 3d AR State Troops, 1861. At Wilson's Creek. Capt., Provence's AR Battery, 1861–62. Elected col., 16th AR, May 8, 1862. Appointed chief of artillery of Hindman's Corps, TMD, Nov. 28, 1862. POW Port Hudson, sent to Johnson's Island. Exch. May 8, 1864. Provost marshal, Dist. of AR, 1865. Paroled Alexandria, LA, June 6, 1865. Returned to his Winnsboro farm postwar. Died Nov. 23, 1874, Monticello, Fairfield Co., SC. Buried in a lone grave on a hill across from Rock Creek Baptist Church, Fairfield Co. A soldier called Provence "the vigilant and watchful little Col."

Pulliam, Andrew Jackson. Born Jan. 21, 1836, Franklin Co., GA. Merchant in Buena Vista, MS, prewar. Unmd. Lt. Co. A, 17th MS, April 22, 1861. Capt., Aug. 26, 1861. WIA and POW Gettysburg, exch. Feb. 24, 1865. Lt. col., Jan. 1, 1864. Col., Feb. 26, 1864. "Commercial traveler" in Chickasaw Co., MS, postwar. Farm manager near Buena Vista. Died June 30, 1910, probably in Buena Vista. Buried Pulliam Cemetery, Buena Vista.

Purdie, Thomas James. Born June 22, 1830, Bladen Co., NC. Prewar farmer/planter at "Purdie Hall," the family plantation in Bladen Co. First cousin of Col. John A. McDowell. Unmd. 1st lt. Co. K, 18th NC, April 26, 1861. Capt., July 26, 1861. Lt. col., March 24, 1862. Col., Nov. 11, 1862. WIA Fredericksburg. KIA Chancellorsville, May 3, 1863, shot through the forehead. Buried in a family cemetery near his home in Bladen Co. Gen. Lane called Purdie "gentle, but gallant and fearless." Some sources credit Purdie with giving the order to fire the volley that accidentally killed Stonewall Jackson.

Pyles, Lewis G. Born c. 1831, FL, son of a prominent planter and politician. Prewar registrar of the federal land office at Newnansville, FL. Md. Mary A. Remington. Major, 2d FL, July 13, 1861. Lt. col., May 11, 1862. WIA Seven Pines. Col., Aug. 28, 1862. Lost race for Confederate Congress in 1863. Retired due to his Seven Pines wounds. To Invalid Corps July 12, 1864. Died Feb. 18, 1866, of his wounds. Buried Newnansville's Old Methodist Cemetery.

Pyron, Charles Lynn. Born May 10, 1819, Marion Co., AL. Moved to TX c. 1840. Rancher in Port Lavaca and San Antonio. Mexican War veteran. Texas Ranger. Md. Octavia Smith. Capt. Co. B, 2d TX MR, April 15, 1861. Major, Feb. 21, 1862. Lt. col., early 1862. Col., 2d TX Cav., Oct. 8, 1862. WIA in 1863 Teche Campaign, which wound unfitted him for field duty. Commanded post of San Antonio, 1864. Dist. commander in West TX, 1864–65. Returned to his ranch, near San Antonio, postwar. Died there Aug. 24, 1869, of consumption. Buried Confederate Cemetery, San Antonio. An English observer thought Pyron "a natural born soldier, and withal a very quiet, unassuming man."

Radcliffe, James Dillard. Born April 17, 1832, Columbia, SC. Grad. SCMA. Headed Deems's military school near Wilmington, NC, prewar. Md. Elizabeth Drane Brown. Col., 18th NC, July 18, 1861. Defeated for reelection at April 24, 1862, reorganization. Col., 61st NC, Aug. 30, 1862. POW Kinston, NC, Dec. 14, 1862. Paroled the next day. WIA by a shell concussion near the Crater, July 30, 1864. Resigned Oct. 11, 1864. Merchant in GA postwar. Died July 16, 1890, New York City. Buried Woodlawn Cemetery, New York City. A junior officer leveled charges of drunkenness and cowardice against Radcliffe after the Battle of Kinston. A court of inquiry cleared Radcliffe. However, when in 1864 that junior officer (Edward Mallett) was promoted to major, Radcliffe resigned, citing a long-standing lack of harmony between himself and his officers. Gen. Branch said the 18th was the best drilled regiment he had ever seen and praised Radcliffe as "a gentleman, a thoroughly educated soldier, and a most faithful and attentive officer. . . . If such men are to be put out of service, we may as well give up the contest."

Radford, Richard Carlton Walker. Born July 8, 1822, Bedford Co., VA. Attd. VMI. Grad. USMA 1845. Cav. officer in US Army, 1845–56. Bedford Co. planter, 1856–61. Md. Octavia DuVal. Col., 2d VA Cav., May 8, 1861. Dropped at April 25, 1862, reorganization. Col., 1st VA State Line, Aug. 22, 1862. Unit disbanded Feb. 28, 1863. Capt. AAIG and AAG to Gens. Jones, Johnston, and Rosser, 1864–65. Bedford Co. planter postwar. Died Nov. 2, 1886, "Rothsay," Bedford Co. Buried St. Stephens Cemetery, Bedford Co. Called by one observer "a narrow foolish Virginian, with little information but honest."

Rainey, Alexis Theodore. Born June 5, 1822, Tuscaloosa, AL. Prewar lawyer. To El Dorado, AR, in 1848. To Palestine, TX, in 1855. State legislator. Delegate to TX Secession Convention. Md. Anne Quarles. Capt. Co. H, 1st TX, June 24, 1861. Major, Oct. 1, 1861. Lt. col., Oct. 21, 1861. Col., Jan. 3, 1862. WIA Gaines's Mill. Returned to TX on a disability furlough and never returned. Assigned to staff duty in TX. Dropped from the army July 15, 1864. Postwar lawyer in Elkhart, TX. State legislator. Died May 17, 1891, Elkhart. Buried Pilgrim Cemetery, Elkhart.

Rains, George Washington. Born April 13, 1817, Craven Co., NC. Brother of Gen. Gabriel Rains. Reared in AL. Grad. USMA 1842. Officer in US Army, 1842–56. Taught at USMA. Chemist and scientist. Resigned in 1856 to become president of an iron works factory in Newburgh, NY. Md. Frances Ramsdell, whose father owned the iron works. Major, PACS, July 10, 1861. Assigned the task of manufacturing the Confederacy's gunpowder, in a country that had no large-scale powder mills. Established a powder works in Augusta, GA, that (against all odds) largely supplied the Confederate army throughout the war. Pioneered new methods of gunpowder purification and production. Also commanded the Augusta arsenal. Lt. col., May 22, 1862. Col., July 12, 1863. Commanded a regiment of LDT in GA in 1864. Stayed in Augusta after the war. Prof. of Chemistry at UGA. Returned to NY in 1894. Died March 21, 1898, Newburgh. Buried St. George's Cemetery, Newburgh. Col. Fremantle called him "a very clever, highly educated, and agreeable officer." Rains wrote a history of the Confederate powder works. Papers at UNC.

Ramsaur, Leander Marcus. Born Aug. 4, 1829, Lincoln Co., NC. Grew up in Marshall Co., MS. Taught school there. Grad. Cumberland U. Law School. Prewar lawyer in Augusta, AR. Md. Mollie Bland. Lt. Co. D, 1st AR MR, 1861. Capt., June 9, 1861. WIA Wilson's Creek. Major, May 1, 1862. WIA (shoulder) and POW Stones River (captured Jan. 5, 1863). To Johnson's Island. Exch. May 1864. Lt. col., Sept. 20, 1863. Col., March 5, 1864, but absent (due to his wounds) the rest of the war. Postwar Augusta lawyer. State legislator. County judge. Died Aug. 14, 1881, Augusta. Buried Augusta Cemetery.

Ramsey, James Newton. Born June 21, 1821, Newton Co., GA. Attd. Randolph-Macon College. Lawyer in Harris and Hamilton Cos. To Columbus in 1857. Lt. in vol. militia. State representative and senator. Delegate to GA Secession Convention. Md. Mary E. Pollard. Col., 1st GA, April 3, 1861. Served in Pensacola and in Western VA. Arrested for granting too many furloughs to his men but never brought to trial. Resigned Dec. 3, 1861, largely due to ill health, but remained in the army through March 1862. Elected to the State Senate in 1863. Columbus lawyer postwar. Died Nov. 10, 1870 (some sources, mistakenly, have

1869), Columbus. Buried Linwood Cemetery. Known as the "Patrick Henry of the South" for his fiery oratory.

Randal, Horace. Born Jan. 4, 1833, McNairy Co., TN. Reared in San Augustine, TX. Grad. USMA 1854. Lt., US Army, 1854–61. Md. Julia Bassett; Nannie E. Taylor. 1st lt., CS Regular Army, March 16, 1861. QM in Pensacola, 1861. ADC on staff of Gen. G. W. Smith (his brother-in-law), 1861. Smith's efforts to promote Randal embroiled both in a long-running dispute with the War Dept. that hampered Randal's promotion. Col., 28th TX Cav., Feb. 12, 1862. Regiment soon dismounted. Led brigade in Walker's Div., 1863–64. Assigned to duty as brig. gen. April 8, 1864, by Gen. Kirby Smith. MWIA Jenkins Ferry, died May 2, 1864. Buried first on the battlefield, eventually in Old Marshall Cemetery, Marshall, TX. A fellow staffer described Randal as "in some respect the most remarkable man I met during the war." A captain in the 28th called him "young, enthusiastic & capable." Randall Co., TX, is named (more accurately, misnamed) after him.

Randolph, Edward Graves. Born July 4, 1829, Fairfield Dist., SC. Educated at Mt. Zion Institute in Winnsboro. Read law and studied medicine. Mexican War veteran of the Palmetto Regt. Merchant in SC. To Bossier Parish, LA, in 1852. Planter. Md. Mary E. Thompson. Capt. Co. D, 9th LA, June 7, 1861. Lt. col., July 7, 1861. Col., Oct. 21, 1861. Dropped at April 1862 reorganization and resigned. Returned to LA. Elected brig. gen. of LA militia in 1863. Commandant of conscripts in LA. Paroled June 8, 1865, Shreveport. Planter in Bossier Parish to 1875, then moved to Grant Parish. State representative 1877–78. Died Sept. 16, 1893, Grant Parish. Buried Rapides Cemetery, Pineville. One of Randolph's men described him as an "excellent disciplinarian and drill-master . . . a rather reserved and studious man."

Ready, Horace. Born March 26, 1838, TN. "Student" in 1860, living with parents in Murfreesboro. Md. Louisiana Cushman. Enlisted July 1, 1861. Lt. and adj., 23d TN, Aug. 23, 1861. Major, probably May 1862. Lt. col., Dec. 16, 1862. WIA Chickamauga. Col., June 30, 1864. WIA Petersburg April 2, 1865. Appmx. Hotel proprietor in Murfreesboro postwar. Died April 17, 1904. Buried Evergreen Cemetery, Murfreesboro. Ready's sister md. Gen. John Hunt Morgan during the war.

Reagan, Wilburn D. Born 1812, Overton Co., TN. To Fayetteville, AR, in 1830. Lawyer and state legislator. Md. Cynthia Bunean. Col. and judge, military court of Dist. of AR, Sept. 1864. Appointed col. and judge, military court of Wharton's Corps, March 23, 1865. Appointed commissioner to meet with Indian tribes, April 15, 1865. Moved to Waco, TX, in 1875. Died March 6, 1893, Fayetteville. Buried Evegreen Cemetery, Fayetteville. A fellow lawyer called him "one of the most eccentric and remarkable characters belonging to the early bar of Arkansas . . . celebrated for curious, remarkable and quaint originality."

Rector, Francis Armstrong. Born c. Jan. 1830, AR, son of a US Army major. Reared in Van Buren, AR. Attd. USMA 1849–50. Miner in Nevada Co., CA, prewar. Md. Laura Nowland. Col. and AAG to Gen. Pearce, AR State Troops, May 1861. VADC at Wilson's Creek. Col., Rector's AR Inf. (a 12-month unit). Col., 17th AR, Nov. 17, 1861. Resigned in 1862 due to ill health. Appointed by Gen. Holmes major and QM Aug. 12, 1862. Served in northwest AR and the Indian Territory. Reappointed by Pres. Davis, Jan. 9, 1864. Clerk in a Fort Smith store in 1870. Died Sept. 10, 1874, in the Choctaw Nation, Indian Territory, "at the mouth of Boggy Creek, on the Red River." Rector was vigorously criticized for his action, or inaction, at Pea Ridge, amid rumors that he had run away. However, Gen. Jackman found him "a most cautious and estimable gentleman."

Reese, Warren Stone. Born Oct. 12, 1841, Sylacauga, AL. Attd. Marion Institute. Clerk for his uncle in Montgomery, AL, when the war started. Md. Mary L. Elmore, 1863. Sgt. Co. E, 1st AL Cav., April 30, 1861. 1st lt. Dec. 31, 1861. Capt., Sept. 10, 1862. Capt. AIG to Gen. Wheeler on Nov. 30, 1862. Col., 12th AL Cav., 1864. Paroled Montgomery May 15, 1865. Postwar merchant and mayor (1885–89) of Montgomery. Lost race for US Senate in 1896. Died Dec. 16, 1897, Montgomery, buried Oakwood Cemetery. One congressman recommended Reese for promotion as "a young man of quickness of parts, great energy, tried courage, and considerable experience as an officer."

Reeves, George Robertson. Born Jan. 3, 1826, Hickman Co., TN. Reared in Crawford Co., AR. Moved to Grayson Co., TX, c. 1846. Rancher and cattleman. County sheriff. State legislator. Md. Jane Moore. Capt. Co. C, 11th TX Cav., Oct. 2, 1861. Promoted to col., Aug. 10, 1863, by Gen. Wharton, as senior capt. of the 11th. Arrested in July 1864 for drunkenness but never brought to trial. He submitted his resignation twice (citing "radical differences between my Brigade Commander and myself," and his arrest without subsequent trial) before it was finally accepted (Jan. 23, 1865). Postwar farmer in Grayson Co. State representative 1873–82. House speaker 1881–82. Died of hydrophobia Sept. 5, 1882, in Grayson Co., after being bitten by a rabid dog. Buried Georgetown Cemetery. Reeves Co., TX, is named for him.

Reeves, Timothy J. Born April 28, 1821, Ashe Co., NC. Moved to Doniphan, Ripley Co., MO, in the 1840s. Farmer. Baptist preacher. Md. Mary Thomas; Ingaleo Hickson; Margaret Hammon; Mary Phelps. Chaplain, 3d Cav., 1st Div., MSG, 1861. Capt. of a scout company, raised in 1862 for local defense. Col. in late 1863 of the 15th MO Cav., a unit formed from companies raised for home guard duty in southeast MO. The 15th rarely if ever operated as a regiment, its companies (up to 20 were organized) serving in their home counties. Paroled June 1865, Jacksonport, AR. Reeves was denied postwar pardon for his role in hanging a Union major accused of atrocities against civilians. Lived in Butler Co., MO, 1865–71, then returned to Doniphan. Baptist minister. Died March 10, 1885, Ripley Co. Buried on his farm, 6 miles northeast of Doniphan. Gen. Jeff Thompson thought Reeves "as good a man and soldier as any in the command."

Reichard, Augustus. Born April 11, 1820, Minden, Hanover, Germany. Officer in Hanoverian Army. Moved to New Orleans in 1844. Commission merchant there prewar. Prussian consul in New Orleans. Md. Mrs. Rosalba (Faure) Prevot; Blanche Bacquie. Major, "Orleans Rifle Regiment," May 1861. Major, the "Lovell" Bn., organized in Sept. 1861, for 12 months service. Col., 20th LA (formed from the Lovell Bn.), Nov. 28, 1861. Led 20th at Shiloh. Regiment consolidated with 13th LA, Nov. 30, 1862. Resigned July 7, 1863, due to a "severe disease" contracted in the KY Campaign. New Orleans merchant postwar. Moved to France after 1880. Cotton planter in Egypt. Died Sept. 7, 1900, La Gardiniere, France. Buried Metairie Cemetery, New Orleans, in the Army of TN tomb.

Reid, John Coleman. Born Dec. 6, 1824, Tuscaloosa Co., AL. Resided in TN and Marion, AL, prewar. Lawyer. AL state representative 1855–57. Author of *Reid's Tramp,* a popular narrative of a trip he took to the Southwest before the war. Filibuster. Md. Alice Coughlin; Adelaide O. Reid; Mary Frances Erwin. 1st lt. Co. A, 8th AL, May 21, 1861. Resigned March 20, 1862. Lt. col., 28th AL, March 1862. Col., Nov. 29, 1862. WIA Stones River. Ordered to north AL in 1864 to organize cavalry. Commanded post of Corinth in Dec. 1864. Paroled May 15, 1865. Postwar lawyer in Marion and Selma. Selma city councilman and active in veterans' affairs. Died Feb. 26, 1896, Selma. Buried Live Oak Cemetery. "An active, energetic officer," said in numerous sources to have been promoted to brig. in 1864 to command cavalry in north AL. However, he was paroled as a colonel.

Reid, Thomas Jefferson. Born Jan. 6, 1838, Caswell Co., NC. Reared in Tulip, AR. Attd. UPA Medical College. Grad. Richmond Medical College in 1861. Md. Carrie Wolcott; Maud Kennicott. Major, 12th AR, July 27, 1861. Authorized in Dec. 1861 to raise a battalion of cavalry. Missed the surrender of the 12th at Island No. 10 because he was absent on recruiting duty. Major, Phifer's AR Cav. Bn. (later the 2d AR Cav.), May 15, 1862. When the 12th was exchanged, Reid transferred back to it. Elected col. at Oct. 2, 1862, reorganization of 12th. POW Port Hudson but escaped in New Orleans and returned to AR. Col., 2d AR Consolidated (formed from the 12th, 18th, and 23d AR), 1864 (probably May, when the unit was formed). Postwar physician in Hot Springs, AR; Chicago; CO; and

Niles, IL. Died Oct. 30, 1907, Niles. Buried Town of Maine Cemetery, Park Ridge, IL. Col. E. W. Gantt of the 12th md. Reid's sister.

Reily, James. Born July 3, 1811, Hamilton, OH. Reared in Lexington, KY. Grad. Miami U. Studied law at Transylvania U. Lawyer in KY and MS. Moved to TX c. 1837, eventually settling in Houston. Lawyer. State legislator. TX minister to the US. Capt. in Indian Wars. Led TX Regt. in Mexican War. Appointed US minister to Russia in 1856. Md. Ellen Hart, niece of Henry Clay. Col., 4th TX Cav., Aug. 20, 1861. In New Mexico Campaign. Sent on a diplomatic mission to Mexico. Shot in the spine and KIA Camp Bisland, LA, April 14, 1863. Buried Lexington Cemetery. An obituary said he was "a good officer and as brave as the bravest."

Reynolds, Arthur Exum. Born Nov. 29, 1817, Alexandria, TN. Attd. Clinton College in TN. Moved to Lawrence Co., AL, in 1838. Moved to Jacinto, MS, in the 1840s. Lawyer. State senator 1850–58. Whig Party leader. Delegate to MS Secession Convention, one of the few delegates voting against secession. Md. Minerva Driver. Although opposed to secession, he was asked by Pres. Davis to raise a regiment. Col., 26th MS, Sept. 10, 1861. POW Fort Donelson; exch. Aug. 27, 1862. Led Tilghman's Brigade in Vicksburg Campaign. Detailed to Conscription Bureau, Aug. 1863. 26th transferred to Joseph Davis's Brigade, ANV, in 1864. WIA Weldon Railroad, Aug. 18, 1864. Sent back to MS to recuperate. Paroled May 21, 1865, Meridian. Elected to US Congress in 1865 but not seated. Lawyer in Jacinto and Corinth postwar. Judge. Died April 18, 1881. Buried Jacinto Cemetery. The "enterprising and gallant" Reynolds was perhaps the heaviest colonel in the Confederate army, weighing over 300 lbs. He is often listed as a Confederate general in postwar writings.

Reynolds, Reuben Oscar. Born Oct. 9, 1832, Columbia Co., GA. Reared in Monroe Co., MS. Grad. UGA, UVA, and LaGrange College. Lawyer in Aberdeen, MS, prewar. Gen. of militia. Md. Mollie English; Sarah B. Young. Lt. Co. I, 11th MS, Feb. 20, 1861. Capt., May 1862. Major, Sept. 25, 1862. Appointed major gen. of MS State Troops late in the war but does not seem to have ever served in that capacity. Col., Dec. 1, 1864. WIA Gaines's Mill and Gettysburg (3d day). Lost right arm March 25, 1865. Captured April 3, 1865, Richmond, while convalescing. Paroled April 21, 1865. Aberdeen lawyer postwar. State senator 1875–87. President of the Senate. Died Sept. 4, 1887, Aberdeen, buried Odd Fellows Cemetery. A wartime inspection report found that Reynolds "displayed all the qualities that constitute an officer."

Reynolds, Samuel H. Born June 1827, VA. Reared in Greenbrier Co. (now WVA). Educated at Lewisburg Academy. Grad. USMA 1849. Lt., US Army, 1849–61. Md. Ellen Douglass. Appointed (from TN) capt. of ordnance, CS Regular Army, Sept. 19, 1861, to rank from March 16th. Col., 31st VA, Sept. 17, 1861. Resigned Nov. 28, 1861. Appointed lt. col., 51st VA (at the request of the officers of the 51st), Sept. 11, 1861, but declined the appointment. Assigned (as capt.) to command the ordnance depot at Knoxville, TN. Promoted to major, Jan. 15, 1863. Chief of ordnance, Dept. of East Tennessee. Later in war OO on Gen. Echols's staff. Relieved from that duty Sept. 29, 1864. Ordered to report to TMD, March 23, 1865, but there is no evidence he made it there before the war ended. Died 1867, Columbia, TN. Gen. Kirby Smith found Reynolds "faithful and efficient."

Rhett, Alfred Moore. Born Oct. 18, 1829, Beaufort Dist., SC, son of US senator Robert B. Rhett, the apostle of secession. Grad. Harvard. Planter on the Ashepoo River prewar. Md. Marie Alice Sparks in 1866. 1st lt., 1st SC Art., Dec. 1860. 1st lt., CS Regular Army, March 16, 1861. 1st lt. Co. B, 1st SC Art. Bn., March 16, 1861. Capt., April 18, 1861. Major, 1st SC Art., March 25, 1862. Lt. col., July 17, 1862. Col., Sept. 5, 1862. Rhett killed his superior officer, Col. W. R. Calhoun, in a duel and succeeded him as colonel. Cashiered for dueling but soon pardoned by Gen. Beauregard. Commanded Fort Sumter for a time. POW Averasboro, while leading a brigade. Sent to Fort Delaware; released July 24, 1865. Postwar planter. Police chief of Charleston in 1880. Died Nov. 12, 1889, Charleston. Buried Magnolia Cemetery, Charleston. A Union captor called the arrogant, aristocratic Rhett a "devil in human shape." Rhett family papers are at USC.

Rhett, Thomas Smith. Born Feb. 25, 1827, Beaufort Dist., SC. Grad. USMA 1848. Lt., US Army, 1848–55. Bank clerk in Baltimore 1855–61. Md. Eliza Eckley. Capt. of artillery, PACS, Nov. 19, 1861. Ordered to Charleston, SC. Col. of art., May 10, 1862, with temporary rank. Commanded batteries in the Richmond defenses. Inspector of ordnance. Sent abroad to purchase arms Oct. 1863. Engineer on Mexican National Railroad postwar. President of an insurance company in Baltimore. Died Dec. 26, 1893, Washington, DC, of injuries suffered when he fell from a ladder. Buried Green Mount Cemetery, Baltimore; soon reburied St. Helena's Churchyard, Beaufort.

Rice, Horace. Born Aug. 4, 1835, at "Marble Hall," near Rogersville, TN. Attd. Centre College and Cumberland U. Lawyer in Hawkins Co., TN, prewar. Md. Rebecca Caruthers. 1st lt. and adj., 23d TN, Aug. 13, 1861. Major, Sept. 30, 1861. Lt. col., May 10, 1862. Col., Nov. 5, 1862. WIA and POW Franklin. Paroled May 2, 1865, Greensboro. Lawyer in Linden and Lexington, TN, postwar. Elected to State Senate in 1871 but died in Lexington Sept. 4, 1871, before he could take his seat. An obituary called Rice "a young man of fine promise, able, eloquent and popular."

Rice, Olin Fletcher. Born Dec. 1839, GA. Dresden, TN, resident. Appointed to USMA from KY, graduating in 1861. Md. Ada D. Talbot of Madison Co., TN, after the war. 2d lt. 9th US, May 6, 1861. Dismissed June 6, 1861. 2d lt., CS Regular Army, appointed June 12, 1861, to rank from March 16. Lt., OO to Gen. Buckner. Capt. Co. E, 1st MO, June 22, 1861. Resigned May 1, 1862. Assigned to Buckner's staff, Aug. 22, 1862. Transferred to Dept. of Gulf, Dec. 23, 1862. Major, Jan. 26, 1863. AAIG to Gens. Maury, Gardner. Appointed col., 63d AL (2d AL Reserves), Aug. 16, 1864. Paroled Grenada, May 19, 1865. Postwar businessman and bookkeeper in St. Louis and Madison Co., TN. Died Dec. 23, 1882, Jackson, TN. Buried Riverside Cemetery, Jackson. Rice was one of the few officers to serve in both armies during the war.

Rice, Patrick Henry. Born 1836, TN. Farmer in Marion Co., TN, and near Guntersville, AL, prewar. Md. Letha Ann Haley; Mary C. Rice. Capt. Co. G, 11th AL Cav. Bn. (later the 3d Confederate Cav.), April 17, 1862. Col., 3d Confederate Cav., Sept. 26, 1863. WIA during the 1864 Atlanta Campaign. Postwar lawyer and newspaper editor in AR, living in Camden in 1870 and Hot Springs in 1880. Died Oct. 16, 1895, Faulkner Co., AR, of Bright's disease. Buried Oak Grove Cemetery, Conway, Faulkner Co.

Rich, Lucius Loomis. Born Sept. 1831, MO. Reared in Liberty, MO. Grad. USMA 1853. Lt., US Army, 1853–61. Md. Mary F. Cosby, sister of Confederate Gen. George Cosby. Capt., CS Regular Army, March 16, 1861. Lt. col., 1st MO, July 1, 1861. Col., May 26, 1862. MWIA Shiloh. Died Aug. 9, 1862, Okolona, MS. Buried Magnolia Cemetery, Mobile.

Richards, William Coolidge. Born Aug. 31, 1828, Shelby Co., AL. Reared in Columbus, MS. Schoolteacher there prewar. Md. Sarah F. Evans. 2d lt., "Lowndes Southrons," March 27, 1861. WIA Booneville while serving as VADC. Major, 9th Bn. MS Sharpshooters, June 1862. WIA and POW Munfordville. Col., 9th MS Consolidated, April 10, 1865. Bank president and mayor of Columbus postwar. Died July 6, 1916, Columbus. Buried Friendship Cemetery.

Richardson, George William. Born Sept. 23, 1819, Hanover Co., VA. Reared in Hanover Co. and Maysville, KY. Grad. William & Mary College. Lawyer in Hanover Co. Commonwealth attorney. Owned a farm. Militia colonel. Delegate to VA Secession Convention. Unmd. Col., 47th VA, May 2, 1861. Dropped at May 1862 reorganization, because the men thought he was too strict a disciplinarian, and because he was not from the Northern Neck of VA, the home section of most of the 47th. VADC to Gen. D. H. Hill during Seven Days. Spent the rest of the war seeking a new post. Commonwealth attorney in Hanover Co. postwar. Militia general. Impoverished, he entered the Confederate Soldiers' Home in

Richmond, where he died Dec. 11, 1891. Buried Hollywood Cemetery. A memoirist remembered Richardson as "[r]ather vain, eager for display."

Richardson, John Harvie. Born June 4, 1828, Richmond, VA. Businessman in Richmond. Worked with streetcar companies in Cincinnati, OH, and St. Louis, MO, prewar. Helped organize a vol. militia company in Richmond. Col., 179th Regt. VA Militia. Md. Catherine C. Hodges. Lt. col., 46th VA, June 24, 1861. Col., May 17, 1862. Almost immediately dropped at reorganization. Organized a corps of scouts/couriers for Gen. Robert E. Lee. Major, 39th (aka 13th) VA Cav. Bn., Sept. 24, 1862, a unit that served as Gen. Lee's personal escort and the ANV's provost guard. WIA Gettysburg. Returned to Richmond postwar and served for 13 years as that city's gas inspector. Thereafter, deputy clerk of the chancery court and streetcar line operator. Died Nov. 29, 1900, Richmond, of paralysis. Buried Hollywood Cemetery. Richardson (the nephew of VA Adj. Gen. Richardson) authored an infantry manual for the Confederate army that was published in 1862.

Richardson, Robert. Born June 29, 1836, Greene Co., AL. Reared in LA. Grad. ULA. Prewar lawyer in Monroe, LA. Md. Mary F. Gaston. Pvt. Co. C, 2d LA, May 11, 1861. Discharged Oct. 4, 1861. 1st lt. Co. D, 17th LA, Sept. 29, 1861. Regimental adj., Oct. 22, 1861. Col., May 23, 1862. POW Vicksburg and exch. Paroled Monroe June 9, 1865. Postwar attorney in Monroe. Masonic Warden. "Prominent because of his ability, eloquence and magnetic character." Died Oct. 12, 1895, Monroe. Buried Monroe City Cemetery.

Riddick, Richard Henry. Born c. 1825, Gates Co., NC. Sgt, 12th US Inf., in Mexican War. Clerk for the Dept. of the Interior in Washington, DC. Lt., US Army, 1855–61. Md. Texana Eugenia Clarke. AAG of NC, May 1861. Lt. col. (NC state rank) and AAG to Gens. Gatlin and J. R. Anderson, 1861–62. Nominated major and AAG, PACS, Aug. 27, 1861. 1st lt., CS Regular Army, March 16, 1861 (nominated Dec. 21, 1861). Col., 34th NC, April 2, 1862. WIA Gaines's Mill. MWIA Ox Hill. Died Sept. 7, 1862, near Fairfax Court House. NC Gov. Clark called Riddick "zealous and capable."

Riley, Amos Camden. Born Jan. 22, 1837, near Louisville, KY. Grew up near New Madrid, MO. Known as "Cam" Riley. Grad. KMI 1855. Prewar farmer near New Madrid. Unmd. 1st lt. Co. I, 1st MO, June 27, 1861. Capt., Oct. 21, 1861. Lt. col., April 4, 1862. Col., Aug. 9, 1862. POW Vicksburg. Regiment consolidated with 4th MO. KIA May 30, 1864, near New Hope Church, GA. Buried Atlanta; reburied in a family cemetery near New Madrid in 1866. One soldier said of Riley that "none possessed higher or more sterling qualities." His wartime letters have been published in the *Missouri Historical Review*.

Rives, Alfred Landon. Born March 25, 1830, Paris, France, son of an American ambassador. Attd. VMI, UVA, Ecole des Ponts et Chaussées in France. Lived in Washington, DC, prewar. Engineer on the Washington aqueduct and the Capitol. Md. Sarah MacMurdo. Capt. of engineers, PAVA, May 2, 1861. Capt., PACS, Feb. 15, 1862. Major, Sept. 23, 1862. Lt. col., May 4, 1863. Col., March 17, 1864. Asst. chief engineer, Engineer Bureau, 1861–65. Acting chief of the bureau, Nov. 1861–Sept. 1862; Aug. 1863–March 1864; April–June 1864. Railroad engineer postwar at various places in the US and Panama. Died Feb. 27, 1903, at his home, "Castle Hill," Albemarle Co., VA. Buried Grace Episcopal Church, Cobham, VA.

Rives, Benjamin Allen. Born May 29, 1822, Buckingham Co., VA. Attd. UVA; Liberty College; and NYU Medical School. Physician in Pittsylvania Co., VA. Moved to Richmond, Ray Co., MO, in 1850. Physician. Farmer. State legislator 1858–60. Md. Eliza C. Townes. Capt. Co. A, 1st Cav., 4th Div., MSG, April 1861. Col., June 21, 1861. Often led the 4th Div. Col., 3d MO (PACS), Jan. 16, 1862. MWIA Pea Ridge, March 8, 1862, died March 11. Buried near the battlefield; reburied Watkins Cemetery near Richmond. A friend called Rives "a thoroughly educated gentleman of decided literary tastes."

Roberts, Oran Milo. Born July 8, 1815, Laurens Dist., SC. Grad. UAL. Lawyer in AL. To San Augustine, TX, in 1840. Judge. State legislator. Law professor. Md. Frances W. Edwards; Mrs. Catherine E. Border. President of TX Secession Convention. Col., 11th TX, June 23, 1862. Elected to TX Supreme Court in 1864. Retired Oct. 19, 1864. Postwar Austin lawyer. Chief justice of TX. Gov. of TX 1878–82. Then professor of law at UTX. Known to his students as "the Old Alcalde." Died May 19, 1898, Austin. Buried Oakwood Cemetery. Roberts wrote the Texas volume of *Confederate Military History.*

Roberts, Philetus Walcott. Born Feb. 2, 1828, Franklin, NC. Attd. Emory & Henry U. Asheville lawyer prewar. City alderman. Clerk of the county court. Md. Selena Corpening. Lt. Co. F, 14th NC, May 3, 1861. Capt., Sept. 20, 1861. Col., April 27, 1862. Died July 5, 1862, in Richmond, of typhoid. Buried Riverside Cemetery, Asheville. A friend remembered, "I have never known a more scrupulously honest and conscientious men." A fellow colonel said Roberts was "endowed with every gift essential to success."

Robertson, James Walthall. Born Aug. 12, 1830, Augusta, GA. Grad. SCMA 1850. Civil engineer. Commandant of cadets, GMI, 1852–54. Superintendent of La Grange College's cadet program 1858–62. Md. Annie Parke. Commanded camp of instruction at La Grange, early 1862. Col., 35th AL, March 12, 1862. Resigned due to illness Nov. 12, 1862. Detailed for engineer duty Jan. 5, 1863. Served at Mobile, Charleston, and FL. Postwar railroad engineer and manufacturer. GA state railroad commissioner. State adj. gen. Died March 5, 1911, Marietta, GA. Buried Citizen's Cemetery, Marietta.

Robins, William Todd. Born Nov. 22, 1835, Gloucester Co., VA. Attd. VMI. Grad. Washington College. Gloucester Co. farmer prewar. Md. Martha Smith; Sally B. Nelson. Pvt. Co. H, 9th VA Cav., June 17, 1861. Sgt. major, July 3, 1861. Lt. and adj., April 15, 1862. Commissioned capt. PACS, Oct. 30, 1862, to report to Gen. W. H. F. Lee as AAG. Detailed to conscript bureau in 1863. Lt. col., 40th VA Cav. Bn., July 15, 1863. Lt. col., 42d VA Cav. Bn. (into which the 40th was merged), Sept. 24, 1863. Col., 24th VA Cav. (formed from the 42d Bn.), June 14, 1864. Injured Feb. 1864 by a falling tree. WIA Samaria Church (arm) and Oct. 26, 1864 (foot). Appmx. Gloucester Co. lawyer postwar. Removed to Richmond c. 1894. Died there Oct. 26, 1906. Buried Episcopal Cemetery, Gloucester Co. A town and air force base in GA are named for his son, Warner Robins, an Army Air Corps pioneer.

Robinson, William George. Born Jan. 1836, Quebec, Canada. Reared in Goldsboro, NC, where his father became editor of the local newspaper. Grad. USMA 1859. Lt., US Army, 1859–61. Md. Gwinthlean McRae. Major and AAG NC State Troops, early 1861. 2d lt., CS Regular Army, March 16, 1861. Lt. col., 2d NC Cav., Sept. 1, 1861. WIA and POW Gillett's Farm, April 13, 1862. Exch. Col., July 23, 1863. Resigned May 25, 1864, having been detailed to the Navy Dept. by the sec. of war. Lived in Covington, KY; St. Louis; Lexington, KY; and Louisville postwar. Clerk in hardware store in Covington. Briefly a civil engineer for the government. By 1876 in the Eastern KY Asylum. Died Dec. 1, 1893, Lexington. Buried Goldsboro. One officer found Robinson "incompetent to command cavalry, and . . . one of the most unprincipled dogs that walk the earth."

Robison, William D. Born June 30, 1840, Murfreesboro, TN. Attd. Union U. in Murfreesboro. Clerk in a Murfreesboro store prewar. Md. Fanny Rice. Corporal Co. F, 2d TN, April 25, 1861. 2d lt., Oct. 19, 1861. Capt., June 20, 1862. WIA Richmond. Col., Dec. 12, 1862, promoted over the heads of senior officers who waived their rights in Robison's behalf. WIA Chickamauga and Ringgold Gap. Severely WIA Jonesboro, the hip wound disabling him for the rest of the war. Grocer and county clerk in Rutherford Co. postwar. Died Sept. 18, 1890, Murfreesboro. Buried Evergreen Cemetery. Gens. Polk and Hardee endorsed his promotion, with Polk praising Robison's "great coolness" in action.

Rodman, William Blount. Born June 29, 1817, Washington, NC. Grad. UNC 1836, at head of class. Prewar lawyer in Washington. Member of a commission to revise NC laws. Plantation owner, whose property was pillaged by Union occupation forces. Md. Camilla H. Croom. Capt. Co. C, 40th NC (3d NC Art.), Oct. 3, 1861. This artillery unit, not having functioning cannon, fought as infantry at the Battle of New Bern. Resigned July 9, 1862. Major, QM, Branch's Brigade, March 13, 1862. Resigned May 21, 1862. Col. and judge of G. W. Smith's Corps, Dec. 16, 1862. Later judge of the military court of Anderson's Corps. Paroled Greensboro, April 26, 1865. Postwar Washington lawyer. Instrumental in drafting postwar state constitution. Justice, NC Supreme Court. Died March 7, 1893, Washington. Buried Oakdale Cemetery, Washington. Rodman family papers are at East Carolina U.

Rogan, James W. Born c. 1835, MD. Reared in Vicksburg, MS. Attd. Sharon College. Prewar bookkeeper in Memphis. 1st lt. Co. C, 15th TN, May 21, 1861. Capt., June 11, 1861. Detached in July 1862 and ordered to report to AR as a mustering officer. Major, 30th AR, Aug. 8, 1862. Lt. col., Nov. 12, 1862. Col., Aug. 6, 1863. Regiment consolidated in 1864. Provost marshal of 4th Dist. of AR. Commanded an unorganized regiment in northeast AR in 1864. Participated in Price's Raid. Postwar Memphis merchant, dealing in groceries, cotton, and cigars. Died May 19, 1873, Somerville, Fayette Co., TN. Buried Somerville Cemetery. An obituary called him "a good citizen, a high-toned merchant and a gallant soldier."

Rogers, George Thomas. Born April 28, 1828, Princess Anne Co., VA. Educated at Kempsville Academy. Farmer in Princess Anne Co. prewar. Officer in vol. militia. Md. Louisa Green; Sally C. Wise. Capt. Co. F, 6th VA, April 22, 1861. Major, Dec. 14, 1861. Col., May 3, 1862. Appmx. Newspaper editor in Norfolk postwar. Entered Richmond Soldiers' Home in 1899. Died March 6, 1901, Princess Anne Co. Buried in a family cemetery at Lynnhaven Farm. A private in the 6th claimed he "would not trade our colonel for any other in the army."

Rogers, John F. Born c. 1828, TN. Merchant in Cleveland, TN, prewar. Md. Catherine Traynor. Col., 1st (aka 5th, Rogers's) TN Cav., Jan. 7, 1862. Dropped at May 1862 reorganization. Very skimpy service record. Merchant in Cleveland postwar. City recorder. Died Oct. 4, 1871. Buried Fort Hill Cemetery, Cleveland.

Rogers, Samuel St. George. Born June 30, 1832, Pulaski, TN. Studied law in Columbus, GA. Prewar lawyer and planter in Ocala, FL. State legislator. Militia colonel. Filibusterer. Fought in Seminole wars. Md. Mary B. Jenks; Josephine A. Baynard. Lt. col., 2d FL, July 17, 1861. Not reelected in May 1862 reorganization and dropped May 11th. Major, commanding FL camp of instruction, July 5, 1862. Col. and judge of military court of Beauregard's Dept., April 23, 1863. Resigned Nov. 21, 1863. Confederate congressman 1863–65. Lawyer/plantation owner in Ocala postwar. Died Sept. 11, 1880, while visiting in Terre Haute, IN. Buried Crown Hill Cemetery, Indianapolis, IN.

Rogers, Sion Hart. Born Sept. 30, 1825, near Raleigh, NC. Attd. Lovejoy's Academy. Grad. UNC. Raleigh lawyer. US congressman 1853–55. State representative 1860–61. Whig Party leader and ardent Unionist. Md. Jane Frances Haywood, sister of Col. E. G. Haywood. Lt. Co. K, 14th NC, May 21, 1861. Resigned Nov. 1861. Col., 47th NC, March 24, 1862. Resigned Jan. 5, 1863, due to ill health and having been elected attorney general of NC. Attorney general 1863–68. US congressman 1871–73. Lost two other races for Congress. Died Aug. 14, 1874, Raleigh. Buried City Cemetery, Raleigh. Papers at Duke U. *Confederate Military History* states Rogers "was never a robust man and had suffered from hemorrhage during his service."

Rogers, William Peleg. Born Dec. 27, 1819, GA. Reared in Aberdeen Co., MS. Attd. medical school in KY. Lawyer and newspaper editor in MS. Capt. in Jefferson Davis's regiment in the Mexican War. Rogers performed great service in that war but felt that Davis slighted his efforts. US consul at Vera Cruz, Mexico, 1849–51. Settled in TX thereafter, practicing law in Washington, Independence, and Houston. Professor of law at Baylor U. Delegate to TX Secession Convention. Md. Martha Halbert. At the start of the war he was offered the colonelcy of the 1st TX but accepted a commission as lt. col., 2d TX, Sept. 23, 1861. Col., June 5, 1862, quickly establishing a reputation for valor and ability. In Aug. 1862 the officers of over 20 regiments petitioned the War Dept. to promote Rogers to major gen. This extraordinary petition (the author has seen none like it) paid Rogers a high compliment but did not move Pres. Davis, his old enemy from Mexican War days. KIA Corinth, Oct. 4, 1862, while leading a charge against Battery Robinette. In a tribute to his bravery, Union Gen. Rosecrans ordered him buried with full military honors near Battery Robinette.

Roman, Alfred. Born May 24, 1824, St. James Parish, LA, son of a governor of LA. Reared in St. James Parish. Attd. Jefferson College in MS. Lawyer. Newspaper editor. Traveled to France just before the war. Capt. of vol. militia. Md. Felicite Aime; Sarah T. Rhett. Col. of LA militia. Major, "Special Battalion" LA Volunteers, Sept. 25, 1861. Lt. col., 18th LA, Oct. 5, 1861. Resigned due to ill health after Shiloh, but while the resignation was pending, elected col., April 16, 1862. Dropped May 10, 1862, at reorganization. Appointed staff lt. col. Oct. 4, 1862. On Gen. Beauregard's staff, 1862–65, as AAIG. Paroled May 1, 1865, Greensboro. Postwar lawyer and planter in St. James Parish. Judge. Died Sept. 20, 1892, New Orleans. Buried first in St. Louis Cemetery No. 1; reinterred in Metairie Cemetery. Roman ("a cultivated gentleman" and "an excellent drill officer") authored a history of Gen. Beauregard (his close friend) after the war, which Beauregard is widely suspected as having written himself.

Ronald, Charles Andrew. Born Jan. 18, 1827, Montgomery Co., VA. Blacksburg attorney prewar. State representative 1855–58. Mexican War veteran. Md. Sallie McCulloch. Capt. Co. E, 4th VA, April 18, 1861. Col., April 23, 1862. Led the Stonewall Brigade at Cedar Mountain, where his "bad management" (in the words of one staff officer) almost cost the Confederates the battle. WIA Oct. 16, 1862, Kearneysville, VA, by a shell. Resigned Sept. 11, 1863, citing this wound and disease. In March 1865, he requested to be restored to rank. Blacksburg lawyer postwar. State representative 1875–77. Died July 1, 1898, Roanoke. Buried Westview Cemetery, Blacksburg. His gravestone bears the inscription, "I Have Suffered."

Rose, James G. Born Sept. 1, 1835, Tazewell, TN. Attd. Emory & Henry College. Hancock Co. lawyer prewar. State representative 1857–59. Md. Virginia J. Thomas. Capt. Co. D, 29th TN, Aug. 13, 1861. Resigned at 1862 reorganization. Lt. col., 61st TN, Oct. 10, 1862. POW Vicksburg. Regiment mounted in the winter of 1863. Col., Aug. 1, 1864. POW Russellville, TN, Oct. 28, 1864. Escaped while en route to the North but recaptured and sent to Johnson's Island. Released May 23, 1865. Morristown lawyer postwar. Briefly lived in MO. Judge. Bank president. Head of school board. Died June 5, 1904, at his Morristown home. Buried Morristown City Cemetery; reburied Jarnigan Cemetery, Morristown. Col. Rowan called Rose "an active and efficient officer."

Rosser, Thomas Henry. Born March 15, 1818, Fayetteville, NC. Prewar merchant in Petersburg, VA. Militia colonel. Took a party of Virginians to settle in KS in 1856. Active in KS-MO border wars. Westport, MO, druggist in 1860. Md. Maria L. Archer. Lt. col., 1st Inf., 8th Div., MSG, June 11, 1861. Col., Sept. 9, 1861. Col., Rosser's Bn. MO Confederates, and Slack's MO Brigade, at Pea Ridge. Commanded posts of Memphis, TN; Gainesville, AL; Selma, AL. Rosser's service record suggests he was at one time col., 62d AL, a reserve unit formed late in the war. Settled in Selma postwar. Farmed near there. Grocer. Died May 22, 1897, Selma. Buried Live Oak Cemetery, Selma.

Rowan, John A. Born Dec. 4, 1820, TN. Monroe Co. farmer prewar. Md. Mary Walker. Capt. Co. B, 4th TN Cav. Bn., June 28, 1861. Resigned due to ill health. Col., 62d TN, Oct. 8, 1862. POW Vicksburg. Exch. Regiment mounted in 1863. Led Vaughn's Brigade often in 1864. MWIA Oct. 12, 1864, in a skirmish at Greeneville, TN, and died the next day. Buried Walker Cemetery, Monroe Co.

Royston, Young Lea. Born June 22, 1819, Perry Co., AL. Grad. UAL. Prewar lawyer in Marion, AL. Prosecuting attorney. Nephew of Sam Houston and brother to Lt. Col. M. H. Royston. Capt. Co. A, 8th AL, May 2, 1861. Major, March 20, 1862. Lt. col., May 5, 1862. Col., June 16, 1862. WIA Frayser's Farm, Salem Church. Retired Nov. 2, 1862, to post duty in Selma. Postwar lawyer and cotton warehouseman in Marion and Selma. Died Dec. 19, 1884, Selma. He owned a lot in Live Oak Cemetery, Selma, but according to cemetery records is not buried there. A postwar history noted Royston's "genial nature, and popular bearing." At 6 feet 7 inches, he was the tallest Confederate colonel.

Rucker, Edmund Winchester. Born July 22, 1835, Rutherford Co., TN. Reared in Wilson Co. Civil engineer in Memphis prewar, working on railroads. City engineer. Md. Mary T. Bentley. Pvt., Pickett's Co. of Engineers, TN State Troops, May 1861. 1st lt. of artillery, CS Regular Army, Nov. 4, 1861. Capt. Co. E, 1st TN Heavy Art., 1862. Commanded a battery at Island No. 10. Major, 16th TN Cav. Bn., Oct. 1862. Col., Rucker's Legion (formed from the 16th Bn.), c. June 1, 1863. Put in command of a brigade in Forrest's Cavalry in 1864. WIA Tupelo. Upon recovery, put in command of Neely's Brigade over the heads of the brigade's colonels, who refused to obey Rucker's orders and were court-martialed. The colonels had no quarrel with Rucker but only with the way he had been promoted. WIA Nashville, eventually losing his arm, and POW. Railroad and bank president postwar, residing in Memphis and later Birmingham. One of the South's leading businessmen and industrialists. Died April 13, 1924, Birmingham. Buried Oak Hill Cemetery, Birmingham. Gen. Thomas Jordan claimed the diminutive Rucker was "formed by nature, except perchance in stature, for a cavalry leader." Often included on postwar lists of Confederate generals.

Rudler, Anthony Francis. Born Antoine-Francois Rudler June 14, 1820, Bitteschwiller, Alsace, France. Came to the US in 1845. Bookkeeper in Augusta, GA. Officer in Mexican War. Filibuster with William Walker. Rudler was Walker's second in command, and his imprisonment in Honduras became a local cause célèbre. Unmd. Capt. Co. G, 3d GA Inf. Bn., Sept. 29, 1861. Major, Oct. 31, 1861. Detached in 1862 to be IG on Kirby Smith's staff. Col., 37th GA (formed from the 3d Bn.), May 6, 1863. WIA Chickamauga and Chattanooga, the latter wound disabling him from further field duty. Arrested Oct. 1864 and sent home to await trial. Ordered to take charge of convalescents in Augusta, Jan. 31, 1865. Commanded posts of Washington, GA, and Columbia, SC, Feb.–April 1865. Active in promoting postwar emigration to Venezuela. Died Aug. 7, 1871, Augusta. Buried Magnolia Cemetery. Rudler was never a popular officer (he was appointed, not elected, major, displacing an officer the troops had elected) but was respected for his "undeniable bravery."

Ruff, Solon Zackery. Born 1837, GA. Reared in Smyrna, GA. Attd. GMI and taught there after graduation. Md. Susan Varner; Irene Arnold. Lt. col., 18th GA, April 25, 1861. WIA 2d Manassas. Col., Jan. 17, 1863. Court-martialed May 10, 1863, for leaving his command and other charges and reprimanded. KIA in the assault on Fort Sanders, Nov. 29, 1863. Buried on the Gibson family farm near Knoxville. Described by a contemporary as "commanding in appearance, a fine tactician, and strict disciplinarian."

Ruffin, Thomas. Born Sept. 20, 1820, Louisburg, NC. Grad. UNC. Prewar lawyer in Goldsboro, NC, and in the Ozark region of MO. Officer of MO volunteers in the Mexican War. US congressman (from NC), 1853–61. Unmd. Confederate congressman in early 1861. Capt. Co. H, 1st NC Cav., May 16, 1861. POW June 29, 1862, near Richmond. Exch. Aug. 5, 1862. Major, June 29, 1863. WIA Gettysburg (saber cut in head and gunshot). Lt. col., July 23, 1863. Col., probably Sept. 28, 1863. MWIA and POW Auburn Mills, VA, Oct. 15, 1863. Died Oct. 18, 1863, at a Union army hospital in Alexandria, VA. Buried on the Ruffin family homestead in Louisburg. Jeb Stuart called Ruffin "a model of worth, devotion and heroism." One of six brothers to die in battle.

Ruffin, Thomas, Jr. Born Sept. 21, 1824, Hillsboro, NC. Grad. UNC 1844. Prewar lawyer in Alamance Co. Md. Mary Cain. Capt. Co. E, 13th NC, April 26, 1861. Capt. Co. H, 6th NC, Jan. 14–April 26, 1862. Lt. col., 13th NC, May 1, 1862. WIA South Mountain. Resigned March 2, 1863. Col. and judge, military court of Dept. of East TN, Dec. 20, 1862. Paroled Greensboro May 2, 1865. Returned to Hillsboro postwar. Lawyer. Justice, NC Supreme Court, 1881–85. Died May 23, 1889, Hillsboro. Buried St. Matthew's Episcopal Church, Hillsboro.

Russell, Alfred Alexander. Born 1827, Johnson Co., AL. Prewar physician in Stevenson, AL. Mexican War veteran. Unmd. Pvt. Co. G, 7th AL (a 12-month unit), April 1, 1861. Major, May 23, 1861. Lt. col., 15th TN PR Cav. Bn., 1862. Col., 4th (Russell's) AL Cav. (formed from his battalion), Nov. 23, 1862. Often led brigade under Forrest and Wheeler and often recommended for promotion. "Cool in action. A man of fine judgment, temperate" with a habit of buttoning and unbuttoning his coat when under fire. Twice wounded during war. Fled to Mexico in 1865, never taking oath of allegiance. Physician and coffee planter in Cordova. Died June 23, 1902, Cordova.

Russell, Daniel Renner. Born 1821, Washington, DC. Grad. Columbian College in DC. Attorney in Carrollton, MS. MS state auditor 1851–55. Officer in Mexican War. Md. Mary E. Booth; Julia P. Hall. MS commissioner to MO, early 1861. Capt. Co. I, 20th MS, April 19, 1861. Col., June 27, 1861. Most of the 20th was captured at Fort Donelson, but due to an ankle injury he missed being captured. Resigned Aug. 8, 1863, due to "indigestion, diarrhea and general disability," and returned home. Died June 6, 1870, Carrollton. Buried Evergreen Cemetery, Carrollton.

Russell, Robert Milton. Born Dec. 15, 1826, Mecklenburg Co., NC. Reared in Middle TN. Grad. USMA 1848. Lt., US Army, 1848–50. Resigned to farm in Gibson Co. Md. Fannie January. Capt. of artillery, TN State Army, May 17, 1861. Capt. Co. E, 12th TN, May 28, 1861. Col., June 3, 1861. Led a brigade at Belmont and Shiloh. Not reelected at May 13, 1862, reorganization. Col., 20th (aka 15th)

TN Cav., Feb. 5, 1864. WIA Tupelo. Paroled Gainesville May 16, 1865. Gibson Co. farmer postwar. Moved to Visalia, CA, after 1880. Died May 5, 1893, Traver, Tulare Co., CA. Buried Visalia City Cemetery.

Russell, Samuel Davenport. Born March 4, 1826, LA. Prewar merchant in Natchitoches. Md. Emily DeRussy Brandt. 1st lt. Co. D, 3d LA, May 9, 1861. Major, May 10, 1862. WIA Corinth. Lt. col., Nov. 5, 1862. WIA and POW Vicksburg. Col., Aug. 22, 1863. Paroled June 10, 1865, Grand Encore. Died Oct. 26, 1866. Buried Russell (aka DeRussy) Cemetery, Natchitoches Parish. A soldier in the 3d called Russell "calm and dignified in bearing, firm, steady, and courageous in battle."

Rust, Armistead Thomson Mason. Born Jan. 18, 1820, near Leesburg, VA. Attd. Georgetown U. Grad. USMA 1842. Lt., US Army, 1842–45. Loudoun Co. farmer 1845–61. Md. Eliza S. Lawrence; Ida Lee. Col., 57th VA Militia at start of war. Col., 19th VA, Nov. 20, 1861. Dropped at April 1862 reorganization. Col. and judge of military court of Jones's Corps, Dec. 16, 1862. Paroled Staunton, VA, May 14, 1865. Postwar farmer near Leesburg. Died July 17, 1887, Loudoun Co. Buried Union Cemetery, Leesburg. Gen. Pickett said Rust "had a high reputation for ability, character and energy" and failed to be reelected colonel only because he lived outside the area the 19th was raised in.

Rutherford, William Drayton. Born Sept. 21, 1837, Newberry Dist., SC. Attd. SCMA and USC. Newberry lawyer in 1860. He was studying in Germany when the war broke out. Md. Sallie H. Fair in 1862. Adj., 3d SC, April 14, 1861. Major, May 14, 1862. POW South Mountain. WIA Fredericksburg. Col., May 6, 1864. KIA Hupp's Hill, VA, Oct. 13, 1864. Buried Rosemont Cemetery, Newberry. A junior officer wrote, "He was gifted with a rare intelligence, and possessed an affectionate nature." Rutherford's wartime letters are at the South Caroliniana Library.

Rutledge, Benjamin Huger. Born June 4, 1829 (some sources say 1828), Statesburg, SC. Grad. Yale. Charleston lawyer prewar. Capt. of vol. militia company, the "Charleston Light Dragoons." Delegate to SC Secession Convention. Md. Eleanor Middleton. Led his old militia company as State Troops in 1861–62. Capt. Co. K, 4th SC Cav., March 25, 1862. Col., Dec. 16, 1862. Served in garrison in SC 1862–64. Regiment ordered to VA in 1864. Attorney in Charleston postwar. State representative 1876–78. Died April 30, 1893, Charleston. Buried Magnolia Cemetery. An obituary called Rutledge "a courteous, accomplished and kindly man . . . a true citizen, a true soldier, a true friend."

Rutledge, Henry Middleton. Born Aug. 5, 1839, SC. Attd. UVA. Henderson Co., NC, resident prewar. Md. Anne M. Blake; Margaret H. Seabrook. Lt. of infantry, PACS, May 21, 1861. Major, 25th NC, Aug. 15, 1861. Lt. col., April 29, 1862. Col., May 17, 1862. WIA Malvern Hill and Antietam. Court-martialed July 22, 1862, and temporarily suspended from command. WIA Petersburg (left arm), June 1864. Appmx. Planter in Georgetown, SC, postwar. Died June 10, 1921, Flat Rock, NC. Buried St. John's in the Wilderness Cemetery, Flat Rock. In 1937 his son wrote a memoir, *My Colonel and His Lady,* that relates many stories of Col. Rutledge.

Saffell, Richard Meredith. Born Feb. 11, 1835, Marysville, TN. Wealthy farmer in Roane Co. prewar. 1st lt. Co. F, 26th TN, July 4, 1861. POW Fort Donelson. Exch. Sept. 1862. Capt., 1862. Major, Oct. 13, 1862 (elected at reorganization). WIA and POW Stones River and again exch. Col., Oct. 26, 1863. KIA Bentonville, March 21, 1865, while leading a cavalry charge. Buried on the battlefield. Saffell has a marker on the battlefield and at Old Gray Cemetery, Knoxville. Saffell's papers are at UTN.

Sale, John Burress. Born June 7, 1818, Amherst Co., VA. Family moved to Lawrence Co., AL, in 1821. Grad. La Grange College, 1837. Lawyer in Moulton, AL. Lawyer and judge in Aberdeen, MS. Md. Susan Turner Sykes; Nannie Mills; Louisa Leigh; Anne Cornelius. Capt. Co. K, 5th MS Bn. (later 27th MS), Sept. 27, 1861. Assigned to duty as judge advocate with Bragg's Army, Feb. 27, 1863. Col. and judge of military court of Hardee's Corps, June 16, 1863. Resigned April 2, 1864. Military sec. (and later chief of staff) to Gen. Bragg, 1864–65. Appointed col. and military sec. to rank from March 15, 1864. Appointed col. and AAG Jan. 23, 1865. Postwar lawyer in Monroe Co. MS. Died Jan. 24, 1876, Aberdeen. Buried Odd Fellows Cemetery. A fellow lawyer called Sale "this compound of frailty and greatness," and Gen. Hardee termed him "a soldier above reproach."

Sanders, Christopher Columbus. Born May 8, 1840, Jackson Co., GA. Grad. GMI 1861. Md. Frances A. Scarborough in 1871. Lt. col., 24th GA, Aug. 30, 1861. Col., Jan. 9, 1864. WIA Spotsylvania. POW Sayler's Creek, released July 25, 1865. Postwar president of the State Banking Co. of Gainesville, GA. Died Aug. 3, 1908, Gainesville. Buried Alta Vista Cemetery, Gainesville. One of nine brothers in Confederate service.

Sanford, John William Augustine. Born Nov. 30, 1825, Milledgeville, GA. Attd. Oglethorpe U. Grad. UAL and Harvard Law School. Pre- and postwar lawyer in Montgomery, AL. Outspoken secessionist. Md. Sallie Taylor. Pvt. Co. F, 3d AL, 1861. Capt. and QM, 1861. Lt. col., 3d Bn., Hilliard's Legion, June 25, 1862. Col., 60th AL, Nov. 25, 1863. Appmx. Postwar attorney general of AL. Clerk of AL Supreme Court. Gen. in the UCV. Died Aug. 7, 1913, Montgomery, buried Oakwood Cemetery.

Saunders, William Hubbard. Born Feb. 28, 1819, Franklin, TN. Prewar lawyer in Monroe Co., MS. Md. Susan Goodwin. 2d lt. Co. K, 27th MS, Oct. 19, 1861. Promoted to 1st lt. and capt. Resigned Feb. 25, 1863. On recruiting duty. Col. and judge, military court of Hood's Corps, April 22, 1864. Postwar farmer in Monroe Co. Died May 21, 1895, near Muldon, MS. Buried Odd Fellows Cemetery, Aberdeen, MS. A relative called him "quiet and studious" with a "hermit-like simplicity of life."

Saunders, William Laurence. Born July 30, 1835, Raleigh, NC. Grad. UNC. Raleigh lawyer prewar. Editor, Salisbury *Banner*. Md. Florida Colten. 2d lt. Co. D, 1st NC Art., May 16, 1861. Resigned Jan. 11, 1862, in order to recruit his own company. Capt. Co. B, 46th NC, April 16, 1862. Major, Sept. 30, 1862. WIA Fredericksburg (mouth). Lt. col., Jan. 2, 1863. Col., Dec. 31, 1863. WIA Wilderness (mouth again). Appmx. Newspaper editor postwar. Founded the Raleigh *Observer*. KKK leader. NC sec. of state 1879–92. Author of books on NC history. Died April 2, 1891, Raleigh. Buried Calvary Episcopal Cemetery, Tarboro. Papers at Duke U.

Savage, John Houston. Born Oct. 9, 1815, McMinnville, TN. Smithville lawyer. US congressman 1849–53, 1855–59. Lt. col. 11th US during the Mexican War. Unmd. Col., 16th TN, June 10, 1861. Court-martialed for disobeying orders, Feb. 1, 1862, and reprimanded. Often clashed with Gen. Donelson, his brigade commander. WIA Perryville (while leading Donelson's Brigade) and Stones River. Resigned Feb. 20, 1863, when a lt. col. (Marcus Wright) was promoted to brig. gen. to command the brigade. Lost race for Confederate Congress in 1863. McMinnville lawyer postwar. State representative 1877–79, 1887–91. State senator 1879–81. Known as "the Old Man of the Mountain." Died April 5, 1904, McMinnville. Buried Riverside Cemetery. In 1863 numerous officers petitioned the War Dept. for Savage's promotion to brigadier, citing his "merit and true worth." Sec. of War Seddon acknowledged Savage's gallantry but doubted his other qualifications. Junior officers thought Savage "corrupt" and "a semi-barbarian."

Scaife, James Wilkes. Born 1828, SC. Prewar farmer/planter in Union Dist., SC. To Phillips Co., AR, c. 1857. Md. Frances Farr. Capt. Co. C ("Trenton Guards"), Johnson's AR Regt., 1861. Capt. Co. E, 2d AR, June 4, 1861. Major, Sept. 2, 1861. Lt. col., Nov. 16, 1861. Col., Nov. 12, 1861 (date of election). Resigned Jan. 6, 1862. Retired, Dec. 16, 1862. Capt. of a local defense company after resignation. Postwar Phillips Co. farmer. Died 1893, AR. Buried Trenton Baptist Cemetery, Phillips Co. Father was lt. col., 18th SC. Middle name also given as "Washington."

Scales, Junius Irving. Born June 1, 1832, Rockingham Co., NC. Brother of Gen. Alfred Scales. Grad. UNC 1853. Teacher and lawyer in Alamance Co., NC. State representative. Moved to Carroll Co., MS, just before the war. Md. Euphemia Hamilton Henderson. Capt. Co. K, 30th MS, Feb. 27, 1862. Lt. col., April 14, 1862. Col., June 6, 1863. WIA and POW Chickamauga. Imprisoned at Johnson's Island the rest of the war. Railroad lawyer and farmer postwar, in Granville Co., then Greensboro, NC. State senator 1877–80. Died July 12, 1880, NY. Buried Green Hill Cemetery, Greensboro. His son remembered him as "always stern against any evil."

Schaller, Franz Emile. Born July 26, 1835, Ostheim, Saxony (now Germany). Educated at a military academy in Saxony. Officer in French army and veteran of the Crimean War. Came to US in 1855. Teacher at St. Timothy's Hall in MD; Columbia, SC; and Hillsboro Military Academy in NC. Md. Sophie Sosnowski; Bertha Klingel. Major, 2d Regt. "Polish Brigade" (aka 3d LA Bn.; 15th LA), June–Sept. 1861. Appointed lt. col., 5th TX, Oct. 2, 1861, but the soldiers of the 5th, dissatisfied with the appointment, drove him out of camp. Reassigned to the 22d MS, Oct. 23, 1861. Col., Dec. 24, 1861. Charged with being cruel to his troops (he manipulated the rations in order to help the sickly) and with paying out regimental funds illegally. A court found him guilty but attached no criminality to the actions and awarded no punishment. WIA in foot and disabled Shiloh. On sick leave thereafter. Dropped Nov. 12, 1862; reinstated Feb. 12, 1863; then dropped again July 31, 1863. Served in Conscript Bureau in 1863. Resigned June 2, 1864. Schoolteacher in Athens, GA, postwar. Professor at colleges in Sewanee, TN, and St. Louis. Prolific author and writer. Died Jan. 16, 1881, St. Louis. Buried Bellefontaine Cemetery, St. Louis. Schaller's wartime letters and diary are at USC. The letters were published in 2007.

Scott, Charles Lewis. Born Jan. 23, 1827, Richmond, VA. Grad. William & Mary College. Lawyer in Richmond. Joined the gold rush to CA in 1849. Lawyer in Sonora, CA. US congressman 1857–61. Md. Harriet Williston. Major, 4th AL, May 7, 1861. WIA 1st Manassas. Resigned July 13, 1862, due to this wound. Col. and judge, military court of Longstreet's Corps, Dec. 20, 1862. Farmer in Wilcox Co., AL, postwar. US minister to Venezuela. Died April 30, 1899, Mt. Pleasant, Monroe Co., AL. Buried Scott family cemetery in Cedar Hill, AL.

Scott, John. Born April 23, 1820, Fauquier Co., VA. Grad. UVA. Editor, Richmond *Whig*. Lawyer. Author. Farmer. Organized the "Black Horse Cavalry" in Fauquier Co. Md. Harriet A. Caskie. Temporarily Capt. Co. H, 4th VA Cav., 1861. Capt. of cav., PACS, March 16, 1861. Major, 24th VA Bn. PR, 1862–63. Battalion disbanded in Jan. 1863. Commanded AR cavalry in northwest AR in April 1863, signing himself colonel and referred to in reports as such. Later served with Mosby's partisans in VA. Fauquier Co. lawyer postwar. Commonwealth attorney. Wrote a book on Mosby. Died May 7, 1907, Warrenton. Buried Warrenton Cemetery. There is no official record of his promotion to colonel, and he called himself "major" in his book.

Scott, John Sims. Born Sept. 21, 1826, Wilkinson Co., MS. Wealthy planter in Feliciana and Pointe Coupee Parishes prewar. Mexican War veteran. Md. Sarah Ann Raiford. Volunteer scout on the VA Peninsula in early 1861. Col., 1st LA Cav., May 4, 1861. Led his regiment and often a brigade, in TN and KY 1862–63. Court-martialed March 16, 1863, and reprimanded. Resigned Oct. 8, 1863, but the resignation was revoked Jan. 25, 1864. Commanded Dist. of Southwest MS and East LA, 1864–65. Charged with neglect of duty and consorting with the enemy. Relieved March 7, 1865. Cotton factor in New Orleans postwar. Died April 16, 1872, New Orleans. Buried Sims Cemetery, Wilkinson Co. Gen. A. S. Johnston called Scott "the best cavalry officer I know of in the Confederate army," although others found him "dangerous." By war's end, the "headstrong" Scott was the most senior serving cavalry colonel. However, personality conflicts with his superiors blocked his promotion.

Scott, William Campbell. Born Nov. 12, 1807, Powhatan Co., VA. Attd. UVA and Hampden-Sydney College. Powhatan Co. lawyer. State representative 1837, 1850–51. Lost race for Congress. Militia general. Delegate to VA Secession Convention. Col., 44th VA, June 14, 1861. Criticized for his actions at Rich Mountain. Resigned Jan. 4, 1863, on surgeon's certificate of disability. Died April 9, 1865, Powhatan. A county history called him "a distinguished man of good education and unblemished private character."

Scruggs, Daniel Edward. Born 1833, Richmond, VA. Lived in De Soto Co., MS, TX, and New Orleans prewar. Bookkeeper. Md. Virginia Pierpont. Enlisted in New Orleans in the Crescent Regt., March 5, 1862. Transferred to the 5th Co., Washington Art., July 16, 1862. Immediately detailed as a clerk to the headquarters staff of Gen. Samuel Jones. Employed in the QM Dept. in Richmond. Capt. Co. A, 2d VA LDT (the "quartermaster battalion"), June 18, 1863. Major, May 10, 1864. Col., Aug. 29, 1864. Returned to New Orleans after the war. Bookkeeper, volunteer fireman, and active Mason. Died Nov. 1, 1871, New Orleans, of tuberculosis contracted during the war. Buried Greenwood Cemetery.

Searcy, Anderson. Born July 26, 1834, TN. Rutherford Co. farmer prewar. Md. Amanda Batey. Lt. Co. C, 45th TN, Nov. 28, 1861. Capt., and col., May 20, 1862. 45th consolidated with 23d TN Bn. in Nov. 1863. Led his men in a brilliant escape from encircling Union forces at Bentonville. Paroled May 1, 1865, Greensboro. Rutherford Co. farmer postwar. Died May 11, 1910, Rutherford Co. Buried Evergreen Cemetery, Murfreesboro.

Searcy, James J. Born Sept. 24, 1830, Clark Co., KY. Grad. UMO. Principal of the Primary Dept. at UMO prewar. Md. Sarah Barrett; Mary Agnes Searcy. 1st lt., Columbia (Boone Co.) Home Guards, MSG, 1861. Left the university in 1862 to join the Confederate army. VADC at Lone Jack, winning praise for activity and courage. Adj., 9th MO, Nov. 9, 1862. Col., Searcy's MO Cav., a regiment raised during Price's 1864 Raid. Regiment dismounted during the winter of 1864–65 and downgraded to a battalion. Lt. col. of this battalion Jan. 24, 1865. Paroled Alexandria, LA, June 7, 1865, as lt. col., Searcy's Bn. of sharpshooters. Postwar teacher in Sturgeon, MO. Died Feb. 20, 1872, Sturgeon, of diphtheria. Buried Rocky Fork Church Cemetery, near Hinton, MO.

Seibels, John Jacob. Born Dec. 8, 1816, Edgefield Dist., SC. Grad. USC, 1836. Moved to Montgomery, AL. Editor of newspaper. Lt. col. in Mexican War. US minister to Belgium, 1854–56. Md. Phillipa Barney. Col. and ADC to governor of AL, Jan.–March 1861. Col., 6th AL, May 14, 1861. Dropped at April 1862 reorganization. Unsuccessful candidate for the Senate in 1863. Died Aug. 8, 1865, at his Montgomery home. Buried Oakwood Cemetery, Montgomery. A staff officer found Seibels "a tall blustering politician, out of his element." Brother of Lt. Col. Emmett Seibels and father-in-law of Col. Charles P. Ball.

Settle, Thomas. Born Jan. 23, 1831, Rockingham Co., NC. Grad. UNC. Rockingham Co. lawyer. State legislator 1854–59. Speaker of the NC House 1858–59. Elected solicitor of the 4th Judicial Dist. in Nov. 1860. Md. Mary Glen. Capt. Co. I, 13th NC, May 3, 1861. Reelected April 1862 but declined. Elected col., 21st NC, April 27, 1862, but declined the appointment and went home. Resumed his solicitor's position. Postwar lawyer. State senator 1866–68 and speaker of the State Senate. US minister to Peru 1871–72. Justice, NC Supreme Court, 1868–71, 1872–76. Chairman of the 1872 Republican National Convention. Lost race for governor in 1876. US dist. judge in FL 1877–88. Died Dec. 1, 1888, Greensboro, NC. Buried Oakdale Cemetery, Wilmington. Papers at UNC.

Seymour, Isaac Gurdon. Born Oct. 1804, Savannah, GA. Distant cousin of Horatio Seymour, wartime governor of NY. Grad. Yale 1825. Moved to Macon, GA, in 1827. Lawyer. Mayor of Macon. Editor, Macon *Georgia Messenger*. Seminole War veteran. Colonel in Mexican War. Moved to New Orleans in 1848. Editor, New Orleans *Bulletin*. Md. Caroline Whitlock. Col., 6th LA, June 4, 1861. KIA Gaines's Mill. Buried Rose Hill Cemetery, Macon. His son's memoirs claim Seymour was "passionately fond of military life." A staff officer considered Seymour "a brave gentleman, but inefficient, slow officer."

Shackelford, Benjamin Howard. Born Nov. 10, 1819, Culpeper Co., VA. Pre- and postwar lawyer in Warrenton, VA. Lt. in vol. militia. Md. Rebecca B. Green. 1st lt. Co. K, 17th VA, April 22, 1861. Capt. June 3, 1861. WIA Blackburn's Ford,

July 18, 1861. Resigned Feb. 20, 1862. Col. and chief judge, military court of the Valley Cav. Corps, March 23, 1865. Died May 18, 1870, Warrenton, while running for the state legislature. Buried Warrenton Cemetery.

Shacklett, Absalom Redmond. Born Dec. 7, 1826, Brandenburg, Meade Co., KY. Farmer in Meade and McLean Cos. prewar. Pvt. in US Army in Mexican War. Md. Minerva Jane Humphrey. Capt. Co. D, 8th KY, Oct. 13, 1861. POW Fort Donelson, exch. Sept. 1862. Lt. col., Sept. 25, 1862. Regiment mounted in 1864. Col., July 29, 1864. Paroled May 1865 at Columbus, MS. Farmer near Island, McLean Co., postwar. State representative. Postmaster. Died Aug. 27, 1910, Island. Buried Island Baptist Cemetery. Shacklett (known as "little Ap") was great-granduncle of Hall of Fame ballplayer "Peewee" Reese.

Shaler, James Riddle. Born Dec. 23, 1830, Allegheny Co., PA. Prewar St. Louis merchant and agent for the Pennsylvania Railroad. Md. Virginia Coons. Captured at Camp Jackson as major, 2d MO Vol. militia. Exch. Oct. 26, 1861. ADC on staff of 7th Div., MSG, early 1862. Briefly led the 7th and 9th Divs. Appointed col., 27th AR, July 2, 1862, by Gen. Hindman. Not elected col. when the regiment had formal elections in 1863. AIG on Gen. Price's staff, 1864. Briefly settled in British Honduras postwar. Moved to Chattanooga, TN, then to New Albany, IN. Railroad superintendent there and in Mexico. Moved to Panama in 1896 to become superintendent of the Panama Railroad. Played a vital role in facilitating the Panamanian Revolution of 1903, which created that country. Died Sept. 7, 1910, at his summer home in Ocean City, NJ. Buried Bellefontaine Cemetery, St. Louis. Shaler was very unpopular with the men of the 27th, being a Missourian, a strict disciplinarian, and not having been elected by the men. Pvt. Turnbo accused Shaler of being a "tyrant."

Shanks, David. Born April 26, 1832, Lincoln Co., KY. Went to CA in 1849 to prospect for gold, returning to MO when the war started. Unmd. Capt. Co. D, 2d Inf., 8th Div., MSG, July 22, 1861. Capt. Co. C, Hays's (12th) Mo Cav., Sept. 12, 1862. Major, Sept. 18, 1862. Lt. col., June 20, 1863. Col., Aug. 20, 1863. Led Shelby's Brigade in Price's Raid. Severely WIA at Moreau Creek near Jefferson City, Oct. 6, 1864. Captured two days later and imprisoned for the remainder of the war. Postwar miner in Wyoming and Colorado. Died 1870, Denver, CO. John N. Edwards called him "the Ney of the division." Wounded 14 times during the war.

Shaver, Robert Glenn. Born April 18, 1831, Sullivan Co., TN. Attd. Emory & Henry College. Prewar lawyer in Batesville and Lawrence Co., AR. Militia colonel. Md. Adelaide Ringgold. Col., 7th AR, July 23, 1861. Led brigade at Shiloh and was stunned senseless by an exploding shell. Not reelected at May 1862 reorganization. Col., 38th AR, Sept. 21, 1862. Often led brigade in TMD.

Provost marshal at Camden, 1865. Paroled Shreveport June 8, 1865. WIA 4 times in war and had 6 horses killed under him. Lived in Center Point, Howard Co., AR, postwar. Lawyer. City alderman. Said to have been head of the state KKK. Gen. of the AR State Guard. UCV official. Died Jan. 13, 1915, at the home of his daughter in Foreman, AR. Buried Center Point Cemetery. Nicknamed "Fighting Bob," Shaver, one veteran averred, "would rather fight than eat." An article in the *Confederate Veteran* asserted that Shaver's promotion to brigadier was blocked in the Confederate Senate by a prewar political opponent.

Shaw, Henry Marchmore. Born Nov. 20, 1819, Newport, RI. Reared in Currituck Co., NC. Grad. UPA Medical College. Indiantown, Camden Co., physician. State senator 1851–53. US congressman 1853–55, 1857–59. Planter. Delegate to NC Secession Convention. Md. Mary Riddle Trotman. Col., 8th NC, May 16, 1861. POW Roanoke Island. Exch. Nov. 10, 1862. KIA Batchelder's Creek, near New Bern, NC, Feb. 1, 1864. Buried Shaw family cemetery, Currituck Co. Although Col. F. M. Parker heard that Shaw had acted cowardly at Roanoke Island, other observers praised his "great courage and coolness."

Shaw, Thomas Pickens. Born June 10, 1828, Edgefield Dist., SC. Farmer near Edgefield prewar. Md. Mattie Lanier. Capt. Co. B, 19th SC, Dec. 28, 1861. Lt. col., May 19, 1862. Col., Dec. 31, 1862. Arrested in 1863 and brought before an examining board. WIA and POW Franklin. Imprisoned until war's end. Edgefield farmer postwar. Died Aug. 2, 1883, at his home near Poverty Hill. Buried Mt. Lebanon Cemetery.

Sheffield, James Lawrence. Born Dec. 5, 1819, Huntsville, AL. Wealthy Marshall Co., AL, farmer. County sheriff. State legislator. Delegate to AL Secession Convention (voted no). Md. Mary Ann Street. Capt. Co. K, 9th AL, July 1, 1861. Col., 48th AL, May 13, 1862, a unit he is said to have spent $57,000 outfitting. WIA Cedar Mountain. Lost race for Congress, 1863. Resigned May 31, 1864. Postwar clerk in the AL State Education office. State senator. Greenback Party candidate for governor, 1882. Died July 2, 1892, Montgomery. Buried Oakwood Cemetery. Not a strong disciplinarian. Lost his fortune in the war.

Shelby, Winchester Bledsoe. Born Jan. 18, 1827, Dixon Springs, TN. Reared in Brandon, MS, and TX. Attd. Lebanon College. Lawyer in Brandon, MS, prewar. Mexican War veteran. Md. Margaret Alexander. 1st lt. Co. I (the "Rankin Guards"), 6th MS, May 4, 1861. Capt., June 1861. Resigned Dec. 27, 1861, due to illness. Col., 39th MS, May 13, 1862. POW Port Hudson, while leading a brigade. To Johnson's Island Prison. Exch. July 24, 1865. Lawyer in Brandon postwar. Died July 9, 1873, Brandon. Buried Brandon Cemetery.

Shields, John Camden. Born Aug. 10, 1820, Rockbridge Co., VA. Prewar publisher of the Lynchburg *Virginian* and the Richmond *Whig*. Capt. in vol. militia. Md. Martha M. Hardy. Capt. 1st Co., Richmond Howitzers, May 10, 1861. Lt. col., 3d VA Art., June 20, 1862. Col., Nov. 13, 1862, but appointment never confirmed by Congress, and he reverted to his former rank. Commandant of conscripts, VA. Commanded "Camp Lee," the camp of instruction in Richmond, 1862–65. Resumed publishing the Richmond *Whig* postwar. Farmer in Rockbridge Co. Died June 30, 1904, at his home in Riverside, Rockbridge Co. Buried Stonewall Jackson Cemetery, Lexington.

Shingler, William Pinckney. Born Nov. 11, 1827, Orangeburg Dist., SC. Prewar planter in Christ Church Parish. Banker, broker in Charleston. Militia colonel. Delegate to SC Secession Convention. Md. Harriet English; Caroline English; Susan Ball Venning. On staff of Gen. Barnard Bee at 1st Manassas. Helped raise the Holcombe Legion. Lt. col., Holcombe Legion, Nov. 21, 1861. Col., Oct. 8, 1862. Took charge of the Legion cavalry. Charged with drunkenness on duty, April 1863. Arrested and relieved of command. On March 18, 1864, the Legion cavalry was re-formed into the 7th SC Cav. Resigned May 30, 1864, after intentionally disregarding an order from the War Dept. to take command of another regiment. Said to have quarreled with Pres. Davis. Returned to SC and commanded militia there. Lived in Mount Pleasant postwar. State senator 1865–67. Died Sept. 14, 1869, Cordesville, SC. Buried Venning Cemetery, near Mount Pleasant. Shingler was often included on postwar lists of Confederate generals. However, on his application for postwar pardon he called himself colonel. A fellow colonel vouched for Shingler's "character, intelligence and integrity . . . and conservatism."

Shivers, William Rabun. Born Oct. 11, 1819, GA. Attd. USMA. Prewar merchant in South Port, then Shreveport, LA. Capt. of TX Volunteers in Mexican War. Md. Sarah E. Trabue. Capt. Co. A, 1st LA, April 28, 1861. Major, May 1861. Lt. col., Oct. 10, 1861. Col., 1862 (probably April 28 or June 8). WIA severely in right arm at Oak Grove during 7 Days' Battles and never returned to regiment. On post duty in Shreveport the rest of the war. Cotton sampler in Shreveport postwar. Mayor of Shreveport briefly in 1871. Died July 3, 1871, Shreveport, at the home of his brother-in-law. Buried Oakland Cemetery, Shreveport. One diarist found Shivers often "drunk & in ill humor."

Shober, Charles Eugene. Born March 24, 1829, Salem, NC. Grad. UNC. Banker and lawyer in Salem, Guilford Co., prewar. State representative 1860–62. Md. Mary A. Gilmer; Letitia Roane; Nannie Hundley. Capt. Co. B, 45th NC, Feb. 15, 1862. Major, Sept. 30, 1862. Resigned Jan. 30, 1863. Lt. col., 2d NC Bn., backdated to rank from Oct. 10, 1862. Resigned June 6, 1863, due to asthma. Col., 7th NC Senior Reserves, July 1864. Resigned Jan. 26, 1865, due to ill health. Chosen a member of the NC Executive Council, Dec. 16, 1864. Banker in Greensboro postwar. Died Nov. 21, 1892, Greensboro. Buried Green Hill Cemetery, Greensboro. Gen. Holmes considered Shober "an officer of the greatest merit."

Shorter, Eli Sims. Born March 15, 1823, Monticello, GA. Grad. Yale. Pre- and postwar lawyer in Eufaula, AL. US congressman 1855–59. Brother of AL Gov. John Gill Shorter. Md. Marietta Fannin. Lt. col., 18th AL, Sept. 4, 1861. Col., Dec. 23, 1861. Resigned April 13, 1862, due to typhoid fever. Aide to Gov. Shorter, 1862–63. In late 1862 he applied for a judgeship on a military court, pledging to avoid the "use of ardent spirits." Died May 6, 1879, Eufaula. Buried Fairview Cemetery.

Shriver, Daniel McElheran. Born Nov. 24, 1835, OH. Worked in his father's wholesale liquor business in Wheeling. Member of vol. militia. Unmd. Capt. Co. G, 27th VA (the "Shriver Grays" of Wheeling, a company he and his family largely equipped), May 16, 1861. Major, May 27, 1862. WIA Port Republic (shoulder and back). Lt. col., Nov. 19, 1862. Resigned Sept. 4, 1863, upon election to the State Senate. Appointed col., Feb. 6, 1864, to raised troops within Union lines in northwest VA. The appointment contained the condition that he raise the regiment within 60 days, and Shriver, who could not accept this condition, refused the appointment. Died July 21, 1865, at the home of William Russell (his brother-in-law) near Wheeling. Buried Greenwood Cemetery, Wheeling.

Simmons, Thomas Jefferson. Born June 25, 1837, Hickory Grove, Crawford Co., GA. Educated at Brownwood Institute in La Grange, GA. Prewar lawyer in Crawford Co. Md. Pennie Hollis; Lucile Peck; Mrs. Ann Renfro. Lt. Co. E, 6th GA, May 27, 1861. Lt. col., 45th GA, March 15, 1862. WIA Gaines's Mill. Col., Oct. 13, 1862. Court-martialed March 22, 1864, and suspended from command. Appmx. Lawyer in Macon postwar. President of the GA State Senate. Justice, then chief justice, GA Supreme Court. Died Sept. 12, 1905, Atlanta. Buried Rose Hill Cemetery, Macon.

Simons, James. Born May 9, 1813, Charleston, SC. Attd. College of Charleston. Grad. USC in 1833. Charleston lawyer. State representative 1842–61. Speaker of the SC House 1850–61, "acknowledged to have been the best presiding officer the State has seen." Brig. gen. 4th brigade, SC Militia. Md. Sarah Wragg. Commanded his militia brigade during the bombardment of Fort Sumter and thereafter. Relieved of command April 29, 1861, by the governor (a political opponent), amid allegations Simons hid out in a hospital whenever the enemy cannon fired. In 1862 Pres. Davis authorized Simons to raise a "legion," but the unit never got off the ground. Appointed col. and judge, military court of Dept. of SC, Sept. 21, 1864, but Simons declined the appointment. Postwar lawyer in Charleston. Trustee of USC. Died April 26, 1879, Charleston, buried Magnolia Cemetery. Papers at South Caroliniana Library.

Simonton, Charles Henry. Born July 11, 1829, Charleston, SC. Attd. College of Charleston. Grad. USC. Charleston lawyer. In state legislature 1858–62. Capt. of vol. militia. Md. Ella Glover. Participated in siege of Fort Sumter, 1861, as capt. of his company, now part of Pettigrew's 1st SC Rifles. Major, 11th SC Bn. (the "Eutaw Bn."), 1861. Col., 25th SC (formed from the 11th Bn.), July 22, 1862. Detached in 1864 to command Fort Caswell, NC. POW (along with most of his regiment) Town Creek, NC, Feb. 20, 1865. Released Aug. 6, 1865. Charleston lawyer postwar. State representative 1865–66, 1876–86. House speaker 1865–66. US dist. judge in the Cleveland administration. Died April 25, 1904, while on a visit to Philadelphia, PA. Buried Magnolia Cemetery, Charleston. His law partner called Simonton "unselfish, sincere, just and true."

Simonton, John M. Born June 17, 1830, Lawrence Co., TN. Merchant in Lawrence Co. in 1850. Moved to Shannon, Itawamba Co., MS, in the 1850s. Businessman in Shannon and Camargo. State senator 1859–61. Md. Ruth Potter; Flora Potter. Capt. Co. I, 1st MS, July 8, 1861. Col., Sept. 19, 1861. POW Fort Donelson, while leading a brigade. Exch. Sept. 1862. Resigned Nov. 26, 1863, due to a hemorrhoidal tumor. Elected to the State Senate in 1863. Col. of MS State Troops at the Okolona rendezvous, Aug. 13, 1864. Businessman and farmer postwar in Itawamba and Lee Cos. Sawmill owner. State senator 1865–69, 1884–88. State agriculture commissioner 1896–98. Died June 24, 1898, at his Jackson home. Buried Whitesides family cemetery, Shannon. A junior officer described Simonton as "a fine specimen of manhood, tall, handsome, and as straight as an Indian . . . a most excellent officer." In 1863 practically all of the officers in the Port Hudson garrison petitioned for his promotion to general.

Sims, William Bradford. Born Dec. 19, 1829, AR. Prewar Clarksville merchant. Md. Jane Brooks. Capt., "Red River Mounted Rangers," TX State Troops, early 1861. Col., 9th TX Cav., Oct. 14, 1861. WIA (arm shattered) at Pea Ridge. Dropped at May 1862 reorganization. Postwar cotton broker in Jefferson, TX. Died Feb. 28, 1889, Jefferson. Buried Oakwood Cemetery, Jefferson. A private in the 9th called Sims "a born commander" with "a voice equal to the modern fog horn."

Sinclair, James. Born July 3, 1821, Tiree Parish, Argyllshire, Scotland. Reared in Nova Scotia and PA. Grad. Western Theological Seminary, Pittsburgh. Presbyterian clergyman in Smyrna, NC, prewar, and antisecession. Md. Mary McPherson; Mary E. McQueen. Chaplain, 5th NC, May 15, 1861. Led that regiment's skirmish line at 1st Manassas. Col., 35th NC, Nov. 8, 1861. Dropped at April 1862 reorganization, amid charges of cowardice at the Battle of New Bern, charges Sinclair hotly denied. Cleared by a court of inquiry. Resigned April 23, 1862. Editor of a Wilmington newspaper. Arrested for "sedition" but released due to the influence of his wife's prominent and pro-secession family. Brother of Lt. Col. Peter Sinclair, 5th NC. Lumberton farmer postwar. State legislator. Died Aug. 5, 1877, Monroe, NC. Buried Lumberton City Cemetery. A "notorious" Reconstruction Republican, reviled as head of the local Union League and thrown out of the church amid charges of drunkenness and adultery. A soldier in the 35th wrote that the men elected Sinclair colonel based on reports of his bravery at 1st Manassas, reports that proved to be false.

Singletary, George Edmund Badger. Born Feb. 27, 1827, NC. Lawyer in Greenville, Pitt Co., prewar. State representative 1854–55. Officer in Mexican War. Militia general. Md. Cora, daughter of Gov. Charles Manly. Capt. Co. H, 27th NC, Aug. 20, 1861. Lt. col., Singletary's Bn., June–Sept. 1861. Col., Sept. 28, 1861. Court-martialed Nov. 18, 1861, for launching an unauthorized attack on Hatteras Island. Sentenced to a suspension of rank and pay for 2 months. Resigned Dec. 16, 1861. Col., 44th NC, March 20, 1862. KIA June 5, 1862, Tranter's Creek, NC. Buried Raleigh City Cemetery. An obituary stated, "A more daring man never lived." Brother of Cols. Richard and Thomas Singletary.

Singletary, Richard William. Born Feb. 10, 1837, Beaufort Co., NC. Reared in Washington, NC. Grad. UNC. Attorney in Pitt Co. prewar. Md. Mary Jane Pitt. Lt. Co. H, 27th NC, April 26, 1861. Capt., July 10, 1861. Lt. col., March 18, 1862. WIA Antietam. Col., Nov. 1, 1862. Resigned Dec. 4, 1862, due to wounds. After recovering, appointed capt. Co. H, 44th NC, Jan. 15, 1863. WIA Spotsylvania. Resigned Sept. 12, 1864. Appointed 2d lt. of artillery, March 21, 1865. Farmer in Edgecombe Co. and Wilson, NC, postwar. Lawyer. Editor, Wilson *Plain Dealer*. State representative in 1876. Moved to Conant, FL, in 1886. Ran store and pharmacy there. Died Sept. 21, 1892. Buried Rose Hill Cemetery, Kissimmee, FL.

Singletary, Thomas Chappeau. Born Aug. 9, 1840, NC. Reared in Washington, NC. Grad. UNC. Lawyer in Pitt Co. prewar. Md. Harriet Eliza Williams. Lt. Co. H, 27th NC, April 19, 1861. Transferred to Co. E, June 1861. Major, Sept. 28, 1861. Lt. col., Jan. 6, 1862. Resigned March 12, 1862. Col., 44th NC, June 28, 1862. Cashiered for drunkenness, Feb. 26, 1864, but the sentence appears to have been suspended. WIA Wilderness (leg) and often absent thereafter. Paroled April 15, 1865, Lynchburg, VA. Resided in Greenville, NC, postwar. Died Jan. 18, 1873. Buried Episcopal Churchyard, Washington.

Skinner, Frederick Gustavus. Born March 7, 1814, Annapolis, MD. Educated in France. Godson of the Marquis de Lafayette (he lived with Lafayette while in France) and said to be "a thorough Frenchman in many regards." Attd. St. Cyr and USMA. Wealthy planter and sportsman. Baltimore resident but often traveled abroad before the war. Md. Martha S. Thornton. Major, 1st VA, May 1861.

Lt. col., Nov. 18, 1861. WIA 2d Manassas (chest) and never returned to active duty. Col., July 3, 1863. Retired to Invalid Corps Feb. 6, 1865. Lived in New York City; Baltimore; Rappahannock Co., VA; and Cincinnati, postwar. Wrote extensively on hunting and horse racing for magazines and newspapers. Died May 22, 1894, Charlottesville. Buried Westminster Churchyard, Baltimore. A contemporary called him "immensely tall, great boned and of tremendous physical strength." On the minus side, one staff officer hinted Skinner drank too much. War letters at VAHS.

Skinner, James Henry. Born Jan. 18, 1826, Norfolk, VA. Attd. UVA. Attorney in Staunton prewar. State representative 1853–54. Col., 160th VA militia. Unmd. Capt. Co. A, 52d VA, July 9, 1861. Lt. col., May 1, 1862. WIA 2d Manassas. Col., June 6, 1863. WIA Gettysburg and Spotsylvania. Retired to Invalid Corps, March 4, 1865. Assigned to command post of Staunton. Staunton lawyer postwar. State representative 1881–82. Died May 19, 1898, Staunton. Buried Cedar Grove Cemetery, Norfolk. "[A] gentleman, in the highest sense of the term."

Slaughter, Philip Peyton. Born Aug. 10, 1834, Orange Co., VA. Grad. VMI. Teacher at VMI, 1857–58. Private tutor to the Fort family in Baton Rouge, LA, after that. Md. Emma Thompson. Volunteer at Harpers Ferry, May 1861. Commissioned capt. and major by Gov. Letcher and ordered to serve in the defenses at Gloucester Point, VA. Lt. col., 56th VA, elected in 1861. Reelected May 3, 1862. WIA Gaines's Mill when shrapnel hit his thigh and drove his field glass into his groin. Col., July 30, 1863. Applied for retirement due to his wound, May 20, 1864. Assigned to duty with the VA Reserves in 1864. Railroad agent in Orange, VA, postwar. Moved to Richmond Soldiers' Home in 1892. Died there April 21, 1893. Buried Orange Co.

Slaughter, William Martin. Born July 28, 1824, Putnam Co., GA. Reared in La Grange. Grad. William & Mary College. Lawyer and planter in Greenville. Moved to Albany, GA, in 1852. State senator. Md. Marcella J. Tinsley. Capt., "Dougherty Grays" (Co. K, 51st GA), March 4, 1862. Col., March 22, 1862. MWIA Zoan Church (Chancellorsville), by a cannon shot that crushed his arm and leg. Died the next day. Buried Oakview Cemetery, Albany. A bar association tribute noted that Slaughter had "no taste for military life and a feeble constitution" and entered the army only from a sense of duty.

Slayback, Alonzo William. Born March 4, 1838, Plum Grove, Marion Co., MO. Reared in Lexington, MO. Grad. Masonic College in Lexington. Prewar lawyer in St. Joseph. Md. Alice Waddell. Col., 5th Inf., 5th Div., MSG, Sept. 23, 1861. Briefly commanded 5th Div. in 1862. Chief of ordnance to Gen. Martin E. Green, mid-1862. Appointed chief of ordnance, Marmaduke's Brigade, Dec.

1862. Appointed lt. col., 1864. Raised a regiment of MO cavalry in 1864 during Price's Raid. Termed "colonel" in wartime correspondence, probably elected in the fall of 1864, but no record of promotion is in his service record. Paroled as lt. col. Fought in Maximilian's Army in Mexico after the war. Said to have been made duke of Oaxaco by that monarch (certainly the only Confederate colonel to have been ennobled!). Returned to MO in 1866. St. Louis lawyer, politician, civic leader, poet. Killed Oct. 13, 1882, in St. Louis. Newspaper editor John Cockerill published an accusation that Slayback was a coward. When Slayback stormed into Cockerill's office to demand an apology, Cockerill shot him. Buried Bellefontaine Cemetery, St. Louis; reburied Machpelah Cemetery, Lexington. John N. Edwards called Slayback "a young and brilliant officer."

Slemons, William Ferguson. Born March 15, 1830, near Dresden, Weakley Co., TN. Grad. Cumberland U. Law School. Prewar lawyer and judge in Monticello, Drew Co., AR. Delegate to AR Secession Convention. Md. Martha S. Howard. 1st lt. Co. A, 2d AR Cav., Aug. 1, 1861. Elected col., 2d AR Cav., May 15, 1862, upon the regiment's formal organization. Led the 2d in MS Campaigns of 1862–63, often leading a brigade. Arrested by Gen. Jackson in 1863 on charges he "tyrannized" his men and appropriated private property. Never brought to trial. Recommended for promotion to brig. gen. Transferred to TMD in early 1864. Led brigade in Price's Raid. POW Mine Creek. To Rock Island Prison. Postwar Monticello lawyer and judge. US congressman 1875–81. Died Dec. 10, 1918, Monticello. Buried Union Ridge Cemetery, near Monticello.

Slemp, Campbell. Born Dec. 2, 1839, Lee Co., VA. Attd. Emory & Henry College. Farmer in Lee Co. prewar. Capt. Co. A, 21st VA Bn., Sept. 16, 1861. Lt. col., mid-1862. Col., 64th VA (formed from the 21st), Dec. 14, 1862. Regiment mounted and stationed in southwest VA. Dismissed Jan. 2, 1864, for dereliction of duty, charged with allowing seized wagons to impede a march. Lee Co. farmer postwar. In mining and lumber business. State representative 1879–82. US congressman 1903–7. Readjuster and Republican Party leader. Died Oct. 13, 1907, at his home in Wise Co. Buried Slemp family cemetery, by his home in the Turkey Cove, Lee Co.

Sloan, John. Born Oct. 22, 1822, Lexington, VA. Merchant in Guilford Co., NC, prewar. Md. Elizabeth P. Graham, niece of US senator William Graham of NC. Capt. Co. B, 27th NC, April 20, 1861. Lt. col., Sept. 28, 1861. Col., Dec. 23, 1861. Dropped at April 24, 1862, reorganization. Merchant in Lexington and perhaps also in TX, postwar. Died Nov. 4, 1877. Buried Stonewall Jackson Cemetery, Lexington.

Sloan, John Baylis Earle. Born March 29, 1828, Franklin Co., GA. Family moved to Pendleton, SC, in 1837. Merchant in Pendleton prewar. Md. Mary

Earle Seaborn. Col., 4th SC, April 14, 1861. Regiment consolidated into the 4th SC Bn. at April 1862 reorganization, with Sloan losing his colonelcy. Appointed collector of the tax in kind in SC, with the rank of major and chief QM of the state. Col. of a regiment of "detailed men" (the Columbia Local Defense Regt., SC State Troops) in 1864. Resigned this colonelcy July 13, 1864. Charleston businessman postwar. State representative 1880–82. Died Feb. 23, 1906, Charleston. Buried St. Paul's Episcopal Church, Pendleton.

Smead, Abner. Born April 4, 1833, Talbot Co., GA. Stepbrother of Col. H. P. Smead. Attd. UVA. Grad. USMA 1854. Lt., US Army, 1854–61. Md. Amanda W. Gordon. Lt. of artillery, CS Regular Army, April 3, 1861. Major, 19th MS, June 10, 1861. Major, 12th GA, June 15, 1861. Lt. col., Dec. 13, 1861. AAG to Gen. Edward Johnson, 1862. Col. of art., Aug. 11, 1862. AIG to 2d Corps, 1862–64. Charged with neglect of duty, Oct. 1864. Relieved of duty Dec. 12, 1864, and ordered to report to Wilmington, NC, for artillery duty. Postwar life insurance agent, then physician in Salem and Harrisonburg, VA. Taught at UVA and in CA. Died July 24, 1904, Salem, buried East Hill Cemetery. The historian of the Doles-Cook brigade called him "an accomplished and brave soldier." The neglect charge stemmed from his introducing an intoxicated officer (Col. Thomas J. Berry) to Gen. Early.

Smead, Hamilton Posey. Born Nov. 28, 1812, Talbotton, GA. Prewar physician and farmer in Talbot Co., GA. State senator 1845–46. To Union Co., AR, c. 1848. Planter there. Md. Bathsheba Walker; Anna Savage; Priscilla B. Hart. Enlisted as private. Elected col., 19th AR, at April 3, 1862, organization of regiment. Not reelected at May 1862 reorganization. Postwar Union Co. farmer. Died Nov. 3, 1878, at his plantation, "Woodville," in Union Co. Buried Mt. Holly Cemetery, Union Co.

Smith, Alexander Davis. Born Nov. 23, 1839, SC. Reared in Marlboro Co. Student at UVA when the war started. 1st lt. Co. G, 46th VA, July 1, 1861. Resigned after the fall of Roanoke Island, where most of the 46th was captured. Capt. Co. D, 9th SC Bn. (part of the Harllee Legion), Feb. 4, 1862. Lt. col., 26th SC (formed from the 9th Bn.), March 24, 1862. Col., Sept. 9, 1862. Suspended by court-martial for 6 months, from Jan. 1, 1864, for conduct prejudicial to good order. WIA the Crater and on disability leave in SC thereafter. Died Dec. 1, 1867. Buried Oak Ridge Cemetery, Bennettsville, Marlboro Co.

Smith, Ashbel. Born Aug. 13, 1805, Hartford, CT. Grad. Yale 1824. Afterward studied medicine at Yale and in France. Physician and teacher in Salisbury, NC, 1824–37. Physician in Galveston, TX. Plantation owner. TX sec. of state. State legislator before and after the Civil War. Unmd. Capt. Co. C, 2d TX, Aug. 13, 1861. WIA Shiloh. Lt. col., June 5, 1862. Col., Oct. 5, 1862. POW Vicksburg. After exchange, returned to TX and commanded forces near Galveston. Assigned to various staff and inspection duties in TX. One of two commissioners who surrendered the state to Union forces in 1865. Postwar Galveston physician. President of Board of Regents, UTX. Died Jan. 21, 1886, at his plantation home on Galveston Bay. Buried State Cemetery, Austin. Smith's papers are at the UTX. Known as "Old Jingle" to his men.

Smith, Baxter. Born March 10, 1832, Davidson Co., TN. Attd. Sumner U. and Cumberland U. Law School. Gallatin lawyer and politician. Md. Bettie Guild. Major, 7th TN Cav. Bn., Nov. 15, 1861. WIA in arm in a skirmish at Woodbury, TN. Col., 8th TN Cav., Nov. 24, 1862. POW May 10, 1863, Carthage, TN. Held at Johnson's Island until Feb. 1865. Led Harrison's Brigade at Bentonville. Paroled May 24, 1865, Charlotte. Lawyer in Gallatin, Nashville, and Chattanooga postwar. State senator 1879–81. Died June 25, 1919, at a hospital in Fort Oglethorpe, GA. Buried Mt. Olivet Cemetery, Nashville.

Smith, Benjamin Burgh. Born May 15, 1835, Summerville, SC. Grad. SCMA and Charleston Medical College. Physician and civil engineer in the Colleton Dist. prewar. Lt. of engineers, Jan. 1861. Capt. Co. B, 11th SC, June 18, 1861. Major, Sept. 19, 1861. Dropped at May 1862 reorganization. Major, 2d SC Bn. Sharpshooters, June 22, 1862. Major, AAG on Gen. Gist's staff, 1863–65. WIA Franklin. Assigned by Gen. Joseph Johnston as col., 16th SC, in March 1865. Col., 16th/24th SC, April 9, 1865. Civil engineer and physician in Charleston postwar. Died there Feb. 7, 1904. Buried St. Paul's Episcopal Cemetery, Summerville, SC. An obituary noted, "His ability as an engineer was unquestioned, and his faith in himself was complete." It was said he was so regular in his habits that people set their watches by his daily walks.

Smith, Charles. Born April 13, 1832, Eastville, Northampton Co., VA. Grad. VMI. Attd. UVA and Jefferson Medical College. Physician in Franktown, Northampton Co., prewar. Md. Margaret Jacob. Col., 39th VA, a unit organized into state service May 28, 1861, and transferred to Confederate service July 1, 1861. The 39th was raised in the eastern shore of VA, cut off from the rest of VA by the Union navy. The unit dispersed in Nov. 1861 when an overwhelming Union force invaded the neck, with only a handful of men making it to the mainland. The 39th officially disbanded Feb. 3, 1862. Appointed asst. surgeon, PACS, Dec. 4, 1862, to rank from Aug. 25. Assigned to duty at Talladega, AL. Paroled there May 18, 1865. Northampton Co. physician postwar. Owned farm. State representative 1893–98, 1904. Died Dec. 30, 1907, Franktown. Buried Wellington Cemetery.

Smith, Dabney Howard. Born Nov. 24, 1821, Georgetown, KY. Attd. Georgetown College and Transylvania U. Law School. Grad. Miami (OH) U. Lawyer in

Georgetown prewar. State representative and senator. Md. Josephine Lemon. Col., 5th KY Cav., Sept. 2, 1862. Captured July 19, 1863, during Morgan's Ohio Raid and imprisoned at the Columbus Penitentiary with Morgan. Exch. March 6, 1864. In Jan. 1865 he applied for transfer to staff duty in TX in order to better care for his family (then in KY). He noted that his regiment numbered fewer than 50 effective men. Paroled May 15, 1865, Columbus. Lawyer in Georgetown postwar. KY state auditor. Died July 15, 1889, Louisville. Buried Lexington (KY) Cemetery. Smith's papers are at the Kentucky Historical Society and the Filson Club.

Smith, Erastus S. Born May 1, 1818, Wilson Co., TN. Wealthy farmer in Wilson Co. State representative. Officer in Mexican War. Md. Fannie Huddleston. Lt. col., 11th TN Cav. Bn., Feb. 1862. Col., 2d TN Cav. (Smith's), April 1862. Regiment disbanded May 1862. Wilson Co. farmer postwar. Died Aug. 24, 1883, Cainsville, TN. In 1862 Gen. Kirby Smith wrote "Colonel Smith should be arrested on the first pretext" and replaced with an "efficient" officer.

Smith, Francis Henney. Born Oct. 18, 1812, Norfolk, VA. Grad. USMA 1832. Lt., US Army, 1833–36. Taught at USMA. Professor at Hampden-Sydney College. Superintendent of VMI, 1839–89. Smith essentially created VMI as the "West Point of the South." Although its emphasis was on molding citizens rather than soldiers, hundreds of VMI cadets used their military training to benefit the Confederate army. Md. Sara Henderson. Col. of art., PAVA, July 1861. Member of the Governor's Advisory Council. Col., 9th VA, July 17, 1861. Often absent. Returned to VMI in late 1861 when it reopened. Appointed major gen. of VA State forces. Dropped as col. at May 8, 1862, reorganization. Died March 21, 1890, Lexington. Buried Stonewall Jackson Cemetery, Lexington. Smith's correspondence is at VMI.

Smith, George Augustus, III. Born Nov. 4, 1824, GA. Candy maker in Macon prewar. Md. Ann Adelphia Cook. Capt. Co. C (the "Brown Rifles"), 1st GA Bn., March 18, 1861. Served in the Pensacola garrison. Lt. col., 1st GA Confederate (aka 36th GA, formed from the 1st Bn.), Dec. 10, 1861. Col., Nov. 25, 1862. Led brigade in the Dept. of the Gulf. Arrested at Kennesaw Mountain for granting a temporary battlefield truce. WIA Atlanta. Rejoined the army before he had fully recovered. KIA Franklin. Buried McGavock Confederate Cemetery near Franklin; reburied Rose Hill Cemetery, Macon. An AL private called Smith "a cross-grained unaccommodating sort of fellow." However, a Macon newspaper called him "an unobtrusive gentleman . . . known for his modesty, his firmness of purpose, integrity and intelligence."

Smith, George Hugh. Born Feb. 3, 1834, Philadelphia, PA, of a Virginia family. Grad. VMI. Taught at VMI 1854–55. Lawyer in Glenville, Gilmer Co., Baltimore, and Alexandria. Lawyer in the Washington Territory in 1859. Md. Susan T. Glassell, widow of Col. George S. Patton and grandmother of WWII Gen. George Patton. 1st lt., 1861. Capt. Co. E, 25th VA, June 11, 1861. POW Rich Mountain June 11, 1861. Paroled July 16, 1861. Exch. in early 1862. Col., May 1, 1862. WIA McDowell (thigh) and 2d Manassas (arm). Col., 62d VA (which included companies from the 25th), Jan. 28, 1863. The 62d served as mounted infantry throughout the 1864 Valley Campaign. Paroled June 7, 1865, Amherst Courthouse. Moved to Mexico postwar. To CA in 1868, residing in San Francisco, then Los Angeles. Attorney. Judge. Authored books on the law. State senator. Died Feb. 6, 1915, Los Angeles. Buried Inglewood Cemetery, Los Angeles. Gen. Imboden called Smith "the bravest man, I sometimes thought, I ever saw."

Smith, Jabez Mitchell. Born Dec. 31, 1826, Calloway Co., KY. Reared in Paducah, KY. Moved to Benton, AR, in the 1850s. Teacher and lawyer in KY. Lawyer in Benton. Capt. Co. B, 11th AR, 1861. Elected col., July 28, 1861, at organization of regiment. POW Island No. 10. To Fort Warren. Exch. Sept. 15, 1862. Not reelected at the Sept. 29, 1862, reorganization of the 11th and returned to AR. Adj. of Crawford's AR Cav., Jan. 1864. Lt. col., Crawford's AR Cav., 1864. Returned to law practice in Benton and Malvern after the war. Delegate to state constitutional convention of 1874. Judge 1874–82. State senator 1885–88. Died March 3, 1888, Malvern. Buried Oak Ridge Cemetery, Malvern. A fellow delegate to the constitutional convention remembered Smith as "an old bachelor, very droll in his mannerisms and unkempt in his dress." Smith alleged he lost reelection due to electioneering by other officers, but Major Poe retorted that Smith lost because of a "great want of energy" and being a poor disciplinarian.

Smith, James Milton. Born Oct. 24, 1823, Twiggs Co., GA. Lawyer in Thomaston, then Columbus, prewar. Lost race for Congress in 1855. Md. Hester Ann Brown; Mrs. Sarah Marshall Welborn. Capt. Co. D, 13th GA, July 8, 1861. Major, July 8, 1861. Lt. col., Feb. 1, 1862. WIA Gaines's Mill (severely). Col., Sept. 17, 1862. Resigned Dec. 14, 1863. Confederate congressman 1863–65. Lawyer in Columbus and later Hall Co., postwar. State representative 1870–72. Speaker of the House. Governor 1872–77. State railroad commissioner, 1879–85. Judge of the Chattahoochee Circuit, appointed 1885. Died Nov. 26, 1890, Columbus. Buried Alta Vista Cemetery, Gainesville. Papers at GDAH. A contemporary history asserted Smith "had active prejudices and resentments, which sometimes resulted in unpleasant and unnecessary antagonisms."

Smith, John Carraway. Born c. 1819, SC. Reared in Leon Co., FL. Prewar planter/lawyer in Madison and Jefferson Cos., FL. State representative. Md. Mary Austin; Sarah Bellamy. Capt. Co. I, 2d FL Cav., March 1, 1862. Col., Sept. 8, 1862. Heavily criticized for mishandling the Confederate pursuit at the Battle of Olustee, his first (and last) pitched battle. However, Smith's personal courage was never questioned. Paroled at Baldwin, FL, May 17, 1865. Madison Co. planter postwar. Died there July 22, 1868.

Smith, John Peter. Born Sept. 16, 1831, Owen Co., KY. Attd. Franklin College in IN and Bethany College in VA. Moved to Fort Worth, TX, in 1854. Prewar teacher, lawyer. Md. Mary E. Fox. 2d lt. Co. K, 7th TX Cav, Nov. 15, 1861. 1st lt. and adj., July 4, 1863. WIA Fort Butler (Donaldsonville). Capt., then major and AAG on staff of Gen. Bagby, 1863–65. WIA Mansfield. Promoted to lt. col. of the 7th, then to col., sometime in 1865, though no official record of such promotion is in Smith's service record. Paroled as col. in Brownsville, July 17, 1865. He returned to Fort Worth after the war to practice law and to deal in real estate. Accumulated great wealth. Civic leader. Mayor of Fort Worth for 6 terms. Known as "the father of Fort Worth," donating land for cemeteries, parks, and hospitals. Died April 11, 1901, St. Louis, MO. Buried Oakwood Cemetery, Fort Worth.

Smith, Levi Beck. Born May 5, 1819, Jones Co., GA. Lawyer and planter in Talbotton prewar. State senator 1859–60. Delegate to GA Secession Convention. Md. Mary Margaret Gullet. Capt. Co. K, 27th GA, Sept. 10, 1861. Col., Sept. 11, 1861. WIA Seven Pines (thigh). KIA Antietam. Gen. D. H. Hill called Smith a "pure, brave, noble Christian soldier."

Smith, Marshall Joseph. Born Oct. 19, 1824, Warrenton, VA. Attd. St. Mary's College in Baltimore 1837–41. Midshipman, USN, 1841–51. Merchant in Mobile 1851–54, New Orleans 1854–61. Md. Mary M. Taylor. Col., 24th LA (Crescent Regt.—at that time a state unit, later transferred to Confederate service), Nov. 30, 1861. At Shiloh. Resigned July 28, 1862 (or May 31) due to ill health. Appointed lt. col. of art., Nov. 15, 1862. Commanded the heavy batteries at Port Hudson. POW there, exch. Aug. 3, 1864. Sent to Halifax, Canada, on special duty. Reappointed lt. col. Nov. 2, 1864, his original appointment never having been confirmed by Congress. Served in the Dept. of the Gulf. In bagging and ties business, then insurance agent, in New Orleans postwar. Died June 19, 1904, New Orleans. Buried Metairie Cemetery. Gen. Gardner praised Smith's "energy, activity, zeal and skill" at Port Hudson.

Smith, Melancthon. Born April 15, 1829, Mobile, AL. Grad. USMA 1851. Lt., US Army, 1851–54. Cotton planter in Clarke Co., MS. State legislator. Militia general. Md. Mary E. Forney. Col. and adj. gen., Army of Alabama, early 1861. Appointed 1st lt., CS Regular Army, April 3, 1861. Declined appointment April 6, 1861, stating that others with his experience were being commissioned captain. Capt. of ordnance, AL state forces, early 1861. In charge of Mount Vernon Arsenal. Capt., Smith's LA Battery, Aug. 26, 1861. Commanded battery at Belmont and Shiloh. Chief of artillery, Cheatham's Div., 1862–64. Major, Aug. 26, 1862. Col., Feb. 20, 1864. Commanded artillery of Hardee's/Cheatham's Corps. Commanded right wing of Mobile defenses in 1865. Paroled Meridian May 10, 1865. Postwar lived in Mobile and later Enterprise, MS. Teacher. Editor, Enterprise *Star.* Died Nov. 1, 1881, Mobile. Buried Church Street Cemetery, Mobile. During the war Smith complained that promotion in the artillery was too slow and requested transfer to another branch of service.

Smith, Moses W. Born c. 1836, York Co., ME. Carpenter in Neosho, MO, in 1860. Capt. Co. A, 6th Cav., 8th Div., MSG, March 12, 1861. Major, July 4, 1861. Major, 2d Cav., 8th Div., MSG. Pvt. Co. D, 6th (aka 11th) MO Cav. PACS, Sept. 12, 1862. Major, Nov. 9, 1862. Col., Dec. 3, 1863. KIA Newtonia, MO, Oct. 28, 1864. Probably buried on the battlefield in a common grave; reburied postwar in Neosho. In common with many MO regiments, the succession to the colonelcy of the 6th is hard to reconcile from surviving records. It is possible the regiment was reorganized in late 1863, with Smith being "jumped" from major to colonel over the head of Lt. Col. Hooper.

Smith, Robert Alexander. Born April 5, 1836, Edinburgh, Scotland. Immigrated to the US in 1850 to join his brother, who owned a hardware store in Jackson, MS. Rich merchant. Officer in vol. militia. Unmd. Capt. Co. A, 10th MS, at Pensacola, a company he equipped at his own expense. Col., May 28, 1861. MWIA in the attack on Munfordville, Sept. 14, 1862. Died Sept. 21, 1862, at a house near the battlefield. Buried on the battlefield; reburied Greenwood Cemetery, Jackson. His brother (who returned to Scotland and became a wealthy stove manufacturer) erected a monument to him at Munfordville, in an Edinburgh cemetery, and in Greenwood Cemetery. Smith's papers are at the MS Archives. Major Sykes said of Smith that "he was always ready to sacrifice his own pleasure, his time and labor to [his men]."

Smith, Robert Anderson. Born Dec. 19, 1824, Clinton, GA. Grad. Oglethorpe College. Macon lawyer prewar. President of the local YMCA. Capt., "Macon Volunteers," 1857–61. Md. Catherine A. Dowdell. Capt. Co. B, 2d GA Bn., April 20, 1861. Col., 44th GA, March 15, 1862. MWIA Mechanicsville, hit three times in the regiment's first action. Died two days later in Richmond. Buried Rose Hill Cemetery, Macon. An obituary called Smith a "Christian warrior."

Smith, Robert Hardy. Born Oct. 21, 1814, Camden Co., NC. Attd. USMA. Lawyer in Dallas Co., NC; Livingston, AL; and Mobile (from 1853). State representative 1849–51. Md. Evalina Inge; Emily Inge; Helen Herndon. Confederate congressman 1861–62. Col., 36th AL, May 13, 1862. Resigned due to ill health March 16, 1863. Appointed chief agent of impressments in the state of AL, Aug.

17, 1864. Lawyer in Mobile postwar. Died there March 13, 1878, buried Magnolia Cemetery.

Smith, Samuel Granville. Born April 15, 1835, Nashville, TN. Attd. WMI/U. of Nashville. In 1860 helping his wealthy father manage a plantation in Arkansas Co., AR. Capt. Co. E, 6th AR, June 5, 1861. Major, April 15, 1862. Col., May 10, 1862. WIA Stones River. WIA and POW Jonesboro. Died (while a prisoner) Sept. 28, 1864 of "remittent fever" in the 20th Corps hospital near Atlanta. Buried near the hospital. A private in his company praised Smith as "a patriot of the purest dye, of the most patrician appearance . . . brave, and invariably gentle in demeanor and address."

Smith, Sumner Jewell. Born Nov. 29, 1823, TN. Farmer in Towns Co., GA, prewar. State representative. Prewar militia colonel. Md. Nancy Neill Todd. Major and QM to GA state forces, Feb. 1861. Major and chief QM, Dept. of GA, appointed May 24, 1861. Resigned May 10, 1862. Col., Smith's GA Legion (later the 65th GA), May 21, 1862. Resigned March 9, 1863. Died April 18, 1869, Burke Co. Buried Hebron Presbyterian Church, Burke Co. A fellow colonel called Smith "a large, powerful man of extraordinary vehemence and volubility in speaking."

Smith, Thomas. Born Aug. 26, 1836, Culpeper, VA, son of future gov. and Confederate Gen. "Extra Billy" Smith. Reared in Warrenton. Grad. William & Mary College. Studied at UVA. Attorney in Charleston (now WVA) prewar. Md. Elizabeth F. Gaines. Pvt. Co. H, 22d VA, early 1861. Major, 36th VA, July 16, 1861. Lt. col., March 30, 1864. WIA and POW Cloyd's Mountain. Col., May 18, 1864. Led brigade, 1864–65. Attorney in Warrenton postwar. State legislator. US attorney in NM, then judge. Died June 29, 1918, Warrenton. Buried Hollywood Cemetery, Richmond, in the same vault as his father.

Smith, William Proctor. Born April 10, 1833, Lewisburg, VA (WVA). Grad. USMA 1857. Lt. of engineers, US Army, 1857–61. Unmd. Capt., PAVA, May 8, 1861. Lt. of artillery, CS Regular Army, appointed July 17, 1861, to rank from March 16, 1861. Capt. of engineers, Feb. 13, 1862. Major, Nov. 3, 1862, serving with Gens. Gatlin and Holmes. Lt. col., April 2, 1863. Chief engineer, ANV, fall and winter of 1863–64. Col., March 28, 1864. Chief engineer for Gen. Early in the Valley, winter of 1864. To Hinton, WVA, postwar. Farmer. Railroad and bridge engineer in Missouri. Civil engineer for US government, mostly involved in improving navigation on the Kanawha River in WVA. Died Aug. 27, 1895, Alderson, WVA. Buried Greenbrier Baptist Church, Alderson. A "kind and courteous gentleman, jovial disposition, unassuming and unpretentious in his manners."

Smith, William Russell. Born March 27, 1815, Russellville, KY. Attd. UAL. Lawyer in Tuscaloosa, AL. Newspaper editor. State legislator. Mayor of Tuscaloosa. US congressman 1857–61. Gen. of militia. Md. Jane Binion; Mary Murray; Wilhelmina Easby. Delegate to AL Secession Convention. Lt. col., 3d AL Bn., Oct. 3, 1861. Col., 26th AL (formed from the 3d Bn.), late 1861. Resigned Feb. 20, 1862. Confederate congressman 1862–65. Lawyer in Tuscaloosa and Washington, DC, postwar. President of UAL. Died Feb. 26, 1896, Washington. Buried first in Tuscaloosa, later in Mt. Olivet Cemetery, Washington. Wrote several books, including poetry and a memoir. Papers at UNC.

Snodgrass, John. Born May 19, 1836, Jackson Co., AL. Educated in Huntsville. Prewar Bellefonte, AL, merchant. Md. Mollie Brown. Capt. 4th (aka 16th) AL Bn., May 1861. Lt. col., May 8, 1862. Col., 55th AL (formed from 6th and 16th Bns.), Feb. 23, 1863. Led Scott's brigade in Hood's TN Campaign. Paroled May 14, 1865. Postwar dry goods merchant in Scottsboro, AL. Active in Democrat party politics. Died Aug. 19, 1888, Scottsboro, buried Cedar Hill Cemetery.

Snyder, Peter. Born Nov. 1829 near Saarbrücken, Germany. Family immigrated to America in 1830. Prewar tailor in Shepherdstown, VA, and Pocahontas, AR. Md. Marietta Ayres. 1st lt. Co. A, 7th AR, July 26, 1861. Major, April 14, 1862. Lt. col., May 14, 1862. 6th and 7th AR consolidated, Dec. 1862. Col., 6/7th AR, Oct. 25, 1863. POW near Jonesboro, GA, Sept. 1, 1864. WIA Nashville. Led Govan's Brigade at Bentonville. Died April 19, 1865, at a hospital in Raleigh, NC, of typhoid. Buried Oakwood Cemetery, Raleigh. His attending physician wrote of Snyder as "a brave man and a most excellent soldier."

Spaight, Ashley Wood. Born Nov. 24, 1821, Prairie Bluff, AL. Grad. UNC. Lawyer and state legislator in AL. To Liberty Co., TX, in 1860, hoping that the climate would improve his wife's health. Veteran of Creek War. Md. Victoria M. Riggs. Capt. Co. F, 11th TX Bn., April 21, 1862. Lt. col., June 17, 1862. 11th merged into 21st TX, Nov. 1864. Col., 21st TX, Nov. 20, 1864. Commanded post of Houston in May 1865. Paroled in Houston June 30, 1865. Resumed his Liberty Co. law practice postwar. Delegate to 1866 Constitution Convention. Moved to Galveston in 1869. Lawyer. Cotton merchant. State commissioner of insurance 1881–83. Died Dec. 23, 1911, Galveston. Buried Lakeview Cemetery. Spaight's papers are at the UTX.

Spalding, Randolph. Born Dec. 22, 1822, near Darien, GA. Attd. UGA. Grad. Oglethorpe U. Planter near Darien prewar. State senator 1851–52 and 1857–60. Md. Mary D. Bass. ADC to Gen. Lawton, Sept. 1861. Col., 29th GA, Oct. 22, 1861. Court-martialed in Dec. 1861 for intoxication. Resigned Dec. 14, 1861. Died March 17, 1862, Savannah, of pneumonia, while serving on Gen. Mercer's staff. Buried Laurel Grove Cemetery, Savannah; reburied St. Andrews Cemetery,

Darien. An obituary labeled Spalding "intelligent and conservative. . . . The soul of honor."

Speer, William Henry Asbury. Born July 6, 1826, Surry Co., NC. Yadkin Co., NC, farmer prewar. Superintendent of a tannery. State representative 1856–60. Militia colonel. Md. Kitty Chamberlain. Capt. Co. I, 28th NC, Aug. 13, 1861. POW Hanover Courthouse, May 27, 1862. To Johnson's Island. Exch. Sept. 1, 1862. Major, Nov. 1, 1862. Lt. col., March 12, 1863. WIA Chancellorsville, Gettysburg. Col., July 8, 1864. MWIA in head, by a shell fragment, at Reams Station. Died Aug. 29, 1864, VA. Buried Methodist Churchyard near Boonville, NC. Speer's wartime letters were published in 1997. The letters indicate he was often ill and wished to resign in 1863.

Speight, Joseph Warren. Born May 31, 1825, Green Co., NC, son of a future US senator. Reared in NC and MS. Lawyer in Aberdeen, MS. Grandmaster of MS Masons. To Waco, TX, in 1854. Farmer near Waco, TX. Md. Josephine S. Prewitt; Mary A. Dockery. Lt. col., 1st (Spaight's) TX Inf. Bn., Feb. 18, 1862. Col., 15th TX (formed from the 1st Bn.), April 16, 1862. Resigned April 15, 1864, due to ill health (diarrhea). Appointed TX cotton agent in 1864. Returned to his Waco area farm after the war. City alderman. Bridge owner. President of Waco U. 1865–66. Newspaper owner. Died April 26, 1888, Waco, buried Oakwood Cemetery.

Spengler, Abraham. Born March 21, 1832, Strasburg, VA. Carpenter in Moorefield prewar and postwar. Md. Mary Welton. Capt. Co. F, 33d VA, May 23, 1861. WIA Cedar Mountain. Lt. col., Feb. 1, 1863. Col., March 21, 1864. Paroled June 5, 1865, Winchester. Lived in Hardy Co., WVA, postwar. Died Feb. 1, 1880, Hardy Co. Buried Mt. Olivet Cemetery, Moorefield.

Spratt, Leonidas William. Born Aug. 3, 1818, Fort Mill, SC. Cousin of Pres. James K. Polk. Grad. USC in 1840. Prewar Charleston lawyer. Editor, Charleston *Southern Standard.* Defended slave trading in court and in the newspapers: Horace Greeley called Spratt "the philosopher of the new African slave trade." State legislator. Teacher in Quincy, FL. Judge in Apalachicola, FL. Md. Caroline Cooper; Mary Ann Wentworth. Delegate to SC Secession Convention. SC commissioner to FL, 1861. Major, commissary, for Gen. Gregg's brigade, April 1, 1862. Resigned Oct. 14, 1862, due to chronic hepatitis. Col. and judge, military court of Longstreet's Corps, Dec. 16, 1862. Paroled Charlotte May 20, 1865. Postwar lawyer in Charleston, Richmond, and Jacksonville, FL. Died Oct. 4, 1903, Jacksonville. Buried Evergreen Cemetery, Jacksonville. Congressman W. P. Miles called Spratt "a gentleman of ability and high character—an excellent lawyer."

Spruill, Samuel Blount. Born Nov. 9, 1808, on his father's plantation near Columbia, NC. Reared in Warrenton. Attd. USMA. Lawyer prewar in Tyrell,

Northampton, and Bertie Cos. Railroad executive. State representative 1832–33, 1840–41, 1852. Delegate to NC Secession Convention. Antisecessionist. Md. Ann T. Cameron; Harriet M. Hardy. Col., 2d NC Cav., June 21, 1861. Resigned March 29, 1862. Bertie Co. lawyer and farmer postwar. "Frank, genial and generous." Died June 12, 1888, Colerain, Bertie Co.

Stacker, George W. Born Nov. 16, 1829, Davidson Co., TN. Stewart Co. farmer and iron manufacturer prewar. Md. Martha West; Blanche Bishop. Capt. Co. B, 50th TN, Sept. 19, 1861. Col., Dec. 25, 1861. Resigned Jan. 20, 1862. Wealthy merchant in Cumberland City, Stewart Co., postwar. Died June 9, 1883, Cumberland City. Buried Greenwood Cemetery, Clarksville. Lindsley's history called Stacker "a man of considerable wealth, who had uniformed his own company."

Stackhouse, Eli Thomas. Born March 27, 1824, Little Rock, Marion Co., SC. Farmer and teacher in Marion Co. prewar. Md. Anna Fore. Capt. Co. I, 8th SC, April 13, 1861. Major, July 5, 1863. Lt. col., Sept. 18, 1863. WIA July 1864, in the chest by a shell fragment. Col., 3d SC Consolidated, April 9, 1865. Paroled May 2, 1865, Greensboro. Farmed near Little Rock postwar. State legislator 1863, 1865–66. US congressman 1891–92. Died June 14, 1892, Washington, DC. Buried Little Rock Cemetery. A junior officer found Stackhouse a mediocre tactician and disciplinarian but a sterling battle leader.

Stanley, Wright Augustus. Born c. 1834, Williamson Co., TN. Attd. WMI. Prewar physician in Dallas and Bonham, TX. TX Ranger. Md. Margaret Emma Campbell. Capt. Co. D, 9th TX, July 6, 1861. Major, Nov. 4, 1861. Col., March 29, 1862. Not popular with his soldiers. Not reelected at May 8, 1862, reorganization. Died 1865, TX.

Stansel, Martin Luther. Born April 23, 1822, Washington Co., GA. Grad. UAL. Pre- and postwar Carroleton, AL, lawyer. Md. Laura Sherrod; Olivia Sherrod. Pvt. Co. C, 41st AL, March 25, 1862. Major, May 16, 1862. Lt. col., Oct. 15, 1862. WIA Stones River. Col., June 27, 1863. Appmx. Postwar state legislator. Active in UCV. President of the AL Bar Assn. Died June 25, 1902, Carrollton, buried Carrollton Cemetery. A fellow veteran called him "profound in law, a polished gentleman, courteous in his demeanor, and distinguished for his literary ability."

Stanton, Sidney Smith. Born April 12, 1829, Jackson (later Putnam) Co., TN. Attd. Cumberland U. Jackson Co. lawyer prewar. Whig Party orator. State representative 1857–59. Md. Martha Apple. Enlisted July 31, 1861. Col., 25th TN, Aug. 10, 1861. WIA Mill Springs. Resigned July 21, 1862, after quarreling with his brigade commander. Col., 84th TN, at its Dec. 1862 organization. The 84th had only seven companies. The War Dept. ruled its organization illegal and ordered that it be consolidated with the 28th TN. Col., 28th/84th Consolidated, March 8, 1863. KIA Resaca, May 13, 1864. Buried Calhoun, GA. Gen. Cleburne heavily criticized Stanton's leadership at Shiloh. A fellow officer proclaimed Stanton "a man of talent and genius" but "too brave" and too genial to impose discipline.

Starnes, James Wellborn. Born July 19, 1817, Wilkes Co., NC. Grad. Louisville Medical Institute (later U. of Louisville Medical School) in 1841. Physician and planter in Williamson Co. Surgeon, 1st TN, in Mexican War. Md. Mary Rudder. Capt. Co. F, 8th TN Cav. Bn., Oct. 30, 1861. Lt. col., Dec. 11, 1861. Col., 4th TN Cav., c. May 26, 1862. MWIA June 28, 1863, near Spring Hill, TN. Died June 30. Buried Starnes (Rudder) Cemetery near Franklin. Starnes was one of Bedford Forrest's favorite subordinates, "a most valuable cavalry officer" who often led a brigade. A descendant has published a slim biography of Starnes.

Statham, Walter Scott. Born July 18, 1832, Wilkes Co., GA. Reared in Grenada, MS. Prewar lawyer. Md. Ann V. Elliott. Capt. Co. G, 15th MS, April 19, 1861. Col., June 6, 1861. Wounded in the shoulder by an accidental gunshot in Sept. 1861 and never entirely healthy thereafter. Led Zollicoffer's brigade at Shiloh. Led a brigade in Breckinridge's Div. in 1862. Died at Vicksburg July 30, 1862, of fever. Buried Odd Fellows Cemetery, Grenada. "All the men loved Colonel Statham." First name given as "Winfield" by several sources. One source says he attended Dartmouth U.

Steedman, Isaiah George Washington. Born Sept. 13, 1835, Lexington Dist., SC. Grad. SCMA and U. of Louisville Medical School. Prewar physician in Wilcox Co., AL. Md. Dora Harrison, 1865. Capt. Co. A ("Wilcox True Blues"), 1st AL, Feb. 9, 1861. Lt. col., March 27, 1862. POW Island No. 10, exchanged Sept. 1862. Col., March 4, 1862. Led brigade at Port Hudson and POW there. Imprisoned for remainder of war. Released June 14, 1865. Postwar physician and manufacturer in St. Louis, MO. Died May 5, 1917, St. Louis, buried Bellefontaine Cemetery. One soldier in the 1st said Steedman was "utterly fearless, but never reckless."

Steedman, John Marcellus. Born Sept. 18, 1833, Lexington Dist., SC. First cousin of Col. I. G. W. Steedman. Grad. SCMA. Planter, surveyor, and merchant in Lexington Dist. Capt., "Pickens Sentinels" from 1860. Md. Henrietta Amanda Spann. Capt. Co. K (his old militia company), 9th SC, July 8, 1861. Major, July 12, 1861. Lt. col., 6th SC, April 22, 1862. WIA Seven Days and 2d Manassas. Col., May 6, 1864. Returned to Lexington Co. postwar. Assassinated by Blacks Jan. 7, 1867, at his home. Buried Batesburg Cemetery, Batesburg.

Steen, Alexander Early. Born 1828, St. Louis, MO. Officer in US Army 1847–

48, 1852–61. Md. Georgia Morrison. Lt. col., MO militia, 1861. Col. and ADC to Gov. Jackson, 1861. Brig. gen., 5th Div., MSG, June 18, 1861. 1st lt., CS Regular Army, Aug. 27, 1861. Capt., CS Regular Army, nominated Dec. 24, 1861, to rank from March 16, 1861. Col., 10th MO, Nov. 10, 1862. Shot in the head and instantly killed at Prairie Grove while leading a charge. Buried National Cemetery, Fort Smith, AR. "[O]ne of the noblest, most gallant spirits in the army." Son of Col. Enoch Steen, US Army. Brother-in-law of Gen. Henry Little.

Stephens, Marquis De Lafayette. Born Nov. 9, 1829, Williamson Co., TN. Studied medicine at U. of Louisville Medical College. Physician and teacher in Calhoun Co. MS. Delegate to MS Secession Convention. Md. Mary Jane Duff. 2d lt. Co. K, 17th MS, April 7, 1861. Granted leave in Feb. 1862 to return to MS. Capt. Co. D, 31st MS, March 7, 1862. Col., March 11, 1864. Often led Featherston's Brigade in 1864. WIA Franklin (thigh shattered) and then invalided out of the army. Merchant in Calhoun Co. and later in Water Valley. State senator 1865–67. State representative 1880–81. Died April 15, 1911, Water Valley. Buried Oak Hill Cemetery, Water Valley. Lt. Col. Rorer called Stephens "a very common looking man to command a brigade."

Stephens, William Henry. Born May 2, 1816, MD (probably Queen Anne Co.). Reared in TN. Grad. U. of Nashville. Lawyer in Jackson, TN, prewar. Bank president. Clerk of the Supreme Court. Md. Barbara Miller. Capt. Co. G, 6th TN, May 15, 1861. Col., May 23, 1861. Led brigade at Belmont and Shiloh. Relieved of command at Shiloh. Not reelected at May 1862 reorganization. Resigned May 18, 1862. Lived in Memphis 1867–75. Moved to Los Angeles, CA, in 1875. Farmer. Died March 8, 1887, San Gabriel, CA. Buried San Gabriel Episcopal Cemetery. Col. J. J. Neely md. Stephens's sister.

Stevens, James G. Born c. 1823, AL. Prewar trader in Hunt Co., TX, and the Indian Territory. County judge. Indian fighter. Md. Elizabeth B. ———. Capt. Co. D, 22d TX Cav., Dec. 15, 1861. Major, Jan. 16, 1862. Col., June 30, 1862. Arrested in Oct. 1862 for cowardice. Resigned Sept. 21, 1863. In his letter of resignation he admitted he was "entirely unable to control the men of the Regiment." The resignation was accepted with relief by his superior officers. To Dallas in 1867. Dallas surveyor, county school superintendent. Died May 24, 1889, Dallas. Buried Greenwood Cemetery.

Stevens, Peter Fayssoux. Born June 22, 1830, FL. Brother of Gen. Clement Stevens. Family moved to Pendleton, SC, c. 1836. Grad. SCMA 1849, first in his class. Railroad engineer on Laurens & Yorkville railroad 1849–51. Brought back to teach at the Arsenal and the Citadel. Superintendent of the Citadel, a post he resigned in Oct. 1861 to enter the ministry. Md. Mary S. Capers, sister of Gen.

Ellison Capers; Harriet Rebecca Palmer. Commanded a battery that fired on the "Star of the West" in Jan. 1861 and another battery that fired on Fort Sumter. Ordained an Episcopal minister in Oct. 1861. The attack on Port Royal caused Stevens to offer his services to the governor. Col., Holcombe Legion (named by Stevens after the governor's wife), Nov. 21, 1861. WIA Antietam (arm). Resigned Oct. 8, 1862, saying he'd volunteered to defend SC, not to fight in VA or MD. He spent the remainder of his life in the ministry, rising to bishop of the Reformed Episcopal Church. Died Jan. 9, 1910, Charleston. Buried Magnolia Cemetery.

Stewart, Francis M. Born c. 1839, KY. Clerk in Columbus, KY, in 1860. Capt. Co. F (the "Kentucky Braves," a KY unit, later part of the 3d KY), 22d TN, July 18, 1861. Major, July 24, 1861. Lt. col., Nov. 4, 1861. WIA severely at Shiloh. Dropped, May 12, 1862. Captured Jan. 27, 1863, near Bolivar, TN, while recruiting. To Fort Delaware. Exch. April 29, 1863. Col., 15th TN Cav., Aug. 27, 1863. Led 15th, and 15th/16th Consolidated, in Bedford Forrest's Cavalry. Relieved of command July 19, 1864, in connection with the dispute over Edmond Rucker's promotion. Paroled May 17, 1865, Columbus. Probably died in MS soon after the war.

Stigler, James Monroe. Born March 8, 1835, Holmes Co., MS. Clerk of Court in Holmes Co. prewar. Md. Mary E. Wilson. Lt. Co. A, 25th MS, May 5, 1861. Capt., May 8, 1862. Major, 1st Bn. MS Sharpshooters, June 15, 1863. WIA Peachtree Creek. Lt. col., 3d MS Consolidated, 1865. Col., April 19, 1865. Farmer in Lexington, Holmes Co., and Alcorn Co. postwar. Died Oct. 26, 1900, Lexington, MS. Buried Odd Fellows Cemetery, Lexington.

Stiles, William Henry. Born Jan. 1, 1810, Savannah, GA. Attd. Yale and Harvard. Lawyer in Savannah. Owned a Cass Co. plantation. US Dist. attorney 1836–38. US congressman 1843–45. Chargé d'affaires in Vienna 1845–49. State representative. Speaker of the GA House 1858–60. Md. Elizabeth Anne Mackay. Lt. col., 4th GA Bn., Sept. 19, 1861. Col., 60th GA (formed from the 4th), July 15, 1862. WIA Fredericksburg. Detached in Aug. 1863 to organize LDT in northwest GA. Resigned Aug. 30, 1864. Died Dec. 20, 1865, Savannah. Buried Laurel Grove Cemetery. A "cultivated man," author of a book on Austria. Papers at Emory U. and UNC.

Stirman, Erasmus Irving. Born April 16, 1839, Fayetteville, AR. Attd. Arkansas College in Fayetteville. Prewar clerk in a dry goods store, while prepping for admission to the US Naval Academy. Md. Miriam Gist. Sgt., "Pike Guards," AR State Troops. Mustered out Sept. 1, 1861. 2d lt. Co. E, 1st AR Cav. Bn., 1861. Capt., 1861. Assigned to duty as lt. col., 1st Bn. of Sharpshooters (the 1st Cav. Bn., renamed and dismounted) in Phifer's Brigade, July 10, 1862. Col., Stirman's Regt. of sharpshooters, Aug. 1, 1862. Regt. broken up c. Oct. 1862. On sick leave in the spring of 1863. His old battalion surrendered at Vicksburg while he was absent, and he reported for duty in AR. Commanded post of Dardanelle, AR, fall of 1863. Formed a new battalion of cavalry in 1864, partly from soldiers of the 1st Bn., which he commanded as lt. col. WIA three times in war. Resumed his academic career after the war ended and graduated in law from the U. of KY. Fayetteville lawyer, judge. Mayor of Fayetteville. Lawyer in Denver, CO, from 1879. Died Jan. 4, 1914, Denver. Buried Fairmount Cemetery, Denver. Stirman's Civil War letters have been published. One private said "Ras" Stirman was "very popular with his men and was a gallant soldier."

Stith, Donald Chester. Born July 21, 1829, Smyrna, Ottoman Empire, of an old VA-MD family. Grad. USMA 1850. Officer in US Army 1850–61. Captured by Texas forces in NM in July 1861 and paroled. Capt., CS Regular Army, Sept. 24, 1861, to rank from March 16. AAG to Gen. Ben McCulloch. Appointed major and AAG, Dept. of Texas, Nov. 13, 1861. On staff of Gen. Van Dorn. Major and IG, staff of Gen. S. D. Lee. POW July 1863, near Jackson, MS. Col., 1st MS PR, to rank from Feb. 11, 1863, with temporary rank, but the officers of the regiment requested that Stith not come, and he never took command of the regiment. On Feb. 8, 1864, he was relieved from duty, his temporary appointment having expired. Capt. on Gen. Elzey's staff, April 1864. Assigned to staff of Gen. Whiting, Sept. 9, 1864. Assigned to staff of Gen. Barton, Oct. 7, 1864. With ANV 1864–65. Appmx as capt. Postwar he sold insurance in St. Louis. Later taught school in TX. Died March 18, 1920, at the veterans' home in Austin, TX, where he had lived for 26 years. Buried State Cemetery, Austin.

Stocks, John Gardner. Born July 27, 1828, Morgan Co., GA. Lived in Talladega Co., AL; LA; Chicot Co., AR; and Memphis prewar. Planter and merchant. Mexican War veteran. Md. Margaret A. Oldham; Fannie Harrison. 2d lt. Co. G, 1st TN Cav. Bn., May 13, 1861. Capt., Nov. 13, 1861. Lt. col., 7th TN Cav., June 10, 1862. Col., Jan. 1, 1863. Resigned Oct. 8, 1863, due to chronic spinal pain. Postwar lived in Red Bluff, CA; OK; Erath Co, TX. Owned a shooting gallery in Red Bluff. Admitted to Confederate Veterans' Home in Austin. Died Feb. 7, 1913, Port Lavaca, TX. Buried Port Lavaca.

Stockton, Philip. Born April 1832, Princeton, NJ. Grad. USMA 1852. Lt., US Army, 1852–61. Md. Katherine Cunningham. Capt. CS Regular Army, March 16, 1861. AAG to Gen. Polk, 1861. Assigned to Gen. Van Dorn's staff, Feb. 23, 1862. Chief of ordnance, Van Dorn's army. Col., April 12, 1862. "A most gallant and brilliant campaigner." Commanded arsenal at Jackson, MS, 1862–63. Commanded arsenal at San Antonio, TX, 1863–64. Sent to Richmond in 1865 to procure funds for the TMD. Insurance agent in Galveston postwar. Government clerk in Washington, DC, 1878–79. Died March 25, 1879, Washington. Body sent to Baltimore for burial.

Stokes, Montfort Sydney. Born Oct. 6, 1810, at "Morne Rouge," Wilkes Co., NC, son of Gov. Montfort Stokes. Attd. USMA. Midshipman, USN, 1829–39. Wilkes Co. planter. Major in Mexican War. Md. Sarah E. Triplett. 1st lt., then capt., "Wilkes Valley Guards" (Co. E, 1st NC), 1861. Col., May 16, 1861. MWIA Mechanicsville. Died July 8, 1862, at a Richmond hospital. Buried in front of his Wilkes Co. home; reburied 2001 in the Presbyterian Cemetery, Wilkesboro. A soldier from MS described Stokes as "a splendid officer, well prepared to drill in regimental or brigade maneuvers." According to a descendant, he was born Algernon Sydney Stokes but changed his first name to his father's.

Stone, Barton Warren. Born Nov. 5, 1817, Georgetown, KY, son of a famous evangelist. Reared in KY and IL. Attd. Georgetown College. Prewar lawyer in IL. Moved south to Memphis, TN, and later Dallas, TX, due to his wife's ill health. Md. Margaret W. Howard; Sue E. Smith. Col., 6th TX Cav., Sept. 12, 1861. Declined reelection at May 1862 reorganization, to concentrate on raising new units. Col., 2d TX PR (a new regiment he raised), spring of 1863. Fought in the 1863 LA campaigns. Resigned Jan. 29, 1864, citing (in a Dec. 14, 1863, letter) his "great weight and age" (46!), which disqualified him "for the active operations of the field." Moved to Howard Co., MO, postwar. Returned to Dallas in 1879. Lawyer, farmer. Died Feb. 26, 1881, Dallas. Buried Pioneer Cemetery, Dallas. In 1862 one previously critical soldier wrote that Stone "is acquitting himself with distinction . . . He ignores whisky entirely."

Stone, John Marshall. Born April 30, 1830, Gibson Co., TN. Steamboat clerk on the Tennessee River; clerk in a store in Eastport, MS; railroad station agent in Iuka, MS. Md. Mary Gilliam Coman in 1872. Capt. Co. K, 2d MS, May 1, 1861. Col., April 16, 1862. WIA Gettysburg. Granted leave to return to MS in Jan. 1865 to collect absentees. Returning to the army, he was captured at Salisbury, NC, April 12, 1865, while directing the defense against Stoneman's Raiders. Discharged from Johnson's Island Prison July 25, 1865. Lived in Iuka, Jackson, and Starkville postwar. Led the fight to redeem MS from Reconstructionist rule. State senator 1869–77. Governor 1877–81, 1889–95. State railroad commissioner. Banker in Jackson 1895–98. President of MS A&M College 1898–1900. Died March 26, 1900, Holly Springs. Buried Oak Grove Cemetery, Iuka.

Stone, William Merk. Born March 20, 1834, TN. Prewar Marion Co., AL, farmer. Md. Elizabeth M. Lloyd; Mary E. Wilson. Capt. Co. D, Jeff Davis Legion, June 29, 1861. Major, Feb. 13, 1862. Resigned 1862 due to ill health. Detailed for conscript duty in AL, Jan. 18, 1863. Lt. col., 1st Bn. AL Reserves, 1864. Col., 65th AL (aka 4th AL Reserves), 1864. Resigned Jan. 22, 1865. Paroled Meridian May 12, 1865. Postwar Sulligent farmer and Lamar Co. commissioner. Died Dec. 18, 1916, Lamar Co. Buried Sulligent City Cemetery.

Stowe, William Alexander. Born Jan. 31, 1832, Lincoln Co., NC. "Manager" in Gaston Co. in 1860. Unmd. Sgt. Co. M, 16th NC, May 1, 1861. Capt., June 17, 1861. Major, April 26, 1862. Lt. col., May 31, 1862. WIA Gaines's Mill and Chancellorsville (head). Col., Dec. 8, 1863. Appmx. Gaston Co. planter postwar. State representative 1872–76. Died June 19, 1908, Gaston Co. Buried New Hope Presbyterian Church, Gastonia. A "gallant and successful commander."

Strange, John Bowie. Born 1823, Fluvanna Co., VA. Attd. Norfolk College. Attorney in Richmond and Norfolk. Professor at Albemarle Military Academy, Charlottesville. Farmer in Louisa Co. in 1860. Md. Agnes Gaines. Lt. col., 19th VA, May 2, 1861. Col., April 29, 1862. KIA South Mountain. Buried Mapleville Cemetery, Charlottesville, in 1867. A niece called him "a very able man, of commanding appearance."

Strawbridge, James. Born Aug. 11, 1821, Philadelphia, PA. Reared in New Orleans. Attd. Georgetown U. and Princeton. Prewar New Orleans lawyer. Lt. in Mexican War. Md. Marie C. Hepburn. Capt. Co. F, 1st LA Regulars, Feb. 6, 1861. Acting IG, Army of Mobile, March 1862. Temporarily assigned to duty as col., 18th AL, April 13 to May 10, 1862. Major, May 23, 1862. Lt. col., Jan. 3, 1863. Col., Feb. 13, 1863. Regiment consolidated, and Strawbridge assigned to staff duty. Commanded post of Madison, GA, winter of 1863–64. Captured at Gibson, GA, Nov. 25, 1864, and sent to Fort Delaware Prison. Released June 14, 1865. Postwar lawyer in New Orleans; Iberia Parish; and St. Landry Parish. Died Feb. 27, 1891, Washington, LA.

Strong, Henry B. Born c. 1827, Ireland. Clerk in New Orleans. Owned coffeehouse. Capt. Co. D, 6th LA, June 5, 1861. Lt. col., May 9, 1862. Col., June 27, 1862. KIA Antietam. Buried on the battlefield, south of the Dunkard Church; reburied Rose Hill Cemetery, Hagerstown, in 1872. Strong led the Louisiana brigade at Chantilly, and Jubal Early criticized him for mishandling the brigade.

Stuart, William Dabney. Born Sept. 30, 1830, Staunton, VA. Grad. VMI. Taught at VMI 1850–53. Then headmaster of schools in DC and Richmond, Md. Frances Harris. 1st lt., PAVA, May 1861. Lt. col., 15th VA, July 1861. Col., 56th VA, Sept. 17, 1861. MWIA (abdomen) Pickett's Charge. Died July 30 (some sources say July 29), 1863, at his Staunton home. Buried Thornrose Cemetery, Staunton. "[A] purer, braver, nobler gentleman never lived." A distant cousin of Gen. Jeb Stuart.

Sturges, John Reynolds. Born Dec. 31, 1827, GA. Grad. Yale. Schoolteacher, then lawyer, in Waynesboro. State senator 1859–60. Unmd. Lt. Co. A, 3d GA, April 26, 1861. Major, April 28, 1862. Lt. col., June 15, 1862. Col., June 19, 1862. KIA Malvern Hill. Buried Confederate Cemetery, Waynesboro.

Styles, Cary Wentworth. Born Oct. 7, 1825, Spartanburg, SC. Lawyer and newspaper editor in Edgefield, SC. Moved to Waresboro, GA, c. 1856–57. Editor of a Waresboro newspaper. Mexican War veteran. Delegate to GA Secession Convention. Md. Frances Jean Evans. Capt. Co. I, 26th GA, April 18, 1861. Col., Aug. 17, 1861. Resigned May 10, 1862. Appointed asst. sec. of the GA Senate in 1863. During the Atlanta Campaign he commanded the artillery battalion of the GA Militia Div. Newspaper editor in Albany; Brunswick; and Atlanta, GA, postwar. Mayor of Brunswick. Moved to TX, where he practiced law and again edited a newspaper. Died Feb. 25, 1897, Stephenville, TX. Buried West End Cemetery, Stephenville. A "tall, muscular, well-built man."

Sugg, Cyrus A. Born Sept. 5, 1833, Logan Co., KY. Received "a military education." Grad. Georgetown College in KY. Farmer in Robertson and Montgomery Cos., TN, prewar. Md. Mattie Snaden. Capt., Montgomery Co. militia, 1861. Capt. Co. E, 50th TN, Nov. 18, 1861. Lt. col., Dec. 26, 1861. Col., Jan. 26, 1862. Reappointed col. to rank from Feb. 24, 1864 (after his death), for reasons not apparent in his service record. POW Fort Donelson. Exch. WIA 4 times at Chickamauga. MWIA Missionary Ridge, died Jan. 25, 1864, of his wounds at the Marietta, GA, hospital. Buried Sugg Cemetery, Robertson Co. Tennessee's Confederate congressmen recommended him for promotion as "a most gallant and meritorious officer." Some family papers are at TSLA.

Sulakowski, Valerian. Born 1827, Poland, of a noble family. Attd. military school in Vienna and served in the Austrian army for 6 years. Officer in Hungarian Revolution of 1848. Fled to the US after the revolt was put down, settling in Houma, LA. Surveyor and civil engineer in New Orleans prewar. Md. Rebecca Simpson. Col., 14th LA, June 1861. Resigned Feb. 15, 1862. Returned to New Orleans, denouncing the war. Col. and chief of engineers to Gen. Magruder, appointed Jan. 22, 1863. Resigned Aug. 27, 1863. Traveled to Cuba on a secret mission, 1864. Postwar civil engineer in New Orleans. Died June 19, 1873, New Orleans, of apoplexy. A portrait of Sulakowski is in the Camp Moore Museum. Sulakowski was called "without a doubt the best colonel in the service" but also the "incarnation of military law—cruel, despotic, and absolutely merciless."

Swanson, William Graves. Born April 26, 1816, GA. Grad. UPA Medical College. Prewar farmer and physician in Macon Co., AL. Md. Mary E. Burney; Anne Gertrude Park; Lucia P. Hand. Capt. Co. C, 3d AL, April 2, 1861. An "excellent" officer. Dropped May 11, 1862. Returned to AL. Major commanding AL conscript camps, 1862–63. Col., 61st AL (a regiment formed largely of new conscripts), April 11, 1864. The 61st was transferred to VA to get them away from their homes and local inducements to desert, in exchange for the 26th AL, an ANV regiment whose colonel had performed poorly. Placed on retired list (due to disability) Jan. 1865. Paroled May 16, 1865, Montgomery, AL. Farmer in Tuskegee, AL, postwar. Moved to Abilene, TX, after 1880, to live near his children. Died Oct. 5, 1890, Abilene. Buried Abilene City Cemetery.

Sweet, George Henry. Born Nov. 28, 1830, Ulster Co., NY. Pvt. in US Army in Mexican War. Settled in San Antonio, TX. Publisher of the San Antonio *Herald*. Md. Fannie Vaughn; Lizzie Thompson; Lena Geering Ross. Pvt. Co. F, 4th TX, 1861. Capt. Co. A, 15th TX Cav., Jan. 1, 1862. Col., April 16, 1862. Led Nelson's Brigade, fall of 1862. POW Arkansas Post. After exchange, appointed inspector, TX militia. Commanded Camp Ford military prison in 1864. Resigned April 15, 1865. Newspaper editor postwar in Galveston and New York City. Died Aug. 7, 1912, at his home in Linden, NJ. Buried Greenwood Cemetery, Elizabeth, NJ. One soldier termed Sweet a "proud, vain and very sensitive man."

Symons, William R. Born Nov. 11, 1812, Devenport, England. Immigrated to Savannah, GA, in 1836. Merchant and tailor in Savannah. City alderman. Helped form the Savannah Gas Light Company. Officer in the "Chatham Artillery." Md. Sarah A. Burr; Jane Ann Miller. Capt. of an independent company (later Co. A, 1st Bn., GA Reserves), Chatham Siege Art., a 6-month unit organized Feb. 24, 1862. Major, 1862. Col., 6th GA Reserves (formed from the 1st Bn.), Oct. 13, 1864. Unit served in the Siege of Savannah. Railroad superintendent in Savannah postwar. Died March 18, 1883, Savannah. Buried Laurel Grove Cemetery.

Sypert, Leonidas Armistead. Born Dec. 15, 1832, Lebanon, TN. Attd. Cumberland U. Lawyer in Christian Co., KY, prewar. Md. Martha D. Henry. Served with Green's KY Battery at Fort Donelson, escaping before the surrender. WIA at Shiloh as a volunteer with an AR regiment. Returned to KY and recruited a company for Woodward's KY Cav. Returned to KY in 1864 to recruit a regiment. Col., Sypert's KY Cav. (3d Regt., Adam Johnson's PR Brigade), Sept. 6, 1864. Lawyer in Hopkinsville postwar. Died March 23, 1893, Christian Co. Buried Cocke Cemetery, Christian Co. Called "a thoroughly brave man and a gentleman" by a local newspaper.

Tabb, William Barksdale. Born Sept. 11, 1840, "The Forest," Amelia Co., VA. Grad. VMI. Attd. UVA. Prewar lawyer. Md. Emily Rutherford; Martha Cocke Masters. 1st lt., PAVA, May 1, 1861. Assigned to Gen. Wise's staff. Capt. and AAG, Aug. 6, 1861. Resigned July 24, 1862, due to ill health. Major, 28th Bn. VA Heavy Art., Sept. 9, 1862. Col., 59th VA, Nov. 1, 1862. WIA Petersburg (thigh), June 15, 1864. Appmx. Lawyer in Amelia Co. postwar. Died Dec. 4, 1874, at "Woodland," Amelia Co. Buried Grub Hill Episcopal Church, Amelia Co. In 1869 an unreconstructed Tabb lamented the passing "of that blissful time . . . when it was lawful to kill Yankees."

Tait, George. Born April 29, 1835, Haddington, Scotland. Immigrated to US and naturalized in 1856. Merchant in Bladen Co., NC, prewar. Md. Sarah R. P. Lesnesne. Capt. Co. K, 18th NC, April 26, 1861. Major, July 20, 1861. Resigned Jan. 16, 1862, citing "an entire lack of good feeling" with his superiors. Capt. Co. K, 3d NC Art., May 6, 1862. Lt. col., Dec. 1, 1863. Appointed col., 7th NC Cav. (69th NC), Jan. 11, 1865. He soon left the 7th in disgust over the mutinous conduct of the men, which included their throwing rocks at him. Seed store owner (florist) in Norfolk and Portsmouth, VA, postwar. Died Nov. 25, 1898, Norfolk. Buried Elmwood Cemetery, Norfolk. Papers at NC State Archives. The junior officers in the 18th praised Tait's "moral worth and military experience" and asked him to withdraw his resignation.

Talbird, Henry. Born Nov. 7, 1811, Beaufort Dist., SC. Educated at Madison U. in NY. Prewar Baptist preacher in Tuscaloosa, Montgomery, and Marion, AL. President of Howard College 1853–63. Md. Mary Tarrant. Capt. Co. K, 11th AL, June 11, 1861. Resigned Aug. 6, 1861. Col., 41st AL, May 16, 1862. Resigned due to disability, June 27, 1863. Minister postwar in Carlowville, AL; Henderson, KY; and Lexington, MO. Pres., William Jewell College in Liberty, MO. Died Oct. 14, 1890, Switzerland, FL. Buried St. Margaret's Episcopal Church, Clay Co., FL. A "student, a successful pastor, and an evangelist of high order."

Talcott, Thomas Mann Randolph. Born March 27, 1838, Philadelphia, PA, son of Andrew Talcott, chief engineer of VA. Known as "Ran" Talcott. Trained in engineering by his father. Prewar civil engineer for Mexican and American railways and for the US Government Mint in Philadelphia. Helped survey fortifications in New York harbor. Md. Nancy Carrington McPhail, 1864. Capt., PAVA, May 24, 1861. Lt. of artillery, PACS, Oct. 7, 1861. Capt. of engineers, PACS, 1861. Engineer on Gen. Huger's staff. POW at Roanoke Island Feb. 8, 1862. Exch. a week later. Major of engineers, April 26, 1862. On Gen. Lee's ANV staff. Lt. col., July 25, 1863. Col., 1st Confederate Engineers, April 1, 1864. Appmx. Postwar engineer and manager for various Southern railroads, living in Richmond. Died May 7, 1920, Richmond. Buried Hollywood Cemetery. Talcott's papers are at the VAHS. In a Nov. 1865 letter, Robert E. Lee praised Talcott's "ability, zeal, devotion and integrity."

Taliaferro, (John James) Alexander Galt. Born Sept. 1808, "Church Hill," Gloucester Co., VA. Attd. William & Mary College. Culpeper lawyer prewar. Wealthy planter and slave owner. Lt. col. in VA Militia. Md. Agnes Harwood Marshall. Capt. Co. G, 13th VA, May 28, 1861. Lt. col., 23d VA, Sept. 12, 1861. Col., April 15, 1862. WIA Kernstown, Port Republic (shoulder), 2d Manassas (head). Post commander at Charlottesville, 1863–65. Retired, due to "debility," March 18, 1865. Paroled May 3, 1865, Richmond. Culpeper lawyer postwar.

Died June 29, 1884, on his Culpeper Co. estate, "Annandale," and probably buried there. Known as the "Fighting cock of Northern Virginia." Taliaferro's war reminiscences are at UNC.

Taliaferro, Valentine Ham. Born Sept. 24, 1831, Oglethorpe Co., GA. Attd. U. of NY Medical College. Prewar physician in Savannah and Columbus. Md. Mary Jones. Pvt. Co. C, 2d GA Bn., April 20, 1861. Asst. surgeon, May 2, 1861. Resigned May 10, 1862. Lt. col., 7th Confederate Cav., May 12, 1862. Col., Sept. 12, 1863. Col., 10th GA Cav. (formed from the GA companies of the 7th), July 11, 1864. Columbus physician postwar. Settled in Atlanta around 1872. Gynecological specialist. Professor, Atlanta Medical College. Died Sept. 17, 1887, Tate Spring, TN. Buried Oakland Cemetery, Atlanta. An obituary called him "full of ambition, singularly careful, bright and intelligent."

Tansil, Egbert Erasmus. Born June 5, 1840 (some sources give May 11, 1839), Dresden, TN. Grad. Cumberland U. Law School in 1861. Md. Jackie Bell. Capt. Co. A, 31st TN, Aug. 21, 1861. Col., May 8, 1862. Transferred to the cavalry in 1864, after the 31st was consolidated with another regiment. On recruiting duty for Bedford Forrest. Organized troops in AL in 1865. Dresden merchant and planter postwar. County clerk. State representative 1891–93. Revenue collector. Moved to New Orleans and to St. Louis, MO. Died June 9, 1919, Dresden. Buried Dresden Cemetery. An obituary called Tansil "as gallant an officer as ever wore the gray."

Tansill, Robert. Born June 12, 1812, Occoquan, Prince William Co., VA. Enlisted in the US Marines, 1833. Rose through the ranks to capt. Resigned May 17, 1861. Md. Frances Weems (granddaughter of Parson Weems, Washington's biographer); Anna L. Bender. Tansill was serving on a US Navy ship when the war broke out. When the ship docked in New York harbor on Aug. 23, 1861, he was arrested. Exch. (as a POW) Jan. 10, 1862. Capt., CS Marines, Jan. 22, 1862. Col., 2d VA Art. (a regiment of 1-year enlistees), Feb. 14, 1862. Unit disbanded May 23, 1862 (the reorganization law forced the soldiers to reenlist for the war, which several companies did not do), with most of the companies going into the 22d VA Infantry Bn. Capt. and AIG to Gen. Whiting, 1862–63. Commissioned col. PACS, May 27, 1863. Served on Whiting's staff. Commanded the land face at Fort Fisher during the first attack. Paroled as col. and IG in NC, April 28, 1865. Lived in Manassas postwar. Mayor. Died Feb. 5, 1890, Alexandria. Buried in a family graveyard at his home, "Vaughnland," near Dumfries. In 1863, when then Capt. Tansill wrote a verbose and florid letter to Pres. Davis asking for promotion, Adj. Gen. Cooper wryly commented that, judging from the letter, captain was as high a rank as Tansill deserved. In 1865 Tansill wrote a little-known, 24-page book on why the South lost. He blamed the loss on lack of men and arms and stated that even if Negro regiments had been formed, the Confederacy could not have armed them.

Tattnall, John Rogers Fenwick. Born Sept. 27, 1828, near Middletown, CT. Son of Flag Officer Josiah Tattnall, USN and CSN. Attd. school in France. Lt., US Marines, 1847–61. Unmd. When his vessel was ordered into service against the South, he threw his sword into the sea and refused to fight against his father and the South. Arrested and imprisoned in Boston, Oct. 7, 1861. Released Feb. 1862. Capt. of Marines, Jan. 22, 1862. VADC to Gen. Robert E. Lee, March 1862. Col., 29th AL, April 17, 1862. Resigned Nov. 24, 1862, to join the Confederate Marine Corps. Capt. Co. E, Marine Corps, a unit he soon raised. Commanded marines at the Savannah naval station. Led marines in siege of Savannah and the Carolinas Campaign. Paroled April 28, 1865, Greensboro. To Halifax, Nova Scotia, immediately after the war. Settled in Savannah in 1869. Cotton businessman. Chairman of county board of education. Died Aug. 17, 1907, at "Walnut Grove" near Middletown, while visiting CT friends. Buried Bonaventure Cemetery, Savannah.

Tayloe, George Edward. Born June 26, 1838, Roanoke Co., VA. Grew up in Big Lick, VA. Grad. VMI 1858. Prewar cotton planter in Marengo Co., AL. Lt. of vol. militia. Md. Delia S. Willis. Capt. Co. D, 11th AL, June 11, 1861. WIA Seven Pines. Lt. col., Sept. 11, 1862. Col., Aug. 21, 1864. Led Sorrell's brigade at Appomattox and paroled there. Lived in Orange Co., VA, postwar. Died there March 9, 1879. Buried first on the Tayloe estate, "Buena Vista," Roanoke Co. Remains removed to Fairview Cemetery, Roanoke, in the 1930s. Tayloe's sister md. Col. Tom Munford. A death notice called Tayloe "a gentleman of high character and intelligence . . . a gallant officer."

Taylor, Ennis Ward. Born Sept. 15, 1839, Greenville, AL. Moved with his family to TX in 1846. Prewar druggist in Jefferson. Md. Fannie Fisher. Capt., TX State Troops, 1861. Enlisted as Pvt. Co. A, 19th TX, March 31, 1862. Major, elected at May 13, 1862, organization of regiment. Lt. col., July 2, 1863. Col., April 30, 1864. Paroled Jefferson May 15, 1865. Postwar druggist in Jefferson and later Fort Worth. Mayor of Jefferson. Banker. Railroad promoter. Died April 3, 1908, Fort Worth. Buried Oakwood Cemetery, Fort Worth.

Taylor, James Rather. Born c. 1838, Fayette Co., AL, son of a future speaker of the Texas State House. Lived in Larissa, TX. Attd. Larissa College. "Student" in 1860. Md. Sarah A. E. Long. Capt. Co. B, 17th TX Cav., March 15, 1862. Col., May 22, 1862. POW Arkansas Post. Exch. April 29, 1863. Organized his regiment's parolees as dismounted cavalry. KIA Mansfield, while leading Polignac's Brigade. Buried Mansfield Cemetery, Mansfield, LA. A college classmate thought "a man of truer spartan courage has yet to be born."

Taylor, Lawrence Berry. Born Aug. 3, 1818, Alexandria, VA. Attd. UVA. Grad. Princeton, 1835. Prewar lawyer. Mayor of Alexandria. State representative 1855–56. Md. Virginia Powell. Col. and judge, military court of the Richmond defenses, March 23, 1865. Paroled April 25, 1865, Fairfax Courthouse. Practiced law in Alexandria postwar. Died Nov. 16, 1873, Alexandria. Buried Ivy Hills Cemetery, Alexandria.

Taylor, Richard Swanson. Born March 18, 1829, Oglethorpe Co., GA. Merchant and planter in Clarke Co. prewar. Md. Susan Lampkin. Lt. col., 2d Bn. GA State Troops, 1861. Col., 24th GA Militia, 1862. Confederate tax collector for Clarke Co. Col., 4th GA Reserves, May 20, 1864. Discharged March 1865. Postmaster of Athens, GA, postwar. Farm manager. Moved to Elberton and later Crawford, GA. Died April 26, 1904, Crawford. Buried Crawford City Cemetery. According to an old lawsuit, Taylor was "a man of violent temper" who lost his fortune in the war.

Taylor, Robert H. Born July 5, 1825, Columbia, SC. A family story has him being born a Russell but taking his mother's name after a fight with his father. Reared in GA and married there. Moved to Bonham, TX, in 1844. Lawyer. State legislator. Outspoken Unionist who opposed recognizing the secession convention but went with his state after it seceded. Capt. in Mexican War. Md. Eppsy Hardaway; Tennessee Gilbert; Delilah Taylor. Enlisted as Pvt., Jan. 1, 1862. Col., 22d TX Cav., Jan. 16, 1862. Dropped in 1862, probably June 30. Postwar Republican Party leader in TX. Justice, Fannin Co. State Comptroller 1865–66. Judge. State legislator. Lost race for lt. gov. in 1873. Died May 10, 1889, Bonham. Buried Willow Wild Cemetery. His gravestone reads, "My Desire is to Be Wrapped in the American Flag."

Taylor, William A. Born March 2, 1832, Cumberland, MD. Prewar postmaster in Cumberland. Moved to Waco, TX, in 1859. Druggist. Owned a book store there. Md. Virginia Ariana; Mrs. B. A. Towns. Pvt. Co. C, 24th TX Cav., enlisted in the winter of 1861. Capt., Jan. 6, 1862. Major, June 27, 1862. POW Arkansas Post, exch. April 29, 1863. Col., Nov. 14, 1864 (appointed Jan. 5, 1865, while in a northern prison). POW Franklin, sent to Johnson's Island Prison. Released June 1, 1865. Returned to Waco after the war. Wealthy real estate agent and banker. Died March 9, 1891, Waco, buried Oakwood Cemetery. Gen. Granbury called Taylor "competent, brave."

Taylor, William H. Born c. 1816, VA. Resident of Raymond and Jackson, MS, prewar. Hinds Co. sheriff. Mayor of Jackson 1852–53, 1855–57. Officer in vol. militia. Md. Margaret Miller; Sarah J. Lancaster. Capt. Co. C, 12th MS, March 13, 1861. Lt. col., May 16, 1861. Col., April 28, 1862. Elected to MS Legislature in 1863. Dropped from the rolls March 19, 1864. Farmer in Madison and Hinds

Cos. postwar. Jackson alderman. Died 1897. Buried Greenwood Cemetery, Jackson. Called the "old war horse" by his men.

Terrell, Alexander Watkins. Born Nov. 3, 1827, Patrick Co., VA. Grew up in Boonville, MO. Attd. UMO. Practiced law in St. Joseph, MO, 1849–52. Moved to Austin, TX. Lawyer, judge. Close friend of Sam Houston and an outspoken Unionist. Md. Ann Bouldin; Sarah Mitchell; Mrs. Ann Jones. For the first 2 years of the war, in between his duties as judge, he volunteered his services to the Confederate army. Capt. and VADC to Gen. Henry McCulloch in 1862. Repeatedly recommended for an officer's commission by Gov. Lubbock, who thought Terrell "had one of the finest minds in the state." Lt. col., Terrell's TX Cav. Bn., March 31, 1863. Col., 34th (aka 37th, Terrell's) TX Cav., June 20, 1863. Led brigade of cavalry 1864–65. Assigned to duty as brig. gen. by Kirby Smith, May 16, 1865. Fled to Mexico in 1865 but soon returned. Lived in Houston, Robertson Co., and Austin postwar. Longtime state legislator. Lawyer, cotton planter, historian. US ambassador to Turkey. Wrote a valuable book on his experiences in Mexico. Called "the Father of the University of Texas" for his efforts on behalf of that school. Died Sept. 9, 1912, Mineral Wells, TX. Buried State Cemetery, Austin.

Terrett, George Hunter. Born Oct. 15, 1807, Fairfax Co., VA. Officer, US Marines, 1830–61. Md. Margaret L. Stuart. Col., PAVA, May 9, 1861. Led brigade in northern VA. Resigned Aug. 22, 1861. Major, Confederate Marine Corps, June 20, 1861. Commanded the Marine Bn. Col., May 23, 1864, with temporary rank, to command the marines at Drewry's Bluff. POW April 5, 1865, near Amelia Courthouse. Farmed near Alexandria, VA, postwar. Died Nov. 27, 1875, at "Oakland," near Alexandria. Buried "Oakland"; reburied Abbey Mausoleum near Arlington Cemetery.

Terry, Benjamin Franklin. Born Feb. 18, 1821, Russellville, KY. Family moved to TX in the 1830s. Prewar sugar planter in Fort Bend Co. Railroad builder. Md. Mary Bingham. Delegate to TX Secession Convention. Major of Texas troops sent in March 1861 to take the surrender of federal garrisons on the Rio Grande. 1st lt. Co. C, 1st TX Infantry (State Troops), May 19, 1861. VADC to Gen. Longstreet in VA in 1861. Organized the 8th TX Cav. ("Terry's Texas Rangers") and commissioned its col. on Sept. 23, 1861. KIA in a skirmish at Woodsonville, KY, Dec. 17, 1861. Buried on his plantation; reburied 1880 at Glenwood Cemetery, Houston. Terry Co., TX, is named in his honor. A member of Longstreet's staff wrote of Terry, "I have never seen a braver man." Brother of Col. David S. Terry.

Terry, David Smith. Born March 8, 1823, Christian Co., KY. Family moved to TX in the 1830s. Prewar Galveston lawyer. Mexican War veteran. To CA in

1849 to mine gold. Lawyer in Stockton, CA, and justice of the state Supreme Court. Killed US senator David Broderick of CA in a famous 1859 duel. Md. Carolina Runnels; Sarah A. Hill. In 1863 Terry left CA, taking a ship to Mexico and going from there to TX. VADC to Gen. Wharton at Chickamauga and WIA there. At war's end he tried to raise a brigade of cavalry in TX to invade NM and CA but succeeded in raising only 1 regiment. Commissioned col. of that regiment. Terry fled to Mexico after the war and ranched there. Returned to Stockton in 1868 and practiced law. Killed Aug. 14, 1889, in an altercation at a railroad station in Lathrop, CA, with Justice Stephen Field of the US Supreme Court. Terry had long feuded with Field, and when he encountered Field at the station slapped his face, whereupon Field's bodyguard shot Terry. Buried Rural Cemetery, Stockton.

Tew, Charles Courtenay. Born Oct. 17, 1827, Charleston, SC. Grad. SCMA 1846 with first honors. Professor at SCMA 1846–59. Superintendent of the Arsenal 1854–59. Founded Hillsboro Military Academy in Hillsboro, NC. Md. Elizabeth Tradewell. Sent north in early 1861 to purchase army supplies for the state of NC. Commanded Fort Macon in early 1861 with the state rank of Major. Col., 2d NC, May 8, 1861. KIA Antietam. Buried on the field of Antietam. "[A] very pleasant and kind hearted man."

Theard, Paul Emile. Born Dec. 20, 1828, New Orleans. Attd. Versailles College in LA. Accountant, newspaper editor, lawyer in New Orleans prewar. State legislator. Enlisted in the Mexican War and in López's filibustering expedition to Cuba. Major of Orleans Guard Militia Art. Md. Margarite Athenaise Pilie. Major, Orleans Art., early 1861. Resigned May 21, 1861. Col., 23d LA, Jan. 30, 1862. Resigned May 1, 1862, after having been defeated for reelection. Served as a VADC to Gen. M. L. Smith at Vicksburg in 1863. Commanded artillery on a war steamer and at Fort De Russy. Commanded a conscript camp at Shreveport until Gen. Kirby Smith determined that Theard had no current PACS rank. Disgusted, Theard returned to New Orleans in 1864 and accepted amnesty. Attorney in New Orleans postwar. Judge 1865–72 under the Reconstruction regime. Author. Died Aug. 27, 1892, New Orleans. Buried St. Louis Cemetery No. 3.

Thomas, Charles Benjamin. Born 1821, Charleston, SC. Family moved to Lexington, KY, when he was young. Attd. Indiana College. Grad. Transylvania U. Law School. Lexington lawyer. Judge of Lexington City Court. Unmd. Joined the Confederate army Sept. 1861. Tried to raise a regiment but failed. Appointed col. and judge of the military court of the Dept. of Southwest VA and East TN, Dec. 16, 1862. Surrendered at Charleston, WVA, May 5, 1865. Lexington lawyer and judge postwar. Died Dec. 14, 1873, Lexington, buried Lexington Cemetery. An obituary called him "a very Chesterfield in dignity, courtesy and polish."

Thomas, Henry Philip. Born May 10, 1810, Gwinnett Co., GA. Brother of Gen. Edward L. Thomas. Grad. UGA. Lawrenceville planter and lawyer. State senator. Officer in Creek War. Delegate to 1860 Democratic National Convention. Md. Ellen E. Burroughs. Major, 16th GA, July 19, 1861. Lt. col., Feb. 15, 1862. Col., Aug. 31, 1863. KIA Fort Sanders. His body was found in the ditch below Fort Sanders, sitting with his back to the fort. Probably buried in Confederate/Bethel Cemetery, Knoxville, along with the other Confederate dead in this assault.

Thomas, Robert Brenham. Born Nov. 20, 1828, KY. Grad. USMA 1852. Lt., US Army, 1852–56. Merchant and cattle shipper in Tampa, FL. Md. Sarah J. McKay; Frances E. Givens. 1st lt., CS Regular Army, March 16, 1861. 1st lt. Co. C, 2d FL, July 13, 1861. On staff of Gen. Mercer, Dec. 1861. Major and AAG, Feb. 17, 1862. On Gen. Finegan's staff, 1862–64. Commanded the garrison at Tampa briefly in 1862. Assigned to duty (by Gen. Finegan) as col. of the newly formed 9th FL, sometime in 1864. Soon resigned, after a dispute with Finegan. Later served in the prison commissary dept., spending part of his time at Andersonville. Postwar steamship company agent in Tampa. Militia general. Civic leader, known as "the social and sporting arbiter of Tampa." Died Jan. 25, 1901, FL. Buried Oaklawn Cemetery, Tampa.

Thomas, Thomas W. Born 1822, Columbia Co., GA. Lawyer in Lincolnton and Elbert Co., GA, prewar. Judge, Northern Circuit of GA, 1855, 1859–63. "A forcible and eloquent speaker." Md. Mary Frances Blackwell; Sallie E. Cade. Col., 15th GA, July 15, 1861. Not popular with his men, due to "a disposition . . . to make people who are subject to his authority to feel it" and a loathing of brigade commander Paul Semmes. Resigned March 26, 1862, due to disability and returned to his judicial duties. While on the bench issued a ruling declaring the Confederate conscription law unconstitutional. Served briefly in the GA State Guard. Died April 24, 1864, Elberton, GA. Buried Elmhurst Cemetery, Elbert Co.

Thomas, William Holland. Born Feb. 5, 1805, Haywood Co., NC. Store owner in Indiantown. Whittier, Jackson Co., resident prewar. Agent of the NC Cherokee Indians in their dealings with the government. Made a chief by the tribe. State senator. Founder of the Western NC Railroad. Delegate to NC Secession Convention. Md. Sarah, sister of Col. R. G. A. Love. Lost race for Confederate Congress in 1861. Major, Thomas's Legion (sometimes mistakenly called the 69th NC—made up of NC's Cherokee Indians), Sept. 19, 1862. Col., Sept. 27, 1862. The legion (essentially an infantry regiment and a cavalry battalion) defended the mountains of western NC for most of the war. Thomas was court-martialed and convicted in Sept. 1864 for insubordination, incompetence, and harboring deserters. Pres. Davis overturned the conviction. Surrendered at Waynesville, NC, May 8, 1865. Thomas went insane in 1867 and spent the remainder of his life in and out of asylums. Died at the Morganton asylum May 10, 1893. Buried Green Hill Cemetery, Waynesville. The "white chief" of the Cherokees was considered "remarkable" but "very shifty." According to his brother-in-law, by 1864 his mind had become unbalanced. Papers at Duke U. and Western Carolina U. Subject of a 1990 biography.

Thompson, Albert Petty. Born March 3, 1829, Green Co., KY. Reared in Calloway Co. Lawyer in Murray and Paducah, KY, prewar. Elected commonwealth attorney of McCracken Co. Md. Mary Jane Bowman; Harriet Harding; Mary Mayes. Lt. col., 3d KY, Sept. 2, 1861. Col., Oct. 18, 1861. WIA Baton Rouge, where he led a brigade. Regiment mounted in 1864. Led brigade in Bedford Forrest's cavalry. KIA by a cannon shot March 25, 1864, in an attack on Paducah, his hometown. Buried Oak Grove Cemetery, Paducah; reburied Bowman Graveyard, near Murray, Calloway Co. A state historical marker is at the site of his death. Often recommended for promotion to general. Gen. Featherston called Thompson "one of the very best Colonels in the service . . . well posted in the drill . . . good disciplinarian."

Thompson, Gideon W. Born Feb. 28, 1823, Todd Co., KY. Reared in Clay Co., MO. Platte Co. farmer and livestock trader. Md. Nancy Hansford. Capt. Co. C, "Extra Battalion," 5th Div., MSG, 1861. Major, 3d Inf., 5th Div., MSG, 1861. Sent to recruit in MO in 1862. WIA at Lone Jack while leading his recruits. Col., 6th MO Cav., Nov. 9. 1862. Paroled as col. at Shreveport, June 15, 1865. Resided in Barry, MO, postwar. Cattle breeder in Platte Co. Died Jan. 8, 1902, Platte Co. Buried Barry Graveyard, Clay Co. John N. Edwards called him "a cool and daring officer."

Thompson, Lycurgus L. Born April 11, 1838, AL. Grew up in AR. Prewar planter in Pulaski Co., AR. Lt. in vol. militia. Md. Elizabeth A. Martin; Mollie Lawson. 1st lt. Co. I, 1st AR MR, June 16, 1861. Resigned May 1, 1862. Lt. col., Carroll's (aka 1st, Gordon's, 9th) AR Cav., Oct. 1862. Col., probably April 12, 1863. Dropped, Sept. 14, 1863. Planter in Pulaski Co. postwar. AR state senator. Moved to Chicago, then to Goldendale, WA. Died July 30, 1905, Goldendale. Buried Goldendale IOOF Cemetery. First name often given as "Lee."

Thompson, Robert. Born Sept. 3, 1833, Fleming Co., KY. Moved to Columbus, GA, just before the war. In livery stable business. Md. Mary Billing in 1866. Capt. Co. A, 3d GA Cav., April 10, 1862. POW New Haven, KY, Sept. 29, 1862. Paroled and exchanged. Promoted to major and lt. col., dates not specified. Briefly captured again during a May 17, 1863, skirmish near Murfreesboro, TN, but soon escaped. Col., July 31, 1863. Cited for gallantry at Battle of Mossy

Creek. WIA in Atlanta and Savannah Campaigns. Kept a livery stable in Columbus postwar. Died May 16, 1880, Columbus. Buried Linwood Cemetery, Columbus. Praised in an obituary as "a brave soldier, kind, good-hearted man."

Thompson, Thomas Williams. Born Jan. 13, 1840, Louisville, KY. Orphaned at an early age and reared by his uncle in Louisville. Worked in his uncle's plumbing business prewar. Md. Ophelia Welch. Capt., KSG, June 7, 1861. Capt. Co. I, 4th KY, Sept. 13, 1861. WIA Shiloh. Major, March 27, 1863. Lt. col., Aug. 31, 1863. WIA Chickamauga. Col., probably Feb. 1864. WIA three times in the Atlanta Campaign. Recommended in 1865 for promotion to general. Paroled at Nashville May 15, 1865, as col. Owner of a wholesale stove and tinware business in Louisville postwar. Clerk of the circuit court in Louisville 1874–80. Died there Aug. 6, 1882. Buried Cave Hill Cemetery. A sketch by a friend called Thompson "quiet, firm, reticent, and self-reliant" (the same sketch says he was born in Philadelphia, PA, Feb. 28, 1839).

Thompson, William Payne. Born Jan. 7, 1837, Wheeling, VA (now WVA). Attd. Jefferson College in PA. Lawyer in Fairmount, VA, 1857–61. Md. Mary Evelyn. Capt. Co. A, 31st VA, May 1861. Major, 25th VA, 1861. Dropped May 1, 1862. Lt. col., 19th VA Cav., April 11, 1863. Col., probably Dec. 19, 1864. Led W. L. Jackson's Brigade 1864–65. Paroled May 20, 1865, Staunton. Lawyer in Chicago and Parkersburg, WVA, postwar. Newspaper editor. Vice president of Standard Oil Co. President of the National Lead Trust. Millionaire businessman. Died Feb. 3, 1896, at his home in New York City. Buried Stone Church Cemetery, Wheeling.

Thomson, Thomas. Born June 5, 1813, Tarbolton, Scotland. Family immigrated to SC in 1818. Lawyer in Abbeville, SC, prewar. State representative 1846–50, 1851–60. Delegate to SC Secession Convention. Md. Eliza Allen; Mrs. Margaret Gomillion Hollingsworth. Capt. Co. A, 2d SC Rifles, Oct. 22, 1861. Major, May 12, 1862. Lt. col., July 6, 1862. Col., Sept. 3, 1862. Resigned Dec. 3, 1863, upon election to the State Senate. Abbeville lawyer postwar. Judge, 1878–81. Died May 12, 1881, Abbeville. Buried Upper Long Cane Presbyterian Church, Abbeville.

Thomson, Thomas David. Born Nov. 8, 1834, Limestone Co., AL. Reared in MO, MS, and AR. Merchant in Ouachita Co., AR, in 1860. Md. Martha Cross. Pvt. Co. C, 15th AR, Oct. 22, 1861. On leave when the regiment surrendered at Fort Donelson. 1st lt. Co. B, 33d AR, July 5, 1862. Capt., July 18, 1862. Assigned to duty as lt. col., Nov. 25, 1863. WIA Jenkins Ferry. Col., probably April 30, 1864. Service record contains no mention of promotion to colonel. Postwar merchant and farmer in Camden, AR. Clerk of circuit court. Active in UCV. Died Aug. 12, 1900, Camden. Buried Memorial Park Cemetery.

Thorburn, Charles Edmonston. Born Nov. 24, 1831, Norfolk, VA. Grad. US Naval Academy in 1853. Officer, USN, 1853–60. Resigned July 21, 1860. Lived in TX and VA after resignation. Md. Rebecca F. Reid. Lt., VA state navy, early 1861. Major, 50th VA, July 3, 1861. Injured at Fort Donelson and thereafter often absent due to illness. Dropped at May 1862 reorganization. AIG on Gen. Loring's staff. Lt. col. of art., PACS, Aug. 1, 1862. Assigned as col., 14th VA Cav., Sept. 5, 1862. Resigned Nov. 11, 1863. Commandant of city of Wilmington, NC, summer 1863. Sent to Europe on a mission for the Confederate government. Returned to VA late in the war. Involved in blockade running out of Wilmington. Thorburn acted as a guide for Pres. Davis's escape party in 1865, barely avoiding capture himself. Broker in New York City postwar. Died there Oct. 26, 1909. Buried Brookside Cemetery, Englewood, NJ. "[O]ne of the most glorious little fellows in the world."

Thorington, Jack. Born Aug. 3, 1810, Co. Armagh, Ireland. Family immigrated to US in 1828, soon settling in Montgomery, AL. Montgomery merchant, lawyer (in partnership with Col. Henry W. Hilliard), bank president, militia colonel. Mayor of Montgomery 1839–40. Md. Mary Parker. Lt. col., 1st Bn., Hilliard's Legion, April 24, 1862. Col., Hilliard's Legion, Dec. 1, 1862. Resigned Dec. 1, 1863, due to age and ill health. Postwar lawyer in Montgomery. Died there Aug. 6, 1871, buried Oakwood Cemetery.

Thornton, John Jones. Born May 10, 1826, Gloucester Co., VA. Physician in Brandon, MS, prewar. Town alderman. Officer in the vol. militia. Unionist delegate to MS Secession Convention. Md. Rachel W. Thornton. Capt., "Rankin Guards," Feb. 1861. Col., 6th MS, Sept. 5, 1861. WIA Shiloh while carrying the 6th's flag. Reelected at reorganization but resigned May 23, 1862. Commanded a camp of MS State Troops at Brandon in 1864. Druggist postwar in Pass Christian, MS. Died Sept. 12, 1886, Pass Christian. Buried Live Oak Cemetery, Pass Christian.

Thruston, Stephen Decatur. Born Nov. 28, 1833, Gloucester Co., VA. Reared in NC. Attd. UVA. Grad. UPA Medical School. Physician, and part-time teacher, in Smithville prewar. In the prewar militia. Md. Annie Everett; Mrs. Ella V. (Wilson) Chappell. Capt. Co. B, 3d NC, May 18, 1861. Major, July 1, 1862. WIA Antietam. Lt. col., Dec. 10, 1862. WIA Chancellorsville. Col., Oct. 3, 1863. WIA Opequon Creek. Hospitalized because of his wounds in late 1864. Detailed to court-martial duty in Wilmington. Declared "permanently disabled for field service" April 10, 1865. Physician in Smithville postwar. Moved to Dallas, TX, in 1872. Died Nov. 15, 1906, Dallas. Buried Greenwood Cemetery, Dallas. A physician in the 3d claimed Thruston "took to military life as one trained to it . . . subordinate, alert, faithful and commanded as he obeyed."

Tillman, James Davidson. Born Nov. 25, 1841, Bedford Co., TN. Attd. WMI/ U. of Nashville. Grad. Cumberland U. Law School in 1861. Md. Mary Frances Bonner. Pvt. Co. F, 41st TN, Nov. 4, 1861. 2d lt., Nov. 6, 1861. POW Fort Donelson. Exch. Sept. 20, 1862. Lt. col., Sept. 29, 1862. WIA Chickamauga. Col., June 3, 1864. Appointed col. 3d TN Consolidated, April 18, 1865. Paroled May 1, 1865, Greensboro. Fayetteville lawyer postwar. Longtime state representative and senator. Ambassador to Ecuador. Died June 16, 1916, Fayetteville. Buried Rose Hill Cemetery. Tillman's father, a prominent politician, remained loyal to the Union.

Timmons, Barnard. Born Jan. 1, 1835, Jefferson Co., KY. Attd. KMI. Moved to La Grange, TX, in 1856. Lawyer. Surveyor. Taught at TX Military Institute. Md. Deborah Gault. Capt. Co. A, Nichols's 9th TX, Oct. 26, 1861. Lt. col., 1st Inf. Bn., Waul's TX Legion, May 29, 1862. WIA Chickasaw Bluff. POW Vicksburg and paroled. Col., Waul's Legion, Sept. 18, 1863. Served in TMD for the remainder of war. Legion may have been numbered the 23d TX Inf late in the war. Resumed his La Grange law practice postwar. Died June 17, 1884. Buried State Cemetery, Frankfort, KY.

Tison, William Henry Haywood. Born Nov. 6, 1822, Jackson Co., AL. Settled in Tishomingo, then Itawamba, Co., MS. Saddler; printer; editor, *Jacinto Republican*. State representative 1850–51. US marshal for the Northern Dist. of MS 1857–61. Delegate to MS Secession Convention. Md. Sarah S. Walker. The Confederate govt. continued Tison as marshal for MS, through 1862. Capt. Co. K, 19th MS, May 6, 1861. Lt. col., 32d MS, April 3, 1862. Detached in 1863 in order to muster in companies of PRs in MS. Col., Oct. 4, 1863. WIA Resaca, Atlanta, and Franklin. Paroled May 12, 1865, Meridian. Farmed in Lee Co. postwar. Dry goods merchant in Baldwyn. State representative 1876–80, 1882. State House speaker. Killed Dec. 4, 1882, in Baldwyn, by a man Tison and his brother had beaten up earlier during a domestic dispute. Buried Baldwyn City Cemetery. A self-made man, of "Spartan" courage.

Tochman, Gaspard. Born Dec. 1797, Letowna, Poland. Grad. U. of Warsaw. Warsaw lawyer. Major in Polish Revolution of 1830. Exiled, came to US. Settled finally in Alexandria, VA. Commissioned col., May 11, 1861, to raise a "Polish Brigade" among his fellow exiles. He helped raise the 14th and 15th LA but was not given the generalship the sec. of war promised him. Others were commissioned to command the regiments; Tochman spent the remainder of the war pressing his claims on the Confederate government. Lived in Richmond and Spotsylvania postwar. Lawyer. Agent of state of VA for encouraging European immigration. Died Dec. 20, 1880, Spotsylvania Co. and buried there. One historian noted that Tochman had a "fertile but essentially muddled brain."

Tomlin, Harrison Ball. Born Oct. 1, 1815, "Clifton," Hanover Co., VA. Grad. UVA. Planter in King William Co. prewar. State representative 1847–65. Militia colonel. Unmd. Major, Tomlin's VA Infantry Bn., c. July 1861. Col., 53d VA (formed from his battalion), Sept. 13, 1861. WIA Malvern Hill. Resigned Jan. 7, 1863, due to ill health. Farmer in King William Co. postwar. State representative 1871–73. Died Aug. 17, 1896, "Queenfield," near Hanovertown.

Tompkins, Christopher Quarles. Born Aug. 4, 1813, "Poplar Grove," Mathews Co., VA. Grad. William & Mary College. Grad. USMA 1836. Officer in US Army 1836–47. Iron manufacturer in Richmond 1847–55. Then farmer and coal mine operator in Kanawha and Fayette Cos., VA (now WVA). Md. Ellen Wilkens. Appointed col. of VA state forces, April 1861. Col., 22d VA, May 3, 1861. Resigned Nov. 23, 1861, after a dispute with Gen. Floyd. Floyd had ordered his artillery to fire on Tompkins's home during an engagement, endangering Tompkins's family. Resided in Richmond thereafter. In coal mining business postwar. Died May 28, 1877, Richmond. Buried Hollywood Cemetery. His half sister, Capt. Sally Tompkins, was the only woman commissioned an officer in the Confederate army.

Toulmin, Harry Theophilus. Born March 4, 1835, AL. Attd. UAL, UVA. Prewar lawyer in Mobile. Md. Mary Henshaw. Pvt. Co. A, 3d AL, April 3, 1861. 1st lt. Co. H, 22d AL, Sept. 28, 1861. Capt. Oct. 25, 1861. WIA Shiloh. Major, Sept. 20, 1863. Lt. col., Dec. 15, 1863. Col., July 28, 1864. Led Deas's brigade at Bentonville. Paroled Greensboro May 1, 1865. Postwar Mobile lawyer. State legislator. US dist. judge 1887–1916. Died Nov. 12, 1916, in Toulminville, near Mobile, buried Magnolia Cemetery. A fellow colonel called him "vigilant and gallant."

Towers, John Reed. Born July 2, 1824, Anderson Dist., SC. Prewar merchant. Moved to Cartersville, GA, in 1849 and to Rome, GA, in 1855. Md. Anna McGhee. Capt. Co. E, 8th GA, May 14, 1861. Lt. col., Nov. 16, 1861. POW Garnett's Farm. Released July 31, 1862. Col., Dec. 16, 1862. WIA 2d Manassas, Gettysburg. WIA June 30, 1864. Appmx. Postwar merchant in Rome. Notary public. Sheriff of Floyd Co. State representative. Superintendent of the GA State Penitentiary. Moved to Marietta in 1886. Died there Sept. 29, 1903. Buried Citizens Cemetery, Marietta. His troops (who nicknamed him "Grand-Ma") found him "a very interesting man and an old soldier."

Townes, Nathaniel Williams. Born Feb. 3, 1827, Pittsylvania Co., VA. Moved to TX in 1851. Farmer in Red River Co. Md. Lucinda Jane Robbins. Capt. of a company later Co. E, 9th TX Cav., Aug. 13, 1861. Major, elected at Oct. 14, 1861, organization of the 9th. Col., May 25, 1862. WIA near Corinth May 28, 1862, by a shell that badly broke his left leg. Resigned March 30, 1863, and returned to TX. Commanded 4th Brigade, TX State Troops, in 1864. Col. and judge of the military court of Buckner's Corps, March 23, 1865. Returned to his Red River Co. farm after the war. Died May 4, 1900, Bogata, TX. Buried Bogata Cemetery. A private in the 9th called him "a fine looking officer and commanded greatest respect among the soldiers." Evidence exists that he was elected to the Confederate Congress in 1865 but never took office.

Townsend, William Purnell. Born Aug. 7, 1822, Lowndes Co., MS. Studied in Philadelphia to be a doctor but never practiced. Lt. Co. K, 1st MS, in Mexican War. Moved to Robertson Co., TX, in 1852. Plantation owner there. Md. Almira R. Jennings. Capt., "Sterling Guards" state cavalry company, March 1861. Capt. Co. C, 4th TX, July 15, 1861. Major, July 10, 1862. WIA 2d Manassas (lost foot). The amputation caused great pain the rest of his life. Resigned Dec. 29, 1862. Col. and judge advocate, military court of Gen. Holmes's army, Dec. 20, 1862. Returned to TX postwar. Farmed in Robertson Co. and near Baytown, TX. Died Oct. 24, 1882, Calvert, Robertson Co. Buried Calvert Cemetery. Of "impetuous courage" with a "strong, clear, highly cultivated" mind.

Trabue, Robert Paxton. Born Jan. 1, 1824, Columbia, Adair Co., KY. Reared in Columbia. Moved to Natchez, MS, in the 1850s. Lawyer. Officer in Mexican War. Md. Hibernia Inge of Natchez. Col., 4th KY, Sept. 13, 1861. Led brigade at Shiloh and Stones River (after Gen. Hanson's death). Died Feb. 12, 1863, of pneumonia, at Richmond, VA, while on a visit there to lobby for promotion to general. Buried Hollywood Cemetery, Richmond; reburied next to his wife in Natchez City Cemetery. Often recommended for promotion and "beloved by the officers and soldiers of his regiment."

Tracy, Carlos Chandos. Born Sept. 1, 1825, near Grahamville, SC. Walterboro lawyer. State representative 1856–58, 1860–62. Md. Emma H. Parker. VADC to Gens. Drayton and Gist, 1861–62. VADC to Gen. Hagood, 1862–64. Found unfit for field duty in 1864 due to bronchitis. Col. and judge, military court of Ewell's Corps, June 24, 1864. Postwar lawyer and planter in Walterboro. SC Senate 1865–67. Died Jan. 1, 1882, Walterboro. Buried St. Helena's Churchyard, Beaufort. Obituaries called him a "bold, outspoken man" of "exceptional bravery" but with a delicate constitution. Gen. Hagood's memoirs published extracts from Tracy's war diary.

Travis, William Edward. Born July 3, 1824, Mecklenburg Co., VA. Reared in Henry Co., TN. Lawyer and farmer in Henry Co. prewar. State representative 1853–57. State senator 1857–59. Md. L. F. Cory; Narcissa E. Hagler. Col., 5th TN, May 20, 1861. Not reelected at May 6, 1862, reorganization. Resigned May 11, 1862, suffering from rheumatism. Confederate commissioner for impressment for Tennessee, appointed April 14, 1863. Paroled May 16, 1865, Columbus. Henry Co. lawyer postwar. State representative 1877–79. Died May 16,

1904, Paris. Buried Johnson Chapel Cemetery, Henry Co. Known as "Buck" Travis. His sister md. TN's war governor, Isham Harris.

Treutlen, John Fletcher. Born Oct. 10, 1828, Cokesbury, SC. Prewar planter and merchant in Eufaula, Barbour Co., AL. Md. Caroline A. Smith. Lt., 1st AL, Jan. 1861. Capt. Co. H, 15th AL (the "Glennville Guards"), July 3, 1861. Lt. col., July 27, 1861. Col., Jan. 8, 1863. Resigned April 28, 1863, due to "bad lungs." Col. of Barbour Co. militia remainder of war. Postwar planter in Barbour Co. Also lived in Abbeville, SC, and Washington, DC. Asst. clerk of the US House of Representatives in 1880. Died Feb. 27, 1908, Eufaula. Buried Fairview Cemetery, Eufaula.

Trigg, Robert Craig. Born Dec. 12, 1830, Christiansburg, VA. Grad. VMI 1849. Cattle merchant and lawyer prewar. Capt. of vol. militia. Md. Emma C. Gardner. Capt., "Wise Fencibles" (Co. G, 4th VA), April 17, 1861. Col., 54th VA (which he raised), Sept. 4, 1861. WIA Kelly's Store, Jan. 30, 1863. Led a brigade at Chickamauga but never received a promotion to brigadier. Injured at Kolb's Farm when his horse fell on him. Submitted resignation Aug. 15, 1864, but this attempted resignation was rejected. On sick leave from the fall of 1864. Ordered to round up deserters in southwest VA and did not return to the 54th. Christiansburg lawyer postwar. Died there Jan. 2, 1872. Buried Craig Cemetery, Christiansburg. Gen. Buckner called Trigg "one of the most gallant and intelligent officers in my command."

Trimble, Edwin. Born c. 1838, KY. Reared in Floyd Co. Attd. Emory & Henry College 1857–58. Clerk in Floyd Co. in 1860. Joined his parents in Bexar Co., TX, just prior to the war. 1st lt. Co. E, 5th KY, Jan. 9, 1862. Mustered out, Oct. 1862. Capt. Co. A, 10th KY Cav, Sept. 25, 1862. Lt. col., 1864. Col., Aug. 3, 1864. KIA Saltville, shot through the head. Buried first in the James Witten Cemetery, later in Maplewood Cemetery, Tazewell, VA. A staff officer called Trimble "a true patriot, an accomplished soldier, a devoted friend, & a good soldier." Trimble's service record has him promoted to col. Aug. 3, 1864, and the next month he signed a receipt using that rank, but the records on promotion of field officers in the 10th are contradictory (see notices of Cols. May and Diamond).

Tucker, Joseph Thomas. Born Aug. 31, 1833, Boston, MA. Grad. Yale and Transylvania U. Law School. Lawyer in Winchester, KY, prewar. City attorney. Md. Mariam W. Hood, aunt of Gen. John Bell Hood. Lt. col., 11th KY Cav., Sept. 10, 1862. Col., July 4, 1863. POW Cheshire, OH, July 20, 1863, during Morgan's OH Raid. Exch. Aug. 3, 1864. Col., 3d Special Bn., Duke's brigade, winter of 1864–65. Surrendered April 29, 1865, Mt. Sterling, KY, while in command of a brigade. Mined in GA 1865–69. Lawyer in Winchester after that. County attorney. State legislator. Died Sept. 28, 1906, Winchester. Buried Winchester Cemetery.

Tucker, Julius G. Born c. 1832, Holstein, Denmark (later Germany). Prewar steamboat capt., residing in Memphis, TN. Md. Bertha Kratzenstein in 1867. 1st lt. Co. E, 10th VA Cav., Aug. 5, 1861. Capt., May 13, 1862. POW Hedgesville, VA, Oct. 22, 1862. Exch. Nov. 10, 1862. ADC to Gen. Fitzhugh Lee in Gettysburg Campaign. Company disbanded, Feb. 28, 1864. Lt. col., 1st Confederate Foreign Bn. (a unit made up of largely foreign-born Union prisoners), Oct. 16, 1864. Col., Tucker's Regt. Confederate Inf. (formed from the 1st Bn.), Feb. 25, 1865. The unit, whose loyalty was not entirely trusted by Confederate authorities, served in rear areas as a pioneer corps and in provost marshal duty. Moved to New York City and Augusta, GA, postwar before settling in Brownsville, TX. Stock raiser. Civil engineer. Traveled the world on business. US consul to Martinique 1895–99. Died Sept. 30, 1905, Hamburg, Germany, of stomach cancer, during a visit to his sister. His superiors uniformly praised Tucker as "a worthy and brave man" of "intelligence and efficiency."

Tucker, Thomas F. Born Feb. 22, 1818, Barnwell Dist., SC. Moved to Shelby Co., TX, in 1841. Later to Harrison Co. Farmer. Mexican War veteran. Md. Frances A. Duncan. 1st lt. Co. E, 17th TX Cav., March 15, 1862. Capt., May 22, 1862. Major, Nov. 1862. Commanded Camp Ford Prison in 1863. Col., 1864 (probably April 8; his service record does not reflect the promotion). Postwar rancher in Harrison, San Augustine, and Haskell Cos. County judge of Haskell Co. Died May 21, 1886, Haskell. Buried Willow Cemetery, Haskell.

Turnbull, Charles James. Born 1827, VA. Said to have had a "military education" at a Southern military school. To CA during the gold rush. Capt. of filibusterers in Nicaragua under William Walker. Lived in Hot Springs, AR, in 1860. Occupation: "gentleman." Appointed capt. and AAAG in northeast AR, Feb. 22, 1862. Lt. col., 11th AR Inf. Bn., May 1862. Col., 25th AR (formed from the 11th Bn.), June 13, 1862. Regiment consolidated Feb. 28, 1863, with Turnbull (now a supernumerary) relieved from duty. Ordered upon recruiting duty. Resigned Sept. 19, 1864. On Gen. Kirby Smith's staff in 1864, in charge of "secret service." Died July 14, 1866, New Orleans. Buried Greenwood Cemetery, New Orleans.

Turner, James Jones. Born June 28, 1830, Sumner Co., TN. Attd. Franklin College. Grad. Cumberland U. Law School. Gallatin lawyer. State representative 1857–59. State senator 1861–63. Md. Adeline Harper. Major, 30th TN, Oct. 22, 1861. POW Fort Donelson. To Fort Warren. Exch. Sept. 1862. Lt. col., Oct. 4, 1862. Col., at an unspecified date late in the war. WIA Chickamauga and Jonesboro. Paroled May 1, 1865, as lt. col. Gallatin lawyer and judge postwar. Died Dec. 4, 1901, Gallatin. Buried City Cemetery, Gallatin.

Turner, Richard Welcome. Born Aug. 23, 1830, GA. Attorney in Forsyth, GA, and Homer, LA. To Bellevue, LA, in 1857. Attorney there. Editor, Bossier *Banner.* Unmd. ADC, 2d brigade, 5th division, LA militia, 1861. Capt. Co. A, 19th LA, May 8, 1862. Major, May 8, 1862. Lt. col., July 17, 1862. WIA Chickamauga (leg). Col., Nov. 25, 1863. WIA Ezra Church. Paroled June 8, 1865, Shreveport. Bellevue lawyer postwar. Judge. Died Jan. 17, 1883, in his home near Bellevue. Buried Bellevue Cemetery. An obituary praised him as "one of the ablest jurists and most efficient Judges who ever sat upon the bench."

Turney, Peter. Born Sept. 22, 1827, Jasper, TN, son of US senator Hopkins Turney. Winchester lawyer prewar. Breckinridge elector in 1860. Md. Cassandra Garner; Hannah Graham. Fathered 15 children. Col., 1st TN (Provisional Army), April 27, 1861. Under arrest in Feb. 1862. WIA Fredericksburg in face and neck. Often absent. Retired May 26, 1864. Assigned to duty in FL and surrendered there May 19, 1865. Winchester lawyer postwar. Justice, TN Supreme Court, 1870–93. Gov. of TN 1893–97. Died Oct. 19, 1903, Winchester. Buried Winchester Cemetery. Turney's papers are at TSLA.

Turnipseed, Richard Augustus. Born June 12, 1830, Richland Dist., SC. Attorney in Clay Co., GA, prewar. Officer in vol. militia. Md. Sarah Marable. Capt., "Fort Gaines Guards" (his old militia company), 1861. Lt. col., 9th GA, June 11, 1861. Col., April 15, 1862. Resigned July 26, 1862. Clay Co. lawyer, farmer, postwar. Judge. State senator 1886–87. Died Nov. 21, 1900, at his home near Fort Gaines. Buried in a family cemetery near Fort Gaines.

Tyler, Charles Humphrey. Born April 20, 1826, Prince William Co., VA. Grad. USMA 1848. Officer in US Army 1848–61. Md. Fiorella Causice; Elizabeth Wright. Lt. col., PAVA, May 25, 1861. AAAG to Gen. Ewell, June–July 1861. Capt., CS Regular Army, June 25, 1861. Captured in Cincinnati, OH, fall of 1861, while trying to bring his family South. Exch. Dec. 17, 1861. Capt., AIG to Gen. Jeb Stuart, 1862–63. Temporarily led the 5th VA Cav. in 1863. Promoted to lt. col., and col. in 1863. Led a brigade of cavalry in East TN in the winter of 1863. Captured again Feb. 13, 1864. Exch. July 22, 1864. Sent to TMD. Led, as colonel, a brigade of newly raised MO cavalry during Price's Raid. Farmed postwar near Cross Keys, VA. Died there March 17, 1882. Buried Massanutten Cross Keys Cemetery No. 2. A fellow staffer thought Tyler was "almost always drunk." His wife's sister married Union Gen. David Stanley.

Underhill, Stephen Edward Monaghan. Born Nov. 9, 1841, Dunse, Scotland. Officer in the British army. He resigned his commission in 1862 in order to join the Confederate army. 1st lt., PACS, July 29, 1863. ADC on Gen. S. D. Lee's staff from Feb. 1863. POW Vicksburg and paroled. Lt. col., 3d Bn. AL Reserves, Aug. 1864. Lt. col., 4th AL Reserves Sept.–Oct. 1864. Col., 65th AL (the renamed 4th AL Reserves), c. March 1865. Paroled May 10, 1865, Meridian. Md. Bessie Lipscomb. Bookkeeper in Mobile postwar. Railroad accountant in Austin, TX. Died Feb. 6, 1904, Austin. Buried State Cemetery, Austin. Gen. Maury called him "a gallant young Scotsman."

Vance, Zebulon Baird. Born May 13, 1830, Buncombe Co., NC. Attd. UNC and Washington College in TN. Asheville lawyer prewar. State legislator 1854–56. US congressman 1858–61. Md. Harriet Espy; Mrs. Florence Steele Martin. Vance, a Whig Party leader and popular stump speaker, opposed secession until Fort Sumter. Enlisted in the "Rough and Ready Guards," Co. F, 14th NC, 1861. Elected capt. at May 3, 1861, organization. Col., 26th NC, Aug. 31, 1861. Resigned Aug. 9, 1862, to become governor of NC. Governor 1862–65. Vance, a noted orator, was in many respects the most effective Confederate governor in supplying his state's troops. But he often clashed with Pres. Davis over states' rights issues. Lawyer in Charlotte postwar. Governor 1876–78. US senator 1878–94. Died April 4, 1894, Washington, DC. Buried Riverside Cemetery, Asheville. Henry Burgwyn, who succeeded Vance as colonel, admired Vance's oratory and popular manners but found him disorganized, "overrated," and "no sort of a commander."

Vandeventer, Alexander Spotswood. Born Nov. 9, 1840, near Jonesville, Lee Co., VA. Farm laborer in 1860. Student at Tazewell Seminar in TN when the war started. Md. Mary Ann Patton in 1866. Capt. Co. B, 50th VA, June 27, 1861. Lt. col., May 25, 1862. Col., Jan. 30, 1863. POW Spotsylvania. Exch. Aug. 3, 1864. Received permission to recruit a squadron of underage boys to scout in southwest VA. Commanded partisan forces in southwest VA, late 1864–65. AWOL from his regiment into 1865 and ordered to be dropped. Moved to Fayetteville, AR, postwar. Lawyer. Mayor of Fayetteville. Chief deputy marshal of the federal court at Fort Smith under Isaac Parker, the famous "Hanging Judge." Died April 26, 1910, Fayetteville, buried Evergreen Cemetery. It is said that after the war Vandeventer shuddered every time he heard a whippoorwill, because the birdcalls reminded him of the funeral dirges played at his soldiers' funerals.

Vason, William Isaac. Born Dec. 13, 1838, Athens, GA. Grad. Cumberland U. Law School, 1860. Prewar lawyer in Albany, GA. Md. Jane Beasley. Pvt. Co. E, 4th GA, April 28, 1861. Elected 2d lt. in 1862. Resigned April 28, 1862. Capt. Co. D, 19th GA Cav. Bn, July 24, 1862. Transferred to Co. I, 10th Confederate Cav. (formed from the 19th Bn.), Dec. 30, 1862. Post officer at Albany, 1863–64. Dropped from rolls by mistake in 1864 but later reinstated. Col., c. 1865. WIA

Bentonville. Paroled Albany May 17, 1865, as col. Postwar lawyer in Tallahassee, FL. Died Sept. 25, 1913, Tallahassee. Buried Old City (Eastern) Cemetery, Tallahassee. Gen. R. H. Anderson found Vason "one of the most gallant & efficient officers in my brigade."

Venable, Calvin Davenport. Born c. 1815, KY. Clerk of Henry Co., TN, court in 1860. Md. Marcy Kendall. Adj., 5th TN, May 20, 1861. Lt. col., Aug. 8, 1861. Col., May 6, 1862. WIA Perryville. Regiment consolidated with 4th TN Dec. 1862, with Venable being relieved from duty and sent to recruit. Died Dec. 27, 1862, at the Ransom family home near Versailles, TN, of his Perryville wounds and congestive fever. Buried Ransom family cemetery. Gov. Porter of TN stated, "No officer of his rank was more distinguished."

Vincent, William Germain. Born Aug. 15, 1828, Norfolk, VA. Reared in New Orleans. Auctioneer. Officer in a NY regiment in the Mexican War. Md. Anna Dellaway. Capt., "Orleans Light Guards," April 28, 1861. Lt. col., 1st LA, April 28, 1861. Col., Sept. 27, 1861. Dropped at 1862 reorganization. Col., 2d LA Cav., Sept. 1, 1862. WIA Fort Bisland. Regiment surprised and routed at Henderson's Hill in 1864. Often led a brigade in the Red River Campaign and after. Paroled June 3, 1865, Alexandria. Merchant in New Orleans postwar. President of the antilottery league. Active in the UCV. Died Oct. 28, 1916, New Orleans. Buried Cypress Grove Cemetery. An obituary called Vincent a "man of brilliant mind, of many attainments," but it appears his brilliance did not include military command. Gen. Richard Taylor was scathing: "I have tried Colonel Vincent for nearly 2 years and overlooked many of his failures. He is one of a class of officers that has done more harm to the service than many good soldiers can repair. Never exactly within reach of a court martial, Colonel Vincent has never done any duty satisfactorily."

Voorhies, William Milton. Born Sept. 15, 1815, Maury Co., TN. Furniture manufacturer in Columbia, TN, prewar. Methodist preacher. Md. Robina Gant; Kate Roy. Pvt. Co. H, 1st TN, May 1, 1861. Sgt. major, 48th TN, 1861. Capt. Co. K, Oct. 1, 1861. Col., Dec. 18, 1861. POW Fort Donelson. WIA and POW Nashville. Released from Northern prison July 25, 1865. Maury Co. farmer postwar. Died May 25, 1896, Maury Co. Buried Rose Hill Cemetery, Columbia. Gov. Harris called Voorhies "an accomplished and excellent officer."

Waddell, James Daniel. Born Dec. 22, 1832, Abbeville Dist., SC. Grad. UGA. Lawyer in Cedartown, Polk Co., prewar. State legislator. "One of the most brilliant men that Georgia ever produced." Md. Medora Sparks. Capt. Co. D, 20th GA, June 1, 1861. Major, June 14, 1862. Lt. col., May 29, 1863. Col., July 2, 1863. Relieved from field service due to ill health and appointed to a board of "slave claims" in Richmond. Paroled May 23, 1865, Augusta. Lawyer and farmer in

Cobb Co. postwar. Newspaper editor. Clerk of state house. Wrote a biography of Linton Stephens. Died Dec. 15, 1881, at his sister's Marietta home. Buried Citizens Cemetery. Waddell's war letters are at Emory U.

Wade, Benjamin Osborn. Born March 24, 1838, Warrenton, NC. Reared in NC and KY. Attd. USMA briefly in 1854. Druggist in Warrenton prewar. Officer of vol. militia. Capt. Co. F, 12th NC, April 18, 1861. Considered by some of his men "efficient and meritorious." Lt. col., May 1, 1862. Col., June 6, 1862. Resigned Dec. 30, 1862, under pressure from his superiors, who were going to cashier him for violations of orders regarding the assignment of conscripts. Died shortly after the war.

Wade, William Bartee. Born Oct. 9, 1823, Bedford Co., VA. Family moved to Columbus, MS, in 1835. Attd. UVA. Officer in Mexican War. Prewar planter. State legislator. Militia general. Md. Ann Weston. Capt., "Lowndes Southrons," Co. D, 10th MS (the original 12-month unit), Jan. 11, 1861. Lt. col., 10th MS, Jan. 17, 1861. Served in Pensacola prior to Fort Sumter. Elected col., 8th Confederate Cav., July 17, 1862. Often led a brigade in Wheeler's Cav. Corps. "[A] remarkable soldier, combining the great skill in handling the brigade . . . and . . . desperate intrepidity" with "an irascible and, at times, uncontrolled temper that led to insubordination," according to an officer in the 8th. Wade quarreled with Gen. Wheeler, who tried to court-martial Wade for disobedience of orders and intoxication. Eventually, Wade got himself and part of the 8th transferred to MS (away from Wheeler) and led a brigade in Forrest's Cav. Corps. WIA Dec. 27, 1864, during Hood's TN Campaign. Paroled May 17, 1865, at Columbus. Killed Oct. 23, 1865, on the streets of Columbus, in a gunfight with Union soldiers. Buried Friendship Cemetery, Columbus. His clashes with superior officers prevented his promotion to general, though he was often called "general" postwar.

Wadley, William Morrill. Born Nov. 1, 1813, Brentwood, NH. Moved to Savannah, GA, in 1834. Started as a blacksmith, rose to railroad president. Md. Rebecca Everingham. Prewar superintendent Vicksburg, Shreveport and Texas Railroad. Lived in Monroe, LA. Early in the war managed railroad transportation in GA. Nominated military superintendent of Confederate railroads, with the rank of Col., Nov. 29, 1862. Congress rejected the nomination May 1, 1863. Later appointed to railway iron commission. Moved to Columbus, then Macon, GA, postwar. Headed Georgia Central Railroad. Died Aug. 10, 1882, Saratoga Springs, NY. Buried Wadley Cemetery, Bolingbroke, GA. UNC has his daughter's wartime diary and papers.

Waggaman, Eugene. Born Sept. 18, 1826, New Orleans, LA, son of a US senator. Grad. Mount St. Mary's College in Baltimore. Planter in Jefferson Parish prewar. State legislator. Md. Felicie Sauve. Raised a cavalry company in early 1861 that was not accepted into Confederate service. Capt. Co. I, 10th LA, July 22, 1861. Lt. col., Jan. 16, 1862. POW Malvern Hill, exch. Aug. 5, 1862. Col., July 23, 1862. WIA Opequon Creek. Commanded the LA Brigade at Appomattox. Sheriff of New Orleans postwar. Planter. Died April 24, 1897, New Orleans. Buried St. Louis Cemetery. In speaking of Waggaman's promotion a fellow soldier called him "the best officer for the situation."

Walker, Calvin Harvey. Born Nov. 11, 1823, Maury Co., TN. Attd. USMA 1840–42. Grad. Jefferson Medical College. Giles Co. farmer and physician prewar. Md. Helen Gordon. Capt. Co. H, 3d TN, May 18, 1861. POW Fort Donelson. To Johnson's Island. Exch. Sept. 1862. Col., Sept. 26, 1862. WIA Chickamauga. KIA Kolb's Farm. Buried first in Griffin, GA, later at Rose Hill Cemetery, Columbia. A fellow soldier said Walker was "born to command . . . the most popular and successful officer in Brown's brigade." Called "Old Ballie" by the troops.

Walker, David. Born Feb. 19, 1806, Christian Co., KY. Moved to Fayetteville, AR, in 1830. Prominent lawyer and Whig Party leader. State senator. Lost race for Congress in 1844. Justice, AR Supreme Court, 1847–55. Md. Jane L. Washington. President of the AR Secession Convention. Antisecessionist but signed the ordinance of secession after Fort Sumter. Col. and judge of the military court, Holmes's Corps, TMD, March 17, 1863. Postwar lawyer. Justice, AR Supreme Court, 1866, 1874–78. Died Sept. 30, 1879, Fayetteville. Buried Walker Cemetery, Fayetteville. Papers at Univ. of AR. Uncle of James Walker, Col. AR State Troops in 1861 and postwar US senator.

Walker, Edward J. Born Dec. 19, 1830, SC. Reared in the Edgefield Dist. Grad. SCMA. Lawyer and alderman in Augusta prewar. Md. Jane G. ——. Capt. Co. G ("Confederate Light Guards"), 3d GA, April 26, 1861. Major, June 15, 1862. Lt. col., June 19, 1862. Col., July 1, 1862. WIA Antietam. WIA badly at Manassas Gap, July 23, 1863, while in command of a brigade. Died Aug. 21, 1864, Augusta, of wounds and disease. Buried Magnolia Cemetery, Augusta.

Walker, Francis Marion. Born Nov. 12, 1827, Paris, KY. Reared in Hawkins Co., TN. Grad. Transylvania U. Lawyer in Rogersville and Chattanooga, TN, prewar. Chattanooga alderman. Attorney general, 4th Dist. Officer in Mexican War. Md. Margaret Kelso Walker. Capt. Co. I, 19th TN, May 20, 1861. Lt. col., June 11, 1861. Col., May 10, 1862. Often led a brigade in the Atlanta Campaign. KIA Atlanta. Buried Citizens Cemetery, Griffin, GA; reburied 1889 in Forest Hills Cemetery, Chattanooga. "He lived a life of truth and integrity." It is often said that Walker was promoted to brig. the day he was killed, but no evidence of such promotion has surfaced.

Walker, James Madison. Born Sept. 15, 1821, Rockingham Co., NC. Known as "Madison" Walker. Farmer in NC. Moved to Kossuth, Alcorn Co., MS, in 1855. Md. Elizabeth J. Young; Frances A. Wheeler. Lt. Co. E ("Horn Lake Volunteers"), 9th MS, March 27, 1861. Capt. (2d) Co. A, 10th MS, early 1862. WIA Shiloh. Lt. col., Sept. 15, 1862. Col., Dec. 11, 1862. Resigned March 1863, due to chronic diarrhea. Farmer in Kossuth postwar. State legislator. Died Nov. 15, 1899, Kossuth. Buried Wheeler Grove Baptist Church Cemetery, near Kossuth. An obituary called Walker "a friend to humanity . . . honored and beloved."

Walker, Joseph. Born May 18, 1835, Spartanburg, SC. Clerk and merchant in Spartanburg prewar. Md. Susan E. Wingo. Capt. Co. K, 5th SC, April 13, 1861. Lt. col., Palmetto Sharpshooters, April 15, 1862. Col., July 22, 1862. Elected state representative in 1864. Wealthy merchant and bank president postwar. Mayor of Spartanburg. Died Jan. 27, 1902, Spartanburg. Buried Oakwood Cemetery, Spartanburg. Gen. Kemper considered Walker "a capital soldier, a good disciplinarian and peculiarly adapted to the command of our citizen soldiers."

Walker, Joseph Knox. Born July 19, 1818, Columbia, TN. Nephew of Pres. Polk, brother of Gen. Lucius M. Walker, and father-in-law of Gen. Frank Armstrong. Grad. Yale. Lawyer in Memphis. Unsuccessful banker. Private secretary to his uncle. State senator 1857–59. Md. Augusta Tabb. Col., 2d TN, May 11, 1861. Led brigade at Belmont. Regiment lost heavily at Shiloh and was soon consolidated with the 21st TN. Resigned May 14, 1862, citing ill health (chronic diarrhea). Died Aug. 21, 1863, Memphis. Buried Elmwood Cemetery. His return to Union-occupied Memphis after his resignation caused some Southerners to question his loyalty.

Walker, Tandy. Born Oct. 11, 1814, in the Choctaw tribal area of modern MS. Mixed-blood Choctaw. Farmer and stock raiser in Scullyville, Indian Territory. President of the Choctaw Senate. Governor of the Choctaw Nation 1857–59. Md. Cillin Krebs. Lt. col., 2d Choctaw & Chickasaw MR, prob. July 31, 1861. Col., Jan. 1, 1863. Cited for "skill and daring" at Poison Spring. Often led a brigade and recommended for promotion to brigadier. Died Feb. 2, 1877, Scullyville. Buried Scullyville Cemetery. A New York *Herald* reporter thought Walker "looks like a full-blooded white man . . . a well-to-do farmer."

Walkup, Samuel Hoey. Born Jan. 22, 1818, Mecklenburg Co., NC. Grad. UNC. Lawyer in Monroe, Union Co., prewar. State representative 1858–59, 1860–61. Militia general. Md. Amelia Price. Capt. Co. F, 48th NC, March 4, 1862. Lt. col., April 9, 1862. WIA Fredericksburg (hip). Col., Dec. 4, 1863. Court-martialed March 2, 1864, and reprimanded. WIA Wilderness. Appmx. Attorney in Monroe postwar. Elected to US Congress in 1865 but not seated. President of Davidson College. Died Oct. 26, 1876, of dysentery. Buried Sunset Cemetery,

Monroe. Although undeniably brave, Walkup was "often laughed at on dress parade and brigade drill for his awkwardness." Walkup's war memoirs are at UNC.

Wallace, George Phillips. Born Nov. 22, 1829, Perry Co., AL. Farmer in Attala Co., MS, prewar. Md. Mary Ann Hodge. Capt. Co. D, 40th MS, May 14, 1862. POW Vicksburg. Assigned to duty by Gen. Baldwin as lt. col., Feb. 5, 1864, to rank from Nov. 11, 1863. Severely WIA Peachtree Creek, eventually losing his left arm. Promoted to col., perhaps March 21, 1865, after W. B. Colbert's death, though Wallace's service record contains no mention of such promotion. Farmer in Anderson Co., TX, postwar. Died Oct. 30, 1881, Anderson Co. Buried Bethel Cemetery, Bethel, Anderson Co.

Wallace, William. Born Nov. 16, 1824, Columbia, SC. Grad. USC. Columbia lawyer prewar. State representative 1854–60. Militia general. Md. Victoria McLemore; Mrs. Fannie C. Means Mobley. Capt. Co. C, 2d SC, April 8, 1861. WIA 2d Manassas (cheek). Major, June 3, 1863. WIA Wilderness. Lt. col., May 6, 1864. WIA Sept. 1864. Col., 2d SC Consolidated, c. April 9, 1865. Lawyer and planter in Columbia postwar. State representative 1865–67. State senator 1882–86. Columbia postmaster. Died Nov. 12, 1902, Columbia. Buried 1st Presbyterian Churchyard, Columbia. A junior officer called Wallace "brave almost to rashness."

Waller, Thomas Conway. Born Dec. 9, 1832, Stafford Co., VA. Farmer and politician in Stafford Co. prewar. Md. Sarah E. Wickliffe. Capt. Co. A, 9th VA Cav., April 21, 1861. Major, Oct. 18, 1862. WIA Brandy Station Oct. 11, 1863. Lt. col., Sept. 16, 1864. Col., Jan. 6, 1865. Appmx. Stafford Co. farmer postwar. Died there Dec. 23, 1895. Buried in "Grafton," near Garrisonville, Stafford Co.

Walton, James Burdge. Born Nov. 18, 1813, Newark, NJ. Grad. Louisiana College. Wholesale grocer in New Orleans. Col. 1st LA Volunteers in Mexican War. Major of the Washington Art., a famed antebellum vol. militia unit. Md. Amelia M. Johnson. Major, Washington Art. Bn., at its acceptance into Confederate service, May 13, 1861. Col., March 26, 1862. Senior col. of artillery in the 1st Corps, ANV. Assigned to duty as "Inspector General of Field Artillery," Jan. 1864. Resigned July 18, 1864, because a junior officer (E. Porter Alexander) had been promoted over him. Lived in New Orleans postwar. Assessor and auctioneer. Died New Orleans Sept. 8, 1885. Buried Cypress Grove Cemetery, New Orleans.

Ward, George Taliaferro. Born c. 1810, Fayette Co., KY. Attd. Transylvania U. Prewar planter and banker in Leon Co., FL. Very wealthy. Active in politics. Delegate (Unionist) to FL Secession Convention, but after the ordinance of secession had passed he signed the document. Md. Sarah Jane Chaires. Appointed to Confederate Congress, May 2, 1861. Resigned to join the army. Col., 2d FL, July 12, 1861. KIA Williamsburg, May 5, 1862. Buried Bruton Parish Church Cemetery, near the battlefield. As he signed the secession ordinance, Ward is credited with saying, "When I die, I want it inscribed upon my tombstone that I was the last man to give up the ship."

Ward, William Walker. Born Oct. 5, 1825, Ward's Crossroads, TN. Grad. Cumberland U. Lawyer in Carthage, TN. State representative 1855–57. Md. Elizabeth Rucks. Pvt. Co. B, 7th TN, May 20, 1861. Discharged May 19, 1862, due to an old ankle injury. Lt. col., 9th TN, Sept. 1, 1862. Col., Dec. 23, 1862. POW Buffington Island, during Morgan's Ohio Raid. Imprisoned at Columbus and Fort Delaware. Exch. Aug. 3, 1864. Appointed col., 1st KY Special Bn., made up in part of survivors of the raid. WIA Bull's Gap (leg) Nov. 13, 1864. Captured at Columbus, GA, May 8, 1865. Carthage lawyer postwar. Chancellor of Smith Co. Died April 10, 1871, Smith Co. Buried Rucks family cemetery near Rome, TN. Basil Duke called Ward "intelligent, zealous and firm." Ward's war diary has been published.

Warfield, Elisha. Born March 2, 1838, MS. Attd. UMS. Prewar planter in Laconia, Desha Co., AR. Capt. Co. C, 2d AR, May 30, 1861. Major, Jan. 6, 1862. WIA Chickamauga. Lt. col., Sept. 20, 1863. Court-martialed March 30, 1863, and reprimanded. Col., Dec. 29, 1863. WIA Atlanta (shot in left elbow). Postwar plantation manager in Concordia Parish, LA, and Natchez, MS. Died Dec. 26, 1894, at his residence near Natchez. Buried Natchez City Cemetery. An obituary memorialized him as "a most excellent, energetic gentleman."

Waring, Joseph Frederick. Born Feb. 13, 1832, Savannah, GA. Attd. Yale. Savannah area planter. City alderman. In vol. militia. Md. Louise Early. Capt. Co. F (the "Georgia Hussars"), Jeff Davis Legion, Sept. 17, 1861. WIA in face Dec. 4, 1861. Lt. col., Dec. 2, 1862. Col., probably July 11, 1864. Returned to Savannah postwar. Forwarding agent for the Georgia Central RR. Died Oct. 5, 1876, of yellow fever, at Whitesville, GA. Buried Laurel Grove Cemetery, Savannah. A "brave and gallant" officer, though unpopular. Waring's papers are at UNC and Georgia Historical Society.

Warren, Edward Tiffin Harrison. Born June 19, 1829, Rockingham Co., VA. Attd. UVA. Harrisonburg lawyer. Officer in vol. militia. Md. Virginia Magruder. Lt. col., 10th VA, July 1, 1861. Col., May 8, 1862. WIA Chancellorsville. KIA Wilderness, May 6, 1864. Buried Woodbine Cemetery, Harrisonburg. "[O]ne of the most efficient regimental commanders in the service and a gentleman of singularly amiable character." Warren's papers are at UVA.

Warthen, Thomas Jefferson, Sr. Born March 18, 1804, Washington Co., GA. Farmer, judge. State legislator. Veteran of Creek and Seminole wars. Militia general. Md. Sarah Faulk Wicker. Lt. col., 8th GA Bn., early 1861. Capt. Co. B, 28th GA, Sept. 10, 1861. Col., Sept. 10, 1861. MWIA Malvern Hill. Died July 3, 1862, Richmond. Briefly interred in Oakwood Cemetery, Richmond; reburied Forest Grove Cemetery, Washington Co. An obituary claimed, "A braver man . . . never fell on the battlefield. By his command he was dearly beloved."

Warwick, Bradfute. Born Nov. 24, 1839, Lynchburg, VA. Grew up in Richmond. Grad. UVA and Medical College of NY. Left the US to join Garibaldi's insurgents in Italy. Soldier of fortune and military surgeon. Unmd. Capt., PAVA, May 17, 1861. Capt. on the staff of Gen. Wise, 1861. Major, 4th TX, Oct. 2, 1861. Lt. col., March 3, 1862. MWIA Gaines's Mill. Died July 6, 1862, at his Richmond home. Promoted to col. posthumously, to rank from June 27, 1862. Buried Hollywood Cemetery, Richmond. A "polished handsome young man . . . [who] would not send a private soldier where he would not cheerfully go himself."

Wasden, Joseph. Born Sept. 21, 1829, Gibson Co., GA. Warrenton lawyer prewar. Md. Mary Ann Wilson. Major, 22d GA, Aug. 31, 1861. Lt. col., June 2, 1862. WIA 2d Manassas. Applied for a judgeship of a military court in late 1862, claiming to be exhausted from continued field duty. Col., April 22, 1863. KIA the 2d day of Gettysburg by canister. Buried on the battlefield; reburied Laurel Grove Cemetery, Savannah. Gen. A. R. Wright's report of Gettysburg claimed, "The service contained no better or truer officer." However, one soldier labeled him "an infidel."

Washington, James Augustus. Born March 8, 1832, Wayne Co., NC. Attd. Wake Forest U. Grad. UNC. Merchant in Wayne Co. prewar. Md. Virginia Pope. Sgt., "Goldsboro Rifles," April 1861. Capt. Co. H, 2d NC, May 16, 1861. Lt. col., 50th NC, April 15, 1862. Col., Dec. 1, 1862. Resigned Nov. 9, 1863, after being censured for conduct during a Union raid on Tarboro. Farmer and clerk in Goldsboro, Wayne Co., postwar. Died Feb. 16, 1911, Goldsboro. Buried Willow Dale Cemetery, Tarboro.

Watkins, Elisha Pinson. Born c. 1826, Coweta Co., GA. Lawyer. GA sec. of state, 1853–61. Md. Martha E. Watts. QM, 9th GA, June 11, 1861. Resigned Aug. 20, 1861. Lt. col., 3d GA State Troops, Oct. 15, 1861. Col., Feb. 24, 1862. Col., 56th GA, May 15, 1862. Commanded Post of Atlanta, summer 1862. WIA Champion Hill. POW Vicksburg and paroled. Resigned Feb. 21, 1865, having been elected to the State Senate. Lawyer in Atlanta postwar. Died June 13, 1868, of consumption, at his father's home in Coweta Co. Buried Watkins Cemetery, Newnan, GA. The surgeon of the 56th called Watkins "one of the best men that lives."

Watkins, George Claiborne. Born Nov. 25, 1815, Shelbyville, KY. Family moved to Little Rock, AR, in 1821. Attd. East TN U. (now UTN) and Yale. Little Rock lawyer. State attorney general. Chief justice, AR Supreme Court, 1852–54. Md. Mary Crease; Mrs. Sophie Fulton Curran. Delegate to AR Secession Convention. Appointed col. and judge of the military court of T. H. Holmes's army, TMD, Dec. 16, 1862. Declined appointment. Died Dec. 7, 1872, St. Louis, MO. Buried Mount Holly Cemetery, Little Rock. Sen. Robert Johnson called Watkins the "ablest judge who ever sat on our Supreme Bench; a gentleman of great diffidence & sensitive modesty." Three sons served in the Confederate army, including Lt. Col. Anderson Watkins, KIA at the Battle of Atlanta.

Watkins, William M. Born c. 1833, Sumner Co., TN. County clerk of Dyer Co. in 1860. Md. Eliza Phillips. Capt. Co. D, 47th TN, Dec. 16, 1861. Col., March 1, 1863. WIA Jonesboro. Led Vaughn's brigade in Hood's TN Campaign. Paroled May 1, 1865, Greensboro. Dry goods merchant in Dyersburg postwar. County clerk. Alive in 1880 but probably died soon after. Buried City Cemetery, Dyersburg. A fellow soldier later stated that Watkins "was a colonel but was willing to become a private."

Watson, Benjamin William Abner Joseph John Frederick. Born June 9 (or 19), 1828, Prince Edward Co., VA. Named for each of his 6 uncles. To Ellis Co., TX, in 1851. Wealthy planter. Md. Mary E. Scott; Margaret Overstreet. Capt. Co. C, 19th TX Cav., March 26, 1862. Lt. col., April 10, 1862. Col., probably commissioned in 1865 to rank from June 7, 1864, though his service record does not reflect that promotion. Paroled July 10, 1865, Ellis Co., as col. Returned to Ellis Co. farm postwar. Died Sept. 16, 1873, Waxahachie. Buried Watson family cemetery, Ellis Co. One soldier asserted that Watson, "although a gallant soldier, and a fine officer, was illiterate." However, another soldier called Watson "the finest civilian officer in the trans-Mississippi," claiming when the war ended he was in line for promotion to brigadier.

Watson, John R. Born c. 1825, GA. Lived in Linden, Cass Co., TX, prewar. Attorney. Clerk of district court. Md. Clementine Connally. Capt. Co. B, 18th TX, April 2, 1862. Major, Feb. 23, 1863. Lt. col., Aug. 10, 1863. Col., April 9, 1864. "A gallant soldier and a fine citizen." KIA Jenkins Ferry.

Watts, George Owen. Born May 17, 1840, Richmond, KY. Attd. KMI. Grad. USMA 1861. Md. Ann E. Ogden in 1865. Lt., US Army, June–July 1861. Resigned from US service Aug. 10, 1861. 2d lt., CS Regular Army, to rank from March 16, 1861. Drillmaster, Cobb's GA Legion, 1861. Engineer on Gen. Buckner's and later Gen. Villipigue's staff, 1861–62. Helped design Fort Donelson and Fort Pillow. Capt., June 6, 1862. WIA four times during war. On Gen. Van Dorn's staff.

Major, Jan. 26, 1863. Transferred to TMD May 16, 1864. Promoted (probably by Gen. Kirby Smith) to col. and chief of artillery, Dist. of AR and West LA. Paroled as such June 1865 at Natchez. Farmed postwar in Rapides Parish, LA, except for 6 years (1870–76) spent in TX. Clerk of district court. Parish superintendent of education. UCV general. Died Dec. 5, 1905, Alexandria. Buried Old St. Landry Church Cemetery, Opelousas. Buckner called him "an officer of great enterprise."

Watts, Nathaniel Green. Born Jan. 25, 1816, VA. Vicksburg, MS, clerk. Deputy US marshal. Sgt. and QM in Mexican War in Jefferson Davis's regiment. Capt., CS Regular Army, March 16, 1861. AQM and ACS to Gen. Clark, June 1861. Major, PACS, Oct. 4, 1861. QM of Griffith's MS Brigade, ANV. Assigned to duty in prisoner exchange bureau, Aug. 4, 1862. Lt. col. (by Nov. 19, 1863). Col., in charge of exchanges in AL and MS, in 1865. Died Jan. 27, 1866. Buried Cedar Hill Cemetery, Vicksburg. His compiled service records contain letters of his signed as lt. col. but contains no record of promotion beyond major.

Watts, Thomas Hill. Born Jan. 3, 1819, Butler Co., AL. Grad. UVA. Lawyer in Butler Co. and Montgomery. Longtime state legislator and Whig Party leader. Lost race for Congress in 1856 and for governor in 1861. Md. Eliza, sister of Gen. W. W. Allen. Delegate to AL Secession Convention. Col., 17th AL, Sept. 5, 1861. Arrested for disobedience of orders March 1862. Resigned March 24, 1862, soon after appointment as attorney general of the Confederacy. Attorney general 1862–63. Elected governor of AL in 1863 in a landslide, despite not campaigning. Governor 1863–65, actively working to maintain morale. Practiced law in Montgomery postwar. State representative. President of the AL Bar Assn. Died Sept. 16, 1892, Montgomery, buried Oakwood Cemetery. In the words of a contemporary, "the faculties of his mind are of a very high order."

Watts, William. Born Dec. 20, 1817, Campbell Co., VA. Grad. UVA. Lawyer in Roanoke prewar. Md. Mary Jane Allen. Major, 19th VA, July 13, 1861. Transferred to 28th VA Aug. 20, 1861. Lt. col., May 1, 1862. Col., July 3, 1863. Absent due to illness, June–Dec. 1864. Paroled May 24, 1865, Lynchburg. Roanoke lawyer postwar. State representative 1875–77. Died May 1, 1877, at "Oakland," near Roanoke. Gen. Hunton thought Watts "not much of a tactician," and a soldier accused him of being drunk "about three fourths of the time."

Way, Charlton Hines. Born Oct. 5, 1834, Fairborn, Liberty Co., GA. Attd. GMI. Read for the law. Commission merchant in Savannah prewar. Officer in vol. militia. Md. Laura Seton: Frances M. Williams. Capt., "Forest City Rangers," July 18, 1861. Mustered out Nov. 1, 1861. AAG to Gen. Francis Capers, GA State Troops, 1861–62. Col., 54th GA, May 16, 1862. Savannah cotton broker and real estate dealer postwar, often traveling to Europe in his business dealings. US consul to St. Petersburg in the Cleveland administration. Died Savannah July 1, 1900, of stomach trouble. Buried Laurel Grove Cemetery. A newspaper called him "a gentleman of classical education, brilliant and witty."

Wayne, Richard Alexander. Born July 23, 1835, Savannah, GA. Commission merchant. Official at the Savannah Customs House in 1860. In vol. militia. Md. Elizabeth L. Cullen. Capt. Co. E, 1st GA Regulars, Feb. 1, 1861. Major, Oct. 3, 1862. Lt. col., Aug. 3, 1864. Col., Sept. 3, 1864. Paroled Greensboro. Employed in the offices of the Georgia Central RR postwar. Died Oct. 14, 1884, Savannah. Buried Laurel Grove Cemetery. A soldier in the 1st described Wayne as "one of the most fearless men I have ever known . . . a gruff man, short and peremptory in manner, in camp disliked by his . . . men, but . . . [in] battle . . . commanding the respect of all."

Webb, Robert Fulton. Born April 25, 1825, Washington, DC. Reared in Baltimore, MD. Orange Co., NC farmer/mechanic prewar. Officer in Mexican War. Md. Amanda Mangum; Henrietta J. Beckwith. Capt. Co. B, 6th NC, May 20, 1861. Major, July 11, 1861. Lt. col., July 11, 1862. WIA Antietam. Col., July 3, 1863. POW Rappahannock Station, VA, Nov. 7, 1863. Released July 25, 1865. Tobacco and furniture merchant in Durham postwar. State representative 1865–66. Died Jan. 11, 1891, Durham, buried Maplewood Cemetery. Gen. Pender considered Webb "a fine man."

Weems, John B. Born Oct. 24, 1824, Wilkes Co., GA. Merchant and lawyer in Washington and Columbus, GA, prewar. Solicitor of the Northern Circuit 1847–55. Mexican War veteran. Md. Mary E. Wingfield; Emily Louise MacCarthy. Capt. Co. B, 10th GA, May 18, 1861. Major, July 4, 1861. Lt. col., Sept. 25, 1861. Col., Oct. 29, 1862. WIA Savage Station and Gettysburg. Retired to Invalid Corps, May 19, 1864. Headed the GA Conscription Bureau. Lawyer, judge in Macon postwar. Sec. of the GA State Senate, 1865–66. Died Nov. 30, 1876, Macon. Buried Washington, GA (probably Rest Haven Cemetery, where his mother is buried). Brother of Col. W. H. Weems.

Weems, Walter Hanson. Born c. 1836, AL. Lawyer in Russell Co., AL, prewar. Md. Ella Ingraham. Capt. Co. F, 6th AL, May 2, 1861. Major, Jan. 1, 1862. Major, 64th GA, May 26, 1863. Lt. col., Feb. 20, 1864. WIA Olustee (leg). Col., June 30, 1864. Druggist in Atlanta postwar, also managing his wife's Lee Co. plantation. Died July 15, 1885, Atlanta. Buried Oakland Cemetery, Atlanta.

Weir, John. Born April 7, 1833, AL. Farmer near Louisville, Winston Co., MS, prewar. Md. Emily Ann Miller. Capt. Co. D, 5th MS, Aug. 12, 1861. Major, March 28, 1862. WIA Shiloh. On June 23, 1862, Gen. Bragg discharged both Weir and

Col. Fant from the service and appointed John Dickins of the 38th MS as col. Weir had been rejected by an examining board. Reappointed major Nov. 10, 1863, as Weir got Bragg's order rescinded. Col., commission backdated to July 8, 1863. WIA Franklin. Paroled May 13, 1865, Meridian. Miller in Choctaw Co. postwar. Founded the town of Weir, MS. Died June 9, 1900. Buried Weir Cemetery, Choctaw Co. Col. Fant praised Weir for his "distinguished gallantry" at Shiloh and urged his promotion.

Wellborn, Maximilian Bethune. Born Jan. 8, 1825, Madison, GA. Reared in Barbour Co., AL. Grad. UAL in 1848. Lawyer in Eufaula, AL. Bought plantation in Lewisville, AR, in 1858. Raised cotton and practiced law there. Md. Emma J. Dent, whose sister md. Col. Whitfield Clark. Lt. Co. E, 1st Trans-Mississippi Confederate Cav. Bn. Said (by family sources) to have served on Gen. Magruder's staff 1862–63. Col. of military court, Dist. of AR, Sept. 1864. The appointment was made by Gen. Kirby Smith—Wellborn has no staff service record. Paroled June 22, 1865. Settled in Houston, TX, in 1865. Returned to Eufaula in 1867. Lawyer. State legislator. Lost race for Congress in 1870. Died May 15, 1885, Eufaula, buried Fairview Cemetery. A newspaper praised Wellborn as "firm in the right, gentle and polite in his manners, brave in spirit, and conservative in all his sentiments."

Wells, Jared W. Born Sept. 1831, VA, probably Frederick Co. Prewar physician in Panola Co., TX. Md. Ora Birdsong. Enlisted in Capt. Holland's local company, 1861. Lt. Co. K, 1st Choctaw & Chickasaw MR. Capt. and AAG on Gen. Cooper's staff, Nov. 1862. Lt. col., Wells's TX Cav. Bn., late in war. Col., 34th (Wells's) TX Cav., 1865. Postwar physician in Panola Co. To Bryson and Jacksboro, TX. Died 1917. Buried Oakwood Cemetery, Jacksboro. Middle name probably "Williams," and first name sometimes given as "John."

Wells, Joseph Morehead. Born Aug. 7, 1811, Giles Co., TN. Methodist minister in Tishomingo Co., MS, prewar. Md. Sarah L. Burns; Mrs. Mary E. Armour. Capt. Co. F (the "Blackland Gideonites"), 23d MS, June 8, 1861. Lt. col., Sept. 5, 1861. POW Fort Donelson, exch. fall of 1862. Col., Sept. 24, 1862. Resigned Sept. 3, 1864, citing age and illness. Minister and farmer in Prentiss Co. postwar. Died Feb. 9, 1896, Prentiss Co. Buried Blackland Cemetery, Prentiss Co. An obituary termed him a "noble old patriot."

Wharton, John Mason. Born Dec. 1, 1832, Towsontown, MD. Commonly called "Jack" Wharton. Attd. St. James College. Prewar lawyer in MD. To KS in 1857, to TX c. 1859. Rancher near the Kaufman and Van Zandt Co. line. Teamster for the US Army during the Utah Expedition of 1858. Unmd. Capt. Co. E, 6th TX Cav., Sept. 7, 1861. Lt. col., Aug. 14, 1863. Col., Dec. 21, 1863. In 1864,

Wharton's regiment mutinied. Wharton fled the camp, in fear of his life, and offered to resign. Instead, he was arrested and charged with cowardice and disobeying an order. Although acquitted, the fiasco ended any chance of his further promotion. Paroled May 1865 in MS. Returned to his ranch in TX after the war. Moved to Shreveport, then New Orleans, LA. Involved in railroad construction. LA sec. of state and adj. gen. US marshal for LA. Died April 7, 1882, New Orleans, of apoplexy. Buried St. John's Episcopal Church, Hagerstown, MD. An obituary called him "the imperturbable and inexhaustible raconteur."

Wheeler, James Thaddeus. Born c. 1826, Giles Co., TN. Farmer in Chickasaw Co., MS, and then Giles Co., TN, prewar. Mexican War veteran. Md. Sallie B. Malone. Pvt., 11th TN Cav. Bn., 1861. Capt. Co. A., late 1861. Col., 6th TN Cav. (aka 1st—formed from the 11th and 2d Bns.), June 12, 1862. WIA in the Dec. 1862 Holly Springs raid. Detached Nov. 1864, to recruit in TN. Paroled at Pulaski, TN, in 1865. 6 feet 4 inches. Farmer in Giles Co. postwar. Died Jan. 12, 1887, at his Giles Co. home. Buried Moriah Church Cemetery. "[A]s brave and daring in war as he was generous and neighborly in peace."

White, David G. Born Oct. 30, 1837, Anne Arundel Co., MD. Grew up in Cecil Co. Attd. USMA, resigning April 22, 1861. 2d lt., CS Regular Army, March 16, 1861. AAG and ADC to Gen. Hardee. Appointed major, 6th Bn. AR Cav., but declined. Capt. PACS, Aug. 1, 1862. Major, AAG, Dec. 31, 1862. Assigned to duty as chief ordnance officer, Hardee's Corps, Sept. 8, 1864. Col., Sept. 20, 1864, to lead the 5th GA Cav. On Feb. 11, 1865, he was transferred back to staff duty. Led Hagan's brigade at Bentonville. Paroled May 1, 1865. Postwar he lived Anne Arundel Co. Officer in Egyptian Army. Explorer in Palestine and Abyssinia for the Egyptian government. In coal and lumber business in West River, MD. Died April 13, 1889, West River.

White, Edward Brickell. Born Jan. 29, 1806, St. John's Parish, SC. Grad. USMA 1826. Lt., US Army, 1826–36, serving in the artillery corps. Resigned to become an engineer and architect in Charleston. Militia colonel. Planter. Md. Delia W. Adams. Turned down commissions as capt. of SC engineers and major of Confederate engineers, tendered him in 1861. Major, 3d SC Art. Bn. ("Palmetto Bn."), Nov. 2, 1861. Lt. col., April 15, 1862. Commanded an artillery brigade in SC, Jan.–Feb. 1863. Col., Jan. 18, 1864. Commanded heavy artillery in the Dist. of SC. Moved to New York City in 1867. Trust manager there. Died May 10, 1882, New York City. Buried Woodlawn Cemetery, the Bronx; reburied St. Michael's Churchyard, Charleston.

White, James Daniel. Born Oct. 23, 1834, SC. Reared in GA. Moved to Morley, Scott Co., MO. Prewar civil engineer in the West. Md. Eugenia B. Froissard.

Capt. Co. A, 3d Cav., 1st Div., MSG, May 5, 1861. Lt. col., Oct. 5, 1861. Mustered out Dec. 27, 1861. Col., 12th (aka Ponder's 9th) MO, Aug. 29, 1862. Unpopular with his men. Submitted his resignation April 28, 1863, but the resignation was never accepted. WIA (arm) at Helena. Departed the regiment Aug. 28, 1863, and became provost marshal of the 2d Arkansas Dist. Paroled as capt. and QM, 10th MO (which the 12th/9th had been consolidated into), June 1865. Fled to Mexico after the war. Returned to US and settled in Arcadia, MO. Contractor with the Iron Mountain Railroad. Died Oct. 13, 1873, near Rondo, Lafayette Co., AR, of malaria. Buried Arcadia. An obituary called him an "energetic business man, noble, generous to a fault."

White, John R. Born c. 1834, Pulaski, TN. Farmer in Giles Co. prewar. Md. Rebecca Smith. Capt. Co. I, 53d TN, Dec. 6, 1861. POW Fort Donelson. Imprisoned at Johnson's Island. Exch. Sept. 1862. Lt. col., Dec. 19, 1862. Col., Feb. 25, 1863. KIA Ezra Church while leading a charge. White's brigade commander reported of White that a "truer and more earnest-hearted patriot never lived."

White, Moses. Born Dec. 19, 1829, Knoxville, TN. Grad. UTN. Knoxville lawyer. State representative 1855–59. Moved to Memphis just before the war. Cherokee War veteran. Unmd. Lt. col., 37th TN, c. Sept. 1861. Col., Oct. 26, 1861. WIA Stones River. 37th consolidated with 15th, June 1863, with the colonel of the 15th leading the combined unit. White, a supernumerary, was assigned to recruiting duty. Commanded post of Eatonton, GA, 1864. POW near Fort McCallister, GA, Dec. 13, 1864. White escaped from Northern prison and made it back South. Paroled May 10, 1865, Meridian. Lawyer in Memphis and Knoxville postwar. Farmer, newspaper editor. Trustee of UTN. Died Nov. 1, 1907, near Knoxville. Buried Old Gray Cemetery, Knoxville.

White, Moses James. Born Oct. 6, 1835, Hinds Co., MS. Reared in Vicksburg. Attd. William & Mary College 1853–54. Grad. USMA 1859 (2d in class). Lt., US Army, 1859–61. 1st lt., CS Regular Army, March 16, 1861. Ordnance officer on Gen. Polk's staff. Appointed col. and commander of Fort Macon, NC, Sept. 30, 1861. Surrendered Fort Macon after a 13-day siege, April 25, 1862. After exchange, transferred to TMD in Sept. 1862 as an artillery officer. Led a brigade of MO Cav. in 1862 but soon relieved of command due to epilepsy that, in Gen. Holmes's words, "seriously impaired" his mind. On sick leave most of 1863–64. Ordered on a purchasing mission to the U.K. Dec. 2, 1864, in the hopes that while there he could obtain medical help. Died Jan. 29, 1865, Natchez, MS, while traveling across enemy lines to New Orleans in order to catch a boat to Europe. Probably buried in an unmarked grave in Natchez City Cemetery. A "very efficient officer" whose disease prevented his promotion.

White, Robert. Born Feb. 7, 1833, Romney, VA (now WVA). Attorney in Romney prewar. Md. Ellen E. Vass in 1859. Capt. Co. I, 13th VA, May 18, 1861. Transferred to duty in the ordnance dept. in Richmond in 1862. Appointed military storekeeper, June 18, 1863. Left this to raise a battalion of cavalry behind enemy lines. Major, 41st VA Cav. Bn. (the unit he raised), Sept. 18, 1863. Lt. col., Dec. 9, 1863. Col., 23d VA Cav. (formed from the 41st Bn.), April 28, 1864. WIA three times. Paroled May 7, 1865, Patterson Creek, WVA. Lawyer in Romney and Wheeling postwar. State legislator. State attorney general. Commander of the WVA division UCV. Wrote the WVA volume of *Confederate Military History.* Died Dec. 12, 1915, near Wheeling. Buried Greenwood Cemetery, Wheeling.

White, Thomas William. Born Jan. 8, 1824, Elbert Co., GA. Attd. UGA. Grad. Harvard Law School in 1846. Lawyer in Hernando, MS, prewar. Militia officer. State representative 1854–55. Md. Mina Barbara Meriwether. MS commissioner to KY in early 1861. 1st lt. Co. A, 9th MS, Feb. 21, 1861. Capt., March 27, 1861. WIA Shiloh. Appointed col., April 11, 1862, by Gen. Bragg, an appointment later declared illegal. However, White headed the regiment while F. E. Whitfield challenged Bragg's appointment. Accused of cowardice (hiding behind a rock) at Stones River. Left out when the regiment was consolidated on Feb. 21, 1863. Detached to Conscript Bureau in MS. Col., 8th MS Cav., Sept. 8, 1864. Paroled May 20, 1865, Memphis. Lawyer in Hernando postwar. Died there July 26, 1889. Buried Hernando Baptist Cemetery. In 1997 White's uniform and sword were put up for auction.

White, William. Born Jan. 7, 1820, Norfolk Co., VA. Attd. the Medical College of VA and said (less reliably) to have attd. Yale. Grad. UPA Medical School. Physician in Deep Creek, Norfolk Co., prewar. Delegate to VA Secession Convention (voting against secession). Md. Henrietta Kemp Turner. Major, 14th VA, May 17, 1861. Lt. col., Aug. 26, 1862. WIA severely in Pickett's Charge. Col., July 3, 1863. Present with his regiment into 1865. Lumber merchant in Portsmouth postwar. Died June 22, 1894. Buried Cedar Grove Cemetery, Portsmouth.

White, William Parker. Born April 18, 1811, Savannah, GA. Attd. UGA. Attorney in Savannah prewar. Militia general. Md. Sarah Berrien Dowse. Major, White's Bn. GA PR, May 7, 1862. Col., 7th GA Cav. (formed from White's Bn.), Jan. 24, 1864. Shot in the knee near Georgetown, SC, March 7, 1864. The shooter, a private, claimed he had been paid by a captain to shoot Col. White, the captain being in trouble with the colonel for disobeying orders. Died April 6, 1864, in a Georgetown hospital. Buried Georgetown; reburied Laurel Grove Cemetery, Savannah, in 1869. Thought to have been the finest horseman in Georgia.

White, William Wilkinson. Born c. 1835, SC. Schoolteacher and lawyer in Cobb Co., GA. Md. Pauline Kirkpatrick (Jan. 12, 1866). Capt., "Cobb Mountaineers" (Co. I, 7th GA), May 31, 1861. WIA 1st Manassas. Lt. col., May 12, 1862. WIA in throat at Garnett's Farm. Col., Aug. 30, 1862. Retired July 27, 1864, due to his wound (he was unable to do more than whisper). Died soon after the war. Perhaps buried in an unmarked grave in Citizens Cemetery, Marietta, where his wife is buried.

Whitfield, Francis Eugene. Born June 22, 1839, Bossier Parish, LA. Reared in Memphis. Attd. WMI; UMS; UVA; and Cumberland U. Law School. Lawyer in Corinth, MS, prewar. Md. Bessie Winifred Whitfield. Lt. Co. A (the "Corinth Rifles"), 9th MS, Feb. 4, 1861. Regimental adj. Capt., fall of 1861. Severely WIA in hip at Shiloh while leading the skirmish line with great distinction. Major, elected April 16, 1862, when the 9th reorganized. Arrested by Gen. Bragg for being AWOL, when he was on medical leave, clearing the way for Bragg to appoint a favorite (T. W. White) as colonel. The War Dept. later declared Bragg's appointment, and the arrest, illegal. Whitfield claimed the colonelcy by seniority over White, a claim evidently recognized by the War Dept., although Whitfield's service record does not give any date of promotion. Bragg's habit of illegally appointing officers, and the subsequent legal challenges to those appointments, demoralized the 9th and many other regiments. Provost marshal of the Army of TN, 1863–64. WIA Resaca and disabled. Commanded post of Meridian, MS. Paroled at Meridian as col., 9th. Lawyer in Corinth and Memphis postwar. Died March 18, 1885, while on a trip down the St. John's River in FL. Buried Elmwood Cemetery, Memphis. His gravestone avers that the "brilliancy of his mind was only equaled by the kindness of his noble nature."

Whitfield, George Franklin. Born June 8, 1831, Duplin Co., NC. Attd. UNC. Farmer in Lenoir Co. prewar. Md. Mary Ann Bizzell. Capt. Co. C, 27th NC, April 17, 1861. Major, Nov. 1, 1862. Lt. col., Dec. 5, 1862. WIA Bristoe Station (right leg) and Cold Harbor (head). Absent due to wounds through Feb. 1865. Col., Jan. 11, 1865. Died Aug. 28, 1869, Lenoir Co. Buried Fairview Cemetery, La Grange, NC.

Whitford, John Nathaniel. Born May 4, 1835, near Vanceboro, Craven Co., NC. Educated at South Lowell School in Orange Co. New Bern merchant prewar. Md. Mary Elizabeth Williamson; Sidney A. Taylor. Capt. Co. I, 1st NC Art., Sept. 20, 1861. Served in the Fort Fisher garrison. Major, 1st Bn. NC LDT, Jan. 1, 1863. Lt. col., July 21, 1863. Col., 67th NC (a unit formed from the 1st Bn. and restricted to state defense), Jan. 18, 1864. WIA Dec. 23, 1864, near Fort Branch, NC. Led brigade at Bentonville. Owned a hardware store in New Bern and a plantation in Jones Co. after the war. State senator 1883–85. Died June 26, 1890, near New Bern. Buried Cedar Grove Cemetery, New Bern. Papers at Duke U.

Whitson, James Monroe. Born Oct. 10, 1825, Currituck Co., NC. Farmer in Currituck Co. prewar. Mexican War veteran. Md. Elvira Dowdy; Sarah Blevins. Capt. Co. B, 8th NC, May 16, 1861. WIA and POW Roanoke Island. Exch. Oct. 4, 1862. Major, April 22, 1863. Lt. col., July 8, 1863. WIA Morris Island. Col., Feb. 1, 1864. WIA and POW, April 13, 1864, while on furlough. Released July 24, 1865. Farmer and schoolteacher postwar in Dare and Elizabeth City Cos. Died March 8, 1899, Elizabeth City. Buried Hollywood Cemetery, Elizabeth City.

Whittle, Powhatan Bolling. Born June 26, 1829, Mecklenburg Co., VA. Attd. UVA. Lawyer in Macon, GA, and (from 1854) Lowndes Co., GA, prewar. Unmd. Pvt., Jackson's (Macon) Art., 1861. Pvt., 2d GA Bn., 1861. Lt. col., 38th VA, June 12, 1861. WIA Williamsburg (arm); Malvern Hill (lost arm). WIA three times and POW Gettysburg. Commissioned col., to rank from July 3, 1863. Resigned Nov. 15, 1863. Col. and judge of the military court of A. P. Hill's Corps, Nov. 15, 1863. Lawyer in Macon and Valdosta postwar. Judge. State representative 1880–81. Died Feb. 21, 1905, South Hill, Mecklenburg Co., VA. Buried Whittle Cemetery, near South Hill. Whittle family papers are at UNC. Brother of Lt. Col. L. N. Whittle and CSN Commodore W. C. Whittle. Named for his ancestor, the Algonquin chief Powhatan, Whittle "was a magnificent looking man. Was six and a half tall and straight as his Indian namesake."

Wickliffe, Charles Arthur. Born June 1819, Bardstown, KY. Grad. USMA 1839. Lt., US Army, 1839–42. Major, 14th US Inf., in Mexican War. Lawyer in Ballard Co., KY. State legislator. County attorney 1851–55. Militia colonel. Md. Martha Eugenia Moore. AAG on staff of Gen. Polk, Oct. 1861. Col., 7th KY, Nov. 1, 1861. MWIA the second day of Shiloh. Praised for "distinguished service and noble conduct" in a report on that battle. Died April 22, 1862, near Jackson, TN, at the home of William Butler. Probably buried in an unmarked grave near there. The city of Wickliffe, KY, is named for him.

Wilbourn, Christopher Columbus. Born Dec. 28, 1834, Union Dist., SC. Attd. UMS and UGA. Physician and planter in Panola Co., MS, prewar. Md. Quince Anne Shaw. 1st lt. Co. E, 1st MS, 1861. Capt. Co. G, Hughes MS Cav. Bn., Aug. 25, 1862. Lt. col., Oct. 2, 1862. Col., 4th MS Cav. (formed from Hughes's Bn.), Sept. 17, 1863. Paroled May 12, 1865, Gainesville. Farmer and physician in Panola Co. and Memphis, TN, postwar. Died Oct. 23, 1892, Memphis.

Wilkes, Franklin Collett. Born Dec. 3, 1822, Pulaski, TN. Methodist minister. Moved to TX in the 1850s. Physician in Washington Co. President of Waco Female College. Md. Ann E. Duvall; Matilda A. Graves. Col., 24th TX Cav., April 24, 1862. POW Arkansas Post, exch. April 29, 1863. Col., consolidated 17th/18th/24th/25th TX, after exchange. Court-martialed in Aug. 1863 for raising the white flag at Arkansas Post and for inciting opposition to his brigade commander (Robert Garland). Found not guilty. WIA Chickamauga. Retired to Invalid Corps June 30, 1864. Captured again in LA in late 1864 and not exch. until March 1865. Methodist minister postwar in Brenham and Austin. Ran a drugstore in Brenham. Died Dec. 8, 1881, Lampasas. Buried Oak Hill Cemetery, Lampasas. A new gravestone mistakenly gives his wife's dates of birth and death. First name sometimes given as "Francis." A "tribute" by his old soldiers called him "a pure and honest man, a gallant soldier."

Wilkes, William Henderson. Born April 8, 1833, Raymond, MS. Reared in Giles Co., TN. Grad. U. of Nashville Medical School. Marshall Co. physician prewar. Md. Malvina Holt. 1st lt. Co. D, 53d TN, Dec. 6, 1861. Capt., 1862. WIA and POW Fort Donelson. Exch. Sept. 1862. Lt. col., Sept. 1862. Col., Sept. 26, 1862. Resigned Feb. 25, 1863, due to consumption. Giles Co. physician postwar. Moved to Waco, TX, in 1868. Physician. Editor, Waco *Telephone*. Mayor of Waco. Died Aug. 12, 1896, Waco. Buried Oakwood Cemetery, Waco. Described by a contemporary as "tall, stately and portly . . . distinguished for his urbanity and social qualities."

Wilkinson, George B. Born July 9, 1819, VA. Attd. William & Mary College and UVA. Lawyer in Petersburg, VA, and Yazoo Co., MS. Judge. Md. Cornelia Perkins. Delegate to MS Secession Convention. 1st lt. Co. D, 18th MS, April 1, 1861. Resigned July 29, 1861. Col. and presiding judge, military court of Pemberton's army, Dec. 16, 1862. Resigned Aug. 10, 1863, due to chronic dysentery. Postwar Yazoo City lawyer. Died Aug. 4, 1870, Elizabethtown, KY. Buried Glenwood Cemetery, Yazoo City. An obituary said he was "distinguished for talents and courage."

Wilkinson, John C. Born c. 1832, NC. Lawyer in Raleigh, Smith Co., MS, prewar. Md. Mary W. ——. Lt. Co. C, 8th MS, Oct. 18, 1861. Elected col., May 7, 1862, after contesting the results of the original election (see G. C. Chandler). WIA (severely in breast) and POW Stones River. Exch. April 1863. KIA Atlanta, July 22, 1864. A soldier in Wilkinson's company found him "a brave man and a strict disciplinarian."

Williams, Charles Jones. Born Oct. 1, 1821, Baldwin Co., GA. Attd. USMA. Columbus attorney, farmer. Solicitor general of the Chattahoochee Circuit 1848–52. State representative 1859–60. State House speaker, 1860. Militia general. Major in Mexican War. Md. Mary A. E. Howard. Appointed lt. col. of a projected (but never raised) 1st GA Regulars, Feb. 1861. Col., 1st GA, March 15, 1861. Died Feb. 3, 1862, at home. Buried Linwood Cemetery, Columbus. "[H]ighly distinguished and greatly beloved."

Williams, Christopher Harris, Jr. Born March 14, 1830, Lexington, TN, son of a US congressman. Grad. Cumberland U. in 1850. Memphis lawyer prewar. Md. Anne Louise Sharp. Appointed asst. IG, Provisional Army of TN, May 16, 1861. Capt. Co. D, 27th TN, Sept. 3, 1861. Col., Sept. 10, 1861. KIA Shiloh, April 6, 1862. Buried Cedar Grove Plantation near Yazoo City, MS. A fellow lawyer called Williams "a noble man." Father of US senator John Sharp Williams.

Williams, David Alexander. Born Oct. 19, 1832, Prince Edward Co., VA. Reared in Livingston and Mercer Cos., MO, where his father, a large planter and slaveholder, had moved. Attd. Grand River College, Grundy Co., MO. Prewar lawyer and merchant in Grundy Co. Md. Louisa Wynn. Lt. Co. A, 3d Cav., 8th Div., MSG, July 4, 1861. Capt., Sept. 20, 1861. Resigned Dec. 15, 1861. AAG 2d Cav. Brigade, 8th Div. Adj., 14th Cav., 8th Div., Feb. 3, 1862. Pvt. Co. D, 6th MO Cav., June 22, 1862. Capt., Jan. 27, 1863. Recruited a regiment of cavalry in MO during Price's 1864 Raid. Elected col., Williams's MO Cav. Escaped to Mexico in 1865. Returned to US and settled in Chicot Co., AR. Farmed there and in Jefferson and Desha Cos. To Dallas, TX, in 1876. Lawyer. Alderman. Dallas Co. attorney. Active in UCV. Died March 29, 1898, Terrell, TX. Buried Oakland Cemetery, Dallas. John N. Edwards found Williams "a splendid officer, devoted, intelligent, skilled, experienced, and courageous."

Williams, Gilbert William Martin. Born Feb. 20, 1818, SC. Physician in McIntosh Co., GA, prewar. Minister. Owned a plantation in MS. Delegate to GA Secession Convention. Md. Esther Cohen. Capt. Co. K, 5th GA State Troops, Oct. 6, 1861. Major, Oct. 25, 1861. Lt. col., 47th GA (formed from the 11th Bn.), March 22, 1862. Col., May 12, 1862. Court-martialed Feb. 26, 1863, for neglect of duty and reprimanded. Contracted dysentery in camp in MS in the summer of 1863 and sent on furlough to recover. Died Sept. 1, 1863, at the home of Rev. Isaac Tichenor in Montgomery, AL. Buried Laurel Grove Cemetery, Savannah; reburied Boggs Cemetery, Ludovici, GA. Williams's papers are at Duke U.

Williams, Horatio Gates Perry. Born Feb. 21, 1827, near Tuscaloosa, AL. Family moved to Hillsboro, Union Co., AR, in 1843. Prewar city magistrate. Farmer. Md. Lovicy Tatum; Mary Smith. Sgt., Union Co. Home Guard, 1861. Enlisted March 1, 1862, in Co. B, 19th AR. Capt. Co. B, 1862. Major, May 12, 1862. WIA three times at Corinth. Lt. col., 3d AR Consolidated (formed from parolees of the 12th, 15th, 18th, 19th, 20th AR), 1864. Led regiment at Jenkins Ferry. Col., c. 1864. Postwar Union Co. merchant. Delegate to 1874 state constitutional convention. Died Nov. 18, 1908, Hillsboro. Buried Hillsboro Cemetery.

Williams, James Harrison. Born Oct. 4, 1813, Newberry Dist., SC. Newberry lawyer prewar. Mayor of Newberry 1848–52. State representative 1858–65.

In Seminole and Mexican Wars. Militia general. Md. Jane W. Duckett. Col., 3d SC, Feb. 6, 1861. Dropped at May 1862 reorganization. Col., 9th SC State Reserves (a 90-day unit), 1862–63. Col., 5th SC State Troops (a 6-month unit), 1863–64. Lt. col., 4th SC Reserves Bn., 1864–65. State senator 1865–67. Moved to AR in 1867 to manage lands inherited through his wife. Planter in AR. Member 1874 AR constitutional convention. Died Aug. 21, 1892, at his home in Rocky Comfort (now Foreman), AR. Buried Holy Cross Cemetery, Little River Co. Some sources give his middle name as "Henderson."

Williams, Jesse Milton. Born Jan. 11, 1831, AL (probably Pickens Co.). Reared in De Soto Parish, LA. Attd. UAL. Clerk in store in Mansfield, LA, prewar. Unmd. Capt. Co. D, 2d LA, May 11, 1861. Lt. col., April 30, 1862. Col., 1862 (probably July 16, upon Col. Norwood's death, though some sources have it June 26). WIA and POW Antietam. Exch. Often led Nicholls's LA Brigade, 1863–64. KIA Spotsylvania, May 12, 1864. Buried Stonewall Cemetery, Winchester, VA.

Williams, Josiah Byrd. Born c. 1834, AL. Merchant in Okolona, MS, prewar. Md. Fannie Darden; Lauren Howe. Capt. Co. C, 11th MS, May 13, 1861. Resigned April 21, 1862, to become an officer in the new 41st MS. Capt. Co. I, 41st MS, 1862. Major, May 9, 1862. Lt. col., Nov. 8, 1862. WIA Stones River. Col., March 1, 1864. KIA Jonesboro. Probably buried Confederate Cemetery, Jonesboro. A wartime examining board found Williams "efficient & competent." Some of his wartime letters are at UNC.

Williams, Lewis Burwell, Jr. Born Sept. 13, 1833, Orange Co., VA. Grad. VMI 1855. Taught at VMI, then practiced law in Lexington. Unmd. Capt. Co. A, 13th VA, April 17, 1861. Lt. col., 7th VA, May 15, 1861. Dropped at April 1862 reorganization. Elected col., 1st VA, April 27, 1862. WIA and POW Williamsburg. Exch. Aug. 1862. Praised for his "coolness and courage." MWIA Pickett's Charge. Died July 5, 1863. Buried Green Mount Cemetery, Baltimore, MD; reburied in the soldiers' section of Hollywood Cemetery, Richmond, in 1896, near his division commander, Gen. Pickett.

Williams, Solomon. Born July 1835, NC. Grad. USMA 1858. Lt., US Army, 1858–61. Md. Margaret Pegram. Col., 12th NC, May 14, 1861. Col., 2d NC Cav., June 6, 1862. KIA Brandy Station. Buried in the Arrington family cemetery in Hilliardstown, Nash Co., NC. A member of the 3d AL called Williams "handsome, dashing, and of gallant bearing."

Williams, Titus Vespasian. Born June 2, 1835, Tazewell Co., VA. Grad. VMI 1859. Taught at a military school in Jeffersonville prewar. Md. Sallie George in 1865. Capt. Co. K, 45th VA, 1861. Major, 37th VA, April 21, 1861 (1862 on his service record, but this is a clerical error). Lt. col. by May 1862. Col., June 28, 1862. WIA Cedar Mountain, Chancellorsville, and Cold Harbor. Led Terry's Brigade at Appomattox. Physician in Edinburg, Grundy Co., MO, postwar. Died May 7, 1908, at his son's home in Valeria, IA. Buried Edinburg (aka Odd Fellows) Cemetery. A staff officer found Williams "a splendid officer."

Williams, William Orton. Born July 7, 1839, Georgetown, DC. Distant cousin of Robert E. Lee and said to have courted one of Lee's daughters. Educated in Alexandria, VA. Worked for US Coast Survey. Unmd., though engaged to a "Miss Hamilton" of Chattanooga during the war. Appointed 2d lt., US Army, March 23, 1861. Promoted to 1st lt. in April. Arrested on suspicion of passing information to the South. Released for lack of evidence, he resigned June 10, 1861. 1st lt., CS Regular Army, July 1, 1861. On staff of Gen. Polk in TN and KY. Capt., Tobin's TN Battery, Aug. 5, 1861. Assigned to Gen. Bragg's staff, March 16, 1862. Asst. chief of artillery to Bragg at Shiloh. Appointed col., Dec. 14, 1862, with temporary rank, on Bragg's recommendation, to collect scattered cavalry units into a regiment. Williams, "tall, blonde, erect, scrupulously groomed, strikingly handsome," was "eccentric to the verge of insanity." In Dec. 1862 he legally changed his name to Lawrence Williams Orton. In June 1863 he rode into Union lines in Franklin, TN, in a Union uniform, pretending to be a US officer. Caught, he denied he was a spy and alleged he had made a bet with a fellow officer that he could penetrate Union lines and borrow $50 from a Union general! He was hanged June 9, 1863. Buried Franklin; reburied 6 years later at Tudor Place, Washington, DC, where his portrait now hangs; reburied Oak Hill Cemetery, Washington, DC.

Williamson, James Adams. Born March 1829, Mecklenburg Co., NC. Reared in Charlotte, NC. Grad. Davidson College, where his father was president. Lived in Chester Co., SC. Moved to Hempstead Co., AR, c. 1855. Lawyer and farmer prewar. Delegate to AR Secession Convention. Md. Carrie Muldrow; Mrs. Annie Pearsall Johnson. 1st lt. Co. H, 2d AR MR, 1861. Capt., Sept. 23, 1861. Lt. col., May 8, 1862. Col., Nov. 8, 1862. WIA Resaca (lost leg). Elected state senator in May 1865. Postwar lawyer, planter in Hempstead Co. and Columbus. State representative 1877–78, 1893–94. Died Nov. 25, 1906, Columbus. Buried Mound Cemetery No. 1, near Columbus. A "comrade" of Williamson's stated, "I never knew a more gallant soldier, a truer patriot, a more loyal gentleman." Some of his wartime letters have been published.

Williamson, Robert White. Born Jan. 11, 1832, Rutherford Co., TN. Reared in Carrollton, MS. Grad. Union U. in TN. Lawyer and teacher in Carrollton prewar. Md. Mrs. Mary E. Howze. Sgt. Co. K, 11th MS, April 19, 1861. 2d lt., April 29, 1861. Capt., May 4, 1861. Dropped April 21, 1862. Pvt., then 2d lt. Co. F, 29th

MS. Capt., Dec. 29, 1862. WIA Stones River, Resaca. Col., 24th MS Consolidated, April 10, 1865. Paroled Greensboro. Lawyer in Carrollton and Winona postwar. Chancellor (judge), 1876–78. Moved to Greenwood, MS, in 1888. Died Jan. 16, 1908, Greenwood. Buried Odd Fellows Cemetery, Greenwood.

Willis, Edward Shackelford. Born Aug. 10, 1840, Wilkes Co., GA. Son of a US congressman and distant relative of George Washington. Attd. USMA, resigning Feb. 5, 1861, upon GA's secession. Appointed junior 2d lt., GA Regular army, Feb. 1861. Lt., CS Regular Army, March 16, 1861. Adj., 12th GA, July 5, 1861. Asst. chief of artillery on Stonewall Jackson's staff, appointed Jan. 1862. Lt. col., 12th GA, Dec. 13, 1862, promoted over the heads of senior officers who waived their rights to allow the promotion. Col., Jan. 22, 1863. Detached with a brigade-size task force to scour southwest VA for deserters, fall 1863. WIA Wilderness (thigh). MWIA Bethesda Church, May 30, 1864, while leading Pegram's VA Brigade in an attack. Died May 31, 1864, near Richmond. Buried Laurel Grove Cemetery, Savannah; reburied Hollywood Cemetery, Richmond, in 1879. Willis won repeated praise from subordinates and superiors: one soldier noted that "no regiment had a better commanding officer than the Twelfth Georgia." It is said that his promotion to brigadier general was delivered on his deathbed. Although the promotion was clearly imminent, and he was commanding a brigade, no firm evidence of that promotion can be found.

Willis, William Henry. Born Feb. 10, 1829, Jones Co., GA. Reared in Talbot Co. Businessman in Oglethorpe, Macon Co., prewar. Md. Isabella Griffin, cousin of Col. Joel Griffin. Lt. Co. I, 4th GA, April 29, 1861. Capt. Co. E, 1862. Major, May 30, 1863. Lt. col., Aug. 15, 1863. Col., Aug. 5, 1864. Oglethorpe merchant postwar. State representative 1873–77. Died Dec. 31, 1889, Oglethorpe. Buried Oglethorpe City Cemetery. A fellow soldier praised Willis as "a splendid officer, careful of the comfort of his men, always at his post and ready for every call of duty."

Wilson, Andrew Neal. Born c. 1829, TN. Farmer in Henderson, TN, prewar. Md. Martha Jane Robins; J. A. Moore. Capt. Co. C, 52d TN, Dec. 3, 1861. Major, May 8, 1862. Lt. col., 51st TN Consolidated, Aug. 20, 1862. Col., 21st TN Cav., Feb. 4, 1864. WIA Tupelo. Paroled May 11, 1865, Gainesville. Farmer in Lee Co., MS, in 1880. Store owner, teacher, state legislator. Died Nov. 1897 on a visit to Guntown, MS. Buried Ellistown Church Cemetery, Union Co., MS. A "brave and chivalrous man."

Wilson, Daniel Allen, Jr. Born June 20, 1823, Cumberland Co., VA. Attd. Washington U. and Hampden-Sydney College. Lynchburg lawyer in 1850. New Orleans tobacco merchant and lawyer prewar. In Mexican War. Unmd. ADC to governor of LA, 1861. Capt. Co. I, 7th LA, June 7, 1861. Capt. and judge advocate, military court of Jackson's Corps, Dec. 16, 1862. Col. and judge, military court of Ewell's Corps, Nov. 1, 1863. Paroled Farmville, VA, April 1865. Railroad agent in New Orleans in 1880. Died May 22, 1893, New Orleans. Buried Presbyterian Cemetery, Lynchburg. Known as "Big Dan" for his "immense size."

Wilson, John Andrew. Born Sept. 21, 1837, Williamson Co., TN. Farmer in Eagleville prewar. Md. Dora Mason. Enlisted in state service July 8, 1861. Capt. Co. D, 24th TN, Aug. 24, 1861. Major, July 15, 1862. Lt. col., July 29, 1862. WIA Stones River. Col., Jan. 4, 1863. WIA Atlanta (leg) and Franklin (side). Paroled May 1865. Resided in Nashville and McMinnville, TN, and Fort Worth, TX. Dry goods salesman. Moved to Bowie, TX, in 1895. Bowie city collector. Died March 19, 1932, at his Bowie home, the last Confederate colonel to die. Buried Elmwood Cemetery, Bowie.

Wilson, Samuel Mazyck. Born Oct. 14, 1817, either in VA or Charleston, SC, son of a naval officer. Reared in Portsmouth, VA. Attd. UVA. Portsmouth lawyer prewar. Farmer and bank president. President of Seaboard and Roanoke Railroad. Md. Myra R. Barraud; Sallie B. Cocke. Lt. col., 7th VA Bn., 1861. Elected col., 61st VA (formed from the 7th Bn.), May 22, 1862, but declined the commission. There was some question whether the 61st had the required ten companies in order to be able to elect a colonel. State representative 1863–64. Postwar farmer in Powhatan Co. Died Aug. 20, 1876, Powhatan Co., of heart disease. Buried "Blemo," Powhatan Co.; reburied Hollywood Cemetery, Richmond, in 1904. Cousin of Gen. Philip St. G. Cocke, whose Powhatan Co. properties he managed after the war.

Wilson, William Tunstall. Born Dec. 15, 1815, Danville, VA. Moved to GA by 1835. Farmer and judge in Houston Co. Mayor of Oglethorpe. Railroad agent in Atlanta 1853–61. Alderman and postmaster there. Mexican War veteran. Capt. of vol. militia. Md. Marion M. Lumpkin. Commissary, 7th GA, May 31, 1861. WIA 1st Manassas. Col., Feb. 13, 1862. KIA 2d Manassas, shot through the head, Aug. 30, 1862. Buried Warrenton, VA; reburied Oakland Cemetery, Atlanta. Wilson's last words were "thank God, I've lived long enough to know that we have whipped the yankees twice on the same field." Gen. David Jones called Wilson "the gray-haired hero."

Wimbish, John. Born May 25, 1812, Surry Co., NC. Attd. USMA. Wealthy merchant in Granville Co., NC, prewar, with a plantation in Coahoma Co., MS. Md. Lucy Ann Townes. Col., 54th NC, May 16, 1862. Resigned Sept. 3, 1862, in order to tend to his MS plantations, which were threatened by Union troops. Later appointed lt. col., 23d Bn. NC Home Guard, organized to protect blockade runners. Merchant in Halifax Co., VA, postwar. Entered Richmond, VA, Confederate Soldiers' Home in 1893. Died May 30, 1905, Richmond. Buried Hollywood Cemetery. Wimbish family papers are at VAHS.

Winans, Wesley Parker. Born Oct. 19, 1825, Wilkinson Co., MS. Grad. 1st in his class at Centenary College, a school his father (a noted preacher) helped found. Grad. ULA law school. Attorney in Shreveport, LA, prewar. Md. Jane Harper. Capt., "Caddo Tenth" company, Feb. 19, 1861. Capt. Co. G (the "Caddo Tenth"), 19th LA, Oct. 21, 1861. Major, Nov. 26, 1861. Lt. col., May 8, 1862. Col., July 15, 1862. KIA Missionary Ridge. Buried on the battlefield (his service record has several letters regarding where, but the spot appears to be unknown). Douglas Cater said Winans was "loved" by his men, and Gen. Gibson called him "a fine specimen, not only of a confident officer, but of a Southern gentleman."

Wingfield, James H. Born Oct. 5, 1826, VA. Accountant in New Orleans, LA, in 1850. Farmed in St. Helena Parish, LA, in 1860. Md. Mary Ann Decker. Capt. Co. G (the "Wingfield Rifles"), 4th LA, May 25, 1861. Lt. col., 9th LA PR Bn., May 28, 1862. POW Port Hudson but broke parole and rejoined regiment. Col., 3d LA Cav. (Wingfield's), at its Sept. 1864 organization. Served in LA and MS. Resided in New Orleans postwar. Died April 2, 1874, New Orleans. Buried Metairie Cemetery.

Winn, William John. Born Feb. 9, 1838, Walthourville, Liberty Co., GA. Attd. GMI. Planter in Liberty Co. prewar. Md. Mary Eliza Fleming. 2d lt. Co. H, 25th GA, Aug. 27, 1861. Major, Sept. 2, 1862. WIA Chickamauga. Col., Nov. 16, 1863. WIA Atlanta. Liberty Co. schoolteacher postwar. Railroad engineer. Moved to Savannah in 1877. City engineer there. Died Nov. 25, 1906, Savannah. Buried Laurel Grove Cemetery.

Winston, John Anthony. Born Sept. 4, 1812, Madison Co., AL. Attd. La Grange College and Cumberland U. Lived in Franklin then Sumter Cos. Moved to Mobile in 1844. Planter, cotton broker, and merchant. State legislator. Governor of AL 1853–57. Md. Mary A. Walker; Mary W. Logwood. Col., 8th AL, June 11, 1861. Resigned June 16, 1862, due to rheumatism. In 1864 he tried to raise reserve forces in AL. Elected to US Senate in 1867 but denied seat. Died Dec. 21, 1871, Mobile. Buried Winston Cemetery, west of Gainesville, AL. Sec. of War Seddon called him a man "of marked individuality, firm and peculiar in his opinions, rather repellent than popular in his manners."

Winston, John Hughes. Born Jan. 22, 1815, Stokes Co., NC. Moved to Platte Co., MO, in 1838. Prewar farmer, militia major. Md. Elizabeth Tibbs. Col., 2d Inf., 5th Div., MSG. Temporarily led the 5th Div. in March 1862. Col., "1st Missouri Rifle Regiment," June–Sept. 1862. It appears this unit was made up of unattached soldiers from his old MSG regiment. It is uncertain whether it organized itself as a PACS regiment. Captured March 22, 1864, in Platte City, while recruiting. Imprisoned at Alton, IL, Military Prison. Sentenced to 5 years imprisonment by a Union military court. Returned to Platte Co. after the war. Farmer. State legislator 1872–76. Died July 25, 1901, at his Platte Co. home. Buried Winston Cemetery, near the present-day Mid-Continent International Airport.

Winston, John Reynolds. Born April 13, 1839, Leakesville, NC. Grad. Trinity College in 1859. Teacher in Reidsville prewar. Md. Marion Long in 1866. Capt. Co. F, 45th NC, March 11, 1862. Major, Feb. 9, 1863. Lt. col., June 26, 1863. WIA and POW Gettysburg. Escaped from Johnson's Island Prison Jan. 1864. Col., May 19, 1864. WIA Spotsylvania (leg) and Sayler's Creek. Appmx. Principal of a school in Memphis, TN, 1865–67. Farmer in Caswell Co., NC. Editor of a Greenback Party newspaper. Lost four races for Congress under three different party labels (Greenbacker, Republican, and "Liberal"). Died March 7, 1888, at his home in Caswell Co. Buried Red House Presbyterian Churchyard, Semora, Caswell Co. "Known as a man of deep piety, stern integrity, and cool courage."

Witcher, William Addison. Born 1820, Pittsylvania Co., VA. Lawyer in Pittsylvania Co. prewar, except for 14 years (1841–55) spent in Clay Co., MO. Editor, *Western Sentinel*. Md. Evelyn Major. Capt., "Turkey Cock Grays" (Co. I, 21st VA), June 29, 1861. Lt. col., Dec. 1, 1862. Col., appointed April 1863, backdated to rank from Dec. 1, 1862. WIA Chancellorsville and in May 1864. Appmx. Farmer in Pittsylvania Co. postwar. State representative 1875–77. Lost races for the State Senate and Congress. Died Jan. 29, 1887, Pittsylvania Co. Buried in a family burying ground near Callands, VA. S. Basset French termed him "a man of commanding talent, sterling courage, and generous qualities."

Withers, Robert Enoch. Born Sept. 18, 1821, near Lynchburg, VA. Grad. UVA Medical school. Physician in Baltimore, Lynchburg, and (from 1858) Danville prewar. Capt. and major of vol. militia. Md. Mary V. Royall. Col., 18th VA, May 23, 1861. WIA in lung at Gaines's Mill and never returned to the army. Retired July 21, 1864, due to his wound. Post commander at Danville thereafter. Moved to Lynchburg in 1866. Active and prominent Mason. Editor of a "Conservative Party" newspaper. Lt. gov. 1873–75. US senator 1875–81. US consul at Hong Kong 1885–89. Wrote an autobiography. Died Sept. 21, 1907, on his Wytheville farm. Buried East End Cemetery, Wytheville.

Withers, Robert Woodson. Born Jan. 18, 1835, "Ivanhoe," Campbell Co., VA. Educated at Piedmont Institute in Liberty. Campbell Co. farmer prewar. Capt. of vol. militia. Md. Blanche T. Payne. Pvt. Co. I, 42d VA, June 11, 1861. Ord. sgt.,

1861. Lt., Sept. 20, 1861. Capt., April 21, 1862. Lt. col., Nov. 30, 1862. WIA Gettysburg. Col., Nov. 29, 1863. WIA (hand) North Anna. WIA (lung) and POW Shepherdstown, Aug. 25, 1864. Exch. Oct. 31, 1864. On sick leave thereafter. Paroled May 27, 1865, Lynchburg. Merchant in Lynchburg postwar. Farmer. Deputy sheriff. Clerk of the county court. Died Nov. 14, 1896, Rustberg. Probably buried in an unmarked grave in the Withers family cemetery at "Ivanhoe," near Rustberg. Cousin of Col. R. E. Withers.

Withers, William Temple. Born Jan. 8, 1825, Harrison Co., KY. Grad. Bacon College in KY. Lawyer in Cynthiana, KY. Lawyer and planter in Jackson, MS. Officer in Mexican War. WIA Buena Vista. Md. Martha Sharkey. Acting general of KY recruits in 1861, while commanding Camp Boone, a training camp on the TN-KY border. Requested by the sec. of war to raise an artillery regiment. Capt. Co. A, 1st MS Art., March 22, 1862. Col., May 14, 1862. Often on sick leave, due to his Mexican War wounds. Distinguished at Chickasaw Bluff, while leading the Confederate right. POW Vicksburg, while commanding artillery there. Later served in the Mobile defenses. Retired to Invalid Corps March 5, 1865. Lawyer in Jackson, MS, postwar. Moved back to near Lexington, KY, in 1871 and bred horses. Died June 16, 1889, Lexington. Buried Lexington Cemetery. An obituary called Withers "a thorough Christian gentleman, a noble and honest man."

Witherspoon, William Wallace. Born c. 1832, MS. Reared in Copiah Co. Grad. UMS. Attorney in Napoleon, AR, in 1860. Pvt. Co. C, 1st AR MR, June 15, 1861. WIA Wilson's Creek, discharged Oct. 15, 1861. 2d lt. Co. A, 36th MS, March 6, 1862. Major, March 12, 1862. Col., May 12, 1862. Often led a brigade. POW Vicksburg and paroled. Cashiered for drunkenness in 1864. The sentence was later voided due to an irregularity by the court. MWIA Franklin, died 1865 near there. Buried McGavock Confederate Cemetery, Franklin. A soldier in the 36th found Witherspoon "a brilliant young officer," but often tipsy, and when tipsy "harsh, overbearing and tyrannical." Nicknamed "Pewterspoon" by the men of the 3d LA.

Witt, Allen Rufus. Born Aug. 17, 1830, Hamilton Co., TN. Reared in AL and Van Buren Co., AR. Attd. Arkansas College in Fayetteville. Elected AR land commissioner in 1857. Took a herd to CA in 1859, remaining there until 1861. Md. Henrietta C. Miller. Pvt., Pulaski Light Art. (State Troops), April–Sept. 1861. Capt. Co. A, 10th AR, July 27, 1861. WIA Shiloh. Col., May 8, 1862. The 10th had a reputation for lax discipline and mutinous conduct, in part due to lack of officers and the conduct of the previous colonel (T. D. Merrick). Witt, a competent officer, struggled with little success to correct this. POW Port Hudson, early in the siege (May 28). He led a daring prisoner escape from the transport *Maple Leaf* while being shipped to a northern prison. Col., 10th AR Cav. (the re-

mains of his old regiment, mounted), c. 1864. The 10th served in Price's Raid
and as a "guerrilla" unit in north AR behind Union lines. Paroled Jacksonport,
AR, June 5, 1865. Postwar lived in Van Buren Co. and (after 1876) Conway,
Faulkner Co. State senator 1866–67. Druggist in Conway. County judge. Militia gen. Died April 29, 1903, Little Rock. Buried Oak Grove Cemetery, Conway.

Wood, Alfred Campbell. Born Nov. 29, 1826, Fayette Co., GA. Prewar merchant in Randolph Co., AL. Md. Emily Pate in 1863. Capt. Co. K, 14th AL, July
22, 1861. Major, May 12, 1862. Lt. col., June 30, 1862. Col., July 8, 1862. WIA
Frayser's Farm. Resigned Oct. 3, 1862, due to ill health. Died July 4, 1866, Randolph Co. Buried High Pines Church, Randolph Co.

Wood, James Hall. Born Aug. 26, 1840, Rowan Co., NC. Living with his half
brother (a physician) in Rowan Co. in 1860. Capt. Co. B, 4th NC, May 16, 1861.
WIA Seven Pines, Gaines's Mill. Major, July 22, 1862. Lt. col., Dec. 23, 1862. Col.,
May 19, 1864. KIA Snicker's Gap, July 18, 1864. Buried at the Ware farm near
the battlefield; reburied Third Creek Presbyterian Church, near Cleveland,
Rowan Co. Col. Osborne called Wood "a most faithful, brave and conscientious
Christian soldier; a lovely gentleman and skillful officer."

Wood, John Taylor. Born Aug. 13, 1830, Fort Snelling, near what is today
Minneapolis, MN. Grandson of Pres. Zachary Taylor; brother of Col. Robert
Crooke Wood Jr. Grad. Annapolis, 1853. Lt., USN, 1847–61. Professor at Annapolis 1855–58, 1860–61. Md. Lola Mackubin. Lt., CSN, Oct. 4, 1861. Served
on the CSS *Virginia* in her fight with the *Monitor*. Col. and ADC to Pres. Davis
(his uncle), Jan. 23, 1863. Commanded several commando raids on Union shipping in VA and NC waters, 1862–64. Commanded CSS *Tallahassee,* a commerce
raider, in 1864. Took 31 prizes. Lived in Halifax, Canada, postwar. Insurance
agent. Died July 19, 1904, Halifax. Buried Camp Hill Cemetery, Halifax. Papers
at UNC. Subject of a biography.

Wood, Robert Clifton. Born Feb. 20, 1828, Charlotte Co., VA. Family moved
to Marshall, MO, in 1842. Prewar merchant in Marshall and New Mexico. Livestock dealer in Sacramento, CA. Rancher, noted Indian fighter. Leader of
Crabbe's filibustering expedition into Sonora, Mexico. Md. Jennie Reynolds. Returned to MO just before the war and became major of Gen. Price's bodyguard,
MSG. col., and ADC to Price in MSG. Lt. PACS and ADC to Price, March 20,
1862. Capt., Feb. 27, 1863, and ordered to raise troops in northern MO. Major,
14th MO Cav. Bn., Sept. 25, 1863. Raised a regiment during Price's Raid. Stabbed
to death Major Lachlan Maclean of Price's staff in Dec. 1864. Tried and convicted of murder, but sentence set aside by military authorities. Paroled July 27,
1865, Columbus, TX, as col. Postwar rancher and miner in TX; Kansas City;
Prescott, AZ; and Tucson, AZ. Died Oct. 12, 1902, Tucson. Buried Tucson City

(Evergreen) Cemetery. Wood's service record contains an extensive transcript of his trial for murder. It is clear that Gen. Magruder voided the sentence because he wished to retain the gallant Wood in command.

Wood, Robert Crooke, Jr. Born April 4, 1832, Fort Snelling, near what is today Minneapolis, MN. Attd. KMI, St. Mary's College, and USMA. Lt., US Army, 1855–58. Lived with his father, a US Army surgeon, in DC in 1860. Md. Mary Trist, of a prominent New Orleans family. Capt., CS Regular Army, March 8, 1861. AAG to Gen. Bragg at Pensacola. Resigned captaincy, Oct. 15, 1861. Lt. col., Wirt Adams's (aka 1st, Wood's) MS Cav., Oct. 15, 1861. POW, May 5, 1862, Lebanon, TN. To Johnson's Island Prison. Exch. Sept. 1862. Col., Wood's Confederate Cav., Sept. 25, 1863. Led brigade of MS Cav. 1864–65. Commander of Central Sub-District of MS, Nov. 1864. Paroled May 17, 1865, Jackson. Sugar planter in LA postwar. Sec. of New Orleans city council. Businessman in Colombia and elsewhere. President of Gatling Gun Co. in Buffalo, NY. Died Dec. 4, 1900, New Orleans. Buried Metairie Cemetery. Gen. Hardee considered Wood "a brave, active and intelligent officer." Wood's grandfather was Pres. Zachary Taylor; Col. John T. Wood was his brother.

Wood, William Basil. Born Oct. 31, 1820, Nashville, TN. Family moved to Florence, AL, in 1821. Attd. La Grange College. Lawyer, judge, Methodist minister. Owned a line of steamboats. Md. Sarah B. Leftwich. Col., 16th AL, Aug. 8, 1861. Frequently led brigade and was "much loved by his men." WIA Stones River. Appointed presiding judge of the military court of Longstreet's Corps April 24, 1863. With ANV rest of war. Resigned as col. of the 16th, June 19, 1863, due to the appointment and his "shattered constitution" (typhoid and rheumatism). Paroled May 19, 1865, Mobile. Judge, railroad president postwar. Died April 3, 1891, Florence, buried Florence Cemetery. Brother of Gen. S. A. M. Wood.

Woodruff, Lewis Thompson. Born March 5, 1816, Farmington, CT. Moved to Winnsboro, SC, in 1834. To Mobile, AL, in 1839. Clerk, merchant. Capt. of vol. militia. City councilman. Unmd. Capt. Co. K, 3d AL, May 3, 1861. Lt. col., 36th AL, May 13, 1862. Col., March 16, 1863. WIA New Hope Church and disabled. Retired Dec. 13, 1864. Mobile grocer postwar. President of Mobile Board of Trade. Killed in Mobile, May 25, 1869, when a wall fell on him during a fire. Buried Magnolia Cemetery, Mobile. His fellow officers stated that Woodruff was "the most efficient and thorough soldier they had seen in the volunteer service."

Woods, Michael Leonard. Born April 1, 1833, Woods Ferry, near Greeneville, TN. Educated at Panther Springs Academy in TN. Lawyer in Montgomery, AL. State legislator. Md. Martha Pickett. Pvt. Co. C, 3d AL ("Montgomery True Blues"), Jan. 8, 1861. Asst. commissary, 13th AL, July 19, 1861. Col., 46th AL (a regiment he raised), May 20, 1862. POW Champion Hill. Imprisoned at Johnson's Island. Exchanged Jan. 6, 1865. Notified of the exchange in March 1865, Woods traveled to Augusta, where he was put in charge of 400 men seeking to rejoin the Army of TN in NC. Fought at Salisbury with this improvised unit. Then put in charge of the reorganized 19th AL. Called "energetic," "willing and competent" by his superiors. Postwar lawyer in Prattville and Montgomery, AL, New York, and Washington, DC. Died Sept. 9, 1911, Montgomery. Buried Oakwood Cemetery, Montgomery.

Woods, Peter Cavanaugh. Born Dec. 30, 1819, Shelbyville, TN. Grew up in Lawrence Co., AL. Attd. U. of Louisville Medical College. Prewar physician in Water Valley, MS; Bastrop, TX; and San Marcos, TX. Md. Georgia V. Lawshe; Ella Ogletree. Capt. Co., A, 32d (aka 36th) TX Cav., March 22, 1862. Col., June 1, 1862. WIA (shot in the arm) Yellow Bayou. Often led brigade. Postwar physician and farmer in San Marcos. Died Jan. 27, 1898, San Marcos, buried San Marcos City Cemetery. A death notice called him "bravest of the brave, tender as the tenderest."

Woodward, John Jefferson. Born Oct. 8, 1808, Fairfield Dist., SC. Grad. USC in 1827. Planter in Talladega Co., AL. Judge. State legislator. Md. Rebecca Pierson. Capt. Co. E, 10th AL, June 4, 1861. Major, Sept. 4, 1861. Lt. col., Dec. 20, 1861. Col., March 14, 1862. KIA Gaines's Mill. Buried Sion Presbyterian Church Cemetery, Winnsboro, SC. A 1919 newspaper article said "his men loved him as a man and idolized him as a commander."

Woodward, Thomas Griffitts. Born July 30, 1827. New Haven, CT, son of an influential newspaper editor. Attd. USMA. Moved to Christian Co., KY, c. 1847–48. Teacher in Garrettsburg. Lawyer. Capt., Woodward's Co. (a 12-month unit, soon attached to the 1st KY Cav.), TN Cav., June 25, 1861. Lt. col., 1st KY Cav., 1861 (probably Dec. 19). Col., March 14, 1862. Lt. col., Woodward's KY Cav. Bn., 1862. Col., Woodward's 2d KY Cav., Dec. 1862. Court-martialed four times during the war, once suspended from command and twice reprimanded. Led forces that captured the Union garrison at Clarksville, TN, in 1862. WIA in the attack on Dover in 1863. Detached on recruiting duty in KY in 1864. Shot and killed while parading around the streets of Union-held Hopkinsville, KY, Aug. 19, 1864. Buried Riverside Cemetery, Hopkinsville. A short man (termed "an insignificant little cuss" by a Union colonel he captured at Clarksville), eccentric, extravagantly dressed, he is said to have ridden into Hopkinsville alone and intoxicated, vowing he would take the town single-handed.

Wooldridge, William Beverly. Born June 27, 1827, Chesterfield Co., VA. Attd. UVA. Chesterfield Co. planter prewar. Md. Martha Virginia Cowan Stanard. Lt. Co. B, 4th VA Cav., April 23, 1861. Capt., April 25, 1862. Major, Sept. 4, 1863. WIA May 9, 1864, near Spotsylvania. Leg amputated. Lt. col., May 12,

1864. Col., Nov. 1, 1864. Collier in Chesterfield Co. postwar. Died there March 15, 1881. Buried Maury Cemetery, Richmond.

Wortham, George Washington. Born c. 1823, NC. Attd. UNC. Lawyer in Oxford, Granville Co., prewar. Elected capt. of the "Granville Independent Grays" in Nov. 1860. Md. Virginia Ridley; Mary A. Watson. Capt. Co. D, 12th NC, April 22, 1861. Major, 50th NC, April 15, 1862. Lt. col., Dec. 1, 1862. Col., Nov. 10, 1863. Under arrest in Feb. 1864. Paroled Greensboro. Attorney in Oxford postwar. Died Sept. 27, 1883, Oxford. Wortham allegedly bolted for the rear during an attack at Bentonville.

Worthington, Edward Stade. Born Oct. 29, 1824, Mercer Co., KY. Grad. Centre College, 1844. Louisville lawyer. State legislator. Md. Ann E. Powell. Capt. and QM, 4th KY, Sept. 1861. Disabled for field duty by a railroad accident Sept. 10, 1862. Col. and judge, military court of Polk's Corps, Dec. 16, 1862. POW at Fayetteville, GA, July 28, 1864. Postwar Louisville lawyer. Died there April 30, 1874, of consumption. Buried Cave Hill Cemetery. Gov. Hawes recommended him for the court as a "man of the best legal qualifications, is sober, industrious."

Wright, Augustus Romaldus. Born June 16, 1813, Wrightsboro, GA. Attd. UGA and Litchfield (CT) Law School. Reared in Crawfordville. Lawyer in Cassville, 1836–55. Judge 1847–49. Moved to Rome in 1855. US congressman 1857–59. Delegate to GA Secession Convention, voting against secession. Md. Elizabeth Richardson; Adeline Allman. Col., 38th GA (often called the "Wright Legion"), Aug. 27, 1861. Resigned Feb. 14, 1862, to enter the Confederate Congress. Confederate congressman 1862–65. Arrested in 1864 by Union forces and sent to Washington, where Pres. Lincoln offered to appoint him gov. of GA. Attorney in Rome postwar. Baptist preacher. Died March 31, 1891, at his home near Rome, of apoplexy. Buried Myrtle Hill Cemetery, Rome. Even though Wright had four sons in the Confederate army, some Confederates doubted his loyalty.

Wright, Daniel Boone. Born Feb. 17, 1812, near Mt. Pleasant, Giles Co., TN. Grad. Cumberland U. Lawyer and farmer in Tippah Co., MS. Veteran of Seminole War. US congressman 1853–57. Delegate to MS Secession Convention. Md. Martha McDonald; Mrs. Mary McDonald Tarpley. Capt., "Dixie Guards" (later Co. K, 34th MS), March 10, 1862. Lt. col., 34th MS, April 16, 1862. Praised for "fearless coolness" at Farmington. WIA (right arm) and POW Perryville. To Camp Chase Prison. Exch. Jan. 13, 1863. Resigned Aug. 5, 1863, due to his Perryville wounds. Col. and judge, military court of Forrest's Corps, April 6, 1864. Paroled May 18, 1865, La Grange, TN. Postwar Tippah Co. and Ashland (Benton Co.) farmer and lawyer. Died Dec. 27, 1887, Ashland. Buried McDonald Cemetery near Ashland.

Wright, Gilbert Jefferson. Born Feb. 18, 1825, near Lawrenceville, GA. Known as "Gid" Wright. Attorney in Albany. Mexican War veteran. Md. Dorothy Chandler. Lt. Co. D, Cobb's GA Legion, Aug. 10, 1861. Capt., May 8, 1862. Major, June 10, 1863. Col., Oct. 9, 1863. Led P. M. B. Young's Brigade, 1864–65. A 6-foot, 4-inch giant known for his "bulldog courage" and "stentorian voice." Lawyer and farmer in Albany and (from 1887) Forsyth. Mayor of Albany 1866–69. Judge, 1875–80. Died June 3, 1895, Forsyth. Buried Town Cemetery, Forsyth. Papers at VAHS and GDAH.

Wright, John Crowell. Born March 14, 1835, Talbot Co., GA. Family moved to Union Co., AR, in 1843. Prewar planter in Union Co. Md. Mary Alabama Newton. Capt. Co. D, 15th AR, Nov. 4, 1861. Lt. col., Jan. 2, 1862. Escaped from Fort Donelson before the surrender. Lt. col., 26th AR, July 7, 1862. Defeated for election as col., Dec. 1863, and resigned. Lt. col., 2d (Wright's) AR Cav. Bn., State Troops, Dec. 17, 1863. Col., 12th AR Cav. (formed from 2d Bn.), Feb. 15, 1864. Unwounded in the war but had four horses shot from under him. Postwar Union Co. farmer. State legislator. County clerk. Died Jan. 18, 1915, El Dorado, AR. Buried Woodlawn Cemetery, El Dorado. Wright's wartime memoirs were published in 1982. They make clear that Gen. Hindman's appointing the original field officers of the 26th and not allowing an election caused much friction in the regiment. His sister md. Col. Asa Morgan of the 26th.

Wright, John Vines. Born June 28, 1828, Purdy, McNairy Co., TN. Brother of Gen. Marcus Wright. Attd. UTN. McNairy Co. lawyer prewar. US congressman 1855–61. Mexican War veteran. Militia colonel. Md. Georgia Hays. Capt. Co. F, 13th TN, May 30, 1861. Col., June 24, 1861. Injured at Belmont when his horse was shot from under him. Resigned Dec. 1, 1861, on being elected to Congress. Confederate congressman 1862–65. Lawyer in AL; Columbia, TN; Nashville; and Washington, DC, postwar. Justice, TN Supreme Court. Lost race for governor of TN in 1880. Died June 11, 1908, Washington. Buried Rock Creek Cemetery, Washington. Gen. A. J. Vaughn said of Wright, "No man ever stood higher in the estimation of his soldiers or was more beloved by them."

Wright, Moses Hannibal. Born Aug. 13, 1836, Liberty, TN. Grad. USMA 1859. Lt., US Army, 1859–61, serving with the ordnance dept. Md. Sallie Sehon. Capt. and ordnance officer, Provisional Army of TN, May 15, 1861. 1st lt., CS Regular Army, March 16, 1861. Operated Nashville Arsenal. Commanded Atlanta Arsenal, 1862–64. Capt. of artillery, PACS, June 9, 1862. Major of ordnance, Sept. 3, 1862. Col., July 14, 1863. Commanded post of Atlanta. Upon the fall of Atlanta in 1864 Wright transferred to the Macon and Columbus arsenals.

Paroled Augusta, GA. Postwar cotton factor in Cincinnati, New York City, and Louisville. Died Jan. 9, 1886, Louisville, when his office building caught fire and collapsed. Buried Cave Hill Cemetery, Louisville.

Yager, William Overall. Born April 3, 1833, VA. Reared in Luray, VA. Grad. VMI 1852. Moved out west. Postmaster, judge in KS. To San Antonio and later Seguin, TX. Md. Mary E. Rhodes. 1st lt. and adj., 1st TX MR, April 15, 1861. Assigned as AAAG, Western Military Dist. of TX, Dec. 18, 1861. Major, Dec. 28, 1861. Assigned Feb. 1862 to 3d TX Cav. Bn. Lt. col., 1st TX Cav. (formed in part from the 3d Bn.), May 2, 1863. Col., April 13, 1864. Paroled Sept. 2, 1865, San Antonio. Returned to Luray (Page Co.) postwar. Manufacturer of "wood goods." County treasurer, school official. State representative 1874–75, 1879–80. Bank president. Died Jan. 20, 1904, at his home near Luray. Buried Yager Cemetery, north of Luray. A private described Yager as "sociable and devoid in the remarkable degree of the arogant [sic] manner that characterized many of the officers."

Yarborough, William Henry. Born March 1, 1840, Franklin Co., NC. Merchant in Franklin Co. prewar. Md. Lucy Massenburg Davis. Lt. Co. L, 15th NC, May 20, 1861. Capt., May 2, 1862. Major, May 2, 1862. Lt. col., Feb. 27, 1863. Col., Nov. 4, 1864. Appmx. Wounded four times during the war. Merchant and farmer in Franklin Co. postwar. Died Aug. 3, 1914, Louisburg, NC. Buried Oakwood Cemetery, north of Louisburg.

Yell, Fountain Pitts. Born 1834, TN, son of Gen. James Yell, AR State Troops, and nephew of Gov. Archibald Yell of AR. Grad. WMI. Attd. Cumberland U. Law School. Prewar attorney in Pine Bluff, AR. State representative 1860–61. Md. Mattie——. Capt. Co. A, Morgan's Bn. (later 26th AR), May 3, 1862. Major, June 4, 1862. Col., 26th AR, Dec. 6, 1863. He tried to resign in 1863, in order to move his family to TX. KIA Pleasant Hill. John C. Wright's memoirs call Yell "a proud, ambitious and gallant gentleman."

Young, Andrew. Born 1814, Grundy Co., TN. Moved to Blairsville, Union Co., GA, in 1841. Attd. Augusta Medical College and Jefferson Medical College. Physician. State representative 1853–54. State senator 1857–58. Md. Sarah Barclay, sister of Col. William P. Barclay. Surgeon, 2d GA, April 27, 1861. Resigned Nov. 19, 1861. Surgeon, Dept. of Savannah, 1861. Pvt. Co. K, 23d GA, Aug. 31, 1861. Capt., Nov. 17, 1861. WIA Seven Pines in lung. Resigned in 1863. Capt. of GA State Guard cav., 1863–64. Lt. col., 30th GA Cav. Bn. (a unit that operated in northern GA), April 7, 1864. Col., 11th GA Cav. (formed from the 30th), Nov. 14, 1864. Moved to Cleburne, TX, in 1867. Physician there and edited the local newspaper. Died Sept. 24, 1889, Cleburne. Buried Cleburne Cemetery. Gen. Howell Cobb described Young as "an excellent officer, brave & energetic."

Young, Overton Stephen. Born Sept. 26, 1826, Lawrenceville, GA. Moved to Brazoria Co., TX, in 1848. Wealthy planter. Md. Mrs. Ann E. (Compton) Manadue. Col., 12th TX, Dec. 1, 1861. Often led brigade. WIA (wrist) Jenkins Ferry. Postwar planter in Brazoria Co. Died Sept. 18, 1877, Galveston. Buried Old Catholic Cemetery, Galveston. Gen. Waul recommended Young for promotion as an officer of "great skill" with "much fitness for command."

Young, William Cocke. Born May 7, 1812 (per his tombstone—some sources give May 12), Davidson Co., TN. Moved to TX in 1837. Lived in Red River, Grayson, and Cooke Cos. prewar. Lawyer, dist. attorney, sheriff. US marshal. Mexican War veteran. Md. Sophia Gleaves Thomas; Ann Hutchinson; Mrs. Margaret Black. Col., 3d TX Mounted Volunteers (a state unit), May 3, 1861. Captured Forts Arbuckle, Wichita, and Cobb in the Indian Territory. Appointed commander, 8th TX militia dist., June 10, 1861. Col., 11th TX Cav., Oct. 2, 1861. Resigned April 16, 1862, due to ill health, and returned to his Cooke Co. home. Murdered Oct. 16, 1862, while leading a posse against an outlaw gang. Buried Black Cemetery, Cooke Co.

Young, William Franklin. Born March 26, 1830, near Bowling Green, KY. Reared in Montgomery Co., TN. Farmer in Montgomery Co. prewar. Militia captain in 1861. Md. Mary P. Shelby; Catherine A. Caudle. Capt. Co. G, 49th TN, Dec. 3, 1861. POW Fort Donelson. Exch. Sept. 18, 1862. Col., Aug. 26, 1863. Lost right arm at Ezra Church and retired to Invalid Corps. Farmer and auctioneer in Montgomery Co. postwar. Died Jan. 12, 1899, at his Clarksville home. Buried Mt. Pleasant Church Cemetery, near Clarksville. "[A]n honored soldier, . . . tested by the fires of many battles and found invariably true."

Young, William Joshua. Born Oct. 18, 1828, Thomasville, GA. Attd. UGA. Thomasville lawyer prewar. Officer in vol. militia. Md. Susan A. Smith. Capt. Co. B, 29th GA, July 27, 1861. Col., May 10, 1862. Lost arm at Chickamauga. Resigned Nov. 10, 1863, due to his wounds. Attorney in Thomasville postwar. Judge. College president. Died Oct. 20, 1883, Thomasville. Buried Laurel Hill Cemetery, Thomasville.

Zacharie, Francis Charles. Born June 11, 1839, New Orleans, LA. Attd. Mt. Pleasant Military Academy in NY, Princeton, Harvard Law School. New Orleans attorney prewar. Md. Anne Tracy. 1st lt., CS Regular Army, June 20, 1861. 1st lt. Co. E, 9th LA, 1861. Major, 25th LA, March 20, 1862. Lt. col., Dec. 31, 1862. Col., 16th/25th Consolidated, Aug. 31, 1864. Paroled Meridian, May 10, 1865. Attorney in New Orleans postwar. State representative. Active in the fight against the state lottery. Died Jan. 6, 1910, at his New Orleans home. Buried St. Louis Cemetery No. 1. An obituary states Zacharie "was recognized far and wide as a man of exceptional attainments."

Zachry, Charles Thornton. Born Feb. 4, 1828, Covington, GA. Farmer. Moved to Henry Co. in 1863. Md. Frances A. Turner; Elizabeth Russell. Capt. Co. H, 27th GA, Sept. 9, 1861. Major, Sept. 9, 1861. Lt. col., Dec. 24, 1861. Col., Sept. 17, 1862. WIA Antietam. Paroled Greensboro. Henry Co. farmer postwar. State representative 1880–83. State senator 1890–92. Died Feb. 19, 1906, McDonough. Buried McDonough City Cemetery. An officer called Zachry "an amiable and very brave officer."

Zinken, Leon Toll von. Born c. 1827, Germany. Said to have been an officer in the Prussian army and the son of a Prussian general. Prewar builder in New Orleans. Md. Elizabeth Miller. Major, Lovell Regt. (20th LA), Nov. 30, 1861. Disabled at Shiloh when his horse fell on him. Lt. col., 20th LA, June 4, 1862. Col., July 4, 1863, 20th and 13th Consolidated. Assigned to staff duty with Gen. Breckinridge, Aug. 17, 1863. Commanded post of Marietta, 1863–64. Commanded post of Columbus, GA, 1864–65. Led an improvised brigade of government employees in siege of Savannah. Retired Nov. 1864. Led Confederate forces in the battle of Columbus, April 19, 1865, the last battle in the eastern theater. Postwar auctioneer, appraiser, and city inspector in New Orleans. Died Aug. 26, 1871, New Orleans, of Bright's disease. Buried Lafayette Cemetery No. 1.

APPENDIX 1

Colonels Who Became Generals

Three hundred and twenty-four of the 425 regularly appointed Confederate generals had been colonels in the Confederate army, and four more had been colonels in a "state" army, at one point in their army service. They are listed below. Biographies of these officers can be found in Ezra J. Warner's *Generals in Gray: Lives of the Confederate Commanders* (Baton Rouge: Louisiana State University Press, 1959) and William C. Davis, ed., *The Confederate General*, 6 vols. (Harrisburg, PA.: Cowles Magazine, 1991).

Adams, Daniel Weisiger (1821–1872), 1st LA Regulars
Adams, John (1825–1864), Cav.
Adams, William Wirt (1819–1888), 1st MS Cav.
Alexander, Edward Porter (1835–1910), Art.
Allen, Henry Watkins (1820–1866), 4th LA
Allen, William Wirt (1835–1894), 1st AL Cav.
Anderson, George Burgwyn (1831–1862), 4th NC
Anderson, George Thomas (1824–1901), 11th GA
Anderson, James Patton (1822–1872), 1st FL
Anderson, Richard Heron (1821–1879), 1st SC Regulars
Anderson, Robert Houston (1835–1888), 5th GA Cav.
Archer, James Jay (1817–1864), 5th TX
Armistead, Lewis Addison (1817–1863), 57th VA
Armstrong, Frank Crawford (1835–1909), 3d LA
Ashby, Turney (1828–1862), 7th VA Cav.
Baker, Alpheus (1828–1891), 54th AL

Baker, Laurence Simmons (1830–1907), 1st NC Cav.

Baldwin, William Edwin (1827–1864), 14th MS

Barksdale, William (1821–1863), 13th MS

Barry, John Decatur (1839–1867), 18th NC

Bate, William Brimage (1826–1905), 2d TN

Battle, Cullen Andrews (1829–1905), 3d AL

Beale, Richard Lee Turbeville (1819–1893), 9th VA Cav.

Bell, Tyree Harris (1815–1902), 12th TN

Benning, Henry Lewis (1814–1875), 17th GA

Benton, Samuel (1820–1864), 37th MS

Blanchard, Albert Gallatin (1810–1891), 1st LA Regulars

Bowen, John Stevens (1830–1863), 1st MO

Branch, Lawrence O'Bryan (1820–1862), 33d NC

Brandon, William Lindsay (c. 1800–1890), 21st MS

Brantly, William Felix (1830–1870), 29th MS

Bratton, John (1831–1898), 6th SC

Brevard, Theodore Washington (1835–1892), 11th FL

Brown, John Calvin (1827–1889), 3d TN

Browne, William Montague (1823–1883), staff

Bryan, Goode (1811–1885), 16th GA

Bullock, Robert (1828–1905), 7th FL

Butler, Matthew Calbraith (1836–1909), 2d SC Cav.

Campbell, Alexander William (1828–1883), 33d TN

Cantey, James (1818–1874), 15th AL

Capers, Ellison (1837–1908), 24th SC

Carroll, William Henry (c. 1816–1868), 37th TN

Carter, John Carpenter (1837–1864), 38th TN

Chalmers, James Ronald (1831–1898), 9th MS

Chambliss, John Randolph (1833–1864), 41st VA, 13th VA Cav.

Chestnut, James (1815–1885), staff

Churchill, Thomas James (1824–1905), 1st AR MR

Clanton, James Holt (1827–1871), 1st AL Cav.

Clark, John Bullock (1831–1903), 6th MO

Clayton, Henry DeLamar (1827–1889), 1st AL, 39th AL

Cleburne, Patrick Ronayne (1828–1864), 15th AR

Clingman, Thomas Lanier (1812–1897), 25th NC

Cobb, Howell (1815–1868), 16th GA

Cobb, Thomas Reed Rootes (1823–1862), Cobb's GA Legion

Cocke, Philip St. George (1809–1861), 19th VA

Cockrell, Francis Marion (1834–1915), 2d MO

Colquitt, Alfred Holt (1824–1894), 10th GA

Colston, Raleigh Edward (1825–1896), 16th VA

Conner, James (1829–1893), 22d NC

Cook, Phillip (1817–1894), 4th GA

Cooke, John Rogers (1833–1891), 27th NC

Cooper, Douglas Hancock (1815–1879), 1st Choctaw & Chickasaw MR

Corse, Montgomery Dent (1816–1895), 17th VA

Cox, William Ruffin (1832–1919), 2d NC

Crittenden, George Bibb (1812–1880), CS Regular Army

Cumming, Alfred (1829–1910), 10th GA

Daniel, Junius (1828–1864), 14th NC

Davidson, Henry Brevard (1831–1899), staff

Davis, Joseph Robert (1825–1896), staff

Davis, William George Mackey (1812–1898), 1st FL Cav.

Dearing, James (1840–1865), 8th Confederate Cav.

Deas, Zachariah Cantey (1819–1882), 22d AL

Deshler, James (1833–1863), Art.

Dibrell, George Gibbs (1822–1888), 8th TN Cav.

Dockery, Thomas Pleasant (1833–1898), 19th AR

Doles, George Pierce (1830–1864), 4th GA

DuBose, Dudley McIver (1834–1883), 15th GA

Duke, Basil Wilson (1838–1916), 2d KY Cav.

Duncan, Johnson Kelly (1827–1862), Art.

Dunovant, John (1825–1864), 5th SC Cav.

Early, Jubal Anderson (1816–1894), 24th VA

Echols, John (1823–1896), 27th VA

Ector, Matthew Duncan (1822–1879), 14th TX Cav.

Elliott, Stephen (1830–1866), Holcombe Legion

Elzey, Arnold (1816–1871), 1st MD

Evans, Clement Anselm (1833–1911), 31st GA

Evans, Nathan George (1824–1868), Cav.

Fagan, James Fleming (1828–1893), 1st AR

Featherston, Winfield Scott (1820–1891), 17th MS

Field, Charles William (1828–1892), 6th VA Cav.

Finley, Jesse Johnson (1812–1904), 6th FL

Forney, John Horace (1829–1902), 10th AL

Forney, William Henry (1823–1894), 10th AL

Forrest, Nathan Bedford (1821–1877), 3d TN Cav.

Frazer, John Wesley (1827–1906), 28th AL

Fry, Birkett Davenport (1822–1891), 13th AL

Gano, Richard Montgomery (1830–1913), 7th KY Cav.

Gardner, William Montgomery (1824–1901), 8th GA

Garland, Samuel (1830–1862), 11th VA

Garnett, Robert Selden (1819–1861), Adj. Gen., PAVA

Garrott, Isham (1816–1863), 20th AL

Gartrell, Lucius Jeremiah (1821–1891), 7th GA

Gary, Martin Witherspoon (1831–1881), Hampton Legion

Gatlin, Richard Caswell (1809–1896), CS Regular Army

Gholson, Samuel Jameson (1808–83), military judge

Gibson, Randall Lee (1832–1892), 13th LA

Gilmer, Jeremy Francis (1818–1883), Engineers

Gladden, Adley Hogan (1810–1862), 1st LA Regulars

Godwin, Archibald Campbell (1831–1864), 57th NC

Gordon, George Washington (1836–1911), 11th TN

Gordon, James Byron (1822–1864), 1st NC Cav.

Gordon, John Brown (1832–1900), 6th AL

Gorgas, Josiah (1818–1883), Ordnance

Govan, Daniel Chevilette (1829–1891), 2d AR

Gracie, Archibald (1832–1864), 43d AL

Granbury, Hiram Bronson (1831–1864), 7th TX

Gray, Henry (1816–1892), 28th LA

Green, Thomas (1814–1864), 5th TX Cav.

Greer, Elkanah Brackin (1825–1877), 3d TX Cav.

Gregg, John (1828–1864), 7th TX

Gregg, Maxcy (1814–1862), 1st SC

Griffith, Richard (1814–1862), 12th MS

Grimes, Bryan (1828–1880), 4th NC

Hagood, Johnson (1829–1898), 1st SC

Hampton, Wade (1818–1902), Hampton Legion

Hanson, Roger Weightman (1827–1863), 2d KY

Hardee, William Joseph (1815–1873), CS Regular Army

Hardeman, William Polk (1816–1898), 4th TX Cav.

Harris, Nathaniel Harrison (1834–1900), 19th MS

Harrison, James Edward (1815–1875), 15th TX

Harrison, Thomas (1823–1891), 8th TX Cav.

Hatton, Robert Hopkins (1826–1862), 7th TN

Hawes, James Morrison (1824–1889), 2d KY

Hawthorne, Alexander Travis (1825–1899), 6th AR

Hays, Harry Thompson (1820–1876), 7th LA

Hebert, Louis (1820–1901), 3d LA

Hebert, Paul Octave (1818–1890), 1st LA Art.

Helm, Benjamin Hardin (1831–1863), 1st KY Cav.

Heth, Harry (1825–1899), 45th VA

Higgins, Edward (1821–1875), 21st LA

Hill, Ambrose Powell (1825–1865), 15th VA

Hill, Benjamin Jefferson (1825–1880), 35th TN

Hill, Daniel Harvey (1821–1889), 1st NC

Hindman, Thomas Carmichael (1828–1868), 2d AR

Hodge, George Blair (1828–1892), Cav.

Hoke, Robert Frederick (1837–1912), 21st NC

Holmes, Theophilus Hunter (1804–1880), CS Regular Army

Holtzclaw, James Thadeus (1833–1893), 18th AL

Hood, John Bell (1831–1879), 4th TX

Huger, Benjamin (1805–1877), CS Regular Army

Humphreys, Benjamin Grubb (1808–1882), 21st MS

Hunton, Eppa (1822–1908), 8th VA

Imboden, John Daniel (1823–1895), 62d VA

Iverson, Alfred (1829–1911), 20th NC

Jackson, John King (1828–1866), 5th GA

Jackson, Thomas Jonathan (1824–1863), PAVA

Jackson, William Hicks (1835–1903), 1st TN Cav.

Jackson, William Lowther (1825–1890), 31st VA

Jenkins, Albert Gallatin (1830–1864), 8th VA Cav.

Jenkins, Micah (1835–1864), 5th SC

Johnson, Adam Rankin (1834–1922), 10th KY PR

Johnson, Bradley Tyler (1829–1903), 1st MD

Johnson, Bushrod Rust (1817–1880), Engineer Corps of TN State Army

Johnson, Edward (1816–1873), 12th GA

Johnston, George Doherty (1832–1910), 25th AL

Jones, Samuel (1819–1887), Art.

Jones, William Edmondson (1824–1864), 7th VA Cav.

Jordan, Thomas (1819–1895), staff

Kelly, John Herbert (1840–1864), 8th AR

Kemper, James Lawson (1823–1895), 7th VA

Kennedy, John Doby (1840–1896), 2d SC

Kershaw, Joseph Brevard (1822–1894), 2d SC

Kirkland, William Whedbee (1833–1915), 21st NC

Lane, James Henry (1833–1907), 28th NC

Lane, Walter Paye (1817–1892), 1st TX PR

Law, Evander McIver (1836–1920), 4th AL

Lee, Edwin Gray (1836–1870), 33d VA

Lee, Fitzhugh (1835–1905), 1st VA Cav.

Lee, George Washington Custis (1832–1913), staff

Lee, Stephen Dill (1833–1908), Art.

Lee, William Henry Fitzhugh (1837–1891), 9th VA Cav.

Leventhorpe, Collett (1815–1889), 34th NC, 11th NC

Lewis, Joseph Horace (1824–1904), 6th KY

Logan, Thomas Muldrop (1840–1914), Hampton Legion

Lomax, Lunsford Lindsay (1835–1913), 11th VA Cav.

Long, Armistead Lindsay (1825–1891), staff

Loring, William Wing (1818–1886), CS Regular Army

Lowrey, Mark Perrin (1828–1885), 32d MS

Lowry, Robert (1830–1910), 6th MS

Lyon, Hylan Benton (1836–1907), 8th KY

MacRae, William (1834–1882), 15th NC

Magruder, John Bankhead (1807–1871), CS Regular Army

Mahone, William (1826–1895), 6th VA

Maney, George Earl (1826–1901), 1st TN

Manigault, Arthur Middleton (1824–1886), 10th SC

Marmaduke, John Sappington (1833–1887), 3d Confederate

Martin, William Thompson (1823–1910), Jeff Davis Legion

Maury, Dabney Herndon (1822–1900), staff

Maxey, Samuel Bell (1825–1895), 9th TX

McCauseland, John (1836–1927), 36th VA

McComb, William (1828–1918), 14th TN

McCown, John Porter (1815–1879), Art. Corps of TN State Army

McCulloch, Henry Eustace (1816–1895), 1st TX MR

McGowan, Samuel (1819–1897), 14th SC

McIntosh, James McQueen (1828–1862), 2d AR MR

McLaws, Lafayette (1821–1897), 10th GA

McNair, Evander (1820–1902), 4th AR

McRae, Dandridge (1829–1899), 21st AR

Mercer, Hugh Weedon (1808–1877), 1st GA

Miller, William (1820–1909), 1st FL

Moody, Young Marshall (1822–1866), 43d AL

Moore, John Creed (1824–1910), 2d TX

Moore, Patrick Theodore (1821–1883), 1st VA

Morgan, John Hunt (1825–1864), 2d KY Cav.

Morgan, John Tyler (1824–1907), 51st AL PR

Mouton, Jean Jacques Alfred Alexander (1829–1864), 18th LA

Nelson, Allison (1822–1862), 10th TX

Nicholls, Francis Redding Tillou (1834–1912), 15th LA

Northrup, Lucius (1811–1894), commissary gen.

O'Neal, Edward Asbury (1818–1890), 9th AL

Palmer, Joseph Benjamin (1825–1890), 18th TN

Payne, William Henry Fitzhugh (1830–1904), 4th VA Cav.

Peck, William Raine (1818–1871), 9th LA

Pegram, John (1832–1865), staff

Pender, William Dorsey (1834–1863), 13th NC

Pendleton, William Nelson (1809–1883), Art.

Perrin, Abner Monroe (1827–1864), 14th SC

Perry, Edward Aylesworth (1831–1889), 2d FL

Perry, William Flank (1823–1901), 44th AL

Pettigrew, James Johnson (1828–1863), 12th SC

Pettus, Edmund Winston (1821–1907), 20th AL

Pickett, George Edward (1825–1875), PACS

Polk, Lucius Eugene (1833–1892), 15th AR

Posey, Carnot (1818–1863), 16th MS

Preston, John Smith (1809–1881), staff

Preston, William (1816–1887), staff

Pryor, Roger Atkinson (1828–1919), 3d VA

Quarles, William Andrew (1825–1893), 42d TN

Rains, Gabriel James (1803–1881), CS Regular Army

Rains, James Edwards (1833–1862), 11th TN

Ramseur, Stephen Dodson (1837–1864), 49th NC

Randolph, George Wythe (1818–1867), Art.

Ransom, Matt Whitaker (1826–1904), 35th NC

Ransom, Robert (1828–1892), 9th NC

Reynolds, Alexander Welch (1816–1876), 50th VA

Reynolds, Daniel Harris (1832–1902), 1st AR MR

Richardson, Robert Vinkler (1820–1870), 12th TN Cav.

Roberts, William Paul (1841–1910), 2d NC Cav.

Robertson, Beverly Holcombe (1827–1910), 4th VA Cav.

Robertson, Jerome Bonaparte (1815–1891), 5th TX

Roddey, Philip Dale (1826–1897), 4th AL Cav.

Rodes, Robert Emmett (1829–1864), 5th AL

Ross, Lawrence Sullivan (1838–1898), 6th TX Cav.

Rosser, Thomas Lafayette (1836–1910), 5th VA Cav.

Ruggles, Daniel (1810–1897), CS Regular Army

Rust, Albert (1818–1870), 3d AR

St. John, Isaac Munroe (1827–1880), Niter and Mining Corps

Sanders, John Caldwell Calhoun (1840–1864), 11th AL

Scales, Alfred Moore (1827–1882), 13th NC

Scott, Thomas Moore (1829–1876), 12th LA

Sears, Claudius Wistar (1817–1891), 46th MS

Semmes, Paul Jones (1815–1863), 2d GA

Sharp, Jacob Hunter (1833–1907), 44th MS

Shelby, Joseph Orville (1830–1897), 5th MO Cav.

Simms, James Phillip (1837–1887), 53d GA

Smith, James Argyle (1831–1901), 5th Confederate

Smith, Martin Luther (1819–1866), 21st LA

Smith, Preston (1823–1863), 154th TN

Smith, Thomas Benton (1838–1923), 20th TN

Smith, William (1797–1887), 49th VA

Smith, William Duncan (1825–1862), 20th GA

Stafford, Leroy Augustus (1822–1864), 9th LA

Starke, Peter Burwell (1815–1888), 28th MS Cav.

Starke, William Edwin (1814–1862), 60th VA

Steele, William (1819–1885), 7th TX Cav.

Steuart, George Hume (1828–1903), 1st MD

Stevens, Clement Hoffman (1821–1864), 24th SC

Stevens, Walter Husted (1827–1867), Engineers

Stevenson, Carter Littlepage (1817–1888), 53d VA

Strahl, Otho French (1831–1864), 4th TN

Stuart, James Ewell Brown "Jeb" (1833–1864), 1st VA Cav.

Taliaferro, William Booth (1822–1898), 23d VA

Tappan, James Camp (1825–1906), 13th AR

Taylor, Richard (1826–1879), 9th LA

Taylor, Thomas Hart (1825–1901), 1st KY

Terrill, James Barbour (1838–1864), 13th VA

Terry, William (1824–1888), 4th VA

Terry, William Richard (1827–1897), 24th VA

Thomas, Allen (1830–1907), 29th LA

Thomas, Bryan Morel (1836–1905), Thomas's AL Cav.

Thomas, Edward Lloyd (1825–1898), 35th GA

Tilghman, Lloyd (1816–1863), 3d KY

Toon, Thomas Fentress (1840–1902), 20th NC

Tucker, William Feimster (1827–1881), 41st MS

Tyler, Robert Charles (1833–1865), 15th TN

Vance, Robert Brank (1828–1899), 29th NC

Van Dorn, Earl (1820–1863), CS Regular Army

Vaughan, Alfred Jefferson (1830–1899), 13th TN

Vaughn, John Crawford (1824–1875), 3d TN

Villepigue, John Bordenave (1830–1862), 36th GA

Walker, James Alexander (1832–1901), 13th VA

Walker, Leroy Pope (1817–1884), military judge

Walker, Lucius Marshall (1829–1863), 40th TN

Walker, Reuben Lindsay (1827–1890), Art.

Walker, William Stephen (1822–1899), staff

Wallace, William Henry (1827–1901), 18th SC

Walthall, Edward Cary (1831–1898), 29th MS

Waterhouse, Richard (1832–1876), 19th TX

Watie, Stand (1806–1871), 1st Cherokee MR

Waul, Thomas Neville (1815–1903), Waul's TX Legion

Weisiger, David Addison (1818–1899), 12th VA

Wharton, Gabriel Colvin (1824–1906), 51st VA

Wharton, John Austin (1828–1865), 8th TX Cav.

Wheeler, Joseph (1836–1906), 19th AL

Whitfield, John Wilkins (1818–1879), 27th TX Cav.

Wickham, Williams Carter (1820–1888), 4th VA Cav.

Wigfall, Louis Trezevant (1816–1874), 1st TX

Wilcox, Cadmus Marcellus (1824–1890), 9th AL

Williams, John Stuart (1818–1898), 5th KY

Wilson, Claudius Charles (1831–1863), 25th GA

Winder, Charles Sidney (1829–1862), 6th SC

Winder, John Henry (1800–1865), CS Regular Army

Withers, Jones Mitchell (1814–1890), 3d AL

Wofford, William Tatum (1824–1884), 18th GA

Wood, Sterling Alexander Martin (1823–1891), 7th AL

Wright, Ambrose Ransom (1826–1872), 3d GA

York, Zebulon (1819–1900), 14th LA

Young, Pierce Manning Butler (1836–1896), Cobb's GA Legion

Young, William Hugh (1838–1901), 9th TX

APPENDIX 2

Colonels of State Armies

This list includes colonels of forces organized by the individual states of the Confederacy. These forces include the 1861 Provisional Army of Virginia (PAVA), the Virginia State Line, and Virginia Reserves; the North Carolina Home Guard; the South Carolina Reserves; the Georgia State Army of 1861, Georgia State Guards, and 1864 Georgia Militia division; the 1861 Mississippi "Army of 10,000," Mississippi State Troops and Reserves; Louisiana state regiments organized to defend New Orleans in 1862; the Arkansas state army of 1861; the Missouri State Guard (MSG); and Texas State Troops.

This list does not include state militia colonels (except for the GA militia division that fought in the Atlanta Campaign) or colonels of "state" regiments who became Confederate colonels or generals and who are listed elsewhere. All units are infantry unless otherwise noted.

Abert, Charles H. (1795–1867), Abert's MS (State) Inf. Regt. in 1861
Alexander, Charles B. (1835–1885), 2d Cav., 6th Div., MSG
Anderson, Charles David (1827–1901), 2d GA Militia
Applegate, Lawrence Martin (1832–1915), MSG staff ADC
Ashmore, John Durant (1819–1871), 4th SC Inf. (when in state service)
Augustine, Joseph Numa (1812–1872), LA Orleans Guards (State) Regt.
Barnes, James William (1815–1892), 4th Inf. TX State Troops
Bartlett, Anthony Wayne (1817–1891), 2d Inf. Regt. MS (State) Army of 10,000
Bartlett, Franklin Adams (1829–1891), Beauregard (LA) (State) Regt.
Baxter, James M. (1825–1881), 10th SC State Reserves
Beattie, George M. (c. 1806–1866), Adj. Gen., 1st Div., MSG
Bell, Caspar Winstar (1819–1898), Adj. Gen., 3d Div., MSG

Bevier, Robert Seymour (1834–1889), 4th Inf., 3d Div., MSG

Blair, William Barrett (1817–1883), PAVA

Bledsoe, Hiram Miller (1825–1899), 6th Inf., 8th Div., MSG

Blythe, Green Lee (1826–1878), 2d MS State PR

Booe, Alexander Martin (1821–1895), 3d NC Home Guard, 3d Class

Brace, Theodore (1835–1921), 3d Inf., 2d Div., MSG

Brand, Horace Holley (1832–1864), Adj. Gen., MSG

Brent, Burr Chinn (1818–1880), Adj. Gen., 2d Div., MSG

Bromley, William Carroll (1827–1887), 4th MS State Troops

Brown, Alexander Henry (1809–1879), 1st SC State Reserves

Brown, Benjamin Johnson (1807–1861), IG, 4th Div., MSG

Brown, William Breckinridge (1828–1861), 1st Cav., 6th Div., MSG

Burney, John Walker (1830–1886), 6th GA Militia

Burr, James Green (1817–1898), 7th NC Home Guard

Burton, William O. (1833–1875), Adj. Gen., 3d Div., MSG

Cabell, Edward Carrington (1816–1896), MSG staff ADC

Camp, Thompson (1818–1889), 2d TX State Troops

Carew, John Edward (1808–1877), 3d SC State

Carroll, De Rosey (1814–1863), 1st AR Cav. (State)

Cawthon,* James (c. 1810–1861), 4th Cav., 8th Div., MSG

Cearnal, James Thaddeus (c. 1829–c. 1866), 1st Cav., 5th Div., MSG

Chastain, Elijah Webb (1813–1874), 8th GA State Troops

Chiles, Christopher Lillard (1835–1862), Chiles's Inf., 8th Div., MSG

Clark, George (c. 1817–1873), LA Continental (State) Regt.

Clarkson, James Jones (c. 1811–1865), 5th Cav., 8th Div., MSG**

Clarkson, John Nicholas (1816–1906), 3d VA State Line

Cole, James Reid (1839–1917), 4th NC Home Guard; 3d NC Home Guard, 1st
    Class

Conrow, Aaron Hacket (1824–1865), Adj. Gen., 4th Div., MSG

Cowart, Robert Jackson (1811–1876), 3d GA State Troops

Cravens, Jesse Lamb (1831–1908), 6th Cav., 8th Div., MSG

Dabney, William Harris (1817–1899), 1st GA State Guard

Darden, Stephen Heard (1816–1902), 5th TX State Troops

Davis, Charles Milton (1819–1902), 10th GA State Troops

---

* Name mistakenly spelled *Cawthorn* in *OR* and every history since.
** Listed in Appendix 3 as well.

Decker, John (c. 1830–1873), AAG, 9th Div., MSG

De Treville, Richard (1801–1874), 1st SC (State) Reserves

DeWalt, Kerr Boyce (1819–1891), 1st TX State Troops

Dills, George K. (c. 1831–1876), 2d Inf., 6th Div., MSG

Dixon, Leonidas Virginius (1816–1878), Memphis (TN) Legion

Dorsey, Caleb (c. 1833–1896), Dorsey's MO Cav. (MSG?)

Draughon, Walter (1811–1870), 3d NC Home Guard

Duncan, Samuel P. (c. 1828–1872), LA Orleans Fire (State) Regt.

Duncan, Theodore (1827–1861), 1st Cav., 5th Div., MSG

Du Val, Gabriel Bertrand (1822–1864), 1st AL Mtd. (State)

Dyer, Randolph Harrison (1825–1890), AQM, MSG

Easterling, William Kennon (1822–1904), 3d MS State Cav.

Erwin, William Hugh (1827–1869), 10th Cav., 8th Div., MSG

Favrot, Henry Mortimer (1826–1887), LA (State) staff

Fisher, Ephraim Stone (1815–1879), 4th MS State Cav.

Floweree, Daniel Walton (1838–1878), Adj. Gen., 5th Div., MSG

Floyd, Henry Hamilton (1817–1873), 5th GA Militia

Floyd, John Julius (1809–1883), 10th GA State Guard Cav.

Fontaine, William Winston (1834–1917), Fontaine's Inf. Regt. VA State Line

Foote, Hezekiah William (1813–1899), 1st MS State Cav.

Fort, William (1820–1875), 2d SC State

Foster, John Allen (1828–1861), 2d Inf., 7th Div., MSG

Fox, Joseph Maurice (1832–1908), Adj. Gen., 5th Div., MSG

Frazier, Julian (1808–1862), 1st Cav., 7th Div., MSG

Fremont, Sewall Lawrence (1816–1886), NC Engineers (State)

Galt, Edward Machen Ballenger (1819–1866), 1st GA State Line; 1st GA State
    Troops

Girault, John Francis (1821–1889), LA Confederate (State) Guards

Goodwin, Artemus Darby (1827–1898), 3d SC Junior Reserves (State)

Gratiot, John Rene (1820–1891), 3d AR (State)

Graves, John Robinson (1830–1902), 2d Inf., 8th Div., MSG

Green, William Furnifold (1828–1898), 1st NC Home Guard, 3d Class

Griffin, James Benjamin (1825–1881), 1st SC Junior Reserves (State)

Gwynn, Walter (1802–1882), NC Engineers (State)

Hale, Stephen Ferguson (1823–1901), 4th Inf., 8th Div., MSG

Hambrick, John Turner (1823–1872), 2d NC Home Guard; 3d NC Home
    Guard, 2d Class

Harbin, Allen A. (1830–1905), 2d NC Home Guard, 2d Class

Haren Jr., Edward (1834–1915), AQM, MSG

Harris, Jeptha Vining (1816–1899), MS State Troops

Harrison, William H. (c. 1825–1880), 1st NC Home Guard

Harriss, Robert Y. (1811–1883), 9th GA State Troops

Henderson, John Thomas (1826–1899), 6th GA State Troops; 8th GA State
    Guard

Henry, Patrick Miller (1815–1873), Henry's VA Reserves

Hill, Henry (1816–1866), PAVA

Hill, James Leslie Stewart (1818–1899), 2d MS State Cav.

Hill, John Meriwether (1827–1894), 9th GA State Troops; 3d GA Militia

Holloway, Edmund Balard (c. 1822–1861), 1st Inf., 8th Div., MSG

Hounshell, David Stuart (1835–1901), 4th VA State Line

Hunter, George Russell (1810–1863), 7th GA State Troops

Hurst, Edgar V. (c. 1835–1862), 3d Inf., 8th Div., MSG

Hyde, Charles P. (c. 1826–1902), 1st Cav., 5th Div., MSG

Hyde, William S. (1827–1862), 3d Inf., 3d Div., MSG

Jackson, Congreve (1803–1869), 2d Inf., 3d Div., MSG

Jamison, James Carson (1830–1916), TX State Troops

Johnson, John Myscal (1826–1874), 3d Cav., 6th Div., MSG

Johnson, Joseph Burton (1816–1874), 4th Cav. TX State Troops

Johnson, Luke Garnett (1825–1903), 3d GA Militia

Jones, Alfred William (1818–1893), MSG staff ADC

Jones, Andrew F. (c. 1822–1862), 1st Cav., 1st Div., MSG

Jones, Tignal W. (1820–1882), 1st Cav. TX State Troops

Kavanaugh, Charles Baxter (1822–1891), 6th Inf., 8th Div., MSG

Kelly, Joseph (1817–1870), 1st Inf., 6th Div., MSG

Kennerly, William Clark (1824–1912), Provisional Inf. Bn., 9th Div., MSG

King, Benjamin (1823–1884), 1st MS Minute Men (State)

Langan, John M. (1838–1904), Adj. Gen., 1st Div., MSG

Langhorne, Daniel Allen (1825–1908), PAVA

Leeds, Charles Jedediah (1823–1898), LA Leeds Guards (State) Regt.

Lester, George Nelson (1824–1892), 7th GA State Guard

Ligon, Robert Burns (1834–1916), 4th SC Junior Reserves (State)

Livingston, Thomas Robinson (1820–1863), 11th Cav., 8th Div., MSG

Lofton, William Alpheus (c. 1829–1896), 6th GA State Guard

Lowe, Aden (1827–1861), 3d Cav., 1st Div., MSG

Maclean, Lauchlan Allen (1820–1864), Adj. Gen., 8th Div., MSG

Maclin, Sackfield (1809–1876), TX State Troops

Maddox, William Alexander (1825–1904), LA (State) Reserve Corps

Magoffin, Ebenezer (c. 1817–1862), 2d Inf., 2d Div., MSG

Manigault, Edward (1817–1874), SC state ordnance officer

Mann, James N. (c. 1827–1895), 5th GA State Troops

Martin, John William (1819–1888), 1st Cav., 8th Div., MSG

Masten, John (1821–1885), 2d NC Home Guard, 3d Class

McCary, Josiah (1807–1899), 2d Cav., 6th Div., MSG

McClain, William Alexander (1816–1878), Adj. Gen., 8th Div., MSG

McDonald, Edward Charles (1803–1862), 1st Inf., 2d Div., MSG

McIntyre, Archibald Thompson (1822–1900), 11th GA State Guard

McKinney, Harvey G. (c. 1826–1863), 6th Inf., 3d Div., MSG

Meek, Samuel Mills (1835–1901), 1st MS State

Meilleur, Jean Simon (1824–1883), LA Chasseurs-a-Pied (State)

Mell, Patrick Hues (1814–1888), 9th GA State Guard

Menifee, Nathaniel McClure (c. 1825–?), 4th VA State Line

Miangolarra, Juan (c. 1820–1878), LA Cazadores Espanoles (State)

Mitchell, Ewing Young (1831–1901), Adj. Gen., 7th Div., MSG

Moore, John Lewis (1832–1881), 3d GA Reserves

Morphis, Joseph Lewis (1831–1913), Morphis's MS (State) Cav. Reserves

Moses, George C. (1820–1885), 2d NC Home Guard, 1st Class

Neely, James Jackson (1818–1889), 4th GA State Troops

Norris, James Madison (1819–1874), TX Frontier Regt. (State)

O'Brien, Patrick Burke (1824–1896), LA Louisiana Irish Regt. (State)

O'Kane, Walter Scott (1832–1908), 4th Inf., 8th Div., MSG

Owens, Winfrey Jackson (1827–1909), 3d MS State Troops

Pallen, Montrose Anderson (1836–1890), Assistant Surgeon General, MSG

Patton, Thomas Jefferson (1822–1898), 2d Inf., 4th Div., MSG

Patton, William S. (1813–1889), 1st Inf. Regt. MS (State) Army of 10,000

Percy, William Alexander (1834–1888), 1st Inf. Regt. MS (State) Army of 10,000

Pettus, John Jones (1813–1867), MS State Troops

Peyton, Robert Ludwell Yates (1822–1863), 3d Cav., 8th Div., MSG

Phelan, William Gerald (1824–1872), 2d Cav., 1st Div., MSG

Poindexter, John A. (1825–1869), 5th Inf., 3d Div., MSG

Pottle, Edward H. (1822–1886), 1st GA Militia

Power, John Logan (1834–1901), MS (State) staff

Price, Edward William (1834–1908), 3d Inf., 3d Div., MSG

Price, John Valentine (1815–1873), 11th GA State Troops

Priest, John William (1826–1899), 2d Cav., 6th Div., MSG

Purvis, John R. (1823–1880), Adj. Gen., 1st Div., MSG

Quinn, Daniel Hillary (1821–1893), 2d MS State Troops

Rand, Oscar Ripley (1833–1904), 1st NC Home Guard, 1st Class

Redding, Abner Flewellen (1826–1864), 7th GA State Troops

Reid, John William (1821–1881), asst. commissary, MSG

Richardson, Thomas J. M. (1826–1884), 3d Cav. TX State Troops

Rion, James Henry (1828–1886), 6th SC Inf. (when in state service)

Roberts, Thomas B. (1821–1885), 1st SC State

Robertson, Francis Marion (1806–1892), 1st SC (State) Reserves

Robinson, Frank Seldon (1828–1896), 3d Inf., 6th Div., MSG

Robinson, Henry Cole (1818–1874), 5th MS State Troops

Robinson, William Heatley (1813–1892), 12th GA State Guard Cav.

Rountree, Charles Napoleon (1817–1900), 8th GA State Guard

Rozell, Blackman L. (1818–1903), 3d Inf. Regt. MS (State) Army of 10,000

Rusk, James Edward (1822–1893), Cherokee Legion, GA State Guard

Ryan, John J. (1817–1869), 11th SC (State) Reserves

Salisbury, William Lewis (1830–1878), 5th GA State Guard

Saunders, James Powers (1827–c. 1912), 1st Inf., 5th Div., MSG

Sayles, John (1825–1897), 4th TX State Troops

Schnable, John A. (1817–1901), 3d Inf., 7th Div., MSG

Scott, John Graham (c. 1826–1873), 3d TX State Troops

Scott, William B. (1825–1879), 8th GA Militia

Secrest, Andrew Jackson (c. 1828–1865), 6th SC (State) Reserves

Sharpe, Silas Alexander (1830–1903), 5th NC Home Guard

Siler, Thaddeus Patton (1823–1894), 6th NC Home Guard

Sims, Richard (c. 1817–1872), 12th GA State Troops

Slover, Thomas Henderson (1835–1907), 5th Cav., 8th Div., MSG

Smith, Alexander (1831–1907), LA Jeff Davis Regt. (State)

Smith, Gideon W. (1815–1892), 2d Cav. TX State Troops

Smith, John Ferguson (1835–1910), 2d MS Cav. State Troops

Smith, John Jackson (1828–1906), 2d Cav., 1st Div., MSG

Smith, Walter (1798–1865), Mobile (AL) "Fire Brigade" Regt. LDT

Snead, Thomas Lowndes (1828–1890), AAAG, MSG

Somerville, James (1828–1877), 3d MS State Troops

Stafford, Samuel Sherrard (c. 1825–1868), 5th GA Militia

Standish, Austin Martin (1825–1865), Adj. Gen., 6th Div., MSG

Stapleton, James (1824–1888), 3d GA State Troops

Stone, Caleb Smith (1810–1873), Adj. Gen., 3d Div., MSG

Storey, Richard Lawson (1823–1892), 2d GA State Line

Stuart, Oscar James Elizabeth (1810–1885), MS State Troops

Szymanski, Ignatius (1806–1874), LA Chalmette Regt. (State), staff

Talbot, Sanford J. (c. 1821–c. 1865), 11th Cav., 8th Div., MSG

Taylor, Henry Clay (1826–1906), ADC, MSG

Thomas, John Peyre (1833–1912), Columbia (SC) LDT (State)

Thomas, Richard (Zarvona) (1833–1875), VA state forces

Thompson, Dexter Booth (1823–1869), 6th GA State Troops

Thompson, James M. (1818–1885), 2d LA Reserves (State)

Tippen, William Jasper (c. 1821–c. 1878), 2d Inf., 1st Div., MSG

Toole, William Thomas (1819–1889), 11th GA Militia

Toombs, Robert (1810–1885), 3d GA State Guard Cav.

Tracy, (John) Charles (c. 1825–?), Tracy's Cav., 8th Div., MSG

Trader, William H. (c. 1835–1885), AR state forces (1864)

Veal, Jesse Thomas (1824–1902), 3d TX State Troops

Von Schmeling, Wedig Franz Alexander (1834–1886), MSG staff

Walker, Benjamin F. (1820–1906), 4th Cav., 8th Div., MSG

Walker, James A. (c. 1818–c. 1869), 1st Inf., 1st Div., MSG

Walker, James David (1830–1906), 4th AR (State)

Walton, Thomas George (1815–1905), 8th NC Home Guard; 1st NC Home
     Guard, 2d Class

Waugh, Alexander (1815–1876), 4th Inf., 1st Div., MSG

Weightman, Richard Hanson (1816–1861), 1st Cav., 8th Div., MSG

White, Martin (1802–1862), 3d Cav., 8th Div., MSG

White, Robert (1805–1898), 4th GA State Guard Cav.

Wilfley, Redman (1825–1910), 2d Cav., 5th Div., MSG

Willcoxon, John B. (1823–1896), 2d GA State Guard

Willis, James Tilman (1836–1887), 1st Brigade, GA Militia

Wilmeth, Joseph Bryson (1807–1892), 3d TX State Troops

Wilson, James D. (c. 1829–1873), 2d GA State Line

Wilson, William Blackburn (1827–1894), 7th SC (State) Reserves

Wingo, Edmund T. (1818–1895), 1st Inf., 7th Div., MSG

Witherspoon, James Hervey (1810–1865), 8th SC (State) Reserves

Wooten, Thomas Dudley (1829–1906), medical director, MSG

Wright, Henry Gregory (1830–1904), 12th GA State Troops

Wright, William Felix (1824–1887), 10th GA State Troops

Yeiser, James Garrard (1826–1895), Floyd Legion GA State Guard

Yerger, William Swan (1833–1868), 3d MS (State) Reserves Cav.

Appendix 3

Other Officers Called "Colonel"

This list includes officers named as PACS colonels in one or more credible sources. It includes some officers with "state" rank who served with the PACS while keeping their "state" rank.

Acee, Erasmus L. (c. 1806–1862), MS PR
Adams, Lysander (1799-post 1879), 33d TN Inf.
Anglade, J. Germain (1831–1870), 1st TN Zouaves
Ashe, William Shepperd (1813–1862), staff
Avery, William Tecumseh (1819–1880), 39th TN Inf.
Bailey, Robert Augustus (1839–1863), 14th VA Cav.
Baker, Thomas Harrison (1836–1908), 55th TN Inf.
Balfour, John W. (1828–1903), "49th" MS Inf.
Barrow, Robert Hilliard (1824–1878), 11th LA Inf.
Bayne, Thomas Levingston (1824–1891), staff
Beckley, Alfred (1802–1888), 35th VA Inf.
Beltzhoover, Daniel M. (1826–1870), Art.
Berry, Thomas J. (1835–1865), 7th VA Cav.
Blair, James Douglas (1828–1874), 2d LA Cav.
Boone, John Coulter (1816–1893), Boone's Regt. MO Mtd. Inf.
Brewer, James Fielding (1836–1864), 1st TN Cav.
Brodie, Robert Little (1829–1913), medical director Western Division
Brooke, Walker (1813–1869), Military Court Judge
Bryan, Joel Mayes (1833–1891), Cherokee PR
Bull, William Izard (1813–1894), staff
Burrow, Reuben (1822–1888), 12th TN Cav.

Burton, James Henry (1823–1894), Ordnance

Candler, Allen Daniel (1834–1910), 4th GA Res.

Childress, James R. (1829–1899), 40th MS Inf.

Chilton, George Washington (1820–1884), staff

Chisholm, Alexander Robert (1834–1910), staff

Clarkson, James Jones (c. 1811–1865), Clarkson's MO Cav.

Clift, Moses Haney (1836–1911), 4th TN Cav.

Cochran, John (1813–1873), staff

Coleman, John Jay (1833–1888), 29th VA Inf.

Collins, Nathaniel Dixon (1830–1874), Collins's TN Cav.

Conn, Raphael Morgan (1805–1887), 43d VA Inf.

Cooper, Duncan Brown (1845–1922), Cooper's TN Cav.

Coupland, Andrew Jackson (1814–1874), 11th TX Inf.

Crews, James Mortimer (1835–1898), 58th TN Inf.

Crisp, John T. (1838–1903), Crisp's MO Cav.

Crow, William C. (1827–1879), 26th LA Inf.

Cuyler, Richard Matthei (1825–1879), staff

Danley, Benjamin F. (1824–1877), staff

Davis, John Foster (1832–1921), 20th AL Cav.

Davis, Nicholas (1825–1874), 19th AL Inf.

Deavenport, Matthew Watson (1828–1911), 34th TX Cav.

De Leon, David Camden (1816–1872), acting surgeon general

Deneale, George E. (c. 1807–1889), Deneale's Choctaws

Duncan, William Hansford (1835–1889), 1st SC Inf.

Echols, William Holding (1834–1909), 29th GA Inf.

Edwards, John Cubbage (1823–1886), 5th SC Cav.

Elliott, James Kelley (1837–1908), 30th AL Inf.

Evans, Stephen B. (1823–1888), 5th NC Cav.

Ficklin, John (1822–1873), Ficklin's Bn. KY Cav.

Field, Joseph Harris (1840–1915), 8th Confederate Cav.

Finley, George Preston (1829–1911), staff

Flournoy, Thompson Breckinridge (1810–1861), 1st AR Inf.

Foard, Andrew Jackson (1826–1868), medical director Army of TN

Forney, George Hoke (1835–1864), 1st Confederate Inf.

Forrest, Jesse Anderson (1834–1889), 21st TN Cav.

Fowler, Pleasant (1831–1924), 14th AR Inf.

Franklin, James Francis (1838–c. 1870), Franklin's TN Cav.

Fry, George Thompson (1843–1897), "7th Confederate Cav. Consolidated"

Fuqua, James Overton (1822–1875), staff

Garnett, Charles Fenton Mercer (1810–1886), Bureau of Iron Impressment

Giddings, Dewitt Clinton (1827–1903), 21st TX Cav.

Gould, Robert Simonton (1826–1904), Gould's TX Cav.

Gray, Gabriel (1831–1902), 22d VA Inf.

Greenwood, Alexander George (c. 1835–1909), 26th AR Inf.

Greer, Henry Clay (1837–1907), Greer's TN PR

Griffin, William Henry (1816–1871), 21st TX Inf.

Guild, Lafayette (1825–1870), medical director ANV

Haden, John Miller (1825–1892), medical director TMD

Hall, Edwin Gilbert (1829–1920), KY PR

Hanks, Joseph M. (1826–1887), KY Cav.

Harrison, Burton Norvell (1838–1904), aide to Pres. Davis

Hartsfield, Wiley F. (1837–1865), 53d GA Inf.

Hodge, Eli (1839–1925), MO Cav.

Holden, William Boyle (1814–1873), 53d TN Inf.

Hollis, William W. (c. 1835–1863), 11th KY Cav.

Holman, James Hardy (1836–1910), staff

Hooks, Robert Warren (1838–1868), 11th TX Cav.

Huey, James K. (1827–1891), 13th KY Cav.

Huger, John Middleton (1808–1894), staff

Hull, Edward Brodie (1839–1921), 2d MO Inf.

Hunley, Peter Forney (1829–1882), 18th AL Inf.

Jackson, Joseph Franklin Ballenger (1832–1912), 39th GA Inf.

Johnston, Josiah Stoddard (1833–1913), staff

Jones, James Henry (1836–1911), 38th MS Inf.

Jumper, John (1820–1896), 1st Seminole Bn.

Kasey, John G. (1839–1902), 58th VA Inf.

Kean, Robert Garlick Hill (1828–1898), War Dept.

Kennard, Perry S. (c. 1812–c. 1874), staff

Kennedy, John Thomas (1824–1913), "7th NC Cav."

Kessler, Joseph R. (1831–1904), 26th VA Cav.

Killgore, Dawson Lea (1823–1893), 9th AR Inf.

King, Barrington Simeral (1833–1865), 9th GA Cav.

Kizer, Thomas Neal (c. 1839–?), Kizer's TN Cav.

Law, Junius Augustus (1839–1881), 63d AL Inf.

Law, George Washington (1828–1873), 1st MO Cav.

Lay, George William (1821–1867), staff

Lee, Philip Lightfoot (1832–1875), 2d KY Inf.

Lee, Richard Bland (1797–1875), staff

Lockert, James William (1828–1912), 14th TN Inf.

Lowe, William Manning (1842–1882), AL "Burr Tailed Regt."

Magee, Turpin Dickson (1824–1879), 46th MS Inf.

Mallet, John William (1832–1912), staff

Marshall, John W. (c. 1814–1889), 17th TN Cav.

Mauldin, Tyirie Harris (c. 1829–c. 1916), 3d AL Cav.

McClellan, James F. (1824–1890), 11th FL Inf.

McCorkle, Matthew Lock (1817–1899), McCorkle's NC Senior Reserves

McCown, George Washington (1828–1880), staff

McGinnis, Noble Lafayette (1829–1898), 2d TX Inf.

McKnight, Moses Waddell (1833–1909), TN Cav.

Miller, C. C. (1828–?), 21st LA Inf.

Mills, Andrew Graham (1839–1894), 7th MS Inf.

Monier, Henry D. (1836–1911), 10th LA Inf.

Morton, Tignal Jones (1843–1871), 53d TN Inf.

Napier, Thomas Alonzo (1837–1862), Napier's TN Cav. Bn.

Napier, Thomas Wilson (1818–1869), 4th Regt., KY PR Brigade

Nichols, Charles H. (1841–1871), Jackman's MO Cav.

Offutt, Nathaniel (1839–1874), 6th LA Inf.

O'Hara, Theodore (1820–1867), 12th AL Inf.

Oury, Granville Henderson (1825–1891), staff and Herbert's AZ Cav.

Parr, Lewis J. (1830–1908), 38th GA Inf.

Peel, Samuel West (1831–1924), 4th AR Inf.

Peery, William Francis (1818–1864), MO Cav.

Pell, James A. (1829–1916), 6th/1st Confederate Cav.

Pickett, John Thomas (1823–1884), "Special Service"

Pickett, William Douglas (1827–1917), staff

Pitchlynn, Peter Perkins (1806–1881), Choctaw chief

Pointer, Marcellus (1841–1909), 12th AL Cav.

Prather, John Smith (1837–1920), 8th Confederate Cav.

Quantrill, William Clarke (1837–1865), MO Partisans

Randolph, Francis Corbin (1841–1905), 7th AL Cav.

Righter, William Harmon (1832–1916), 15th MO Cav.

Robins, Josiah (1825–1901), 3d AL Cav.

Roy, Thomas Benton (1838–1910), staff

Rudulph, John Barrett (1835–1910), 10th Confederate Cav.

Sandidge, John Milton (1817–1890), staff

Saunders, James Edmonds (1806–1896), staff

Shannon, Alexander May (1839–1906), Wheeler's Scouts

Shuster, Jacob Powhatan (1826–1869), Art.

Shy, William Mabry (1838–1864), 20th TN Inf.

Sims, Milton Walker (1831–1912), Sims's TX Cav.

Smith, Charles Henry (1819–1879), acting surgeon general

Smith, Larkin (1814–1884), staff

Smith, Stokes Anderson (1815–1872), medical director TMD

Stafford, Fountain Pitts (c. 1835–1864), 31st TN Inf.

Standifer, Thomas Cunningham (1827–1897), 12th LA Inf.

Steele, Theophilus (1835–1911), 7th KY Cav.

Stewart, Richard A. (c. 1816–1880), Stewart's LA Legion

Thomas, Francis John (1824–1861), staff

Thompson, Jacob (1810–1882), staff

Todhunter, Ryland (1840–1921), Regt. of supernumerary officers

Upson, Christopher Columbus (1829–1902), staff

Vaughan, Edwin L. (c. 1835–1884), 10th AR Inf.

Waddell, James Fleming (1826–1892), 20th AL Art. Bn.

Wade, William (1819–1863), MO Art.

Walker, Cornelius Irvine (1842–1927), 10th SC Inf.

Walker, John G. (c. 1829–1869), 8th TX Cav.

Walker, William Clay (1820–1864), Thomas's NC Legion

Waller, Ed, Jr. (1825–1878), Waller's TX Cav.

Ware, Josiah William (1802–1883), 34th VA Inf.

White, John D. (c. 1816–1869), White's TX Cav.

Willey, William J. (c. 1802–1868), 31st VA Inf.

Williams, Hazael Joseph (1830–1911), 5th VA Inf.

Williams, Thomas Greenhow (1828–1885), staff

Williamson, Thomas Hoomes (1813–1888), staff

Wilson, Lawrie (c. 1838–1866), 32d VA Inf.

Winn, Samuel James (1837–1919), 13th GA Cav.

Wisdom, Dew Moore (1836–1905), 18th TN Cav.

Withers, John (1827–1892), AAG War Dept.

Wood, Joseph G. W. (1836–1896), 18th TX Inf.

Woolfolk, George William (1832–1878), KY Cav.

Wortham, William Amos (1830–1910), 35th TX Cav.

Yandell, David Wendell (1826–1898), medical director TMD

Printed in the United States
147598LV00001B/2/P

9 780826 218094